The Daily Telegraph
Chronicle of Rugby

Compiled and edited
by Norman Barrett

GUINNESS PUBLISHING

Published in Great Britain by Guinness Publishing Ltd,
33 London Road, Enfield, Middlesex

Reprint 10 9 8 7 6 5 4 3 2 1 0

Front cover illustrations courtesy of Allsport UK Ltd:
François Pienaar *(David Rogers)*, Will Carling *(Clive Brunskill)*

Design and layout by Mitchell Associates, Hertford

Printed and bound in Great Britain by The Bath Press, Bath

"GUINNESS" is a registered trademark of Guinness Publishing Ltd

A catalogue record for this book is available from the British Library

ISBN 0-85112-626-x

Contents

Introduction

Rugby was first reported in *The Daily Telegraph* on a regular basis in the 1870s, although initially the coverage was scant, a single paragraph of 150 words, say, on an international, plus the lists of players and their clubs. For the sake of a comprehensive history of the sport, matches and other events before this have been compiled from book sources and the headlines manufactured. Indeed, apart from the general heading 'Football' (which included the Association game), and perhaps a sub-heading England v Scotland, say, headlines did not begin to creep in until the turn of the century.

Although 'Our Special Correspondent' reported regularly from abroad a few years earlier, it was 1908 before by-lines were introduced for matches at home, and that's when the prolific and ubiquitous Major Philip Trevor's name first appears in the *Telegraph* sports columns – under cricket reports as well as rugby. The Major was everywhere, it seemed, filing reports from all parts of the British Isles and from the Colonies, too. After World War I, it was Colonel Trevor and his by-line boasted a CBE, and we are indebted to him for reports right to the end of the twenties.

The year 1930 marked the debut of Howard Marshall as the *Telegraph*'s chief rugby correspondent, another who covered cricket in the summer. Marshall continued until just before World War II, when Peter Lawless and then JP Jordan took over. Rugby and cricket, of course, complemented each other, with the public schools and universities connection, and two more great cricket writers began to contribute rugby articles and reports, EW Swanton in the late forties and Michael Melford in the mid fifties. Other correspondents to be acknowledged over these years include the former Welsh centre Wilf Wooller, Tony Lewis, JA Bailey and Reg Sweet (from South Africa). John Reason, who made his first contribution in the latter sixties, became chief rugby correspondent for *The Sunday Telegraph*, and continued his pungent analysis and criticism into the early nineties. John Mason also began reporting in *The Daily Telegraph* in the late sixties, became its chief rugby man and is still going strong, as fresh as ever and with a matchless reputation in rugby circles. Paul Ackford, the former Quins and England lock, has now added his considerable weight to the *Telegraph* list of rugby scribes, recently taking over as the top Sunday man. Other contributors whose articles are reproduced in this book include former England fly-half Richard Sharp, Justin Rogers, Michael Austin, Edward Bevan, Charles Randall, Brendan Gallagher, Peter Fitzsimons and Michael Calvin.

In most years, deciding what to include has been difficult, but the diary for each year has been used to complement the reports, and hopefully nothing of great importance has been omitted altogether. Space has rarely permitted complete reports to be reproduced, and in many instances background material or sequels (in italics) have been provided at the end of the reports.

The final International Championship table has been included since 1900, together with results of the matches. Results of all Tests between the full IB member countries are also listed from that year, but lack of space has made it impossible to include results involving associate members. However, the rapid spread of the game throughout the world is reflected by the number of reports and diary entries

One of modern rugby's great heroes, the talismanic Dean Richards of England, takes on the Springboks at Pretoria in 1994.

in more recent years relating to countries such as Romania, Italy, Argentina, Canada, Western Samoa and Japan, and nor has women's rugby been forgotten.

Thanks are due to Alex Erskine, head of the Telegraph cuttings and microfilm department, for her generous co-operation, Simon Barrett for cuttings research, David Prole for reading the proofs, and Charles Richards at Guinness Publishing for his contributions on all fronts.

Norman Barrett
July 1996

Photographic Acknowledgments

Allsport UK Ltd 166, 182
Shaun Botterill 165, 181, 184, 187
Howard Boylan 163
Simon Bruty 167, 186
David Cannon 140, 157, 159, 169, 176
Russell Cheyne 144, 145, 148, 150, 152, 162, 164
Mike Hewitt 173
Michael King 135
Gary M Prior 177 (top)
David Rogers 4-5, 155, 174, 175, 177 (bottom), 178, 180, 185
Dan Smith 161
Billy Stickland 143, 168
Associated Press 85
Colorsport 95, 97, 99, 100, 103, 104 (left), 104 (right), 106, 107,

108, 111, 113, 114, 116, 119, 121, 122, 123, 124, 125, 126, 127, 129, 130, 131, 132, 133, 134, 138, 141, 153, 160, 170, 172, 189
Hulton Getty Picture Collection 40-1, 44, 67, 84, 86, 93
The Illustrated London News Picture Library 22, 25, 31, 32-3, 34, 35, 36, 38, 39, 47, 49, 50, 57, 73, 79, 83, 87, 91
Popperfoto 40 (inset), 45 (top), 52-3, 75, 77, 88, 94, 101
The Daily Telegraph 183
Western Mail & Echo 90
Norman Barrett Collection 6-21, 26, 42, 45 (bottom), 51, 54, 60, 66, 136, 151

Early Days

F orms of football have been played for hundreds, perhaps thousands, of years. Some of the earliest references to football go back to ancient China and Japan, and it is possible that the conquering armies of ancient Rome brought the game to Britain.

Scheduled, if disorganised, games took place all over Britain in the Middle Ages, particularly the Shrovetide gatherings. But most of the officially recorded references to football are to be found in the statutes banning the 'mob football' that endangered life and limb as players stampeded through the streets of towns and villages ostensibly in pursuit of a ball. As this pastime also threatened to take the minds of able-bodied men off archery practice, many of the anti-football edicts were of royal origin, in France as well as in England and Scotland.

The seeds of rugby football were sown in games such as 'hurling to goales' and the very similar 'camp-ball' that emerged and flourished in various parts of Britain over hundreds of years. But it was in the English public schools in the 19th century that such games took on a regular shape, and then in the universities that the disparate games were unified.

The part played in the evolution of rugby football by the 16-year-old Rugby schoolboy William Webb Ellis in 1823, when he caught the ball and rushed forward with it instead of kicking it, has never been clearly established. He did not suddenly change a kicking game into a carrying game, for most types of football to that time had more in common with present-day rugby than with soccer – it was the Football Association that diverged from the norm, soccer that broke the mould.

But after the contentious Ellis incident, the football at Rugby School gradually developed into a running game, and it was the rules drawn up at the School in 1846 that later formed the basis of rugby union. The withdrawal of the Blackheath club from the newly formed Football Association in 1863 was the springboard from which the game was launched.

Main picture: **Football at Rugby School as seen by an artist in the late 1860s.** *Inset:* **The commemorative plaque to William Webb Ellis, unknowing 'founder' of a major sport, who later took Holy Orders and died in France in 1872, a year after the formation of the Rugby Football Union. The plaque was erected at the school in 1895.**

THIS STONE
COMMEMORATES THE EXPLOIT OF
WILLIAM WEBB ELLIS
WHO WITH A FINE DISREGARD FOR THE RULES OF FOOTBALL
AS PLAYED IN HIS TIME
FIRST TOOK THE BALL IN HIS ARMS AND RAN WITH IT
THUS ORIGINATING THE DISTINCTIVE FEATURE OF
THE RUGBY GAME
A.D. 1823

30 BC – 1869

***c*.30 BC** A ball game called *harpastum*, probably derived from a Greek game called *episkyros*, is played by the ancient Romans, and from descriptions was a carrying game with many similarities to modern rugby.

AD 217 Although there is no positive evidence that the Roman invaders introduced football to Britain, legend has it that a game played to celebrate the slaying of a cohort of Roman troops at Derby in 217 was the forerunner of the celebrated match played annually at Derby on Shrove Tuesday.

1175 The 'famous game of ball' takes place in London (probably Smithfield) on Shrove Tuesday.

1314 Edward II bans football in London.

1331 Edward III bans football as 'public nuisance'.

1319 Philippe V bans football in France.

1365 Edward III orders able-bodied men to use bows and arrows or pellets or bolts in leisure time, forbidding other sports such as football under pain of imprisonment.

1388 Richard II orders use of bows and arrows on Sundays and holidays, banning football and other games.

1396 Size of ball limited by clergy in Auxerre, France, for their ritual game of football.

1400s Many references in documents to a game called 'camp-ball', played in the Eastern Counties, a game of football that evidently took its name from being played in open country (Latin *campus*).

1410 Henry IV imposes fine of 20 shillings on mayors and bailiffs in towns where 'misdemeanours' such as football occur.

1414 Henry V issues further proclamation ordering archery and banning football and other games.

1424 James I of Scotland issues act specifically banning football.

1477 Edward IV twice issues statutes banning football and ordering archery.

1491 James IV is fourth Scottish king this century to ban football for its interference with military exercises.

1527 Statutes of Galway, in Ireland, exempt the 'great foote balle' from general ban on sports.

1533 Football replaced as traditional Shrove Tuesday sport in Chester.

1583 Puritan pamphleteer Philip Stubbes castigates football in particular in his vitriolic campaign against all sports.

1608 Broken windows lead to ban on football in Manchester.

1618 Football officers appointed to deal with football-playing in Manchester streets.

1618 James I issues his Declaration of Sports, a counterblast to Puritanism, which, although not mentioning football specifically, encourages sport on the Sabbath.

London: 1175

Football played in Shrovetide festival

Several sporting festivities took place in London on Shrove Tuesday in the year 1175. The morning was spent in cock-fighting and other boyish pastimes. Then, after dinner, all the youth of the city proceeded to a level piece of ground just outside town for the famous game of ball.

The students of every different branch of study had their own ball, as did the various tradesmen. The older men, the fathers and the men of property, arrived on horseback to watch the contests, and in their own way shared the sport of the young men. These elders were filled with excitement at seeing so much vigorous exercise, and participated vicariously in the pleasures of unrestrained youth.

The common practice of 'hustling over large footballs': banned in London in 1314.

London: 13 April 1314

Football banned by proclamation of the King

The Lord Mayor of London, Nicholas de Farndone, has issued a proclamation, in the name of King Edward II of England, banning the playing of football in the city.

The game and its inherent clamour has been upsetting merchants and other solid members of the community for some time, and they petitioned the king to put it down.

The proclamation reads: 'Forasmuch as there is great noise in the city caused by hustling over large footballs in the fields of the public from which many evil rights might arise which God forbid, we command and forbid on behalf of the king, on pain of imprisonment, such game to be used in the city in future.'

1647 Beginning of Winchester College Football.

1717 Wall built at Eton College, used for Eton Wall game.

1734 With football no longer frowned upon, Dr George Cheyne recommends, in a popular essay on health, the playing of tennis and football every day.

1746 The Mayor of Derby tries unsuccessfully to suppress the Shrove Tuesday football match on the grounds that it was likely to spread foot-and-mouth disease among cattle.

1823 William Webb Ellis catches and then runs with the ball at Rugby School, setting a trend, initially frowned upon but gradually accepted, which leads later to separate codes of football.

1839 What is possibly the first rugby club is set up at Cambridge University by Arthur Pell (later an MP), who came up from Rugby School.

1841 Eleven-a-side football introduced at Eton.

1843 A rugby club is formed at Guy's Hospital, London.

1845 The laws of football as played at Rugby School are codified, with terms including many still in use today, such as 'try', 'knock on', 'off side', 'place kick', 'fair catch' and 'touch'. The goals are H-shaped, with scoring by kicking the ball between the posts and over the bar.

1848 Rules are drawn up at Cambridge University which become the basis of those used for association football.

1850 The Rev Rowland Williams, a former Fellow of King's College, Cambridge (where Arthur Pell is said to have started rugby), becomes vice-principal of St David's College, Lampeter, in Wales, and introduces rugby there.

1851 A 'Rugby School football', its oval shape originating from the pig's bladder mainly in use, is on view at the International Exhibition in London.

1854 Trinity College (Dublin) RFC is founded, with an old Rugbeian, RH Scott, as its first secretary.

1857 Edinburgh Academicals RFC is founded.

1858 The Blackheath Football Club is founded. Edinburgh Academicals meet Merchiston Castle School in what is claimed to be the world's oldest fixture (still played today).

1862 JC Thring draws up 10 rules of *The Simplest Game* for use at Charterhouse School. Blackheath draw up their own rules, which include the outlawing of 'throttling' in the scrum. The first match on record in South Africa takes place at Capetown, Civilians v Military.

1863 The Football Association is founded and Blackheath withdraw over a rules dispute, marking, probably, the point when the association and rugby games begin to diverge.

1864 The game spreads to Australia, where a club is formed at Sydney University, and Canada, at Trinity College, Toronto.

Mayor puts stop to Shrove Tuesday football

Henry Gee, Mayor of Chester, has finally put a stop to the ceremonial game of football played every Shrove Tuesday in the city. This tradition, carried out for as long as anyone can remember, with a ball presented in homage by the Shoemakers' Company to the Drapers' Company before the game began, had, thanks to the participation of 'evil disposed persons', become an excuse for violence. Many players finished up bruised and battered, some with broken legs, arms and even heads, or otherwise maimed or in peril of their lives.

The mayor, instead of banning the festivities completely, substituted other sports, including a foot-race for the football match, a horse-race and a shooting competition.

The popular traditional Shrovetide game of street football, as played at Kingston-upon-Thames in the 1840s. Going back to at least the 1100s, the tradition was threatened many times over the centuries, but survived and flourished.

West Country sports

A chronicler called Carew describes games played in Cornwall, called 'hurling to goales' and 'hurling over country', with rules resembling those of modern rugby.

An 'off side' rule is employed in 'hurling to goales', in which teams strive to carry or throw a ball into goals.

'There are 15, 20, or 30 players, more or less, chosen on each side, who strip themselves to their slightest apparel, and then join hands in ranks one against another; out of these ranks they match themselves by payres, one embracing another and passe away, every of which couple are especially to watch one another during the play.

'After this they pitch two bushes in the ground some 8 or 10 feet asunder, and directly against them, 10 or 12 score paces off, other twain in like distance, which they term goales, where some indifferent [neutral or impartial] person throweth up the ball, the which, whomsoever can catch or carry through the adversaries' goales hath won the game.'

In hurling over country, two or three parishes play each other between goals three or four miles apart. In what is essentially a carrying game, the players catch and carry the ball 'by force or slight' [stratagem] to the place assigned to gain victory.

'The hurlers take their way over hilles, dales, hedges, ditches, yea, and thorow bushes, briars, mires, plashes, and rivers whatsoever, so as you shall sometimes see 20 or 30 lie tugging together in the water, scrambling and scratching for the ball.'

[From its description, hurling over country had many of the characteristics of the great Shrovetide games played in Derby and other places.]

Headmaster lauds educational values of football

Richard Mulcaster, headmaster of St Paul's School in London and former head of the Merchant Taylors School, claims that football has positive educational values in school if properly used. In his treatise *Positions,* Mulcaster argues that, as football is so widely played, it must have some good qualities.

While recognising the abuse and violence associated with the game, he feels that it could be used to promote health and strength. Mulcaster, known to be a keen student of Italian works on the subject, goes so far as to advocate the introduction of a 'trayning maister', or referee.

Calcio, the traditional football played in Florence.

Football as a political safety valve?

The publication of an English translation of an Italian work dealing with the game of calcio, similar to our football, praises the game as a political safety valve. The author, Boccalini, commends it as 'very good to breed up youth to run, leap and wrastle'.

Calcio, which dates back to the 15th century, is highly regarded in Florence, where it is played every night from Epiphany to Lent in the Piazza di' Santa Croce by teams of 27 known as the Red and the Green. The sides, who wear their respective colours, are led by young cavaliers of the Florentine aristocracy.

1866 Blackheath join Richmond in a move to abolish 'hacking', and the practice eventually dies out.

1867 According to some sources, the first Richmond v Blackheath match takes place on 26 Jan (others place it sooner, as early as 1863), probably the oldest surviving club fixture.

1869 The first game of inter-collegiate football takes place in the United States when Rutgers beat Princeton at New Brunswick, New Jersey, on 6 Nov in a 25-a-side match played under rugby-like rules adopted from the London Football Association.

Modern rugby evolved not only from the game played at Rugby School, but also from the other great public schools of England. Many still play their own individual version of football, and similarities to rugby are easily seen.

Right: A 'fifteen hot' at Winchester.
Below: A throw-in at Harrow.
Bottom: The inimitable Eton wall game.

Description of camp-ball by Moore: 1823

Camp-ball: How it is played

Each party has two goals, 10 or 15 yards apart. The parties stand in a line, facing each other, about 10 yards distance midway between their goals and that of their adversaries.

An indifferent [neutral or impartial] spectator throws up a ball about the size of a cricket ball midway between the confronted players, and makes his escape. The rush is to catch the falling ball.

He who can first catch or seize it, speeds home, making his way through his opponents and aided by his own sidesmen. If caught and held, or rather in danger of being held – for if caught with the ball in his possession he loses a snotch – he throws the ball (he must in no case give it) to some less beleaguered friend more free and more in breath than himself, who, if it be not arrested in its course or be jostled away by the eager and watchful adversaries, catches it; and he in like manner hastens homeward, in like manner pursued, annoyed, and aided, winning the notch or snotch if he contrive to carry or throw it within the goals.

At a loss or a gain of a snotch a recommencement takes place. When the game is decided by snotches, seven or nine are the game; and these, if the parties be well matched, take two or three hours to win.

Sometimes a large football is used; the game is then called 'kicking camp'; and if played with shoes on, 'savage camp'.

[It has been suggested that camp-ball might have been the same game as the 'hurling to goales' described by Carew in 1602, and that both are obviously forms of football similar to rugby.]

Rugby School: 1846

Football laws codified at Rugby School

The rules of football at Rugby School, in a state of flux ever since 1823, when William Webb Ellis is said to have caught the ball and then run with it, have finally been codified in a set of decisions on certain disputed points. 'Hacking' is permitted, but not above the knee. Holding a player carrying the ball is permitted, but with one arm only. 'Running in' – the Ellis method – is permitted, but passing with the hands is banned. And if no decision is reached after five afternoons' play, a match will be declared drawn.

Below: A Bigside at Rugby. Old Bigside was the field on which the boys of Rugby School played, and a Bigside was a major match. The Rugby game, which was immortalised by Thomas Hughes in Tom Brown's School Days, featured goals, with posts and crossbar, much like those used today. Up till the late 1850s, all those who were not 'caps' had to stand in goal during Bigsides, while only those who were awarded caps (the origin of the custom) were allowed to 'follow up' and take part in the play.

London: 8 December 1863

Blackheath withdraws from Association

On Monday 26 October, at a meeting convened in the Freemason's Tavern, Great Queen Street, a dozen London and suburban football clubs formed a Football Association. But it has taken another six meetings to formulate a set of rules for the game.

The problem has been co-ordinating the disparate codes of football played around the country. There was a strong body of opinion in favour of banning some of the practices allowed by the Rugby (School) code, already outlawed by the Sheffield (1857) and Cambridge (1862 and 1863) Rules. But representatives of the Blackheath club, strong advocates of the Rugby game, have been unyielding.

They have insisted on the inclusion of two clauses in the rules: firstly, that 'A player may be entitled to run with the ball towards his adversaries' goal if he makes a fair catch', and, secondly, 'If any player shall run with the ball towards his adversaries' goal, any player on the opposite side shall be at liberty to charge, hold, trip or hack him, or wrest the ball from him'.

Now, the dispute has come to a head. Blackheath's proposal to adjourn the meeting was defeated by 13 votes to 4, and they have withdrawn from the Association.

[Oddly enough, it was not over handling or carrying that Blackheath defected, but because of the refusal of those favouring the dribbling game to countenance hacking, the practice of kicking an opponent's shins.]

The Late 1800s

The structure of the game and its organisation as we know it today took shape in the latter part of the 19th century, and the game spread to the 'colonies', who would one day become its foremost strongholds.

The Rugby Football Union was founded in January 1871, and until the establishment of a strong International Board in the 1890s was the biggest influence on the rules, both on and off the field, a staunch guardian of the sanctity of the amateur status.

The seventies saw the first internationals, County and Varsity matches, and the standardisation of a 15-a-side game. The first points system of scoring was not introduced until 1886.

Fixtures between all four home countries were established in 1883, which marked, in retrospect, the beginning of the International Championship, although disputes of one kind or another were to plague it until the end of the century. England and Scotland shared the honours until Wales won their first title in 1893, after which Ireland surprisingly won three championships.

New South Wales and New Zealand exchanged tours in the early 1880s, but it was 1888 before a British side ventured forth – to the Antipodes. The Native New Zealand side, mostly Maoris, undertook a Herculean tour of the British Isles and Australia in 1888-89, and teams representing the British Isles visited South Africa twice and Australia in the 1890s.

Among the greatest influences on the style and tactics of the game were the Oxford University players Harry Vassall, a forward, and Alan Rotherham, a half-back. Together, they revolutionised rugby in the early 1880s, linking the forwards with the backs and establishing passing movements as a weapon of attack.

Another great innovator was Welsh three-quarter Arthur Gould, perhaps the greatest player of this era, but who is remembered more for the furore his 'testimonial' caused in the late 1890s. This, and the 'broken time' dispute that led to the Northern Union breakaway in 1895, were two great focuses of the battle between the diehard amateurs and those who wanted to relax the 'professionalism' rules. That rugby survived was due in no small part to the sane and sensible influence of Rowland Hill, whose service to the RFU and to rugby in general should never be underestimated.

Play at Richmond in 1891 when Scotland beat England 9-3 to win their first Triple Crown. The England captain in this match was the tall three-quarter FHR Alderson *(inset left)*, and one of the forwards who won the match for Scotland was RG Macmillan *(inset above, left)*, who played in all 19 matches of the unofficial British tour of South Africa later that year which included a match versus Cape Colony *(inset above, right)*.

The 1870s

1870 The first county match in England takes place at Leeds between Yorks and Lancs.

1870 Rugby is introduced to New Zealand by Charles John Monro, who learnt the game at public school in England, and the first club match takes place at Nelson on 14 May between Nelson FC and Nelson College.

1871 Neath RFC are the first senior club to be formed in Wales.

1872 The Rev William Webb Ellis, unknowing 'founding father' of rugby, dies on 24 Jan in the south of France and is buried in Menton.

1872 England beat Scotland in the return

international at Kennington Oval on 5 Feb by a goal, a dropped goal and two tries to a dropped goal.

1872 The first Varsity rugby match takes place on 10 Feb, with Oxford beating Cambridge by a goal to nil.

1872 The first French club is formed at Le Havre by British residents.

1873 The Scottish Rugby Football Union is founded in Glasgow on 3 Mar by the Universities of Edinburgh, St Andrews and Glasgow, the Academicals of Edinburgh and Glasgow, the Royal High School, the West of Scotland and the Merchistonians.

London: 26 January 1871

Foundation of the Rugby Football Union

On the evening of 26 January 1871, a party of 32 members of London and suburban football clubs following Rugby School laws assembled at the Pall Mall Restaurant, Regent Street, under the presidency of EC Holmes, captain of the Richmond Club, and resolved unanimously to form what they called the Rugby Football Union.

They drafted a set of bye-laws and elected a president, Algernon Rutter, and a secretary and treasurer, Edwin H Ash, both of Richmond, along with a committee of 13 who were entrusted the drawing up of the laws of the game upon the basis of the code in use at Rugby School.

The names of the clubs present on this auspicious occasion were: Blackheath, Richmond, Civil Service, Marlborough Nomads, West Kent, Wimbledon Hornets, Gipsies, Clapham Rovers, Law, Wellington College, Guy's Hospital, Flamingoes, Harlequins, Queen's House, King's College, St Paul's School, Lausanne, Addison, Mohicans, and Belsize Park.

Scotland v England: Raeburn Place, Edinburgh, 27 March 1871

The first rugby international: Scotland beat England by a goal and a try to a try

The Scottish XX *(left)*, winners of the historic first rugby international, and the vanquished English side *(above)*.

The first International match between England and Scotland was played at the Academy Ground in Raeburn Place, Edinburgh. The weather was magnificent and the turf in excellent order, and an attendance of some 4,000 spectators showed that Rugby football had already attained considerable popularity north of the Tweed. The ground measured some 120 yards in length by 55 in breadth, and its narrowness compared with English grounds materially handicapped the excellent running of the English half-backs.

It was arranged before kick-off that the match should be played for two periods of fifty minutes each, that no hacking-over or tripping-up should be allowed, and that the ball should not be taken up for a

run unless absolutely bounding, as opposed to rolling. There were other points, too, upon which the Scottish fashion of playing the Rugby game had to be followed.

The match was very evenly contested until half-time, after which the combination of the Scotsmen, who knew each other's play thoroughly, and their superior training began to tell a tale, and after a maul just outside the English goal-line the umpires ordered the ball to be put down in a scrummage five yards outside the line. It was taken out accordingly, but, instead of putting it down, the Scottish forwards drove the entire scrummage into goal, and then grounded the ball and claimed a try. This, though illegal according to English laws, was allowed by the

umpires, and a goal was kicked by Cross.

England then penned their opponents for some time, and ultimately RH Birkett ran in close to touch, but the captain's place-kick, a long and difficult one across the wind, failed. Scotland gained another try just before 'no side', Cross touching the ball down after an unintentional knock-on by one of his own side. His place-kick, however, was unsuccessful.

The English twenty in this match averaged 12st 3lb per man, and the Scotch probably about the same. JF Green and F Tobin for England and M Cross for Scotland played splendidly behind the scrummage. The Scotch forwards were distinctly quicker on their feet, and in better training than their opponents.

In this match an extraordinary charge was made by Osborne. Finlay had got well away with the ball, and was sprinting towards the English goal at hundred yards' speed, when Osborne, folding his arms across his chest, ran full tilt at him, after the fashion of a bull charging a gate. Both were very big, heavy men, and the crash of the collision was tremendous, each reeling some yards and finally falling on his back. For a few seconds players and spectators alike held their breath, fearing terrible results, but the two giants promptly resumed their places, apparently none the worse.

[The above extract is from Football: The Rugby Union Game, edited by Rev F Marshall and published by Cassells in 1892.]

1874 The first rugby match takes place in the USA, at Cambridge, Massachusetts, Harvard Univ entertaining McGill Univ of Montreal.

1874 The Irish Rugby Union is formed, without Ulster.

1874 Laws: Captains are the sole arbiters of disputes, and results are to be decided on goals scored, and failing that on tries, the Rugby Union having ruled that 'A side having touched the ball down in their opponents' goal shall "try" at goal either by a "place kick" or a "punt out".'

1875 Oxford persuade Cambridge to play the Varsity match 15-a-side and win by a try to nil. Scotland's proposal for 15-a-side international matches comes too late for acceptance this season.

1875 In England, the Inter-Hospitals Challenge Cup is inaugurated, with Guy's beating St George's in the final by a goal to nil.

1875 Rugby is introduced in South Africa by British troops garrisoned in Cape Town, and clubs are formed, Hamilton FC having the strongest claims to being the first.

1875 Ireland play their first home international on 13 Dec, losing to England by a goal and a try to nil at Leinster Cricket Ground, Rathmines.

1876 The number of players in all matches is reduced to 15, although there is no mention of this in the laws (until 1892).

1877 In the first match between the two countries, Scotland beat Ireland by 6 goals to nil at Belfast.

1877 In the first 15-a-side international, on 5 Feb, England beat Ireland at the Oval by 2 goals and 2 tries to nil.

1877 Scotland's HH Johnston is the first to play as a single full-back.

1878 Broughton v Swinton, on 22 Oct, is the first floodlit match, played by 'electricity'.

1878 Newport beat Swansea by a goal to nil in the first South Wales Cup.

1879 Scotland (1 dropped goal) and England (1 goal) draw at Raeburn Place on 10 Mar in the first match for the Calcutta Cup.

1879 The Irish Rugby Union is re-formed to include Ulster.

1879 The first Unions are formed in New Zealand, in Canterbury and Wellington.

England v Ireland: Kennington Oval, 15 February 1875

England outplay their new opponents

The first match ever played between England and Ireland took place yesterday under the auspices of the Rugby Football Union at Kennington Oval. The England twenty included four players from Oxford University, while Ireland had no fewer than six players from Dublin University in their team.

Play began at a quarter to three. Ireland won the toss, and chose to kick off from the Harleyford Road end. The ball was quickly returned, and several scrimmages took place in the Irish half of the ground. R Galbraith, one of the Irish backs, made a good attempt to get the ball away to the middle of the play. He was checked, however, by Collins. Some sharp play followed, and Bell ran the ball into touch.

So far, the Irish players, though they worked very well, had not succeeded in getting the ball far away from their goal. A scrimmage by the goal-line now took place, and Ireland had to touch down in self-defence. Soon after the ball had been returned into play, Collins made an attempt to drop a goal, but failed owing to a plucky charge by Cronyn.

Several attempts were made about this time by the Irishmen to force the ball into the centre of the ground, but without success. A scrimmage by the Irish goal-line resulted in a second touchdown. Cronyn, who was very conspicuous throughout for Ireland, was thrown down in trying to carry the ball up the ground, and for the third time the Irish had to touch down.

Just after this Collins and Nash each failed to drop a goal, but another touchdown was scored against the visitors. A fifth touchdown was the only feature of the play for some little time after this.

The Irishmen now got the ball a little further from their goal, but Michell soon took it back, and obtained a try in brilliant style. The place-kick, however, entrusted to Fraser, altogether failed. Ireland again touched down, and then, half-time having been called, ends were changed.

The character of the play, however, remained the same, the visitors repeatedly touching down. At last, Nash made a fine run, and dropped the first goal for England in grand style.

Towards the close, Cheston ran the ball in, and got a try. Pearson had an easy place-kick, and succeeded in obtaining a second goal for England. At a quarter past four 'no side' was called, England being victorious by two goals, a try and fifteen touches down to nothing.

Although over-matched, the Irishmen deserve credit for their pluck and endurance. The play of the English twenty was excellent throughout.

[At this time, matches were decided by a majority of goals, or, if equal in that respect, by a majority of tries. 'Touches down' were worth nothing, a proposal in 1874 that three touches down should count as one goal having been rejected. The Irish side, composed of men from the Northern and Southern Irish Unions, many of whom had never met before, was haphazardly put together and not all those chosen to play did so. The final line-up included nine from Dublin University and six from North of Ireland.]

The British influence spread rugby to all parts of the world, and here the natives of Yokohama, in Japan, are treated to a demonstration of what must have seemed a curious activity in 1874.

The 1880s

1880 The RFU agree travelling expenses for international matches.

1881 The Welsh Rugby Union is founded at a meeting on 12 Mar at the Castle Hotel, Neath, between representatives from 11 clubs: Bangor, Brecon, Cardiff, Lampeter, Llandilo, Llandovery, Llanelli, Merthyr, Newport, Pontypool and Swansea. Swansea president CC Chambers is elected the first president, and Richard Mullock, whose 'private team' playing as Wales were humiliated by England last month, becomes the first hon. sec.

1881 Scotland, playing with 3 three-quarters against Ireland at Belfast, lose by a goal to a try after an internal dispute weakens their team.

1881 The laws provide for the appointment of neutral umpires.

1882 In their second international, Wales chalk up their first win, beating Ireland by 2 goals and 2 tries to nil at Lansdowne Road on 28 Jan.

1882 The first overseas tour takes place when New South Wales visit New Zealand; the boat journey takes 5 days.

1882 In what is later accepted as the first match in the first International Championship, England beat Wales at St Helen's, Swansea, on 16 Dec by 2 goals and 4 tries to nil, with CG Wade *(pictured right)*,

1883 Local butcher Ned Haig of Melrose, Roxburgh, organises the first 7-a-side rugby.

1883 Coventry play 4 three-quarters in a match at Stratford-on-Avon.

1884 England beat Scotland at Blackheath on 1 Mar by a goal to a try, to achieve the Triple Crown again. But the dispute over England's try – for a knock-back on the Scottish side that would have given England an advantage anyway – holds the game up for 10 minutes, before the referee disallows it because no Englishman had appealed over the illegal knock-back. The repercuss-ions are of greater historical significance, with Scotland denying the right of the RFU to be sole interpreters of the laws of the game, leading eventually to the setting up of the International Rugby Football Board.

1884 Cardiff pioneer the 4 three-quarters system, which spreads to all the Welsh clubs as well as many in the west of England.

1884 The first New Zealand tourists win all 9 matches in New South Wales.

1884 The first rugby in Fiji – the local soldiers play European soldiers at Ba.

1886 Wales employ 4 three-quarters for the first time, on 9 Jan against Scotland at Cardiff.

1886 The RFU adopt a points system (not accepted by other unions) for the first time, a try worth 1pt, a goal 3pts (ie a conversion 2pts).

INTERNATIONAL CHAMPIONSHIP

Year	Winners	Points
1883	England	6
1884	England	6
1885	*incomplete*	
1886	England/Scotland	5
1887	Scotland	5
1888	*incomplete*	
1889	*incomplete*	

England v Wales: Richardson's Field, Blackheath, 19 February 1881

Crushing defeat for Wales in first International

A match under Rugby rules between England and Wales was decided on Saturday at Mr Richardson's Field, Blackheath. In anticipation of seeing some first-rate play, a large number of people assembled on the ground, but had to put up with a complete disappointment, the match being utterly devoid of interest. From the 'kick-off' to the call of 'no side', the Englishmen showed them-selves in every way superior to their opponents, and in the end they gained a ridiculously easy victory by eight goals [including one drop] and six tries to nothing. Ten of England's tries were scored by forwards, including four by GW Burton and three on his début by Harry Vassall, the Oxford University captain.

[Ten years after England's first match, Wales entered the international scene, and this 'disgraceful defeat' led less than a month later to the foundation of the Welsh Rugby Union. England used 5 backs

Harry Vassall, one of rugby's most influential players: scored a hat-trick of tries on his England début.

and 10 forwards, Wales 6 backs, including 2 full-backs, and 9 forwards. The match was refereed by Arthur Guillemard, president of the Rugby Union.]

International Championship: Edinburgh, 3 March 1883

England's first victory on Scottish soil

The annual football match, under Rugby rules, between teams representing England and Scotland was decided at Edinburgh on Saturday in charming weather and before nearly 10,000 spectators. Throughout, the match was a fast one, but from a very early period it was evident that the Englishmen would have the best of it, and they obtained a victory by two tries to one.

The game was for the most part a forward one, and the home team, being much the lighter of the two, had a hard struggle to maintain their ground, and it was, generally speaking, only in the loose scrimmages, where some good dribbling was shown, that they were able to make some headway.

The passing of the visitors was at times splendid, com-pletely outstripping anything their opponents could do in that line. Rotherham obtained the first try for England about twenty minutes after the kick-off, and the only other point scored in the first half was a touch-down in favour of Scotland.

Early in the second half, C Reid got behind for the home team, but the try was kicked under protest, and about fifteen minutes later, Bolton, after a splendid run, obtained the second try for his side, Evanson failing to convert an easy 'place' into a goal.

[This match, England's first victory in Scotland, became, in retrospect, the decider of the first generally accepted Inter-national Rugby Champion-ship, with England winning the first 'Triple Crown'; only Ireland and Wales did not play each other, but both had lost their two matches.]

International Championship: Edinburgh, 8 January 1883

Scotland win first match with Wales

An international match, under Rugby rules, between teams representing respect-ively Scotland and Wales, was decided yesterday at Raeburn Place, Edinburgh. Overhead the weather was favourable, but owing to a frost which had set in on Sunday night the ground was not in good condition for the game.

Nevertheless, a most exciting contest was witnes-sed, and after a very obstinate struggle Scotland won by three goals (and one not allowed) to one.

[Wales played a single full-back for the first time in an international, their captain CP Lewis.]

1886 The Rugby Union refuse to participate in a meeting at Manchester in which the other home unions set up an International Board to deal with disputes and policies concerning international matches.

1887 The other home unions, having refused to play England until a four-nation International Board is formed, hold the first meeting of the International Rugby Football Board at Manchester on 5 Dec.

1888 England again (4 Feb) decline to join the International Board, and consequently do not play the other home

countries again until 1890.

1888 The captain of the first (unofficial) British touring side, RL Seddon, is drowned while sculling in Australia on the Hunter River. AE Stoddart, **(pictured right)** their centre three-quarter, who had joined them after representing England in the cricket Tests, takes over the

captaincy and is the star of the team.

1889 The RFU establish a close season, 1 May to 31 August in the Northern Hemisphere.

1889 In the match against England at Blackheath on 16 Feb, three of the Maori touring team walk off the field when the referee allows what they feel is a third highly dubious try. They are eventually

persuaded to return, and England win 7-0, with 1 goal and 4 tries.

1889 Touch judges are introduced in the laws ('appointed at the request of either of the contending Unions') as optional to umpires, but to deal only with the touch line, the referee having the power to override their decisions.

1889 The South African Rugby Football Board is formed.

1889 In England, the County Championship receives official recognition, and Yorkshire, who win all their matches, are declared champions.

International Championship: Edinburgh, 26 February 1887

Depleted Wales crushed by Scotland

This annual match under Rugby rules, which was postponed from New Year's Day owing to frost, was decided at Edinburgh on Saturday before about 6,000 spectators. The Scotchmen early showed their superiority in a one-sided game, and ten minutes after the start a judicious pass by Reid allowed Don Wauchope to get behind pretty far out. Berry took the kick but failed to improve on the try. A rush by the Scotch forwards gave an opportunity to Lindsay, who, by a fine dribbling run, passed the backs and secured a try which Berry, amid cheers, converted into a goal. Within

a few minutes Orr got the ball from a scrimmage, and got behind, enabling Berry to kick another goal. Just on half-time, Lindsay again crossed the Welsh lines, but the ensuing kick failed.

The play in the second half was a repetition of that in the opening portion, and Scotland won by no fewer than four goals and eight tries to nil.

[Scotland ran in a record 12 tries, 5 of them from London Scottish back George Lindsay, who had not been chosen for the original, postponed match. Wales were unlucky to lose one man for the whole second half, another playing most of the match as a virtual passenger.]

Rest of England v Yorkshire: Halifax, 23 February 1889

The Rest beat champion county

Much interest was taken in this new fixture, as evidenced by the 12,000 spectators who gathered on the ground of the Halifax Club on Saturday. Yorkshire is undoubtedly the champion football county, and the fixture was instituted to see what their chance would be against a picked fifteen of all England. Both sides were well represented, but the Tykes were beaten by three goals to nil.

The home side took the

best of the game in the first half, but Alderson by a splendid run managed to gain a try which Mason-Scott converted into a goal. After the interval, Jowett and Bedford by good play carried the ball to the visitors' 'twenty-five' where Sutcliffe gained possession and ran in, but the referee disallowed the point. Afterwards, Valentine and Evershed ran in for the visitors, Mason-Scott placing a goal each time.

Rugby Union Meeting: 7 March 1888

The Rugby Union and professionalism

A hastily summoned committee meeting of the English Rugby Football Union was held last evening at the Queen's Hotel, Leeds. The meeting was convened by Yorkshire County in consequence of the novel point arising out of the conviction of Clowes, Halifax, as a professional, the committee desiring to have an authoritative decision on the status of the team chosen to commence the journey to Australia today.

Proceedings were strictly private, and Mr JA Miller, hon. sec. Yorkshire, laid the case before the meeting. W Stadden and R Lockwood, Dewsbury, gave evidence respecting the transaction between Mr Turner (Messrs Shaw, Shrewsbury and Lilly-

white's manager) and GP Clowes, and after careful consideration the meeting passed the following resolution: 'The Rugby Football Union have decided, on evidence before them, that GP Clowes is a professional within the meaning of their laws.'

On the same evidence, they have formed a very strong opinion that others composing the Australian team have also infringed these laws, and they will require from them such explanations as they may think fit on their return to England.

[When the team returned, each member was required to make an affidavit that he had received no pecuniary benefit from the tour, and there the matter ended.]

Tour Match: Southern Counties v Maoris, Leyton, 27 March 1889

Maoris finish with a victory

The Colonists played their final contest in England yesterday, when at Leyton they were opposed by a team under the above title. Although a weak one, the Southern Counties started the scoring, Stamp scoring a try, but before half-time the Maoris had placed two tries to their credit. In the second portion, F Warbrick added a further try, and the Englishmen, failing to increase their points, were defeated by three tries to one try.

The tour of the visitors has proved successful from a playing standpoint, and although there will be no profit to speak of, the trip has paid its way. Of the 74

matches played they have won 49, lost 20 and drawn 5. They have obtained 92 goals, 115 tries, as against 43 goals, 59 tries secured by their opponents. They leave tomorrow for Australia, where they play before returning home to New Zealand.

[The tourists could legitimately be called the New Zealand Native team because, although they contained four 'pakehas' ('white' men), every member was born in New Zealand. After playing 16 matches in Australia, they completed their arduous programme with 17 games in New Zealand – making a total of 107, the greatest number ever played by a rugby touring side.]

The 1890s

1890 The Barbarians, founded on 9 Apr at the Alexandra Hotel, Bradford, beat Hartlepool Rovers 9-4 on 27 Dec in their first fixture.

1890 The International Rugby Football Board, now established with 6 places for England (who have most clubs) and 2 each for the other Home Unions, is empowered to ensure one code of laws for international matches.

1891 The British team for the first ever tour of South Africa is composed of English and Scottish players, captained by WE Maclagan. All 19 matches are won, including 3 internationals, with a points aggregate of 224 against 1.

1891 The Currie Cup is inaugurated in South Africa.

1892 An extra point is added for each method of scoring, making tries 2pts, conversions and penalty goals each 3pts, and dropped goals and goals from a mark 4pts each. Mauls in goal are abolished, and the RFU decrees that all matches should be played 15-a-side.

1892 The New Zealand RFU is founded.

1893 Wales beat Ireland 2-0 at Stradey Park, Llanelli, to clinch their first Triple Crown, with a memorable try scored by GH 'Bert' Gould, who runs through a defence expecting him to pass to his illustrious brother Arthur.

1894 The scoring values are changed so that a try is now worth 3pts and a conversion 2pts, instead of vice versa.

1895 Referees are given sole charge of matches, with no appeal against their decisions.

1896 In January, the Welsh RU donate a house to mark the retirement of their great captain and centre three-quarter Arthur Gould, setting in train a dispute that drags on until 1899.

1896 Johnny Hammond's GB team win 19 and draw 1 of their 21 matches in South Africa, winning the first 3 Tests and losing the last.

1897 Numbering of jerseys is adopted.

1897 Scotland and Ireland refuse to play Wales because of the Gould affair.

1899 The term 'Triple Crown' is used for the first time to signify a clean sweep of all 3 International Championship matches by one country.

1899 Managed and captained by the Rev Mathew Mullineux, himself not an international, the British Isles side touring Australia is far from fully representative, but is the first to contain players from all four home countries. They win 18 of 21 matches, and the Test series 3-1 after losing the first.

SMJ Woods: Historic move for England.

WJ Bancroft: Historic kick for Wales.

International Championship: Wales v England, Cardiff, 7 January 1893

Welshmen beat England in exciting finish

In the first International match of the season, the Welshmen scored their second victory over England's representatives as the outcome of ten engagements, in front of fully 20,000 spectators. Wales had four three-quarter backs, while the visitors started with the usual three played by English clubs. After half-time, however, it was found desirable to increase the number, and SMJ Woods was brought out of the pack, in order, if possible, to check the onward career of the Welsh quartet.

Within five minutes of the start, Lohden grounded the ball in the corner for England, who continued to play an open game, but were unable again to beat the excellent defence of M'Cutcheon and Gould until Marshall snapped up the ball from the heels of the forwards and landed a splendid try. Lockwood converted to give England a lead of 7 points to nil at half-time.

The Welshmen began to play their characteristic game in the second half, but they soon received a decisive check, as a splendid pass by De Winton enabled Marshall to get clear away and score a third try for England. In the scrimmaging which followed the drop out, Graham, the Newport captain, got away with a dribble, picked up and passed to Hannan, who reached English territory and then passed to A Gould, who raced the English backs and obtained the first try for Wales. Bancroft made no mistake at the place-kick, and reduced the Englishmen's lead to one of 4 points.

Encouraged, the home division put England unmistakably on the defensive, and some combined play enabled Biggs to secure their second try. But Marshall scored another for England, his third. Then Gould scored his second for Wales. None of these tries was converted, so England still led, by 11 points to 9.

Soon after, Conway Rees punted to within a few yards of the English line, where the Welshmen were awarded a penalty kick. Bancroft, taking a drop in preference to a place-kick [according to some reports, in direct defiance of his captain Gould's instructions], landed a beautiful goal from near the touch line. This proved the deciding point, and the Welshmen won by 12 points to 11 – 2 goals (1 penalty), 2 tries to 1 goal, 3 tries.

[Billy Bancroft's was the first penalty goal scored in an international. Had the Welsh system of scoring been in force, they would have only drawn, 14-14.]

International Championship: England v Scotland, Richmond, 7 March 1891

Decisive defeat of the Englishmen

The great Rugby football contest of the season, that between representatives of the Rose and the Thistle, was duly decided on Saturday afternoon, on the Athletic Ground, Richmond, and will long be remembered for the decisive manner in which the Scotchmen defeated England, the margin being 3 goals to 1. Both had beaten Ireland and Wales somewhat easily, and by their win against England the Scotch representatives take the leading position.

The rain had made the turf slippery, but this hardly excused the weak play of the home side, who were kept very busy in their own twenty-five. In the first half, however, they restricted the visitors to just one dropped goal, magnificently kicked by Clauss after ten minutes.

After the interval, the Scots went to work with a will, and JE Orr got right away to land a try behind the uprights, and then the youthful three-quarter back Neilson, showing his rivals a clean pair of heels, obtained a try between the uprights, M'Gregor easily converting both. With eight minutes remaining, Lockwood registered a try for the Englishmen, from which Alderson obtained a goal.

[This win clinched Scotland's first Triple Crown.]

INTERNATIONAL CHAMPIONSHIP

Year	Winners	Points	Year	Winners	Points
1890	England/Scotland	4	1895	Scotland	6
1891	Scotland	6	1896	Ireland	5
1892	England	6	1897	*incomplete*	
1893	Wales	6	1898	*incomplete*	
1894	Ireland	6	1899	Ireland	6

Rugby Football Union AGM: London, 20 September 1893

Cheering greets defeat of motion to legalise 'professionalism'

At the Westminster Palace Hotel, Victoria Street, London SW, last evening, the annual September general meeting of the Rugby Union was held, under the presidency of Mr W Cail (Northumberland County). The meeting was largely attended, chiefly because it was to be called upon to decide the question of legalising professionalism, the advocacy of which emanated from Yorkshire, who were receiving partial support from Lancashire. On the other hand, the Midland Counties, the West Country, Cheshire and the South signified their intention of opposing the proposition.

Mr JA MILLER, Yorkshire County, proposed: 'That players be allowed compensation for bona-fide loss of time.' This proposition was brought forward because of the changed conditions under which football is now played, a change brought about by the Union itself, who, in order to popularise the game, had brought into the field a type of player vastly different from that of years gone by. They were no longer confined to the Universities, public schools and more favoured classes of the people. The Union had urged the game upon the people of the country, particularly the young workingmen of the manufacturing centres of the North. But it had not been realised in the South what difficulties the North had to contend with. In calling upon a player to leave his work and lose his wages to play football they did him an injustice. According to the present interpretation of the laws, they were debarred from making him any recompense for his loss of time. In the England and Ireland match, several Yorkshire players lost three days' work and pay through going there. The amateurs, however, lost nothing. If his resolution were carried it would remove this injustice. In conclusion, he believed that if his proposition were carried it would raise the strongest barrier against professionalism that had yet been brought

forward. (Loud cheers from the Yorkshire delegates.)

Mr CAIL (president) proposed as an amendment: 'That this meeting, believing that the above principle is contrary to the true interest of the game and its spirit, declines to sanction the change.' He described the argument for compensation for loss of time as increasingly fallacious, and it was generally recognised that the legalisation of payment for loss of time was tantamount to the introduction of professionalism.

Mr G ROWLAND HILL believed most emphatically that if Mr Miller's resolution were adopted it would in the end professionalise the game and divide the Rugby Union. He did not believe that any man could devise a scheme to meet the payment for broken time.

Mr THORPE (Cheshire County) supported Mr Cail's proposition, asserting that the pseudo working-man and bastard amateur did not represent the working-men of this country. He did not believe in the working-man who got a transfer from one club to another, which placed him in a public-house. (Hear, hear, and laughter.)

The Rev FRANK MARSHALL strongly opposed the scheme. He knew one club in Yorkshire where there were seven publicans in the team (laughter). It was an open secret in Yorkshire that there were many players in receipt of funds, either from the clubs or from their supporters.

Mr MILLER, in reply, said that it had been stated that the proposal, if passed, would be the thin end of the wedge of professionalism. All he could say was that the end had been inserted years ago, and they knew it, and were powerless to prevent it.

The CHAIRMAN put the amendment, for which a majority of hands were held up, but Mr Miller challenged a division. The figures were announced a few minutes past ten, as under: For Mr Miller's motion 136, Against 282, Majority against 146. The result was received with vociferous cheering, which lasted fully five minutes.

Huddersfield: 29 August 1895

A Rugby professional union

For many years past there has been an uneasy feeling about the Northern Rugby clubs, who doubtless have seen with not a little envy the large sums of money that Association football teams have been handling. More than one attempt has been made to introduce 'broken time' payments. Recently a new set of rules has been drawn up, which will provide the most stringent penalties to deal with this subject of professionalism.

Many of the Yorkshire and Lancashire clubs maintain that the tax upon the time of their players is one that no longer can be borne without recompense,

and they have decided to form a Union of their own, on the basis of 'payment for bona-fide broken time'. To this end, a meeting was held at the George Hotel, Huddersfield, last evening, when it was decided to form a Northern Union.

In all, twenty clubs resigned from the English Rugby Union. Senior competitions for Lancashire and Yorkshire were resolved on, with a Northern League for twenty-two clubs.

[It was 1906 before the new organisation reduced the number of players from 15 to 13 per side, and 1922 before it took its present name, the Rugby Football League.]

Rugby Football Union: London, 16 September 1897

The Gould controversy

There will be a widespread feeling of satisfaction amongst those interested in Rugby football that the Union, at the annual meeting last evening at the Westminster Palace Hotel, London, adopted Mr Rowland Hill's resolution in connection with the Gould case, recommending that, in view of the exceptional circumstances, Mr Gould should be allowed to play against English clubs. The motion was strongly opposed by three past presidents, and all the Yorkshire representatives who spoke were almost fierce in their denunciation of the proposition.

It was contended that, Gould having been pronounced guilty of an act of professionalism, the English Union would stultify themselves by permitting English clubs to play against him. On the other hand it was pointed out that Gould belonged essentially to a Welsh organisation, and that in what he had done he had not only broken no law of his Union, but in all his actions had enjoyed the support of the governors of the game in the Principality.

Another reason, too, for passing the resolution was that of expediency. Was it worth while for the sake of appearing consistent to inflict such an injury upon the game

Gould: May play.

as would result from an abolition of not only international engagements between the two countries, but of fixtures between English and Welsh clubs?

After all, the laws against professionalism were framed to prevent men receiving pecuniary reward for playing football, or for people offering inducements to men to leave one club for another. To the lay mind, they do not apply to the case of Mr Gould, who, towards the close of a football career unique in its brilliancy, was, in a spontaneous outburst of enthusiasm on the part of the Welsh people, presented with a handsome testimonial in recognition of the fame he had gained for his country.

The course adopted last evening may not be entirely logical, but is certainly a common-sense one, and may be regarded as a step towards the resumption of the International matches. Mr Rowland Hill is to be congratulated not only on his statesmanlike action in dealing with a very awkward matter, but upon a great personal triumph.

[This cause célèbre, however, was far from over, as Scotland still refused to play Wales, and it would be 1899 before the International Championship was again completed.]

The Early 1900s

The early part of the 20th century, before The Great War, was a golden age for Welsh rugby, some say the golden age. In the first decade, they were never out of the first two in the International Championship, winning it five times, sharing it once with Ireland and finishing runners-up to Scotland in the other four seasons. Each time they won the title they took the Triple Crown with it, and in those ten years they won 24 of their 30 Championship matches, including all 15 played at home. Only Scotland (three times) and Ireland (twice) beat them, and England, who conversely suffered a wretched period in their history, won but a solitary point from their ten clashes with the all-conquering Welshmen, from a draw at Leicester in 1904.

Above: **The 1905 All Blacks.**

Among the men responsible for this glorious age of Welsh rugby were that 'immortal' three-quarter line of Willie Llewellyn, Gwyn Nicholls, Rhys Gabe and Teddy Morgan. Behind them, the legendary full-back WJ Bancroft retired in 1901, to be followed in 1903 by Bert Winfield and later by his brother Jack, all brilliant goal-kickers. The versatile Billy Trew played in the centre, on the wing and as outside half, and also captained Wales. The outstanding half-backs were Swansea scrum-half Dicky Owen, tireless and full of tricks, and, perhaps the most talented of all, the Cardiff outside half Percy Bush, said to have been 'a veritable team on his own'. Stars of the great Welsh packs are too numerous to mention, but Newport prop forward Jehoida Hodges stands out, not only for his 23 caps, but for the hat-trick of tries he scored as an emergency wing three-quarter against England in 1903.

Yet however much the home scene was dominated by the 'Principality', touring 'Colonial' teams gave notice in this era that rugby in the Southern Hemisphere had developed apace – indeed had already overtaken the game in the British Isles. The All Blacks (1905) made the biggest impact, introducing a revolutionary approach to the game that featured specialist forward play, supreme fitness and teamwork, and creative tactics – all of it technically decades ahead of the British game. Just as effective in their own way, the Springboks (1906), full of pace and power, steamrollered over most of the sides they met. And even the Wallabies (1908-09), virtually a New South Wales side, also made an impression, with victory over England and the Olympic title to their credit.

The interest created by the All Blacks tour might have been one of the reasons for a revival in club fortunes, with a marked increase in gates reported by secretaries around the country. This was certainly not due to any noticeable improvement in the standard of play. 'The four three-quarters still chased each other into touch and spoiled the game as a spectacle,' as one critic complained.

The early 1900s also saw France playing internationals with the home countries in the latter part of the decade, and the opening of Twickenham at the end of it.

Right: **Scotland inflicted the Springboks' first defeat on their 1906 tour, winning 6-0 at Hampden Park in front of 40,000 spectators.**

1900

7 Aug The Arthur Gould affair is finally closed when the Welsh professional laws are brought into line with those of England.

28 Oct The 'first Anglo-French Rugby match of the season', as reported in the following day's *Telegraph* at the end of the 'Paris Day by Day' column, takes place at Vincennes and proves 'a remarkable surprise', the home team 'pronounced victorious by 27 points to 8'. It turns out that this match is part of the Olympics programme, in which the events of a rambling, farcical Games, lasting from 20 May to 28 Oct, are constantly confused with the concurrent Paris Universal Exposition. [The team representing Great Britain were not internationals and almost certainly did not know they were taking part in the Olympics, but they were awarded the bronze medal. In the only other match, France beat Germany (a Frankfurt XV) 27-17, and these teams won the gold and silver medals, respectively.]

Rugby Union meeting: Westminster Palace Hotel, London, 20 September

Union 'No' to league competition

A spirited effort by Bristol to secure the sanction of a League to foster junior football was doomed to failure. Of what was referred to as the 'bugbear' of football the Union would have nothing. The young representative from the West Country pointed out that with Association professional competitions holding the public so firmly, the Rugby game continually lost ground. What his district desired was the alteration of a Cup competition into a League.

But though holding his own well in argument with his elders, the young gentleman with his radical views could not carry weight against the fathers of the Union.

Delegates spoke with one accord against the evils they knew must spring from the introduction of this system; and the meeting ended with solemn words from Mr FH Fox, the new president; and Mr JWH Thorp, the retiring president; and Mr Rowland Hill, as to their determination to uphold the purity of the game as they always had done.

International Championship: Ireland 0 Wales 3, Belfast, 17 March

Welshmen complete third victory of season

After an extremely interesting contest, the annual Rugby encounter between Ireland and Wales – the last of the International series – at Belfast, on Saturday, ended in a victory for the representatives of the Principality by a try to nothing. It is doubtful whether the Welshmen played as well as against either England or Scotland, and the falling off in form may be attributed to the fact that several of the side had a bad passage over.

Though the distinction of scoring the Welsh try fell to George Davies, the Swansea centre three-quarter, the chief merit rested with Guy Nicholls, who, taking a pass from Phillips, opened the way for his comrade in masterly fashion. Once more Nicholls, who, by the way, was born in Gloucestershire, emphasised his greatness as a centre three-quarter.

As in the season of 1892-93, the Welshmen have won all three Internationals and, on the score of sheer merit, they are deservedly champions.

England came second this season [3pts], Scotland are third [2], and Ireland [1], who were the champions last year, have dropped to the bottom.

INTERNATIONAL CHAMPIONSHIP											
	E	I	S	W	P	W	D	L	F	A	Pts
1 WALES	-	-	12-3	-	3	3	0	0	28	6	6
2 ENGLAND	-	15-4	-	3-13	3	1	1	1	18	17	3
3 SCOTLAND	0-0	-	-	-	3	0	2	1	3	12	2
4 IRELAND	-	-	0-0	0-3	3	0	1	2	4	18	1

Varsity Match: Oxford 10 Cambridge 8, Queen's Club, 12 December

An exciting finish: Victory for the Dark Blues

After a keenly contested and intensely exciting contest, the annual Rugby match between Oxford and Cambridge, at the Queen's Club, yesterday, ended in a remarkable win for the Dark Blues by the narrow margin of two goals (10 points) to a goal and a try (8 points). After only twenty minutes Oxford had the misfortune to lose Crawfurd, who put out his right shoulder in tackling an opponent. For the remainder of the struggle the Oxonians had, of course, to play a man short, Hammond being withdrawn from the pack and placed on the left wing.

When half-time arrived neither side had scored, and the play up to that point had left the impression that Cambridge had had the best of it and had not turned their superiority forward to proper account.

The second half was full of exciting incidents, and the spectators were worked up to a high pitch of enthusiasm.

Cambridge continued to maintain the upper hand, their forwards once rushing the ball fully forty yards before being pulled up near the Oxford line.

Sagar, the Cambridge full back, came within an ace of dropping a goal, and then, after some capital passing, Hind raced away and gained Cambridge's first try.

This success was soon followed by another, and Hind was once more the scorer. Sagar placed a beautiful goal, and having then a lead of eight points, Cambridge looked to have victory well assured.

However, soon afterwards there came a startling change. When well in their own half the Oxford halves initiated a movement which ended in complete success. The ball was passed along the three-quarter line to Hammond, who, realising he had not

Scrummage action from the Varsity match at the Queen's Club.

sufficient pace to get round, returned it to Terry, who, in turn, handed it on to Walton. The last-named momentarily hesitated, and then, clearing two opponents with a delightful swerve, he raced right away under the posts, and Rogers easily placed a goal.

This infused fresh life into the contest, and clearly had a disconcerting influence upon the Cambridge men. Five minutes from the finish Hind, failing to field the ball, let in Oxford. The ball was kicked past Frank Jones, and Crabbie, dashing up and securing it, ran right behind, Rogers once more placing a goal.

Altogether it was a great game, one of the best played between the two Universities for some years past.

1901

9 Mar The International Board rules that, in the case of injury to a player, the game shall not be stopped for more than 3 minutes.

30 Mar Devon win the County Championship, beating Durham by a goal and 3 tries to a try at West Hartlepool, thus continuing the sequence of the away side winning the final ever since the competition was first played on its present basis in 1896. [Durham take this curious sequence to 7 the following year when they win at Gloucester, but break it themselves in 1903 by beating Kent at West Hartlepool.]

Apr The Barbarians make their first 4-match Easter tour of Wales.

INTERNATIONAL CHAMPIONSHIP

	E	I	S	W	P	W	D	L	F	A	Pts
1 SCOTLAND	-	9-5	-	18-8	3	3	0	0	45	16	6
2 WALES	13-0	10-9	-	-	3	2	0	1	31	27	4
3 IRELAND	10-6	-	-	-	3	1	0	2	24	25	2
4 ENGLAND	-	-	3-18	-	3	0	0	3	9	41	0

International Championship: Wales 10 Ireland 9, Swansea, 16 March

Bancroft's last International

Narrow victory for Welshmen

After a contest that was at once interesting, exciting, and yet disappointing, the Welsh fifteen managed to snatch a victory, beating Ireland by the narrow margin of 2 placed goals (10 points) to 3 tries (9 points).

The unsatisfactory feature about the game was that on the afternoon's play the better side lost. No disinterested spectator could arrive at any other conclusion. The Welsh team themselves would probably be the first to admit that they were fortunate to win. The crowd clearly recognised the fact, for, though at the close they cheered heartily enough, they did not reach that point of enthusiasm that Welshmen usually display after the success of their own men. They were happy that Wales had won, but clearly realised that the occasion did not warrant any marked outburst of feeling. As was suggested in this column might prove the case, the turn of the luck decided the issue. The Irishmen were unfortunate in that all their place-kicks were at a more or less awkward angle, and that two of the attempts only just failed to come off successfully. On the other hand, the Welsh tries were gained under the goal-posts, and Bancroft, the most deadly of place-kicks, had no difficulty in adding the extra points.

After having on so many occasions referred in terms of praise to Bancroft, it is a matter for regret to have to record the fact that on Saturday he was a conspicuous failure. His career as an International full-back has come to an end. Even if given the chance, Bancroft would be ill-advised in running the risk of again marring one of the greatest of reputations ever achieved by a full-back. He has taken part in more International matches [33] than any Rugby player, and his record may possibly never be surpassed.

International Championship: England 3 Scotland 18, Blackheath, 9 March

Fight for the Championship

Decisive defeat for English XV

No surprise was in store for the many thousands of Englishmen who journeyed to the Rectory Field, Blackheath, on Saturday afternoon. The great game between England and Scotland took the course that the previous international matches this season had suggested would be the case. The Scotch fifteen proved themselves to be much the superior side, and won by 3 goals and a try (18 points) to 1 try (3 points).

This is the most decisive defeat England has sustained at the hands of Scotland in the course of the 28 games that have taken place between the two countries, and at the same time it is only proper to observe that never was a victory more genuinely deserved. The score in no way flattered the Scotsmen.

The prestige of English Rugby football has received a severe shock. At Cardiff, early in January, the English team, though beaten, made a creditable fight of it, and against Ireland at Dublin a month later, they had rather the worst of the luck. On Saturday, however, it would be idle to pretend that they were unfortunate in any respect. In a word they were outclassed.

Whether it is possible to pick a stronger side from the many English clubs must be, more or less, a matter of opinion. It certainly is remarkable that, with such a wide field of selection, the Rugby Committee are unable to find a better fifteen than the men who took the field on Saturday. Possibly they selected the best available talent, though that is a point open to question. English Rugby football has deteriorated. Two years ago England, for the first time, lost all their international games, and this season the same painful fact has to be admitted. Possibly, the committee are out of touch with the modern development of the game, or the method of selection needs some alteration. Whatever causes may have been at work, the plain fact remains that the English Rugby players, more especially the backs, have not kept pace with the change in the style of play, and in the struggle for supremacy have fallen considerably in the rear. The Rugby Committee will do well to give the whole matter their very serious consideration.

England were badly let down by their half-backs, Oughtred and Kendal. Possibly they were not too well served by their forwards in the matter of heeling out, but when the ball did come out of the scrummage they often allowed the opposing halves to get on to it and were singularly weak in their efforts to open the game for their three-quarters. They were outplayed by Gillespie and Neill. The Scotch pair worked together admirably, Gillespie playing an exceptionally fine game.

Having won all three international matches, Scotland carry off the International Championship, which was won last year by Wales, and, whatever the result of the Wales and Ireland match next Saturday, England, as was the case two seasons ago, occupy the last position. Saturday's match proved a great attraction, with a crowd of nearly 20,000.

1902

8 Mar In rugby's first all-ticket international, Wales beat Ireland at Lansdowne Road to claim the Triple Crown, the 15-0 defeat being Ireland's heaviest at home since the start of the Championship.

14 Sep The Ranfurly Shield, the challenge trophy for New Zealand's provincial rugby championship, is inaugurated. Presented by the Governor of New Zealand, the Earl of Ranfurly, it has to have its embossed centrepiece altered at the last minute, to a scene depicting a game with an oval ball rather than an Association game, before it can be awarded to the unbeaten Auckland team, the first recipients.

13 Dec Canada begin their 23-match first tour of the British Isles with an 11-8 victory over Ulster on the Balmoral Grounds, Belfast. [They go on to win 8 matches and draw 2, but play no internationals.]

INTERNATIONAL CHAMPIONSHIP

	E	I	S	W	P	W	D	L	F	A	Pts
1 WALES	-	-	14-5	-	3	3	0	0	38	13	6
2 ENGLAND	-	6-3	-	8-9	3	2	0	1	20	15	4
3 IRELAND	-	-	5-0	0-15	3	1	0	2	8	21	2
4 SCOTLAND	3-6	-	-	-	3	0	0	3	8	25	0

Varsity Match: Oxford 8 Cambridge 8, Queen's Club, 13 December

International Championship: England 8 Wales 9, Blackheath, 11 January

A keen struggle
Interesting and exciting contest:
Welsh XV victorious

After a most interesting and exciting contest at Blackheath on Saturday, Wales gained a narrow victory over England, winning by 9 points to 8. In many particulars the game resembled the historic and dramatic struggle at Cardiff in 1893, when in the last five minutes Bancroft dropped a remarkable goal from near the touch-line, that feat winning the match for the Principality by the bare margin of a single point. Curiously enough, on Saturday a dropped penalty goal by Strand-Jones, who is Bancroft's successor as the Welsh full-back, determined the issue.

In some respects England were perhaps the victims of misfortune and had they been in luck might easily have won. It certainly was exasperating that a foolish piece of off-side play by Oughtred a quarter of an hour from the finish should have lost them the lead and, as it turned out, the match. It was a very heavy penalty to pay for one individual blunder. Still, regarding the match as a whole, a sense of common fairness compels the frank admission that the Welshmen deserved their victory.

Despite the fact that a light drizzle prevailed, making the ball wet and somewhat difficult to hold, the play all round was of admirable quality. The match was one of the brightest international encounters witnessed in recent years.

Though they just failed to achieve success, the England fifteen as a whole came through a severe ordeal much better than was expected, and the selection committee have little to reproach themselves with in their choice of players.

The Englishmen made a much closer fight and played better football than any of the fifteens who took the field last season, and they might with two or three exceptions be given another chance against Ireland.

Of course, should Daniell be back in time for that engagement a place for him must be found, but otherwise there is no need to disturb the pack. All the three-quarters were excellent, Raphael, about whom some fears had been entertained, fully justifying his selection. As full-back Gamlin was in great form, giving a display that hardly could be surpassed. Not once did he make a mistake, and on several occasions he saved his side under circumstances of difficulty.

With regard to the Welsh-men, it must be said that they left the impression of not being quite up to the standard of some past Welsh fifteens. Their forwards were admirable, but the halves and three-quarters did not display that finished combination former teams have shown.

A drawn game
But Light Blues should have won

Quite in accordance with expectations based upon the form the teams had shown in their trial games, the Rugby match between the rival Universities at the Queen's Club, West Kensington, on Saturday, produced a close struggle. A hard battle, extending over eighty minutes of actual play, ended in a draw, each side scoring a placed goal and a try.

The result was barely satisfactory. On the afternoon Cambridge were the better side, and should have won. Indeed, a little steadiness on the part of their three-quarters in the last ten minutes would probably have secured for them a victory.

At one point the chances seemed to be that the Dark Blues would win comfortably. They scored a try in the first half, and five minutes after changing ends they added a goal, thus leading by 8 points. The game then looked to be practically over, but, as it happened, it then underwent a complete change. In no way dismayed by the position of affairs, the Cambridge men infused more life into their play, their forwards quite carrying all before them. For the remainder of the game, or the best part of it, the attack rested with the Light Blues, and, though none too skilfully conducted, it was successful on two occasions. Amid a scene of great excitement and enthusiasm, Cambridge drew level, and afterwards they were twice within an ace of adding to their score.

It is true the Oxford three-quarters displayed the better combination when their chances came, but when their forwards were overpowered their work was almost entirely of a defensive nature. Further, they were unfortunate in the fact that early in the second half Raphael fell lame, and was placed on the wing, Sandford coming inside. This change naturally made some difference, though it probably did not materially affect the issue.

Though he obtained Oxford's first try, Raphael was not seen at his best, making more than one bad mistake. He certainly jeopardised his chances of playing for England this season. To Walkey fell the distinction of gaining both tries for Cambridge, but, though he did not score, Pumphrey, the left wing three-quarter, made admirable use of the few opportunities that fell to him, twice being pulled up only a stride or two from the goal-line.

The record now stands: England 11 wins, Wales 7 wins, and one drawn game.

[The single-point victory in the first international of the season determined the Championship, as both sides went on to win their other two matches.]

1903

10 Jan A downpour at St Helen's, Swansea, before the start of the Wales-England game fills the band's instruments and they have to stop playing.

15 Aug In their first international, New Zealand, with their revolutionary 2-3-2 scrummage, beat Australia 22-3 at Sydney Cricket Ground, dazzling the 30,000 crowd as full-back Billy Wallace kicks 12pts. This is the only international in the 10 matches played, and won, by the tourists in New South Wales and Queensland.

26 Aug In the drawn 1st Test at Johannesburg, the British Isles are captained by Mark Morrison, who had the opposing captain, Alex Frew, under him in the 1901 Scottish Triple Crown XV, and played in the same 1896 Scottish side as referee Bill Donaldson.

12 Sep South Africa beat the British Isles 8-0 in the deciding test at Newlands, Cape Town, the first two having been drawn (10-10 and 0-0). The full tour record is P22, W11, D3, L8, Pts 231-138.

INTERNATIONAL CHAMPIONSHIP

	E	I	S	W	P	W	D	L	F	A	Pts
1 SCOTLAND	-	3-0	-	6-0	3	3	0	0	19	6	6
2 WALES	21-5	18-0	-	-	3	2	0	1	39	11	4
3 IRELAND	6-0	-	-	-	3	1	0	2	6	21	2
4 ENGLAND	-	-	6-10	-	3	0	0	3	11	37	0

TOURS (Internationals)
New Zealand in Australia: A3-NZ22
British Isles in South Africa: SA10-BI10, SA0-BI0, SA8-BI0

International Championship: Wales 21 England 5, Swansea, 10 January

A great Welsh victory

To the satisfaction of some 30,000 spectators, the Welsh fifteen at Swansea on Saturday gained a notable triumph, beating England by 3 goals and 2 tries to 1 goal. The decisive nature of the result came as a surprise, a close game having been anticipated by both sides.

However, it may at once be said that the victory was rendered all the more meritorious from the fact that after the first quarter of an hour Wales played one man short. The Welsh captain, Tom Pearson, the left-wing three-quarter, was hurt in a collision with Gamlin and was compelled to leave the field. Jehoida Hodges was withdrawn from the front rank to go on the left wing, and scored three tries.

Though their backs did all the scoring, the chief honours of the victory rested with the forwards. The seven scrummagers proved quite equal to the occasion, fairly and squarely beating the English eight, in the first half at all events.

In the first half Wales had the advantage of playing with a wind which blew very strongly for some time, but towards half-time abated. Settling down to their work in rapid fashion, the Welsh scrummagers very soon bustled the English forwards off their legs, and for a prolonged period held the upper hand. Only once during the first half did England reach their opponents' line.

The match had been in progress less than ten minutes when a bout of passing, in which Owen, Rees and Gabe took part, ended in Pearson gaining a try, which Strand-Jones converted into a goal. The ball was repeatedly with the Welsh backs, and the England defence was sorely taxed. Rees missed a good chance of scoring, and directly afterwards came the injury to Pearson, who was tackled by Gamlin just outside the line. Though Hodges came out of the pack, the Welsh scrummagers continued to have the best of matters, and a neat piece of work by the Welsh halves resulted in Owen scoring, Strand-Jones placing another goal.

By this time it was obvious that the Welshmen were the superior side, and they very soon materially added to their lead. After a brilliant bout of passing, in the course of which the ball passed through several hands, Hodges gained a try near the corner, and a little later a blunder by Taylor gave Gabe a chance, and the Welsh centre cleared the way for Hodges to score again.

Then for a brief period England attacked, but without success. Hesitation on the part of the English forwards enabled Strand-Jones to initiate a movement which ended in Hodges gaining his third try. Strand-Jones kicked a fine goal, and at half-time

---

International Championship: Scotland 6 Wales 0, Inverleith, 7 February

History repeats itself

History repeated itself at Edinburgh on Saturday. Four years ago the Welshmen easily overcame England and subsequently lost to Scotland, and now this season Wales, after administering a bad beating to the English fifteen, have once more succumbed to the men over the Border. To put the result briefly, Scotland defeated Wales by a penalty goal and a try to nothing.

In passing it may be observed that the various Scotch fifteens have always won against the representatives of the Principality on the Inverleith ground. Saturday's game was a most unsatisfactory affair. It was played under conditions in which the element of luck preponderated too largely. Several hours of rain in the morning had left the ground little better than a quagmire, and, to make matters worse, something approaching a hurricane prevailed, while during the progress of the game rain fell more or less smartly at intervals.

It was a tremendously hard struggle in which at times a little unnecessary roughness was introduced, but it was not much better than a rough-and-tumble scramble, productive of plucky saving and numerous blunders.

Scotland first had the assistance of the gale which blew from corner to corner, but they did not make full use of their luck in winning the toss. They had all the best of the play in the opening half, and led at the interval by three points. The game had been in progress less than ten minutes when Scotland obtained their penalty goal, Timms, with a beautiful kick, dropping it from nearly forty yards distance.

About ten minutes from the finish came the best play in the match. By another rush, the Scotch scrummagers reached the mid-field, and a minute later the ball went into touch in the Welsh twenty-five. From the line-out the Scotchmen broke away and bore down on their opponents' line. In the fierce struggle that ensued, Morrison tried to get over, but lost the ball. Happily for Scotland, Kyle picked it up, and went over the line. The game was as good as over.

Wales held the formidable lead of 21 points.

There is no need to enter into any detail of the play in the second-half, as all real interest in the match had vanished. England's score came about twenty minutes after the interval. There was some passing between the backs, and Taylor, finding himself unable to break through, kicked across. In the scramble that ensued, Dobson picked up and dashed over, Taylor placing a goal.

The Welsh backs' swift passing movements enthralled the 30,000 spectators at Swansea.

1904

2 Jul Captained by the Scotland and Cambridge wing-forward "Darkie" Bedell-Sivright, the British Isles win the 1st Test with Australia 17-0 at Sydney. With Bedell-Sivright injured, the Welsh three-quarter Teddy Morgan takes over the captaincy, and the side, enjoying a substantial Welsh contingent for the first time, and inspired by the tactical genius Percy Bush at fly-half, go on to win all 14 matches in Australia, with a 265-51 points record.

13 Aug The British Isles play their first Test in New Zealand, the only one on their Antipodean tour, losing 9-3 at Wellington in front of a 25,000 crowd. After their successful tour in Australia, this is a warning of things to come for the British side, who are also beaten by Auckland and, in an unofficial match, by a Maori XV, finishing the NZ leg of their tour with a W2-D1-L2 record.

25 Oct Former Oxford Blue Percy Coles, an original member of the Barbarians, is appointed the first paid secretary of the RFU.

INTERNATIONAL CHAMPIONSHIP

	E	I	S	W	P	W	D	L	F	A	Pts
1 SCOTLAND	6-3	-	-	-	3	2	0	1	28	27	4
2=WALES	-	-	21-3	-	3	1	1	1	47	31	3
2=ENGLAND	-	19-0	-	14-14	3	1	1	1	36	20	3
4 IRELAND	-	-	3-19	14-12	3	1	0	2	17	50	2

TOURS (Tests)
British Isles in Australia: A0-BI17, A3-BI17, A0-BI16
British Isles in New Zealand: NZ9-BI3

International Championship: England 14 Wales 14, Leicester, 9 January

Exciting struggle ends all square

After an extremely exciting struggle, the match at Leicester on Saturday ended in a draw, each side scoring 14 points. It was a curious and bewildering kind of game, and one that, as to the respective merits of the teams, will always be a matter of controversy. A draw, though arrived at by unusual scoring, was perhaps the most appropriate result.

Paradoxical as the statement may seem, each side should have won. With accurate place-kicking, England should have obtained a lead in the first half sufficient to have put the result beyond reasonable doubt, but they succeeded with only one of their many penalty kicks.

On the other hand, there was a strong element of luck in all three tries gained by the Englishmen, while the two that fell to Wales were the outcome of delightful and well-judged passing by the backs, the wing man on each occasion scoring after the ball had gone through several hands. Still, Wales were fortunate that Winfield managed to kick two exceptional goals, one from a difficult angle and the other from a long distance.

For a time the game was marred by the frequency with which the referee had to award penalty kicks, the majority of them against the Welshmen. Though Elliott gained two tries, he clearly should not have been in the England team, as he has not sufficient pace for a wing three-quarter. He had three fine chances after the centres had cleared the way for him, but he failed to get through. Finally, the forwards got through and, coming across from the left, Elliott joined in the rush and picked up to score close to the posts. Vivyan failed at the easy place-kick. But a couple of minutes later Wales were again penalised, and this time Gamlin placed a good goal to give England a half-time lead of 6 points to nil.

The play after the interval was of quite a remarkable kind, brimful of interesting incidents. The spectators, among whom was a strong contingent of Welshmen, were kept in a state of excitement. The Welsh XV began in excellent style, and soon Llewellyn scored, Winfield placing the goal. But then Gamlin got on the ball, and the spectators witnessed the unusual spectacle of a full back making a long and clever dribble. The ball was kicked across, and Elliott scored his second try, Gamlin just failing to place the goal. This put England ahead by 4 points.

The Welsh team, however, were playing much the better, and a movement carried on by their halves and three-quarters ended in Morgan scoring. Winfield kicked the goal from the touch line, and Wales led for the first time, by

---

The international at Edinburgh: England are in white.

International Championship: Scotland 6 England 3, Edinburgh, 19 March

Scotland retain the Championship

In the presence of probably 20,000 spectators, on the Inverleith Ground, Edinburgh, on Saturday, the Scotch fifteen defeated England by 2 tries to 1 try. The game was the last of the Internationals, and by their victory Scotland not only retain possession of the Calcutta Cup, but of the championship itself.

It is many years since England won the first place among the Unions, and a draw would have sufficed for that purpose. Three seasons ago, at Blackheath, a penalty goal lost them the championship, and on Saturday, within a few minutes of time, a blunder cost them the game.

The match for the most part was confined to the forwards, and while due allowance must be made for the accident to the England captain Daniell, it cannot be denied that the Scotch scrummagers lasted better than their opponents.

Scotland had the benefit of the wind in the first half, and for the greater part of the time kept the play in the English half. Gillespie opened up the game, and McLeod cleared the way for Crabbie to gain a capital try, the only score of the first half.

Early in the second half, Hancock picked up in the loose and threw the ball out to Dillon. The latter cleared the way for Vivyan, who scored under the posts, but then hit the cross-bar with his hurried kick.

After that, the game was fought out, for the most part, a few yards from the England line. The English defence was splendid and looked like holding up during the last ten minutes, Gamlin doing great work. Then came the fatal blunder. Vivyan's attempted punt was charged down by MacDonald, who went on, gathered the ball, and scored near the corner.

---

10 points to 9. England looked in more trouble until Vivyan intercepted a pass and made a long run before kicking the ball over the Welsh line. Brettargh got to the ball first to score, and Stout kicked a capital goal, placing England 4 points in front. But 3 minutes later the lead disappeared when Winfield scored a goal from a mark just inside the England half.

Just before the end, England were lucky to escape with a draw when Morgan crossed their line but was adjudged to have knocked on.

1905

16 Sep The newly named 'All Blacks' beat Devon at Exeter 55-4 (8 goals, 4 tries, 1 pen goal against 1 drop goal), but fail to impress the British critics, the Daily Telegraph observing: 'Much of the New Zealand passing was slow and faulty, the ball often being parted with in a somewhat reckless manner; and although at times their general combination was admirable, it unquestionably fell short of the Welsh standard,' while the sub-editor on a London daily paper confidently corrects the incoming score to 5-4 in favour of the tourists. [The All Blacks eventually leave the British Isles after winning 31 of their 32 matches (830-39pts), losing only the controversial match with Wales, but outplaying both England and Ireland by 15-0 and beating Scotland 12-7.]

Laws Goal from a mark reduced from 4pts to 3

INTERNATIONAL CHAMPIONSHIP

	E	I	S	W	P	W	D	L	F	A	Pts
1 WALES	25-0	10-3	-	-	3	3	0	0	41	6	6
2 IRELAND	17-3	-	-	-	3	2	0	1	31	18	4
3 SCOTLAND	-	5-11	-	3-6	3	1	0	2	16	17	2
4 ENGLAND	-	-	0-8	-	3	0	0	3	3	50	0

TOURS (Tests)
Australia in New Zealand: NZ14-A3
New Zealand in British Isles: S7-NZ12, I0-NZ15, E0-NZ15, W3-NZ0

International Championship: Wales 10 Ireland 3, Swansea, 11 March

Struggle for the Championship

Tour Match: Wales 3 New Zealand 0, Cardiff, 16 December

New Zealand's first reverse

Memorable conflict

After a tremendous conflict, which will be memorable in the annals of Rugby football, the New Zealanders suffered the first defeat of their tour at Cardiff on Saturday, the Welsh fifteen beating them by one try to nothing. Never, perhaps, has an international aroused such widespread interest, and in view of defeats sustained by Scotland, Ireland, and England at the hands of the Colonials, the result is very welcome.

The remarkable series of successes gained by our visitors – they had prior to Saturday's encounter won 27 games off the reel – had created quite a feeling of dismay which had penetrated even into the Principality. The Welshmen realised to the full that they had a great task before them, and that they were the last defenders of the prestige of Rugby football on this side of the globe. Happily, they were equal to the occasion.

That the Welshmen deserved their win and were on the afternoon the better side cannot be disputed. Whether they are as good football players as the New Zealanders have shown themselves to be is quite another question, and, the Principality apart, would be answered by most good judges of the game in the negative.

The chief honours of the Welsh victory rested with their forwards. For perhaps the first time during the tour the New Zealand 'hookers' found, if not their masters, at least their equals in the art of obtaining possession of the ball in the scrummage. But perhaps the most outstanding feature of the game was the singularly accurate fielding and kicking of Bert Winfield, the Welsh full-back. He gathered the ball beautifully, and rarely failed to find touch some fifty yards away.

Cliff Pritchard, who was mainly concerned in watching Gallaher, performed his duties so well that the New Zealand wing forward was not seen to anything like his customary advantage. Owen worked the scrummage cleverly, and to his astuteness Wales were largely indebted for their try, and Bush, the half to stand away, accomplished a lot of good work. As was expected, Gabe and Morgan on the left made the stronger and more dangerous pair, and it was in every way fitting that the solitary try should be gained by Morgan, who is still the finest wing three-quarter in the kingdom.

In dealing with the play of the New Zealanders, one must confess to a feeling of surprise. Their forwards were sluggish, and their backs, mainly through the frequent blundering of Mynott and Hunter at five-eighths, were all at sea. Possibly the men, feeling the strain of the tour, have grown stale, but whatever the cause, they failed to do themselves

After a severe game at Swansea on Saturday, the fight for the international championship resulted in a triumph for the Welsh fifteen by 10 points to 3. The game was largely made up of hard scrummages, rapid forward rushes, and determined tackling.

There was a complete absence of any suspicion of rough play, both sides fighting out their great battle in a thoroughly sportsmanlike manner.

For the first forty minutes Wales played with the wind – a big advantage. But the Irish forwards went off, as usual, at a great pace, and in five or six minutes the visitors had scored their try. After a scramble, the ball went over the line, and Robinson was first on it.

Half an hour slipped by, and Ireland were still holding their own. But five minutes later the game had undergone a complete transformation, Wales in that brief space of time scoring twice. Wyndham Jones, after a neat run, slipped over near the posts, and Davies placed a goal. Directly afterwards, the Welsh scrummagers, with a really magnificent burst half the length of the ground, reached the goal-line, and Morgan, who was up with them, pounced on the ball and scored, Davies kicking a fine goal.

Thus, Wales crossed over at the interval leading by seven points, and their defence, even with the wind against them, were rarely in serious trouble.

justice. Roberts played a great game at half, but most of his swift passes were either knocked on or missed by the five-eighths. Deans was an unsatisfactory centre, and Gillett was an indifferent full-back.

The first serious movement was started by Harding getting in a useful cross-kick, which was well followed up by Llewellyn. This took the game right on to the Colonial line, and led up to the scoring of the try.

In the second half, the Colonial forwards worked much harder, but were usually sent back by the fine kicking of Winfield. Wallace did cross the Welsh line, but, unfortunately for his side, had just gone into touch in doing so. Once the game went on right under the Welsh posts, and several desperate efforts were made to break through.

After an anxious period Wales managed to clear, and Bush very nearly dropped a goal with a long shot. Once more the New Zealanders made a fine attempt to save the match, and must have scored had not a pass by Deans to McGregor been a forward one. That trouble over, the Welshmen took the game into their own hands, and during the last four or five minutes the New Zealanders were on the defensive.

[A controversy of legendary proportions grew up out of an incident in this match, the All Blacks claiming that centre Bob Deans had scored a try. It was not given, apparently, because he grounded the ball when tackled a few feet from the line. It is still argued about today, whenever New Zealand fans visit Cardiff Arms Park, even though the protagonists are long dead.]

1906

13 Feb The All Blacks play in North America on their way home from Europe, and in their last match, at Berkeley, California, the Taranaki wing three-quarter Bunny Abbott plays for the Canadians in an emergency and scores a try against the New Zealanders.

22 Mar The first official international between France and England takes place at the Parc des Princes, Paris, with England winning by 35-8 (4G, 5T to 1G, 1T). There are upwards of 5,500 spectators who pay a French record of £277 at the gate (except for the £480 that came in for the match v the All Blacks, but then the charges were doubled!). English visitors at the match express the opinion that after a few more years' practice the French team will be a match for anyone.

League The Northern Union, the breakaway Rugby League, diverges further from its mother code with the reduction of the number of players to 13.

Tour Match: France 8 All Blacks 38, Parc des Princes, 1 January

Losers intoxicated with triumph

From Our Own Correspondent

This has been a great day for football in France, the greatest day ever known. France scored eight points against the 'All Blacks'! Think of it! The New Zealanders' 38 points (4 goals and 6 tries) are relatively nothing to the French goal and try under the circumstances.

I came back from the game in a delirious crowd of young Frenchmen. They dreamt of the day when football shall become a national game in this country. They were intoxicated with triumph, measuring the distance between what France showed this afternoon and the miserable achievements of but half a dozen years ago. Young Frenchmen, all of whom seemed to have in England dreamt of a time when the street boys in Paris shall practise gutter-football and pavement-cricket, in winter and summer, as they do with us, and today's match gave them a great hope that that time may now not be so far off after all.

The spirit of outdoor sport is more alive among French boys than we often suppose. One had only to see and hear the delight of all young boys, and elderly boys as well, when France scored a try, then actually a second try, and converted it, to understand what strides athletics have made in France within the last few years.

Eight points against the 'All Blacks', the same score as Cardiff – it was wonderful. France actually equalled the top score recorded against New Zealand during the entire tour. It was, indeed, a great day for football in France, and all the greater because the French crowd appreciated thoroughly how great it was.

[This was France's first official rugby international.]

Tour Match: Scotland 6 Springboks 0, Hampden Park, 17 November

South Africans' tour: Their first defeat

The South Africans, after winning fifteen games off the reel, sustained their first defeat, the Scotland XV beating them by 2 tries to 0. It may at once be said that the success of Scotland was a thoroughly genuine one, and that, on the afternoon, they were unquestionably the better side.

Owing to recent wet weather, the ground was very soft and heavy, and rain fell during the greater part of the game. It has to be said that the home fifteen's style of play was more suited to the conditions, but the Scotchmen won fairly on their merits and indeed were unlucky not to have won by a larger margin.

Kenneth McLeod, who was on the wing, was quite the hero of the afternoon, fully maintaining his high reputation. Displaying great versatility, he not only gained one of the tries, but came very near dropping a goal and helped his side by his judicious kicking and general tactics.

[This was South Africa's first Test in the British Isles. They did not lose another until 1965!]

INTERNATIONAL CHAMPIONSHIP										
	E	I	S	W	P	W	D	L	F	A	Pts
1=WALES	-	-	9-3	-	3	2	0	1	33	25	4
1=IRELAND	-	-	6-13	11-6	3	2	0	1	31	17	4
3=SCOTLAND	3-9	-	-	-	3	1	0	2	19	24	2
3=ENGLAND	-	6-16	-	3-16	3	1	0	2	18	35	2

TOURS (Tests)
New Zealand in France: F8-NZ38
South Africa in British Isles*: E3-SA3, I12-SA15, S6-SA0, W0-SA11
* Tests played in 1906, but tour finished New Year's Day 1907

International Championship: Ireland 11 Wales 6, Belfast, 10 March

Depleted Irish deny Wales Triple Crown

Beating Wales at Belfast on Saturday by a goal and 2 tries to 2 tries, the Irishmen inflicted the first defeat the representatives of the Principality have had to admit since the encounter on the same ground two years ago.

The Welshmen entered into the contest with the confidence born of triumphs this season over New Zealand, England and Scotland, and their success was generally anticipated; but Ireland played their traditional game in brilliant style, and were rewarded with a well-deserved victory.

But when, shortly before the interval, their half-back Purdon had the ligaments of a knee so badly torn that he had to be carried off the field, the spectators, despite the fact that Ireland led at the time by 8 points to 3, were quite prepared to see the home side lose their advantage. After a try apiece in the second half, the Welsh were still a goal behind, but the Irish redoubled their efforts and were pressing in the Welsh twenty-five when their other half, Caddell, had to be carried off, in this case with a leg broken just above the ankle.

Thus they had to contest the closing stages of the match with only six forwards against the Welsh eight. They bravely held out, and there was no further scoring. The thirteen men gained a memorable victory, enabling Ireland to draw level with Wales in the championship.

[Ireland and Wales shared the title.]

Tour Match: Ireland 12 Springboks 15, Belfast, 24 November

Colonials just win
Irishmen's grand recovery

After a remarkable struggle and an intensely exciting finish, the South Africans won their second international engagement, defeating Ireland by 1 penalty goal and 4 tries to 1 penalty goal and 3 tries.

Almost throughout, the play was of a stirring nature, being fast, bright, and open, but the most dramatic incidents came in the last twenty minutes, when the Irishmen, apparently a well-beaten side, made an heroic attempt to pull the match out of the fire. After being 9 points to the bad, and facing a fairly strong wind, they actually drew level. But they could carry their stupendous effort no further and the South Africans scored again. Defeat, however, was deprived of nearly all its bitterness.

Basil Maclear stood out for Ireland as the commanding figure, and his try, obtained after running three-fourths the length of the ground, would in itself have sufficed to have made the match memorable in the annals of great games.

[On the following Saturdays, the Springboks beat Wales 11-0 and drew 3-3 with England.]

1907

3 Jan The Springboks, smarting from their shock defeat by Cardiff two days earlier, thrash a representative French side (composed of 9 players from Stade Français and 6 from Racing Club de France) 55-6 at the Parc des Princes.

16 Mar Scotland beat England 8-3 at Blackheath to take the Triple Crown for a record 5th time and condemn the hosts to the Wooden Spoon for the 3rd time in succession.

The all-round sportsman William Williams selects a site for the new Rugby Union headquarters, 10 acres of market garden at Twickenham, which they purchase for £5,572 12s 6d.

International Match: England 41 France 13, Richmond, 5 January

Visitors' plucky effort

Though there was no likelihood of a close struggle some 7,000 spectators assembled at Richmond on Saturday to welcome the French fifteen on the occasion of the first international encounter between the two countries in England. The match, as was practically inevitable, ended in an easy victory for the Englishmen, who scored 6 goals (one dropped) and 4 tries, as against 3 goals (one penalty).

The game was, however, much more interesting to watch than the score would indicate, as, with England taking a grave liberty, the French team, seizing upon two or three chances, drew level before half-time after being 13 points to the bad.

Early in the proceedings Lee, the Blackheath full back, had the misfortune to break a rib in stopping a hard forward rush, and, after making a plucky effort to keep his place, was ultimately compelled to retire. At that point England were leading by 13 points, and for some time dispensed with a full back. A very proper penalty was paid for holding their opponents thus lightly, as the visitors quickly gained a couple of capital tries, both of which were converted, and a third goal was kicked from a penalty.

Subsequently Mills was withdrawn from the pack to full back, and, taking matters more seriously, the English team had not the least difficulty in winning the game a second time. The chief factor in England's victory was the brilliant combination of the three Harlequins – the dazzling Stoop (AD) at half-back and the left wing of Birkett and Lambert, the latter making splendid use of his chances to score five tries.

It would be discourteous to our visitors to subject their play or their methods to such close or severe criticism as might with propriety be employed in the case of more experienced players.

Rugby is in its infancy in France, but it is progressing steadily.

International Championship: Scotland 6 Wales 3, Edinburgh, 2 February

Keen game at Edinburgh: Principality beaten

After a keen fight and an exciting finish on Saturday, Scotland defeated Wales by 2 tries to 1 penalty goal, thus gaining their thirteenth victory over the Principality. The Scotch fifteen quite deserved their success, if for no other reason than from the simple fact that, while their own defence was impregnable, they twice succeeded in crossing their opponents' line.

Having regard to the different styles of the two countries, it is a little strange that the solitary Welsh score should have been a brilliant individual effort, a splendid penalty goal from close to the touch line by full back Winfield in the first half, and that the Scotchmen should have gained two tries, by Purves and Monteith, the second after Winfield had retired injured.

The failure of the Welsh fifteen to carry through successfully any one of their many attacks was perhaps the most notable fact in connection with the game. It is true they came desperately near doing so in the last five minutes, but their inability to overcome a defence that, though good and steady, was in no way exceptional, was significant.

While Scotland played the customary formation, Wales, encouraged no doubt by their success against England, relied on seven forwards and eight backs, one of whom – Gibbs – was entrusted with a roving commission. Lest there may be any misconception on the point, it may be said that the Welsh methods were not those adopted by the New Zealanders.

The latter also played seven forwards and eight backs, but their scrummage formation and distribution of the backs division differed materially from those of the Welshmen. It was the compromise between two styles that was on trial on Saturday.

Tour Match: Cardiff 17 South Africans 0, Cardiff, 1 January

South Africans' defeat
Surprise end of the tour:
Welshmen's great game

After losing only one game in 27, the South Africans, at Cardiff, yesterday, in the last match of their tour sustained a heavy reverse, the Cardiff fifteen defeating them by 2 goals (1 penalty) and 3 tries to 0. The result is, of course, a great surprise, as on the form that has been shown so far this season there seemed no reason to anticipate that the Cardiff team would prove themselves capable of doing any better than the other Welsh sides that had met the Colonials. As it was, however, the Cardiff men rose to the occasion in a superb manner, and were rewarded with a great triumph that will do much to restore the prestige of Welsh Rugby.

It was extremely unfortunate that the conditions yesterday were about as unfavourable for football as could well be imagined. A strong wind blew down the field, and with rain falling more or less throughout the match, the ground, already very soft, was soon in a terrible state, being for the greater portion of its surface nothing else than a muddy swamp. The Welshmen more readily adapted themselves to the conditions, playing indeed much better football than one would have deemed possible, while the Colonials floundered about a good deal, being seemingly helpless in the sea of mud.

Perhaps the most gratifying feature of the game was the superb play of Gwyn Nicholls. At Swansea the famous three-quarter was so much below his best form as to suggest that his day for serious football was past, but yesterday he was his old self, exhibiting great generalship and running with a rare pace on the heavy going. Naturally, with Nicholls in such a happy mood, Gabe, his partner in the centre, also acquitted himself far better than for Wales, and both in attack and defence they made a splendid pair. Each had the satisfaction of gaining a try, and between them contributed largely to the general success.

	E	I	S	W	P	W	D	L	F	A	Pts
INTERNATIONAL CHAMPIONSHIP											
1 SCOTLAND	-	15-3	-	6-3	3	3	0	0	29	9	6
2 WALES	22-0	29-0	-	-	3	2	0	1	54	6	4
3 IRELAND	17-9	-	-	-	3	1	0	2	20	53	2
4 ENGLAND	-	-	3-8	-	3	0	0	3	12	47	0

TOURS (Tests)

New Zealand in Australia: A6-NZ26, A5-NZ14, A5-NZ5

1908

14 Mar By their 11-5 defeat of Ireland in Belfast, Wales not only gain their fifth Triple Crown to equal Scotland's record, but are the first to beat the other three home countries and France in the same season, although this is not a Grand Slam because France are not yet in the International Championship.

25 Jul New Zealand win the last Test 29-0 at Auckland to take the series against the British Isles by 2-0 with one drawn. With the other countries declining to lend their support, the Anglo-Welsh touring party, captained by Cardiff and London Welsh

forward AF 'Boxer' Harding, having won 7 of their 9 games in Australia (no Tests played), finish the NZ leg with a W9-L7-D1 record.

22 Oct France, due to play Cornwall (representing the UK) in the first match of the Olympic tournament at the White City Stadium on Monday (26 Oct), are unable to get together a XV from the 44 names submitted to the Olympic Council and withdraw from the competition, leaving the other two entrants, the UK and Australia, to contest the final.

INTERNATIONAL CHAMPIONSHIP

	E	I	S	W	P	W	D	L	F	A	Pts
1 WALES	-	-	6-5	-	3	3	0	0	45	28	6
2=SCOTLAND	16-10	-	-	-	3	1	0	2	32	32	2
2=ENGLAND	-	13-3	-	18-28	3	1	0	2	41	47	2
2=IRELAND	-	-	16-11	5-11	3	1	0	2	24	35	2

TOURS (Tests)

British Isles in New Zealand: NZ32-BI5, NZ3-BI3, NZ29-BI0

International Championship: England 18 Wales 28, Ashton Gate, Bristol, 18 January

Another Welsh victory: Game played in fog

After a singular match, played amid exasperating surroundings, Wales defeated England by 5 goals (1 dropped and 1 penalty) and 2 tries to 3 goals and 1 try, and by their success take the lead of England in the matter of wins. Practically everything had been done to ensure the success of the game, which, being the first Rugby international played in Bristol, had aroused great local interest, but, unhappily for all concerned – and there were some 25,000 present – fog set in and quite spoiled the match. At no time was it possible to see distinctly the width of the field of play, and in the later stages the occupants of the stands frequently lost sight of both teams.

Though regret will be felt at the failure of the England fifteen to break the long run of ill-success, some

consolation may be derived from the fact that they crossed the Welsh line four times. Such a feat had not been accomplished by an England side since 1898, and in a sense the Englishmen could regard themselves as the victims of misfortune in scoring 18 points and then being beaten. In all the games played between the four countries, there is no previous instance of the kind.

Percy Bush, the Cardiff half, with whom Vile worked well, was a source of great trouble to the English. He laid down the foundation of the victory by dropping a goal in the first few minutes, later on gaining a clever try, while he had a hand in nearly all the good work accomplished. Bush is a player of great gifts, and as an outside half he has on his day no superior.

Olympic Games Final: Australia 32 United Kingdom 3, White City, 26 October

Big colonial victory: English outplayed

By Major Philip Trevor

The Australians beat Cornwall [representing the UK] very badly indeed at the Stadium by 32 points to 3, and the victory was a remarkable one for several reasons. It will be remembered that less than a month ago there was a match played between Australia and Cornwall at Camborne, and although the Australians also won on that occasion, the beaten side then played, on the whole, a very good game. Yesterday the champion English county was practically at full strength, but from start to finish they were outplayed.

The methods by which this victory was gained were even more creditable to the

winners than the completeness of the victory itself, and it is only fair to the Australians to speak of their play in terms of unqualified praise. The ground was very slippery and very heavy, and as a result of several hours' continuous rain the ball was very greasy. The continued excellence of the play of the Australian backs therefore surprised the spectators agreeably. They gave a display of football which would have done credit to a Welsh international side at their best. They scored eight tries, and so good was the play which led up to each of them that it would be hard to say which was the best.

Tour match: Wales 9 Australia 6, Cardiff, 12 December

Twenty-second match of tour: Colonials just beaten

By Major Philip Trevor

The Welshmen deserved to win the big match played at Cardiff on Saturday. They made football history by defeating the Australians in their first international on British soil.

In Winfield the Welsh had a man capable of taking advantage of an opponent's error. During the first fifteen minutes, he made a couple of bad mistakes himself. But they were his only mistakes, and they went unpunished. He soon began to atone for them by kicking the ball dead when

it seemed that Richards must score after dribbling the ball across the Welsh goal-line.

Some three minutes later came the first score, Travers crossing the Australian line after good work by Owen and Hopkins. Five minutes later was seen the gem of the match. A bout of passing, begun by the Australian backs, was taken up by their forwards, and it was in midfield that the movement was left under the direction of Craig and Richards. A superb exhibi-

tion of that short passing in which the Australian forwards excel ended in these two men finishing alone under the goal posts for Richards to score. The Welsh crowd greeted this denouement with the loud cheering which it well deserved. But to the surprise of everyone, Carmichael's place-kick failed, and the scores stayed equal at 3 points each at half-time.

Nine minutes after the restart, the Welshmen scored again. Charging down a kick, three of the Welsh forwards, travelling

fast, controlled the ball well with their feet; and, dashing up as it went over the line, Hopkins just managed to touch it with his hand. Again a place-kick failed.

Eleven minutes later, Winfield scored with a penalty kick, and then – and not till then – did the Australian backs play with something like their customary dash. Russell gained a try in the extreme right-hand corner to reduce the lead, but the Welshmen bravely held out in the last fifteen minutes.

1909

9 Jan England, in their last international at Blackheath, go down 9-3 to the Australians, who are playing the 29th match of their England/Wales tour, having lost to four Welsh sides (including Wales) and the Midland Counties. The Wallabies, whose side includes 13 NSW players (plus 2 from Queensland), eventually finish with a P31-W25-D1-L5 record.

13 Mar Wales beat Ireland 18-5 at Swansea and become the first country to win back-to-back Triple Crowns.

20 Mar At the Athletic Ground, Richmond, in their last home international before the opening of their permanent home at Twickenham, England suffer their sixth successive home defeat to

Scotland, 18-8 after leading 8-3 at half-time.

11 Dec England international Ronnie Poulton, arguably the most dangerous attacking three-quarter back in the country, is originally left out of Oxford's team for the Varsity Match and plays only because of the late withdrawal of Henry Vassall, nephew of the great Harry Vassall. Playing on the left wing, Poulton scores a record 5 tries in Oxford's record 35-3 victory over Cambridge, H Martin on the other wing scoring the other 4 - this despite Oxford losing their centre FN Tarr with a broken collar-bone after only 14 minutes when they were leading 8-0. Oxford forward DG Herring is the first American to play in the Varsity Match.

INTERNATIONAL CHAMPIONSHIP

	E	I	S	W	P	W	D	L	F	A	Pts
1 WALES	8-0	18-5	-	-	3	3	0	0	31	8	6
2 SCOTLAND	-	9-3	-	3-5	3	2	0	1	30	16	4
3 ENGLAND	-	-	8-18	-	3	1	0	2	19	31	2
4 IRELAND	5-11	-	-	-	3	0	0	3	13	38	0

TOURS (Tests)
Australia in England/Wales: E3-A9, W9-A6

13 December

Substitutes and malingering
By Major Philip Trevor

An interesting letter from an American on the subject of substitutes is on hand. He raises a point which has, of course, been raised before. Why, he asks, when a player has been injured in a game, should not a substitute be allowed to take his place?

Granted that ethically it is desirable that a man injured in a game should be replaced by another man. But is such a practice feasible in Rugby football? It is with a certain amount of shame that we have to admit that it is not. There is one insuperable objection to the system of the substitute. It would put a premium on malingering.

To substantiate this, a single illustration will suffice. It used to be the law that when a player was hurt the referee blew the whistle and stopped the game. Malingering ensued, as players would deliberately lie prostrate when an opposing attack threatened in order to have the game stopped. Nowadays, when a man is thought to be hurt, the whistle is not blown so long as the ball is in play, unless a continuation of play is, in the opinion of the

referee, dangerous to the prostrate man.

We should, I fear, have in certain places and among certain players malingering with a vengeance if the introduction of the substitute system again opened the sort of door which it has been found necessary to close and lock.

The reason for this kind of moral deterioration is easy enough to recognise. Day by day and week by week the tendency increases to think more of the result of a game than of the game itself. 'Win somehow' is the motto. The unspoken argument seems to be something to this effect: 'We have reached the limit of our skill and we are not prevailing; we must look in other directions for the gaining of an advantage.'

These evils are to be deplored; but as they exist, they have got to be faced. It will, then, be time enough seriously to consider the substitute suggestion when we notice a return in the general tone to those more robust and healthier days when even a referee was not needed.

Club Match: Harlequins 14 Richmond 10, Twickenham, 2 October

New ground opened

It has been rather unkindly said of the old-time Rugby Unionist that never in his active days did he hug an opponent with the effective tenacity which he now shows in hugging a grievance. I am afraid that we armchair critics are more than a little inclined to grumble, and so, when we approve, we make a great point of letting people know that we do approve. I proceed to duly record the fact that I heard praise that was practically universal expressed on the subject of English Rugby Union's new ground at Twickenham, which is, of course, the Harlequin Club's new home.

It is a magnificent football ground, though not in all respects perfection. The grass, like the hair of some of our clever friends, was at the opening performance a little too artistic in the matter of length, while more cinders or asphalt could be put with advantage in certain places. But these little defects are remediable. The stand accommodation is splendid, and sight from each stand is interfered with as little as possible by the strong yet slender pillars supporting the roof.

The public have practically nothing to complain about in regard to the ground, except perhaps on the score of inaccessibility. It is said to be a bare half-mile from Twickenham railway station. Perhaps that is so – as the crow flies; but to those of us who have not yet developed any Bleriot or Latham like tendency what the crow does

in this case is not supremely interesting. Addressing myself to the mere walker, I would say that I have lived in the neighbourhood in question off and on since I was a baby, and certainly this particular half-mile is a longer one than any of the other half-miles in that part of the world.

The weather was fine, and so were both the attendance and the game. Indeed, it was a case of congratulations all round. In the end the visitors were beaten by the rather narrow margin of 4 points.

Under the able guidance of AD Stoop, whose resource on Saturday last was practically never at fault, the Harlequin backs gave a most welcome exhibition of clever as well as strong play in attack. At half-

time the score was 9 points to nil in favour of the home side, the result of tries gained by AD Stoop, Birkett, and Lambert. After half-time, Odgers, who always played superbly, scored a couple of

Harlequins play Richmond at the new Twickenham ground.

tries for Richmond, which Terry converted. Harlequins' fourth try was the result of a superb movement. All the men who were supposed to act

in combination did so, and FM Stoop, in fine style, put the finishing touch to a really great exhibition of Rugby football.

The 1910s

Before the last five years of the decade were effectively lost to World War I, France joined the home unions to make the International Championship a five-nation competition, although they did not gain representation on the International Rugby Football Board. England gave up two of their seats on the Board in 1911, leaving themselves with four and the rest of the home countries with two each. The 'Colonials' were as yet not represented, even if they were, in the form of the Springboks and the All Blacks, riding roughshod over anything the home countries could produce on the field. The second Springboks (1912-13), indeed, brought off the first Grand Slam by a touring side.

The proliferation of international matches was not universally accepted as a good thing for the game, and Major Philip Trevor, the chief rugby correspondent of The Daily Telegraph, sounded a cautionary note:

'Personally, I would rather see England continue to lose matches played against other countries if I were convinced that deterioration of club football was the price we had to pay for international success. Improve county football if you can; let us win international games if possible; but, above all things, keep the clubs the splendid institutions which, without help from headquarters, they have made themselves. Indeed, wherever and whenever any suggestion for the improvement of Rugby football is made, I do not think it would be applying to it a test which was either irrelevant or unfair if we promptly asked the question, "How will this affect club football?"'

Wales carried on their 'Golden Age' into this decade, although England took the Championship in 1910 by a point thanks to their defeat of Wales in the first International at Twickenham, and they remained unbeaten at headquarters in Championship matches until 1926. Wales won another Grand Slam in 1911 – the first in the Five Nations Tournament – before England took firm hold of the reins, sharing the title in 1912 before registering back-to-back Grand Slams. The men that made England great at this time would have been outstanding in any era – Ronnie Poulton, whose twinkling runs had the crowd on their feet and the opposition on the floor, and who, but for a sniper's bullet, would have captained his country for many years more; the incomparable CH 'Cherry' Pillman, who defined wing-forward technique, but never played again after breaking a leg in 1914; and Cyril Lowe, prolific try-scoring right wing, and elegant stand-off half WJA 'Dave' Davies,

whose careers spanned the war.

Major Trevor put the improvement in English rugby down to the public schools, and, in summarising the 1913-14 season, the last before the war, wrote: 'It is my firm conviction that from London clubs alone could be chosen at the moment at least half a dozen fifteens, any one of which on its merits could be demonstrated to be superior to any English international side of eight or ten years ago.' He also attributed the increasing popularity of the

game to a dramatic improvement in refereeing. In discussing the subject of 'cleanliness of methods', he referred to the existence of 'dirty tricks', and wrote: 'Rugby Unionists will be justified in insisting that public opinion shall help individual referees in stamping out what is practically the only blot on the fair page of Rugby football ....'

Strangely enough, crowd hooliganism also reared its ugly head briefly before the war, with French and Welsh spectators the chief culprits.

An artist's representation of the first international played at Twickenham – between England and Wales in 1910. England won 11-6 at their new headquarters.

1910

22 Jan In the first ever match between the two countries, Scotland beat France 27-0 at Inverleith.

12 Mar With 5 tries in their 19-3 victory over Ireland at Lansdowne Road, Wales create new records of 21 tries and 88 points in the International Championship (albeit with five nations now competing),

marks set to stand for many, many years.

19 Mar With the Stoop brothers, Adrian and Frank, playing together in the side for the first time, England beat Scotland 14-5 at Inverleith to win the first five-nations International Championship and their first title for 18 years.

The French team, in white shorts, in action at Swansea.

International Championship: Wales 49 France 14, Swansea, 1 January

France join the Championship: Easy Welsh victory

By Major Philip Trevor

At Swansea on Saturday was played the first of yet another international series of matches, and, as we read the history of our game, we can scarcely fail to be struck by the evidence of progress which this playing of international matches provides. It is not yet forty years since the first of these fixtures – England v Scotland – took place, and at that time there were two competitors, and two only. Now, with France joining in regular competition, there are eight.

That Wales would beat France with a good deal of ease had been generally expected, and the margin of 35 points by which victory was gained surprised no one. Such surprise, indeed, as there was, was furnished by the Frenchmen. As usual, they played with splendid pluck, and they never showed any signs of discouragement. When the teams changed ends the Welshmen led by only seven points, 21 to 14.

Most people expected that directly the game began again the Welsh scoring would begin in real earnest. However, for twenty minutes after half-time there was nothing practical done.

At length the desirability of

making their victory complete seemed to impress itself upon the winners, and when they had once begun to resort to cleverness and method, try-getting was frequent – so frequent, indeed, that no fewer than 28 points were added in less than twenty minutes. The final score was 9 goals (one of which was a penalty goal) and 2 tries to 3 goals (two of which were penalty goals) and a try. All the Welsh goal-kicking was done by Bancroft, and, seeing that it rained persistently throughout the match, his performance must be accounted a very good one.

Easily beaten as they were, their experience at Swansea should rather encourage the Frenchmen than dishearten them. In several essential particulars they showed not merely promising but very distinctly improved form. Their tackling is certainly infinitely better than it used to be.

The visitors must have been pleased with their reception. Indeed, all the applause in which the large Welsh crowd indulged was reserved for the Frenchmen.

[Jack Bancroft made a record 8 conversions in this match.]

International Championship: England 11 Wales 6, Twickenham, 15 January

England successful: A great game

By Major Philip Trevor

The thing has been done at last. An English fifteen, officially chosen by an English Selection Committee, have beaten the Welshmen. Rugby Unionists will scarcely need to be reminded that it was as far back as 1898 when England last beat Wales.

Now, in the first international at their new headquarters, England have won fairly and squarely by play that was not merely worthy and respectable, but

really dashing and clever.

On Saturday last in The Daily Telegraph I ventured to predict the success of England if only Adrian Stoop's bold finesse was in evidence. The match was only two seconds old when a most reassuring instance of it was forthcoming. Stoop caught the ball at kick-off, and very characteristically omitted to do the stereotyped thing. A dash, a swerve, and he was off, with the result that the Welshmen *[contd p.35, opposite]*

INTERNATIONAL CHAMPIONSHIP

	E	F	I	S	W	P	W	D	L	F	A	Pts
1 ENGLAND	-	-	0-0	-	11-6	4	3	1	0	36	14	7
2 WALES	-	49-14	-	14-0	-	4	3	0	1	88	28	6
3 SCOTLAND	5-14	27-0	-	-	-	4	2	0	2	46	28	4
4 IRELAND	-	-	-	0-14	3-19	4	1	1	2	11	36	3
5 FRANCE	3-11	-	3-8	-	-	4	0	0	4	20	95	0

Five nations competing for the first time.

TOURS (Tests)
New Zealand in Australia: A0-NZ6, A11-NZ0, A13-NZ28
British Isles in South Africa: SA-14-BI10, SA3-BI8, SA21-BI5

Tour Match: South Africa 14 British Isles 10, Johannesburg, 6 August

Colonial football: Rugby 'Test' lost

The British Rugby team this afternoon engaged in the first international match of their tour, and after a strenuous and exciting struggle were defeated by 14 points to 10. Glorious weather prevailed, and the crowd numbered 15,000.

After 25 minutes the South African three-quarters got going, and Devilliers succeeded in crossing the visitors' line with a brilliant try. Following this, the British fifteen played up in splendid style, and a clever, combined run by their backs ended in Foster getting over.

Early in the second half Hirsch was injured, but the Colonials continued to play a dashing game. From a splendid forward rush, Douglas Morkel raced over the British line, and shortly afterwards Luyt secured the ball from a scrum and

scored a fine try, which was converted by Douglas Morkel. Then the British side took up the attack, and in the midst of an exciting struggle in the South African '25', Jones got the ball and dropped a fine goal.

Encouraged by this success, the British team were soon pressing again, and after a brilliant bout of passing by the back division Spoors scored a try, thus reducing the South Africans' lead to 1 point. Both sides then played up desperately, and amid great excitement, Hahn got over the British line for the last try of the match.

[The British Isles went on to win 8-3 at Port Elizabeth, but lost the decider of this first official series in South Africa 21-5 at Cape Town after their influential Newport full-back Stanley Williams had to retire hurt with only 20 minutes played.]

Happy English supporters enjoy their victory over Wales.

[contd] were subjected to a sudden attack. There was a scrummage, and then in a flash Stoop made an opening for Birkett, who drew the defence on to himself, and gave his wing man, Chapman, a beautiful pass, which was very neatly taken. Chapman dashed over the line, and so, one minute after the start, England were three points ahead. To say that the Welshmen were surprised is to considerably understate the case.

Chapman then kicked a neat goal. The annual match, to which England are accustomed to be a losing side from start to finish, had been in progress only a quarter of an hour, and poor old England were actually six points ahead.

Then once again did the success of their opponents stimulate the Welsh forwards, and following a line-out Evans, a forward, scored a try. Two minutes after Bancroft's kick at goal had failed, Stoop set his three-quarter line going and Solomon made a capital run. On his right Chapman kept his position beautifully. The threatened pass was never given. Instead there was a feint, an inward swerve, and another try for England, which an extremely good place-kick by Chapman turned into a goal. And so England led by 8 points to 3 at the interval.

The Welsh back division did not appear to be playing with their customary confidence, and only one bout of passing was successful. It came after four minutes' play in the second half, and resulted in Gibbs, on the right of the three-quarter line, beating Poulton, and scoring after a capital run. The try was not converted.

Practically all the English forwards played well, and if one mentions Johns and the ever-reliable Chambers especially, it is not to be inferred that the others were not absolutely International form. It was a great game for Pillman, and few young forwards can have distingui-shed themselves as well in their first International match.

Of Adrian Stoop enough has been said. He is a great player and a great captain, and to him do we primarily owe the gaining of a victory which was very badly needed.

1911

28 Jan England record their biggest Championship win, 37-0 against an injury-hit France at Twickenham, with right-wing Douglas Lambert scoring a Championship record 22 points with 2 tries, 5 conversions and 2 penalty goals.

12 Mar In the first match between teams representing the two capitals, London win 21-17 (3G, 2T to 1G, 4T) in Paris.

International Championship: Wales 16 Ireland 0, Cardiff, 11 March

Wales champions: A record crowd

By Major Philip Trevor

In the presence of a huge crowd at Cardiff, Wales beat Ireland on Saturday by 3 goals, one a penalty goal, and a try to nothing. To say that the crowd was a record one is to understate the case. The order was given to close the gates 45 minutes before play was due to start. This very necessary proceeding led to much wall climbing, and many hundreds obtained admission to the ground in this way. It was not an especially attractive game from the spectacular point of view, nor was the issue in any real doubt. The Welshmen distinguished themselves as usual by their capacity to seize chances.

Wales thus regain the championship, which they lost last year to England, and our English team alone in the season which is all but over have given the champions a fright [Wales won 15-11]. Since then things have gone consistently well for Wales. Scotland they completely vanquished [32-10]; France they beat comfortably [15-0], though not badly; and now, by a quite respectable margin of points, they have defeated the Irishmen, who until the day before yesterday were undefeated. Certainly the Welshmen have the best side in the four – or, indeed, in the five – countries, and they deserve those honours which now return to them.

[This was the championship's first 'Grand Slam', a term not yet in use.]

International Championship: France 16 Scotland 15, Paris, 2 January

France defeats Scotland: An exciting finish

From Reuter

For the first time in the history of these international contests, the match resulted in a victory for the French team over a British team. No finer match has ever been seen in France. The French victory, which was hailed with wild enthusiasm, proves the remarkable progress which is being made in the game on this side of the Channel.

The Scotsmen, preceded by a piper in Highland costume, appeared on the ground amid great cheering punctually at half-past two, and the Frenchmen came out a few minutes later. France started one man short, one of the players arriving late. McCallum marked the first try, which was not converted.

The French at first remained on the defensive, but soon carried the attack into the enemy's camp. A successful movement ended in a try being marked by Laterrade, which Decamps converted. The French continued to attack with renewed vigour, and frequently menaced the Scottish goal. Failliot scored another try, which was not converted, and almost immediately afterwards Peyroutou marked a third try, which Communeau again failed to convert.

Scotland now resumed the offensive, and Munro marked a try, which Turner converted. This was the final addition before half-time, and the score then stood at 11 points to 8 in favour of France.

In the second half the Scots again began with a vigorous attack, but the cleverness of the defence, especially Lane and Combe, prevented scoring on several occasions when the visitors looked dangerous. Ultimately Pearson scored a dropped goal. The French retaliated quickly with a try, scored by Failliot, which Decamps converted. The concluding part of the match was very fast, though perhaps less brilliant than the earlier stages. Abercrombie marked a try, which was contested, but which was accorded by the referee. It was not converted. A splendid contest came to an end with the score: France 16 points (2 goals and 2 tries), Scotland 15 points (1 goal, 1 dropped goal, and 2 tries).

The victors and vanquished were both tremendously cheered as they left the field.

	E	F	I	S	W	P	W	D	L	F	A	Pts
1 WALES	15-11	-	16-0	-	-	4	4	0	0	78	21	8
2 IRELAND	3-0	25-5	-	-	-	4	3	0	1	44	31	6
3 ENGLAND	-	37-0	-	13-8	-	4	2	0	2	61	26	4
4 FRANCE	-	-	-	16-15	0-15	4	1	0	3	21	92	2
5 SCOTLAND	-	-	10-16	-	10-32	4	0	0	4	43	77	0

INTERNATIONAL CHAMPIONSHIP

1912

20 Jan Dicky Owen's record 34th cap is marked with the captaincy of Wales at Twickenham, but England win 8-0. [Owen, who beats Billy Bancroft's Welsh and British record, wins 1 more, against Scotland, but forsakes another 2 when, with Trew, he withdraws from the matches against Ireland and France to go on Swansea's tour of Devon.]

8 Apr England beat France by 18-8 in Paris to earn a share in the Championship with Ireland. Harlequin centre JGG Birkett, making the last of his 21 appearances for England, scores their first try.

23 Nov Freddie, Dick and John Luyt are in the Springbok side that beat Scotland 16-0 (and later beat Wales and England), the only cases of three brothers playing together in internationals.

INTERNATIONAL CHAMPIONSHIP

	E	F	I	S	W	P	W	D	L	F	A	Pts
1=ENGLAND	-	-	15-0	-	8-0	4	3	0	1	44	16	6
1=IRELAND	-	-	-	10-8	12-5	4	3	0	1	33	34	6
3=SCOTLAND	8-3	31-3	-	-	-	4	2	0	2	53	37	4
3=WALES	-	14-8	-	21-6	-	4	2	0	2	40	34	4
5 FRANCE	8-18	-	6-11	-	-	4	0	0	4	25	74	0

Tour Match: Wales 0 South Africa 3, Cardiff, 14 December

Narrow colonial victory: Keen forward battle

By Major Philip Trevor

South Africa beat Wales at Cardiff on Saturday by a penalty goal to nothing. The match was played in the rain, and the weather had been bad for days before it began. The ground, therefore, was more or less a quagmire, and the ball so greasy that the backs seldom succeeded in gathering it without fumbling. Such conditions were, of course, all in favour of the Welshmen, who have long since established their reputations as smart bad-weather players. Yet it was certainly the better side that won, close as was the fight and narrow as was the victory gained.

The game had lasted a quarter of an hour when Douglas Morkel, with a good kick, scored the penalty goal which won the match. Subsequently there were several cases of 'all but, but not quite'. On the majority of these occasions it was the Colonials who threatened to score and just failed to do so. However, twice at least were the Welshmen unlucky. Once Green, after what was perhaps the best bout of passing of the afternoon, made a splendid run. On reaching the full-back, he kicked, and there was a great race for the ball. For a moment it looked as if Green had won it, but in the nick of time McHardy had saved the situation. Later Thomas made a fine attempt to drop a goal, and the crowd, under the impression that he had succeeded, cheered wildly.

The smaller (and no doubt physically weaker) men lasted well; and, though the game ended with desperate scrummaging on the home goal-line, the Selection Committee of Wales should have been pleased with the quickness and indomitable energy of their eight forwards.

Tour Match: Newport 9 Springboks 3, 24 October

Seventh match: Colonials suffer first defeat: Birt's success for Newport

By Major Philip Trevor

Thanks to the play of W Birt, who was the bright star of the match, Newport succeeded in beating the South Africans by a goal from a try and a dropped goal to a try. Newport played extremely well, but the gaining of the victory was the work of one man. Birt dropped the goal, he got the try, and it was his place kick by which that try was converted.

From start to finish it was a splendid match, and the huge crowd of some 25,000 persons that watched the play loudly cheered Birt when it came to an end. Quite apart from what they may have failed to do in any other department of the game, the South Africans did weakly where they are wont to succeed, their kicking at goal being many degrees below their established form. The try obtained for them by Douglas Morkel was scored behind the goal posts; but the easy kick ended in failure. Also on four occasions the visitors were awarded what should have been very useful penalty kicks, but Douglas Morkel (who took three of these) was not by any means in his best form, and no goal resulted from any of them.

[This was the Second Springboks' first defeat, and they suffered only two more, in the return match with London Counties and against Swansea.]

1913

11 Jan The South Africans beat France 38-5 in an unofficial international at the end of their tour, and, as usual, the Daily Telegraph's Own Correspondent in Paris turns overwhelming defeat into triumph for France, who 'does not feel herself disgraced' as 'only four teams have scored more heavily against the Springboks' and 'France, with her 5 points, heads the four international teams, only one of which – England – with an unconverted try, succeeded in crossing the visitors' lines at all.... To have scored a goal against the redoubtable Springboks is a fine feather in her cap.'

15 Mar In front of the Prince of Wales and a crowd of 25,000 at Twickenham, a try by Oxford University's Australian forward LG 'Bruno' Brown is sufficient to give England a 3-0 victory over the Scots and with it the Calcutta Cup, the Triple Crown and their first Grand Slam. Thus England finish the Championship season with a 50-4 points record, their defence beaten only once, by a dropped goal from Ireland's Dicky Lloyd.

Tour Match: England 3 South Africa 9, Twickenham, 4 January

The great International: A Colonial victory

By Major Philip Trevor

The South African tourists and the England XV before the international at Twickenham.

Cape Town, 15 January

Welsh football crowds: A South African attack

From Central News

Some scathing remarks are made by the correspondent of the Cape Times with reference to the Rugby match at Neath, during the South African tour.

'Yesterday,' he says, 'I witnessed the foulest and dirtiest football that I have ever seen, and heard the most unsportsmanlike, bigoted, partisan, and ignorant lot of spectators giving tongue, like a pack of yelping dogs, right through the game, abusing in the vilest language the referee and our players, and by their conduct directly contributing to the rotten football and the unpleasant recollections of Welsh football and Welsh manners that we shall carry back with us to South Africa.

'Readers will remember that I drew particular attention to the crowd at Llanelly, the lack of control, and the license permitted them, and made it quite clear that when trouble arises, as it frequently does, it is almost entirely due to the way in which players are encouraged to bring into operation those dirty tricks which mar the good reputation of Rugby football. The Llanelly people, however, are plaster saints in comparison with the alleged sportsmen at Neath, who care nothing for the game, or the way in which it should be played, provided that their own team wins. Talk about "win, tie, or wrangle", these are the people who wrangle even when winning, and to whom the name of sportsman is apparently an abomination.... I had no idea that partisanship could go to such extremes. The crowds at these places are the curse of Welsh football.'

INTERNATIONAL CHAMPIONSHIP

	E	F	I	S	W	P	W	D	L	F	A	Pts
1 ENGLAND	-	20-0	-	3-0	-	4	4	0	0	50	4	8
2 WALES	0-12	-	16-13	-	-	4	3	0	1	35	33	6
3 SCOTLAND	-	-	29-14	-	0-8	4	2	0	2	50	28	4
4 IRELAND	4-15	24-0	-	-	-	4	1	0	3	55	60	2
5 FRANCE	-	-	-	3-21	8-11	4	0	0	4	11	76	0

TOURS (Tests)
South Africa in British Isles & France: E3-SA9, I0-SA38, S0-SA16, W0-SA3, F5-SA38
Australia in New Zealand: NZ30-A5, NZ25-A13, NZ5-A16

The fine place kicking of Douglas Morkel, who captained the winning side, enabled South Africa to beat England at Twickenham on Saturday by 9 points to 3. Each side got an unconverted try, and it was left to Morkel to win the match for the South Africans by scoring a couple of very fine penalty goals.

A record crowd of more than 30,000 witnessed what was, in some respects, a disappointing match. The impartial but critical spectator left the ground more impressed with the shortcomings of the losers than with the merits of the winners. Behind the English scrummage, only full back WR Johnston and centre three-quarter Ronnie Poulton, the best and cleverest player on the field, came out with credit. Poulton's early brilliancy gave England the lead after five-and-twenty minutes, when he threaded his way through the opposing defence to score behind the posts, Wodehouse missing the easy conversion. A few minutes later, the crowd went wild with delight as Poulton ran from his own half, beating man after man before being hauled down some four feet from the line.

Never again did an English player look really likely to score. R Luyt scored a try for the visitors under the cross-bar, which Morkel failed to convert. But he made amends with his two kicks in the second half.

Thus the Springboks are the first Colonial side to beat all four countries of the Union, and they are the first side to bring disaster at Twickenham to an England fifteen in an international match.

[The impressive South African tour record reads W 23, L 3, Pts 403-96, and Poulton's try was the only one they conceded in the four Tests.]

International Championship: France 3 Scotland 21, Parc des Princes, 1 January

Victory of the visitors

By Major Philip Trevor

Scotland beat France by three goals and two tries to a try, but the score rather exaggerated the merits of the winners. The Scotsmen quite deserved their victory, but it was not a one-sided game. The Scots owed their superiority to their back division. Stewart, on the right of the three-quarters, secured three tries, Gordon two.

Mr John Baxter was the referee. He was exceptionally strict, but his awarding of a very large number of penalty-kicks against France was not to the liking of sections of the crowd, many of whom were presumably quite unacquainted with the technicalities of Rugby football.

[Following representations made by the Rugby Football Union, it was reported on 10 Jan that the French football authorities had issued an appeal to the public to refrain from demonstrations against referees, which 'are calculated to do great harm to the cause of sport in France'.]

Scottish-French trouble: 3 February

L'Entente Cordiale – a plea for generosity

By Major Philip Trevor

The news that the Scottish Union have declined to renew their international fixture with France next year has come as an unpleasant surprise to all Rugby unionists. [It will be remembered that the referee, Mr Baxter of the English Union, and the Scottish players were mobbed and assaulted.] We had thought that the little trouble that existed had died away. Now, however, at an interval of a month, it has – more's the pity – cropped up again.

I was present at the Parc des Princes on New Year's Day, and saw the fracas. I purposely refrained at the time from adding my mite towards giving publicity to an incident, comment on which seemed to me (in the interest of peace and of good fellowship) to be thoroughly undesirable. Unfortunately, others have taken a different view.

To palliate or extenuate the action of a large section of what was necessarily an ignorant holiday crowd is quite impossible. I frankly allow that the situation that day at Paris was, for about a couple of minutes at any rate, an exceptionally ugly one. But in a very real sense the French themselves were the chief sufferers in consequence. Their officials and their Press were mortified beyond measure at what happened, while in the noisy and disgraceful conduct of the malcontents the quiet good sportsmanship of thousands of peaceful spectators was not noticed.

Now, however, in spite of French apologies, the Scottish Union have decided that they cannot make a fixture with France for next year. They say that French crowds, as well as players, need to be educated. But is the rupture – even the temporary rupture – of friendly relations the best way of educating them? Personally I prefer the method recently adopted at Twickenham. In the England and France match it was not by any means a stupendous performance that the Frenchmen gave. Yet were they cheered with exceptional enthusiasm. I was not the only one who recognised design in that hearty applause. It was a reply to the Paris crowd of New Year's Day. The English way was the way a crowd should behave.

I do not say that the Scottish Union have not been strictly just in their recent action; but their strongest supporters will scarcely claim for them that they have been generous, while the anti-Scotch people in England and Wales are already making the most of their lack of generosity. I hope it is not too late for the Scotchmen to reconsider.

[Scotland did not play France in 1914.]

1914

21 Mar 1914 A 7-try spectacular at Inverleith in the last international played in the British Isles before World War I sees England hold out to edge Scotland 16-15 and win the Triple Crown despite losing that greatest of forwards Cherry Pillman with a broken leg in the latter stages.

13 Apr The records tumble at Stade Colombes, Paris, as England, 8-3 down at one time to the usual French opening surge, clinch their second Grand Slam in a row with a 39-13 victory which includes a record 9 tries to take their season's total to 20. The diminutive right wing three-quarter Cyril Lowe is the first player to score a hat-trick of tries in successive matches, and his Championship tally for the season is 8. Ronnie Poulton (now Poulton Palmer since becoming a beneficiary in his uncle's will earlier this month) scores 4 tries. There are more signs of the crowd misbehaviour, with barracking of the referee, that led to Scotland's refusal to play France, although the loss of this fixture is irrelevant to the Championship as the two countries lose all their matches.

4 Aug War breaks out and there are no more official internationals until 1920.

INTERNATIONAL CHAMPIONSHIP

	E	F	I	S	W	P	W	D	L	F	A	Pts
1 ENGLAND	-	-	17-12	-	10-9	4	4	0	0	82	49	8
2 WALES	-	31-0	-	24-5	-	4	3	0	1	75	18	6
3 IRELAND	-	-	-	6-0	3-11	4	2	0	2	29	34	4
4=SCOTLAND	15-16	-	-	-	-	3	0	0	3	20	46	0
4=FRANCE	13-39	-	6-8	-	-	3	0	0	3	19	78	0

TOURS (Tests)
New Zealand in Australia: A0-NZ5, A0-NZ17, A7-NZ22

International Championship: England 17 Ireland 12: Twickenham, 14 February 1914

English victory: Fine Irish forwards

By Major Philip Trevor

As mentioned on another page, the King and a number of other distinguished visitors were amongst the huge attendance [40,000] at Twickenham on Saturday, and witnessed a great game between England and Ireland, which the home country won.

The prowess of the Irish pack was early in evidence, and RA Lloyd, the Irish captain, dropped a clever goal after only six minutes. Two minutes later, the forwards made a try for Quinn which went unconverted.

Then the Englishmen woke up. Poulton cut through the defence in inimitable style and made an ideal opening for his winger Roberts, who scored in the corner. Lowe, skirting the touch line at great speed, did the same on the other wing. Both tries went unconverted, so, at change of ends, the visitors led by a point.

After a fierce Irish onslaught was beaten off, Poulton made another typical run which would have been wasted but for the handiness of the handiest forward of modern times. It was Pillman who put his head back and raced away to support his captain on the left flank. Poulton drew the Irish full back, and tossed the ball to the emergency man, who made no mistake.

So the Englishmen took the lead (9-7), which never afterwards were they in serious danger of losing. But it was some time before a bout of passing enabled Lowe to score again, a try that probably only he could have scored. Near the end came the gem of the afternoon, a brilliant individual try by the stand-off half-back WJA Davies, who had spent the game unselfishly playing for the men in rear of him, but this time fooled the entire Irish defence by going right through alone, feinting and swerving before speeding over under the goal-posts. Chapman converted. Hardly had the cheering died, however, when Jackson scored from a long line out and, as Lloyd kicked the goal, it was only by five points that England won.

[The match was front-page news not only for the presence of King George V, at Twickenham for the first time since his accession in 1910, and Prime Minister Asquith, but also because of the passionate debate in Parliament over Home Rule for Ireland.]

International Championship: England 10 Wales 9, Twickenham, 17 January 1914

England's lucky win: Fine finish at Twickenham: A record crowd

By Major Philip Trevor

It was a lucky victory which England scored on Saturday at Twickenham. Two goals from tries to a goal was the final score, and so the favourites just, and only just, succeeded in doing what had been expected of them. A one-point victory was theirs.

In what is nowadays probably the most important item of forward play, namely the getting possession of the ball in the scrummage, there was no comparison at all between the two packs. Indeed, not so many as half a dozen times in the whole match did the Englishmen give a successful exhibition of hooking and heeling.

It follows, therefore, as a matter of course that Wood and Taylor, the half-backs, had a very difficult task. The ordeal was altogether too much for Wood, the scrum half. His immediate opponent, Lloyd, of Pontypool, pounced upon him time after time, and he was even more worried by the Welsh forwards.

Play had lasted a quarter of an hour when Hirst, the left wing three-quarter, doubled and turned inwards to send the ball over the cross-bar with a fine drop kick. This Welsh success had the effect of waking the Englishmen up, and, when only three minutes remained for play in the first half, Poulton zigzagged through the Welsh defence as only he can and passed to Brown, dashing forward to support his captain. Brown took his pass well, and hurled himself over the goal-line with three Welshmen clinging to him. As Chapman's place-kick was accurate, England led at half-time by 1 point. But only for a few minutes did they hold their lead. A punt from Poulton was charged down and Watt gathered it, scoring almost without difficulty. This try Bancroft converted. England, however, instituted a dribbling rush which the fleet Pillman headed. The ball was kicked over the line, and a desperate race was just won by the most famous forward of modern times.

There ensued a scene of great excitement. Men and women rose in their seats, hats and sticks were waved, and Pillman rejoined his comrades amid a hurricane of cheers. It was a scene to be remembered. Chapman made no mistake with the place-kick, and England therefore led by 1 point again. A quarter of an hour, however, still remained for play, and the ascendancy of the Welsh pack was as marked as ever, but the sterling defence of the Englishmen held, and there was no further scoring.

The crowd was a record one, and before the match began a certain notice was placed on the gate: 'Ground full: a view of the game is not guaranteed.' There were probably 30,000 persons present, and it was when the time came to go that one realised how great was the multitude which filled the place in which (in the British Isles Tournament) England has never lost a match. Half a mile of humanity went at less than a snail's pace from the headquarters of Rugby football to the Twickenham railway station.

England wing Lowe watches his forwards in action.

1915 – 1919

17 Apr 1915 In what is termed a 'military international' between Wales and 'England' at Cardiff, Wales lose 10-26 to what is in effect a Barbarians team, which includes two Irishmen and a London Welsh player. The match, arranged to boost recruitment for the Welsh Guards, raises £200 in gate receipts for local military charities, but the stirring half-time speeches inspire the conscription of fewer than 200 of the 1,000 sought to join the Colours.

19 Mar 1919 In their second game in the King's Cup, the Inter-Services Tournament, New Zealand beat South Africa 14-5 at Twickenham – the first clash of the two giants of world rugby (not counting some matches played by New Zealand servicemen in South Africa in 1902 for the Boer War).

16 Apr 1919 New Zealand beat the Mother Country 11-3 at Twickenham in the final of the Inter-Services Tournament.

25 Dec 1919 Watsonians win at Swansea, becoming the first side from England, Ireland or Scotland (including the Barbarians) to beat them on their own ground for 20 years.

Obituaries

Of the hundreds of rugby players who gave their lives in the war, 111 were internationals. These included the following:

JHD 'Bungy' Watson, England three-quarter capped 3 times in 1914, drowned in action when HMS Hawke was torpedoed by a German submarine (15.10.1914)

RW Poulton Palmer *(pictured above)*, one of England's great sporting heroes, a three-quarter capped 17 times, killed by a sniper's bullet in a trench in Belgium (5.5.1915)

D 'Daniel' Lambert, holder of England scoring records with 5 tries (v France 1907) and 22pts (v France 1911), killed in action near Loos while serving with the Buffs (13.10.1915)

CM Pritchard, Newport forward, capped 14 times for Wales (1904-10), killed in a raid on German trenches (1916)

Edgar Mobbs, DSO, English three-quarter, refused a commission at start of war, so raised his own company of 250 sportsmen for the Northamptonshire regiment, rising to command his Battalion with rank of Lt Col, fell in action at Zillebeke (29.7.1917). [Still commemorated by an annual match between East Midlands and Barbarians]

Dave Gallaher, Irish-born captain and wing-forward (the 'rover") of the formidable 1905 All Blacks, killed in action in France (4.10.1917).

Wales 3 New Zealand Army 6: Swansea, 21 April 1919

Welshmen beaten
New Zealand servicemen outdo famous All Blacks

By Our Special Correspondent

The New Zealand Services team yesterday at Swansea followed up their many recent triumphs with a crowning achievement in beating Wales by 6 points to 3. In ordinary circumstances victory by the margin of a penalty goal would be nothing to enthuse about. Special interest, however, was involved in yesterday's encounter. Success against Wales was denied to even the famous All Blacks combination of 1905, and naturally the present team were desperately anxious to accomplish what their far-famed predecessors had failed to achieve. Two attempts – in non-official contests, so far as the Welsh Union were concerned – on the part of the New Zealanders to lower the colours of the Principality were made at Christmas time, but a narrow defeat and a draw were all that happened.

Recently the interests of the New Zealanders have, of course, been bound up more with their chances of winning the Services Championship than in any meeting with Wales. For the Services matches New Zealand went 'all out', and it seemed hard luck that within five days of their desperate struggle with the Mother Country – not to mention the contest with the French Army last Saturday – they should be called upon to take part in a match the result of which meant so much to them. New Zealand, after finding themselves 3 points in arrear within ten minutes of the start, played up with such tenacity that before the interval they in turn were 3 points ahead and that lead they maintained to the final score.

As upon nearly all others associated with New Zealand triumphs this season, the Dominions team owe success to their splendid scrummagers. The New Zealand forwards won the Services Tournament, and with it the King's Cup, and yesterday they again attained to great heights.

Ideal weather prevailed, the ground was in splendid condition, and the company numbered about 25,000.

[The WRU recognised this as an official match and awarded caps, 13 of the side making their international débuts.]

Varsity Match: Cambridge 7 Oxford 5, Queen's Club, 9 December 1919

Victory of Cambridge: The King present

By Colonel Philip Trevor CBE

The King yesterday honoured the University match at the Queen's Club with his presence, and witnessed the narrow victory of Cambridge, who won by a dropped goal and a penalty goal to a placed goal – 7 points to 5.

It was a desperately exciting match that the King saw, and both in method and result it came as a surprise even to those who had reason to know something about respective form. Oxford may consider themselves unlucky to have lost. In the second half of the game they only had fourteen men, for their stand-off half back, FA Waldock, was injured just prior to the interval. Also, when Oswald Jenkins made a fine attempt to drop a goal, the ball hit the cross-bar and rebounded into the field of play.

Furthermore, they did more actual attacking than Cambridge did; and whereas their own goal line was uncrossed, they pierced the Cambridge defence on one occasion.

The 1920s

Without dominating the game at home, England achieved four Grand Slams in the 1920s, in 1921–23–24–28. Wales won the title outright only once (1922). Their rugby subsequently declined to such an extent and the public's confidence in the Welsh Union dropped so low that a special selection panel was formed in 1924.

Despite almost monopolising the Wooden Spoon, or at least a share of it, France made great strides in this decade, chalking up their first wins over both England and Wales. But it was Scotland who challenged England's superiority. They won the title twice and shared it on three other occasions. They celebrated the opening of their new ground, Murrayfield, in 1925 by beating England to seal the Grand Slam, and the following year they became the first home country to beat England at Twickenham.

Scoring increased in the 1920s, chiefly as a result perhaps of the better quality ball coming from the set-pieces. There was no very great difference between the home countries. England had not yet found the successors of those who established the honour of Twickenham – no second Poulton or Davies, no ready replacements for Lowe or Pillman. Scotland's great all-Oxford three-quarter line broke up and Wales were still looking backwards at their glory days. Ireland had their moments, but usually found someone to beat them, and their best seasons were two shared titles with Scotland (1926–27).

Domestic skirmishes, however, were put into perspective by the great Springboks and All Blacks, who at times seemed to be playing a different game. Their scientific approach to all aspects of the game, particularly to the formation and play of the packs, with specialised positions of the forwards – the South Africans with their 3–4–1 scrum, the New Zealanders using seven forwards (2–3–2) and a 'rover' – was a revelation, and began to influence the home countries.

But there was very little inter-continental contact in the twenties. The only All Blacks (1924-25) won all 30 of their matches in the home countries and France, comfortably beating England at Twickenham despite playing with 14 men for most of the game after Cyril Brownlie sensationally became the first player ever to be sent off in an international. The Springboks did not come at all, and the only British Isles side to tour lost the series in South Africa 3-0 with one drawn. They were unfortunate to come up against new fly-half Bennie Osler's boot for the first time. Osler became the 'Great Dictator' of South African rugby, controlling the game with his

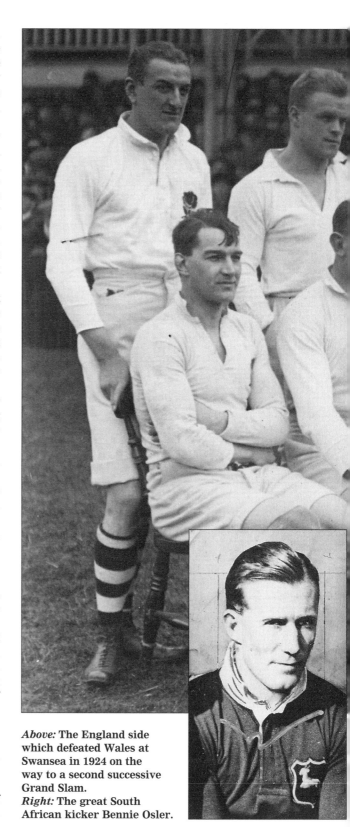

Above: **The England side which defeated Wales at Swansea in 1924 on the way to a second successive Grand Slam.**
Right: **The great South African kicker Bennie Osler.**

kicking. He was often criticised for using the boot too much, sometimes by his own team-mates, but his match-winning tactics and unsurpassed drop-kicking became legendary.

The first ever clashes of the Colonial 'Titans' took place in the twenties, in New Zealand in 1921 and South Africa in 1928, and both series finished with honours even. The former tour, in which the Springboks lost only two matches (both Tests), was marred by racial tensions that came to the fore when the visitors played a Maori side, presaging events half a century later.

1920

1 Jan France resume fixtures with Scotland after the split in 1913 over crowd behaviour and the treatment of the referee, and after this last international played at the old Parc des Princes the English referee Frank Potter-Irwin is carried shoulder-high from the field, despite their 5-0 defeat

5 Sep The USA, represented by a team from California, the only rugby-playing state, beat France 8-0 in the Olympic rugby final in Paris, these being the only teams contesting the tournament. [The British unions had declined to enter teams because it was out of season, while Czechoslovakia and Romania had withdrawn their entrants because of the ease with which France had won the continental championship.] Daniel Carroll (USA) wins his second rugby gold medal, having played in 1908 for Australia.

10 Oct The Californian Olympic champions, having agreed to a short tour of France and having beaten teams representing the South-East 26-0, the

South 14-3 and the South-West 6-3, go down in their last match 14-5 to a team selected from all France.

11 Oct The Fédération Française de Rugby (French Rugby Union) is formed to take over rugby affairs from the Union des Sociétés Française des Sports Athlétiques.

7 Dec In the last Varsity match played at the Queen's Club, Kensington (the venue since 1887), King George V sees 9 tries as Oxford beat Cambridge 17-14. The game, henceforth known as 'Neser's match', is a triumph for VH 'Knoppie' Neser, the South African wing-forward who at the last minute is a controversial replacement for the injured stand-off half FA Waldock, hitherto the mainstay of the side. Oxford's South African captain Denoon Duncan's calculated gamble on Neser, who has never played stand-off before, comes off as he has a creative hand in their first two tries and scores the fourth himself with a classic stand-off move.

Action from the 1920 Olympic rugby final in Paris, contested by the United States and France.

International Championship: France 5 Wales 6, Stade Colombes, 17 February

Close rugby match

From a French Critic

Wales defeated France at Colombes today in the presence of a vast crowd by two tries (six points) against a placed goal (five points). The receipts for the match exceeded 125,000F.

Wales kicked off with the wind against them but the interval arrived without any scoring having taken place. When play was resumed, the Welsh clearly assumed the mastery, and two tries were quickly obtained. The first was secured by Bryn Williams after some fine passing by the forwards. The second was due to the work of Wick Powell, who accepted a pass from Albert Jenkins and carried the ball behind Jaureguy.

The Welsh continued to attack, but suddenly Struxiano intercepted a pass to Jenkins and transferred to Crabos. The latter gave to Jaureguy, who, swiftly evading all opposition, carried the ball between the posts. Struxiano, the captain of the French fifteen, converted the try to the accompaniment of wild enthusiasm.

It was now the turn of the home side to dominate the play, and Jaureguy all but got over. Immediately afterwards

Chilo became dangerous. Following a line-out, Cassayet secured and passed to Struxiano, who crossed the visitors' line. The touch judge, however, raised his flag, and the try was not awarded. Soon the whistle was heard announcing the end.

The Welsh victory was due almost entirely to the scientific methods of their pack, who overshadowed the French forwards in all phases. Had their backs displayed a little more decision and speed, their success would have been more substantial. The best of the Welsh back division were JP Jones, in the centre of the three-quarter line, F Reeves, at half, and full-back J Rees, who never made a mistake. For France, Struxiano, Cambre, and Jaureguy did best.

[After the match the French captain Struxiano claimed his disallowed try was valid, and it did not help that it was the Welsh touch judge who was responsible for changing the referee's mind. This was France's 17th championship defeat in a row, a record run they thankfully ended in their next match, a 15-7 victory over Ireland in Dublin on 3 April.]

International Championship: Wales 19 England 5, Swansea, 17 January

How England lost
Shea the star performer

By Colonel Philip Trevor, CBE

Once again, on Saturday last, did England lose an international match at Swansea, for Wales won by a goal from a try, two dropped goals, one penalty goal, and a try to a goal from a try – 19 points to 5.

Certainly the Welsh victory was well deserved, and it could easily have been greater, seeing that after half-time, although they held a lead of 2 points, England played like a beaten side. Despite that lead, the Welshmen were superior to their opponents all through the match, and even if the weather had been good – it rained steadily most of the afternoon – the chances are that the superiority of the home fifteen would have been equally noticeable.

So far as the scoring was concerned it was more or less a case of 'England versus Jerry Shea'. Shea was responsible for 16 of

the 19 points scored by his side, and had he chosen to run a small risk he could have got the try which he elected should be got by Powell. Magnificently as he played, some of the Welsh experts condemned him for being over-individualistic, for, true to Welsh conviction, they held that he should have done more for his wing-men.

I cannot myself agree with that criticism. The ball was greasy, the ground was very muddy, and the wing players did not impress one with the idea that they were up to the best Welsh standard. Shea excels as a dropper of goals, and the laws of football still say clearly that a dropped goal is to count more than a try. Moreover, as a side-stepper on slippery ground, Shea has no superior among modern centre three-quarter backs. I doubt, indeed, if he has his equal in that art.

INTERNATIONAL CHAMPIONSHIP											
	E	F	I	S	W	P	W	D	L	F	A	Pts
1=WALES	19-5	-	28-4	-	-	4	3	0	1	58	23	6
1=SCOTLAND	-	-	19-0	-	9-5	4	3	0	1	37	18	6
1=ENGLAND	-	8-3	-	13-4	-	4	3	0	1	40	37	6
4 FRANCE	-	-	-	0-5	5-6	4	1	0	3	23	26	2
5 IRELAND	11-14	7-15	-	-	-	4	0	0	4	22	76	0

1921

5 Feb In a match very nearly abandoned because of stoppages caused by overspills of the 50,000 crowd, Scotland beat Wales 14-8 at Swansea, their first victory in Wales since 1892.

9 Apr After their sternest examination of the season, England emerge 10-6 victors (2 goals to 2 penalty goals) at the Stade Colombes to clinch their third Grand Slam, but concede twice as many points as in their other three matches. France finish joint 2nd in the Championship and for the first time score more points than they concede (33-32).

7 Sep On their first Antipodean tour, the Springboks beat a Maori team 9-8 at Napier in a heated match, which leads to an inflammatory cable (whether leaked by a telegraphist or deliberately handed out by its author, it is never established) from a correspondent (CWF Blackett) travelling with the South Africans, stating, among other things, that it was 'bad enough having to play a team officially designated New Zealand natives, but the spectacle of thousands of Europeans frantically cheering on a band of coloured men to

defeat members of their own race was too much for the Springboks, who were frankly disgusted'. When published in the Napier Daily Telegraph, the report causes an international furore.

17 Sep The last Test of the Springboks' tour, played at Athletic Park, Wellington, on mud and in driving rain, is drawn 0-0, leaving the series tied. Full-back PG 'Gerhard' Morkel, the Springboks hero, saving them time and again, is one of five of the famous rugby-playing family on the tour – WH 'Boy', HJ 'Henry', HW 'Harry' and JA 'Royal' also playing in Tests, Gerhard and Boy in all three. The Springboks finish with a W15–D2–L2 record in New Zealand, having won all 4 matches in Australia.

8 Dec Oxford beat Cambridge 11-5 at Twickenham, the new home of the Varsity Match, despite the dominance of a powerful Cambridge pack which includes England internationals Wavell Wakefield, R Cove-Smith and GS Conway.

Laws The player making the 'fair catch' has to take the kick.

INTERNATIONAL CHAMPIONSHIP

	E	F	I	S	W	P	W	D	L	F	A	Pts
1 ENGLAND	-	-	15-0	-	18-3	4	4	0	0	61	9	8
2=FRANCE	6-10	-	20-10	-	-	4	2	0	2	33	32	4
2=WALES	-	12-4	-	8-14	-	4	2	0	2	29	36	4
4=SCOTLAND	0-18	0-3	-	-	-	4	1	0	3	22	38	2
4=IRELAND	-	-	-	9-8	0-6	4	1	0	3	19	49	2

TOURS (Tests)

South Africa in Australia: No Tests

South Africa in New Zealand: NZ13-SA5, NZ5-SA9, NZ0-SA0

International Championship: Scotland 0 England 18, Inverleith, 19 March

Scots beaten pointless: England's supremacy

By Colonel Philip Trevor, CBE

England beat Scotland at Edinburgh on Saturday by three goals and a try to nothing, and by so doing won the championship of the British Isles.

By degrees the England forwards found their game, and ever afterwards their loose rushing was done in the way that has made them famous in the last three months. Nineteen minutes passed, however, before the first of England's four tries was obtained, when Gardner, the smallest of the sixteen forwards on the field, won a scramble for the ball on the French line. Another forward, Woods, then scored from a line-out, and Hammett kicked the goal. The teams changed ends with England leading by 8 points to 0.

England's second-half tries, scored by the ever-watchful Brown, another

forward, and King, who ran half the length of the field unopposed, were somewhat lucky. Hammett converted both.

England's victory in the British Isles tournament is, of course, pronounced and unmistakable. Not only has the team beaten in turn Wales, Ireland, and Scotland, but it has beaten them decisively, both arithmetically and technically. There are those who will go so far as to say that the 1921 team is the best that has represented England. Possibly, but the opposition has not been desperately difficult to beat. *[Although the fixtures with France appeared of no consequence to the writer, England's 10-6 victory in Paris 10 days later clinched the Championship and the Grand Slam, with France 2nd on 4pts.]*

Ring scored a somewhat lucky try, allowed after consultation even though he struck the corner flag.

The effect of this was to re-stimulate the English side, and four minutes later Smallwood scored his second. Another five and the whistle blew for 'no-side'.

It was the splendid play of the English forwards which made the try-getting possible. They were the surprise – the welcome surprise – of the afternoon. In the tight scrummaging they were almost, if not quite, the equals of the Welshmen, and in the loose play they were infinitely

superior to them.

It is almost impossible to draw distinctions in merit between the eight men who formed the England pack. Brown, the linker-up-in-chief, was as brilliant as usual. Edwards, Wakefield and Woods were indomitable. It generally took a couple of men to pull Mellish down. Gardner was trained to the ounce and worked like the proverbial Trojan. Blakiston did his scrummaging well and was resourceful in the loose. Voyce was speedy and anticipatory, and made the most brilliant individual run of the afternoon.

International Championship: England 18 Wales 3, Twickenham, 15 January

England's great win: Triumph of forwards against the Welsh

By Colonel Philip Trevor, CBE

England won a great victory over Wales at Twickenham on Saturday afternoon, beating them by 2 goals (one dropped) and 3 tries to a try, 18 points to 3. It is 24 years since England has beaten Wales as badly.

They immediately opened up the game. The forwards helped the backs, and loud and long was the cheering as it was recognised that the Englishmen were determined to begin to win early, and were prepared to run legitimate risks in order to do so. We had the long pass, the return pass, the feint, and the swerve. We had forwards, half-backs, and three-quarter backs in combination and very early was the genius of Kershaw and Davies in evidence.

The dazzling attack of the Englishmen went on, and the game was only seven minutes old when, after a brilliant

movement, Kershaw scored a try near the posts. Hammett duly kicked a goal, and again the swift and brilliant attack of the English backs was renewed. Five minutes later Davies dropped a clever left-foot goal, and after the lapse of another three minutes a bout of passing ingeniously exploited by Myers and Hammett gave Lowe one of the few chances of distinguishing himself which he got during the game, and he scored a capital try. So England were 12 points ahead after only fifteen minutes, and Wales were already a badly beaten side.

There was no further scoring prior to half-time, but ten minutes after the change of ends England increased their lead, Smallwood following up a kick by Hammett to score.

For a long time there had been indications that Wales would be beaten pointless, but

1922

2 Jan Sprinter Eric Liddell (of Chariots of Fire fame) makes his début on the left wing for Scotland, who draw 3-3 with France at the Stade Colombes, the gate receipts of 253,000F setting a record for any sporting event in France.

25 Feb A last-minute try by forward AT Voyce, converted by HLV Day, who also kicks 2 penalty goals, enables England to draw 11-11 with France and save their unbeaten Championship record at Twickenham. This is the third Championship tie this season (the most until equalled in 1962).

Laws: No more than three players to form or become part of front row of scrummage.

International Championship: France 3 Wales 11, Stade Colombes, 23 March

Triumph of Wales

From our Special Correspondent

Under a dull, grey, threatening sky, with a cold blizzard blowing across Colombes, Wales triumphed over France today to the extent of 11 points (one goal and two tries) to 3 points (one try). The better side undoubtedly won. The result came as a bitter disappointment to all supporters of France. However, the Frenchmen took their defeat as real sportsmen should do. To use René Crabos, the French captain's own words, 'We were beaten by better players all round.'

As generally expected, the Welsh forwards were mostly responsible for the victory. They showed better form, better judgment, and more 'go' than their rivals. Very few scrummages ended without one of the red sweaters being in possession of the ball. And, moreover, the much eulogised French three-quarter line appeared to be almost at sea and played much below the standard which they have set up, barring one magnificent run, by which Jaureguy scored the solitary try registered for his side.

The first half was the more interesting. As usual, the French full back, Clement, played splendidly, saving his side many times.

Half-time was whistled with the score board untouched. On resuming, Wales, who played with the wind in their favour, took the initiative, starting so vigorously that the French seemed to be quite taken aback. After Bowen had come very near scoring a try, a rather confused piece of play led to half-a-dozen men falling near the French line, and Cummins emerged just in time to plant the ball down in rival territory. Less than ten minutes later another try was registered at the Frenchmen's expense under almost similar conditions, except that Whitfield was the scorer on this occasion. However, a more brilliant success was in store for the visitors. After a series of splendid passes Islwyn Evans happened to find a road almost clear in front of him, and going through he planted the ball right behind the posts. Jenkins had no difficulty in converting the try.

With Wales leading by 11 points to nil, the Frenchmen made one last desperate attempt to score. And they were eventually rewarded, for with only two minutes to play that magnificent three-quarter, Jaureguy, obtained a try after a superb run across the field.

[This win clinched the Championship for Wales, but France, who had promised so much, went on to lose their remaining game to Ireland, with whom they shared the Wooden Spoon.]

International Championship: Wales 28 England 6, Cardiff, 21 January

England pack routed

By Colonel Philip Trevor, CBE

The unexpected happened at Cardiff on Saturday, for Wales beat England there – in the mud – by two goals and six tries to two tries – 28 points to 6. The afternoon was fine, but the ground was a quagmire. However, even if it had been a morass that fact would not have excused the display given by the England pack *(pictured)*. They were routed, although they were half a stone per man heavier.

The Welsh pack who did the deed, they deserve to be given the fullest and fairest credit for what they achieved. The Welsh backs supported them capitally, but the game was one long, unbroken series of victories for the Welsh forwards.

The England back division never looked like atoning for the sins of their forwards. Kershaw got very little help from comrades in front or in rear of him. Two Welsh wing forwards were told off to look after him. They leaned on the fringes of the scrummage (sometimes, as it seemed to me, they were in prolongation of the front rank), and they pounced. Some day, I would remark incidentally, we shall have to settle this vexed question, and the laws of the game will have to say definitely and arithmetically how packing is to be done, and how it is not to be done.

By half-time the score was 17-3 in favour of Wales, whose tries were scored by Whitfield, Bowen, Hiddlestone, Palmer and Tom Parker, only the last of them converted. England's solitary reply was a try by the most famous wing player of the day, Cyril Lowe.

In the second half, with the result of the match a foregone conclusion, the Welshmen decided to exploit their back division, and further tries were scored by Palmer, Richards and Islwyn Evans before Day scored England's second just prior to 'no-side'.

[The 8 Welsh tries were the most conceded by England in any match, and this was the first time that both sides wore numbers in an international.]

INTERNATIONAL CHAMPIONSHIP

	E	F	I	S	W	P	W	D	L	F	A	Pts
1 WALES	28-6	-	11-5	-	-	4	3	1	0	59	23	7
2 ENGLAND	-	11-11	-	11-5	-	4	2	1	1	40	47	5
3 SCOTLAND	-	-	6-3	-	9-9	4	1	2	1	23	26	4
4=FRANCE	-	-	-	3-3	3-11	4	0	2	2	20	33	2
4=IRELAND	3-12	8-3	-	-	-	4	1	0	3	19	32	2

1923

10 Feb In a match experimentally played at Leicester to reintroduce Championship rugby to the provinces, England score a record number of points against Ireland, beating them 23-5, but the gate of under 20,000 is disappointing and thereafter England's home internationals return permanently to Twickenham.

7 Mar In the last international played at Inverleith, with the Triple Crown at stake, England beat Scotland 8-6 (a goal and a try to a try), an exciting game and England's 6th victory in a row over the Scots. Gloucester forward Tom Voyce dives over for the equalising try with two opponents clinging to him, WGE Luddington converting for the winning points.

2 Apr A record French crowd of 35,000 gathers on Easter Monday to see England beat France 12-3 to clinch the Championship and win the Grand Slam with 9 points in the last 8 minutes. England's forwards win them the match, not only by their superiority in both the loose and in the scrummage but by scoring both tries, through Wakefield and Conway. It is the last international for

three great England players, wing three-quarter Cyril Lowe (25 caps), and the brilliant half-back pairing of Kershaw (16) and Davies (22), who drops a late goal.

6 Oct Humbled 20-5 by Ranfurly Shield holders Hawke's Bay only a fortnight ago, Auckland turn the tables when a return is arranged at short notice to produce funds for a war memorial, and, in a match that has gone down in New Zealand folklore as an exhibition of classic rugby football, win 17-9 to claim the Shield.

1 Nov In an exciting mixed international to commemorate the centenary of the game, played before a privileged few at the historic Close of Rugby School, where 100 years ago the schoolboy William Webb Ellis is said to have first run with the ball with a 'fine disregard' for the rules, England-Wales beat Ireland-Scotland 21-16. As Col. Trevor remarks in the Daily Telegraph, referring to England's WJA Davies and GA Kershaw, 'the boys of Rugby School saw enough to make them understand how and why they had become the greatest pair of half-backs the game has seen.'

The victorious Scottish XV: Gracie holds the ball.

International Championship: Wales 8 Scotland 11, Cardiff, 3 February

INTERNATIONAL CHAMPIONSHIP

	E	F	I	S	W	P	W	D	L	F	A	Pts
1 ENGLAND	-	-	23-5	-	7-3	4	4	0	0	50	17	8
2 SCOTLAND	6-8	16-3	-	-	-	4	3	0	1	46	22	6
3=WALES	-	16-8	-	8-11	-	4	1	0	3	31	31	2
3=FRANCE	3-12	-	14-8	-	-	4	1	0	3	28	52	2
3=IRELAND	-	-	-	3-13	5-4	4	1	0	3	21	54	2

Varsity Match: Oxford 21 Cambridge 14, Twickenham, 11 December

Oxford victory
Wickes's try for Cambridge
By Colonel Philip Trevor, CBE

Oxford beat Cambridge at Twickenham yesterday by three goals and two tries to two goals (one of which was a penalty goal) and two tries. But the match will be remembered primarily for the try scored by the Cambridge captain, RH Hamilton-Wickes *(right)*.

Wickes, on the right wing, took a pass and ran obliquely for a moment or two, but, hampered by the touch-line, turned inwards, and then, to the amazement of the crowd, proceeded to beat his opponents one by one. He went into the thick of it; various pairs of dark blue arms were stretched out towards him; they scarcely touched him. 'Tackle him!' screamed the Oxford partisans. But Wickes was not tackled. Once again he turned, but as he did so he went over

the goal-line. It was a rare, fine individual try. But, although the much-despised Cambridge team had actually established a lead, Oxford proceeded to show why they had won all their matches and soon put the score beyond doubt.

Scotland's fine win
Gracie's great performance
By Colonel Philip Trevor, CBE

It is 33 years since the Scots beat the Welsh at Cardiff, but on Saturday they did it again. They did it handsomely, too, though not easily, for the final score was a goal and two tries to a goal from a try and a penalty goal – 11 points to 8.

Moreover, three or four minutes before 'no-side' Wales were again leading, as they had been for about half an hour. Then it was that Gracie got the wonderful try that won the game for his side. But it was not for that reason alone that he was the hero of the match. From the very beginning he had shown himself to be the best player on the field, and the longer play continued the more did those who watched have cause to appreciate his exceptional value, both in defence and in attack.

Great, then, was the general dismay when, with the second half some twenty minutes old, he was injured. The Welsh forwards at that moment made the best loose rush they made all the afternoon. Down the field they swept, with the ball at their toes, and the Scots forwards gave way before them. It was no time for half measures, and gallantly did McQueen and Gracie sacrifice themselves.

The rush was stopped, but at a price. McQueen lay prone, but as Gracie got up it was not immediately realised that he too was hurt. Soon, however, it was seen that his face was

covered with blood, and he would not retire, even for temporary treatment, to the dressing room.

For a while he was content to instantly toss the ball to Liddell when it was tossed to him. The minutes passed, and at last he ventured to trust himself. Fortunately he had cause to be reassured, and thence onward to the end he dominated the situation. Once he was tackled six yards from the Welsh goal line. He made a similar effort three minutes later and got to within a couple of yards of it.

Gracie tried a third time. Swerving, dashing, dodging, he went through the defence and finished at a walk behind the posts. That try, gained amid cheering that was universal as well as tumultuous, won the match.

Nor did the Welshmen subsequently regret their spontaneous offering of tribute to great play by a great player. When the end came shortly afterwards they surged onto the field and carried shoulder-high to the dressing room the opponent who at the last moment had so dramatically robbed them of victory. It was a sight to be remembered. Let us hope that when in after years Gracie's great performance at Cardiff in 1923 is appraised (as it deserves to be), the great performance of the Cardiff crowd will be appraised as well.

1924

9 Feb On their first (and only) visit to Belfast, England, fielding five consecutive Cambridge captains – GS Conway, R Cove-Smith, WW Wakefield (capt), RH Hamilton-Wickes (scoring a try on his début) and AT Young (currently Cambridge capt) – beat Ireland 14-3.

1 Sep The first 'Big Five' – a special panel for the selection of Welsh international teams – is chosen, in an effort to restore lost glories and as a result of the 'Ossie Male affair', for which the selection committee were vilified for suspending

their full-back on the train journey to France because he had played for his club at the weekend instead of standing down for the six days prior to an international.

29 Nov After four balls are rejected before the start, the All Blacks avenge their 1905 defeat, beating Wales 19-0 and recording the 20th straight win of their tour.

2 Dec Just 3 days after Wales's rout by the invincible All Blacks, Llanelli bring some pride back to the Principality but go down valiantly 8-3.

INTERNATIONAL CHAMPIONSHIP

	E	F	I	S	W	P	W	D	L	F	A	Pts
1 ENGLAND	-	19-7	-	19-0	-	4	4	0	0	69	19	8
2 SCOTLAND	-	-	13-8	-	35-10	4	3	0	1	60	47	6
3 IRELAND	3-14	6-0	-	-	-	4	2	0	2	30	37	4
4 WALES	9-17	-	10-13	-	-	4	1	0	3	39	71	2
5 FRANCE	-	-	-	12-10	6-10	4	0	0	4	23	47	0

TOURS (Tests)
British Isles in South Africa: SA7-BI3, SA17-BI0, SA3-BI3, SA16-BI9

Olympic Final: USA 17 France 3, Stade Colombes, 18 May

America's Olympic win

(Item in the American column, 20 May)

'If the team representing the Stars and Stripes is going to be hissed every time it wins an Olympic title, it would be better for the Americans to return home and concern themselves no longer with international athletics.' Such is the comment representing the feeling aroused in the United States by the reports printed here of the hostile demonstration that was made when America won the Rugby championship at the Olympic Games, and this feeling is all the more acute because the Paris despatches, in almost every instance, emphasise that 'the victors played as clean a game as was ever contested' and did not once, to quote a Paris cable to the New York Times, 'resort to undue roughness'. The hissing of the American team by the French is the chief feature of America's newspaper Press today, and the situation is relieved only by the information, cabled later, indicating that the French in general are disgusted with the action of the crowd at the Colombes Stadium.

[The US team played 3 matches in England on their way to France, losing in turn to Devonport Services, Blackheath and Harlequins. The only other entrants in France were the Romanians, who lost 61-3 to France and 39-0 to the USA. In the final the USA shocked a full-strength France 17-3, and, not for the first time, an unsportsmanlike French crowd gave vent to their disappointment. With never more than three countries entering the four Olympics in which rugby figured, it is not surprising that this was the last Games to include the sport.]

International Championship: England 19 Scotland 0, Twickenham, 15 March

England's victory in the Rugby Championship

By Colonel Philip Trevor, CBE

The King witnessed the remarkable victory which England gained over Scotland on Saturday at Twickenham by three goals from tries and a dropped goal (19 points) to nil. By this victory England win the championship.

It was a Homeric battle that the King saw. It was certainly one of the greatest games any one of us has been privileged to witness. As readers of The Daily Telegraph may be aware, I had anticipated the victory of England, but not the margin by which they would win.

It was the England forwards who won the match. Wakefield was superb, Conway fine, and admirable were Cove-Smith and Robson. Both Voyce and Blakiston worked hard in the scrums as well as in the open; Luddington was back in his old form and that remark applies with equal force to Edwards.

The game had lasted half an hour ere England scored – from the too seldom seen cross-kick. Corbett essayed it with excellent judgment, and the ever-ready Wakefield gathered the ball and forced his way over the goal line. Conway converted this try as he did the other two tries that were gained by Myers and Catcheside. In between, Myers dropped a very clever left-foot goal.

Tour Match: Swansea 11 Barbarians 9, Swansea, 21 April

Barbarians are beaten

The hopes raised after the victories at Penarth and Cardiff that the Barbarians would repeat their triumph of last Easter when for the first time in their history they won three consecutive matches in Wales were destroyed at Swansea yesterday, when, although they scored as often as their opponents, a successful place kick enabled Swansea to claim a victory by two points – a goal and two tries to three tries. Twelve internationals were included in the visitors' team, while Swansea were not quite at full strength. Play ruled fast and very keen, a try by AC Wallace being equalised by Rowe Harding. IS Smith and JLF Steele afterwards crossed for the Barbarians, but Rees and J Jones got over for Swansea, and one of these tries being converted by A Lewis.

[There was no space in the paper to describe the famous Barbarian try scored by Ian Smith. It started from a missed Swansea penalty kick when Aitken and Wallace set the 'Flying Scot' off on a remarkable 85-yard run that finished under the Swansea posts. Unfortunately, the conversion that would have tied the match was missed.]

Tour Match: South Africa 7 British Isles 3, Durban, 16 August

Rugby Test match: British team lose to South Africa

The first of the Rugby Test matches between the touring British side and South Africa was today won by South Africa by 7 points to 3. Twelve thousand people were present at the start.

After eighteen minutes Osler, the African half, opened the scoring with a magnificent dropped goal. Twelve minutes later Clarkson broke away cleverly and gave to Aucamp, who crossed the British line for a try, which was not converted. There was no further scoring before half-time.

On the resumption the British set up strong pressure, the forwards bringing off some dangerous dribbles. It was not until the second half was 23 minutes old, however, that they succeeded in breaking through, and then Blakiston scored a try, which was not converted. A final effort by the visitors in the last few minutes proved futile.

[For South Africa, this was the start of the 'Bennie Osler era', dominated by the tactical genius and remarkable kicking of the fly-half. The injury-ridden Lions salvaged a solitary 3-3 draw at Port Elizabeth from the 4 Tests, and finished with an unimpressive tour record of W9–D3–L9, Pts 175–155.]

1925

18 Jan With 115 journalists covering the match – 15 from Britain, 20 from Paris and 80 from the rest of France – the all-conquering All Blacks, Cliff Porter's 'Invincibles', finish their tour with a 30-6 victory over France, having beaten Ireland 6-0, Wales 19-0 and England 17-11, and won all 30 of their matches, with a 721–112 points record. The Daily Telegraph rugby correspondent heaps praise upon the New Zealanders, especially on the young Maori George Nepia, who has played in all their matches – 'Nepia stands alone among modern fullbacks. His pluck is equal to his play, and that is saying a great deal' – and on Maurice Brownlie – 'I should imagine ... quite the best forward in the world.' It is a pity the All Blacks were not invited to play Scotland, Grand Slam champions-to-be,

the reason being the SRU's refusal to allow the RFU solely to organise the tour.

7 Feb The Scottish selectors pick the speedy Oxford University three-quarter line en bloc to play Wales at Swansea and are rewarded with a fine 24-14 victory, right-winger Ian Smith, 'the Flying Scot', scoring four tries for the second international in a row (his 4 v France had equalled the Scottish record) and left-winger AC Wallace (later to lead the Waratahs) the other two, 6 tries being the most Scotland have ever scored in Wales. Smith's 8 tries (he fails to score in the remaining two matches) equals the Championship record of Cyril Lowe (England). The two Oxford centres are GPS Macpherson (capt) and GG Aitken (a Rhodes Scholar who had already captained New Zealand!).

Tour Match: England 11 All Blacks 17, Twickenham, 3 January

'All Blacks' win the Rugby International
England's great effort: An unpleasant incident

By Colonel Philip Trevor, CBE

The referee orders the New Zealand forward Cyril Brownlie off the field during the match at Twickenham.

The Prince of Wales saw New Zealand beat England on Saturday at Twickenham by a goal from a try, a penalty goal, and three tries, to a goal from a try, a penalty goal, and a try – 17 points to 11. The Prince received a rousing reception from the record crowd – there were some 60,000 persons on the ground.

Unfortunately the opening of this really great match was marred by unusual and excessive unpleasantness. Scrapping in the scrummage began immediately, and in a minute or two blows were struck. Twice did Mr Freethy,

the referee, warn an Englishman, and twice did he warn a New Zealander. His warnings having apparently no effect, he blew his whistle and told both sets of forwards that on the next occasion he would send the offender off the field. The next occasion came all too quickly, when the game was only ten minutes old.

Mr Freethy said that he saw Cyril Brownlie 'deliberately kick a player lying on the ground', and he ordered him off the field in consequence. Mr Freethy had issued his warnings, and he had to be as good as his word. Never

before have I seen such action taken in an international match, and in justice to the punished player, I ought to say that he had a reputation of being a very fair one. Mr Freethy refereed magnificently, and in less capable hands than his this game would have become just chaos.

The absence of Cyril Brownlie from the pack made it necessary for Parker, the wing forward, to go into it, and this arrangement, besides handicapping the New Zealanders numerically, militated against the tactical efficiency of their back division. For

International Championship: Scotland 14 England 11, Murrayfield, 21 March

Scotland champions: England fail to stay

By Colonel Philip Trevor, CBE

Scotland beat England at Edinburgh on Saturday by three goals (one of which was dropped) to a goal from a try, a penalty goal and a try – 14 points to 11. So the new ground at Murrayfield was happily christened from the point of view of its owners.

It is indeed a fine ground, and in this matter at any rate the Scottish Rugby Union have shown themselves up to date. It will hold approximately 90,000 persons – nearly 70,000 watched this game – and the arrangements made for entrance and egress border on perfection.

The turf is 'well and truly laid', and all who are admitted can see the game. Incidentally, the Press seats are the farthest removed of any from the field of play. The Press of Scotland, to say nothing of that of England, has not of late seen eye to eye with the officials who control the game in Scotland; so those of us who like to think we retain a sense of humour ought to appreciate this little touch of silent irony.

But that is a detail. It is a

rare good ground, and its institution, if it heralds an era of Scottish enterprise, all the better. It certainly had a great opening. The sun shone on it, and Scotland won the Calcutta Cup for the first time for 13 years.

It was a desperate tussle, and up to the last few seconds of a very exciting match the issue of it was in doubt. Near the end, with England leading by 11 points to 10, to the general amazement it was seen that nearly all of the England forwards were 'done'. Some actually could not get out of a walk; a few managed to trot. It is true that most of the Scottish pack had also had all the exercise they wanted. But some of them retained a little life. About ten minutes or so remained for play when the ball was tossed to Waddell. His tired opponents left him alone and he proceeded to drop the goal which won the match.

By this victory Scotland, who have in turn defeated France, Wales, Ireland, and England, win the international championship.

that reason alone they are to be much congratulated on winning the match.

[In a leader, The Daily Telegraph showered praise on the all-conquering All Blacks: '...the match itself proved worthy of the rapturous anticipation with which it had been awaited. We congratulate New Zealand on the achievement of her heart's desire, and her team upon the victory which set the crown upon a wonderful tour.... Their skill has roused immense enthusiasm and admiration and the crowds have been most generous and sportsmanlike in their applause.']

1926

13 Mar Championship favourites Ireland go to Swansea with 3 wins behind them, but in front of nearly 55,000 spectators are beaten 11-8 by a Welsh side largely inspired by 19-year-old outside-half Windsor Lewis in his first international. [Deprived of the Grand Slam, Ireland later have to settle for a share of the Championship when Scotland beat England.]

27 Dec The Maoris win the only Test (unofficial) of their 1926-27 tour to the British Isles and France, beating France 12-3 in Paris.

Laws In a general revision of the laws,

'Time' is mentioned for the first time, the duration of International matches being set at two periods of 40min, with a maximum of 5min for the interval; the referee is confirmed as the sole judge of Law and of fact; the free-kick and penalty kick are defined respectively as 'a kick allowed for a fair catch' and 'a kick awarded to a non-offending side by reason of an infringement of the Laws by their opponents', and both 'may be taken by a place kick, drop kick or punt'.

IRFB Australia, New Zealand and South Africa gain full representation on the International Rugby Football Board.

INTERNATIONAL CHAMPIONSHIP

	E	F	I	S	W	P	W	D	L	F	A	Pts
1=SCOTLAND	-	-	0-3	-	8-5	4	3	0	1	45	23	6
1=IRELAND	19-15	11-0	-	-	-	4	3	0	1	41	26	6
3 WALES	3-3	-	11-8	-	-	4	2	1	1	26	24	5
4 ENGLAND	-	11-0	-	9-17	-	4	1	1	2	38	39	3
5 FRANCE	-	-	-	6-20	5-7	4	0	0	4	11	49	0

International Championship: England 9 Scotland 17, Twickenham, 20 March

The Twickenham record

(Leader article, 22 March)

The whirligig of time brings its revenges in sport as in other things. It is not for Englishmen to be glad that the ground of the Rugby Union at Twickenham has lost its proud record. But those who love the game above the prize will be able to believe without affectation that it is no bad thing that Scotland won on Saturday. Records of victory or of immunity from defeat are of very doubtful benefit, and a tradition of the invulnerability of England on the Twickenham turf is not likely to serve the English game. That the countries which play each other should share the honours of victory and change places year by year in the unofficial table of the championship is in the interests of one and all. Thus the interest of each rising generation in the United Kingdom and in France is turned to the Rugby game, and without any slur upon the other games of winter it may be said that the influence of Rugby on national physique and morale is the highest value. Moreover, the fascination of Rugby, both for player and spectator, depends upon a mingling of diverse elements in which the different nationalities excel. The peculiar prowess of the Irish forward and of the Scottish forward are proverbial, but they are not the same, and the game is in need of both. There was a time when Wales taught all the other nations how backs should play. That lesson having been more or less thoroughly learnt, the Welsh are now undertaking to teach us all the importance of old-fashioned scrummaging, and it seems more than possible that next year the lesson may be grimly enforced. Therefore without pretending to enjoy our humble position with but one victory and a bare balance of points against us, we may heartily congratulate the Scots on their Twickenham victory, and while we salute Scotland and Ireland as dividing the honours of the championship, sincerely declare our satisfaction with the result.

International Championship: Ireland 19 England 15, Dublin, 13 February

Ireland's triumph in rugby international: Why England lost

By Colonel Philip Trevor, CBE

In the presence of the Governor-General of the Irish Free State, who went onto the field of play before the match began and shook hands with the members of the two teams, Ireland beat England at Dublin on Saturday by two goals from tries, a penalty goal, and two tries to three goals from tries – 19 points to 15.

This is the first time since 1911 that Ireland have beaten England. For one reason alone Ireland deserved their victory, namely because of George Stephenson's superb place-kicking, the practical reward of which was a matter of seven points.

It must not, however, be inferred that apart from the effect this had on the issue of the match England were the better side.

The Irish pack outstayed the English pack, and after change of ends they outplayed them too.

Middlesex Sevens Final: Harlequins 26 St Mary's Hospital 3, Twickenham, 24 April

Seven-a-side tournament: Victory of the Harlequins

By Colonel Philip Trevor, CBE

The Harlequins won the seven-a-side Rugby tournament, the concluding games in which were played at Twickenham on Saturday afternoon, and very thoroughly did they deserve their victory. Of the 43 teams which took part in the competition they were easily the best. They had played and won one tie before Saturday's events, and between 2.30pm and 5.55pm the same seven men – VG Davies, RH Hamilton-Wickes, JC Gibbs, JRB Worton, WW Wakefield, JS Chick, and WF Browne – took part in no fewer than four matches of 15 minutes' duration each. During the tournament the Harlequins scored 80 points, 22 being scored against them.

Not a man on the ground had expected that St Mary's Hospital would reach the final of the competition. The last proposition of all, however, was too much for them, and their famous opponents did very much what they chose. Harvey, by getting a try, prevented the losers from being beaten pointless, but an easy victory for the Harlequins was always a certainty. Gibbs (two), Wakefield, Hamilton-Wickes (two) and Davies got tries, in each case by piercing the heart of the defence, and the final score – 26 points to 3 – was indicative of the only defeat approaching a rout seen all the afternoon.

Undoubtedly the tournament was a pronounced success, but it is fairly obvious that the majority of the sides and the large majority of the individuals who took part did not practically realise the special opportunities which seven-a-side Rugby provides. There was too much automatic kicking into touch.

Most of the tries gained were individual efforts, and as that was so it was more common than not for the try-getter to go over the goal-line under the crossbar. There was, of course, very little off-side play. The forward pass was also pleasantly conspicuous by its absence.

A very large crowd watched the games, and on all sides favourable opinions were expressed as to the possibility and desirability of the development of seven-a-side Rugby.

The whole tournament was admirable organised. To Mr Russell Chapman much is due, and he was splendidly assisted by the officials of the Middlesex Rugby Union, who came forward in great style to aid their county hospital.

1927

15 Jan The French Rugby Federation confirms reports that the Scottish RU has decided not to send any more referees to officiate in matches organised by them – a sequel to incidents attending the France-Ireland encounter on 1 Jan at Colombes, when Mr RL Scott was subjected to most unsportsmanlike treatment by the crowd and needed police protection after the game.

15 Jan England, with 5 new caps, beat Wales 11-9 at Twickenham, thanks largely to the performance of their new captain LJ Corbett, the Bristol centre, who drops a goal from a mark, scores a memorable try under the posts and, after

replacing the injured outside-half HCC Laird (at 18yr 134d, England's youngest international), repels the late Welsh surge with fine defensive kicking, although Wales must be regarded as unlucky after playing with only 7 forwards for most of the game. [This is the first rugby match broadcast by the BBC – see photograph.]

24 Aug The British team, managed by James 'Bim' Baxter, depart from Buenos Aires after a successful tour of Argentina, on which they win all 9 matches, including 4 unofficial Tests (37-0, 46-0, 34-3, 43-0) and finish with a 295-9 points record and their line uncrossed.

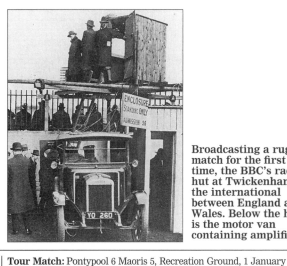

Broadcasting a rugby match for the first time, the BBC's radio hut at Twickenham for the international between England and Wales. Below the hut is the motor van containing amplifiers.

International Championship: France 3 England 0, Stade Colombes, 2 April

Great French victory in Paris: England are beaten pointless

By Colonel Philip Trevor, CBE

France beat England here today by a try to nothing, and most thoroughly did the winners deserve their victory. Rugby Unionists should scarcely need reminding that this is the first occasion on which France have ever beaten England at Rugby football.

It is just 21 years since the infant France was introduced to international Rugby, and it has certainly celebrated in style its coming of age by defeating the predominant partner. Wales is now the only country of the British Isles which has consistently beaten France every time the two teams have met.

There were four factors in the victory – quickness, pace, three-quarter back play, and team work. In each one of these the winners were distinctly superior to the losers. The day was fine, the ground was in good order, the ball was dry, and there was very little wind. The conditions, then, were in favour of speed and accuracy, and in those two particulars (I had almost called them essentials) France beat us. For

the first time in their history the Frenchmen played like an evenly balanced team in an international match. Their forwards were together, their backs were together, and, best of all, there was an understanding between their backs and their forwards.

The Frenchmen found their form at once. I lay especial stress on that fact. When the match was only a few minutes old they were attacking, and when I say attacking I do not mean just pressing. For twelve minutes – a long period in a game of Rugby football – this distinct attack was sustained, and then it was practically rewarded. In the England half the ball was heeled out to Dupont, and it went via Verger, Gerald and Behoteguy to Vellat, who made his dash for the line successfully. It was this try that won the match.

[This ended France's run of 15 successive Championship defeats and they shared the Wooden Spoon with Wales. It was the great WW Wakefield's 30th and last match for England.]

Tour Match: Pontypool 6 Maoris 5, Recreation Ground, 1 January

Maoris' narrow reverse

So narrowly victorious at Cardiff on Tuesday, when a successful place-kick enabled them to claim a win by 5 points to 3, the Maoris lost at Pontypool by 6 points to 5, the Welshmen putting on two tries and the tourists a goal. About 7,000 people gathered to witness what proved to be a desperately hard struggle.

Early on, James and Matthews each came very near to scoring for Pontypool, and eventually Callis, getting away, sold the dummy and finished with a pass to Richards, who

gained a try in the corner.

Rather severely pressed for a time after change of ends, Pontypool increased their lead, James intercepting and sending in Thomas. Again the place-kick failed, but not until the concluding minutes did any success attend the Maoris. Eventually Falwasser scored under the posts, and Pataka converted, so the tourists finished only one point in arrear.

[The Maoris finished with a tour record in the British Isles & France of P31–W22–D2–L7.]

Tour Match: Pontypool 6 New South Wales 3, 2 December

Second defeat of NSW: How Pontypool won

By Colonel Philip Trevor, CBE

At Pontypool, yesterday, New South Wales suffered the second defeat of their tour, the Pontypool club beating them by a penalty goal and a try to a try – 6 points to 3. The Welshmen thoroughly deserved the victory. Their forwards outplayed the tourists' forwards, and the sound tackling of their backs made the attack of the visitors innocuous.

Mistakes of all kinds were made by both teams. A Beddington penalty goal for the home side was the only score in the first half; indeed, it was practically the only noteworthy incident.

In the second half, after only the second passing movement in their back division, Mann scored a

capital try for the visitors to bring the score to 3 points all. But with only three minutes left, after a successful forward rush the ball was flung to Cormac, who, amid wild cheering, scored the try which won the match.

The afternoon was foggy, and there was semi-darkness during the last ten minutes of the game. There was a huge crowd present, and there was, not unnaturally, a scene of great excitement when all was over. Little Pontypool had succeeded where all other Welsh sides had failed.

['Little Pontypool' had also become the only club to beat two touring teams in the same year.]

INTERNATIONAL CHAMPIONSHIP

	E	F	I	S	W	P	W	D	L	F	A	Pts
1=SCOTLAND	21-13	23-6	-	-	-	4	3	0	1	49	25	6
1=IRELAND	-	-	-	6-0	19-9	4	3	0	1	39	20	6
3 ENGLAND	-	-	8-6	-	11-9	4	2	0	2	32	39	4
4=WALES	-	25-7	-	0-5	-	4	1	0	3	43	42	2
4=FRANCE	3-0	-	3-8	-	-	4	1	0	3	19	56	2

TOURS (Tests)
Maoris to E, W, F: No official Tests

1928

7 Jan England beat the Waratahs (representing Australia, as NSW are currently the country's only Union) 18-11 at Twickenham in front of a 50,000 crowd, their first victory over a touring Dominion side since they beat the Maoris in 1889. [The tourists' record in the BI and France was P31–W24–D2–L5.]

17 Mar England beat Scotland 6-0 at Twickenham to achieve their sixth Grand Slam.

9 Apr Despite playing an hour with 14 men, France beat Wales for the first time, 8-3 at the Stade Colombes, after 13 Championship defeats, to share the Wooden Spoon with their opponents and Scotland.

Rules: The four Home Unions ban players and officials contributing articles to newspapers and magazines.

INTERNATIONAL CHAMPIONSHIP

	E	F	I	S	W	P	W	D	L	F	A	Pts
1 ENGLAND	-	18-8	-	6-0	-	4	4	0	0	41	22	8
2 IRELAND	6-7	12-8	-	-	-	4	3	0	1	44	30	6
3=WALES	8-10	-	10-13	-	-	4	1	0	3	34	31	2
3=FRANCE	-	-	-	6-15	8-3	4	1	0	3	30	48	2
3=SCOTLAND	-	-	5-13	-	0-13	4	1	0	3	20	38	2

TOURS (Tests)

New South Wales in British Isles & France: I3-NSW5, W8-NSW18, S10-NSW8, E18-NSW11, F8-NSW11

New Zealand in South Africa: SA17-NZ0, SA6-NZ7, SA11-NZ6, SA5-NZ13

John, the Welsh scrum-half, is dragged to the ground.

International Championship: Wales 8 England 10, Swansea, 21 January

Thrilling struggle as England resist splendid Welsh pack

By Colonel Philip Trevor, CBE

England just beat Wales on Saturday at Swansea by two goals to a goal and a try (10 points to 8), after one of the most desperate struggles ever witnessed in international football. Also, it was in some essentials the most amazing game I ever saw. The superiority of the Welsh pack was so pronounced that in the end it became almost laughable.

The game was played on a quagmire. Indeed, but for the timely aid rendered by the Swansea fire brigade in pumping work, it might not have been possible to play the match.

Well it was for England that they scored the points that gave them their victory while it was just possible to use feet and hands with some degree of accuracy. Their first try came after seven minutes when Aarvold both deluded and eluded the Welsh captain Rowe Harding on the right and drew their back before putting Taylor in. Richardson converted.

A similar chance was missed when Laird decided to kick for touch, but luckily one more chance (and one more only) did the English back division get, after 18 minutes, when good work by Aarvold

and Taylor enabled Laird to get home under the crossbar, Richardson again kicking a goal.

Never again were the English backs in combined action. Wales gained their first try through their right wing Bartlett, following up a forward rush. It failed to produce a goal, and at half-time England led by 10 points to 3.

Soon after the interval the Welsh forwards initiated the siege which was never raised, and this was the amazing part of the match. I do not recall ever having seen anything like it. For roughly half an hour practically without a break there was scrummaging and forward rushing in the England twenty-five. It was all sheer frontal attack – naked and

unashamed. Practically no attempt was made by the Welsh forwards or backs to elude the defence. It was clearly intended to break it down – to batter it to pieces.

Yet the only practical success, after 13 minutes of the second half, came when Ivor Jones took a chance and flung a wide pass out to the right for D John to dash over near the corner flag, for Jones himself superbly to convert.

Then the Welsh attack was renewed with ever increasing severity, and pluck alone saved the Englishmen. It was invariably individual bravery which robbed the Welshmen of some seemingly certain try. And I say without hesitation that in England's dire hour of need full back Sellar was a marvel.

Obituary: Sir G Rowland Hill

Rowland Hill: Rugby Union pioneer

By Colonel Philip Trevor, CBE

With Sir George Rowland Hill, whose death was announced in the later editions of The Daily Telegraph yesterday (25 April), the greatest figure Rugby Union has produced has passed away. He was an uncompromising antagonist, yet I doubt if he ever had an enemy. Even those who differed most strongly from him could not but recognise his selflessness and his unswerving integrity. He championed Rugby football – amateur Rugby football – at a time when its fortunes were at their lowest ebb. 'No compromise' was then his motto, and whether by reason or in spite of it the game won through.

The present generation can scarcely understand the fierceness of the storm which raged when the suggestion of payment for broken time was officially made. Obviously, had

the concession been made, it would have led to any amount of 'wangling'; indeed, to absolute fraud. Equally obviously, the working man was severely handicapped in his competition with the more fortunately situated player. The inevitable happened – there was a split. Rowland Hill was just the one man who could have led with success an opposition which declined even to entertain without wrath what it regarded as an abominable suggestion. He had then earned not merely the admiration and respect of his colleagues, but also their deep and sincere affection.

[Rowland Hill was, in 1926, the first man to be knighted for services to rugby. First elected to the RFU committee in 1879, he served until his death, including 23 years as Hon Sec and three as president.]

Tour Match: South Africa 5 New Zealand 13, Cape Town, 3 September

Test match in South Africa: All Blacks finish strongly

From Reuter

South Africa lost in the fourth and final Test match to the New Zealand All Blacks by 13 points to 5, their first defeat at Newlands since 1891, when McLagan's English XV were victorious. The attendance was a record 25,000.

Frequent showers made both ground and ball slippery, and the play throughout was largely confined to the forwards, although New Zealand employed their backs at every possible

opportunity. Towards the close of the first half the All Blacks began to gain the whip hand, and they unquestionably deserved their victory of one dropped goal, two penalty goals, and one try to one placed goal.

[On this, their first visit to South Africa, the All Blacks shared the Tests 2-2 – after being routed 17-0 in the 1st – and finished with a tour record of P22–W16–D1–L5, Pts 339–144.]

1929

27 Jul Having already clinched their first ever series triumph over New Zealand with 9-8 and 17-9 wins in Sydney and Brisbane, respectively, Australia make it a clean sweep back in Sydney with a 15-13 victory. Both sides finish with 6 tries from the series, and the decisive factor is the 20 points from the boot of stand-off half Tommy Lawton, from 6 penalty goals and a conversion.

31 Aug The 100th Ranfurly Shield match throws up arguably the biggest shock in the history of the competition as Southland (Canterbury), with only 4 All Blacks in their side to the 11 of Wairarapa, beat the holders and overwhelming favourites 19-16 at Carterton. So confident of winning are the Wairarapa RU that they do not bring the trophy to the ground, and after the match an official has to drive 20 miles to Masterton to retrieve the shield from a shop window, where it has been on display.

Representative Match: Hants 5 Barbarians 9, Southampton, 14 September

Hampshire lose: Opening of Trojans' new ground: Bunney in form

From Our Special Correspondent

Even though one could detect lack of practice in much that was done, the football in the match at Banister Court Stadium, Southampton, was always very jolly and enjoyable. The occasion was a memorable one for Rugger in the great Southern seaport, teams representing Hampshire and Barbarians meeting formally to open the new ground of the Trojans' Club. Formerly devoted to greyhounds and now to speedway racing, the enclosure forms an ideal spot for Rugby, with ample seating and stand accommodation, and once the turf recovers from the present prolonged drought, the playing area ought to be very good indeed. The only fly in the ointment is the shortness of the dead-ball line.

Many well-known international players were included in the Barbarians' fifteen, while there were three in that of Hampshire.

The Barbarians won by three tries (9 points) to a goal (5 points). Bunney showed himself to be in first-rate form thus early in the season, while Aarvold played extremely well, not only handling accurately, but giving his passes just at the right time. He was responsible for both the Barbarians' tries towards the end.

International Championship: Scotland 12 England 6, Murrayfield, 16 March

Scotland win the Championship
England outplayed: Macpherson & Smith in form

By Colonel Philip Trevor, CBE

Scotland beat England at Edinburgh on Saturday by four tries to two (12 points to 6) and by so doing won the international championship, and incidentally the Calcutta Cup. It was a great game, and most thoroughly did the Scots deserve their handsome victory.

It has been deliberately decided that in international matches two 'forties' shall be played. Intentionally, therefore, does staying power count. England were outplayed because they were outstayed, and long before the end came they were a rather badly beaten side.

The third Scottish try was a great one. The ball changed hands six times, and Ian Smith successfully finished off the movement. And before the end came, Smith did the same sort of thing once more. Indeed, the whistle for 'No side' came to the relief of the outstaged Englishmen.

No international side this season has played so well as a team as the Scots did in this match. Macpherson in attack was great, and certainly it was his rare combination of ingenuity and daring (for there was always 'method in his madness') which made Smith so dangerous. It was good to be reminded that hand-to-hand passing does pay, and pay right well, too, when you have men doing it who know their job.

Bannerman, who captained the winners, had his now usual experience of being the best forward in the field. It was his 38th consecutive international match, and I do not see how this marvellous record of his can ever be equalled. When all was over he was carried shoulder high in triumph to the dressing-room.

[This was the last international played by Lord Bannerman (Glasgow High School FP), and he retired at the early age of 27. Although they had lost to Wales, Scotland won the title outright thanks to the 5-5 draw between Ireland and Wales, who both finished on 5 points.]

INTERNATIONAL CHAMPIONSHIP

	E	F	I	S	W		P	W	D	L	F	A	Pts
1 SCOTLAND	12-6	6-3	-	-	-		4	3	0	1	41	30	6
2=WALES	-	8-3	-	14-7	-		4	2	1	1	30	23	5
2=IRELAND	-	-	-	7-16	5-5		4	2	1	1	24	26	5
4 ENGLAND	-	-	5-6	-	8-3		4	2	0	2	35	27	4
5 FRANCE	6-16	-	0-6	-	-		4	0	0	4	12	36	0

TOURS (Tests)
New Zealand in Australia: A9-NZ8, A17-NZ9, A15-NZ13

Rowland Hill Memorial Match: Scotland-Ireland 20 England-Wales 13, Twickenham, 5 October

Scotland-Ireland XV triumph: Winners' superior forwards

By Colonel Philip Trevor, CBE

In the Rowland Hill memorial match, played at Twickenham on Saturday, the Scotland-Ireland XV beat the England-Wales XV by three goals (one of which was dropped) and two tries to two goals and a try – 20 points to 13. The winners were undoubtedly the better side and thoroughly deserved their victory.

Before the match began an interesting ceremony was performed when Mr WT Pearce, the president of the English Rugby Union, unveiled a bust of the late Sir G Rowland Hill and opened the new gates erected in memory of him. Mr Pearce's appreciation of the man who did so much throughout his life for Rugby football was to the entire liking of all who heard it.

Many prominent personalities in Rugby football were present when the memorial was opened. Before the ceremony wreaths were laid at the base of the monument from the unions of England, Scotland, Ireland, Wales, France, South Africa, New Zealand, New South Wales, and the Kent County Union, of which Sir Rowland was president.

The memorial consists of a stone column 30 feet high, upon which is the inscription:

'He devoted his life to the service of our game throughout the British Empire.'

On either side of the memorial are oaken gates, which will be reserved for the use of Royal visitors.

Mr Pearce referred to the world-wide significance of the work of the late Sir Rowland Hill and his colleagues. The keynote of the work in the past had been the subordination of trophies or prizes to the game itself. They had built upon an atmosphere free from compulsion, which the Rugby Union strove to maintain today. The memorial was one, not only to Sir Rowland, but

Sir George Rowland Hill.

to all who worked with him and to the game in all parts of the world.

The 1930s

Just as France were beginning to blossom as an international force – two wins in each of the first two seasons of the decade and within one match of winning the title in 1930 – they found themselves frozen out of the Five Nations Championship, excluded because of the inability of their Federation to contain professionalism at club level. It would be 16 years before they returned to the fold.

Honours in the International Championship were spread fairly evenly in the thirties, with England just having the edge, their three outright titles including two Triple Crowns. Scotland blew hot and cold, their two Triple Crowns being offset by five Wooden Spoons!

However, this domestic rivalry continued to be put in its place by the global scene. The British Lions, as they became known in 1930, played attractive football, but were no match for the All Blacks and Springboks in the two tours undertaken during the decade. The 1930 Lions lost the series in New Zealand 3-1 and lost their only Test in Australia, and the 1938 tourists lost 2-1 in South Africa. And although England and Wales both beat the 1935-36 All Blacks, the Springboks made a clean sweep of the Home Countries on their only visit, in 1931-32, and their 2-1 triumph in New Zealand in 1937 (and 2-0 victory over Australia) earned them the unofficial title of world champions.

Howard Marshall, writing in *The Daily Telegraph* on England's defeat by the Springboks at Twickenham in January 1932, made this salient point: 'Here we come to a fundamental difference in the theory of scrummaging. The South Africans have retained their belief in the virtue of combined shoving as the ball comes in – on the principle that the pack which then moves forward will either secure the ball or prevent its opponents from heeling cleanly. In England, on the other hand, specialisation has gradually sapped the strength of scrummaging.

'Three forwards in most English club packs – the hooker and the outside men in the back row – do little or no work, and everything is left to what was once called derisively "the forest of scraping legs". In the English pack on Saturday the front-row forwards were hooking specialists, accustomed to allowing other members of the pack to push while they concentrate on heeling the ball. Is it surprising, therefore, that they buckled up against the strength of Mostert, Kipling and Boy Louw, three hard-working forwards of the highest quality?

'The truth is that South Africa taught us a badly needed lesson. We must return to honest

scrummaging before we can hope to improve the standard of Rugby football in England.'

Compare the same correspondent's report on the defeat of the All Blacks by Swansea in 1935: 'The truth is that the All Blacks do not seem to have appreciated the importance of sound scrummaging as the essential foundation of Rugby football tactics. In earlier matches they packed 3-4, and then, as at Swansea, 3-4-1, but both these formations are quick heeling expedients against inferior packs in dry weather. For all-round scrummaging purposes they are unsound, and on Saturday a heavy drizzle set in and made forward control of a slippery ball imperative.'

The great Wilf Wooller kicks ahead for Wales against England at Cardiff.

Nevertheless by the end of the decade, the Springboks' 3–4–1 scrummaging system had been almost universally adopted. But what did the South Africans do with the ball when it came back out of the scrum? Two of the most significant figures in their supremacy of the early thirties were Danie Craven and Bennie Osler. Scrum-half Craven invented the dive pass, stand-off Osler perpetrated the monotonous punt upfield. Sadly, this latter tactic, although hugely unpopular, produced results – and copyists.

The Lions finished their decade on a high note, winning the last Test against South Africa in 1938. Beset as they were with injuries on that tour – full-back Viv Jenkins, for one, missed the second half of it – and without such stars as Cliff Jones, Wilson Shaw and Wilf Wooller, the Lions, with eight Irish internationals, still impressed with their attractive, offensive style, encouraging the Springboks to open up their own game. It was a wonderful tour, but the end of an era. As war in Europe broke out, there were to be no more major tours for a dozen years.

1930

19 Mar In the 50th Hospitals Cup, Guy's chalk up their 24th success, beating Bart's 18-9 in the final at Richmond, a drop goal and a brilliant try by Windsor Lewis being the highlights.

21 Apr Having beaten Scotland and Ireland, France need to beat Wales in Paris to take their first International Championship, but they go down 11-0, leaving England as champions and finishing joint 2nd with Wales and Ireland. Had Scotland managed to win at Twickenham last month instead of drawing 0-0, the Championship would have finished in a 5-way tie!

Laws: All matches now to be played under International Board rules.

Windsor Lewis: scored brilliant try.

Tour Match: New Zealand 3 Great Britain 6, Dunedin, 21 June

Britain win: Last-minute victory over New Zealand: Ivor Jones in form

From Reuter

For the first time in the history of New Zealand rugby, the famous All Blacks had to admit defeat on the Carisbrook ground, where Britain today won the first of the four Test matches by 2 tries (6 points) to a try (3 points).

Six previous victories at Carisbrook and a team including seven former internationals encouraged the Dominion to look forward to another victory, but, for the most part, Britain had the measure of the New Zealanders, and the crowd of 30,000 saw a hard game and thrilling finish. In the last minute Ivor Jones dodged his way through and gave a perfect pass to Morley, who ran hard from the half-way line and scored a great try.

The British forwards played magnificently throughout and only for one short period early in the second half did the All Blacks hold the upper. Ivor Jones, whose breakaways were a feature of the game, Rew and Beamish, who were both great spoilers, were outstanding in a fine pack which had much the best of all the tight scrums. Bassett's steadiness was equal to that of the famous Nepia; Bowcott's screw-kicking relieved many an awkward situation, and the

heroic defence of Spong held up more than one promising movement. The recently formed Spong-Murray combination was a great success and the British have to thank them for the effective way in which they evaded the attention of that relentless spoiler, Cliff Porter.

Britain won the toss and New Zealand kicked off in real wintry weather, the thickly falling snow being driven across the ground by a stiff wind. Britain at once took up the attack, and Spong, with a clever short punt, sent Reeve away to get over in the corner for the first try of the match.

The cessation of the snow and a freshening wind made the conditions more favourable for New Zealand after the interval, and Hart found an opening in the corner to equalise with a try.

Almost at the end of the game New Zealand were battling to hold their ground when suddenly Ivor Jones nipped in and intercepted a pass. He raced up to Nepia, who was standing just over the half-way line, and, feinting cleverly, drew the full-back, and set Morley up for the dramatic winning try.

[The Lions lost the other three Tests 13-10, 15-10 and 22-8.]

Obiter Dicta (5 February)

French Rugger

H.C.B.

A stern test of English manhood is soon to come. Before the month is out France will play us at Rugger. I doubt if our players, our selectors, even the Olympian wisdom of the Rugby Union itself, is awake to the perils of that encounter.

It is not necessary to have any very intimate acquaintance with the game – always a handicap in criticising players – in order to admire the heroism of men who, in the depth of winter, proceeded from France to Belfast, and defying the ravages of two channels, wore down an Irish pack. But how was the victory won? How were the physique and morale maintained? That is the question for the Rugby Union.

When Panurge wished advice on how to face the perils of life he went on a

voyage to the Oracle of the Divine Bottle, and was answered in the one word, 'Trinq'. The priestess said it was the most gracious and intelligible rule of conduct she had ever heard. They still know their Rabelais in France. When the French fifteen went to Belfast they took with them four kegs of wine. Of course they won.

Now they are coming to Twickenham, and it is not concealed that they are again to be accompanied by wine. I might say it is threatened. This time they have ordered six kegs.

What is the policy of the Rugby Union?

[Whether or not it was too much wine, the French faded after taking the lead at Twickenham and England won 11-5.]

INTERNATIONAL CHAMPIONSHIP

	E	F	I	S	W	P	W	D	L	F	A	Pts
1 ENGLAND	-	11-5	-	0-0	-	4	2	1	1	25	12	5
2=WALES	3-11	-	12-7	-	-	4	2	0	2	35	30	4
2=IRELAND	4-3	0-5	-	-	-	4	2	0	2	25	31	4
2=FRANCE	-	-	-	7-3	0-11	4	2	0	2	17	25	4
5 SCOTLAND	-	11-14	-	12-9	4	1	1	2	26	30	3

TOURS (Tests)
British Isles in New Zealand: NZ3-BI6, NZ13-BI10, NZ15-BI10, NZ22-BI8
British Isles in Australia: A6-BI5

Tour Match: Australia 6 Great Britain 5, Sydney, 30 August

Tourists fail: Australia's single point victory: British injuries

From Reuter

Australia beat Great Britain for the first time in a Rugby Test since 1899 on the Sydney Cricket Ground today by two tries (6 points) to a goal (5 points).

The Australian side for the first Test contained no fewer than ten of the New South Wales team, which the British had defeated so decisively on the same ground a week previously. TS Lawton's presence in the Australian side was a great factor in their success, for, apart from his inspiring play and generalship, there was his ability to hold the elusive Spong.

The British backs made the most of their chances, and the speed of Aarvold and Novis was always a source of considerable anxiety to the Australian defence. Murray

and Spong were excellent, but the attentions of Lawton prevented Spong from making the best of the many fine passes he received.

The game was hard and fast, and it was not until five minutes before half-time that Australia took the lead, Malcolm scoring a brilliant try following a three-quarter movement. From a scrum five minutes after the interval Lawton passed out to Malcolm, who sent his three-quarters away in splendid style for McGhie to score far out.

Then the British team scored. Murray ran round the blind side of the scrum and sent the three-quarters away, Reeve finally sending Novis over for a try, which Prentice converted.

1931

21 Mar In a record-breaking (47 points) Calcutta Cup match, Scotland beat England 28-19 in front of 75,000 at Murrayfield, by 5 goals and a try to 2 goals, 2 tries and a penalty goal.

6 Apr France beat England 14-13 in Paris to leave England without a win for the first time since 1907. More importantly, this is France's last appearance in the International Championship until 1947, the four home unions having severed relations with the French Federation because of the state of French club rugby and the Federation's inability to control a dozen rebel clubs (the 'Douze') which had split away.

INTERNATIONAL CHAMPIONSHIP

	E	F	I	S	W	P	W	D	L	F	A	Pts
1 WALES	-	35-3	-	13-8	-	4	3	1	0	74	25	7
2=SCOTLAND	28-19	6-4	-	-	-	4	2	0	2	47	44	4
2=IRELAND	-	-	-	8-5	3-15	4	2	0	2	17	28	4
2=FRANCE	14-13	-	3-0	-	-	4	2	0	2	24	54	4
5 ENGLAND	-	-	5-6	-	11-11	4	0	1	3	48	59	1

TOURS (Tests)
Australia in New Zealand: NZ20-A13

Paris, 11 February

British clubs and French 'rebels': Current fixtures to stand

British Rugby clubs who have fixtures with any of the French 'rebel' clubs need not fear that these fixtures will have to be cancelled.

Ordinarily British clubs could not meet unaffiliated French clubs, but tonight the French Federation, with the motive of not allowing private quarrels to influence the international side of Rugby, resolved to inform the English Rugby Union that they have no objection to English clubs playing any of the French clubs who have broken away.

They express the hope that the quarrel in France will not in any way affect the cordial relations which have always existed between the French and English Rugby Unions.

[Rumours of professionalism at club level persisted, and the Home Unions severed relations with France.]

International Championship: Ireland 3 Wales 15, Ravenhill, 14 March

Wales win Championship in classic game at Belfast

Gallant Irish struggle with weakened pack

By Howard Marshall

In a game that will take its place with the great games of Rugby history, Wales beat Ireland at Belfast by a goal, two tries, and a dropped goal to a try. Wales thus win the International Championship for the first time since 1922, and unquestionably they are the best side of the year. But if Wales deserve congratulations on their victory, no less do Ireland merit recognition as the most gallant losers of the season.

At the beginning of the second half, with the score 4-3 against them, they unluckily lost Crowe, injured in a tackle, but despite the Welsh try which immediately followed, Ireland, with 14 men, settled down to one of the most magnificent and violent onslaughts I have ever seen. Their seven forwards overwhelmed that great Welsh pack, and for 25 minutes Wales were battered by a sustained attack, which slashed and ripped through their desperate defence with the fury of inspiration.

I shall never forget those glorious Irish rushes – the berserk rage of Beamish, and the venomous raids of Clinch, and Siggins and Pike smashing their way yard by yard with the ball at their feet. Behind these heroic forwards Sugden played like a man possessed, and then Arigho, taking Crowe's place in the centre, went on a series of brilliant glancing runs, stabbing through the gaps to set the crowd aflame with excitement. Three times Arigho flashed between Davey and Williams, on his last thrust being caught and crushed only two feet from the line. That was a great moment, but it marked the end of the Irish effort. The valiant 14 could not stand that pace and gradually Wales took the game in hand, to score two more tries before the end.

Tour Match: Leics & E Midlands 30 Springboks 21, Leicester, 14 November

Surprise defeat of Springboks

Young Midland player hero of amazing game: Slow scores 10 points in first half

By Howard Marshall

At last the Springboks have been beaten. In the 13th match of their tour a combined Leicestershire and East Midlands team trounced them fairly and squarely by six goals (one dropped, one penalty) and a try to two goals (one dropped) and four tries.

They must be a little disappointed at losing their unbeaten record, though we must admit that they were not at full strength.

What a glorious game it was! For the first time the Springboks were thoroughly outplayed in the tight and the loose. The Midland pack was tremendous, but what are we to think of the backs? First Gadney, a fighting scrum-half, and Brumwell, of Bedford, thick-set and springy. And then an unfamiliar face – this is young Slow, of Northampton, pale and slightly built, who a year ago was playing in junior football; Slow – what a name for him! – who is to prove at stand-off half the hero of the match.

I wonder if Slow dreamt at all the night before, dreamt that he would drop a goal and score two tries and pave the way for another? Perhaps he did, and perhaps when the game was over he pinched himself to make certain that his fantastic dream had come true.

[The hero Charles Slow won just a solitary cap as stand-off half for England when they beat Scotland in 1934 to win the Triple Crown. He was killed in a motor accident while serving with the RAF Volunteer Reserve in April 1939.]

Tour Match: Wales 3 Springboks 8, Swansea, 5 December

Springboks' gallant victory in torrential rain: Triumph of Craven

By Howard Marshall

We humbly eat our words this morning, those of us who rashly prophesied that Wales would beat South Africa at Swansea on Saturday. South Africa won, and thoroughly deserved to win, by a goal and a try to a try. Rain fell in torrents throughout the game, and the tail-end of a gale whipped icily across the water-logged playing surface.

The Springbok forwards were magnificent; their vitality, and the speed at which their heavy men followed up on that slimy ground were most impressive, especially during a fiery twenty minutes in the second half when both the Springbok tries were scored.

Then there was Craven at scrum-half, and here is a young player who will surely represent South Africa many times again. He went down to the Welsh foot rushes as if he liked it; he passed, when passing was possible, with speed and accuracy, and frequently he drove the Welshmen back with well-judged kicks to touch.

Wales were ahead through a Davies try when there was a sudden change in the game. Osler kicked ahead, Bassett slipped, and Nel dribbled on for Daneel to score. Then, after a Welsh rally, Nel took a huge fly-kick, there was a scramble on the line, and Bergh hurled himself over for the winning try, which Osler converted.

1932

16 Jan The Springboks complete their 'Grand Slam' against the home countries with a 6-3 win over Scotland at Murrayfield with tries by Osler and Craven, having beaten Wales 8-3, Ireland 8-3 and England 7-0, completing their tour with a W23–D2–L1, Pts 407–124 record.

2 Jul Packing 3–4–1 for the first time in a Test, New Zealand lose 22-17 to Australia at Sydney.

23 Jul Having levelled the rubber by

beating Australia 21-3 in Brisbane on 16 Jul, New Zealand win the final Test at Sydney 21-13, and, after the 30 players join hands and sing 'Auld Lang Syne' in the centre of the field, the winners receive the new trophy, the Bledisloe Cup, presented by the Governor-General of New Zealand for competition between the two countries. *[The Bledisloe Cup was first played for the previous year, but the actual trophy was not available until 1932.]*

Tour Match: England 0 Springboks 7, Twickenham, 2 January

Springboks defeat England by magnificent forward work: South African pack win nearly every scrum

Losers' heroic resistance in second half

By Howard Marshall

It is all over, the great match, and South Africa have beaten England at Twickenham by a dropped goal and a try to nil. Sitting in the stand there afterwards, while the huge crowd slowly eddied away – nearly 70,000 people watched the game – our feelings were curiously mixed. We had seen what we expected to see – the South African forwards smashing the English pack, and Osler's kicking driving England back to their line – but with our admiration was mingled a sense of disappointment.

The splendid South African scrummaging, the heroic English resistance in the second half, Brand's superb dropped goal, these were compensations indeed, and yet we are bound to set against them the weakness of South Africa in constructive play behind the scrummage, the collapse of the English front-row forwards, and a disturbing amount of half-hearted tackling by England.

But first let us pay tribute to South Africa. Their forwards were magnificent. From the 28 set scrums in the first half South Africa heeled 23 times, and we shall not soon forget the way their pack walked over the ball, pushing England as they pleased.

De Villiers, the South African scrum-half, was definitely good, and Waring ran brilliantly now and again, but Zimmerman was held by

Aarvold, van der Westhuizen was too slow, and Osler was not at his best.

Osler, indeed, was disappointing. Certainly his kicking was valuable, though it was not as accurate as usual, and it may be that he was rightly so anxious that South Africa should win that he did not feel justified in taking any chances.

The fact remains, however, that no stand-off half can ever have had the ball so regularly in an international match and done so little with it. Osler rarely opened up the game, preferring to kick or run on his own.

After 15 minutes came a curious try, for a Springbok forward fly-kicked after a line-out, the ball slithered over the line through Barr's upstretched hands, and Bergh followed fast and touched down before the unfortunate Barr could save.

Brand failed to convert, but South Africa were three points ahead and they clung desperately to their lead. In the second half, South Africa worked their way to the English twenty-five and remained there. This was the period of England's heroic resistance, for the Springboks were pounding at the defence with terrible venom, but time after time the Englishmen tackled and fell and cleared. It was stirring football, this, and Osler seemed to decide that the only way to score was over

---

Wales robbed of rugby honours in dramatic game: Last-minute kick fails

By Howard Marshall

In a game so desperately close that the result hung upon the very last kick of all, Ireland beat Wales at Cardiff by four tries to a dropped goal and two tries, thus deservedly sharing the honours in the International championship.

A glorious victory it was, and a glorious game, and when in the final minute, with Ireland leading by five points, Ralph took a long pass from

Powell and raced through a scattered defence to score near the posts, we were certain that Bassett would kick a goal and force a draw.

A mighty groan went up as he failed, only to be drowned by a still mightier cheer when the referee immediately blew his whistle for 'no-side', and the sporting Welsh crowd realised that Ireland had won.

INTERNATIONAL CHAMPIONSHIP

	E	I	S	W		P	W	D	L	F	A	Pts
1=IRELAND	8-11	-	-	-		3	2	0	1	40	29	4
1=WALES	12-5	10-12	-	-		3	2	0	1	28	17	4
1=ENGLAND	-	-	16-3	-		3	2	0	1	32	23	4
4 SCOTLAND	-	8-20	-	0-6		3	0	0	3	11	42	0

TOURS (Tests)
South Africa in British Isles: E0-SA7, I3-SA8, S3-SA6, W3-SA8
New Zealand in Australia: A22-NZ17, A3-NZ21, A13-NZ21

---

2 September

Rugby football bombshell
Board's censure of modern tactics
By Howard Marshall

The International Rugby board last night issued one of the most revolutionary statements in connection with Rugby football which has appeared since the war.

It consists of a wholesale condemnation of modern scrummaging methods, and it takes the form of a plea to players, referees, and club officials to abolish specialisation among forwards in order that the spirit and standards of the game may be preserved.

The statement is highly controversial in itself, but particularly significant are the implications it contains. There can be no doubt that the International Board are

most seriously concerned for the future welfare of Rugby football, for only real perturbation could have forced them to publish so sweeping an attack on present tendencies.

At first sight the manifesto seems to be making a large mountain out of a small molehill, though no one will deny that the board have reason for many of their conclusions. At any rate, it is certain that they have taken an unprecedented step in thus attempting to check the evolution of the game, and their action will cause widespread discussion in Rugby football circles.

---

the heads of the English defenders. Five times he dropped at goal, and five times he missed, until slowly England relieved the pressure.

So it went until there were two minutes to go, and England were awarded a penalty on their own line. Barr took the kick, and a long

kick it was to half-way, but it did not find touch. Brand caught it, ran a few yards, paused, and took a drop with his left foot, and there was the ball, driven with superb power and accuracy high between the posts. A great kick, and a worthy vindication of South Africa's hard-earned victory.

1933

4 Mar JA Crawford scores 4 of the Army's 5 tries in their 19-0 defeat of the Navy at Twickenham. [The Army later beat the RAF 12-3 to win the Triangular Services Tournament.]

1 Apr The Ireland-Scotland match at Dublin, postponed from February because of snow, turns out unusually to be the Championship decider, and Scotland beat Ireland a little luckily by 2 dropped goals to 2 tries, 8pts to 6, while clinching the

Triple Crown (the other three countries finish on 2pts). Ian Smith, appointed captain after last season's débâcle when they lost all three internationals, plays his 32nd and last match for Scotland.

2 Sep The Wallabies beat South Africa 15-4 at Bloemfontein, and although they lose the rubber 3-2 are acclaimed for their fine performance against the powerful Springboks.

International Championship: England 3 Wales 7, Twickenham, 21 Jan

England are fairly and squarely beaten by the Welsh at Twickenham

Wooller's great promise: A doubtful try

By Howard Marshall

A line-out during the international at Twickenham.

Most appropriately, The Prince of Wales was present on Saturday to see the first victory of a Welsh team at Twickenham, where England were fairly and squarely beaten by a dropped goal and a try to a try.

Unfortunately, the game was marred by a serious injury to Gerrard, the English centre, who left the field early in the second half after colliding with Davey.

Then there were two incidents during the match which aroused considerable controversy. To begin with, did Elliot score a try for England? For the purposes of the record book, he did, though he is not entirely convinced about it himself. He was tackled heavily as he flung himself over the line, and to many of us it seemed that the ball was jerked

forward out of his hands before he could touch it down.

But about the other incident there is no doubt whatever. This occurred when Wales scored, and Jenkins' kick at goal sent the ball at least a yard outside the right-hand post. The Welsh touch-judge put his flag up, but the English touch-judge signalled that the kick had failed, and the referee did not blow his whistle. To our surprise the score-board registered a goal to Wales, and as this mistake was never corrected, many people must have left the ground believing that the Welshmen had made themselves virtually safe by gaining a six-points lead.

And now, after congratulating Wales on a thoroughly well-earned victory, we are bound to admit, I think, that the game itself was disap-

---

Varsity Match: Oxford University 5 Cambridge University 3, Twickenham, 12 December

Oxford win by two points: Great full-back display by Owen-Smith

By Howard Marshall

By the skin of their teeth – a goal to a try, to be exact – Oxford beat Cambridge at Twickenham yesterday, and never has a victory been more hard earned.

There were long, agonising periods when the battle swayed perilously upon the Oxford line, and there were Cambridge drop kicks and penalties which shaved the posts. I will not have it, though, that Oxford were lucky to win. Cambridge had the better of the play, but the object of Rugby football is to score points, and there Cambridge failed.

In a sense it was a sterile game; the backs from whom we had hoped so much were frustrated. Not once was CW Jones able to show us that dazzling run of his. Cranmer did jink inwards to pave the way for the Oxford try, but, after that, defence was his lot.

Warr, the Oxford right wing, was pegged to the touchline, Rees-Jones spent his time stopping Johnston, and of all the men behind the scrummage Owen-Smith, the Oxford full-back, was the only one who found it possible to give final and positive proof of his worth.

Owen-Smith is a great player, there is no doubt of that. He was as safe as a sandbank, with his intelligent positioning, his perfect fielding, and those long spinning kicks which time

and again sent the Cambridge forwards panting back thirty, forty, fifty yards.

Cambridge were soon into their stride, and we gasped as a drop by Wooller fell just below the bar. Then came two exquisitely judged kicks by Owen-Smith, and Cambridge were defending for a change. A drop by Jackson, a glorious forward rush by Cambridge, a line-out, and there was Cranmer, going right-handed, turning inwards, through and away, with only Parker to beat. A great moment; Cranmer kicked ahead, the ball skidded over the line, and Nicholson, most persevering of hookers, was up to touch down. Jackson kicked the goal, but before the Oxford cheers had died away Cambridge heeled on the Oxford twenty-five, Dick slipped through a badly aligned defence, went straight as a bullet, and fell over the line as Owen-Smith took him round the ankles. A glorious try, but Fyfe missed a difficult kick, and Oxford still led.

In the second half, Cambridge launched a tremendous assault, and Oxford were penned in their own twenty-five, tackling, tackling, tackling, but unable to escape. Then Fyfe missed a penalty in a relatively easy position for Cambridge, before they were driven back and held until the end of a magnificently hard game.

INTERNATIONAL CHAMPIONSHIP

	E	I	S	W	P	W	D	L	F	A	Pts
1 SCOTLAND	3-0	-	-	3-7	3	3	0	0	22	9	6
2=ENGLAND	-	17-6	-	-	3	1	0	2	20	16	2
2=IRELAND	-	-	6-8	10-5	3	1	0	2	22	30	2
2=WALES	-	-	3-11	-	3	1	0	2	15	24	2

TOURS (Tests)
Australia in South Africa: SA17-A3, SA6-A21, SA12-A3, SA11-A0, SA4-A15

---

pointing. Still, Wales may look to the future with considerable confidence. If Bowcott was not constructive, his beautiful kicking and his saving and his general alertness were extremely valuable, and, even more important, I believe young Wooller is a great player in the making.

It is plain enough that Wooller has the big match temperament, and though he made mistakes and found Burland rather too much of a

handful, he did his job for the most part with an impressively steady efficiency. He had few opportunities in attack, but now and again he got off the mark with a burst of speed and a long stride which suggest that he will be awkward to stop when he has filled out in a year or two's time. What is more, he saved a certain and possibly decisive try by overhauling and tackling Elliot when he had broken clear away.

1934

Jan FIRA (Federation of Amateur Rugby) is founded by Czechoslovakia, France, Germany, Holland, Italy, Portugal, Romania, Catalonia (Spain) and Sweden. Belgium join in March.

10 Mar East Midlands win the County Championship for the first time, beating Gloucestershire 10-0 in the final at Northampton.

25 Aug Australia win the Bledisloe Cup (inaugurated 1931) for the first time, holding New Zealand to a 3-3 draw at Sydney Cricket Ground, having won the first of the two-Test series 25-11 a fortnight earlier.

Paris, 17 May

No rugby with France: The British unions are unanimous

From Reuter

The four British Rugby Unions, in their reply to the French Federation, have decided that the time is not yet ripe for a resumption of international matches with France.

A translation of an extract of the letter, just received by the French Federation, reads: 'If your federation has done much for the recovery of Rugby, we consider it has not yet done sufficient.

'As long as Rugby, as practised in France, is not played in the right spirit and in accordance with the traditions of the game long ago laid down by the home unions, and, above all, as long as the present system of competition exists in France, it will not be possible to consider the arranging of international or inter-club matches.'

This negative reply has caused much disappointment in France.

'A masterly slap in the face,' is the comment of the Paris Soir.

M. Dantou, President of the French Federation, who was a member of the delegation which recently visited London, expressing his personal opinion, said:

'I consider that we have no lessons or suggestions to receive from the British Unions. We have done without them for three years, and we shall continue to do without them in the future. As for suppressing competitions, like the French championship, I reply, speaking for myself, that this is our business.'

Tour Match: Blackheath 13 Barbarians 16, 26 December

Christmas spirit at Blackheath
Barbarians triumph in last five minutes

By Howard Marshall

No fog; no mist; clear, bright, jovial, stirring; the Barbarians playing Blackheath at the Rectory Field and beating them on the post by 2 goals and 2 tries to 2 goals and a penalty goal. Oh, glorious, glorious!

If you know your Dickens, you will have recognised his touch by now, and since he simply will not keep out of this little account of a Boxing Day football match he may as well continue. 'Wonderful party, wonderful game, wonderful unanimity, won-der-ful happiness.'

I could almost imagine that the reformed Scrooge was with me, and that I heard the old gentleman chuckle and shout, 'Hullo! Whoop! Hullo there!' when we met Major BC Hartley dressed up as Father Christmas, collecting for the Kent Playing Fields Association.

It was certainly Scrooge who chortled, 'An intelligent boy! A remarkable boy! It's a pleasure to watch him run,' when Shaw flashed into attack so brilliantly for the Barbarians in the second half.

Never mind the blunders and mistakes. Never mind the famous players who cherished, I dare say, hopes of English caps and corresponding fears of premature injury. They were

International Championship: Wales 13 Ireland 0, Swansea, 10 March

Wales win in desperate rally
Three tries in last ten minutes: Ireland are gallant losers after having most of game

By Howard Marshall

Wales must be pleased with their victory over Ireland by two goals and a try to nil at Swansea, for now they may share the international championship, that mythical honour, if Scotland should happen to win the Calcutta Cup match next week.

Ireland, on the contrary, must be bitterly disappointed. They went desperately near to winning at Swansea for the first time since 1888, and there is little consolation in the fact that they were only beaten in the last ten minutes of a remarkable game.

Everyone agreed, and Welshmen were particularly generous in their comments after the match, that Ireland deserved a kinder fate. For the first hour of play there was no scoring, but Ireland definitely held the upper hand. They missed tries by inches; their forwards were magnificent; their inexperienced backs did better than even their own supporters could have expected.

Ireland's reward seemed certain when Bailey intercepted, broke clear, and was racing for the line. But Bassett shot across and brought him down with a crash. This actually was the turning point; Jenkins kicked the ball over the stand; CW Jones began his bewildering running, with the new ball; and Wales had suddenly found themselves. By scoring three times in five minutes, they proceeded to turn possible defeat into brilliant victory.

Jenkins dived over for a try, which he converted himself with a glorious kick. Fear managed to wriggle over and score. And then CW Jones rubbed it in by swerving through the defence and sending Cowey away for the last try of the match, a try which Jenkins converted from the touch-line with another superb kick.

[The Welsh efforts were in vain, as England won the Calcutta Cup – and with it the mythical Championship and Triple Crown – beating Scotland 6-3 at Twickenham.]

INTERNATIONAL CHAMPIONSHIP

	E	I	S	W		P	W	D	L	F	A	Pts
1 ENGLAND	-	-	6-3	-		3	3	0	0	28	6	6
2 WALES	0-9	13-0	-	-		3	2	0	1	26	15	4
3 SCOTLAND	-	16-9	-	6-13		3	1	0	2	25	28	2
4 IRELAND	3-13	-	-	-		3	0	0	3	12	42	0

TOURS (Tests)
New Zealand in Australia: A25-NZ11, A3-NZ3

excused by Bob Cratchit's plea, 'It's only once a year, sir. It shall not be repeated. I was making rather merry yesterday, sir.'

And, truth to tell, the Barbarians were rather at sixes and sevens. GS Cottington cried off at the last moment, so they took the field with only seven forwards. And then, just before half-time, Hordern hurt his right ankle, and had to leave the field.

Singing 'Good King Wenceslas' with what little breath remained to them, the Barbarians faced their troubles, but soon after the interval were 13-5 down. Suddenly Logan slipped away again, and put Cowey in, and then Shaw, running beautifully, circled round the right wing, cut inside, and found Cowey up to take the scoring pass. Forrest converted this excellent try, the scores were level, and five minutes to go.

This was a match-winner's moment, and Heaton, they say, has won matches before now. He won another yesterday, whipping crack through the centre, and sending Shaw away to dash over the line and give the Barbarians every reason for remarking, like Scrooge, 'We will now discuss our affairs cheerfully this very afternoon over a Christmas bowl of smoking bishop.'

1935

8 Mar Lancashire, three times losing finalists in the last six years, win the County Championship for the first time since before the 'split' of 1895, beating Somerset 14-0 at Bath.

16 Mar England, throwing away chances galore, go down 10-7 at Murrayfield, leaving Ireland outright winners of the International Championship for the first time since 1899.

14 Apr Cambridge University beat Eastern Universities 23-9 in New York to complete their 4-match tour of the USA with a 100% record, having played the last 3 games in 4 days.

27 Apr Harlequins I beat London Welsh

10-3 at Twickenham to win the 10th Middlesex Sevens, their sixth success in the tournament.

4 May In Jubilee Trust Fund matches (King George V's Silver Jubilee) breaking into the close season, the Barbarians beat London 34-3 with ridiculous ease at Twickenham and Wales beat the Rest 13-5 at Cardiff.

28 Sep The All Blacks suffer only their second defeat in Europe (the first was at Cardiff in 1905 at the hands of Wales), losing 11-3 to a superb Swansea side served well by a dominant pack and brilliant young half-backs in Tanner and Davies.

INTERNATIONAL CHAMPIONSHIP

	E	I	S	W	P	W	D	L	F	A	Pts
1 IRELAND	-	-	12-5	9-3	3	2	0	1	24	22	4
2=ENGLAND	-	14-3	-	3-3	3	1	1	1	24	16	3
2=WALES	-	-	10-6	-	3	1	1	1	16	18	3
4 SCOTLAND	10-7	-	-	-	3	1	0	2	21	29	2

Services Tournament: The Army 11 Royal Navy 8, Twickenham, 2 March

Army's gallant victory over Navy: Champions finish without Cowey and Kendrew

By Howard Marshall

In the presence of the Duke of York, the Army beat the Royal Navy at Twickenham by a goal, a penalty goal and a try to a goal and a try.

Put thus, baldly, it would seem that the result leaves us with little cause for enthusiasm. You may even argue that it is always unsatisfactory when a match is won by the margin of a penalty goal, to which I reply that if back-row forwards persist in lurking off-side, these things will happen.

A plague upon back-row forwards, anyhow. The salient point about this match is that the Army won their fourth successive victory with two of their best players off the field. Cowey, their international

right wing, was hurt after five minutes, much to the chagrin of one of the Welsh selectors who had come to watch him, and 20 minutes later the great Kendrew smashed a shoulder, and very reluctantly had to retire.

Sayers was put out on the wing, therefore, and with 13 men the Army plugged away indomitably, and by a mixture of splendid defence and intelligent opportunism were able to turn misfortune into triumph. The six Army forwards stuck to their guns heroically, and behind the scrummage such players as Dean, Cole, Unwin and Novis – particularly Novis – were a class better than their opponents.

Tour Match: Wales 13 New Zealand 12, Cardiff Arms Park, 21 December

Wales' greatest rugby triumph

Wooller the hero of historic match: A palpitating finish

By Howard Marshall

When New Zealand had made their last furious onslaught, and Wales had won by a single point at Cardiff, I saw a man part with his bowler hat for ever. He flung it far into the swirling crowd, and I was sorry to see it go.

That bowler had suitably punctuated a glorious game for me. When New Zealand scored in the first half it tilted lugubriously over its owner's nose. Then came that astonishing second half.

Two goals to Wales in six minutes, and the bowler was so prodigiously thumped that it became a billycock. A great dropped goal by Gilbert, another converted try which gave New Zealand the lead again, and the billycock swayed perilously upon its shattered brim.

The last Welsh try, three minutes before the end, and a hand like a ham descended from the row behind and turned the billycock into an opera-hat which would never open again.

What a game, what players, what prodigious excitement! They will still be telling the story of it all in 50 years' time. It will have become a little exaggerated by then, I dare say. The frosty December afternoon will grow colder; the players will increase in stature.

Our grandchildren, I do not doubt, will hear of a giant Welsh centre three-quarter brushing the New Zealand backs aside like flies.

This giant Wooller, their fathers will explain, was nearly seven feet high, and one of the greatest centres who ever smashed a desperate defence. And upon my word, where the question of Wooller's greatness is concerned, I do not think they will be exaggerating unduly.

A wintry afternoon right enough, with patches of frost showing, and bundles of straw round the playing pitch, and 50,000 spectators overcoated and muffled and rather red-nosed. I never saw a more splendid match, fine in spirit

and performance and strong endeavour.

An extraordinary match, too, for all the Welsh tries followed punts ahead, and how often do we see the punt ahead which bounces kindly for the attacking team?

Then Gilbert dropped a goal from 40 yards' range and a wide angle, with a low, raking shot which never seemed likely to carry the distance. Somehow, though, the ball bored its way through the air, and 50,000 Welshmen watched in horrified silence as it fell over the bar.

It was from another drop at goal, moreover, that Ball snatched an unexpectedly easy try after Wales had fumbled, so that opportunism was the order of the day.

The New Zealanders, I believe, thought little of Jones and Wooller before the game, but I expect they have changed their minds now. All the Welsh backs, indeed, played up to their reputations, and if Idwal Rees, the Welsh captain, was less spectacular

than the others, his football sense and his beautiful kicking saved Wales time and again.

It was Idwal Rees, with Wales trailing by two points and Tarr having been carried off with concussion, who shot the ball across from the wing for Wooller to stride round the defence again. The Cambridge man straightened and then kicked ahead, leaping for the ball as it bounced over the line, missing it, only to find the faithful Rees-Jones there once more to touch down for his second try.

At that, pandemonium broke loose, for there were only three minutes to go. As New Zealand spared neither themselves nor their opponents, twice more Idwal Rees was called upon to field long, high punts down the middle, with the New Zealand forwards pounding up on him. And twice more Rees made his catch and found his touch before the whistle went to end as grand and historic a match as ever was played.

1936

14 Mar Fire hoses are turned on the crowd at Cardiff Arms Park as an attempt is made to rush the barriers at the match against Ireland, when the gates are closed two hours before the kick-off with a record 60–70,000 inside. Spectators spill onto the pitch, and at one time are standing 15 deep along the touch-line. One man collapses and dies. Ireland lose their chance of the Triple Crown as Wales snatch the Championship from them with a penalty kick.

31 Aug On the way home from Argentina, the British touring side stop off to play a Brazilian XV in Niteroi, winning 82-0, with Prince Alexander Obolensky scoring 17 tries, a record for a representative match.

Tour Match: England 13 New Zealand 0, Twickenham 4 January

Obolensky's two historic tries: Twickenham sees England's first triumph over All Blacks

By Howard Marshall

So England have beaten New Zealand at last! A clear-cut, decisive victory at Twickenham by a dropped goal and three tries to nil, and the 70,000 spectators will remember it for the rest of their lives.

Again and again this great match will be discussed. As we talk of it smoking our pipes, we shall see once more the white figure of Obolensky, running gloriously, and Peter Cranmer, smashing his way through the centre, and the English forwards, solid as a wall against which the black waves of New Zealand broke in vain.

It does not greatly matter that this is the first time any combination of English players has beaten a New Zealand team. What does matter is the quality of the game itself, and this was higher than we had any reason to expect.

England played magnificently – let there be no mistake about that. The English selectors had summed up the New Zealand methods, and picked their men accordingly. New Zealand would concentrate on midfield attack. Very well, Hamilton-Hill, Candler, Cranmer and Gerrard would be there to stop them, and stop them they did, with a vengeance. Never has Caughey been so ruthlessly put down, and even Oliver, most dangerous of runners, was given short shrift.

England harried the New Zealand attack with merciless vigilance, with a proper bulldog tenacity which never lost its grip.

Then, said our selectors, these New Zealand forwards must be pounded and shaken – and pounded and shaken they were. The tight scrummaging ran fairly level, but the tearaway loose rushes of New Zealand were steadily controlled and held and worn down by the strength and weight of this grand English pack.

With the sting thus taken out of the New Zealand attack, the next problem was for England to score, and Cranmer was the man to find that gap in the New Zealand midfield defence. Twice he found it, and went thundering up the centre to pave the way for tries, and once he checked suddenly and dropped a beautiful goal. The rest is Obolensky.

New Zealand must have been painfully surprised by the brilliance of Obolensky's running, though they had played against him on a miserably wet day at Oxford.

Obolensky has the most deceptive change of pace. He fades past his opponents like a ghost. I shall never forget how Gilbert raised a hand helplessly, with a look of almost comical resignation on his face, as Obolensky lengthened his stride and raced round him to score England's first try.

Obolensky has a genius for the game. The instinct which took him inwards from the right wing to run diagonally across the field and score his second try in the left corner showed the real player. Here is no mere sprinter, but a footballer who uses the weapon of exceptional speed with intelligence and precision.

This has, indeed, been a rich season, and we must be grateful to New Zealand for the stimulus they have given to our game. They will not begrudge us our victory, I am sure, disappointed though they must have been.

Obolensky scores his second try against the All Blacks.

Middlesex Sevens Final: Sale 18 Blackheath I 6, Twickenham, 25 April

Sale triumph in 'sevens' tournament

By HALF-BACK

Sale, weary but happy, toiled up the steps to the committee box at Twickenham and received the Kinross Arber Cup for winning the Middlesex Seven-a-Side Tournament.

It was the first time Sale had competed, and they were easily the best side on view. They defeated Blackheath in the final by three goals and a try to two tries before the biggest crowd I have ever seen for the event.

They were the most colourful side entered, with Claude Davey, W Wooller and KC Fyfe running beautifully. These three combined in some of the cleverest movements of the day, and although Blackheath rallied, Sale never really looked like losing.

Tour Match: Combined Argentine XV 0 British XV 27, Buenos Aires, 20 July

British XV again win easily: Combined Argentine side routed

From Reuter

Playing the second match of their Argentine tour, the British Rugby Union team, under the captaincy of BC Gadney, defeated a combined Argentine team by 27-0. HJM Uren, the Waterloo full-back, played a great game for the British side, and Gadney was conspicuous all through.

After a thrilling opening, in which the Argentine side held their own well, the visitors gradually gained the upper hand. Their tries were scored by JA Tallent (3), CV Boyle (2), and RW Shaw (2), the last-named, who played on the wing during the latter stages of the game, converting three of them.

[The tourists went on to win all 10 of their matches in what was a 'demonstration' of how the modern game is played. They scored 399 points, conceding only 12, and Belgrano were the only side to cross their line. The British XV beat Argentine Pacific Athletic Club 62-0, a record score against an Argentine side, and beat Argentina 23-0 in an unofficial international.]

1937

20 Mar The International Board announce changes to the scrummage law, which has been a subject of debate for some time and resulted in the setting up a year ago of a sub-committee to recommend simplifications. The main change states that the ball shall be put in 'fairly at a moderate speed so that it first touches the ground beyond one foot of the nearest player of each front row'. Another change affects the penalty try, which must now always be awarded between the posts irrespective of where the offence occurs. The Board also express dissatisfaction with the refereeing in international matches and insist they must be refereed 'in full accordance with the laws of the game'.

24 Mar St Mary's win the Hospitals' Cup for the fourth season in a row, beating Guy's 11-4 in the final at Richmond, thanks largely to their strong, fast forwards.

International Championship: Scotland 3 England 6, Murrayfield, 20 March

England win championship: Keep Calcutta Cup & beat Murrayfield hoodoo

By Howard Marshall

They carried Owen-Smith triumphantly to the dressing-room after the match. They tried to carry Sever. A small boy with an autograph book sprang mysteriously from every tuft of grass. By two tries to a penalty goal England had beaten Scotland at Murrayfield for the first time, after six successive defeats, and this historic victory carried with it the Calcutta Cup, the international championship, and that grandiose but mythical distinction, the Triple Crown.

Championships, caps and crowns you may keep, for all I care, but humble the Scotsmen at Murrayfield and every English player becomes a hero.

If the reverberations of England's triumph were to be heard at the Waverley station later that evening, who shall complain? England had beaten the Scotsmen in their own lair, thumped and spreadeagled them properly at last. They had conquered the Murrayfield hoodoo, and English throats, already raw, shouted themselves hoarse for life.

Swansea 3 Cardiff 4: St Helen's, 20 March

Wooller and referee booed at Swansea – but Cardiff win

By Rowe Harding

Cardiff beat Swansea for the fourth time this season, winning at Swansea by a dropped goal to a penalty goal.

It was a singularly unpleasant game, completely spoilt, for me at any rate, by the disgraceful conduct of a section of the crowd, who booed either Wooller or the referee almost unceasingly throughout the game.

Referee-baiting is unfortunately common enough, but this singling out of a star player for hostile criticism of the most offensive kind, merely because he is a star player, is an unusual and most unwelcome departure from the principles of fair play.

I saw no justification for the crowd's attitude, either to Wooller or to the referee, who was both competent and impartial.

The game itself was disappointing, though Swansea did much better than expected and were unlucky to lose in the last few minutes after holding on grimly to the slender lead they had gained early in the first half when G Jenkins kicked a penalty goal.

With only a few minutes left, Cardiff forced a scrum on the Swansea line. They heeled the ball, and Morgan passed back to Wooller, who dropped a goal and so won yet another match for Cardiff.

International Championship: England 9 Ireland 8, Twickenham, 13 February

Brilliant Sever scores the try of a lifetime
Remarkable run wins game for England: Real rugby at last

By Howard Marshall

Another addition to our rich store of Rugby memories – five minutes to go – Ireland two points ahead in a desperately close game at Twickenham – suddenly the thickset figure of Sever breaking clear – pounding along the left touch-line – running 60 yards – 60 miles it seemed – Boyle racing across to cut him off – Sever swinging inwards – Malcolmson and Boyle hitting him like thunder – Sever swinging left again – driving forward with his powerful thighs – plunging over to score the great try which gave England victory by a single point.

It was the sort of try which the hero of a school story scores in the last chapter, and it enabled England to scrape home by a penalty goal and two tries to a goal and a try.

Were you there, in that yelling crowd? Did you see that tremendous run? And did you wonder, as I did, how Sever found the strength to reach the line and hurl himself over with Boyle and Malcolmson clinging to him, when all the afternoon he had taken such a hammering from the 13-stone Moran?

Sever, with his pale, determined face, is swiftly becoming one of the game's great characters. As we waited for play to begin, Irishmen were apprehensively recalling his smashing try in Dublin last year, when he ploughed through the Irish pack and left two massive Irish forwards stretched out for dead. And it was Sever, you will remember, who dropped the decisive goal against Wales a month ago.

Now it is not often that we have a chance to talk about a match like this. I dare say there have been better matches, from the purists' point of view, matches with more brilliant football to raise them above the ordinary. This match, though, had a quality of its own, a vitality which silences, temporarily at least, all critical mugwumpery.

It was a convincing answer, anyway, to the demand for new legislation. We do not need new laws, but a revival of the old spirit, a revival which took place in this particular game.

INTERNATIONAL CHAMPIONSHIP											
	E	I	S	W		P	W	D	L	F	A	Pts
1 ENGLAND	-	9-8	-	4-3		3	3	0	0	19	14	6
2 IRELAND	-	-	11-4	5-3		3	2	0	1	24	16	4
3 SCOTLAND	3-6	-	-	-		3	1	0	2	20	23	2
4 WALES	-	-	6-13	-		3	0	0	3	12	22	0

TOURS (Tests)
South Africa in Australia: A5-SA9, A17-SA26
South Africa in New Zealand: NZ13-SA7, NZ6-SA13, NZ6-SA17

Tour Match: New Zealand 6 South Africa 17, Auckland, 25 September

South Africa win test rubber

South Africa gained a decisive victory by 17 points to 6 over New Zealand in the final Rugby Union test match here today, and won the rubber by two matches to one.

There was no doubt about the superiority of the Springboks, who dominated the scrums, and New Zealand's only points came from two penalty goals by D Trevathan (Otago), one in each half.

South Africa's tries were scored by L Babrow (Western Province) (2), FG Turner (Transvaal), DO Williams (W Province) and WF Bergh (Transvaal), GH Brand (W Province) converting one.

1938

5 Feb Scotland beat Wales 8-6 at Murrayfield in a match that proves to be the deciding one of the Championship. The points tally is the lowest of a season where all four-nation Championship records are smashed, 176 points and 35 tries against 142 points and 32 tries in 1908 and 1904 respectively. England, in third place, register 60 points

6 Aug Playing their first Test in South Africa for 14 years, the British touring team three times lose the lead to go down 26-12, 4 goals and 2 penalty goals to 4 penalty goals, in front of a record South African crowd of 36,000 at Ellis Park, Johannesburg.

22 Dec Cardiff full-back Alban Davies is expelled from the game by the Welsh Rugby Union for contravening the laws on professionalism, namely for claiming £3 for loss of work when 'assisting' Major RV Stanley's team at Oxford.

INTERNATIONAL CHAMPIONSHIP

	E	I	S	W	P	W	D	L	F	A	Pts
1 SCOTLAND	-	23-14	-	8-6	3	3	0	0	52	36	6
2 WALES	14-8	11-5	-	-	3	2	0	1	31	21	4
3 ENGLAND	-	-	16-21	-	3	1	0	2	60	49	2
4 IRELAND	14-36	-	-	-	3	0	0	3	33	70	0

TOURS (Tests)
British Isles in South Africa: SA26-BI12; SA19-BI3; SA16-BI21
New Zealand in Australia: A9-NZ24, A14-NZ20, A6-NZ14

Tour Match: South Africa 16 British Isles 21, Cape Town, 10 September

Britain's recovery: South Africans fail in third test

From Reuter

A fine second-half recovery enabled Great Britain to win the third and final Test against South Africa here today by 21 points to 16.

South Africa led by 13-3 at half-time, and many thought that Britain was due for another heavy defeat. But the tourists fought back in grand style and scored 11 more points without reply, to take the lead at 14-13 midway through the second half.

In spite of desperate South African attacks, the British clung on to their one-point lead until, six minutes from time, FG Turner gave South Africa the lead with a penalty goal.

The British, however, did not give up, and CF Grieve, their full-back, dropped a great goal from 40 yards to make the score 18-16 in Britain's favour. Just before the end PL Duff made certain by scoring a try.

For the first time, the British were really successful in the scrums, which were very even throughout. The British forwards gave a grand display in the loose, with Walker and Dancer outstanding.

International Championship: England 16 Scotland 21, Twickenham, 19 March

Scotland again rugby champions: Dramatic victory against England

By Howard Marshall

In a magnificent match, played before their Majesties the King and Queen, Scotland beat England well and truly at Twickenham by 2 penalty goals and 5 tries to 3 penalty goals, a dropped goal and a try.

Scotland thus most deservedly won the Calcutta Cup, the international championship, and the Triple Crown, which is a romantic way of saying that Scotland have defeated Wales, Ireland and England in turn.

If there were any more honours available, Scotland would deserve them all. The score is sufficient evidence of that, for Scotland crossed the English line five times, whereas England could snatch only one try and a dropped goal. The penalty goals we will omit as redundant frivolities, though they were beautifully kicked by the respective champions, Parker and Crawford.

Taking it by and large, I cannot remember a more interesting and remarkable match. It was a fitting climax to a season of phenomenally high scoring, and I am quite prepared to swallow my national pride – what is left of it, that is to say – and welcome the fact that attack so decisively beat defence.

What an afternoon it was, to be sure! The sun shone with summer benevolence, and the gates were shut at 2.30, with a mile-long queue of optimists waiting to get in, and approaching cars inextricably tangled on the roads of half a county.

A gusty, swirling, powerful wind blew behind England in the first half, and yet Scotland managed to score four tries to two penalty goals and a try. The second half was extraordinary. Scotland, we thought, with the wind to help them, must surely go romping through the English defence, but with the true perversity of Rugby football, England monopolised the ball in the tight and actually did most of the pressing.

There was the crux of the matter. The England forwards did enough to win the match four times over. If they had kept the ball, and used the wheel and the straight shove, they probably would have won it.

As it was, they heeled from nine scrums out of 10, but their backs were helpless. Duff bottled Giles, and Crawford went straight up on Reynolds like a shot out of a gun, and the English attack was smothered and smashed.

The Scottish backs were like a steel spring, waiting for release. Whenever the ball did come to them, and it came so rarely, they threatened to score. Ironically enough, the first really quick Scottish heel occurred in the last five minutes, and Shaw promptly flashed through the English defence like a knife through butter.

How brilliantly Shaw played, and the whole three-quarter line behind him! The running of these Scottish backs was so swift, so intelligent and beautiful that I almost wished they had the English forwards to give them the ball, for we do not often have a chance of enjoying such glorious attack.

When all is said and done, though, it was a superb match, and my only regret is the thought of those unfortunates who travelled all the way from Scotland to find the Twickenham gates closed when they arrived there.

Scotland led by only two points with 10 minutes to go. What a match, and how England piled into it then! A punt ahead by Cranmer sent Sever hurling himself for the line, to be pulled down inches short by four desperate Scotsmen, and Reynolds and Cranmer both tried drops which were carried wide by the wind.

Again and again the English backs went crashing at the Scottish centre, and Unwin was nearly over and a try seemed inevitable, when England were penalised and their furious onslaught relaxed. But for the check England might have scrambled home, but Shaw scotched their hopes just on time with a run of such speed and darting cleverness that it carried him clean through to score on his own. England will not grudge him that try, for it crowned an afternoon of great endeavour, and no captain ever led a team to victory more worthily than Shaw.

[This was the first international to be televised.]

1939

11 Mar Ireland are denied their first Triple Crown for 40 years yet again as Wales trample their hopes in the Belfast mud, scoring all the points in their 7-0 win in a frantic last six minutes.

18 Mar England win 9-6 at Murrayfield in the last international played before the war to earn a share of the Championship and condemn Scotland to the Wooden Spoon.

7 Jul A meeting of the four Home Unions in London agrees to the resumption of friendly relations with France, with internationals to resume in the 1939-40 season (an eventuality postponed for seven years owing to World War II).

6 Dec One competition not cancelled for the war is the Varsity match, although it is moved from Twickenham, Oxford winning the first of these 'unofficial' matches 15-3 at Cambridge. [Two matches, at the respective universities, are played in each season of the war, Cambridge winning 9, Oxford 2, with one drawn.]

Rugby Union statement: 14 September

Union wish game to go on: Helpful financial concessions

The Rugby Union yesterday announced that with the exception of those between schoolboys, all fixtures for the current season were to be considered cancelled. At the same time they hoped that games would be played provided they did not interfere with national duties or Government regulations.

Many clubs will be relieved to learn that the Union also declared a moratorium on all outstanding loans due to them – 60 clubs, with loans aggregating £47,579, are the debtors.

Immediately the Rugby Union gave their permission for the clubs to carry on, Harlequins announced that they will hold trial games tomorrow week at Fairfax Road, Teddington, instead of tomorrow as originally planned. They hope to be able to organise games of some description throughout the season.

The first Rugby in Scotland since war began will be played tomorrow, when Selkirk Club are holding their annual seven-a-side tournament.

Australian Tour: 15 September

King receives rugby team: Talk to Australians

The King yesterday received the 29 members of the Australian Rugby football team, whose visit to this country has been curtailed by the war. All the men shook hands with the King and Queen, and the King expressed the hope that the war would be of such short duration that they would be able to come back soon.

Rugby Union statement: 13 November

Rugby Union lifts professional ban: Players in services

The strictest rule of peacetime Rugby Union football, which bars any player connected with the professional organisation, the Rugby League, has been lifted for the duration of the war.

A statement by the Union yesterday says that League players in the Forces will be allowed to take part in matches between affiliated clubs and Services teams. A proviso is that the players must have had no connection with the Rugby League since their enlistment.

Wales, as in the last war, will follow England's example.

Mr HM Simson, Scottish Rugby Union secretary, stated yesterday that his Union would not be removing the ban on professionals in the Services.

International Championship: England 3 Wales 0, Twickenham, 21 January

England's rugby team shock Wales
Forwards smash way to thrilling win
By Peter Lawless

A storming pack carried England to victory over Wales at Twickenham by a try to nil. So are the critics derided, and the lessons of many trial games set at naught. A crowd of 70,000 watched the game, and the gates had to be closed before the kick-off.

Of its kind the match was a great one, a robust struggle of ceaseless aggression between two powerful sides. Some of those present may have longed for more open play, for fast wings in action, and for Welsh midfield artistry luring the defence into wrong-footed impotence.

A treacherous surface and a greasy ball blurred the edges of the finer arts, so that passing movements broke down, to be renewed immediately as fierce forward rushes or mauls of swirling fury.

Every man of the winning fifteen played his part. If the forwards took the honours it was because the conditions gave them their chances to prove what a grand eight they were. They took them wholeheartedly, and it seemed only fitting that they should score the vital try.

This came after 17 minutes of thrilling play in the second half. Marshall, who had made some glorious bursts, forced his way clear again. Two Welshmen pulled him down, but Watkins, ever in the right place, was there to carry on, and before the defence could hold up the attack Teden had booted on over the line and dived over to score as Wooller arrived beside him.

INTERNATIONAL CHAMPIONSHIP

	E	I	S	W		P	W	D	L	F	A	Pts
1=WALES	-	-	11-3	-		3	2	0	1	18	6	4
1=IRELAND	-	-	12-3	0-7		3	2	0	1	17	10	4
1=ENGLAND	3-0	0-5	-	-		3	2	0	1	12	11	4
4 SCOTLAND	6-9	-	-	-		3	0	0	3	12	32	0

TOURS (Tests)
Australia in British Isles: Tour aborted (war)

Representative Match: England/Wales 17 Scotland/Ireland 3, Richmond, 16 December

Strong pack: England's win
By Our Special Representative

Despite the icy-cold wind, the large crowd at the Richmond Athletic Ground saw a splendid game in which the score of a goal, a penalty goal and three tries to a try, by which England and Wales beat Scotland and Ireland, did not do justice to the splendid fight put up by the losers.

It was most pleasant to find such a big crowd. The proceeds go to the Red Cross Fund.

England and Wales won because they were better served by their forwards in the tight, Travers' skill as a hooker being a tremendous asset, and they also held the whip hand at half, particularly at the base of the scrum, where Ellis was allowed a lot of latitude in dancing away or putting in touch-finding kicks that often gained valuable ground.

In the centre, too, the powerful thrusts of Davey took a lot of stopping and the combined movements of the England and Wales backs were more effective than those of their opponents. At full-back, however, Scotland and Ireland had a splendid bulwark in Penman, a much more finished player than he was last season.

Teden opened the scoring and Jenkins followed with a penalty goal to give England and Wales a 6 points lead at half-time.

Soon afterwards came a try by Obolensky, and Scotland and Ireland retaliated with a try by Sampson, a great forward rush paving the way.

In the closing stages England and Wales hit back hard, and first Unwin and then Cranmer put them further ahead with tries.

The 1940s

The first casualty of the outbreak of war in Europe at the end of the 1930s was the tour of the Second Wallabies, who, no sooner had they arrived, were on their way home again. The authorities did their best to keep rugby alive during the war and the Dominions played a major role to this effect, especially 'the Kiwis' of the Eighth Army.

Many clubs kept going, largely to provide servicemen on leave with a game, and Red Cross and Service Internationals drew large crowds. Oxford and Cambridge Universities continued to play each other, in home and away matches each year, the Middlesex Sevens went on without interruption, and a Hospitals Sevens tournament was introduced.

What first, perhaps, brought the exigencies of war sharply into the focus of rugby fans was the death in March 1940 of the former Russian Prince, Alexander Obolensky, lionised for his exploits against the 1935-36 All Blacks. 'Obo' was a pilot-officer in the RAF, and was killed in a flying accident in Norfolk.

No international fixtures of any kind were arranged in the critical period of the 1940-41 season, although a New Zealand Expeditionary Force XV played some matches in Britain. International rugby came under the jurisdiction of an Inter-Services Committee in March 1942, and did not revert to civilian control by the various Unions until the first post-war season, 1945-46.

A series of 'Victory' internationals (no caps awarded) was arranged for this first season, and huge crowds flocked to see some scintillating football. The Kiwis – All Blacks in all but name – made a popular and successful tour, winning 23 and drawing two of their 27 matches, and France were welcomed back into the fold of international rugby.

The International Championship (still not recognised officially!) restarted in 1946-47 as a five-nations affair for the first time since 1931 and was shared by Wales and England. But the rest of the decade, what was left of it, belonged to the Irish, who won consecutive titles for the very first time, including, in 1947-48, their first ever Grand Slam and first Triple Crown since 1899.

The success of the Irish in 1947-48 was matched by the Third Wallabies, who not only beat the champions-to-be but England and Scotland too, and went through their five-month tour in the British Isles and France with the loss of only six matches in 35. Their accent on attack helped them compile exactly 500 points while conceding 243, while their masterly cover defence kept their line intact in all four British Isles Tests.

Admittedly, the Australians had gained recent valuable experience against New Zealand – losing all

four Tests in 1946 and 1947 – but the Wallabies manager Arnold Tancred hit the nail on the head when he said of British rugby that too much attention seemed to be given to spoiling and too little to constructive play in the open.

The Wallabies went on to enjoy their first Bledisloe Cup success in New Zealand in 1949, albeit against third-string All Blacks fifteens, for the New Zealanders had undertaken a tour of South Africa at the same time – and proceeded to lose all four Tests against the Springboks, who thus maintained their reputation as champions of world rugby.

Ireland achieved their first ever Grand Slam in 1948, a campaign which included victory over England *(above)* at Twickenham by 11 points to 10. Here the loose ball eludes English winger Cyril Holmes *(Photo: Sport & General)*

1940 – 1945

10 Feb 1940 The Army beat the Empire 27-9 at Richmond, and Monday's report is punctuated, in the interests of wartime security, by the notice: 'In common with other newspapers, The Daily Telegraph will henceforth make no announcements of the cancellation of racing, football matches and other sporting events.'

9 Mar 1940 In front of a crowd of 50,000 at Cardiff for the Red Cross International, England storm to an impressive 18-9 victory over Wales, scoring 3 goals and a try to 2 penalty goals and a try.

13 Apr 1940 In the second Red Cross International, England beat Wales 17-3 at Gloucester.

2 Jan 1941 The new grandstand at Cardiff Arms Park is wrecked by a landmine.

26 Apr 1941 Cambridge University win the Middlesex Sevens, beating the Welsh Guards 6-0 (two tries) in the final at Richmond.

1 Nov 1941 The Army gain an unexpectedly easy victory over the RAF XV at Richmond by 4 goals, a dropped goal and 2 tries to a try (30-3), with W Wooller, AJ Risman, Haydn Tanner and FG Edwards being provided with plenty of ball and Risman kicking 3 goals.

11 Apr 1942 England lose their fourth services international of the season, their second to Scotland, by 8-5 at Wembley.

30 Jan 1943 After being 11 points in arrears at half-time against Ireland at Belfast, the Army XV, inspired by scrum-half J Ellis, snatch a win by a goal, a dropped goal and a try (12) to a goal and two tries (11).

17 Apr 1943 Harlequins, returning after two seasons without playing, beat Rosslyn Park 8-6 at Old Deer Park.

25 Sep 1943 In the first match to celebrate the centenary of Guy's Hospital, the Present XV beat the Past 33-3.

Representative Match: French Army XV 3 British Army XV 36, Paris, 25 February 1940

Runaway win for the Army XV: Frenchmen outplayed in Paris match

From Peter Lawless

In the first representative match to be played between Britain and France since the unfortunate break in 1931, a British Army XV, selected from the Forces at present at home, won a smashing victory against a French Army XV at Parc des Princes this afternoon by six goals and two tries (36 points) to a penalty goal (3 points).

Beaten fore and aft as they were, the French side played from start to finish in the finest of sporting spirit. Admirably led by their captain, Thiers, from the back row of the scrum, they kept trying to the very last against a team of all the talents, in which Travers hooked with magic feet and the long-legged Wooller strode through a bewildered but ever courageous defence.

It was but a shadow of the French sides of many years, but the British Army did play the most delightful football on dry turf and in any company they would have taken a lot of stopping.

Behind a tight binding but mobile scrum, in which Horsburgh, Walker and the mercurial Sayers were ever helping to open up the game, Ellis worked all sorts of individual marvels yet managed to get Reynolds going at top speed. I have rarely seen the stand-off play better.

If Wooller, scorer of three brilliant and spectacular tries, was the outstanding player, he was in admirable company, and with Cranmer deciding that the straight burst is greater than the punt ahead, the wings had their chances and the defence was kept perpetually busy.

As the final whistle went, both teams rushed to shake hands. Every man changed jerseys with his fellow and the 30 men left the field bare-chested, with their new colours flung around their necks.

[The British Army XV were all internationals – 7E, 4W, 3I, 1S.]

---

29 March 1940

Obolensky dies in air crash: Famous rugby star

Daily Telegraph Reporter

PRINCE ALEXANDER Obolensky, the Rugby International, who was a pilot-officer in the RAF, was killed in a flying accident yesterday.

He was landing at an East Anglian aerodrome, when his machine overturned. His neck was broken.

The Prince, who was 25, was a member of the English team which beat Wales in the international match at Cardiff on March 9.

Obituary

PRINCE OBOLENSKY will figure throughout years to come as one of the legendary figures of the Rugby football world.

He earned fame in a day when he played on the right-wing for England against New Zealand at Twickenham in 1936 and scored one of the most remarkable tries ever seen on that historic ground.

'Obo', as he was called by his friends, was a Russian Georgian Prince, son of Prince Alexis Obolensky, an officer in the Tsarist cavalry before the 1917 revolution. Alexander came to this country when two years old.

Educated at Trent College and Brasenose, Oxford, Obolensky quickly made a name for himself as both runner and Rugby player. He got his Blue in 1935, and was mainly responsible for Oxford's draw with their Varsity rivals in that year.

Tours of the United States and the Argentine, where he was fêted, 'caps' for England against Ireland, Scotland and Wales, all came 'Obo's way. He played for Rosslyn Park, London, and for Leicester, and wherever he played crowds came to watch him.

He became a naturalised British citizen in 1936, soon after his triumph against the All Blacks.

Services International: Wales 17 England 12, Swansea, 7 March 1942

Great Welsh rally to beat England

Wales made a magnificent recovery to defeat England by 17 points to 12 in the Services international at Swansea, after being 12 points down at half-time.

A crowd of 20,000 (the receipts were £1,959) saw England start like winners, scoring a try, a goal and a dropped goal before the interval.

Wales' wonderful revival was inspired by AJF Risman, the Rugby League international, with a penalty goal. He also started the movement from which Alan Edwards went over for a try. Haydn Tanner, after a grand run, added another try, this time converted by Risman, who then put Wales ahead with his second long-range penalty goal. WTH Davies completed the scoring.

29 Apr 1944 In a special match for servicemen arranged by Northern Command, a Rugby League XV beat a Rugby Union XV 15-10 at Bradford's Odsal Stadium after being 10-0 down at the interval, and the 18,000 gate provides £1,350 for Service charities.

1 Jul 1944 The West Stand of Twickenham is damaged by the blast of a German V-bomb which falls nearby.

21 Oct 1944 Newport's first wartime visit to London draws a big crowd at Sudbury, where the Wasps just manage to maintain their unbeaten record by 8-6.

11 Nov 1944 South African Services beat New Zealand Services 11-8 after a hard-fought match at Richmond in the Inter-Dominions Tournament.

20 Jan 1945 St Mary's beat Coventry 8-3 at Teddington to bring to an end the Midland club's remarkable 72-match winning streak in which they scored 1,712 points to 254.

21 Apr 1945 St Mary's, four times winners of the Middlesex Sevens in the last five years, are surprisingly beaten 6-3 by Notts in the final at Richmond.

28 Apr 1945 The British Empire Services outclass the French Services at Richmond, overwhelming them by 3 goals and 4 tries (27) to a penalty goal and a try (6) in what is the first visit to Britain of a French XV since 1931.

Services Match: RNZ Air Force 8 SA Services 3, Richmond, 22 Jan 1944

South Africa's fine start

By Half-Back

The South Africans, on their first war-time appearance in England, gave a splendid account of themselves against the Royal New Zealand Air Force at Richmond. It took them a little time to settle down, and they crossed over a goal and a try behind. They played up with spirit in the second half, prevented the New Zealanders from adding points, and scored a penalty goal themselves.

Ackermann, the South African full-back, gave a fine display of lengthy kicking. Hewitt, at scrum-half, and E Grant, in the centre, were the pick of a fast and clever New Zealand back division.

Inter-Dominion Series: RAAF 8 NZ Forces 6, Richmond, 21 Oct 1944

Australian airmen win at Richmond

By Our Special Correspondent

Australians and New Zealanders provided a large crowd at Richmond with one of the finest games for a long time. The tremendous pace, beautifully accurate handling and fielding at top speed, and grim tackling were worthy of a miniature international.

The RAAF won by 8-6 because they had the more incisive backs, with an outstanding centre in MJ Young, and a greater share of the ball from the scrums, thanks to the hooking of K Kearney and the service of BR Miles at scrum-half.

[This was the opening match of the Inter-Dominion Series.]

Inter-Dominion Series: French Forces 6 RAF 26, Paris, 11 Nov 1944

RAF victory in Paris

By Our Special Correspondent

Superior all round, the RAF Rugby team experienced no difficulty in defeating the French Forces in Paris on Saturday by 4 goals (all kicked by KI Geddes) and 2 tries to 2 tries.

The 20,000 spectators enjoyed the game and, anticipating a heavier defeat, were thoroughly pleased with the display of the home team, especially when General Jacques Delmas gained the Frenchmen's two scores.

This 29-year-old leader of the Resistance Movement is the first of his rank ever to play in a Rugby match.

Victory International: England 3 NZ Army 18, Twickenham, 24 Nov 1945

Kiwis outplay England XV
Plucky defence breaks down

By JP Jordan

An England XV, by sheer tenacity and a full measure of luck, had their line crossed only once until the last 10 minutes of this hectic game at Twickenham on Saturday – a game distinguished more by physical energy than polished football.

Then the brave England defence broke down and the Kiwis added a couple of tries, both converted, to win by the significant margin of three goals and a penalty goal to a penalty goal.

Had the Kiwis not blundered more than once, and had it not been for Marriott's brilliant turn of speed in overhauling opponents who had got clear away, the margin must have been greater.

The Kiwi forwards, with Finlay, Arnold, Rhind and Simpson outstanding, were terrific. They beat England in the tight scrums by getting the ball 28 times to 12, they beat them in the lines-out 36 times to 21, and their crashing tactics in the loose, combined with the straight and determined running of their backs, kept England on the defensive for nearly all the afternoon.

Victory International: Wales 8 France 0, Swansea, 22 Dec 1945

Williams at his best
France threw away chances

By JP Jordan

Bleddyn Williams: Brilliant play.

Wretched conditions prevailed at Swansea where France made their first appearance since 1931 against one of the four Home Unions. Driving wind and rain made the ball extremely difficult to handle and the turf soon became a morass.

Much of the football was of the kick-and-rush order, but towards the end of the game the Welsh backs triumphed over the conditions. Brilliant play on the part of Bleddyn Williams led to Wales winning by a goal and a try to nil.

The display of the Frenchmen surprised the crowd – the smallest I remember ever having seen at an international. The weather and the fact that 3s was charged for admission to the ground, with stand tickets costing 15s, were doubtless the cause.

France, with one of the best packs that has done duty for them and an attacking full-back in Rouffia, dominated the game in the first half. Their forwards, splendidly built and fast, dribbled in first-class fashion, and Prat, Matheu, Basquet and Sorot pestered the defence to the full.

But although their backs tackled magnificently, and Junquas, the captain, kept a watchful eye on Williams, they exhibited their traditional weakness in failing to seize a scoring chance.

Twenty minutes from the end, the persistence of Williams in trying to find a gap in the French centre met with its reward. A beautiful cut through on his part put Matthews through for a try and another brilliant opening and a perfectly judged cross-kick found the Welsh forwards up to rush the ball over for Davies to gain the try and James to convert.

1946

26 Jan France pull off a surprise 4-3 victory over Ireland in the 'Victory International' in Dublin, winning by a dropped goal to a penalty goal. The mighty kicking of back-row forward Jean Prat, the outstanding forward on the field, is the feature of a disappointing game.

2 Feb Dr Kevin O'Flanagan plays soccer for Ireland against Scotland in Belfast a week after representing his country at rugby on the left wing against France in

Dublin. [But for missing a plane connection because of fog, O'Flanagan, who was Arsenal's leading goalscorer this season, would have played rugby again for Ireland the following Saturday.]

22 Apr Wales, playing the last of their 8 victory internationals, complete a disappointing season with their fifth defeat, going down 12-0 to France in Paris.

VICTORY INTERNATIONALS 1945-46

	E	F	I	S	W	Kiwis*
ENGLAND	-	-	-	12-8	0-3	3-18
FRANCE	-	-	-	-	12-0	-
IRELAND	6-14	3-4	-	-	-	-
SCOTLAND	27-0	-	9-0	-	13-11	11-6
WALES	13-25	8-0	6-4	6-25	-	3-11

* The Kiwis, a touring party of New Zealand soldiers from the Eighth Army, finished with a P27-W23-D2-L2 record in the British Isles, and went on to play a further six matches in France, winning them all, including 14-9 and 13-10 victories over France.

TOURS (Tests)
Australia in New Zealand: NZ31-A8, NZ14-A10

Victory International: Scotland 27 England 0, Murrayfield, 13 April

Scotland's biggest rugby win at Murrayfield: England crack after Uren's injury

By JP Jordan

Allowing for the fact that they lost their full-back Uren with a slipped knee cartilage after the first 12 minutes, and while Moore was having a cut eye patched up had only 13 players on the field, it was a dismal display that England gave against Scotland.

So heavily did the Englishmen allow their misfortunes to weigh upon them that they could make no reply to Scotland's three goals, a penalty goal and three tries, their biggest victory at Murrayfield.

It was difficult to believe

that the teams were practically the same as those that had met a month previously at Twickenham. This time it was England who fell completely to pieces in inexplicable fashion. The loss of a player should not have knocked the stuffing out of them to this extent.

Only a fortnight before, Wales had met with the same bad luck – oddly enough in the same position, in the same manner and in the same part of the field. But Wales rose magnificently to the occasion and nearly won.

Victory International: Wales 3 NZ Army 11, Cardiff, 5 January

Miskick beats Wales
Kiwis avenge 2 All Black XVs

By JP Jordan

Despite an heroic defence Wales lost to a better team at Cardiff Arms Park, the New Zealand Army winning by a goal and two penalty goals to one penalty goal.

Incidentally, the Kiwis avenged two defeats of the All Blacks by Wales, and are the first New Zealand team to beat a Wales XV at Cardiff. Wales beat the All Blacks there in 1905 and 1935. The 1924 New Zealand tourists, who went through unbeaten, played Wales at Swansea.

Nothing could have been better than the Welsh tackling. Every single man, with Hale and WE Williams on the wings in particular, went for his man whole-heartedly.

For most of a terrific struggle the fast and clever Kiwi backs not only found themselves checked but seemed to be at a loss to know how to penetrate the stubborn opposition.

But defence alone does not win matches even if it may save them. Had the Welsh attack been of the same superlative standard it would have been a different story. Their magnificent forwards played the game of their lives. Jones, Manfield, Travers and the two Thomases were in grand form in the loose. Travers got more of the ball in the scrums than Haigh, and the heeling was clean and swift.

Wales held the lead until 10 minutes from the end. Then Lloyd Davies made a hurried kick that failed to find touch. Sherratt gathered the ball and raced for the line 50 yards away. Hale and Lloyd Davies gave chase, but the long-striding Kiwi out-distanced them and Scott converted the try. That sealed Wales's fate.

Scott kicked two splendid penalty goals afterwards, but the Kiwis had already won a great match.

Varsity Match: Oxford 15 Cambridge 5, Twickenham, 10 December

Great Oxford win is inspired by Donnelly:
Big varsity crowd watches handsome victory

By JP Jordan

Oxford crowned their invincible career with a handsome victory over Cambridge by a goal, a dropped goal and two tries to a goal before a record crowd for a University Rugby match. Over 50,000 divided partisans watched the game at Twickenham yesterday in perfect weather, though the evening mist nearly blacked out the closing stages.

The play followed expectations. The almost uncanny skill of Gilthorpe as

hooker, the definite superiority of the Oxford halves, Newton-Thompson [the captain] and Donnelly (which I had stressed), and magnificent team-work, gave Oxford the spoils.

Donnelly was the hero of the day. He had a perfect understanding with his captain, who also was in splendid form, and he dictated Oxford's tactics behind the scrum in masterly fashion, sometimes setting his three-quarters going, at others

either employing the short punt or cutting through on his own, but always doing the right thing.

His defensive kicking, too, was of immense help, while he had the personal satisfaction of giving his side the lead with the neatest of dropped goals, and played a big part in all three tries. His was indeed a display of high polish and brilliance, the only error he committed being his failure to convert Oxford's last try.

In contrast, Bruce-Lockhart

had a poor day at stand-off half for Cambridge. It was not the fault of Gatford who, while not a Newton-Thompson, performed creditably at the base of the scrum. But Bruce-Lockhart could do little right, and his three-quarters suffered accordingly.

[Arguably the world's finest left-hand batsman of the post-war period, Martin Donnelly played only 7 cricket Tests for his native New Zealand, and also represented England at rugby.]

1947

19 Apr England, with two tries, scrape a 6-3 win over France at Twickenham to earn a share of the Championship with Wales, France's only score being a dropped penalty goal by Jean Prat from the halfway line and close to touch.

1 Oct The Third Wallabies (the Second returned home in 1939 without playing a match) beat Combined Services at Twickenham 19-8 in the sixth match of their tour, but suffer a serious blow as their captain, the great Queensland forward WM McLean, breaks a leg.

International Championship: France 8 Scotland 3, Colombes, 1 January

Surprise for Scotland: French forwards win match

From Our Special Correspondent

France surprised and delighted a crowd of 25,000 at the Colombes Stadium here to-day when they won the first Rugby international of the season, and their first against Scotland for 16 years, by a goal and a try to a penalty goal.

French opinion before the game inclined towards a Scottish victory, but as play went France were clearly the better side. The fact that they crossed Scotland's line twice while keeping their own intact emphasises their superiority.

Chief credit for France's triumph belongs to their forwards, a magnificent pack with great shoving power and also speed in the open. They carried most of the set scrums and also beat the Scots in the line-outs.

INTERNATIONAL CHAMPIONSHIP

	E	F	I	S	W	P	W	D	L	F	A	Pts
1=WALES	6-9	-	6-0	-	-	4	3	0	1	37	17	6
1=ENGLAND	-	6-3	-	24-5	-	4	3	0	1	39	36	6
3=IRELAND	22-0	8-12	-	-	-	4	2	0	2	33	18	4
3=FRANCE	-	-	-	8-3	0-3	4	2	0	2	23	20	4
5 SCOTLAND	-	-	0-3	-	8-22	4	0	0	4	16	57	0

TOURS (Tests)
New Zealand in Australia: A5-NZ13, A14-NZ27

International Championship: England 24 Scotland 5, Twickenham, 15 March

Oddest rugby game ever
England triumph at Twickenham

By JP Jordan

One of the oddest games in the 68 years' history of the Calcutta Cup ended in an absurdly easy triumph for England, before a crowd of about 65,000 at Twickenham, by four goals and one dropped goal to a goal.

Had not Jackson in the last minutes raced in with a try for Scotland that Geddes converted, the margin of victory would have established a new record for the series.

As it was, it made form in this season's international matches quite insoluble, since Ireland had beaten England by 22 points to nil and Scotland by a bare try. But the Englishmen gave a vastly different exhibition from that in Dublin.

In contrast to the Scots, whose over-long journey from the North doubtless left its effects, there was a refreshing liveliness about the play of the England forwards that was missing against Ireland, although the conditions were as bad – a bitterly cold wind in the first half and a snowstorm afterwards.

These England forwards, Steele-Bodger and White in particular, with Weighill and the others in close support, were always on the ball or crashing into their opponents

---

Tour Match: Scotland 7 Australia 16, Murrayfield, 22 November

Injury upsets Scots against Wallabies

By JP Jordan

All the honours of the first Rugby International of the season, in which Australia beat Scotland before 50,000 at Murrayfield by two goals and two tries to a dropped goal and a penalty goal, did not go to the winners.

Until losing Wright with a dislocated shoulder midway through the second half, Scotland's experimental team had not only enjoyed more of the play, but were leading by 7 points to 3.

The loss of Wright meant the moving of McDonald into the centre and the withdrawal of Elliot from the scrum on to the wing. This lessening of their numbers proved too much of a handicap for the gallant Scottish forwards and the Australians quickly found the weak spot.

The Australians deserve every credit for the way they played in conditions new to them. Heavy going and a greasy ball upset the normal smoothness of their passing movements, but their splendid teamwork and magnificent covering in defence pulled them through.

Tour Match: Wales 6 Australia 0, Cardiff, 20 December

Wallabies lose in Wales
Tamplin's kicks win the day

By JP Jordan

England's Rugby selectors sat yesterday to pick a team they hope will emulate, at Twickenham on Saturday week, the feat of Wales, the first national fifteen to beat the Australian tourists.

Two penalty goals kicked by their captain, WE Tamplin, a 14∞ stone local policeman, were the extent of Wales's triumph on Saturday in a game which, though singularly devoid of incidents, thrilled an all-ticket crowd of 45,000 at Cardiff Arms Park.

It was the first time the Australians, who had previously defeated Scotland and Ireland, had failed to score in the 26 matches they have played on the present tour. They have kept their line intact in all three internationals.

Wales deserved their triumph over the Wallabies because they took their chances of turning penalty kicks to the best advantage. Tamplin was more accurate that either Piper or Allan, and that settled the titanic struggle between two hard scrummaging packs, with the attacking skill of the backs completely subordinated by deadly tackling and intensive covering up.

Tamplin had three shots at goal and scored with two; Piper and Allan had five between them and failed with all. Otherwise, there was nothing to choose between the teams.

---

with a zest that thrilled the huge crowd. Valentine was the only Scot who seemed imbued with the same spirit and he was just as big a success when he deputised on the wing.

Where England held the winning advantage, however, was at half back. Here Scotland were completely outplayed. The presence of Newton-Thompson at the base of the scrum made all the difference to the smooth working of England's back division, his passing out to Hall being accurate and swift.

Hall could not find a way through the defence, but he served Heaton and Bennett most successfully, while his smothering of Bruce, with similar treatment accorded Munro by the English centres, reduced the Scottish backs to a negligible factor in attack.

Guest's opportunism and neat picking up brought him a try late in the first half after Hall had opened the scoring with a dropped goal and Holmes had intercepted at halfway to sprint in unopposed. Heaton converted the tries for England to lead at the interval by 14 points. Heaton converted two further opportunist tries afterwards by Henderson and Bennett and finally came Scotland's solitary score.

1948

7 Feb Cardiff set a British record by supplying 10 players for Wales, against Scotland at Cardiff.

21 Feb France gain their first victory in Wales, after nine successive defeats, winning 11-3 at St Helen's, Swansea.

IRFB The RFU give up two of their four seats on the Board, and Australia, New Zealand and South Africa are admitted, with one seat each.

Laws The dropped goal is reduced in value from 4 to 3pts.

INTERNATIONAL CHAMPIONSHIP

	E	F	I	S	W	P	W	D	L	F	A	Pts
1 IRELAND	-	-	-	6-0	6-3	4	4	0	0	36	19	8
2=FRANCE	15-0	-	6-13	-	-	4	2	0	2	40	25	4
2=SCOTLAND	6-3	9-8	-	-	-	4	2	0	2	15	31	4
4 WALES	-	3-11	-	14-0	-	4	1	1	2	23	20	3
5 ENGLAND	-	-	10-11	-	3-3	4	0	1	3	16	35	1

TOURS (Tests)
Australia in British Isles & France: S7-A16, I3-A16, W6-A0, E0-A11, F13-A6

Tour Match: England 0 Australia 11, Twickenham, 3 January

England XV beaten for energy and speed: Classic Australian try by Walker

By JP Jordan

Superior energy, greater speed and brilliant opportunism gave Australia victory over England's Rugby team at Twickenham by a goal and two tries to nil.

Australia have thus beaten Scotland, Ireland and England and lost to Wales without having had a try scored against them, a feat unparalleled by any touring side.

Until the last quarter of an hour Australia held only a three points lead and England were having a full share of the game. But the Australian attack carried more punch, their passing was brisker and their determination such that often it took two Englishmen to pull down an opponent.

The inclusion of Walker strengthened the Australian three-quarter line considerably, as I anticipated, and to him fell the distinction of scoring one of the finest tries I have seen at Twickenham.

From 60 yards out Walker short-punted, gathered the ball in his stride, slipping past Scott and Bennett, and, pulling out every inch of speed he had in him, raced past Newman and dived over the line.

Allan also chose the occasion to play his best game of the tour. It was through his initiative that Australia took the lead a minute before the interval.

Windon scored the first try after Allan had fielded Newman's miskick, run down the touchline and passed inside.

Half an hour after the interval came Walker's grand score, and in another three minutes Windon picked up a dropped pass near half-way, broke clear of the defence and showed astonishing speed to beat all pursuers. Tonkin, who had failed at the other two attempts, managed to convert this try.

International Championship: Ireland 6 Wales 3, Belfast, 13 March

Irish forwards beat Wales
Decisive speed and tackling

By JP Jordan

Ireland made Rugby history before a capacity crowd at Belfast when they beat Wales by two tries to one.

Not only did they win the Triple Crown for the third time after a lapse of 49 years, but for the first time they have beaten all four other countries in the international championship.

The enthusiasm and excitement of a crowd of 32,000, including a large Welsh contingent, were intense. From start to finish there was one perpetual roar of 'Ireland', which rose to a yell as B Mullan and Daly scored their tries.

Ireland's victory came through a splendid display by their forwards, admirably supported again by Kyle. Karl Mullen so inspired his pack that what they lacked in weight they more than made good by speed and relentless

---

Tour Match: France 13 Australia 6, Paris, 11 January

Three tries against Wallabies: France spoil their record

From Reuter

Australia failed to produce their usual passing accuracy in three-quarter movements against France in Paris yesterday, and were soundly beaten by two goals and a try to two penalty goals.

The Wallabies had the advantage of a heavier pack, but their backs often fumbled. When they did manage to break through they were brought down by keen French tackling.

France's captain, Guy Basquet, proved a brilliant opportunist. He charged over the line within five minutes for a try, which Alvarez converted. Before half-time Basquet and Pomathios scored tries, the latter converted by Alvarez. Tonkin kicked Australia's two penalty goals.

Tour Match: Barbarians 9 Australia 6, Cardiff, 31 January

Wallabies' fine rally, but too late

By JP Jordan

If not in a blaze of triumph, at least amid the cheers of a crowd of 45,000 in raptures over the brilliant display of Rugby football provided, the Australians wound up their tour at Cardiff, where the Barbarians won the best game seen on the ground for many years by three tries to a penalty goal and a try.

The Australians leave for home on February 12. They have had a strenuous five months in this country and France, and their record of 29 wins against six defeats in 35 matches is one with which they have every reason to be pleased.

Three minutes from the finish the score stood at 9-3 against the Wallabies. Then a beautiful passing movement ended in Tonkin diving across for a try to make it 9-6. With only two minutes left they returned to the attack for Shehadie, Hardcastle and Windon to almost force their way over by sheer physical strength. But the Barbarian defence just managed to hold out.

Tonkin also scored a penalty goal for the Wallabies, and the Barbarians' tries were obtained by Steele-Bodger, Holmes and Tanner.

[Arranged as an extra match at the end of the Wallabies' tour, this was the first time the Barbarians met an overseas touring side, and set the pattern for the traditional open rugby played in this now regular closing fixture.]

tackling. They were so quick on to G Davies, BL Williams and Cleaver that all Tanner's efforts to start a passing movement broke down in the middle. Particularly was that the case in the second half when Ireland dominated the play.

Kyle received a slow and poor service from Strathdee, but he clenched his claim as the best stand-off half in the five countries. It was from one of Kyle's shrewdly placed kicks that B Mullan scored 14 minutes from the start. Thirteen minutes later Wales carried out their single successful round of passing and BL Williams cut inside for a try. Daly's crowning try came seven minutes after the interval.

1949

16 Jul The All Blacks lose the first Test in South Africa 15-11, all the Springboks' points coming from the prodigious boot of prop forward 'Okey' Geffin, who kicks 5 penalty goals.

3 Sep An extraordinary day of humiliation for the All Blacks – they lose two Tests. With 30 players in South Africa, the side taking on the Wallabies at Athletic Park, Wellington, is regarded in many quarters as a third-string XV, although they boast the talents among others of three Maori backs – Vince Bevan, Ben Couch and Johnny Smith – ineligible on racial grounds for the South Africa tour party. Nevertheless, they lose 11-6, and, as the sun swings towards the West, the All Blacks lose the third Test against the Springboks 9-3 in Durban.

24 Sep Australia win 16-9 at Eden Park, Auckland, to annex the Bledisloe Cup in New Zealand for the first time and complete a miserable year for the All Blacks, who have lost all six Tests played, four in South Africa and two against the Wallabies.

26 Nov The Australian Rugby Union is founded, taking over the control of the game in Australia from the New South Wales RU.

INTERNATIONAL CHAMPIONSHIP

	E	F	I	S	W	P	W	D	L	F	A	Pts
1 IRELAND	14-5	9-16	-	-	-	4	3	0	1	41	24	6
2=ENGLAND	-	8-3	-	19-3	-	4	2	0	2	35	29	4
2=FRANCE	-	-	-	0-8	5-3	4	2	0	2	24	28	4
2=SCOTLAND	-	-	3-13	-	6-5	4	2	0	2	20	37	4
5 WALES	9-3	-	0-5	-	-	4	1	0	3	17	19	2

TOURS (Tests)

New Zealand in South Africa: SA15-NZ11, SA12-NZ6, SA9-NZ3, SA11-NZ8

Australia in New Zealand: NZ6-A11, NZ9-A16

International Championship: Wales 0 Ireland 5, Swansea, 12 March

Triple Crown goes to Ireland once again: Why Wales lost

From EW Swanton

Ireland by beating Wales here yesterday by a goal to nil became the Rugby international champions of 1949, though Scotland will share the pedestal with them if they beat England next Saturday. What is more, Ireland's victory gave them, once again, that mythical and romantic emblem, the Triple Crown.

To beat the other three countries two years running is one of the rarest achievements in international sport. How has it happened?

Briefly, the Irish have owed almost everything to the fire and fury of their forwards under Mullen's admirable leadership, especially to their wing forwards, McCarthy and McKay, supported by Kyle's magnificent all-round play at stand-off, and added, of course, to the grand esprit of the whole side.

That they have been able to win without the slightest constructive assistance from their three-quarters reflects the general state of back play among their opponents and, in particular, upon that of Wales yesterday.

The Welsh lost for two reasons, first because there were generally three Irish forwards on the ball before the first Welshman joined issue in the loose, secondly because the theoretical advantage in running and passing which should have brought tries to Wales was thrown away by glaring and elementary errors in technique.

It was, as always, a stirring emotional experience to watch an international on St Helen's Field. Before the game began every chord of 'Land of My Fathers' was a prayer for victory.

From start to finish the struggle was fierce and gruelling. Just before half-time a quick dash by Kyle on the blind side, a short cross-kick, and a great leap to catch the ball by McCarthy gave Ireland the one and only score. Norton made the try worth five points.

Hospitals' Cup Final: St Mary's 6 Guy's 5, Richmond, 23 March

Clever try wins Rugby Cup for St Mary's: Rarest of all moves

By EW Swanton

St Mary's won the Hospitals Cup at Richmond yesterday by two tries to a goal, and when their captain, Summerskill, received it from Dr LG Brown, the Rugby Union president, he may well have clung on tightly to assure himself that the prize was really his. For St Mary's, so to speak, won the game twice and lost it once, and the final snatching of the victory, when time was almost up, came from the rarest of all moves in Rugby.

From just before half-time until a few minutes from the end St Mary's led by the only score of the match, a try by Whittingham. Gradually in the second half Guy's pressed more and more strongly until a movement on the right left Gray overlapping the defence, and he scored wide out. D Le Clus now brought all the friends of Guy's to their feet by kicking an excellent goal, the ball clearing the bar by a foot or so. That, we felt, was that.

Nothing seemed less probable when St Mary's were awarded a penalty in a last desperate rush than that Beatson would kick a goal against the breeze. He had to take the shot from near touch and just inside the 25 line. With great care he made the preparations. Then, before Guy's could guard against his intentions, and with their players strung out thinly along their goal-line, he tapped the ball a yard forward, caught it, and streaked over for a try at the corner-flag.

When his kick at goal just failed my watch made it time, allowing generously for stoppages. But the referee was of a different mind, and the game swayed horrifyingly to and fro for five everlasting minutes before he blew the final whistle.

Justice was served by the result, for so long as they had 15 sound men St Mary's were always better.

They weakened somewhat when Robins, the hooker, was hurt at the beginning of the second half. He hobbled about gamely but to little purpose, and a more distinguished set of backs than those of Guy's must have made the issue safe.

[St Mary's controversial winning try caused much debate, as it appeared to contravene Law 24, and it was felt that, had Guy's formally appealed against the referee's ruling, there might have been a reversal of the result.]

---

5 September

250 Rugby Union clubs will insure players

Mr E Watts Moses, president of the Rugby Union, outlined at a Press conference in London last night the insurance scheme which the Union has introduced for its clubs and referees.

A premium of 10s will cover all the members of one team from the financial hardships of injury for one year, and provide a lump sum in case of fatal accident. The Union will pay 3s 6d of this premium, and clubs may insure as many teams as they like. Already 250 clubs have joined the scheme and the Union hopes that all their 1,000 clubs will come in.

The 1950s

The fifties were notable for the rise of French rugby. In 1951 the Tricoleurs chalked up their first win at Twickenham and won three matches in the International Championship for the first time. Only a 9-8 defeat in Dublin, as Ireland won their third Championship in four seasons, prevented them from winning their first title. They did, indeed, share the title in 1954, with England and Wales, the latter beating them at Cardiff, although again they won three matches as well as beating the All Blacks for the first time.

France again won three matches in 1955, but once more had to settle for a share in the title, this time with Wales, who beat them in the last match, in Paris, in what was a sad farewell for the French captain Jean Prat, one of the great forwards of all time. Finally, France achieved their goal, in 1959, winning the Championship outright, paradoxically with only two wins and five points.

The architect of France's development from 15 talented individuals to the smooth-working unit that won the Championship was second-row forward Lucien Mias, whose last season this was in international rugby. He had achieved even greater heights in 1958, when, miracle of miracles, he led France to victory on their first tour of South Africa – the Springboks' first defeat in a home series this century. Other French stars of this historic era included full-back Pierre Lacaze, wing-forward François Moncla and prop Aldo Quaglio.

Throughout the fifties Wales were consistently to the fore in the International Championship. With Grand Slams in 1950 and 1952, another title in 1956 and two shared titles, they were only once out of the first two. Stars of those early triumphs included inspirational captain John Gwilliam, three-quarter Lewis Jones, who made his international début at 18 as a full-back in 1950 and turned professional in 1952, wing three-quarter Ken Jones, an Olympic sprinter, and fly-half Cliff Morgan, whose brilliant international career spanned the years 1951 to 1958.

England, too, enjoyed their share of success in the fifties, winning the Championship three times, including a Grand Slam in 1957, the year when the term is thought to have originated. Captaining England was Eric Evans, prop or hooker, and other outstanding players included scrum-half Dickie Jeeps, three-quarters Peter Jackson and Jeff Butterfield, and forwards John Currie, David Marques and Peter Robbins. Scotland, on the other hand, were going through a period in the doldrums, without ever coming close to the title and finishing with the Wooden Spoon on five occasions. They led

the way in one respect, however, when Murrayfield introduced undersoil heating in the summer of 1959.

On the world scene, South Africa confirmed their acknowledged No.1 position with a devastating tour of the British Isles and France in 1951-52, beating all five countries and winning 30 of their 31 matches, their mainstay being a magnificent, rampaging pack that boasted the likes of Hennie Muller, Salty du Rand and Basie van Wyk. The Springboks, however, fell away in the latter fifties, being held to a tied rubber by the 1955 Lions, losing the next year in New Zealand and then suffering that home reverse in 1958 by the French.

The All Blacks enjoyed a successful decade, with home triumphs over the Lions at the beginning and end of it, and that 1956 success over the Springboks – winning three of the four Tests each time, although Stuart's Fourth All Blacks lost to Wales and France in 1953-54. It was against the Springboks that New Zealand introduced full-back Don Clarke, a goal-kicking phenomenon who enabled them to play what became known as '55-yards rugby' or 'ten-man rugby', in which the backs appeared on the field to make up the numbers and the tries v penalty goals controversy was brought into sharp focus once again.

It was, perhaps, this sterile trend in the game that led EW Swanton to eulogise in *The Daily Telegraph* about the Twickenham Jubilee match at the end of the fifties: 'There took the field 30 of the finest players in the four countries, obviously determined to show that they are fit to be compared with any past generation.... The game they showed us (won by England and Wales by four goals and two tries to a goal, three tries and a penalty goal) was brilliant almost beyond the conception of many who have become used to accepting international football as a desperately hard, tight-locked battle, with perhaps just one or two fleeting individual escapes from the tenacious grip of the respective defensive systems.

'The swiftness, in conception and execution of move and countermove, the quality of the passing and backing-up, the daring nature of so much that was attempted and brought off, kept a crowd that was little short of 60,000 in perpetual explosions of cheering and applause.... The key to the whole robust and stimulating picture was the emphasis on attack.

'The match showed beyond all quibbling that Rugby football under the present Laws is as fine a game for the young and the fit as the wit of man has devised – so long as the accent is put in the right place and the balance of effort and ingenuity maintained in favour of attack.'

Above: The championship match at Twickenham between England and Ireland in 1958 turns into something of a mudlark. England's 6-0 victory set them on their way to a second successive Five Nations title, their third of the decade outright, while fly-half Jackie Kyle made his 45th appearance for Ireland to set a new international record.

1950

21 Jan In front of a record crowd of 75,532, Wales beat England at Twickenham for only the second time, their 11-5 victory due largely to a pack superior to England's in every department and led brilliantly by JA Gwilliam, while the impressive international début of 18-year-old full-back Lewis Jones 'marks him out for a great future' according to Daily Telegraph correspondent EW Swanton.

11 Mar After a wait of 73 years, Cheshire win the County Championship for the first time, beating the star-studded East Midlands 5-0 in the final. Their try, scored 5 minutes after the interval by GD Hill, is converted by Uren, whose diagonal kick made it.

19 Aug The British Isles beat Australia by 19-6 in Brisbane, Lewis Jones dominating the game, scoring 16 of their points with a try, a brilliant dropped goal, two conversions and two penalties. BL Williams scores the other try.

International Championship: Ireland 3 Wales 6, Belfast, 11 March

Welsh Rugby owes much to Gwilliam

Triple Crown success is reward for skipper's plan

By EW Swanton

MC Thomas's try, scored only two minutes from the end of the match between Ireland and Wales at Belfast on Saturday, achieved for Wales at a single stroke their two dearest ambitions. It won both the Triple Crown and the international championship of 1950, the game with France still to be played in a fortnight's time.

Two tries to a penalty goal: it could hardly have been a closer business, but the answer was a just one.

Wales have indeed shown themselves the best of the five countries, with their tough, irrepressible pack as the striking force and every man on the side playing to a directed plan. Gwilliam has had much to do with the success, not only during the games, but by precept and attention to detail in the Friday afternoon practices.

It is a happy illustration of luck in the best-laid sporting schemes that he captained Wales this year only by the accident of BL Williams's unfitness.

Ireland, as all the portents suggested, chased their opponents right home with the utmost tenacity and unsparing endeavour. The play epitomised all that is most rugged and sheerly elemental in the game of football.

In sad and sober fact, the Welsh tries both came after Irish passing had broken down. For three years now the Triple Crown has been won by a pack of forwards, and if a counter-revolution is to come it will need to be introduced by a set of backs more competent and more ingenious than is nowadays to be seen, served, above all, by an exceptionally strong scrum-half with a really long pass.

The first score came after seven minutes of the second half. Kyle threw the ball somewhat rashly into the centre. Matthews gathered and made a long pass to K Jones, whom there was no stopping. L Jones, who had been at hand if needed, missed the conversion from two-thirds of the way out.

A tragic if understandable error this seemed when 10 minutes later Norton, from about the same angle, kicked a penalty given for off-side, to level the scores.

Then, when eyes were turning repeatedly to the clock, came the vital moment. The ball went loose as Kyle was tackled on his own 25. Matthews, Cleaver and Lewis Jones handed expertly, and Thomas finally hurled himself over in the left corner for the winning try.

So the reproach of 39 years was wiped away, and at least it had been a hint of Welsh back-play which had brought the victory.

Tour Match: New Zealand 9 British Isles 9, Dunedin, 27 May

Rugby Test drawn in New Zealand

From Reuter

The British Isles Rugby touring team gave an excellent display here yesterday and drew the first Test with New Zealand, each side scoring a penalty goal and two tries.

It was only a late New Zealand rally which earned them a draw, for the British team, playing much better than many thought possible, led by nine points to three well into the second half.

The British team took command straight from the kick-off and only twice in the first half did the powerful All Blacks penetrate far enough into their half to become dangerous.

The British side went ahead after 10 minutes with a penalty goal by J Robins, the Birkenhead Park front-row forward. After the interval J Kyle, Belfast stand-off half, received a fine pass from A Black, of Edinburgh, and eluding all defenders went over for a try near the posts.

New Zealand then came more into the picture and RA Roper went over for a try, but Ken Jones, Newport three-quarter, regained the British advantage of six points by another try. In a New Zealand rally RWH Scott kicked a penalty goal and RR Elvidge scored a try.

Tour Match: New Zealand 11 British Isles 8, Auckland, 29 July

New Zealand win Rugby Test: British rally just fails to snatch victory

From Reuter

New Zealand won the fourth and last Rugby Union Test here yesterday, beating the British Isles touring team by a goal, a dropped goal and a try (11 pts) to a goal and a penalty goal (8). They had already gained the rubber, winning two of the three previous Tests, the first being drawn.

The British team made a great rally in the final stages of a fast, exciting game and almost snatched victory, but the better side won. New Zealand took the honours in all-round forward play and at back.

J Matthews (Wales) was one of the best men on the field, clever in attack and strong in defence. JW Kyle was not allowed to show his usual brilliance and R John and PW Kininmonth were effectively held in the lineouts.

Lewis Jones kicked a penalty for the touring team and K Jones scored their try which Lewis Jones converted.

PA Johnstone, New Zealand's captain, said afterwards it was the most exciting match in which he had ever played.

INTERNATIONAL CHAMPIONSHIP

	E	F	I	S	W	P	W	D	L	F	A	Pts
1 WALES	-	21-0	-	12-0	-	4	4	0	0	50	8	8
2 SCOTLAND	13-11	8-5	-	-	-	4	2	0	2	21	49	4
3=IRELAND	-	-	-	21-0	3-6	4	1	1	2	27	12	3
3=FRANCE	6-3	-	3-3	-	-	4	1	1	2	14	35	3
5 ENGLAND	-	-	3-0	-	5-11	4	1	0	3	22	30	2

TOURS (Tests)
British Isles in New Zealand: NZ9-BI9, NZ8-BI0, NZ6-BI3, NZ11-BI8
British Isles in Australia: A6-BI19, A3-BI24

1951

17 Feb A record crowd for a club match of 48,500 at Cardiff Arms Park sees Newport beat Cardiff 8-3.

24 Feb France lay the Twickenham bogey after 44 years, beating England there by 11-3, with forwards Jean Prat, scorer of 8pts (try, conversion and dropped goal) and Guy Basquet and scrum-half Gérard Dufau their heroes.

10 Mar Ireland, held 3-3 by Wales at Cardiff, miss out on the Grand Slam but clinch the Championship. Cliff Morgan, just out of school, makes a splendid début at fly-half for Wales.

24 Mar Michel Pomathios becomes the first French player to represent the Barbarians, who lose 13-3 at Cardiff.

22 Dec In a match of incidents decided by inches, the Springboks beat Wales by 6-3, a dropped goal and a try to a try.

The Springboks begin their tour of the British Isles with a comfortable victory over Hants & Sussex at Bournemouth.

International Championship: Scotland 19 Wales 0, Murrayfield, 3 February

Young Scots XV rout mighty Welsh

From JP Jordan

More than 80,000 enthusiasts, the biggest crowd ever to watch a Rugby Union match, saw Scotland spring the sporting surprise of the season at Murrayfield here yesterday, confounding the critics and exceeding the wildest hopes of the most rabid Scotsman with a smashing victory over Wales. Two goals, a dropped goal, a penalty goal and a try (19 points) was the measure of their totally unexpected triumph.

Magnificent forwards and young backs who chirpily assumed the role of Davids against the Welsh Goliaths shattered Wales's fond hopes of retaining the Triple Crown, for which mythical emblem they were hot favourites. Their brilliant exhibition against England a fortnight ago brought 25,000 exultant Welshmen to the Scottish capital in anticipation of another dazzling display and the rout of the Scots.

The Welshmen cheered loudly enough in the early stages, but dismay arose in their ranks as Scotland's grand forwards gradually assumed complete control.

Getting splendid support from their young outsides, the Scottish forwards knocked the famous Welsh backs right out of their stride and reduced their opponents to such a degree of impotence that in the last 20 minutes Scotland piled on 16 points.

The Welsh backs had no answer to the crash tackling of Elliot, who was in superb form, to the fierce onslaughts of Taylor, Kininmonth, Inglis and indeed of the whole Scottish pack.

Nor could L Jones or Matthews ever elude the low and splendidly timed tackling of Sloan and Scott, the two Scottish centres, neither of whom was an original choice.

Two of the three tries were due to Welsh blunders, as was Kininmonth's amazing dropped goal from 40 yards out, after which Wales began to go to pieces.

Scotland's new 20-year-old full-back, Thomson, who came into the side at almost the last moment, deserves every praise for his part in the victory. He played like a veteran of a dozen caps, and he kicked two goals. Like another 20-year-old, Gordon, who scored two tries, Thomson was carried off the field shoulder-high at the finish.

Play did not run much to Rose's wing, but this 19-year-old never allowed the speedy KJ Jones to beat him. Scotland have every reason to be proud of their young three-quarter line whose combined ages totalled only 73 years.

Tour Match: London Counties 11 South Africans 9, Twickenham, 10 November

Hall's goal began rally which beat Springboks
London hold out in hectic finish
By EW Swanton

The South African footballers surrendered their Springbok mascot to London after a memorable game by the same two-point margin as their predecessors of 1912 lost to the same Counties.

They made many friends on their first visit to Twickenham both by their method of play and by the manner in which they accepted defeat, typified by the spontaneous gesture of carrying their victors from the field. First Koch and du Rand hoisted Matthews, the London captain, onto their shoulders, whereupon others of the team, led by Muller, followed suit.

It was an admirable ending to a match which had been full of excitement and interest from the moment that Hall's dropped goal opened the London score, and which rose to an agonised climax in the last quarter of an hour after Grimsdell's excellent long penalty had put London ahead for the second and final time.

In this last phase the London side really rose above themselves. It said much for the fitness of the London forwards, whose working hours are prosaically spent in City offices, that, though outweighted by as much as a stone a man – and, incidentally, for eight of these most hectic minutes reduced by Bland's injury to seven – they were able to hold their ground in this last period.

[This was the 4th Springboks' only defeat – they won their other 30 matches.]

Tour Match: Scotland 0 South Africa 44, Murrayfield, 24 November

South Africa give Rugby lesson to the Scots: Brilliant and conclusive victory
By EW Swanton

The South Africans have many triumphs to their name on the Rugby football field, but they surely have never won a game against opponents of international class so brilliantly and so conclusively as that against Scotland at Murrayfield on Saturday.

The score, made up of seven goals, one dropped goal, and two tries, has no parallel in an international match since WA Millar's South Africans made 10 tries against Ireland in 1912.

Almost from the moment of the first try there appeared between the two sides such a wide and ever-growing disparity that the game developed merely into an exhibition. In this spectators, as soon as the first disappointment was behind them, seemed to revel in a detached, unemotional way oddly out of keeping with an international occasion.

The tries were scored by du Rand, Van Schoor, Koch (2), Delport, Van Wyk, Muller, Lategan and Dinkelmann. Geffin converted seven and Brewis dropped a goal.

INTERNATIONAL CHAMPIONSHIP

	E	F	I	S	W	P	W	D	L	F	A	Pts
1 IRELAND	3-0	9-8	-	-	-	4	3	1	0	21	16	7
2 FRANCE	-	-	-	14-12	8-3	4	3	0	1	41	27	6
3 WALES	23-5	-	3-3	-	-	4	1	1	2	29	35	3
4=SCOTLAND	-	-	5-6	-	19-0	4	1	0	3	39	25	2
4=ENGLAND	-	3-11	-	5-3	-	4	1	0	3	13	40	2

TOURS (Tests)
New Zealand in Australia: A0-NZ8, A11-NZ17, A6-NZ16

1952

5 Jan England go down with honour to the all-conquering Springboks, matching them try for try in their 8-3 defeat at Twickenham.

12 Jan France win at Murrayfield for the first time, with flanker Jean Prat, scorer of a try, two conversions and a penalty goal, the hero of their 13-11 victory.

22 Mar In a surprisingly low-key match, devoid of both excitement and good play, Wales gain a singularly lucky and unimpressive 9-5 victory over France at Swansea to clinch the Championship with a Grand Slam. [This was the last international of the great Lewis Jones, for he was to turn professional with Leeds for a record £6,000 in October after only 10 matches for Wales.]

5 Apr England fly-half Nim Hall turns back the clock to drop-kick a penalty from just inside the French half in England's 6-3 victory at the Stade Colombes.

International Board Statement: 17 March

Rugby Board and games with France: Decision in April

By EW Swanton

The relations between the Unions comprising the International Rugby Football Board and the Federation Français de Rugby have been brought into the open by a statement issued yesterday by the International Board. The statement says:

The International Rugby Football Board, at its meeting in Edinburgh on March 14, 1952, considered the report of the conference in Dublin between representatives of the Home Unions and the French Federation of Rugby Football.

The Board noted the information conveyed to it that the Committee of Direction of the FFR had decided unanimously on December 22, 1951, that the French Club Championship should be abolished.

The Board is gravely disturbed by the actions and tendencies of some French clubs which are in conflict with the statutes and regulations of the French Federation itself and with the spirit of the amateur game of Rugby Football.

The Board has decided to await the notification to it of the effective measures of reform, to be determined by the General Assembly of the FFR to be held in the month of April, 1952, before reaching a final conclusion as to whether or not relations between the Unions represented on the International Rugby Football Board and France can be maintained during the season 1952-53.

It is hard to see what good purpose has been served by the publication of the present statement. The fact that the French themselves appreciate the need to put Rugby football on an unequivocal amateur basis is made clear by their suppression of the club championship that engenders the excess of enthusiasm from which professional practices spring.

The International Board obviously have a duty to protect the principles round which the great game of Rugby football has been built up. Yet, frankly, there is a hint of something smug and self-righteous about some of the phrases they have thought fit to publish.

It is the FFR who should be, and apparently are, 'gravely disturbed'.

Tour Match: Barbarians 3 South Africans 17, Cardiff, 26 January

Springboks finish tour with 14 points in 12 minutes

By EW Swanton

The Springbok tour, so far as the British Isles is concerned, ended on an appropriately satisfying note at Cardiff on Saturday, for in their last match before they cross to France the South Africans beat the Barbarians convincingly, by a goal, three penalty goals and a try to a try.

Up to the point, 18 minutes after half-time, when Keevy celebrated his promotion to stand-off by putting them ahead with the first of the penalties, little had been seen of the positional skill and mutual support which normally distinguish their football.

But from then onwards the Springbok movements gradually regained their habitual sweep and stride. And though in this period they only once crossed the Barbarian line, the Springboks scored 14 points in 12 minutes.

That was that, and the proceedings thereafter were mainly of academic appeal. Cardiff being Cardiff, the 50,000 spectators to a man remained till the last whistle, and were rewarded by some of the best of the football.

After the match, Dr D Craven, joint-manager of the touring team, presented a springbok head to the Cardiff club as best losers of the tour. Cardiff were beaten 11-9, the score by which London Counties inflicted the only defeat on the tourists at Twickenham on November 10. The Springbok record is: P27-W26-L1-F499-A143.

Paris, 6 April

French championship abolished

From Our Own Correspondent

Confronted with the choice of abolishing the French Rugby Championship or breaking off relationship with the other Rugby Unions the French Rugby Federation, by 19 votes to six, today decided to bring the national competition to an end. A congress will be held in Paris early in May to ratify the decision.

Because of complaints of violation of the amateur rule the French Federation on December 22 decided at a private meeting that the only way to enforce respect for the rule in France was to abolish the championship.

A storm of protest arose in the South-West, the home of Rugby in France, when the decision became known, and many local federations threatened to withdraw. The French Federation, however, today stood by its guns.

If this measure had not been taken the next step – a cessation in international games, such as occurred between 1931 and 1939 – would most probably have been decreed by the International Board for the same reason as the pre-war break, namely, violations of the amateur rule.

The big clubs will make their own match arrangements as in the United Kingdom, and local federations will arrange fixtures for the small clubs. But there will be no more knock-out tournaments.

Rugby men in Britain and the Dominions will welcome the decision taken, particularly because, since the war, matches with French sides have always been fought out in the best possible spirit.

INTERNATIONAL CHAMPIONSHIP

	E	F	I	S	W	P	W	D	L	F	A	Pts
1 WALES	-	9-5	-	11-0	-	4	4	0	0	42	14	8
2 ENGLAND	-	-	3-0	-	6-8	4	3	0	1	34	14	6
3 IRELAND	-	-	-	12-8	3-14	4	2	0	2	26	33	4
4 FRANCE	3-6	-	8-11	-	-	4	1	0	3	29	37	2
5 SCOTLAND	3-19	11-13	-	-	-	4	0	0	4	22	55	0

TOURS (Tests)
Australia in New Zealand: NZ9-A14, NZ15-A8
South Africa in British Isles & France: S0-SA44, I5-SA17, W3-SA6, E3-SA8, F3-SA25

Paris, 11 May

French clubs keep championship

From Our Own Correspondent

French Rugby clubs yesterday rejected by 745 votes to nil (with one abstention) their executive's decision to suppress the national championship. They decided:

(1) To enforce the amateur rules and conform strictly to the spirit of the game.

(2) To maintain the championship in the various categories.

(3) To hold a congress in June to set up a commission responsible for international relationships.

1953

22 Aug South Africa beat the Wallabies in the first Test, at Ellis Park, Johannesburg, by 25-3, a record margin for a home Test.

5 Sep The Newlands crowd give the Wallabies a prolonged standing ovation after the visitors come back from 14-3 down just after the interval to win 18-14 with a converted try in injury time to level the series 1-1 – the vital move starting 10 yards from the Wallaby line and finishing with a 70-yard run by left-wing Gareth Jones, who just manages to outpace the formidable Hennie Muller. At the final whistle, the limping Australian captain John Solomon, who played a part in the move, is chaired off the field by team-mates and opponents. [The Springboks comfortably win the last two Tests to take the series 3-1.]

19 Dec A month after Cardiff's great victory over the All Blacks, the tourists are beaten again on the same ground, this time by Wales, claiming their third triumph over New Zealand in four tours, débutant Gwyn Rowlands kicking them level with 10 minutes to go and then Ken Jones scoring the winning try, Rowlands converting to make the final score 13-8.

International Championship: England 26 Scotland 8, Twickenham, 21 March

How Regan has improved England's rugby: Old-style play at Twickenham

By EW Swanton

To be champions in very deed as well as name, England needed to beat Scotland handsomely at Twickenham on Saturday. The score, made up of four goals and two tries to a goal and a try, reflects the degree of their success.

What must first be added is that the general pattern of the game was something much nearer the old style of play than has been seen of late. Both sides decided that running with the ball was better than kicking it. The spectators, all 60,000 of them, must have enjoyed the result richly, and so assuredly did the players.

Full tribute is due to Hall and to his team for bringing home the championship after Wales and Ireland have monopolised it so long. England were lucky last month to snatch a draw at Dublin, but it must be realised how much harder is England's task in the alternate years when they have to begin operations in Wales and thence proceed to Ireland.

The forwards, with Wilkins in command, have played consistently well, as indeed they did last year. The chief improvement has derived from Regan, and Shuttleworth's service against Scotland gave him the chance to show fully just what impetus means in a stand-off half. The English three-quarters were fairly striding out when they took the ball, and the wings accordingly had time and room to work in.

The best thing about these backs is that they are all distinctly on the upgrade, and apart from Shuttleworth, who will unfortunately be less agreeably engaged in Korea, they may be expected to be even better players next season.

[England's six tries, a record for them against Scotland, were scored by Bazley (2), Adkins, Butterfield, Stirling and Woodward, and four of them were converted by captain and full-back Nim Hall.]

INTERNATIONAL CHAMPIONSHIP

	E	F	I	S	W	P	W	D	L	F	A	Pts
1 ENGLAND	-	11-0	-	26-8	-	4	3	1	0	54	20	7
2 WALES	3-8	-	5-3	-	-	4	3	0	1	26	14	6
3 IRELAND	9-9	16-3	-	-	-	4	2	1	1	54	25	5
4 FRANCE	-	-	-	11-5	3-6	4	1	0	3	17	38	2
5 SCOTLAND	-	-	8-26	-	0-12	4	0	0	4	21	75	0

TOURS (Tests)
Australia in South Africa: SA25-A3, SA14-A18, SA18-A8, SA22-A9

Tour Match: Cardiff 8 New Zealanders 3, Cardiff, 21 November

Magnificent Cardiff give All Blacks a lesson: Virtues of the open game extolled

By EW Swanton

Two years ago a crowd surged sadly out of Cardiff Arms Park sick at heart at seeing the Springboks snatch the narrowest and luckiest of victories in the last moments of the match. On Saturday, before 56,000 of their countrymen, Cardiff gave another wonderful game to a Dominion team, and this time justice was done beyond question or argument.

The All Blacks were beaten by a goal and a try to a penalty goal, and while the Cardiff players carried in their captain, Bleddyn Williams, to a final roar of admiration and delight from the crowd, there must have been just a few present whose minds could turn back to two other historic successes on the same field.

In 1906 Cardiff beat the Springboks, in 1947 the Wallabies – and now this. South Africa, Australia and New Zealand. No country, let alone any other club or combina-

Collins of Cardiff leaps highest in the line-out.

tion, can point to such a trinity of victories.

This in fact was the 98th match played by the All Blacks on British tours. They have won 92 of them, and their only conquerors hitherto have been Wales twice, England once and Swansea. Ulster once fought them to a draw.

Every since Haydn Tanner commanded the first famous post-war Cardiff sides the club have led Welsh Rugby football, and their influence has spread far beyond the borders of Wales.

The great lesson that Cardiff have taught, in an age where so much of the emphasis has been on heavy forwards, thick defensive screens and an abundance of kicking, is that the open game can still pay best, just as it is the most attractive to watch and the most enjoyable to play.

The game was only five minutes old when Cardiff took a lead that they were never to lose. Morgan burst through the centre just in his own half, punted ahead and caught the ball as it bounced back off a defender. He passed to Williams beside him, who in turn gave to Rowlands, who cross-kicked high under the All Blacks' goal for Judd to dive over. Rowlands converted.

The next score though was to the All Blacks, Jarden kicking a magnificent long goal.

Within two minutes Cardiff scored again, from a set scrum. Bleddyn Williams, at first centre, made the perfect short kick over the All Blacks three-quarter line, and it bounced just right for Alun Thomas, who took the ball in his stride and, after drawing Jarden, sent Rowlands in at the corner.

In the last 10 minutes the All Blacks tried several high kicks towards the Cardiff line with every man following up for dear life.

A side less gallant or less shrewdly marshalled by Willis and Judd must have fallen, but Cardiff were not to be wrested from the prize. When the last whistle went the crowd acclaimed them as only a Welsh crowd can.

1954

10 Apr Jean Prat leads France to an 11-3 victory over England in Paris which, after more than 40 years of striving, gives them their first share in the International Championship, with England and Wales, who beat Wooden-Spoonists Scotland – pointless for a record third time in a row – 15-3 at Swansea.

Laws The International Board make it illegal for any player intentionally to fall or kneel in a scrummage, to cause it to collapse or for either team to delay the formation of a scrummage, and the player putting in must ensure that the ball touches the ground immediately beyond the nearer second foot. Several other changes are made, including measures to curb the activities of wing forwards who merely lean on the scrummage and break away directly the ball is put in and of players who push, charge, hold or bind with other players in the line-out

---

Tour Match: England 0 New Zealand 5, Twickenham, 30 January

Brave England XV go down with colours flying

Only numbers could stop Woodward

By JP Jordan

Fighting bravely to the last, England's Rugby team went down with colours flying after a desperate game at Twickenham in which the sheer physical strength and immense determination of New Zealand's forwards, coupled with magnificent covering in defence, proved the decisive factors. New Zealand won by a goal, from a try scored by Dalzell after 18 minutes, to nothing.

Stripped of its warm coat of straw the ground was in good condition and the 70,000 spectators were able to watch one of the very few Rugby games that were possible between those played at Aberdeen and Penzance. No other first-class matches were played.

A bitingly cold north-east wind appeared to have little effect on the players, much of England's passing, especially when they were making their grand rally in the last quarter of an hour, being exceedingly well done. That was the most stirring period of the afternoon.

Time and again, with New Zealand keeping up the pressure in an effort to make the match secure by scoring a second try, England turned defence into attack, even from their own goal-line.

Woodward, Regan or Butterfield would break away and play would be carried to midfield, but New Zealand's cleverly planned defence in depth could not be penetrated, and remorselessly England would be driven back.

The English defence itself is deserving of the highest praise for limiting New Zealand's success to five points. Woodward's complete subjection of Jarden saved many a threatening situation.

Just as Woodward reached the heights for England, so did Scott for New Zealand. A more polished full-back display has not been seen at headquarters.

The result of the game meant the fulfilment of the fourth All Blacks' ambition. More than anywhere else they wanted to win at Twickenham, the Mecca of the game, as Stuart described it. So overjoyed was the New Zealand captain when the final whistle blew, that he fell flat on his face and embraced the turf.

INTERNATIONAL CHAMPIONSHIP

	E	F	I	S	W	P	W	D	L	F	A	Pts
1=WALES	-	19-13	-	15-3	-	4	3	0	1	52	34	6
1=ENGLAND	-	-	14-3	-	9-6	4	3	0	1	39	23	6
1=FRANCE	11-3	-	8-0	-	-	4	3	0	1	35	22	6
4 IRELAND	-	-	-	6-0	9-12	4	1	0	3	18	34	2
5 SCOTLAND	3-13	0-3	-	-	-	4	0	0	4	6	37	0

TOURS (Tests)
New Zealand in British Isles & France: W13-NZ8, I3-NZ14, E0-NZ5, S0-NZ3, F3-NZ0

Tour Match: Barbarians 5 All Blacks 19, Cardiff

Scott and RA White are too good for Barbarians

All Blacks wind up tour on top note

By JP Jordan

Wearing down the strongest team the Barbarians could put into the field, the All Blacks, after being led at half-time, gave their brightest display of the tour and concluded their official programme in the British Isles on the top note, running out easy winners by two goals, a dropped goal, and two tries to a goal.

The capacity crowd of 56,000 at the Cardiff Arms Park saw a splendid exhibition of Rugby. Scott, the tourists' full-back, was the hero of the afternoon. His superlative form so captured the imagination of the knowledgeable Welshmen that at the close they shouted, 'We want Scott.'

The relentless pressure of the magnificent All Black pack, in which RA White was pre-eminent, supported by the superb skill of Scott, won the match.

Scott and his captain, Stuart, were carried shoulder-high, and as a tribute to a great band of sportsmen the crowd sang the Maori song of farewell, 'Now is the Hour'. It was a memorable and fitting conclusion to a long and successful tour.

Out of 28 matches the All Blacks won 24, drew two (against Swansea and Ulster) and lost two with an aggregate of 417 points to 102. As the defeats were at the Arms Park, the All Blacks were doubly pleased that their third visit proved lucky.

Tour Match: France 3 New Zealand 0, Colombes, 27 February

New Zealand stopped by French tackling

By JP Jordan

Badly beaten for the ball, France nevertheless gained their first victory over New Zealand at Colombes. The score in their favour was only a try to nothing, but it was a thoroughly deserved success, as they were always the livelier team, their swiftness in defence completely nonplussing the All Blacks backs.

France have now beaten Scotland, Ireland and New Zealand without a point scored against them, a remarkable feat. On Saturday the odds were against them, since they were so seldom in possession, but they seized their one chance of scoring a try.

In a long experience I do not think I have ever seen a side so completely outhooked – New Zealand won 32 scrums out of 42 – nor so beaten in the line-out as were the Frenchmen. But that did not seem to worry them.

The longer the game went on the more obvious it became that New Zealand had no answer to the first-time tackling of Domec, who gave Bowers no rope, and of Martine and M Prat in the centre.

Scott did his utmost to get his backs moving. Frequently New Zealand were playing without a full-back, as Scott was up in the three-quarter line and sometimes even taking the ball from his scrum-half. But every time he had the ball, down he went. Never on the whole tour has Scott been kept in such subjection.

The French forwards, inspired by Jean Prat, who had grand supporters in Bienes, Baulon, Domec and Chevallier, played their part admirably in the loose, and it was Baulon who initiated the movement that led to the winning try, scored by Jean Prat, who hurled himself over with a cluster of All Blacks on top of him.

1955

5 Feb Inspired by captain and full-back A Cameron, Scotland beat Wales 14-8 at Murrayfield to end their run of 17 consecutive defeats.

26 Mar Wales beat France 16-11 in Paris to share the Championship with them and deprive the great Jean Prat of the honour of leading them to their first outright title in his 38th and last international.

16 Apr Italian rugby makes its début at Twickenham with the 22-11 defeat of an Italian XV by London Counties.

24 Sep The Springboks recover from a 5-point deficit to beat the Lions 22-8 at Port Elizabeth in the 4th and last Test and tie the rubber, although it is the first time they have failed to win a home series for 27 years.

6 Dec The Varsity match comes back into its own as a great sporting fixture, as the 55,000 crowd (a total exceeded only once before) at Twickenham thrill to Oxford's 9-5 victory over Cambridge in a match that epitomised the determination of the respective captains, RCP Alloway and JW Clements, at the beginning of term to keep the emphasis on attack. It is Oxford's good fortune that to this end they could call upon the alliance at half-back of DO Brace and MJK Smith, who at times have the crowd in laughter as they feint and twist and turn, almost always finding someone to pass to in the end. Cambridge are helpless in the face of Oxford's famous 'switch' tactics, and there are moments of real brilliance when Oxford are passing back and forth, through many hands, keeping the ball for what seems minutes as they probe for a way through the opposing defence. Scorers – Oxford: tries, JC Walker, IL Reeler; penalty goal, JD Currie. Cambridge: try, ME Kershaw; conversion, JGG Hetherington.

INTERNATIONAL CHAMPIONSHIP

	E	F	I	S	W	P	W	D	L	F	A	Pts
1=WALES	3-0	-	21-3	-	-	4	3	0	1	48	28	6
1=FRANCE	-	-	-	15-0	11-16	4	3	0	1	47	28	6
3 SCOTLAND	-	-	12-3	-	14-8	4	2	0	2	32	35	4
4 ENGLAND	-	9-16	-	9-6	-	4	1	1	2	24	31	3
5 IRELAND	6-6	3-5	-	-	-	4	0	1	3	15	44	1

TOURS (Tests)
British Isles in South Africa: SA22-BI23, SA25-BI9, SA6-BI9, SA22-BI8
Australia in New Zealand: NZ16-A8, NZ8-A0, NZ3-A8

Tour Match: Northern Transvaal 11 British Isles 14, Pretoria, 27 August

Great try by Butterfield

From a Special Correspondent

'Wonderful' was the one-word comment of Mr F Mellish, chairman of the South African Rugby selectors and a former England and Springbok forward, on the British Isles' 110-yard passing attack from their own line to beat Northern Transvaal 14-11 here yesterday.

A crowd of 40,000, a record for Pretoria, saw the British forwards heel from a scrum near their own posts, scrum-half Williams feint to kick to touch, sending the defence the wrong way, and then give Morgan a perfect pass.

Morgan ran 30 yards before handing on to England and Northampton centre Butterfield. With two men outside him for a double overlap, Butterfield raced up to the Northern Transvaal full-back, half dummied and then swung inside to leave his would-be tackler flat-footed and finish a 75-yard run by scoring the winning try under the posts.

The try was not converted but the British team, who had played through the last hour without their captain, Thompson, held out to win by a goal and three tries to a goal, a try and a penalty goal. Butterfield's try was certainly the finest in the British teams' 19 games. Veteran Springboks go so far as to say it was the greatest try ever scored in South Africa.

Tour Match: South Africa 22 British Isles 23, Johannesburg, 6 August

Lions backs best in SA for 50 years
Triumphant XV carried off the field

From a Special Correspondent

An earthquake has shaken the foundations of South Africa's world Rugby supremacy. It was witnessed by a near 90,000 record crowd for the game here yesterday, when the British Isles defeated the Springboks by four goals and a try to two goals, two tries and two penalty goals.

It was a desperately close affair. South Africa, 12 points behind with a quarter of an hour left, made a storming finish against courageous opponents who were handicapped by losing blindside forward Reg Higgins for the last 35 minutes.

The seven-man British pack, magnificently served by the all-Welsh front row of WO Williams, B Meredith and C Meredith, had not only held but beaten the Springbok forwards in tight and loose.

It was an astonishing performance remembering South Africa's traditional forward power and the fact that the British team were unaccustomed to Johannesburg's mile-high altitude which takes heavy toll on stamina.

Getting more of the ball as the sands of the game ran out, the Springboks got within two points of victory with ten seconds left. Now it was left to Jack van der Schyff to win the game with a conversion midway between the goal and the touchline. There was hushed silence, then a groan from the crowd as the full-back lifted his head and hooked the ball to the right of the posts.

Next instant the referee blew for no-side, and the field was black with thousands of spectators who lifted all the British players on their shoulders and carried them to their dressing room. It was a wonderful tribute to a wonderful team.

Winning with 14 men, the red-jerseyed British Lions ended South Africa's 59-year-old record of success in the first Test of a home series. Yet another record was broken, the highest score against Springboks in South Africa.

What was the pattern of the victory? It was superb forward play with the Scottish flanker, Greenwood, outstanding in defence and attack, supported by the finest backs seen in South Africa for 50 years. And Welsh outside half, Cliff Morgan, dominated the attacking play.

Morgan's tactics were just what was wanted to wear down the opposition. He 'softened' van der Schyff, notoriously unreliable with a rolling ball, with diagonal kicks. The result was that Greenwood and O'Reilly crossed for easy tries as the full-back failed to clear off the ground.

So from 8-11 at half-time the Lions were leading by 12 points, Cameron having converted all three tries – Morgan got the other – scored in eight minutes of this second-half burst.

The South Africans had no real counter to the inside breaks by the centres, Butterfield and the powerful Davies, who simply ran through the tackles. Butterfield got a first-half try, converted by Cameron, after Pedlow had opened the British scoring with a try.

Cliff Morgan leaves South Africa's Van Wyk trailing as he scores for the Lions.

1956

24 Mar Ken Jones (Wales) makes his world-record 43rd international appearance in the 5-3 defeat of France in Paris as Wales win at least a share of the Championship. [Wales win the title outright when France beat England next month in their postponed fixture. Jones plays once more for Wales.]

14 Jul New Zealand beat South Africa

10-6 at Dunedin, their first win over the Springboks since 1937.

21 Jul The Springboks lose 9-6 to New Zealand champions Canterbury at Christchurch, the winning points coming from a hotly disputed penalty for offside after a protracted ruck, and the tourists' manager, Dr Danie Craven, lodges an official complaint against the standard of refereeing in the South Island.

International Championship: France 14 England 9, Colombes, 14 April

Flatfooted England beaten by France: Forwards are tossed about like rag dolls
Wales are Rugby Champions

By JP Jordan

Two bad blunders within a yard of their line at Colombes ruined England's expectations of sharing the Rugby championship. As it is, that honour goes alone to Wales.

France, quick as ever to profit by errors, snatched eight points from these two to win the jubilee match of the series by a goal, two penalty goals and a try to two penalty goals and a try. The irony of it lay in the fact that Thompson was England's solitary try getter, and it was he who was responsible for both the mistakes.

But it would be quite wrong to shoulder England's defeat entirely on Thompson. Not an English back played up to form.

They had plenty of the ball from the line-outs and set scrums, but they could do little right with it. Compared with the French they looked flatfooted and stale.

The forwards were having a rare set-to, with the French using their superior strength to toss the Englishmen about like rag dolls, and England dominating the line-outs through Marques and Currie. These two took a rare battering, but, like the other six, they remained undaunted.

France had splendid forwards in the massive Celaya and Chevallier. Baulon, Domenech and Bienes were also outstanding, and Lazies most ably filled the role Domec has so long occupied as France's number eight.

It was after the interval that real disaster befell England. With France pressing, Thompson ran back. He was partly tackled and dropped the ball a few feet from the line, where Pauthe grounded it without having to move. The second blow fell as Thompson fumbled Stener's kick ahead and Dupuy was at hand to score.

INTERNATIONAL CHAMPIONSHIP

	E	F	I	S	W	P	W	D	L	F	A	Pts
1 WALES	-	5-3	-	9-3	-	4	3	0	1	25	20	6
2=ENGLAND	-	-	20-0	-	3-8	4	2	0	2	43	28	4
2=FRANCE	14-9	-	14-8	-	-	4	2	0	2	31	34	4
2=IRELAND	-	-	-	14-10	11-3	4	2	0	2	33	47	4
5 SCOTLAND	6-11	12-0	-	-	-	4	1	0	3	31	34	2

TOURS (Tests)
South Africa in Australia: A0-SA9, A0-SA9
South Africa in New Zealand: NZ10-SA6, NZ3-SA8, NZ17-SA10, NZ11-SA5

Tour Match: New Zealand 11 South Africa 5, Auckland, 1 September

Springboks lose Test rubber

From Reuter

South Africa were beaten by 11 points to 5 in the final Rugby Union Test against New Zealand here yesterday and so lost a series for the first time since 1896. New Zealand gained the rubber by three Tests to one.

South Africa's previous defeat in a Test series was by J Hammond's British Isles touring side in 1896, when the game in the Union was still in its infancy. Since then they have been almost unrivalled, though the touring British Lions held them to a 2-2 draw last year.

Yesterday's match, the final one of the Springboks' tour, was a magnificent forward struggle between two evenly matched packs. There were few three-quarter movements, but the quality of the forward display more than made up for the shortcomings of the backs.

Hero of the day for New Zealand was Don Clarke, the 16st 1lb full-back, who scored eight points, kicking two penalty goals and converting a try scored by Peter Jones.

Roy Dryburgh scored South Africa's try, which was converted by Basie Viviers.

Tour Match: London Clubs 6 South African Universities 6, Twickenham, 26 December

Weakened London hold out against Sables
Universities' pack deserve better reward for late effort

By Michael Melford

The South African Universities remain unbeaten and by the end of yesterday's excitements at Twickenham were playing really well. Not quite well enough, however, to overcome the London Clubs XV, which hung on bravely with a depleted pack and somehow earned a draw, scoring a penalty goal and a try against two tries.

On paper London, with 10 internationals, were formidable opposition at this stage of the tour. But Harding was carried off before half-time with a broken shin and afterwards their other seven forwards had to struggle desperately against a heavier pack which was becoming a more cohesive and menacing body all the time.

London twice led – just after half-time by a penalty goal, and 10 minutes from the end by a brilliant half-back try by Baker and Williams. But each time the Sables hit back with a try at once. The kick that would have won the match came back off the post.

In the first half, Pfaff suffered a wicked-looking and sounding kick in the face from Harding's boot. Miraculously he rose, bleeding, but not seriously damaged, while Harding, who had tried to halt the kick in mid-air, lay with a broken leg.

Roberts kicked the penalty goal early in the second half. The Sables replied with a try after the London defence became involved in a chapter of accidents. Grant, trying to kick, had to dodge the posts and miskicked; Calvert, trying to avoid being off-side, slipped; and Holmes scored in isolation.

Only once after that did London break out of their own half. A foot rush by the centres ended in a scrum 10 yards from the line. The seven forwards heeled, Williams broke wide and gave a reverse pass to Baker, who jinked through to give London a 6-3 lead.

It would have been a fantastic victory, but there were still 10 minutes left. Back went the South Africans, and Pfaff broke round the blind side to sent Coetzee over on the left.

1957

19 May In front of 93,000 spectators at the August 23rd Stadium, Bucharest, France come back dramatically in the last 15 minutes from 15-6 down to win 18-15 and maintain their 100% record against Romania in this first post-war fixture between the two countries.

10 Dec Oxford beat Cambridge 3-0 with a try by scrum-half SG Coles, both universities having beaten the touring Wallabies within the space of five days last month, Oxford by 12-6, Cambridge by 13-3.

International Championship: England 16 Scotland 3, Twickenham, 16 March

Handsome victory earns England the Grand Slam
Finest pack for years routs Scots in closing minutes

By Michael Melford

If England were to win their fourth victory of the season and all the glory that went with it, the ideal always was that they win it handsomely and conclusively in a game worthy of the presence of the Queen, Prince Philip and 72,000 others.

Two goals, a penalty goal and a try to a penalty goal seemed an unlikely end after an even first half. With 10 minutes to go, England still only led 6-3. Yet on those last minutes, the margin was fair enough. The longer the match lasted, the more England must have scored.

The grand slam of four victories, last achieved by England in 1928, would not have been possible without a captain of character in Evans and selectors who built carefully over two seasons and, once satisfied, were prepared to back their judgment. They have needed only 17 players this season.

Mostly, Saturday's events confirmed reputations. They confirmed that this was the

finest England pack for a long time and that Robbins and Marques in their respective spheres were the outstanding English forwards of recent years. Currie had one of his best games for England yet, joining Marques in some brilliant line-out play; Evans, among other things, heeled three times against the loose head. For all the successes of this Scottish pack, it had always seemed that their back row must suffer in comparison with England's great combination of Robbins, Ashcroft and Higgins. Thus it was, and Higgins rubbed it in by instigating the second try and scoring the third.

And no one has contributed more to the season's success than Jeeps, so often a ninth forward or a second full-back. Now, with his rare speed in gathering and dispatching the ball, with his accuracy of service and general appearance of knowing exactly what was going on, he showed his talents as an attacking scrum-half as well.

INTERNATIONAL CHAMPIONSHIP

	E	F	I	S	W	P	W	D	L	F	A	Pts
1 ENGLAND	-	9-5	-	16-3	-	4	4	0	0	34	8	8
2=WALES	0-3	-	6-5	-	-	4	2	0	2	31	30	4
2=IRELAND	0-6	11-6	-	-	-	4	2	0	2	21	21	4
2=SCOTLAND	-	-	3-5	-	9-6	4	2	0	2	21	27	4
5 FRANCE	-	-	-	0-6	13-19	4	0	0	4	24	45	0

TOURS (Tests)
New Zealand in Australia: A11-NZ25, A9-NZ22

Representative Match: Welsh XV 17 International XV 16, Cardiff, 6 April

Welsh team triumph in classic
Welter of high-class, open play

By EW Swanton

The match for the 1958 Empire Games Fund produced football of much brilliance at Cardiff on Saturday, and since the Welshmen won narrowly but deservedly it is safe to say everyone went home completely happy. This will certainly have included the organisers, for the crowd mustered 50,000, which means for the Fund a sum of around £12,000.

If this sort of response reflected the magnetic pull of Rugby football in Wales, the play itself, after the local disappointments of the season, emphasised that there is little basically wrong with the quality. The selectors of the side comprising England, Scotland and Ireland had everyone to call upon, and were able to fit the best of the Scots and Irish into a framework supplied by the victorious England team.

Yet in the second half the

quicker wits of the Welshmen behind the scrum put them very much in the ascendant, and it was not until the last minute that the Rest scored their third try and so almost caught up.

There have been some great games of the same open kind on this field between Cardiff and the Barbarians; but these perhaps apart, I cannot think such a welter of high-class open football, carried on for the full 80 minutes at an unrelenting pace, has ever been seen here – or for that matter anywhere, except possibly on the Lions' tour of South Africa.

[Scorers - Welsh XV: tries, RH Davies, B Meredith, C James, G Wells; drop goal & conversion, TE Davies. International XV: tries, AR Smith (2), AJ O'Reilly; conversions (2) & penalty goal, PJ Berkery.]

Tour Match: Cardiff 0 Barbarians 40, Cardiff, 20 April

Display that crowns 67 years of Rugby: Cardiff are turned into bedraggled team of second-raters

By Arthurian

The humiliation of the famous Cardiff Rugby club on their own ground by the equally famous Barbarians by 40 points without reply is an astonishing event. For the 20,000 Welshmen at the Arms Park on Saturday it was a tragedy, and something they will want to forget.

Cardiff, unwisely taking the field without the combined attacking genius of C Morgan, G Wells and G Griffiths, paid a heavy penalty. They were outplayed so completely they were made to look a bedraggled collection of second-class performers. The Barbarians played magnificently while producing a superb exhibition of open football.

In all their 67 years of endeavour to foster the best in the game and fulfil the ideals of their originator, they have never played better. From Davies at full-back to Robson at wing forward, the whole side performed with swift precision. Winn, the only non-international in their ranks, played as well as any England

centre has done this season.

It was a remarkable day for Smith, the Scottish wing, who led the Barbarians. He scored three tries and converted the tenth and last scored by his side with a beautiful kick from the touchline.

O'Reilly showed his power at exploiting the smallest gap, and Winn and Thompson were stars in their own right. Baker at outside-half was strong and quick to bring his three-quarters into action, while Mulligan thoroughly enjoyed himself, playing against a back row which had little ability and less speed.

The pack was well drilled under Evans, and in the second half opened out to join the backs in an all-out attacking effort. The sight of 15 men running and handling in unison and at top speed to bewilder defenders was something new in the history of a great ground.

One Welshman leaving the ground remarked: 'Well, Dai, I couldn't make out whether it was no-side or they declared.'

1958

8 Feb Fly-half Jackie Kyle makes his 45th appearance for Ireland in their 6-0 defeat at Twickenham to set a new international record.

22 Feb Veteran forward Nick Shehadie, dropped by the Wallabies after playing against Wales and Ireland, plays against his own side for the Baa-Baas, who beat the tourists 11-6 at Cardiff.

10 May The 60,000 spectators at Ellis Park take the Baa-Baas to their hearts as great tries by AJF O'Reilly and AR Smith in the last 10 minutes earn the tourists a 17-all draw with Transvaal in their first match.

28 May On the way home from their highly successful, if not in results (W1-D1-L3), tour of South Africa, the Baa-Baas beat an East African XV 52-12 in Nairobi, the Irish three-quarter Tony O'Reilly scoring 7 tries. Their captain, Welsh fly-half Cliff Morgan, 'whose name in South Africa remains synonymous with

British Rugby at its best', reaffirms that this is his last match.

16 Aug On their first official visit to South Africa, France beat the Springboks 9-5 at Ellis Park, Johannesburg, to win the series 1-0 with one drawn. The French victory creates a sensation back home, elevating the sport onto a new level.

Laws The several changes include the following: Scrummage – Near foot of tight-head hooker allowed to strike at ball on equal terms with far foot of loose-head hooker. Tackle – Players, after regaining their feet, are permitted to play the ball after a tackle in any lawful way (rather than only with their feet). Knock-on – An unintentional knock-on direct from a kick is no longer an infringement, provided the player recovers the ball before it touches the ground or another player.

IRB Overseas countries' vote on Board increased to two each, now on par with Home Unions.

Tour Match: Ireland 9 Australia 6, Dublin, 18 January

Untried Irish forwards shatter the Wallabies

Captain's agonising victory run

By Michael Melford

You could not find many people in Dublin on Saturday morning who fancied Ireland's chances or who expected to see much of a game. Yet a famous Irish victory was won, and the game abounded in excitement, climaxed with a dramatic winning try.

When before has an Irish captain, with three minutes to go and the score level, been offered the chance of a clear run in from half-way? The start which Hewitt's interception gave Henderson was such that any other Irish back must have scored with time to spare. But speed is not one

of the heavily built Henderson's virtues, and all Ireland suffered agonies as he lumbered on, with the pursuit rapidly closing on him.

In fact, he was caught a yard from home. But the tackler glanced off, like a destroyer off a battleship, and he fell over the line amid a din which must have echoed from Kerry to Donegal.

Thus, Ireland, with two tries scored inside five minutes, against a half-gale, came from behind to win their first international against a touring side in modern times.

INTERNATIONAL CHAMPIONSHIP

	E	F	I	S	W	P	W	D	L	F	A	Pts
1 ENGLAND	-	-	6-0	-	3-3	4	2	2	0	26	6	6
2 WALES	-	6-16	-	8-3	-	4	2	1	1	26	28	5
3 FRANCE	0-14	-	11-6	-	-	4	2	0	2	36	37	4
4 SCOTLAND	3-3	11-9	-	-	-	4	1	1	2	23	32	3
5 IRELAND	-	-	12-6	6-9	-	4	1	0	3	24	32	2

TOURS (Tests)
Australia in British Isles & France: W9-A3, I9-A6, E9-A6, S12-A8, F19-A0
France in South Africa: SA3-F3, SA5-F9
Australia in New Zealand: NZ25-A3, NZ3-A6, NZ17-A8

Tour Match: England 9 Australia 6, Twickenham, 1 February

England snatch most dramatic of victories to foil Wallabies: Great run by Jackson to climax amazing recovery

By EW Swanton

The game at Twickenham on Saturday, wherein England beat the Wallabies by a magnificent try scored by Peter Jackson in the last moments, will be remembered as one of the more extraordinary in the history of the Rugby Union ground.

England had twice pulled up from behind in spite of the loss of their stand-off half, Horrocks-Taylor, and the consequent strain on a depleted pack. Yet in these final minutes the 14 men summoned their very last reserves of energy to mount a surging attack. Jackson completed it with a weaving, feinting run that deceived at least three men in his path before he threw himself over in the extreme

right corner.

The climax would have been unforgettable in any circumstances. What made it especially so was that the crowd had been roused to an unusual fervour of partisanship, not only by the gallant recovery of a depleted side, but also, sad to say, by a feeling of resentment brought about by two or three foolish, hot-headed things which caused injuries, happily not serious, to several of the English backs.

This built up as the second half progressed, and finally expressed itself in hat-waving, cushion-throwing, and a thunder of applause such as one scarcely remembers at Twickenham.

International Championship: Wales 6 France 16, Cardiff, 29 March

Magnificent France are too fiery for Wales

Hollow championship for England

By EW Swanton

France won the game of the season at Cardiff on Saturday by two goals and two dropped goals to a penalty goal and a try.

So at one blow they deprived Wales of the championship and made clear to 60,000 subdued but appreciative Welshmen that they, the French, at their best were more than a match for all comers.

The title stays with England on the strength of two wins and two draws; a hollow victory, it may be thought, in an international season which has produced a reasonable amount of good football but no one team with the stamp of champions.

Except France! In this match they touched heights of skill beyond attainment of any of the other countries in any of their matches.

Their forwards, with their captain Celaya, and the pack

leader, Mias, making a magnificent pair of locks, swept and stormed their way over the Arms Park, making a cracking pace and sustaining it for the full 80 minutes.

In rear, Danos, dangerous on his own, a good kicker, and with a fine long pass, played perhaps the game of his life, and certainly gave the scrum-half performance of the season.

Labazuy made him a cool, tactically-sensible partner, while the Lourdes three-quarters, without throwing up any one match-winning hero, contributed a lively all-round performance, and in defence contained the Welsh efforts with the utmost ease.

To top off all these virtues, Vannier, at full-back, was truly magnificent.

Panache, with a capital P, is the word which best expresses the French performance. How unpredictable they are!

1959

4 Mar In a match played under floodlights at the White City as part of the Blackheath centenary celebrations, the Barbarians beat 'The Club' by 21-8.

18 Apr Ireland's 9-5 victory over an unmotivated France, already crowned as champions, is the last match of the International Championship, in which only 93 points and 12 tries are scored,

all-time record lows with five nations competing.

17 Oct England & Wales beat Scotland & Ireland 26-17 in the Twickenham Rugby Jubilee, a match which, according to Daily Telegraph correspondent EW Swanton, was brilliant almost beyond compare and kept the crowd in perpetual explosions of cheering and applause.

International Championship: France 11 Wales 3, Colombes, 4 April

French are Champions at last

By EW Swanton

On an afternoon of blazing hot sunshine, France beat Wales fair and square before a crowd of 55,000 by 11 points to 3, and so for the first time became [outright] champions.

All true enthusiasts in the British Isles must be very happy for them to have won at last, although Saturday's match was the reverse of spectacular. The French supposed quite correctly that their forwards could win the day for them. The Welsh kept the game even tighter than their opponents, so that their centres played virtually no part in the picture except in defence.

A stranger newly arrived on the football scene after, say, 30 or 40 years' absence would have found the sight a strange one, with both packs

keeping possession largely to themselves and the halves either playing the ball back to the forwards or more frequently booting for touch as deeply as possible into enemy territory. To go back even farther to the beginning of things, William Webb Ellis himself might almost have wondered whether his revolution had been achieved in vain, for there was certainly not a great deal of picking up the ball and running with it.

However, within the policy laid down, the French acquitted themselves admirably, and their forwards, with Mias leading to equal effect both by precept and example, were simply magnificent.

Scorers – France: F Moncla 2T, A Labazuy 1C, 1PG; Wales: TJ Davies 1PG.

Action from the Stade Colombes: Bouquet to Marquesuzaa.

INTERNATIONAL CHAMPIONSHIP

	E	F	I	S	W	P	W	D	L	F	A	Pts
1 FRANCE	-	-	-	9-0	11-3	4	2	1	1	28	15	5
2=IRELAND	0-3	9-5	-	-	-	4	2	0	2	23	19	4
2=WALES	5-0	-	8-6	-	-	4	2	0	2	21	23	4
2=ENGLAND	-	3-3	-	3-3	-	4	1	2	1	9	11	4
5 SCOTLAND	-	-	3-8	-	6-5	4	1	1	2	12	25	3

TOURS (Tests)
British Isles in Australia: A6-BI17, A3-BI24
British Isles in New Zealand: NZ18-BI17, NZ11-BI8, NZ22-BI8, NZ6-BI9

Tour Match: New Zealand 18 British Isles 17, Dunedin, 18 July

Strange decisions rob Lions of victory

By Our Special Correspondent

In quite the most remarkable Test match in living memory, New Zealand defeated the British Isles here yesterday by six penalty goals to a goal, a penalty and three tries.

It will remain unique, for never before in representative Rugby have a side been so outplayed in all departments except goal kicking and won despite the fact that the opposition scored four tries.

In kicking six goals to give his side victory, DB Clarke, the New Zealand full-back, did remarkably well and created a new record for Test matches, passing Geffin's five for South Africa against New Zealand in 1949. He had 10 kicks at goal altogether, three from difficult positions.

The awards by the referee for three of the goals were clearly understood, but the others will remain a mystery.

Obviously the standard of the New Zealand refereeing will come in for considerable criticism after this match, following upon the unhappy Test series of 1956 when the South African management complained officially that

New Zealand referees were not good enough.

There is cause to think that neutral referees are needed for Test Rugby or that the value of the penalty goal should be reduced to two points.

In this match, Referee Fleury bewildered the British Isles team with many of his decisions, particularly those in the closing 10 minutes which changed the whole course of the match. It will be an unhappy tour if the British Isles team suffer as they did in this match from refereeing which, if unbiased, falls well short of Test standards.

Though defeated, the British Isles side enjoyed a moral victory, for their play was far superior to that of New Zealand. The heaviest All Black eight was held and outplayed in the loose, and behind the scrum the speed and quality of the British backs brought several delightful scores.

The British points were scored by Hewitt (penalty) and tries by O'Reilly, Price (2) and Jackson. Risman converted Price's second.

Tour Match: New Zealand 6 British Isles 9, Auckland, 19 September

Lions show what might have been

From Our Special Correspondent

This was a wonderful occasion here at Eden Park, the Lions' tour ending with an impressive crescendo. For the first time in 29 years a New Zealand side was defeated at home by a British team.

Never before on the tour has a New Zealand crowd so readily supported a British victory. The singing of 'Now is the hour', a Maori song of farewell, by the vast crowd before the players left the field created an appropriate atmosphere of goodwill.

For the British team this was a victory for superior skill in the finer arts of the game. The British forwards were on top for most of the play, and by containing the New Zealand pack were able to make things considerably easier for their backs.

As a result the British backs took their chances readily, and three brilliant tries were scored. O'Reilly's

try took his tour total in New Zealand to 17 – one more than the number scored by KJ Jones in 1950 – Jackson's, the best of the three, to 16.

Fly-half Risman's control of the play was a valuable asset, and Mulligan at scrum-half and Davies at full-back have never given better performances in difficult conditions. Davies, through injury, did not reveal his greatness until the second half of the tour. In this match he was far superior to Clarke, who in the four Tests has scored 39 points out of the New Zealand tally of 57. Without him the series would have been lost.

Clarke put New Zealand ahead with a 35-yard penalty, but a try by Jackson made the half-time score 3-3. Early in the second half O'Reilly scored his try, and though Clarke replied with an easy penalty, Risman finished the scoring 15 minutes from time.

The 1960s

International fixtures proliferated in the sixties, with the Home Countries making individual short visits to the 'colonies' in addition to the Lions' tours. South Africa entertained 11 touring parties, nine from International Board countries and two from the British Isles. The Springboks also made major and short tours of Britain and France and paid a return visit to New Zealand. They began another tour of the British Isles and France in 1969, but this was beset by protests and demonstrations and was to be their last major tour to the Northern Hemisphere for more than twenty years.

Taking the results of all these fixtures as a whole makes it painfully obvious that the Springboks and All Blacks were still a class apart from the rest, virtually unbeatable at home and suffering few setbacks abroad. The Springboks started as 'world champions' and at first confirmed their status. But by the end of the decade, with flaws beginning to appear in South African rugby for the first time, the All Blacks, instead of just disputing their mantle, took it over comprehensively.

New Zealand had a wonderful decade. They played 42 Tests, of which they won 35, drew three and lost four. No country from the Northern Hemisphere beat

Wilson Whineray: All Black skipper.

them, and indeed only Scotland, at Murrayfield in January 1964, managed to avoid defeat. The only series the New Zealanders lost was in South Africa in 1960, when they went down by two Tests to one with one drawn. They amply avenged this in 1965 when they beat the visiting Springboks 3-1, and after losing the third Test of this rubber 19-16 at Christchurch won the rest of the internationals they played in the sixties – 17 in all.

Wilson Whineray's 5th All Blacks (1963-64), who lost only one and drew one of their 34 matches in the British Isles and France, were one of the most popular sides ever, but this tour marked the end of defensive New Zealand rugby. Fortunately, New Zealand grew tired of the physical nature of their successful tactics, and manager Charles Saxton and coach Fred Allen, both lovers of handling rugby, put their ideas into practice, and had the 6th All Blacks (1967) playing 15-a-side balanced rugby. They were undefeated, winning 14 of their 15 matches, including all four Tests, and their sustained attacking play earned them the highest praise from British and French critics.

Earlier in the sixties, Wilfred Wooller had written in The Sunday Telegraph: 'As the game stands in this year of grace 1961, the balance of power lies too strongly in the hands of the eight forwards. Some redress is necessary to swing back the balance towards the seven backs.' He referred to the 1960-61 Springbok tour as a 'tragedy of success' and their tactics as an emotionless and unimaginative 'steam-roller of massive forward play'. This sort of criticism did not go unnoticed in South Africa, where the 1962 Lions tour proved a great disappointment and where rugby attendances were beginning to dwindle, especially in the face of increasing competition from professional soccer. Rugby supremo Danie Craven was not slow to spot this reaction against the traditional South African game and devised and introduced in 1963 experimental laws to bring attacking backs into the game. His ideas, which included no kicking on the full into touch from outside the 25, and backs lining up 10 yards back from shortened lineouts, proved immensely popular, and the International Board were eventually to accept some of them. However, unfortunately for South Africa, these innovations resulted in a sharp decline in their forward play, leading to their unprecedented slump in 1965. First, they failed to win a match on their five-match tour of Ireland and Scotland, losing both Tests. Then they lost both Tests in Australia, suffering their first ever series defeat by the Wallabies. And finally they lost their rubber in New Zealand by three Tests to one.

France and Wales dominated the Five Nations Championship in the 1960s, with seven outright wins between them. They shared the points in this match at Cardiff in 1964, an 11-all draw.

Meanwhile in the Five Nations, France were capitalising on their new-found pre-eminence – joint first in 1960, followed by two outright wins to give them four titles on the trot, and another two near the end of the decade. Only Wales came anywhere near this record, with three outright wins and one shared Championship. After winning the title in 1966, Wales finished the following season with the Wooden Spoon, but in their last match unleashed an 18-year-old boy, Keith Jarrett, who destroyed England's title chances at Cardiff with 19 points on his début in what was perhaps the most sensational match of the sixties. But in 1969, Wales were on the receiving end at Auckland, when All Black Fergie McCormick set a new individual Test record with 24 points.

A revolutionary development took place in British rugby towards the end of the sixties, a shift in thinking that led to the acceptance of coaches at international level. The 1966 Lions tour to the Antipodes was the first to take an official coach, John Robins. The Welsh Rugby Union pioneered the change at home amid some controversy at the start of the 1967-68 season, but it was not until Clive Rowlands accepted the post as official coach for the tour of Argentina in 1968 that it became established, and Wales won the Championship undefeated in 1969. England adopted a squad system in 1969, and thirty players met monthly under coach Don White for four months before their victory at Twickenham over South Africa, their first ever against the Springboks.

This was an unhappy campaign for the Springboks, with demonstrators taking every opportunity to show their abhorrence of the apartheid laws operating in South Africa. Feelings had been building up for some time – the All Blacks should have toured South Africa and not the British Isles in 1967, but cancelled because of South African leader Verwoerd's speech on the Maori issue made at the end of the Springboks' 1965 tour of New Zealand, and the D'Oliveira affair erupted in cricket in 1968. Sport could no longer turn a blind eye to the policies of oppressive regimes, and matters were soon to come to a head.

1960

12 Mar Warwickshire complete a hat-trick of County titles, beating Surrey 9-6 in the final at Coventry, Peter Jackson scoring the only try of the game.

9 Apr France beat wooden-spoonists Ireland 23-6 at Colombes to earn a share with England in the Championship, and their 3 drop goals, all kicked by fly-half Pierre Albaladejo, is a record for any team in the Championship.

15 Apr Penarth beat the Barbarians 10-8, their first victory over the tourists in 40 years.

1 May Scotland, the first of the Home Unions to undertake an overseas tour, with several caps unable to make the party, lose only 18-10 to a largely experimental South African side in their first match, played in front of 24,000 spectators at the new Erasmus Stadium, Port Elizabeth. [Scotland go on to win their other two matches, beating Griqualand West 21-11 (4 May) and East Transvaal 30-16 (7 May).]

Jun Romania beat France for the first time, after six defeats, 11-5 in Bucharest.

13 Aug Fine kicking under pressure in the last 6 minutes by full-back Don Clarke earns the All Blacks an 11-all draw in the third Test at Bloemfontein to keep the series with South Africa level. A penalty from 5 yards inside his own half puts them within striking distance of the Springboks, and a conversion 5 yards in from touch in the last seconds equalises the scores.

27 Aug A gruelling forward battle at Port Elizabeth is resolved by a converted try by HJM Pelser early in the second half to give the Springboks an 8-3 win and victory by 2-1 in the rubber over the All Blacks.

3 Dec The Springboks beat Wales 3-0 in a sea of mud at Cardiff Arms Park, thanks to a Keith Oxlee penalty goal. Welsh captain Terry Davies declines the referee's offer to call the game off 15 minutes from the end, but Avril Malan's powerful pack holds out against the fierce gale.

INTERNATIONAL CHAMPIONSHIP

	E	F	I	S	W	P	W	D	L	F	A	Pts
1=FRANCE	3-3	-	23-6	-	-	4	3	1	0	55	28	7
1=ENGLAND	-	-	8-5	-	14-6	4	3	1	0	46	26	7
3 WALES	-	8-16	-	8-0	-	4	2	0	2	32	39	4
4 SCOTLAND	12-21	11-13	-	-	-	4	1	0	3	29	47	2
5 IRELAND	-	-	-	5-6	9-10	4	0	0	4	25	47	0

TOURS (Tests)
Scotland in South Africa: SA18-S10
New Zealand in South Africa: SA13-NZ0, SA3-NZ11, SA11-NZ11, SA8-NZ3

International Championship: Scotland 12 England 21, Murrayfield, 19 March

Pace & Sharp's sagacity bewilder Scots: 20 prolific minutes give England grip on Triple Crown

By Michael Melford

Speed, savoir faire and Sharp are three of the best reasons for England's 13th Triple Crown. A remarkable capacity for taking their chances is another, and it was never more evident or important than at Murrayfield on Saturday.

The strong wind, which winning the toss gave England behind them in the first half, had to be used swiftly. The fiery Scottish forwards, and for that matter their 60,000 fervent compatriots, could not be allowed to gather confidence.

For 20 minutes the Scottish forwards performed well up to expectations, having at least an equal share of the play. And in that period England scored 16 points.

Sharp's second attempt at

a dropped goal just missed, but nothing else did. His first went over; so did Rutherford's long penalty goal; and in between them so did Rutherford's conversions of two tries scored within six yards and a yard of the touchline. This was opportunism in the grand manner.

To their great credit the Scottish pack lost none of their spirit. Their occupation of enemy territory allowed KJF Scotland to kick three penalty goals, and near the end led to a good orthodox three-quarter try. But by then Phillips and Young, at a speed Scotland could not match, had contrived a brilliant try. Rutherford had converted it – once again from the touchline – and England had moved out of reach.

International Championship: England 14 Wales 6, Twickenham, 16 January

England's new vitality ends try-less era
Brilliant Sharp harries Wales in a day to remember

By Michael Melford

An England team with a new aggression and vitality; a Twickenham international which sent even Welshmen home with a sense

Richard Sharp: Brilliant.

of having had their money's worth; a young fly-half, brilliant in thought and deed. These were just three of the good things which made Saturday a day to remember.

How England won is a question soon answered. They won by having the more constructive half-backs and much the livelier and more cohesive back row, by their greater speed on the wings and by the more accurate place-kicking of Rutherford.

These advantages helped them to build a lead of a goal, two penalty goals and a try in the first half; and to yield only two penalty goals when under severe forward pressure later.

Perhaps the decisive moment was when Sharp received the ball from the scrum for the first time. No exploratory diagonal kick for him, no hurried pass. He made a swift outside break deep into the Welsh defence and sent Roberts racing for

the left corner. It was from Roberts's inside pass that Phillips crashed against the corner flag, injuring a shoulder which was to restrict him for the remaining 75 minutes.

Sharp has always looked of international calibre from his early days – as scrum half – at Blundell's. It was thought then that he might lack the speed for an outside-half in the highest company and eventually become a full-back. He is taller, longer of leg, than the usual conception of a great fly-half.

However, at 21, he has not only acquired the necessary turn of foot, but also the speed of thought - indeed, the most vivid impression of his play is that, like a great batsman, he has so much time to spare.

His hands pick up the bouncing ball like magnets: he is a beautiful kicker. Yet his most valuable gift is the knowledge of how, when and where to pass. Not until you see it done perfectly do you realise how an opening can be contrived by a pass when all possible recipients seem closely marked.

Jeeps made a substantial contribution to Sharp's success by his accurate service, which Sharp took surging forward, and by not letting the ball out when there was no future to it.

Sharp's arrival, the greater speed on the wings and the establishment of a back row with more aspirations to attack than last year's, made certain that the try-less days of 1959 would not be repeated.

1961

18 Feb France prevent the South Africans from making their third clean sweep of all 5 internationals, holding Avril Malan's Springboks to a pointless draw at Colombes.

15 Apr Already assured of the Championship, France beat Ireland 15-3 at Lansdowne Road, for the first time winning the title both outright and undefeated.

13 May Emulating Scotland's short tour last year to South Africa, Ireland go down 24-8 to the Springboks at Cape Town in their first match, the only Test, all their points being scored by full-back Tom Kiernan, from a try, a conversion and a

penalty goal. [They win their other 3 matches.]

22 Aug France end their first tour of the Antipodes with a victory, winning at Sydney in the only Test against Australia by 15-8, with tries by Lacroix, Pique and Bouguyon and two drop goals by Pierre Albaladejo. France had lost all 3 Tests in New Zealand, as well as 4 of their other 10 matches, but this victory makes it 2 out of 2 in Australia.

2 Sep In their centenary match at Twickenham, Richmond lose 29-19 to Major-General RGS Hobbs's XV, which contains 14 internationals. The President's captain, AR Smith (Scotland), scores 5 tries.

No way out of this Barbarian tackling for the Springboks.

Tour Match: Barbarians 6 South Africans 0, Cardiff, 4 February

Barbarians' shock for those proud Springboks

By Michael Melford

At the last hurdle of 30, the Springboks have been brought down. The Barbarians scored two tries in the first 25 minutes and hung on to their lead under tremendous pressure in a second half which was fought out almost entirely around their 25. For once, it was the opposition who took their chances, not the Springboks. For once it was the speed on the ball of the opposing forwards which provoked mistakes and turned them to account.

For once, in fact, the Springboks met a back row in

the same class as their own and a pack as shrewdly directed by Dawson. This was no exhibition in the manner so often associated with the Barbarians. If this was a 'gala' as Mr Bergh suggested during the week, then the two contests between Mr Patterson and Mr Johansson have been cultural displays of physical fitness.

Yet this was a game which for skill and excitement lived well up to the high standard expected.

The Barbarians scored their first try after 12 minutes when a long kick by Watkins

over his pack reached touch in the Springboks 25. From the line-out the ball came out to Uys, but W Morgan charged down his kick, picked up and dived over.

The Barbarians had a bad moment soon afterwards when the Springboks heeled and Uys ran 30 yards before putting in a short kick which seemed to leave Stewart clear. He was caught by Sharp, however, and the first of many menacing threats to the Barbarians line was survived.

It was from Sharp's drop-out that the attack developed which brought the second try. This time Dawson put a foot to the ball as it momentarily eluded Uys from the line-out.

H Morgan darted after it at great speed and slid over the line with it.

Some minutes before the end there came that moment when a Welsh crowd instinctively knows that victory is safe. As the singing welled up the Springboks went on launching attack after attack and the Barbarians, into the wind going back in the tight now and with a low sun shining in their eyes from over the Taff, went on repelling them.

So at last a famous record was broken. It stands now at 30 matches played, 28 won, one drawn (against Midland Counties in November) and one lost, points 476–110.

International Championship: France 8 Wales 6, Colombes, 25 March

France take the Championship: Brilliant Boniface is the hero

From Michael Melford

The French are champions again, having played in the second half at Colombes today as well as they or any other side have played for a long time. Yet a great share of the glory was earned by the new Welsh XV with its seven changes and three new caps. To be beaten only by a goal and a try to two tries was a considerable feat, and for a period of eight minutes midway through the second half Wales actually led 6-3.

France had every reason to be rattled then, for the second Welsh try by Bebb had come out of the blue at a time when the French were playing with a stride and rhythm which lifted the game to a new level.

For a few minutes they faltered and then they won the match with a magnificent try by Boniface, who gave an exhibition today which establishes him beyond doubt among the one or two best centres in the world.

From a line-out on the left the ball came out to Boniface

just outside the 25. He broke between the Welsh centres, turned back to catch Davies on the wrong foot, shook off the tackles of the covering defence, and dived over near the posts.

Not long before this he had sprinted in behind the posts from 35 yards out after a brilliant run by Bouquet from the French 25. But he had touched another Frenchman slightly in front of him as he took the pass and was thus accidentally off-side.

This was one of many perfectly reasonable decisions which made an Englishman, Dr.Parkes, easily the most unpopular in the department of Seine-et-Oise. He was alive to the less legitimate French activities in scrum and line-out, but a French crowd is not concerned with the finer points of the laws. Mercifully, for public order, France won, wrath turned to amiable disagreement and the massed ranks of the gendarmerie relaxed.

INTERNATIONAL CHAMPIONSHIP

	E	F	I	S	W	P	W	D	L	F	A	Pts
1 FRANCE	-	-	-	11-0	8-6	4	3	1	0	39	14	7
2=WALES	6-3	-	9-0	-	-	4	2	0	2	21	14	4
2=SCOTLAND	-	-	16-8	-	3-0	4	2	0	2	19	25	4
4 ENGLAND	-	5-5	-	6-0	-	4	1	1	2	22	22	3
5 IRELAND	11-8	3-15	-	-	-	4	1	0	3	22	48	2

TOURS (Tests)
South Africa in British Isles & France: W0-SA3, I3-SA8, E0-SA5, S5-SA12, F0-SA0
Ireland in South Africa: SA24-I8
France in New Zealand & Australia: NZ13-F6, NZ15-F3, NZ32-F3, A8-F15
Australia in South Africa: SA28-A3, SA23-A11

1962

30 May The All Blacks beat Northern New South Wales by 103-0 at Quirindi, a record score in a first-class match, scoring 22 tries, 17 of which are converted, and one penalty goal. Sprint champion Rod Heeps (Wellington) scores 8 of the tries from the left wing.

5 Dec The Canadian tourists break their losing run, drawing 3-3 with an international Barbarian side at Gosforth.

[The Canadians later beat Welsh Counties 8-3 at Llanelli and finish with a W1-D1-L14 record.]

17 Nov Last season's International Championship is completed when Ireland and Wales draw 3-3 at Lansdowne Road in a match postponed originally from 10 Mar (owing to an outbreak of smallpox in the Rhondda Valley) but which has no effect on the title.

INTERNATIONAL CHAMPIONSHIP

	E	F	I	S	W	P	W	D	L	F	A	Pts
1 FRANCE	13-0	-	11-0	-	-	4	3	0	1	35	6	6
2 SCOTLAND	3-3	3-11	-	-	-	4	2	1	1	34	23	5
3=ENGLAND	-	-	16-0	-	0-0	4	1	2	1	19	16	4
3=WALES	-	3-0	-	3-8	-	4	1	2	1	9	11	4
5 IRELAND	-	-	-	6-20	3-3	4	0	1	3	9	50	1

TOURS (Tests)
New Zealand in Australia: A6-NZ20, A5-NZ14
British Isles in South Africa: SA3-BI3, SA3-BI0, SA8-BI3, SA34-BI14
Australia in New Zealand: NZ9-A9, NZ3-A0, NZ16-A8

Ken Jones dives over for the try which drew the game.

International Championship: France 11 Ireland 0, Paris, 14 April

France's fitful brilliance sets the seal on another title

From Michael Melford

France are champions again – for the fourth successive year – and no one is likely to grudge them the honour, even if they sparkled only spasmodically today. Ireland were not outplayed as England were here in February, but were brought down by occasional shafts of French brilliance and the modern French flair for taking chances.

In the first half, when a strong wind blew behind France, Ireland had an equal share of the game territorially. In the second, they had much more of it, though they were reduced by injuries. Hewitt pulled a muscle when France scored their second try soon after half-time and retired limping to the wing.

Midway through the second half Gilpin was led off apparently concussed and was replaced at full-back by Kavanagh.

In some ways today was an anti-climax for the French. It is late in the season, when their thoughts are very much occupied with their domestic championship.

Tour Match: Northern Transvaal 14 Lions 6, Pretoria, 16 June

Sharp out of Test: Breaks cheekbone

From Tony Goodridge

Richard Sharp, the British Lions' fly-half, will be out of the first Test match against South Africa next Saturday. Today he was carried off on a stretcher with a broken cheekbone after five minutes in the match against Northern Transvaal.

The Lions, so heavily handicapped, were beaten by a goal and three tries to a dropped goal and a penalty goal. It was their first defeat in seven games.

Credit must go to the Northerns. They had a fast and remarkable rugged pack, supported in the main by a back row of Du Preez, Schmidt and Prinsloo.

Some 50,000 enjoyed the success, as they were fully entitled to do, but they also must have got a great deal of pleasure out of a courageous effort by the Lions, who battled ferociously to overcome their handicap. But it was asking too much, and they went down fighting with the depleted pack playing itself into the ground.

Sharp's injury was sustained in a tackle with Roux.

REG SWEET, the leading South African Rugby correspondent, writes: Cover defences of the provincial sides have been manifestly unable to blunt the thrust of the England stand-off half, and it is true, in fact, to say that something of a 'Sharp complex' has been engendered by all this, which the shrewd Arthur Smith, planning his tactical approach, will have noted with satisfaction.

Now all plans have been thrown into the melting pot, and any intentions the Lions' captain may have had of using Sharp as a decoy – for the Lions deploy plenty of running elsewhere – must be abandoned.

Tour Match: South Africa 3 British Isles 3, Johannesburg, 23 June

Spectacular try by Ken Jones saves Lions: Electrifying run

From Reg Sweet

What a glorious climax to a Rugby Test match, and what magnificent prospects there now are for this series. The British Lions, three points in arrears with only ten minutes to go, snatched the cake from the burning before a capacity 75,000 crowd here today, to draw the first international.

How spectacularly they achieved it, too. Little Ken Jones earned the Lions their draw in a manner which may well be remembered so long as Rugby Tests are played.

Yet one must be fair. If there were medals to be minted for the heroes of fine matches, they would be striking them in the British Isles tonight for those grand Lions forwards, led by Bill Mulcahy, who held the Springboks.

They broke even from the set scrummages, where Meredith heeled five times against the head and conceded a similar number. They also levelled the question of possession from the line-out, where Rowlands and Mulcahy, with admirable assistance from Pask and Campbell-Lamerton, proved a far sterner proposition than had once seemed likely. And in the loose play Pask and Rogers often matched the fiery Springbok breakaways.

As Test Matches go this one was fast and open. The Springboks happily played the running game in which little Roux was a constant threat to the British defence, and their first-half try by Gainsford, initiated as it happened by a swerving run from Roux, was well deserved.

The admirable Waddell, content in the first half to probe for weaknesses with tactical kicks, had found full-back Wilson in the best of form. So in the early stages of the second half, Waddell gave Jones his head two or three times, and with each run Jones looked more dangerous.

When Willcox dashed upfield and put him in possession, Waddell knew precisely where the next move lay. As he broke for the centre line he drew the defence toward him. He had Jones coming up on his outside under full sail, and he knew it. With the defence, all except Wilson, committed, he put Jones away, and with an in-field swerve which left the Springbok full-back diving and grasping for his heels, Jones made for the corner flag.

Not for a second did he look like being cut off, and 55 yards later he was across the line. It was as fine a try as we have seen in a Test in South Africa for many years.

The Springboks lined the exit from the field and cheered the Lions off – as well they might.

1963

2 Feb Wales chalk up their first win at Murrayfield for 10 years, 6-0, but are universally criticised for scrum-half Rowlands' touch-kicking tactics. The game, televised to millions on a day in one of the worst winters on record – (the 'big freeze') – produces 'the ultimate in non-handling rugby'.

28 Feb In the first Mobbs Memorial match to be played outside the Midlands,

the Barbarians beat the East Midlands 23-21 at Richmond. In a match of 9 tries, East Midlands score two late goals to get within 2 points of the BaaBaas.

30 Oct Newport inflict what turns out to be the only defeat of Whineray's 5th All Blacks, 3-0, in only their third game, the points coming from a drop goal by JR Uzzell – and Don Clarke does not get a single shot at the Newport goal.

International Championship: France 6 Scotland 11, Colombes, 12 Jan

Scotland triumph over France with the last move: Lucky – but win deserved

From Michael Melford

In the last few minutes of a hard, exciting match on this arctic afternoon, Scotland scored twice and came from behind to give France their first beating at Colombes in five years. The winning try, scored from the last move of all, may have owed something to providence. But Scotland won on merit, without any doubt. Only masters of opportunism, such as the French, would have led them for so long.

Scotland had not long drawn level at a penalty goal and a dropped goal apiece when, from what was clearly the last line-out, the ball was kicked back to Laughland perhaps 45 yards out on the right touchline.

The wind was behind him and his captain had dropped a goal from the same spot earlier. So he dropped in hope. The ball achieved little elevation and was hooked, but it bounced on and on along the bone-hard ground over the French right wing Besson, and into the hands of Thomson who had appeared on the left wing. Thomson scored, KJF Scotland converted well and a famous victory was won.

Tour Match: New Zealand 9 England 6, Christchurch, 1 June

Tourists fail with honour

From Our Special Correspondent

England were beaten by a goal from a mark in the last five minutes of their second and final Rugby Union international against New Zealand here today. England had scored a penalty goal and a try in answer to two tries, when New Zealand full-back Don Clarke snatched victory.

Clarke marked five yards inside his own half and calmly he put the ball over the bar to seal England's fate and clinch the rubber.

But even then England were not finished. They stormed the New Zealand line, got the put-in and attempted a pushover try. It was not awarded, so the crowd, restless and unhappy with their team, cheered the

gallant Englishmen off the field at the end.

The match was a pulsating affair, far exceeding the expectations of the pundits and prophets. England will leave pleasant memories in this country after today's performance.

England's lightning five-match tour is over – four losses and a win, and a 45-73 deficit in points – and they have acquitted themselves well on and off the field.

Not every experiment works first time and most believe that they took on too much.

[England lost their one match in Australia, a Test, by 18-9, coming back from 18-0 with 3 tries.]

International Championship: England 10 Scotland 8, Twickenham, 16 March

Sharp's flash of genius is enough: England's crown

From Michael Melford

England have the Calcutta Cup and the Championship – by the slim margin of two goals to a goal and a dropped goal – and the crowds who watched in the sunshine here and on television have a match to remember. It may not have been classical stuff, but as a spectacle and an even, exciting game it must have answered nearly everyone's hopes. Moreover, it was won by a piece of great brilliance by the England captain.

With a boisterous south wind behind them, Scotland led by eight points after 17 minutes, but Sharp's try put England 10-8 ahead five minutes after half-time.

But for another wonderful performance by Willcox, England must have conceded more than the eight points, and but for his two conversions, one from the touchline, one from half-way out, they might not be

champions tonight.

Sharp's try came from a scrum near the right touchline on the Scottish 25. England heeled respectably and Clarke sent Sharp racing away left. Sharp gave a dummy-scissors pass to Weston, which made a little room, and raced for a gap in the centre. It was a slim one, non-existent for most, but his speed took him through and he raced towards the full-back with Roberts outside.

Here he departed from the text-book and, instead of passing, gave a dummy with devastating effect. A second later he was diving triumphantly over the line.

He rose and walked back as placid as ever to a tumultuous ovation, which was renewed when the faithful Willcox kicked the goal.

The rest was relative anti-climax, though it had many palpitating moments before England were home.

INTERNATIONAL CHAMPIONSHIP												
	E	F	I	S	W		P	W	D	L	F	A	Pts
1 ENGLAND	-	6-5	-	10-8	-		4	3	1	0	29	19	7
2=FRANCE	-	-	-	6-11	5-3		4	2	0	2	40	25	4
2=SCOTLAND	-	-	3-0	-	0-6		4	2	0	2	22	22	4
4 IRELAND	0-0	5-24	-	-	-		4	1	1	2	19	33	3
5 WALES	6-13	-	6-14	-	-		4	1	0	3	21	32	2

TOURS (Tests)
England in New Zealand & Australia: NZ21-E11, NZ9-E6; A18-E9
Australia in South Africa: SA14-A3, SA5-A9, SA9-A11, SA22-A6

Tour Match: South Africa 9 Australia 11, Johannesburg, 24 August

Wallabies shock South Africa

From Reg Sweet

Australia today set the seal on her most successful Rugby tour. In winning the third international at Ellis Park by 11 points to 9, the Wallabies went one up in the four-match series and cannot lose the rubber.

In the process they became the first side ever to inflict two Test defeats in a row on South Africa in a home international series

in this century and they will be favoured now to win at Port Elizabeth.

Scorers – South Africa: CM Smith 3PG; Australia: TV Casey DG-PG-C, JL Williams T.

[South Africa, having made 8 changes for this Test, made another 7 for the decider, and won 22-6, albeit with 16pts coming in the last 8 minutes.]

1964

14 Mar Warwickshire complete their second hat-trick of County Championships in 7 years, beating Lancashire 8-6 in the final at Coventry, one of their tries scored by Peter Jackson, in his last season. The great England right winger is one of five players to have taken part in all six triumphs.

21 Mar Scotland beat England 15-6 at Murrayfield to bring back the Calcutta Cup for the first time in 14 years and earn a share of the Championship for the first time in 26 years – with Wales, who on the same afternoon, at Cardiff, register their first ever draw with France, thanks to a late try by Stuart Watkins converted from far out by K Bradshaw.

14 May The celebration of the 75th Anniversary of Rugby Football in South Africa, having produced an orgy of points-scoring, which serves to demonstrate how open the game could become under the new Laws to take effect officially from next season, culminates at Cape Town when, in the third match, the President's XV beat The Rest by 44 points (7G-3T) to 24 (3G-2T-1PG).

23 May On their first overseas tour, Wales lose the only Test, 24-3 to South Africa. *[They finish with a W2-L2 record.]*

29 Aug Australia inflict the biggest defeat on the All Blacks in the series between the two nations, 20-5 in Wellington, and it is their highest score in a Test in New Zealand, but they had already lost the rubber.

Laws: Changes to come into effect on 1 Sep, made in the expectation that greater freedom of movement, with consequent added enjoyment in playing the game, will result, include: Set scrummage – no foot of any front row player may be raised or advanced before the ball has touched the ground, and when it has, any foot of any front row player may be used to gain possession of it; touch – an opponent of the player carrying the ball and forced into touch shall bring the ball into play, and when the ball is thrown in, a clear space shall be left between the two lines of players until the ball leaves the hand of the throw-taker.

Tour Match: South Africa 6 France 8, Springs, East Transvaal, 25 July

France too fast for Springboks

From Reg Sweet

Along the boulevards, around the Place de la Concorde and throughout the fair land of France I dare say they will surely celebrate tonight. Well they might, for France gained an 8-6 Rugby Test victory here today which was as comprehensive for them as it was calamitous for South Africa.

A 55,000 crowd at this first international played at Springs saw Michael Crauste, Lira and Herrero lay the foundations in the loose for South Africa's eclipse. They waited for the error, pounced upon it and made handsome capital.

Albaladejo put France three points up within two minutes with a 40-yard penalty goal from a wide angle and, although Stewart landed an equalising penalty in the same half, South Africa did

not suggest that they might take the lead.

A minute from half-time came calamity for the Springboks. Engelbrecht dropped a pass from Du Preez and, Voila!, Darrouy had conjured the ball from nowhere and raced nearly half the length of the field for a runaway try. Albaladejo converted from wide out.

Not until the last 10 minutes did South Africa produce the type of rugby which had beaten Wales. Then Walton heeled for the 10th time against the head, Lawless put in a diagonal attacking punt and Stewart picked up the ball at pace to cut through and score. He took the kick himself from a tricky angle and missed. Justice had been done.

TOURS (Tests)
New Zealand in British Isles & France: I5-NZ6, W0-NZ6, E0-NZ14, SO-NZ0, F3-NZ12
Wales in South Africa: SA24-W3
France in South Africa: SA6-F8
Australia in New Zealand: NZ14-A9, NZ18-A3, NZ5-A20

Tour Match: Barbarians 3 All Blacks 36, Cardiff, 15 February

All Blacks go out in blaze of glory

From Wilfred Wooller

Barbarians' play in the first half flattered to deceive and from near-equality they fell away after the interval to the level of a supporting team to an exhibition, and to their worst defeat ever by six goals and two tries to a dropped goal.

Seldom if ever on this tour have the New Zealanders played with such carefree abandon. One was left exhilarated, and wondering at the quantity of points that could have been amassed by the visitors had this been standard policy. In the closing minutes, when Whineray crowned a magnificent after-

noon's work, a fitting epilogue to a fine tour's leadership, with a great try between the posts, the crowd burst spontaneously into the Maori tune 'Now is the Hour' – an automatic, emotional response to a wonderful exhibition of Rugby.

This quality of Rugby had been signally absent from the visitors' previous games in Wales – the dour defeat at Newport by a drop goal, the narrow 6-5 victory against Cardiff, the touchline tactics of the 6-0 win over Wales. But this display must rate as one of the best executed pieces of Rugby ever seen on this famous ground.

The Fijian fly-half Barley is intercepted by Prothero.

Tour Match: Welsh XV 28 Fiji 22, Cardiff, 26 September

Fijians win 55,000 friends in defeat

From Michael Melford

On the other side of the world in Suva it is already Sunday morning as I write, and the early risers in that friendly and fascinating capital will be learning of the feats of their countrymen who had 55,000 Welshmen standing, singing and cheering themselves hoarse here today.

Fiji lost to the Welsh XV, but in defeat they won admiration and affection such as few visitors to Wales can have won before.

Wales scored two goals, a penalty goal and five tries

against two goals and four tries, and for most of the match made fewer mistakes and knew rather too much.

The score was level at a try apiece when, after 10 minutes, the Fijian lock, Nalio, retired with a dislocated shoulder. Yet the Fijians kept on attacking until, miraculously, the Welsh 15, not the Fijian 14, flagged, and the Fijians scored three tries and 13 points in the last 10 minutes.

Their last try, the 13th and best of the match, was greeted by a din such as Cardiff Arms Park can seldom have known.

1965

6 Feb Welsh captain Clive Rowlands, scrum-half and master tactician, is carried shoulder-high from the field as Wales beat Scotland 14-12 at Murrayfield thanks to a late try by NR Gale, in what eventually proves to be the crucial match in the Championship.

13 Mar In the match that determines not only the Triple Crown, but the Championship, Wales beat Ireland 14-8 at Cardiff Arms Park despite losing the influential London Welsh centre John Dawes for much of the first half.

13 Mar Warwickshire come back from 9-3 down at the interval to beat Durham 15-9 at Hartlepool and win their seventh County Championship in eight seasons, their fourth on the trot. Nine of their second-half points – two drop goals and a penalty – come from the boot of scrum-half GH Cole, one of 12 Coventry players in the side. Two of them, Cole and PE Judd, have now played in all seven of the county's triumphs, along with SJ Purdy (Fylde).

27 Mar Triple Crown winners Wales see their Grand Slam hopes dashed in Paris as France go 22-0 up – unprecedented for the Tricoleurs against an International Board country – before they bring a semblance of respectability to the score with 3 tries and 13 points.

17 Apr South Africa's 8-5 defeat by Scotland at Murrayfield completes a miserable short tour of Ireland and Scotland for them. Amazingly, the hitherto almost invincible Springboks have failed to win a match, losing four and drawing one. Yet again they are beaten by a last-minute score, this time by DH Chisholm's drop goal, which gives Scotland some recompense for the record hammering they took here in 1951.

19 Jun South Africa's season of disasters continues with their first ever defeat on Australian soil – they go down to Australia 18-11 before a crowd of 46,000 in Sydney, where the referee awards the home side 18 penalties and the Springboks only 5. On the same day, at Ellis Park, Johannesburg, the Junior Springboks lose to the Pumas from Argentina. [A week later, the Springboks lose the second Test, in Brisbane, to suffer their first ever series defeat by Australia.]

18 Sep A final black day for the Springboks – their 20-3 defeat at Eden Park, Auckland, is their most comprehensive in a Test, the biggest score compiled against them by the All Blacks, and it completes a 3-1 loss of the series and a year in which they lose 7 of 8 internationals. Their 8 defeats in 30 matches in the Antipodes is the worst record of any Springbok team on a long tour.

INTERNATIONAL CHAMPIONSHIP

	E	F	I	S	W	P	W	D	L	F	A	Pts
1 WALES	14-3	-	14-8	-	-	4	3	0	1	55	45	6
2=FRANCE	-	-	-	16-8	22-13	4	2	1	1	47	33	5
2=IRELAND	5-0	3-3	-	-	-	4	2	1	1	32	23	5
4 ENGLAND	-	9-6	-	3-3	-	4	1	1	2	15	28	3
5 SCOTLAND	-	-	6-16	-	12-14	4	0	1	3	29	49	1

TOURS (Tests)

South Africa in British Isles: I9-SA6, S8-SA5

South Africa in Australia & New Zealand: A18-SA11, A12-SA8, NZ6-SA3, NZ13-SA0, NZ16-SA19, NZ20-SA3

Tour Match: Combined Irish Universities 12 South Africans 10, Limerick, 6 April

South Africans fall to Irish Univs: Jubilation at famous win

By Roy Standring

Amid scenes of high jubilation at Thomond Park, Limerick, last night, Combined Irish Universities scored an historic and memorable victory over the South Africans by two tries, a dropped goal and a penalty goal to two goals. This was the first defeat of any South African team in Ireland.

It need hardly be said that the Universities played well above themselves. Their covering was superb, the spirit of their forwards unquenchable.

Maguire was outstanding in a tremendously effective back-row, tackling, spoiling and generally making a nuisance of himself all over the field.

The scrum-half, Whiteside, with his intelligent building up of attacks with the back-row, and his harassing of de Vos, was another key man for the Universities, and Murray and Hickie, the full-back, refused to be intimidated in the face of fearsome pressure.

[A few days later, the Springboks lost to Ireland for the first time, going down 9-6 at Lansdowne Road, the winning points coming from a remarkable penalty goal by Tom Kiernan 5 minutes from the end. This was only South Africa's second-ever defeat in the British Isles – their first, back in 1906, was by Scotland.]

International Championship: England 3 Scotland 3, Twickenham, 20 March

It's Hancock's hour with late 85-yard try

From JA Bailey

Never can the cup of victory have been dashed so dramatically from the lips of any side. With the last seconds of injury time ticking away and Scotland, leading by Chisholm's dropped goal, looking for all the world assured of their first victory of the season and their first at Twickenham since 1938, Hancock ran 85 yards down the left wing to score an incredible, amazing try for England.

It may have been the greatest, it was certainly the most unexpected try scored at Twickenham for many a long day. Throughout the last quarter, indeed for nearly all the second half, England had been trying desperately to break clear of relentless Scots pressure.

Another abortive attempt failed when Weston's kick had been gathered by Whyte who had halted deep in the English 25. The resultant loose ball was scooped up by Weston

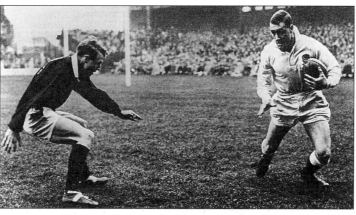

The hero of the hour: England's left wing AW Hancock evades his Scottish opponent DJ Whyte before setting out on his remarkable run at Twickenham.

and immediately given to Hancock. The Northampton wing, by sheer speed, broke clear of the 25 as the Scottish forwards, wrong-footed, were still following Whyte's incursion into the centre of the field.

Still it seemed a forlorn hope. Laughland made a despairing tackle and checked Hancock's stride. Hancock faltered, but went on. Wilson was there just on the halfway line, and it seemed that at the very least he must push Hancock into touch.

But as Hancock checked and looked inside, so Wilson hesitated and Hancock was past him on the outside. Now a try was England's if only Hancock could keep going to the corner. Although his stride got shorter, keep going he did, to beat a bevy of coverers and score near the flag.

Rutherford's kick, the last of the match, failed as well it might. It would have been a grave injustice for Scotland had it gone over. But so great was the excitement at Hancock's try, that I doubt whether some of the 65,000 crowd even noticed.

1966

10 Sep The All Blacks' 24-11 victory at Auckland, where 58,000 pay a record £43,000 in gate money, completes the first whitewash (4-0) ever suffered by the British Lions on a major tour. The All Blacks, playing less spectacular rugby

than the tourists in the four Tests, are lucky enough to complete the rubber using only 16 players.

Laws: The International Board propose the standard numbering of players.

International Championship: Wales 9 France 8, Cardiff, 26 March

Wales hail Watkins the hero as Morgan checks Gachassin

From JA Bailey

Welsh hearts must still be thumping! By the slimmest of margins, in a game which swung this way and that and was in doubt right up to the final kick, Wales, with a stirring try by Stuart Watkins, snatched a hard won but well deserved victory after being three points down in the first minute and eight points down before the game was 12 minutes old. It was a fine performance.

They thus have won the championship outright for the second successive season, and in storming back to beat this potentially brilliant French side they have in large measure atoned for that defeat in Dublin which saw the Triple Crown disappear from view.

They could hardly have made a more dispiriting beginning than that which saw France deliver first a body blow and then, as it were, a punch full to the point of the jaw, as one French try followed another.

Both owed much not only to loose play by Wales but to brilliant opportunism by Rupert, the French flanker.

Yet Wales never gave any

sign of reaction other than a seeming determination to attack harder and carry the fight to the French.

Had their backs been able to handle the ball with their usual efficiency, despite the high wind, Wales might have had more than Bradshaw's two penalties to show for their efforts at the interval.

It was from one of France's really promising attacks that Wales scored the try which brought them this narrow victory.

For once, Gachassin eluded Morgan and, with that magnificent acceleration of his, sped through a gap near the Welsh 25. France had an overlap of two men and a try seemed almost certain.

And a try there was, but not to France. Gachassin lobbed a long pass out towards his left wing only to see S Watkins intercept and his huge frame make off at great speed along the 70-yard route to the French line.

Twice Lacaze came within a whisker of tackling Watkins, twice Watkins evaded him. His stride lengthening and cheered on by a mighty roar from the crowd, he made it to the corner.

INTERNATIONAL CHAMPIONSHIP

	E	F	I	S	W	P	W	D	L	F	A	Pts
1 WALES	-	9-8	-	8-3		4	3	0	1	34	26	6
2=FRANCE	13-0	-	11-6	-	-	4	2	1	1	35	18	5
2=SCOTLAND	6-3	3-3	-	-	-	4	2	1	1	23	17	5
4 IRELAND	-	-	-	3-11	9-6	4	1	1	2	24	34	3
5 ENGLAND	-	-	6-6	-	6-11	4	0	1	3	15	36	1

TOURS (Tests)
British Isles in Australia & New Zealand: A8-BI11, A0-BI31; NZ20-BI3, NZ16-BI12, NZ19-BI6, NZ24-BI11

Tour Match: Australia 0 British Isles 31, Brisbane, 4 June

The Lions are kings for a wonderful day
Humiliation for Wallabies

From Terry McLean

At last they have found themselves; at last their dreams have come true. No matter what terrors await the British Rugby Union tourists when they next week begin their hard and rugged programme of 25 matches in New Zealand, just for today they know what it is to be kings of rugby.

Their defeat of Australia's Wallabies by five goals, a dropped goal and a penalty goal before 15,000 people at Lang Park today was more than shattering: it was humiliating.

It took a long time for the Lions to strike, for the first-half yielded them only a fine 40-yard penalty goal by Wilson, and the first 18 minutes of the second half contained only a David Watkins dropped goal after a line-out in the Wallabies 25.

But then - excelsior! In 22 amazing minutes, no fewer than five tries were scored, principally by pace, pace and yet more pace, and to each and every one Wilson

unfailingly placed the goal.

Wilson was superb in every phase, Weston and Bebb scarcely less so. Those dodgers supreme, Jones and David Watkins, were like eels, and Young, for the first time, was the player of his reputation. Then there were Murphy, Pask and Telfer in the back row.

But they were all kings for the day, and with their play the tour, so to speak, came vibrantly alive. Will there be many days in New Zealand when they will be kings again?

Well before no side, a crowd which had stayed largely to jeer the tired and dispirited Wallabies remained to cheer the triumphant Lions.

And so, after eight matches, a fair share of travail and a good deal of travelling, the Lions have come out of a hard programme in Australia with seven wins and a draw and a highly respectable scoring record of 26 goals and 12 other tries in a points score of 202 against 48.

Tour Match: Wales 11 Australia 14, Cardiff, 3 December

Matilda waltzes over Wales

From Michael Melford

They won – the maligned, long-suffering Australians of 1966, who have struggled in vain against lesser opposition, beat the might of Wales today in the most exciting international match for a long time. From the first they matched Wales in almost every phase forward, and with a very good try they went ahead 9-6 just before half time.

In the second half they went on attacking and eventually scored again to lead 14-6. Only then did their line yield again to allow Wales to score once more and draw within range.

By now the Australians were making all sorts of immature mistakes in their

excitement, such as moving in front of a kicker, but if their judgment sometimes failed them, their hearts did not, and they held on bravely to win by a goal, a dropped goal, a penalty goal and a try to a goal, a penalty goal and a try.

It was one of the great games of rugby football, and perhaps Wales did not deserve to lose it. But somehow today you did not have to hail from many miles over the Bristol Channel to be a dinkum Aussie, and an Australian victory seemed the proper outcome.

[The Wallabies had come to this, the first Test on their tour, with a W6-D1-L6 record.]

1967

28 Jan With two fine tries in the last 5 minutes, the Wallabies become the first Australian side to beat the Barbarians, their 17-11 victory climaxing the British Isles part of their tour (P30-W15-D2-L13) in which Catchpole and Hawthorne were among the finest pairs of half-backs to visit this country.

11 Feb The Camberabero brothers score all France's points (Lilian 1T, Guy 4PG-1DG-1C) in their 20-14 victory over the Wallabies.

22 Apr Surrey, after beating Cornwall at the third attempt in the semi-finals, finish their County Championship saga with another draw (0-0) in the replayed final with Durham at Hartlepool, and the two counties share the title.

29 Apr Harlequins celebrate their centenary season by winning the Middlesex Sevens, coming from behind in all four rounds of the last day, culminating in their 14-11 victory over Richmond in the final.

13 May Irish captain Tom Kiernan equals the world record for a full-back of 33 caps and reaches 100pts in internationals as Ireland win the only Test on their Australian tour (record W4-L2).

12 Aug An anticlimactic 6-6 draw at Newlands means France lose the series against South Africa 2-1 on a tour arranged to replace the cancelled visit of the All Blacks. [French tour record W8-D1-L4.]

29 Oct England and Bedford centre Danny Hearn, 27, is dangerously ill in Stoke Mandeville Hospital with serious spinal injuries incurred yesterday playing for Midland, London and Home Counties against the All Blacks. [Hearn eventually recovers sufficiently to resume teaching at Haileybury School, his courageous fight against total paralysis earning him universal admiration.]

13 Dec The All Blacks lose their 100% record and are, by all accounts, lucky to draw 3-3 with East Wales at Cardiff.

16 Dec The All Blacks – with their two-match tour of Ireland called off because of an outbreak of foot and mouth disease in England – finish with an 11-6 victory over the Barbarians at Twickenham, after being 6-3 down with 2 minutes to play, and become only the second touring team to the British Isles and France to remain undefeated – their record W14-D1-L0.

---

19 October

Watkins turns pro for a record £13,000: Welsh star joins Salford

By John Reason

David Watkins, the British Lions, Wales and Newport outside-half, has turned professional. He signed for the Salford Rugby League club yesterday. The fee was reported to be £13,000, which comfortably exceeds the record £10,000 Bradford Northern paid for Terry Price. Watkins, captain of Wales, and of the British Lions in New Zealand last year when Campbell-Lamerton was injured, won 22 Welsh caps, and as a sevens player he must have been the greatest of all time.

Tour International: Scotland 3 New Zealand 14, Murrayfield, 2 December

Meads' dismissal mars All Blacks' fine tour

From Michael Melford

You can't have caviar all the time. The All Blacks won again, and though this was the least spectacular of their victories they won convincingly by a goal, two penalty goals and a try to a dropped goal. But two minutes from the end of their last international there occurred an incident which will inevitably tarnish the memory of a wonderful tour – the sending off of Colin Meads *(pictured left)* by the Irish referee, KD Kelleher.

The offence was not in itself as heinous as many one sees, and it came at the end of what was a vicarage tea party compared with last Saturday's battle in Paris.

But as Meads, emerging from a maul, aimed a kick in the rough direction of Chisholm and the ball, missing both comfortably, Mr Kelleher did not hesitate and Meads at once walked the 30 yards to the tunnel amid a storm of cheers and boos.

For one with Meads's world-wide reputation for robust play, this was like sending a burglar to prison for a parking offence.

Some may think that he has been lucky to sail near the wind for so long and survive, but there is a stigma attached to being sent off which made the decision at this stage of an orderly match seem desperately harsh, especially to a member of a team which has overall done all it can to advertise the skills of New Zealand rugby rather than the toughness.

That said, in the first half Mr Kelleher had warned Meads for dangerous play and the law says that once he has cautioned a player he has no alternative but to send him off for what he considers to be a similar offence.

International Championship: Wales 34 England 21, Cardiff, 15 April

Genius Jarrett – a great Welsh find

From Michael Melford

There can never have been anything quite like today's extraordinary match in which Wales robbed England of a share in the championship and the Triple Crown. Five goals, a dropped goal and two penalty goals to Wales, four penalty goals and three tries to England, and 19 points to an 18-year-old boy playing in his first international. It was all like some wildly improbable school story.

The hero of heroes, of course, was Keith Jarrett, lately of Monmouth School. He had been brought in here in the unaccustomed position of full-back to kick goals, and he kicked seven out of eight, mostly from the touchline. When he failed, the ball hit the post.

More than this, he scored a brilliant individual try at a vital moment in the game when it seemed as if England, recovering well from a shaky start, could triumph after all.

Wales, with much the better of the first half, led 14-3 at one time, but by midway through the second half England had drawn up to within four points at 19-15. Hosen was kicking goals almost as regularly as Jarrett, the England forwards were shoving forward and handling superbly, while one or two Welsh forwards seemed to be wilting a little under the tremendous pace.

Then it was that McFadyean, from his own 25, kicked diagonally to the right. Jarrett, near half way, judged the bounce perfectly and ran into it at full-stretch. In a flash he was round Savage and Hosen and racing 50 yards to the left corner amid a din which few Welsh crowds of the past can have bettered, even in moments of supreme emotion.

He kicked the goal, with the help of the top of a post, and Wales, suddenly, were going away again. They scored two more tries in the next five minutes and were well out of range before England finished the scoring with a penalty goal and a try.

INTERNATIONAL CHAMPIONSHIP												
	E	F	I	S	W	P	W	D	L	F	A	Pts
1 FRANCE	-	-	-	8-9	20-14	4	3	0	1	55	41	6
2=ENGLAND	-	12-16	-	27-14	-	4	2	0	2	68	67	4
2=IRELAND	3-8	6-11	-	-	-	4	2	0	2	17	22	4
2=SCOTLAND	-	-	3-5	-	11-5	4	2	0	2	37	45	4
5 WALES	34-21	-	0-3	-	-	4	1	0	3	53	55	2

TOURS (Tests)
Australia in British Isles & France: W11-A14, S11-A5, E11-A23, I15-A8, F20-A14
Ireland in Australia: A5-I11
France in South Africa: SA26-F3, SA16-F3, SA14-F19, SA6-F6
Australia in New Zealand: NZ29-A9
New Zealand in British Isles & France: E11-NZ23, W6-NZ13, F15-NZ21, S3-NZ14

1968

13 Jan The teams at Murrayfield for the Scotland-France international wear black armbands to mark the tragic loss in separate road accidents of two French internationals: the great centre three-quarter Guy Boniface, 30, and Jean Michel Capendeguy, who had been chosen to win his second cap on the right wing.

20 Jan Wales's first coach, David Nash, sees his first side come back from an 8-point deficit and scrape a lucky 11-all draw with England at Twickenham, as two failed penalty attempts by Jarrett are knocked on by England defenders and lead to scores.

22 Jun A controversial penalty try 2 minutes from time gives the All Blacks a 19-18 victory over Australia at Brisbane in the second Test, and takes their winning sequence to 11 internationals and 33 matches.

10 Aug Colin Meads wins his 47th cap for the All Blacks at Auckland in their 19-12 win over France, beating the world record held jointly with Jackie Kyle (Ireland).

14 Sep A Welsh XV lose 9-5 to Argentina in Buenos Aires on their first tour of South America. [They later draw the second unofficial international and finish with a W3-D2-L1 record.]

Laws: Replacements for injured players are allowed in international matches.

International Championship: Wales 9 France 14, Cardiff, 23 March

Voila! Grand slam for France

From Michael Melford

Where more brilliant French sides have failed, the French of 1968 have succeeded at last in bringing off the clean sweep of four victories in the championship. The last enemy, Wales, led them 9-3 at half-time but, with the wind behind in the second half, France scored three times more to win by a goal, a penalty goal, a dropped goal and a try to two penalty goals and a try.

There is nothing like an international match at Cardiff Arms Park to end a drought, and the last two days have been the wettest of the year here. Though the rain stopped just before the start and the mud dried during the match, this was not the sort of day when the French are wont to be seen at their best.

Yet this French side, based, except for one match, on the Camberabero brothers, has not been in the usual tradition. Confronted with a wet, rolling ball, they were as prone to the wildly speculative fly-kick as ever today.

Guy Camberabero, reversing the usual procedure, tended to pass only when he had no time to kick.

However, as the inclusion of the brothers committed France to kicking and not handling whatever the weather, the conditions handicapped them less than a French side relying on speed and sleight of hand – and as against England the brothers directed the operation supremely well. I liked particularly the last try, scored by Lilian Camberabero round the blind side, while all Wales – especially the back row – seemed to be expecting a drop at goal by one of the brothers.

By their rather dilettante standards, the French scrummaged hard and well, neutralising many Welsh heels. The big forwards Cester, Plantefol and Spanghero, were a great force in loose and line-out and the French speed on the ball and into the tackle had many Welshmen, of whom O'Shea cracked a rib in the first maul but played on, seeming slow and hesitant by the end.

INTERNATIONAL CHAMPIONSHIP

	E	F	I	S	W	P	W	D	L	F	A	Pts
1 FRANCE	14-9	-	16-6	-	-	4	4	0	0	52	30	8
2 IRELAND	-	-	-	14-6	9-6	4	2	1	1	38	37	5
3 ENGLAND	-	-	9-9	-	11-11	4	1	2	1	37	40	4
4 WALES	-	9-14	-	5-0	-	4	1	1	2	31	34	3
5 SCOTLAND	6-8	6-8	-	-	-	4	0	0	4	18	35	0

TOURS (Tests)
British Isles in South Africa: SA25-BI20, SA6-BI6, SA11-BI6, SA19-BI6
New Zealand in Australia: A11-NZ27, A18-NZ19
France in New Zealand & Australia: NZ12-F9, NZ9-F3, NZ19-F12; A11-F10
Australia in Ireland & Scotland: I10-A3, S9-A3
South Africa in France: F9-SA12, F11-SA16

---

25 January

Wales give captaincy to Gareth Edwards

By Tony Lewis

The Welsh selectors last night announced six changes in the team to meet Scotland at Cardiff on 3 February – five at forward. The team includes a change of captaincy, Gareth Edwards taking over from Norman Gale, who is dropped. Wheeler, D Williams, James, Mainwaring and Wanbon also lose their places.

Edwards, 20, a student at the Cardiff College of Education, is the youngest player ever to captain Wales. He recently led the East Wales side which drew with the New Zealand tourists.

Scrum-half Edwards: new Welsh captain.

Tour International: South Africa 25 British Isles 20, Pretoria, 8 June

Kiernan saves Lions from a mauling

From Reg Sweet

Despite magnificent kicking by the captain, Kiernan, who collected 17 points, the British Isles made rugby history here today of a type they would sooner have done without – losing the first international of a series against South Africa for the first time.

And in going down by two goals, a try and four penalty goals to a goal and five penalties before a crowd of 75,000, the Lions failed to make adequate use of a fair share of the opportunities offered.

The Lions were 16-11 behind at half-time, then threatened to lose their grip entirely. But superlative goal-kicking by Kiernan twice enabled them to narrow the gap in the second half to five points, and this in the end was the winning margin.

Kiernan's monumental share was only one point fewer than the Test scoring record which stood to the credit of Don Clarke before Jarrett came along.

The British Isles had possession enough to have brought into play their strong-breaking three-quarter line, the factor it was generally thought would prove decisive in a Lions' win. They had the misfortune to lose fly-half John in the first half with a broken collar-bone, and yet the advent of Gibson as his substitute still did not produce material results in the shape of incisive back-play.

At the line-out, too, the Lions held a working advantage, but seemed unable to mount telling thrusts from this phase.

In one phase, however, the British Isles did surprise. This was at the set scrummages where they held at bay any threatened Springbok dominance.

The potential Springbok weak link at half-back did not materialise. De Villiers and Visagie had their best game together in five internationals.

Mostly, however, this was a victory for quicker mastery of the loose ball and better use made of it by the Springbok breakaways, with Bedford and Ellis constantly at the spearhead.

Two phenomenally long penalties by Naude played their part, but it was Bedford's loose forwards who cracked the whip.

1969

22 Feb Captaining England in place of the injured Greenwood, Budge Rogers celebrates his 32nd cap, beating Wavell Wakefield's long-standing England record, by leading them to a 22-8 victory.

8 Mar Ireland, going for the Grand Slam, suffer defeat after their record 6 international wins in succession, going down 24-11 at Cardiff to Wales, the eventual Championship winners.

24 May The Barbarians, having lost three of their four previous matches, score a magnificent 32-22 victory at Pochefstroom in their last match over the strongest side they have met, South African County Districts, who include the Springbok captain Dawie de Villiers and his half-back partner Piet Visagie – this

despite losing flanker Budge Rogers with concussion at the end of the first half.

14 Jun Fergie McCormick sets a new Test points scoring record with 3 conversions, 1 dropped goal and 5 penalty goals (24pts) as New Zealand beat Wales 33-12 at Eden Park, Auckland, to win the series 2-0, while the previous joint holder with 19pts, opposing centre three-quarter Keith Jarrett, scores a try and 2 penalty goals, but is otherwise wayward with the boot. [Wales later beat Australia and a Fijian XV for a W4-D1-L2 record on their short tour of the Antipodes.]

2 Dec In the Oxford University Centenary match at Iffley Road, an OU Past & Present XV are beaten 18-16 by the Barbarians.

INTERNATIONAL CHAMPIONSHIP

	E	F	I	S	W	P	W	D	L	F	A	Pts
1 WALES	30-9	-	24-11	-	-	4	3	1	0	79	31	7
2 IRELAND	17-15	17-9	-	-	-	4	3	0	1	61	48	6
3 ENGLAND	-	22-8	-	8-3	-	4	2	0	2	54	58	4
4 SCOTLAND	-	-	0-16	-	3-17	4	1	0	3	12	44	2
5 FRANCE	-	-	-	3-6	8-8	4	0	1	3	28	53	1

TOURS (Tests)
Wales in New Zealand & Australia: NZ19-W0, NZ33-W12; A16-W19
Australia in South Africa: SA30-A11, SA16-A9, SA11-A3, SA19-A8

International Championship: Wales 30 England 9, Cardiff, 12 April

England thrashed: Superb Richards

By JA Bailey

The championship and the Triple Crown to Wales. A storming second-half display, which tore England apart, left no doubts about their worthiness to wear the Crown in 1969. It was a magnificent performance by forwards and backs alike; a triumph for hard work both on and off the field. It was the final accolade.

The whole Welsh team will dine out on this victory for a long time to come. None of them will remember it with a greater sense of pride, though, than Maurice Richards, the Cardiff left wing three-quarter.

In a Welsh tally of three goals, two tries, two penalties and a dropped goal, Richards scored four fine tries, three of them coming during a bewildering period of eleven minutes in the game's final quarter, when England were finally cracked asunder.

Richards *(pictured)* shared the Welsh points with Jarrett – who kicked three conversions and two penalties – and John, who besides scoring a brilliant try and a dropped goal, gave one of his best attacking displays at fly-half.

England, who crossed over on level terms having played with the wind in the first half, owed their three penalties to

the foot of Hiller, who played a stalwart part throughout.

The lineout, dominated by Davies, John Taylor and Delme Thomas, was another source of supply denied the English backs. In the second-half we saw the full fruits of intensive coaching and training throughout the season. The power of this Welsh pack really made itself felt. In every phase, and particularly, and most important, in the rucks, their forwards were dominant.

Edwards's immaculate service to John, John's elusive running, the sure handling and passing of the centres, the frequent appearances of Williams in the line, and the speed of Richards, on the wing, proved all too much for the England defence.

Tour Match: Oxford University 6 South Africans 3, Twickenham, 5 November

Springbok defeat as protest flops

By Guy Rais

The anti-apartheid demonstration at the opening game of the Springboks' tour fizzled out at Twickenham yesterday as Oxford University gained a surprise 6-3 victory.

More than 400 policemen were at the ground and parts of the stadium were wired off. But the game was played without interruption, unaffected by the occasional chanting and slow handclapping by about 300 demonstrators.

The stadium looked like a besieged citadel. The east and north wings were wired off and only the west wing, with a capacity of about 12,000, was open. Rugby Union officials said they had never witnessed such a bizarre scene.

A detachment from Scotland Yard's commando squad were on duty, as well as

mounted police. There were a dozen Black Marias in the car park behind the West stand, and plain clothes officers mingled with the crowd.

The demonstrators, mostly from Oxford University, paid the 5s admission charge for standing and stood in three different groups. As soon as they started chanting a wall of policemen moved in front of them.

Before kick-off an announcement over the loudspeakers told the crowd that the pitch was out of bounds: 'Please leave all control to our friends the police.'

As the South African team took the field the demonstrators shouted 'Sieg Heil' and gave the Nazi salute but their chanting was drowned by applause.

Laidlaw inspires Oxford to bring down the mighty Springboks

JOHN REASON writes: Oxford produced a demonstration at Twickenham yesterday of which everyone approved, whatever the length of their haircuts. Those who went to watch the football thought it marvellous and those who went to make a noise ended by agreeing.

Oxford thoroughly deserved to beat the South Africans in the first match of the tour. Laidlaw led his team quite beautifully, and with his forwards showing

a priceless ability to win mauls going backwards he was able to drive back the Springboks with a whole stream of spin kicks which went rifling through the crisp autumn sunshine.

The margin of victory was two penalty goals to one. That told nothing of the efforts of the Oxford forwards in the loose, of their truly valiant effort in the line-out and perhaps, above all, of their dogged rearguard action in the tight.

Tour International: England 11 Sth Africa 8, Twickenham, 20 December

England forwards pave way to historic victory

By John Reason

No-one watching South Africa's forbidding forward domination in the first quarter of an hour of this international in the gloom and the mist of Twickenham would have given England any chance of overhauling a lead of eight points.

After half an hour South Africa led by a goal and a penalty goal, and yet

England forwards fought back so magnificently that they scored two tries themselves and gave Hiller the chances to kick a penalty goal and conversion to win the match.

It was the first time that England had beaten South Africa since the two countries first played each other, 63 years ago.

The 1970s

With the Springboks in virtual exile during the seventies, the All Blacks might well have been expected to dominate world rugby. That they won 'only' 28 of 46 Tests played, losing 14, was, compared with past achievements and the very high standards always expected of New Zealand rugby, regarded with dismay by all their followers. Indeed, that doyen of New Zealand rugby correspondents, TP McLean, in his definitive chronicle *The All Blacks*, described the seventies as the 'Decade of Disasters'.

It was not only the loss of their two series in South Africa (both by three Tests to one) and their first ever series defeat by the British Lions that gave rise to such a sweeping statement. More significant, perhaps, were the cracks appearing in the All Blacks machine, the serious decline in player-management relations that eventually saw the controversial sending-home of prop Keith Murdoch, who scored the only try in their narrow victory over Wales at Cardiff in December 1972.

These All Blacks proved to be the least popular to tour the British Isles. They won three Tests, but were disappointed when Ireland held them to deny them the Grand Slam, and they lost to France. However, they are remembered most of all for their defeat in the last match of the tour by the Barbarians, who scored the most memorable try of the decade, or arguably of any decade.

The Barbarians, coached by Carwyn James, were very much representative of the British Lions triumphant in New Zealand in 1971. And what a decade it was for the Lions, successful for the first time since official tours began in 1910. James masterminded that tour, knitting a team packed with individual talent into a force that swept through New Zealand losing only one of 24 matches. At last, with the revolution in forward play that had been taking place over the last few years, a Lions back division was supplied with decent possession. And what a back division it was – the supreme half-back partnership of fly-half Barry John, dubbed 'The King' by the hosts themselves, and elusive scrum-half Gareth Edwards, with dashing wingers Gerald Davies and David Duckham flanking John Dawes, the captain, and Mike Gibson in the three-quarter line, and behind them JPR Williams, one of the finest full-backs of all time, in both defence and attack. This team shattered the complacency of the All Blacks, but at the same time won unprecedented acclaim, goodwill and support from the New Zealand public wherever they went for their attractive, winning rugby.

The 1974 Lions, with many of those names missing, reached the high point of British Isles rugby abroad. Captained by Willie-John McBride, they swept through South Africa, winning every match but the last, the final Test when the Springboks managed to scrape a controversial draw. And the Lions threw away the chance of a tied series in New Zealand in 1977 when they conceded a late try in the final Test.

Wales, with the likes of John, Edwards, JPR, Dawes, Davies and later Phil Bennett and JJ Williams, were the dominant force in the Five Nations Championship, achieving three Grand Slams to surpass England's total of seven, and five Triple Crowns, including an unprecedented four in succession at the end of the decade. In all, Wales were champions or joint champions eight times in the seventies. Ireland and France were the only other countries to win the title outright, once each, while 1973 produced a quintuple tie for the first time.

It was in the seventies that the first real threat to the sacrosanct IRB rules relating to amateurism emerged. Towards the end of the decade, the formation of a professional travelling 'circus', drawn from top players of all the leading countries, was very nearly accomplished, but in the end it fizzled out.

The intrusion of politics, of course, was evident throughout the seventies, as rugby unions fought the ever-increasing, losing battle to keep sporting contacts with South Africa open. The unrelenting South African governments made this impossible, however, and the Springboks made only two tours – to Australia in 1971 and France in 1974.

Partly as a result of this significant loss of a major force, international rugby saw a marked increase in short tours. England, Ireland and Scotland in turn made single-Test tours to New Zealand in the mid-seventies (England were successful), and Wales undertook a short tour of Australia in 1978, which, however, at nine matches, was the longest yet to that country by any of the Home Unions. This was an unsuccessful venture in more ways than one, as they lost four matches, including the two Tests. And there were problems with team discipline, including bickering with referees both on and off the field, often to mask the players' own shortcomings.

However, assistant manager John Dawes made some salient points about the system of refereeing and short tours in general. He was particularly outspoken about Australian referees: 'I'd be a liar if I said I wasn't unhappy with them. You must have neutral referees for international matches, otherwise it's unfair to both sides.' He added that most referees in the Southern Hemisphere were several years out of date in their interpretation of the laws, and

The British Lions enjoyed a triumphant tour of South Africa in 1974. Led by Willie John McBride, they matched the Springboks sometimes blow for blow as the two packs became involved in some epic, violent confrontations.

concluded: 'There have to be more players on these short tours, and neutral referees. If administrators can't see that, they've got to resign.'

No account of the seventies would be complete without mention of the emergence of a world-class star, another fly-half, to rival the reputation of Barry John, from the most unlikely place – Argentina. Hugo Porta captivated crowds in the British Isles when he captained the Pumas on an eight-match tour in 1978, in which they beat a Welsh 'B' side and drew with a strong England XV. A prolific scorer of drop goals, he was outstanding in every phase of the game, from his

phenomenal goal-kicking to his elusive running and ability to join in running attacks. He was equally impressive the following year when he scored 84 points and 10 drop goals in eight matches in New Zealand, where Argentina, who lost both Tests by only nine-point margins, took a further step towards full international recognition.

Romania, too, demonstrated their credentials, and after a single-point defeat by a Wales XV at Cardiff in 1979, their tour manager Viorel Morariu prophetically looked forward to a time when there would be a Rugby Union World Cup.

1970

14 Mar After taking a first-half hammering, the veteran Ireland XV destroy Wales's Triple Crown ambitions with a 14-0 victory in Dublin, all their points coming in 16 devastating second-half minutes, when they produce 'a brand of football which no team could have lived with, full of Celtic fury'. Ireland captain and full-back Tom Kiernan, who wins his 47th cap, beating Jackie Kyle's international record, is carried off shoulder-high at the end.

2 May In what immediately becomes known as 'Fielding's Day', England right wing Keith Fielding inspires Loughborough Colleges to victory in the Middlesex Sevens, scoring 11 tries in their four ties, including 4 in their 26-11 win over Edinburgh Wanderers in the final, in which he eschews a fifth, waiting under the posts for his hooker Gray to arrive and touch down.

6 Jun Scotland are comprehensively beaten 23-3 by Australia at Sydney in the final match and only Test of their short tour, to finish with a W3-L3 record.

3 Oct The celebrations of the RFU Centenary open at Twickenham with an entertaining encounter between England/Wales and Scotland/Ireland which results in a 14-all draw.

17 Oct Wales put on a vintage performance at Cardiff in an RFU Centenary match, beating a strong RFU President's XV, made up from the other Home Unions and France, by 26-11.

Laws: If the ball is kicked into touch on the full from outside a player's '22', the line-out is brought back level with where the ball was kicked from.

Tour International: Wales 6 South Africa 6, Cardiff, 24 January

Injury-time try stuns Springboks: Wales hail a super fight

By Wilfred Wooller

In mist, rain and mud this contest reached heroic heights. Trailing by 6-3, Wales fought back after a terrific hammering in the first 20 minutes of the second half to score the equalising try, a brilliant effort by Gareth Edwards, in the first minute of injury time.

Wales have yet to beat South Africa, and this was their seventh attempt, but on this showing they could still prove to be the best team in the home championship.

The great feature of the Welsh forwards was their fine comeback after a tremendous battering in the rain and mud. It is invidious to mention any by name but Morris, Davies and Hughes were particularly

skilful in coming away in the loose to relieve pressure.

Edwards, at scrum-half, was, as usual, superb and no more need be said, but Barry John was not at his best with the slippery ball and at times his kicking lacked accuracy. He nevertheless came in at the vital moments.

Williams, at full-back, was on great form and the whole team tackled magnificently.

It was looking like a South African victory when Barry John kicked into an attacking position. Barry Llewellyn somehow got the ball back to Edwards, who raced away to score in the corner.

The final kick of the match failed. But it would have been an injustice had it succeeded.

INTERNATIONAL CHAMPIONSHIP

	E	F	I	S	W	P	W	D	L	F	A	Pts
1=FRANCE	35-13	-	8-0	-	-	4	3	0	1	60	33	6
1=WALES	-	11-6	-	18-9	-	4	3	0	1	46	42	6
3 IRELAND	-	-	-	16-11	14-0	4	2	0	2	33	28	4
4=SCOTLAND	14-5	9-11	-	-	-	4	1	0	3	43	50	2
4= ENGLAND	-	-	9-3	-	13-17	4	1	0	3	40	69	2

TOURS (Tests)
South Africa in British Isles: S6-SA3, E11-SA8, I8-SA8, W6-SA6
Scotland in Australia: A23-S3
New Zealand in South Africa: SA17-NZ6, SA8-NZ9, SA14-NZ3, SA20-NZ17

Tour Match: Barbarians 12 South Africans 21, Twickenham, 31 January

Dawie leads grand finale to South African tour

By JA Bailey

A happy ending! The manner of their victory in a spanking game will help to ease from the Springboks' memory many of the tribulations of a disappointing tour. The spirit and skill they displayed in coming from behind after conceding two tries in the first 10 minutes will be long remembered by all at Twickenham.

The South Africans won by three goals, a dropped goal and a penalty to four tries. They did so because they tamed a formidable looking, but loosely knit Barbarians' pack in something like the old Springbok manner.

The Springboks took their chances well. Equally important was the decision of Dawie de Villiers to replace his namesake, full-back HO, who had already missed four penalties, as place kicker. The captain's kicking, responsible for the conversion of three tries from near the touchline and a penalty, made all the difference, not only to the result, but to the confidence of his team.

The Baa-baas played their

part to the hilt. Three of their tries followed movements which were gems of their kind, and the all-round virtuosity of Edwards, his understanding with John, the sheer determination of Spencer and the flowing surge of Duckham in full flight all made their mark on a game of high excitement.

Edwards initiated the most spectacular try of the match, the Baa-baas' second. His speed and strength took him clear on their 10-yard line, before he drew the wing and sent Duckham away at full stretch on the half-way line. Duckham's smooth acceleration took him past all attempts to cover, and his sidestep inside HO de Villiers, made at colossal speed, brought art into the game of rugby.

Demonstrators, smoke bombs and tin-tacks notwithstanding, it was a triumph for rugby football and for the Springboks in particular.

They finish with a record of played 25, won 16, drawn 4, lost 5.

International Championship: England 13 Wales 17, Twickenham, 28 February

Sub cracks England
Triple Crown denied by Welsh victory

By JA Bailey

When England play Wales at Twickenham it is always a very special event. And when a match produces a finish such as this, with Wales emerging from the slough of despondency to seize victory at the last gasp after England had for all the world laid fingers on the Triple Crown, then 70,000 people who were there will be in no doubt that this was a once-in-a-lifetime occasion.

Gareth Edwards, captain and architect of this Welsh team, limped off the field midway through the second half. He was replaced, with 15 minutes to run, by R Hopkins of Maesteg who was winning his first cap. Wales were

trailing 6-13 and their play was shot with desperation.

As English eyes blinked in disbelief this 'intruder' Hopkins made a nonsense of all that had gone before. With immaculate rolling kicks he set Wales up for the kill. In no time he had put in Williams for a blind-side try. Then as the last seconds of normal time were ticking away he scored a try himself.

With Williams's conversion putting Wales ahead for the first time and John's dropped goal rubbing salt into the wound, Wales were assured of an astonishing breathless win by a goal, three tries and a drop goal to two goals and a penalty.

International Championship: France 35 England 13, Paris, 18 April

France just unforgettable

By Michael Melford

The French on their day play rugby football with a mastery and a brilliance all their own – and yesterday was their day. In all the history of international rugby no one has ever scored 35 points against England before, and the margin of four goals, two drop goals, a penalty goal and two tries to two goals and a penalty goal if anything flattered England.

By three minutes after half-time France had already scored more points – 19 – than they had ever scored before against England, and were worth every point of their lead. Not often are virtues so completely on one side.

They then gave away eight easy points to which England added another five through a superb try by Spencer from almost their only organised attack of the match.

Thus, within nine surprising minutes, England found themselves only 19-13 down, a score which Frenchmen could with reason regard as one of the great travesties of justice of the age. However, the French soon went away again, finishing with two tries near the posts in injury time.

The French command of the line-out through Cester, Dauga and Le Droff was almost absolute and their speed on the loose ball and their backing-up was in their very finest tradition.

Two weeks ago against Wales, with whom they now share this year's championship, they were kept at a distance by the Welsh forwards and were in one of their muddled, undisciplined moods.

Yesterday the forwards dominated the English pack so completely from the start that it was half an hour before one of the dangerous English centres had the ball in hand. Everyone knew this time what he was trying to do, and the substitute fly-half, Berot, whose four previous caps were won as a scrum-half, conducted the attacking operation with authority and flair. Pebeyre gave him a fast, accurate service.

Dauga and Carrere were at their best in a talented back row and the centres, Lux and Trillo, produced some bewildering runs.

Of England one can only say that when the three-quarters, and indeed Finlan, had the ball occasionally in the second half, they did enough to recall happier days. Full-back Jorden, after a fair start, was inevitably forced into error in the end and was unlucky to be picked for such a day.

Dauga: commanding performance in the French back row.

Tour International: South Africa 20 New Zealand 17, Johannesburg, 12 September

South Africa win the series

By Reg Sweet

It seems entirely fair to say that Springbok rugby is back among the ranking powers in the game. One would rate a 3-1 victory in any rubber an achievement of some magnitude. Against a side of this New Zealand calibre it enjoyed a relatively higher rating.

It was a quite momentous climax to a series only equalled here in modern times by the classic qualities of the British Lions of 1955 and as close a call as you could ask for.

Justice was seen to be done, no doubt, but, by jove its scales were delicately poised. At 20 points to 17 the margin comprised a Springbok goal, try and four penalty goals to New

Zealand's goal and four penalties and in all conscience this was close enough.

New Zealand staged a rousing recovery after trailing 3-14 at half-time, but nine minutes from time the rubber was decided without a final shade of doubt.

It was then that Springbok centre three-quarter Jansen, a notable success throughout this series, crash-tackled as New Zealand sought a breakout from their own quarter with full-back Kember in the line. Roux pounced as the ball came clear, made good ground and sent Muller racing through at the corner flag.

Tour Match: Barbarians 9 Fijians 29, Gosforth, 24 October

Radiant Fijians consume humble Barbarians

By JA Bailey

'Oh, what a fall was there, my countrymen!' The Barbarians, containing the probable nucleus of the British Lions touring team, were humbled, fragmented and finally totally vanquished by the Fijians, whose radiant faces at the finish told how much this victory meant to them.

What meant even more to the 12,000 crowd was that the Fijians should be capable of playing in such glorious, all-consuming fashion.

The running, passing, feinting and dodging of these natural athletes – and especially the speed and skill of the giant forwards in the open - had the stadium in uproar long before the end. The Barbarians just did not know which way to turn. The story is briefly told in the scoring analysis: four goals and three tries to the Fijians; two tries and a penalty goal to the Barbarians.

Not apparent though is the nervous start by the Fijians. They had to wait until the dying moments of the first half before equalising through Nasave's try. For all their obvious potential, they had

not yet given away any hint of the holocaust to come.

Then, in the second minute of the second-half, came the crucial try. It came from a movement which set the pattern for the rest of the game and it left the onlookers shaking their heads in disbelief at the sheer power and speed of the Fijian forwards.

The Fijians began a passing movement which quickly sent play to the other side of the field. Ravouvou, 6ft 3in and 15 1/2 stone, sliced through the defence, with his head thrown back, leaving Gareth Edwards in his wake. Visei was up for the scoring pass, Batibasaga at last found the target – and the rout had begun.

Less than five minutes later, Racika added another try and the list was completed by Qoro, Batibasaga, Tuiese and Ravouvou. Batibasaga added three more conversions.

Williams kicked a penalty goal and Duckham scored a last-minute try for the Barbarians. But by now the Fijians were so happy they were past caring.

1971

20 Mar Scotland's 16-15 win over England is their first at Twickenham since 1938.

27 Mar Scotland beat England for the second Saturday in a row, humiliating them 26-6 at Murrayfield in the match to commemorate the first ever rugby international at Raeburn Place exactly 100 years ago.

27 Mar The first victory (9-5) for Wales in France since 1957 clinches the Championship and their first Grand Slam for 19 years. Wales have to come back from 5-0 down, and do so thanks to an interception and 70-yard run by John Williams to put Gareth Edwards over for a try, and a second-half penalty goal and try from a bloodied Barry John, whose 31 points in this season's Championship equals Keith Jarrett's Welsh record.

17 Apr In the last of the RFU Centenary matches, England lose 28-11 at Twickenham to the President's Overseas XV.

7 Aug Thanks largely to a splendid individual performance by goal-kicking outside-half Piet Visagie (12 pts from 1T, 1PG and 3C), the South Africans win the

3rd Test 18-6 at Sydney, to complete their tour of Australia with their 13th win in 13 matches (396pts to 102), and become the first Springboks to return home undefeated.

14 Aug The British Lions win their first series abroad, drawing 14-all with the All Blacks at Eden Park to clinch the rubber 2-1.

2 Oct A Welsh XV run in 10 tries as they beat the Canadians 56-10, the new experimental value of 4 points for a try having applied throughout their 5-match tour (record W2-L3).

8 Oct England conclude their 7-match tour of the Far East with their 7th win, a second victory over Ceylon, having also beaten Japan (twice), Singapore and Hong Kong.

20 Nov Australia come back from 11-0 down to beat France 13-11 at Toulouse in the first Test in which tries are worth 4 points.

Laws: The value of a try is increased from 3 to 4 points.

Tour International: South Africa 8 France 8, Durban, 19 June

French foiled in Durban

By Reg Sweet

rEight-all in the second international here, and so the honours in the two-match rubber go to South Africa. But in case there is any room for doubt, this was very clearly France's day. They gave full rein to their devastating flair for incisive running, and drew on the full magic of their handling.

France led three-nil at half time by way of a dropped goal from 45 yards by Cantoni, who played at full back with results that were spectacular. Cronje put South Africa ahead with a good try when he probed a midfield gap and McCallum goaled.

But McCallum, who missed not a goal kick at Bloemfontein the week before, had meagre pickings here. Six times he tried and missed and when France stormed back it was Dauga, their captain of the day and certainly the dominating personality of this match, who started the rolling movement that brought Bertranne through magnificently well for a try goaled by Berot.

Visagie staved off what might have been a Springbok shipwreck with a final dropped goal from 45 yards. South Africa were lucky to salvage something from the wreckage.

INTERNATIONAL CHAMPIONSHIP

	E	F	I	S	W	P	W	D	L	F	A	Pts
1 WALES	22-6	-	23-9	-	-	4	4	0	0	73	38	8
2 FRANCE	-	-	-	13-8	5-9	4	1	2	1	41	40	4
3=ENGLAND	-	14-14	-	15-16	-	4	1	1	2	44	58	3
3=IRELAND	6-9	9-9	-	-	-	4	1	1	2	41	46	3
5 SCOTLAND	-	-	5-17	-	18-19	4	1	0	3	47	64	2

TOURS (Tests)

British Isles in (Australia) & New Zealand: NZ3-BI9, NZ22-BI12, NZ3-BI13, NZ14-BI14

France in South Africa: SA22-F9, SA8-F8

South Africa in Australia: A11-SA19, A6-SA14, A6-SA18

Australia in France: F11-A13, F18-A9

Wonderful Wales win match of a lifetime!

By JA Bailey

This was one of the great games of a lifetime. It had everything; skilful football, high excitement, the lead changing hands with the swelling tide of play, the hopes of both sides raised, dashed, and raised again until finally Wales, with a try in the dying minutes and a conversion by Taylor which required nerves of steel, stole victory just as all Scotland were preparing to acclaim their heroes. Even this impartial onlooker finished with a thumping heart. The lead changed hands no less than five times.

Scotland were four points in the lead with only ten minutes remaining. Wales attacked. They gave all they had. Somehow Scotland held on. Welsh movements broke down, passes went astray, until they once more sent the ball along the line. Gerald Davies took a long pass, and his great speed left Taylor a conversion ten yards in from touch with all Wales depending on him. Taylor did not fail and the Welsh tally of two goals, two tries and a penalty saw them home.

John was once again the significant weapon in the Welsh armoury. His eye for the slim-mest of openings and the incredible balance of his running were the catching part of his performance. Added to these, however, was the precision kicking of both him and Edwards, which served Wales equally well in attack and defence.

After half-an-hour Scotland were ahead by two Peter Brown penalties against one from John. Not until the 42nd minute did Wales go into the lead for the first time. Then Williams burst through the centre, turned inwards and found Taylor inside him as he was tackled. Show Taylor the line, with the ball in his hands, and he needs no urging. His burst over 15

Nerveless: Taylor kicks for victory.

yards left John with an easy conversion.

Welsh elation at this somewhat unexpected turn of events was increased further when Edwards brushed aside all opposition in a 25-yard run for the line on the short side of a ruck. Now, Scotland were really up against it.

They came back through a try by Carmichael. He seized on a Welsh tap-down from a line-out near the Welsh line, and hurled himself over from five yards, Brown's conversion curled just wide of the far post, but he was on the mark again when Scotland were awarded a penalty in front of the Welsh posts.

Almost unbelievably, Scotland had regained the lead. It was short lived. John intruded himself upon the scene midway through the second-half to score a try which ranked high even by his standards. It was the result of a 25-yard run, made incredible by the way he kept his feet after being hit first one way and then the other by converging defenders.

Another penalty by Brown and a fine opportunist try by Rea saw Scotland in the lead by a clear four points. The stage was set for that remarkable climax.

Tour International: New Zealand 3 British Isles 9, Dunedin, 26 June

Champagne for proud Lions
Barry John inspires fine victory in New Zealand
By a Special Correspondent

The British Isles beat New Zealand by nine points to three in the first international of the series. It was a victory of which Wellington would have been proud. It was close – damned close – but the thin square of red shirts never wavered.

The All Blacks came at them like an avalanche in the first quarter of an hour and they came at them again in a series of pounding assaults in the last 20 minutes. Each time the Lions threw them back.

The tackling close to the scrum, the tackling as the All Blacks poured round the back of the line-out, the cover defence and the tackling of John Williams at full-back were beyond praise.

The Lions had stuck out their chins last Sunday after the carnage against Canterbury at Christchurch [a 14-3 victory, but with half a dozen players injured], and they stuck them out a bit further when scrum-half Gareth Edwards went off the field at the very beginning of the match with an injured hamstring.

Ray Hopkins came on and immediately set about proving Bob Hiller's assertion that the players in his midweek side are as good as this Saturday lot any day.

Hopkins found himself pitched into the middle of a battle in which there were so many All Blacks coming at him that he must have felt he was fighting the Zulu wars all over again at Rorke's Drift.

Colin Meads was in such tremendous form from line-out peels that twice within 10 seconds Barry John was faced with the great man bearing down on him in open country in front of his posts.

It would be stretching a point to say that John tackled him, but at least he got in his way long enough for somebody else to finish the job. The great point about the Lions defence was that always there was somebody else standing by.

Once that first desperate assault of the All Blacks was repulsed the Lions worked their way upfield and created three chances of scoring. Barry John missed two penalty goals well within his capabilities before Ian Mc-Lauchlan, looking like the Nobby Stiles of British rugby, first caught Fergie McCormick and then followed up as the New Zealand full-back scraped away a hurried pass to Sutherland.

He charged down the latter's attempted clearance and, as the ball cannoned back over the line directly in the path of his touchdown, he enveloped it in his loving bosom. It was his first try on the tour and he grinned all the way back to the halfway line.

McCormick equalised with an easy penalty goal when John Dawes was penalised for what amounted to not playing Sid Going after a tackle.

McCormick had already missed a dolly from in front of the posts and he missed another in the second half. By then, though, his nerves must have been in shreds. Barry John positively taunted him with his tactical kicking, and made him look like a pensioner. All that was missing was the wheelchair.

John pulled him from one side of the field to the other, and if it had not been for the memory of what he did in the Canterbury match the previous week the Lions might have felt sorry for this old man fumbling across the field. John put the Lions ahead again with a penalty goal early in the second half when the All Blacks were offside at a ruck, and he kicked another four minutes from the end when he was late-tackled by McNaughton. After that, there was nothing to do but order the champagne.

It was the first time the Lions had won an international match in New Zealand or South Africa for 12 years. Bill McBride, the Lions lock, has been on all three of the losing tours in the meantime, and as he said: 'Now I can die happy.'

Tour International: New Zealand 3 British Isles 13, Wellington, 31 July

Earth-shattering Rugby
John the architect of wonder win
By a Special Correspondent

New Zealand has been expecting a major earthquake in Wellington for some years and the 1971 British Lions have certainly done their best to provide one. They have scored 81 points in this fair city, and they have just ended up by beating the All Blacks in the third of the four internationals.

Their 13-3 triumph has given the Lions a 2-1 lead in the series and is the first time the British Isles have ever won two matches in an international series in New Zealand. It has also shaken the All Blacks' faith in themselves.

The British Isles cannot lose the series now. They scored 13 points in 17 minutes and were then playing so emphatically that an anxious New Zealand voice said, 'Jeez, they're gonna score fifty.'

First John dropped a goal. Then Gerald Davies forced his way over in the corner and somehow got the ball down before he hit the flag. John's kick nudged the inside of the far post and bounced down over the bar.

Midway through the first half Edwards picked up a loose ball and knocked Burgess out of the way with a ferocious hand-off. He then thrust past Cottrell before giving the ball to Barry John a couple of yards outside him, and

John touches down for the Lions' second try in Wellington.

John scored by the posts with a fastidious little jab before walking back calmly to convert the try.

At that stage it really did seem as if the Lions might score 20 or 30 points. But, playing into the wind in the second half, they were committed to 40 minutes of almost uninterrupted defence. They managed this admirably, though they had their shaky moments.

1972

12 Feb Ireland beat England 16-12 at Twickenham, but the refusal of the Scots and Welsh to fulfil their fixtures at Lansdowne Road robs Ireland of the opportunity to win the Triple Crown and Grand Slam at home.

26 Feb France, playing their last match at Colombes, register their highest score against England with a 37-12 victory.

18 Mar England's 23-9 defeat at Murrayfield means they have lost all four Championship games for the first time.

29 Apr Ireland beat France 24-14 in a non-Championship match in Dublin, arranged to compensate for the loss of Ireland's two home games in the Championship.

6 May Neath, in their centenary year, win the inaugural WRU Challenge Cup, beating Llanelli 15-9 in the final at Cardiff.

7 May The 'King' abdicates – Wales and Lions fly-half Barry John, 27, announces his retirement. In 25 appearances for Wales, he scored a record 90pts (13PG, 8DG, 6C, 5T), and his 35pts in three Championship matches this season is another Welsh record.

25 Jun France complete their first full-scale tour of Australia with a 16-15 victory at Brisbane in the second Test, having drawn the first, and finish unbeaten, with a W8-D1-F254-A122 record. Scorers: Australia – Fairfax 5 penalty goals; France – Maso (2) and W Spanghero tries, Villepreux and Cabrol conversions.

16 Dec Georges Domercq is the first French referee to take charge of a UK international with a touring side when he officiates at Murrayfield over Scotland's 14-9 defeat by the All Blacks.

International Championship: Wales 20 France 6, Cardiff, 25 March

Welsh tackling snuffs out French brilliance

By John Reason

Roy Bergiers led a display of such uncompromising tackling by Wales at Cardiff Arms Park that France were restricted to only two of the handling movements with which they are capable of bewildering their opponents.

There were a few occasions when the powerfully built Bergiers tackled two men in the same movement. Once he even brought down three.

Shorn of the leadership of Walter Spanghero, and of his command at the back of the forwards, France struggled vainly against the constraints imposed by Bergiers and by the impregnable defensive organisation of the Welsh.

France were pinned near their 25 for much of the game, and all the time they were there Barry John was waiting for mistakes. In the first half the French made four and John kicked three penalty goals and hit a post, which did not please him.

He kicked a fourth penalty goal in the second half, and those 12 points brought his career total for Wales to 90, which broke Jack Bancroft's 50-year-old record.

Wales also scored two tries, both in the second half, and against that France could kick only two penalty goals. Both were superb efforts by Villepreux from inside his own half.

INTERNATIONAL CHAMPIONSHIP

	E	F	I	S	W	P	W	D	L	F	A	Pts
1 WALES	-	20-6	-	35-12	-	3	3	0	0	67	21	6
2=IRELAND	-	-	-	*	*	2	2	0	0	30	21	4
2=SCOTLAND	23-9	20-9	-	-	-	3	2	0	1	55	53	4
4 FRANCE	37-12	-	9-14	-	-	4	1	0	3	61	66	2
5 ENGLAND	-	-	12-16	-	3-12	4	0	0	4	36	88	0

Cancelled because of terrorist threats.

TOURS (Tests)
England in South Africa: SA9-E18
France in Australia: A14-F14, A15-F16
Australia in New Zealand: NZ29-A6, NZ30-A17, NZ38-A3

International Championship: France 9 Ireland 14, Paris, 29 January

Well-drilled Irish demolish French with iron display

By John Reason

France's need of a national squad was made desperately apparent by Ireland's thoroughly well-organised victory in a bitterly cold diagonal wind at Stade Colombes, in Paris. Hope has very little chance against homework these days.

France, with infinitely greater resources of playing talent than Ireland, were beaten out of sight in all aspects of match planning, rucking, support play, and in control of the loose ball.

They were also out-scrummaged and out-generalled and they were outplayed in the key positions closest to the ball.

Poor Astre had a disastrous day at scrum-half and the French back row flickered only briefly when Skrela came on in place of Boffelli, who injur-ed a knee in the second half. The French lumbered where once they leapt. They kept dropping the ball and they were even prevented from taking any profit from the abundant line-out possession that ought to have won them the match.

Ireland led 11-3 at the interval, with tries by débutant John Moloney and Ray McLoughlin – his first in 10 years of playing for Ireland – and a penalty by Kiernan.

Against the wind in the second half, they defended so well and counter-attacked with such spirit and common-sense that they were able to increase their lead with another penalty kicked by Kiernan, while France did not score their goal until the seventh minute of injury time.

RFU Club Knock-out Competition: Gloucester 17 Moseley 6, Twickenham, 29 April

Knock-out becomes mockery: Moseley are brave to the end

By John Reason

Moseley had to play the last 20 minutes of this rain-swept final of the Rugby Union's first club knock-out competition with only 12 men, and yet the match went into injury time before Gloucester made sure of winning it.

This was a scathing commentary on the inflexibility of the tactics Gloucester used at Twickenham. They had no back row at all against them in the last quarter, and yet they did not take advantage of it.

Either Micky Booth or Tom Palmer kicked the ball high to where Sam Doble was playing a magnificent game at full-back, or John Bayliss took a crash ball into the centre to the one other place where Moseley could muster some defence.

Close-passing rushes by the Gloucester loose forwards, or quick passing to the wing supported by the back row, must have brought tries as fast as Gloucester could have run them in. However, instead of shoving Moseley off the ball at a pace they could control, Gloucester hurled them off it at a run and then dissolved in such confusion that they kept Moseley in the game almost to the end.

Gloucester did not pull away until injury time when Palmer and Booth dropped goals to add to the tries by Dix and Roy Morris and the penalty goal by Stephens with which they had overhauled Moseley's first-minute goal.

Moseley had scored their try from the first scrum. It was the only time in the match when they were at full strength.

Almost from the kick-off an eruption in the front row following a biting incident led to Nigel Horton, Moseley's international lock forward, being sent off for punching Dick Smith. They lost Tim Smith through injury just before half-time and his fellow flanker Ian Pringle in the second half.

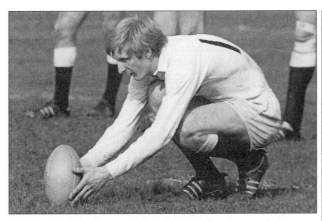

England full-back Sam Doble: kicked fourteen points.

Tour International: South Africa 9 England 18, Johannesburg, 3 June

England are first to tour South Africa unbeaten in 81 years

By John Reason in Johannesburg

When the Springbok team and its management failed to turn up at the official reception after being beaten by England at Ellis Park, members of the South African Board were obviously considerably embarrassed.

The Springboks had good cause for feeling despondent. They had just been beaten by a goal and four penalty goals to three penalty goals, and were obviously aware that they had contributed to one of the worst performances ever put up by South Africa.

It was their own fault that they lost. The referee launched such an assault on the England front row that South Africa were given nine fairly easy chances of kicking penalty goals, yet their goal-kicking was so bad that they could take only three of them.

Piet Greyling, the Springbok captain, was so uncertain about his choice of kicker that he dodged from Snyman, to Sauerman to Ellis, and then back again. This helped to destroy his team's confidence, while the game was being won and lost.

England's new full-back Sam Doble kicked four penalty goals out of five, and converted England's try from the right touchline. He missed three penalty goals at the end of the game, two of them quite easy by his standards, but by then England were safe.

England's try was the crux of the match, just after they

had taken the lead for the first time with Doble's third penalty goal. Jan Webster put up a kick wide of the Springbok full-back. Carlson over-reached himself, fell as he ran to gather the ball, and threw it at Webster's feet. Webster's pick-up was a marvellously sure reflex. He passed to Alan Morley who scored in the corner.

Doble's conversion, and his final penalty goal, gave England an 18-6 lead which South Africa were never able to threaten. Their only other score was a third penalty goal by Snyman.

Webster was in great pain throughout after Sauerman had trodden on his toe, but he played magnificently. His service was sharp and sure. He darted among the Springbok loose forwards. He covered and tackled and kept chipping the ball down the blind-side to keep the game tight and he had an unerring eye for an opening.

Chris Ralston thoroughly justified himself, and the combination of Andy Ripley and Tony Neary at the back of the lineout also turned in a useful profit.

England conceded only two tries on tour, and they became the first touring team since 1891 to leave South Africa unbeaten. They won six matches out of seven and drew the other against Northern Transvaal. This was the second time in succession that they have beaten South Africa.

SRU Centenary Match: Scotland/Ireland 30 England/Wales 21, Murrayfield, 14 October

Gibson exploits weaknesses of Welsh half-backs

By John Reason

An uncharacteristic tangle at half-back in the England and Wales team provided Mike Gibson and Tom Grace with enough chances to score five tries for Scotland and Ireland in the Centenary match at Murrayfield.

Ray Hopkins, the Wales and Lions scrum-half, had difficulty in establishing contact with the ball won by his forwards, and the problems which this gave Phil Bennett were compounded by others of his own making. The result was that England and Wales made their opponents a present of three tries.

Gibson was supreme. He constantly threatened poor Bennett in defence and once charged down a kick of his and ran away to beat a tackle by John Williams and score in the corner. Gibson scored three tries, Grace two, and AR Brown kicked two conversions and two penalty goals. For England and Wales, TGR Davies, Lloyd, Williams and Neary scored tries, Bennett kicked one conversion and Taylor a penalty goal.

Tour International: Wales 16 New Zealand 19, Cardiff, 2 December

Gallant Wales can kick themselves for Cardiff defeat

By John Reason

Wales will kick themselves for all eternity about this match, but, from what we saw at Cardiff Arms Park, they will not do it with quite the precision with which Joe Karam, the New Zealand full-back, applied his right boot to the ball.

Karam kicked five beautifully struck penalty goals out of six attempts as Wales destroyed themselves with a succession of sickeningly trivial mistakes.

Two of these, in the first eight minutes, gave New Zealand the start they prayed for; and another before half-time was added to a try by Keith Murdoch to give them a lead of 13-3.

This was such a healthy position for the All Blacks, and it was so thoroughly deserved by their monopoly of the good ball – and by their unashamed 10-man rugby – that the crowd was dazed.

However, the first eight minutes of the second-half were even more productive for Wales than the first eight minutes of the match had been for New Zealand.

Wales also scored twice, but one of their scores was a try by Bevan; and as they also smashed the New Zealand scrum for the first of

several times, they achieved a dominance of the field play which they never lost.

The contrast with the first-half could not have been more complete. New Zealand were still playing 10-man rugby, but now it looked totally barren as Wales roared at them.

However, each time Wales got into a position to challenge for victory, they made another mistake – and Karam dampened the enthusiasm of the crowd by stretching New Zealand's lead to six points again.

Even then, Wales could have won. But they failed to score a try which was there for the taking, and they took a tapped penalty instead of kicking an easy goal. This would have made the score 19-16, with time enough still to win the match.

After all that Wales could still have drawn, but with the score 19-16 and one final chance of kicking a penalty goal, Phil Bennett missed from a fairly comfortable 35 yards to the right of the posts.

So New Zealand won by a try and five penalty goals to a try and four penalty goals. Truly, the name of a close game at this level is goal-kicking.

1973

15 Jan France beat Scotland 16-13 at the magnificent new Parc des Princes stadium in Paris thanks largely to the kicking of new cap Jean-Pierre Romeu (3PG, 1DG). Ken Pattinson, just appointed to England's panel of referees, tears a calf muscle after only 15 minutes of his first international, and is replaced by the French international referee François Palmade.

10 Feb A weary 7th All Blacks, bedraggled in the rain and mud of Parc des Princes, never threaten to beat France in the last match of their tour, going down 13-6.

24 Apr The Barbarians' extraordinary 60-15 victory over Newport not only gives them only their third 'grand slam' since the war on their Easter tour of Wales, but is the most points they have ever scored in their 83-year history, and Newport's heaviest-ever defeat. Three of the Baa-Baas' 12 tries are scored by their captain, right wing three-quarter JS Spencer.

30 Jun After losing the first international last week by 30-12, the touring Tongans beat Australia (whose players are awarded full caps) at Brisbane 16-11 in the second and last Test.

7 Jul Transvaal register a record score in the Currie Cup, beating Far North 99-9 at Ellis Park, and Gerald Bosch breaks the individual scoring record with 36pts (1T-2DG-13C)

6 Oct Wales outclass Japan 62-14 at Cardiff Arms Park, as fly-half Phil Bennett amasses 26pts, converting 9 of their 11 tries, 2 of which he scores himself. [The tourists later lose only 19-10 to England Under-23s and 30-18 to France, and finish with a W2-L9 record.]

10 Nov Ireland avenge their two 1970 defeats in Buenos Aires with a 21-8 victory at Lansdowne Road over Argentina.

Tour International: Ireland 10 New Zealand 10, Lansdowne Road, 20 January

Kiernan denies All Blacks their clean sweep

By John Reason

A defiant run by Tom Kiernan that had its origins in a distinctly uncomfortable moment inspired Ireland to snatch two scores in 90 seconds and save their game against New Zealand, thereby denying the tourists a clean sweep in the internationals.

After a near bungle by his own 25, Kiernan weaved 30 yards upfield with an impromptu mixture of jink and dummy before setting up a good ruck, which eventually led to a line-out. Though Ireland's throw was not straight, neither was Sid Going's feed into the subsequent scrum, and Barry McGann kicked a penalty goal.

This made the score 10-6 with five minutes to go, and within 90 seconds the Irish forwards had come roaring to such a boil that they won a scrum and a ruck from which Tom Grace scored the equalising try by the right touchline.

McGann, who had played a beautifully astute game throughout, hit the kick so well that the crowd cheered it three-quarters of the way home before it eventually faded just past the far post. So the match was drawn.

Tour Match: Barbarians 23 New Zealanders 11, Cardiff, 27 January

Carwyn James plots memorable Barbarians win

By John Reason

Carwyn James *(pictured)* talked to the Barbarians for 20 minutes and in that time he convinced them that they could go out at Cardiff Arms Park and play just as they had when they were Lions in New Zealand.

He convinced them that they could beat the All Blacks in the last match of the tour, despite their crippling lack of match practice, and he convinced them they could do it with no compromises to their own supreme brand of 15-man football.

The 12 Lions in the team believed him and, with Tom David, Phil Bennett and Bob Wilkinson, they went out and did exactly what he said they could do.

To Phil Bennett, Carwyn James said: 'You can sidestep these people off the park.' To John Williams he said: 'Relax.' Those words came true, too, in only the second minute of the game when Bryan Williams cross-kicked deep into the Barbarians' 25.

Bennett went back, turned, sidestepped Alistair Scown, sidestepped Ian Hurst, sidestepped Ian Kirkpatrick and sidestepped Ron Urlich. Then he passed to John Williams, who calmly rode a tackle and gave a swivel pass to John Pullin.

He moved the ball to John Dawes, who sold a gorgeous dummy on the left touchline. Coming up to the halfway line, Dawes passed inside to Tom David – what a game he had as a late inclusion – who fed Derek Quinnell, playing as emergency No.8, and then came a final, exquisite touch.

As Quinnell's pass went to John Bevan on the left wing, Gareth Edwards burst through to take it as Bevan scissored inside. Whoever the All Blacks' last defender was, he must have been cross-eyed as Edwards accelerated past him and dived over to score amid a thunderous eruption of ecstasy.

As a statement of an opening theme, it could not have been more definitive than Beethoven's Fifth Symphony, and from that point the Barbarians went on to play a first-half of such lyrical magnificence that they scored a goal, two tries and a penalty goal to lead 17-0 and leave the All Blacks aghast.

It was one of the great passages in the history of rugby football. It compared with the first half of the All Blacks against England in 1967, or the first half of the Lions against New Zealand in Wellington in 1971.

Above all, it put what has been one of the most mundane tours of modern times into its proper place – and no one did more to restore our sense of proportion than David Duckham, whose running from deep counter-attack positions was superb.

This level of inspiration could not continue because only a touring team can achieve the fitness to sustain such running. Peter Whiting took control and the tourists fought to save their country from the most humiliating defeat in its history, scoring two tries and a penalty goal.

But Williams scored the final try, fittingly initiated by Duckham. Quinnell supported him; Dawes and Williams moved the ball out to Gibson; Slattery came through on the inside, and Williams wrong-footed Karam with the greatest of ease to score in the corner. Bennett converted from the touchline. Nothing less would have sufficed!

Edwards (2nd right) lurks as the great move gets underway.

International Sevens: Murrayfield, 7 April

Preece key man in England's triumph

By John Reason

A piercing try scored most fittingly by Keith Fielding in the slippery wetness of a snow shower enabled England to catch Ireland in the last minute and take the international sevens tournament at Murrayfield. England won 22-18.

Because of live television commitments, England had to play the final of the climax of the Scottish centenary celebrations only 16 minutes after beating Wales 24-10 in the most demanding match of the tournament. Ireland had a rest of more than an hour.

Fielding did not set up the ball well on the rare occasions he was tackled, but his pace and his knowledge of sevens were such that he scored nine tries – easily the highest individual total. Once he even held off Gerald Davies to score against Wales in a memorable kick-and-chase.

England were well equipped. With Fran Cotton, Steve Smith and John Gray making notable contributions, their positional play was excellent. Their line-out and scrum were the best and their discreet use of the kick-ahead was most effective.

Apart from that, Peter Preece was only a yard slower than Fielding, and once he got moving Andy Ripley's huge stride was too much for the fastest men in Wales and Ireland.

This enabled England to shrug off the loss of David Duckham after the first round against France, who were sadly out of their depth. He pulled his hamstring, just as he thought he would, and was replaced by Peter Rossborough.

But Ireland went so close. As Mike Gibson said, they were not exactly crushed by the weight of being overwhelmingly favourites. With his own strength and pace and footballing skill supported magnificently by the tackling and mauling of Fergus Slattery, Ireland were able to win the easier pool.

Scotland were poor collectively and individually. New Zealand were much better, and even Ireland only overhauled them at the last gasp.

To start with, Wales looked as if they would swamp everyone. Mervyn Davies was superb, and with John J Williams and Gerald Davies running outside Gareth Edwards they demolished France (36-4) and the President's VII (30-10).

In the end, though, the exceptional pace and defence of Preece gave England a priceless advantage at fly-half, and their forwards were just that much better equipped.

Tour International: New Zealand 10 England 16, Auckland, 15 September

Webster inspires historic victory for England

By A Special Correspondent

John Pullin and his England team claimed a place in rugby history at Auckland on Saturday when, after losing all three provincial matches on their four-match tour, they defeated the mighty All Blacks in splendid fashion.

England were 10-6 in arrears at half-time, but fought back magnificently, particularly through their loose forward play, to inflict on the All Blacks their second successive international defeat. France had previously beaten them at the end of their European tour.

Architect of England's unexpected success was Jan Webster, the Moseley scrum-half, who completely overshadowed the great Sid Going.

Webster had a hand in all three England tries and was a constant source of worry to the New Zealand defence, in support of an England pack that played well above the form they showed in the provincial matches.

They beat the All Blacks at their own game, destructive forward play. And the men who did the most damage were Tony Neary, Andy Ripley and, particularly, John Watkins.

So England, although only gaining a share in the Home international championship last season, have had the distinction of beating two of the world's rugby giants – South Africa and New Zealand – on foreign soil in successive summers.

International Championship: Ireland 6 France 4, Lansdowne Road, 14 April

French chance of outright Championship lost by Romeu

By John Reason

The goal-kicking of Jean-Pierre Romeu, which has been so deadly this season, collapsed in the wind at Lansdowne Road on Saturday and allowed Ireland to hang on and win the last match of the international championship.

This means that all five teams have won both their home matches and finished level with four points each for the first time in history.

Romeu's confidence was badly shaken the day before the game when he practised some kicks and found that he could not get on at all with the different shape of the Irish ball, which has more pointed ends than the French one.

This ebb and flow of confidence was emphasised even more by an enormous 60-yard penalty goal kicked by Tony Ensor, the Irish full-back. That and another tricky one kicked across the wind by Mike Gibson, after Ensor had been dazed by a head-high tackle by Esteve, enabled Ireland to lead 6-0 going into the last quarter.

France then mounted a whole series of assaults and might have scored five or six tries, but they were restricted to just one, scored by right-wing Jean-François Phliponeau at the beginning of injury time. It was not a difficult conversion by Romeu's normal standards, but he knew that it would give France a draw and the international championship, and again he hooked the kick past the far post.

INTERNATIONAL CHAMPIONSHIP

	E	F	I	S	W	P	W	D	L	F	A	Pts
1=WALES	25-9	-	16-12	-	-	4	2	0	2	53	43	4
1=IRELAND	18-9	6-4	-	-	-	4	2	0	2	50	48	4
1=FRANCE	-	-	-	16-13	12-3	4	2	0	2	38	36	4
1=SCOTLAND	-	-	19-14	-	10-9	4	2	0	2	55	59	4
1=ENGLAND	-	14-6	-	20-13	-	4	2	0	2	52	62	4

TOURS (Tests)
New Zealand in Brit. Isles & France: W16-NZ19. S9-NZ14, E0-NZ9, I10-NZ10, F13-NZ6
England in New Zealand: NZ10-E16
Australia in England & Wales: W24-A0, E20-A3

Talking Rugby, 18 April

Line-out changes far from perfect, says John Dawes

By John Reason

John Dawes, the British Lions' captain, is so doubtful about the practicality of the changes in the line-out laws that he thinks that initially they may prove a farce.

'I am all in favour of the thinking behind the changes,' says Dawes, 'but the forwards say that in their present form the laws are unworkable, and I am inclined to agree with them.

'If forwards go on tapping the ball the opposition will be able to pour through one-yard gaps so easily that you will need volunteers to play scrum-half.

'I can see the dangers of some serious injuries. Clubs may even have to think of taking out a special insurance on their scrum-halves.'

Dawes knows full well that the biggest impetus to revise the line-out laws came from his 1971 Lions, who went to New Zealand with the deliberate intention of making an outrageous mockery of the local interpretation of the line-out, and succeeded well enough to win the series.

'We know that the line-out was a shambles,' says Dawes, 'and that it needed fresh thinking, but I think that these changes will need some amendments before they make it any better.'

1974

16 Feb Led by Willie John McBride, whose 56th cap is a new world record (beating Colin Meads), Ireland chalk up their third win in succession over England, 26-21 at Twickenham, equalling their record score in internationals (at Murrayfield in 1953). Mike Gibson scores two splendid tries, converting both himself, but Alan Old's goal-kicking and some tremendous surges by Andy Ripley help England to 12 points in a rousing finish that leaves them just short.

23 Mar Gloucestershire's 22-12 victory in the Counties' final at Blundellsands (Lancs) gives them their 11th Championship, beating the record they held jointly with Yorkshire.

10 Apr The postponed match between the two leaders of Scotland's new national league having finally been rearranged, the destination of the first club championship in the British Isles is decided – the previously unbeaten Hawick, despite losing 13-9 at home to West of Scotland, win the title on a superior points difference (West needed a 13-point margin to succeed).

1 May The All Blacks register a world record score for a major touring side, beating South Australia 117-6 at Adelaide, with full-back Joe Karam scoring a record 41 points.

1 Jun Owen Stephens, capped once for the All Blacks in 1968, now faces them on his début for Australia, and launches their recovery in the last 15 minutes that sees them make up a 10-point deficit for a 16-all draw in the second Test, at Brisbane.

19 Oct The Tongans finish their first tour (W1-L9) of Britain with a 26-7 defeat by Wales at Cardiff, an improvement on their heavy defeats by Scotland (44-8) and England Under-23s (40-4), thanks in part to coaching received from Carwyn James.

23 Nov The All Blacks dominate Ireland's centenary match in Dublin, winning far more easily than the 15-6 scoreline suggests.

30 Nov The All Blacks, having won the first 7 matches of their first short tour to the British Isles, outplay the Barbarians at Twickenham in their final game for all but the last 5 minutes, when Andy Irvine, scorer of 3 penalty goals (2 from 50 yards), cross-kicks for Mervyn Davies to scoop up and go over to earn a 13-all draw.

30 Nov The Springboks retain their unbeaten international record on French soil with a narrow and rather lucky 10-8 victory over France in Paris, to win the rubber 2-0, a huge boost after their defeats by the Lions. *[They finish their 9-match tour 4 days later with a 6th win out of 7 against French Regional XVs.]*

INTERNATIONAL CHAMPIONSHIP

	E	F	I	S	W	P	W	D	L	F	A	Pts
1 IRELAND	-	-	-	9-6	9-9	4	2	1	1	50	45	5
2=SCOTLAND	16-14	19-6	-	-	-	4	2	0	2	41	35	4
2=WALES	-	16-16	6-0	-	-	4	1	2	1	43	41	4
2=FRANCE	12-12	-	9-6	-	-	4	1	2	1	43	53	4
5 ENGLAND	-	-	21-26	-	16-12	4	1	1	2	63	66	3

TOURS (Tests)
New Zealand in Australia: A6-NZ11, A16-NZ16, A6-NZ16
British Isles in South Africa: SA3-BI12, SA9-BI28, SA9-BI26, SA13-BI13
New Zealand in Ireland (& Wales): I6-NZ15
South Africa in France: F4-SA13, F8-SA10

International Championship: England 16 Wales 12, Twickenham, 16 Mar

England scuttle Wales: Ireland champs without playing

By Rupert Cherry

John J Williams, Wales' left-wing, claims he scored a try towards the end of the game that would have robbed England of their first triumph over Wales at Twickenham for 14 years and given Wales the championship, or at least a share of it.

No doubt all Wales support him, so that this becomes one of those dramatic incidents in international rugby which will be debated as long as memories last.

It is ironic that John West, the referee in charge of his first international, who decided against the try, is an Irishman.

By his decision, Ireland take the championship title; a thought which would not occur to anyone, least of all, I am sure, to Mr West, until considerably later in the day.

My view of the incident from 70 or 80 yards away leaves me in doubt whether Williams grounded the ball properly. Three times I have watched the re-run of the BBC television film and even that did not resolve my doubt.

Meanwhile, at Murrayfield, Scotland comprehensively beat France 19-6, and made certain that Ireland became international champions.

Irvine: Scotland's match winner at Murrayfield.

International Championship: Scotland 16 England 14, Murrayfield, 2 February

Magnificent Irvine snatches victory from England

By John Reason

Andy Irvine savoured the most joyful moment of his burgeoning international career when he kicked an immensely difficult penalty goal, from 45 yards and far out on the right, to win the Calcutta Cup match for Scotland at Murrayfield.

The pressure on Irvine could not have been greater. He knew it would be the last kick of the match, and apart from the forbidding range, it was from the wrong side of the field for a kicker who bends the ball to the left as he does.

What is more, he had missed an easy penalty goal which would have taken Scotland 12 points clear, and put them in complete command after only 18 minutes; and he had seen England come back so hard and so strongly that they had taken the lead twice in the second half, and seemed certain to win.

The kick hung in the air for what seemed an eternity, but the crowd behind it on the open terracing were roaring it home long before Norman Sanson, the Scottish touch judge, leapt in the air with his flag jack-knifing aloft in triumph, and the English touch judge dolefully followed suit to signal that they were right.

So Scotland won by a goal, a try and two penalty goals to two tries, a penalty goal and a dropped goal, and Irvine scored 12 of their 16 points.

Rugby Union Sevens: Richmond 34 London Welsh 16, Twickenham, 4 May

Richmond's highest winning score

By John Reason

Long before the final of the Middlesex Sevens at Twickenham it was obvious that Richmond would stop London Welsh winning the tournament for the fourth year in succession.

When it came to the point, the Welsh were overwhelmed. Richmond led 24-0 soon after half-time and although the Welsh scored two goals and a try to pull up to 24-16, Gerald Davies missed the conversion that would have put them a goal away.

Richmond then raised their game again and added another goal and a try to the four goals they had scored previously to win 34-16. It was the highest winning final score in the history of the tournament.

Tour International: South Africa 9 British Isles 28, Pretoria, 22 June

Bennett inspires biggest-ever win over Springboks

By John Reason

South Africa suffered the worst defeat in their rugby history when the British Isles beat them in the second international of the four-match series at Loftus Versfeld. It was the worst defeat to their pride, too, because they played so badly the Lions must feel they are now in the position of being two up with no-one to play.

The extraordinary thing is that the Lions did not have to play particularly well to win. The business of scoring five tries to nil was accomplished with such ease, it looked like an abrupt encounter between the Lions and the lambs.

Mercifully for South Africa, Phil Bennett had a poor day with his goal-kicking, otherwise the Lions would have scored over 40 points. He missed two easy penalty goals and four conversions.

The Lions won by a goal, a dropped goal, a penalty goal and four tries to two penalty goals and a dropped goal. Sadly, the game seemed to confirm our earlier suspicions that South Africa are now a second-class rugby power.

By the end, the Lions were in such control, Mervyn Davies was standing rocking the ball gently under his foot at the back of the scrum and Gareth Edwards was indulging in his own form of razzle-dazzle by letting the ball fall over his shoulder and flicking it up with his heel.

As Dr Danie Craven said afterwards: 'It was a massacre.'

[Scorers: South Africa - Bosch 2PG, DG; Lions - JJ Williams 2T, Bennett C, T, PG, Gordon Brown T, Milliken T, McGeechan DG.]

JJ Williams scores under the posts for the Lions.

Tour International: South Africa 9 British Isles 26, Port Elizabeth, 13 July

Lions' great triumph breaks 78-year record

By John Reason

The British Isles, to their everlasting credit, took command of the third international against South Africa and made sure of winning the series when Gordon Brown scored a try at the end of the first half and Andy Irvine kicked a huge penalty goal at the beginning of the second half.

They were mortal thrusts, because the Springboks had attacked for almost the whole of the first half, and their forwards had played with such spirit and such resolve, that they deserved to be in the lead.

South Africa looked as if they had scored in the first five minutes, only to be re-called for a five-yard scrum, and Bill McBride, the Lions' captain, confessed afterwards that the Springbok forward effort worried him.

However, instead of leading, South Africa found themselves approaching half-time with the scores level at 3-3. Suddenly the Lions broke out of defence and forced a lineout near the Springboks' left corner flag.

Brown correctly anticipated that the Springboks would throw the ball short, but even he must have been surprised when his opponents left a gap at the front of the lineout and Muller obligingly threw the ball straight to him so that he could dive over to score.

So South Africa were 7-3 down at half-time and immediately afterwards they were penalised for kicking at a man on the ground just inside the Lions' half. The penalty kick was at sea level and from something like 60 yards out, Irvine rose magnificently to the occasion kicking a splendid goal.

Leading 10-3 and knowing that the Springboks would have to score twice to overhaul them, the Lions expanded the range of their play and South Africa just collapsed.

JPR Williams started joining the line for almost the first time in the series, and the Lions scored two more fine tries so easily that they raced away to an historic victory by a goal, two tries, two penalty goals, and two dropped goals to three penalty goals.

It is the first time the British Isles have won a series in South Africa since 1896, and the first time the Springboks have lost an international at Port Elizabeth for 64 years - truly a great occasion.

[Scorers: South Africa - Snyman 3PG; Lions - Irvine 2PG, C, Brown T, JJ Williams 2T, Bennett 2DG.]

Centenary Match: Ireland 18 President's XV 18, Dublin, 7 September

Slattery the star as friendly Lions share spoils

By John Mason

The President's XV, comforted by some devastating contributions from their Lions and sustained by the hard work of Esteve and Azarete, drew with Ireland at Lansdowne Road in this centenary match. Each side scored two goals and two penalty goals.

Ireland, marginally, were the better team, and, until a couple of decisions went against them in final surges to the line, looked to be pulling away early in the second-half when the scores were already level.

In Slattery, Ireland possessed the outstanding player. But even he, slowed slightly by a couple of knocks, appeared content to settle for the draw as wind and rain drove fiercely into Irish faces for a long time.

For a time the match was a private contest between 1974 Lions. Bennett began with a simple penalty goal following an off-side in midfield at a line-out. Slattery's try in retaliation came despite a horrid pass. He barely broke stride as he reached low for the ball. Gibson converted and followed with penalty goals from 40 yards (line-out) and 35 yards (scrum) before half-time.

Another line-out offence allowed Bennett a second penalty before Edwards set up a try for Williams. An angled kick to the blind-side corner over his forwards as they broke up was perfectly judged.

Another splendid drive by the pack, McLauchlan and Neary to the fore, immediately after half-time – and instant possession when stopped – enabled Edwards to skip away from the ruck unimpeded for the President's second try. Bennett again converted with a minimum of fuss.

Ireland levelled at once. The alert McKinney, who has benefited from the South African tour, collected the try, Gibson's conversion being his last tidy offering before limping off with a damaged hamstring.

1975

1 Mar The Five Nations is thrown wide open again as the joint leaders both go down, Wales 12-10 at Murrayfield and France 25-6 at Lansdowne Road, where Ireland's captain Willie John McBride scores his first try for his country on his 62nd [and penultimate] appearance. It equals Ireland's best score against France, made at Cork in 1911. The 80,000-plus gate at Murrayfield is a record for British rugby (some estimates, disputed by the police, are as high as 104,000), and thousands are turned away. [Many inside the ground, including those allowed to sit on the grass behind the in-goal areas, see little of the game, and the SRU issue an apology later for underestimating the attendance.]

22 Mar In beating the RAF 41-13 at Twickenham, the Army record the highest ever score in the Triangular Tournament (surpassing the Navy's 36-0 defeat of the RAF in 1934), which nevertheless results in a triple tie.

22 Mar Holders Gloucestershire chalk up their 12th County Championship triumph, beating Eastern Counties 13-9 at Gloucester in their sixth consecutive appearance in the final.

19 Apr Ireland and Scotland seal the Irish Centenary celebrations, with a 17-10 victory over England and Wales in Dublin.

21 Jun Norman Sanson (Scotland) is the first neutral referee to handle an international in South Africa, the 38-25 defeat of France by the Springboks at Bloemfontein, where the 63 points scored is the highest ever total recorded in a Test involving either country.

28 Jun Fly-half Gerald Bosch scores 22 points as the Springboks beat France 33-18 at Pretoria to set a new South African record (beating Keith Oxlee's 16 against the Lions at Bloemfontein in 1962).

International Championship: France 10 Wales 25, Paris, 18 January

Edwards sets Welsh pack to crush French

By John Mason

So all that pre-match gloom among the French was justified. France, playing remarkably badly at times, were roundly beaten by Wales on a soggy, clinging pitch at the Parc des Princes, Paris.

Wales were a calm, efficient unit. They began forcefully, rode out the one period of sustained French pressure and, long before the finish, had won easily.

Though it would be wrong to reach for superlatives, Wales did score five tries to one. This was possible because they controlled matters up front with a sturdy authority that France barely challenged.

John Dawes and Mervyn Davies, involved in their first championship match as coach and captain respectively, have good cause to be well-pleased. Commitment, endeavour and resourcefulness attended every effort; the squad had been well-prepared.

Edwards watched these events – the growing strength of his forwards; the increasing disarray of his opponents – with a benevolent eye. Every so often, dipping into his extraordinary range of skills, he reminded everyone quite how good he can be.

His repertoire included a try – of course – and at least three Frenchmen must be still wondering how he stepped out of their eager embraces on or near the line. His was a cunning path.

If there are reservations about the performance of Wales, they would be, I suggest, about the questionable quality of the opposition and, less important overall, perhaps, the indifferent place kicking. Fenwick will land those goals on another day.

International Championship: Wales 32 Ireland 4, Cardiff, 15 March

Wales are champions to a man in Irish destruction

By Rupert Cherry

Wales played the rugby of real champions in Cardiff. They pulverised Ireland, inflicting the heaviest defeat the Irish have suffered from anyone in the five nations tournament for 68 years.

Ireland were beaten 29-0, also by Wales in Cardiff, in 1907 during the days of one of the many Welsh legendary figures, Rhys Gabe. Had Wales not given away a soft try in injury time on Saturday, even that record would have been surpassed.

This performance, which must be rated as the best rugby in this year's series, not only made the vast crowd delirious with delight, but, as England had beaten Scotland, it brought Wales the championship outright.

Every man in the Welsh team was at his best, and Edwards was positively superb. His kicking, whether it was for the touchline, high for his forwards, or diagonally to disorganise the Irish defence, was as accurate as I have seen by any player.

Equally thrilling was the fielding of JPR Williams. It did not seem to matter where the Irish kicked, he was under the ball and, in his characteristic way, initiated the Welsh counterattacks.

These were the jewels

Welsh prop Charlie Faulkner battles over for his try.

which sparkled most brightly through the dazzling display of everyone in a red jersey. The forwards won so much of the ball and supplied it so quickly to their backs that Wales had time to construct attacks in any way they wished.

The Welsh backs handled with great speed and much skill. Gerald Davies ran with tantalising wizardry on the beautifully firm turf, Bergiers

marked his recall with many determined thrusts, and while the ball was moved constantly along the line scarcely a pass was dropped.

Edwards set the pattern, and his own seal on the game, with a try after he had stolen away from a ruck with such determination and speed that the Irish back row seemed unaware that he had gone.

Other tries were scored by Gerald Davies, JJ Williams,

the loosehead prop Faulkner and Bergiers. Bennett converted three tries, hit a post with two other attempts, and scored two penalty goals.

Edwards took on so much that Bennett had little need to do more than act as link man. Even so, he was in four scoring moves and contributed as much as anyone to the 'hywl' on which Wales soared to a great victory.

INTERNATIONAL CHAMPIONSHIP

	E	F	I	S	W	P	W	D	L	F	A	Pts
1 WALES	20-4	-	32-4	-	-	4	3	0	1	87	30	6
2=SCOTLAND	-	-	20-13		12-10	4	2	0	2	47	40	4
2=IRELAND	12-9	25-6	-	-		4	2	0	2	54	67	4
2=FRANCE	-	-		10-9	10-25	4	2	0	2	53	79	4
5 ENGLAND		-	20-27	-	7-6	-	4	1	0	3	40	65	2

TOURS (Tests)

England in Australia: A16-E9, A30-E21
Scotland in New Zealand: NZ24-S0
France in South Africa: SA38-F25, SA33-F18

Tour International: Australia 30 England 21, Brisbane, 31 May

Burton sent off and cautioned as England slump

By John Reason

Mike Burton, the England prop, has been severely cautioned after being sent off the field for a late tackle on Doug Osborne, the Australian winger, at the beginning of the second international between England and Australia in Brisbane on Saturday.

A minute earlier, Burton had been warned by the referee after widespread fighting had broken out in the first line-out of the match.

The Australian Rugby Union convened a disciplinary committee to consider the case yesterday. It consisted of Bill McLoughlin and Barrie Ffrench, the president and deputy chairman of the Australian union, and Alec Lewis, the England manager.

Afterwards, Mr McLoughlin said Burton had been given a severe caution and added: 'The fact that he was sent off in an international match was regarded as sufficient punishment.'

There is no doubt that Burton's dismissal lost England any chance they may have had of winning the match and saving the two-match series. There is not much doubt either that the referee's decision which led to it must have been as embarrassing for Australia as it was sickening for England.

What made England so indignant was that Australia clearly made up their minds before the series began that they were going to make their presence felt physically. They did it in such a welter of flying boots and fists at the beginning of the match at Brisbane that a brawl was inevitable.

England, therefore, felt it was unfair of the referee to single out Burton for a warning when, as the television replay showed quite clearly, Australia had started the fight and when most of the forwards of both sides were involved.

Anyway, within three minutes, England were short of the prop who has been the key man in their scrummage since the injury to Fran Cotton early in the tour, and they had to move Billy Beaumont up into the front-row.

They had to wait even to do that, because Beaumont had to go off the field after the first fight to have a deep cut in his head bandaged. So for a time, England had to play with six forwards and then with seven – and they did surprisingly well.

Thanks to some fine goal-kicking by Alan Old, and some poor goal-kicking by Australia, England led 15-9 at half-time.

In the end, Australia overhauled England and won by two goals, three tries and two penalty goals to two goals and three penalty goals, but the game was empty of any real meaning.

Tour match: Western Australia 3 England 64, Perth, 10 May

Bennett's spree makes it hard for Wordsworth

By John Reason

John Burgess, the England coach, hopes that the Sydney game will be a more valid test of ability than the overwhelming victory against Western Australia. England won by eight goals, a try, three penalty goals and a dropped goal to a penalty goal.

It was disappointing, the negative way Western Australia played. They were still kicking at goal when they were 50 points down, and they exerted none of the pressure which will be necessary before anyone can make a proper evaluation of the ability of the new England players.

To that extent, therefore, the new players are not much further on than they were, though it will obviously be difficult now for Alan Wordsworth to displace Neil Bennett at fly-half in the England team to play New South Wales.

Apart from scoring 36 points, and making that world record tremble, Bennett kicked to touch against Western Australia as accurately as he kicked at goal. He timed his maximum effort perfectly, too.

He settled England with an early dropped goal and his two tries and two conversions in those crucial moments on either side of half-time turned the game into a rout.

The other England tries were scored by Alan Morley (4), Peter Squires, Dave Rollitt and Peter Preece. Bennett also kicked eight conversions, three penalty goals and a dropped goal.

Tour International: New Zealand 24 Scotland 0, Auckland, 14 June

All Blacks water babies punish Scots

By John Reason

The concept of amateurism in rugby football was made to look distinctly shabby by the thinly disguised commercial pressures which dictated that this international match should be played, even though most of the pitch was under water. It may have been terribly inconsiderate of a complex low pressure area to dump millions of gallons of storm water on Auckland in the 12 hours preceding the match, but it unquestionably did, and it flooded almost the entire city.

It would also have been heartbreaking to return all the gate money paid in advance, but the pitch at Eden Park was unplayable and no referee in the world could have pretended otherwise. Half of one in-goal area and part of the field in front of it was covered by a lake so deep in parts that the ball could be submerged.

The All Blacks, much assisted by a near tornado which changed the direction of the wind so that it was blowing behind them in both halves, proved very much more capable at this particular water sport than Scotland and they won it by four goals to nil. We shall never know what would have happened if the two teams had been required to play rugby football.

The game, such as it was, consisted largely of kicking the ball as high as possible into the biggest of the lakes near the goal-lines so it would stop dead and sometimes even float back a few inches on the waves made by the impact.

This enabled Sid Going and Duncan Robertson to gain plenty of height on their kicks and that, in turn, gave Grant Batty and Bryan Williams time to follow up.

Batty was particularly successful at this. Being such a short and explosive little fellow, he was able to dash off in such a rush of spray, few noticed he was at least two yards offside every time he started running.

The referee did not seem to notice, either, when Bruce Hay, the Scottish full-back, caught one of these kicks early in the game and called for a mark. It was not given, Hay was swept off his feet and he was kicked so blatantly, his arm was broken.

1976

21 Feb Wales take the Triple Crown with a 34-9 win in Dublin, their biggest score against Ireland (beating last year's 32 points at Cardiff), and Phil Bennett's 19 points (1T-3C-3PG) equals the Welsh record held by Jack Bancroft (1910) and Keith Jarrett (1967).

20 Mar England go down 30-9 in Paris – despite a display by the French backs so appalling that it leaves them disconsolate in their dressing-room – for their fourth defeat of the season, only the second time they have suffered such ignominy (the first was in 1972), while in a boring match at Lansdowne Road Scotland chalk up their first away win for five years and Andy Irvine's 12 points gives him a Scottish record of 82 (beating Ken Scotland's 71).

12 Jun Jean-Pierre Romeu sets a new French international record with 25 points

(1T-3C-5PG) as the Tricoleurs climax their 3-match mini-tour of the USA with a 33-14 victory over the Americans.

30 Oct France beat the Wallabies 34-6 in Paris, their biggest score against any International Board country, despite squandering several chances.

4 Nov After their disappointing tour of France and their thrashing in Paris, the Wallabies just stave off a final indignity as they edge Italy 16-15 in Milan, where blinding rain reduces the crowd to 3,000.

7 Dec Cambridge, with a record fifth consecutive victory, beat Oxford 15-0 at Twickenham to attain parity in the Varsity series for the first time since 1899, and win the new handsome silver trophy, the Bowring Bowl, put up by City firm CT Bowring & Co, the first sponsors of the match.

Tour International: USA 12 Australia 24, Los Angeles, 31 January

Wallabies beat ball ... and US

From Reuter

Australia overcame high temperatures, an incorrectly marked field and a deflated ball to beat the United States 24-12 in a rugby union international in Los Angeles.

With the temperature over 80 degrees Fahrenheit, the match could not begin because the ball was not inflated.

Finally a pump was found after an appeal had been made over the public address system, and the game started.

Then the Wallabies found themselves up against some rangy forwards and fast, hard-tackling backs on a pitch that was neither long enough nor quite wide enough.

[This was the Americans' first international since they beat France in the final of the 1924 Olympics.]

Tour match: Transvaal 52 Gloucestershire 19, Johannesburg, 12 June

Gloucestershire put to rout by Transvaal

By John Mason

For more than a fortnight on tour Gloucestershire have bumbled and fumbled their way about South Africa. On Saturday at Ellis Park the muddles and mistakes multiplied majestically, defeat turning to rout.

Transvaal, containing, subduing and then annihilating, won by seven goals, a try and two penalty goals to a goal, a try and three penalty goals. In the last 20 minutes or so, they scored 30 points and Gloucestershire's defence disintegrated.

Gerald Bosch, the

Springbok outside-half who attracts as much criticism here as he does praise, kicked 20 points and caused huge groans of disbelief when missing a conversion attempt from the left-hand touchline immediately before half-time. He had nine kicks and landed eight.

Watkins and Chris G Williams scored Gloucestershire's tries, Butler kicking the goals. Besides 20 points by Bosch, Transvaal's tries came from Ellis (2), Fourie (2), Symons (2), Pypers and Van Wyngaardt.

International Championship: Wales 19 France 13, Cardiff, 6 March

Touch-and-go but brave Wales make it a grand slam

By John Reason

The whole Welsh nation watched in anguished silence as France took command of the end of this match at the Arms Park and fought to snatch a victory that would have deprived Wales of the international championship and a grand slam.

Gourdon was bundled into touch by JPR Williams in the corner on one side of the field, and the referee decided that Aguirre had not grounded the ball properly for a try on the other flank.

The referee brought France back and gave them a scrum after they had broken through with an apparent advantage and Jacques Fouroux, the French captain, was held near the line.

Wales missed touch far too frequently and more of their kicks were charged down as the Welsh scrum came under pressure. The French backs ranged the field with swift, incisive running.

Bertranne's strength and speed was always evident in this, but in the end, the ease

with which he broke past opponents proved France's undoing because instead of playing the ball out to the two powerful wings he came inside and squandered overlaps.

This helped Wales to hang on so that the remarkable penalty goal which Allan Martin had kicked from 50 yards in the first half proved the decisive blow in a scrappy, tumultuous contest.

Thanks to that kick, and to two very much easier ones which Romeu missed, France had to run a point-blank kick at goal which otherwise might have made sure of victory.

The result was that although France scored two tries to one, Wales scraped home by a try and five penalty goals to a goal, a try and one penalty goal. The sigh of relief echoed up the valleys.

Wales again owed an enormous debt to the line-out play and leadership of Mervyn Davies and to the strength of JPR Williams in defence.

INTERNATIONAL CHAMPIONSHIP

	E	F	I	S	W	P	W	D	L	F	A	Pts
1 WALES	-	19-13	-	28-6	-	4	4	0	0	102	37	8
2 FRANCE	30-9	-	26-3	-	-	4	3	0	1	82	37	6
3 SCOTLAND	22-12	6-13	-	-	-	4	2	0	2	49	59	4
4 IRELAND	-	-	-	6-15	9-34	4	1	0	3	31	87	2
5 ENGLAND	-	-	12-13	-	9-21	4	0	0	4	42	86	0

TOURS (Tests)
Australia in British Isles: S10-A3, W28-A3, E23-A6, I10-A20
Ireland in New Zealand: NZ11-I3
New Zealand in South Africa: SA16-NZ7, SA9-NZ15, SA15-NZ10, SA15-NZ14
Australia in France: F18-A15, F34-A6

Tour match: Canada 4 Barbarians 9, Toronto, 12 June

Barbarians beat Canada

From AP

The Barbarians scored the sixth win of their North American rugby union tour with a 29-4 victory over the Canadian national team in Toronto on Saturday.

They took the lead after 30 seconds through the first of four penalty goals by Phil Bennett. Dave McKay scored two tries in the first half and, with Bennett's one conversion and two penalties, and a drop goal by Andy Irvine, the

Barbarians had a 19-4 lead at half-time. Canada's only points came just before half-time, from a try in the corner by Spence McTavish of British Columbia.

The second half saw the Canadians camped in their own half. It was a disappointing display, with infringements breaking the flow of the game. Steve Fenwick scored the only try of the half, Bennett adding two more penalties.

Phil Bennett: rescued his team with injury-time penalty.

Tour International: Wales 20 Argentina 19, Cardiff, 16 October

Bennett's coolness rescues Wales at last gasp

By John Reason

Wales were all but beaten by Argentina at Cardiff Arms Park before Phil Bennett gave them victory with a penalty goal from the last kick of the match in the fifth minute of injury time.

Argentina had recovered from the apparent hopelessness of losing 17-6 in the second half, to the point where they actually regained the lead at 19-17.

The match was already in injury time when Gonzalo Beccar Varela calmly ignored what looked like an old soldier's trick to make him lose concentration, and kicked the penalty goal which put Argentina ahead again.

At that point not many Welshmen would have given much for their country's chances, because the Argentines had played so well in an eventful second half that they had scored two spirited tries, and had heaped all sorts of unaccustomed indignities upon their opponents.

However, the huge centre, Travaglini, foolishly cut down

JPR Williams in midfield with a dangerous high stiff-arm tackle, and Bennett summoned up enough composure to kick the winning goal from 40 yards.

Bennett's task was made crucially easier because the referee, in following Travaglini to lecture him, gave the kick at least six yards nearer the posts than the offence had been committed.

The All Blacks beat Wales when Bennett missed a similar kick in 1972, but he made no mistake this time, and a roar of relief split the skies as Wales scraped home by two tries and four penalty goals to a goal, a try and three penalty goals.

It had been an anxious afternoon for Wales. Argentina led 6-0 in the first half from penalty goals kicked by Porta and Gonzalo Beccar Varela.

It is not often that Gareth Edwards, Bennett and JPR Williams, individually and collectively, are worsted in an international match, but all

three were outplayed by Etchegaray, Porta and Sansot.

Etchegaray did not have quite as much ball to play with at scrum-half as Edwards, but he hardly made a mistake.

The Argentines produced some brilliant counterattacks, and on four occasions they had the Welsh defence all but in ruins when they gave the ball away with wild passes.

No one could have begrudged Argentina victory, because after they had taken the lead initially, Wales had only drawn level with a second penalty goal kicked by Bennett after Wheel had flattened the excellent Fernandez with a punch. It was surprising that the referee did not at least reverse the penalty kick, or even send Wheel off the field.

Tour International: South Africa 15 New Zealand 14, Johannesburg, 18 September

'All Blacks should have won' says Dr Danie Craven

By John Reason

Dr Danie Craven, the President of the South African Rugby Board, and never a man afraid to express an opinion, said unequivocally after this final Test at Ellis Park on Saturday that New Zealand should have won.

Speaking at the reception after the match, he said he had no doubt that the All Blacks should have been awarded a penalty try after Bruce Robertson had been obstructed by the Springbok centre, Johan Oosthuizen, in the second half.

'If ever there was a penalty try, that was one,' said Dr Craven. This unprecedented criticism of an international referee by the most powerful man in South African rugby was thoroughly justified in my view, but it will be scant comfort to the All Blacks.

The New Zealanders now go home having lost the series by three matches to one when, if they had accepted South Africa's offer of neutral referees, they could just as easily have won it by a similar margin.

They were beaten in this match partly by the refereeing and partly by the accurate goal-kicking of Gerald Bosch, who kicked four goals in four attempts as South Africa scored a goal, a dropped goal and two penalty goals.

New Zealand, on the other hand, managed to kick only two goals out of five attempts as they scored two tries, a dropped goal and a penalty goal.

The final Test of this series was, sadly, a game which is becoming all too typical of international rugby. It was a brutally hard, bludgeoning business, repeatedly interrupted by stoppages for deliberately inflicted injuries.

It contained very little movement, the seemingly inevitable fist fight, a disgracefully prolonged affair, and the kicking of goals turned out to be more important than the scoring of tries.

The losers were justifiably incensed by an almost unbelievable refereeing decision. Even so, the All Blacks should have made more of their superiority than they did.

They won enough ball and achieved enough attacking positions to have won the match twice over, but instead of moving the ball quickly to their wings to stretch the Springboks' hopelessly ponderous back-row, they kept bringing it back inside.

The All Blacks should also have been awarded a penalty kick in front of South Africa's posts when Bruce Robertson and Morgan were obstructed as they broke through onto a kick by Bruce.

A penalty goal by Bosch put South Africa ahead 12-11, although it was bitterly contested by the All Blacks. They pointed out that Bush was penalised in trying to stop the Springboks lifting de Klerk.

It was at that point that New Zealand should have been awarded their penalty try. The referee told the All Blacks' captain that he 'did not see it' – though he saw enough to award a penalty kick.

This contradiction left the All Blacks with three points instead of six, because Williams kicked the goal.

For what it is worth, South Africa's final penalty kick at goal was awarded for barging in the line-out. Bosch took it successfully.

1977

15 Jan England's 26-6 victory at Twickenham is their biggest ever over Scotland, while at Cardiff the talk is not about Wales's 25-9 victory, but the sending off by referee Norman Sanson of Irish No.8 Willie Duggan and Welsh second-row forward Geoff Wheel.

19 Mar France beat Ireland 15-6 in Dublin to become the first country to win the Grand Slam with an unchanged side and the first since 1913 to complete the season without conceding a try, while Wales's 18-9 victory at Murrayfield makes them the first country to win the Triple Crown and finish second.

31 May South African domestic records are smashed as Orange Free State beat Eastern Free State 132-3 at Boerbok Park, Senekal, with De Wet Ras amassing 48 points.

2 Jul After six comfortable wins on their short tour of Argentina, including 26-3 in the first Test, France, in their last match, fail to beat the Pumas for the first time, the 18-all draw being described in one French paper with the heading 'Porta 18,

Aguirre 18, Rugby 0', a commentary on a bad-tempered encounter that elicits 37 penalties, the respective place-kickers converting six each.

27 Aug In the match launching the new Loftus Versfeld stadium in Pretoria, South Africa beat a strong World Invitation XV under the captaincy of Willie John McBride 45-24.

10 Sep In a new fixture, rugby's chief contribution to the Queen's Silver Jubilee celebrations, the Barbarians lose 23-14 at Twickenham to the British Isles on their return from New Zealand.

18 Sep Scotland complete their 5-match Far Eastern tour with a 74-9 victory over Japan, their 5th win, Bill Gammell scoring 4 tries and Colin Mair notching 30 points (9C-4PG).

Nov The South African Rugby Board reconstitutes itself under a new format, encompassing itself, the SA Rugby Federation (Coloured) and the SA Rugby Association (Black).

INTERNATIONAL CHAMPIONSHIP

	E	F	I	S	W	P	W	D	L	F	A	Pts
1 FRANCE	-	-	-	23-3	16-9	4	4	0	0	58	21	8
2 WALES	14-9	-	25-9	-	-	4	3	0	1	66	43	6
3 ENGLAND	-	3-4	-	26-6	-	4	2	0	2	42	24	4
4 SCOTLAND	-	-	21-18	-	9-18	4	1	0	3	39	85	2
5 IRELAND	0-4	6-15	-	-	-	4	0	0	4	33	65	0

TOURS (Tests)
British Isles in New Zealand: NZ16-BI12, NZ9-BI13, NZ19-BI7, NZ10-BI9
New Zealand in France: F18-NZ13, F3-NZ15

International Championship: England 3 France 4, Twickenham, 19 February

Disciplined France hang on grimly to beat England

By John Reason

Discipline, self-control and an unyielding defence – qualities not traditionally associated with French rugby – enabled France to beat England in a clamorous, intensely exciting game at Twickenham and take the second step towards the 'grand slam' in the international championships.

The French forwards were outraged to have one after another of their attacking positions lost to an avalanche of penalty kicks as they turned to play down a strong, gusty wind in the second half.

They were even more incensed when England were given penalty kicks at goal in crucial scrummage and ruck situations. Midway through the second half, when England had been given 13 penalty kicks against two to France, the French forwards seemed on the point of mutiny.

Jacques Fouroux, the tiny French captain, more than made up in diplomacy and powers of leadership whatever he may lack in size, and the indignation of his players was slightly mollified by the fact that Alastair Hignell, the England full-back, missed all but one of his six kicks at goal.

Near the end, though, France were so disconcerted and England so encouraged by the turn of events that even with the wind behind them France again had to rely on the strength of their defence to contain a spirited English rally and win by a try to a penalty goal.

France scored their try early in the second half when Hignell dropped the ball after Romeu had kicked ahead from a quick line-out and Beaumont had been dispossessed in the ruck. Fouroux worked the ball to the left, where Averous and Aguirre gave Sangalli the chance to beat Smith and score.

---

7 February

French rule out Sanson as referee

By John Reason

France have not accepted England's nomination of Norman Sanson of Scotland to referee the international match between England and France at Twickenham on Saturday week.

The match will now be refereed by Jeff Kelleher, of Wales.

M Albert Ferrasse, the president of the French Federation, said that as Mr Sanson lived in London, France feared that he might not be impartial. 'We feel his refereeing is too strict, too harsh,' he added.

'He came with us on our tour of South Africa two years ago and awarded so

many penalties that there was hardly any rugby.'

If M Ferrasse has been quoted fairly, this is an extraordinary statement for a man in his position to make. It is not difficult to envisage thoroughly justified outrage, both in the Scottish Rugby Union and in refereeing societies everywhere, followed swiftly by an unreserved apology from the French Federation.

Norman Sanson sent both Geoff Wheel and Willie Duggan off the field for foul play in the match between Wales and Ireland at Cardiff last month.

Tour International: New Zealand 9 British Lions 13, Christchurch, 9 July

Brave Lions triumph in Test brawl to level series

By John Reason

The British Lions simply had to win this second Test match to save the series, and to do it as they did in this implacable city, where they had never won before, gave them a satisfaction beyond words.

Victory tasted even sweeter because it was gained in the face of late tackles and trips,

so disgraceful and so persistent that they could not have been a coincidence, being so obviously aimed at the Lions' most brilliant and most physically vulnerable backs.

Making every tackle count is one thing – that was one of the great strengths of New Zealand's play in the first Test – but going through with

tackles long after the ball has gone is another thing entirely.

Even in the first game of the series in Wellington, when the All Blacks' play was largely above reproach, there were a couple of incidents which left a lingering suspicion that New Zealand wanted to take Phil Bennett and Andy Irvine out of the game by whatever means they could.

Those suspicions were confirmed in a badly refereed match here but, fortunately for Irvine, the All Blacks did not kick well enough to get at him. But they got at Bennett and JJ Williams, and they did it often enough to turn the

match into a brawl as the Lions rushed to retaliate.

By then, though, New Zealand were struggling to retrieve a losing cause, and on a pitch ankle-deep in mud, they found mistakes far easier to make than scores. Scrum-half Sid Going, in particular, made so many expensive mistakes and played such an ill-judged game that he may well have come to the end of his 10-year career as an All Black.

The Lions won by a JJ Williams try and three penalty goals kicked by Bennett to three penalty goals by Bryan Williams.

Tour International: New Zealand 10 British Isles 9, Auckland, 13 August

Lions throw away chance to save series

By John Reason

The British Isles threw away a wonderful chance of winning the final Test at Eden Park and saving the 1977 series against New Zealand.

The Lions' forwards had played so well, and scrum-half Doug Morgan so sensibly to keep them in command, that midway through the second half the game was there for the taking.

At that point, though, the Lions suddenly loosened their grip and abandoned the game that had given them a 9-3 lead. Instead of sticking to their policy of keeping the ball in front of their forwards and kicking for touch, they began some almost suicidal speculations in midfield.

This was quite unnecessary, because the Lions' forwards had control of the line-out. However, Phil Bennett, the Lions' captain, threw out a couple of passes that caused his centres considerable embarrassment and gave renewed life to the All Blacks.

Their forwards had been given the most humiliating pounding, but they hauled themselves off the floor and chased after the Lions in the hope of exploiting a mistake which might give them a chance to save the match.

That mistake was duly made. The All Blacks duly exploited it and in the first of five minutes of injury time, Lawrie Knight, the All Black

Lions scrum-half Doug Morgan, scorer of their try, gets his pass away.

No.8, scored a try which won both the match and the series for New Zealand.

At that point, the British Isles were leading by a goal and a penalty goal to two penalty goals kicked by Bevan Wilson. Knight's final try gave New Zealand victory by one point.

Even then, the Lions nearly won the match, because in the last four minutes they forced an attacking five-yard scrum and then another a yard from the New Zealand line.

On the first occasion, the All Blacks saved themselves only by collapsing the scrum, which is never penalised, as it should be, in New Zealand; and on the second occasion, Andy Irvine, the Lions' full-back, dropped a poor pass in midfield.

The Lions' only try was scored by Morgan after an excellent line-out peel initiated by Duggan was carried to a successful conclusion by Cotton, Beaumont, Price and Fenwick.

Morgan converted the try, and also kicked a penalty goal.

Obituary: 19 September

Sam Doble, man of firm views

By John Mason

Sam Doble, of Moseley, a goal-kicking full-back of immense ability, died in a Birmingham hospital on Saturday after a long illness. He was 33. Though he played only three times for England, he was a regular leading points scorer.

Doble was a splendidly articulate man whose views about the game were as firm and decisive as his goal-kicking. He believed the game was to be enjoyed, and made light of his own ability.

Though it was as a full-back that he will be remembered with sad affection – he scored fourteen points in his first

international when England beat South Africa in Johannesburg in 1972 – Doble could also play wing, centre or outside half.

In student days at St Paul's, Cheltenham, he often appeared at No.8. He was a tall, gangling young man with a mass of fair hair, and was blessed with unusually large feet that suggested clumsiness – until he started running.

Illness struck a year ago and, though it became apparent that recovery was unlikely, Doble carefully maintained his link with Moseley.

Tour International: France 3 New Zealand 15, Paris, 19 November

Accurate kicking levels series for All Blacks

By John Reason

Brian McKechnie and Gary Seear would not exactly leap to mind as match-winning goal-kickers at international level, but the four goals they landed on Saturday enabled New Zealand to give France the slip at Parc des Princes.

Jean-Pierre Romeu, on the other hand, had such a poor day that he kicked only one goal out of five attempts and also for once found himself outmanoeuvred by the touch-kicking and tactical kicking of Doug

Bruce, the All Blacks' fly-half. Bruce kicked so well that the All Blacks were able to keep far closer than is usually possible to the sensible game they had so obviously prepared, and New Zealand sailed home by a goal, a dropped goal and two penalty goals to a penalty goal.

The game was almost exactly the reverse of that in Toulouse last week when France won the first international of the two-match series.

1978

18 Feb Scotland lose 22-14 to Wales, but register their highest ever score in Cardiff.

Mar France are admitted as full members of the International Rugby Football Board.

11 Jun Wales suffer only their second defeat by the Wallabies, their first in Australia, 18-8 at Brisbane.

14 Oct The touring Argentinians hold a strong England XV to a 13-all draw at

Twickenham, their outstanding captain and fly-half Hugo Porta equalising with a penalty goal 10 minutes from no side.

16 Dec The All Blacks, playing carefree rugby for the first time since they suffered their only defeat, at Munster, climax their Grand Slam tour of the British Isles with a thrilling 18-16 win over the Barbarians at Cardiff, Eddie Dunn dropping a goal to snatch victory in the dying seconds.

International Championship: Wales 16 France 7, Cardiff, 18 March

Martin plays key role as Wales land grand slam

By John Reason

Allan Martin played probably his most effective game for Wales, both as line-out jumper and lock, and it was his work, above all others, which enabled his country to beat France at Cardiff on Saturday.

He checked the obvious menace of the French midfield by winning a stream of ball in the first 15 minutes and then, after France had taken a 7-0 lead, he gave Wales the opportunities to make three scores in 10 minutes and win the title and the Grand Slam.

First, Martin helped Wales to wheel a scrum, after France had put the ball in and hooked it 10 yards from their line, and then he fed the ball back from the confusion to put Bennett in for a try which Bennett converted himself.

Then, because of the line-out success he had enjoyed, Martin caught Bastiat in two minds and a long Welsh throw sailed over him to Squire, who knocked the ball down to Price. He gave the ball to Edwards, who dropped a goal.

From the kick-off Edwards kicked into France's left corner, and there Martin won another French throw to set Wales up again.

Gravell attacked the open side, and laid the ball back when he was tackled. Fenwick hesitated, then moved the ball back to the short side, where Edwards made ground before lobbing it out to JJ Williams.

Williams flung the ball back inside as he was swept into touch, and Bennett backed up to score his second try. Martin could not convert, but Wales went on to win by a goal, a try, and two dropped goals to a try and a dropped goal.

Bastiat knocked on a kick-ahead by Gallion with an open field in front of him, and Bustaffa disastrously chose to go inside when he had enough room to go for the corner.

On top of all that, France missed seven kicks at goal – four of them quite easy – and their tactical kicking was deplorable.

Romeu, the deposed French fly-half and goal-kicker, sat in the North Stand and watched it all with a rueful smile. The point was rubbed in even more unkindly by the obvious relish Bennett and Edwards took from the superiority of their kicking.

International Championship: Ireland 16 Wales 20, Dublin, 4 March

Welsh spirit takes them to remarkable treble

By John Mason

The indelible mark of this remarkable Welsh side is the priceless ability to go on creating scoring opportunities irrespective of opposition pressure and, on Saturday in Dublin, uncharacteristic errors in their own ranks.

The magnitude of the achievement in becoming the first country to win the Triple Crown three years in succession would be difficult to exaggerate. To continue winning means many things – consistency, of course, though I prefer heart and spirit.

Ireland came at Wales with a ferocious relish which, from the safety of the stand, was marvellous to see. At closer quarters other views prevail, for a couple of Welsh voices sounded askance later. Distinguished former players present also winced.

Yet if there was a degree of sourness, most of it arose late in the first half after a delayed body-check on Gibson by JPR Williams. Referee Domercq took no action, presumably because he was following the ball that Gibson had kicked.

Gibson was groggy from that point, and twice had attention, though he stayed on

the pitch. Each time JPR was in possession thereafter he was roundly booed, the crowd relenting only a fraction in the final minutes.

The barrage had its effect. JPR made errors, the like of which might be par for the course for lesser individuals but not for him. He was at fault initially when Ireland scored their try, and there were other mistakes that could have forced Wales off their determined course to another victory.

To have beaten Ireland by two tries and four penalty goals to a try, dropped goal and three penalty goals may not have been the jewel in the Crown, but it was a cornerstone of near excellence, of authority, of teamwork – and all mostly shaped by Edwards.

When for a while – the scores were level for more than 20 minutes in the second half – the possibility of an Irish surge for victory was not moonshine, Edwards was superb. His brain, agility and strength were all shrewdly employed. And he declined to be rattled, despite the constant attentions of the dogged Slattery.

Allan Martin (second from right) in the thick of the action.

INTERNATIONAL CHAMPIONSHIP

	E	F	I	S	W	P	W	D	L	F	A	Pts
1 WALES	-	16-7	-	22-14	-	4	4	0	0	67	43	8
2 FRANCE	15-6	-	10-9	-	-	4	3	0	1	51	47	6
3 ENGLAND	-	-	15-9	-	6-9	4	2	0	2	42	33	4
4 IRELAND	-	-	-	12-9	16-20	4	1	0	3	46	54	2
5 SCOTLAND	0-15	16-19	-	-	-	4	0	0	4	39	68	0

TOURS (Tests)

Wales in Australia: A18-W8, A19-W17
Australia in New Zealand: NZ13-A12, NZ22-A6, NZ16-A30
New Zealand in British Isles: I6-NZ10, W12-NZ13, E6-NZ16, S9-NZ18

Tour International: Australia 19 Wales 17, Sydney, 17 June

'Thugs' outburst by Rowlands

By John Mason

The unacceptable face of rugby violence was scathingly condemned by Clive Rowlands, the manager of Wales, in a dinner speech at the Randwick Club in Sydney on Saturday evening. His words were echoed by Bill McLaughlin, the Australian RU president.

Amid the normal pleasantries of these occasions and the sundry presentations that mark the final night of a tour, Mr Rowlands paused dramatically, then said:

'If I've got something on my mind, I say it. I have no wish to offend, but if I've a complaint to make, I'll make it – as I've done previously. I will never condone thuggery.

'One of my players is tonight in a Sydney hospital with a double fracture of the jaw. If we rugby people condone thuggery, then I want no part of it.'

These firm words, which later Mr McLaughlin, who had spoken first, announced that he entirely endorsed, were prompted by an incident in the third minute when, the ball won and Wales attempting to counter a high short kick ahead by McLean, Graham Price, the Welsh tight-head, was felled by a blow from behind.

The punch that broke Price's jaw was not seen by the referee, who correctly was following the ball. As the scrum was breaking up and the bulk of forwards were turning at the time, not all the players were absolutely certain what had happened.

No one in Australia's team on Saturday has been left out of the Wallaby party to tour New Zealand next month. But one member of that party, without doubt, hit Price from behind as he levered himself from his scrummaging position. To identify the culprit would be legally unwise, though the tourists have no reservations among themselves. Nor, I imagine, have many Australians.

Tour International: New Zealand 16 Australia 30, Auckland, 9 September

All Blacks hit by 5 Wallaby tries – record 4 by No. 8

By John Reason

John Hipwell, Australia's former captain who was flown out to join the team as a replacement scrum-half, combined shrewdly with another replacement player, fly-half Tony Melrose, in Australia's extraordinary 30-16 victory over the New Zealand All Blacks in the final Test in Auckland.

New Zealand won the three-match series 2-1, thanks to scraping home 13-12 in a controversial game in the first Test, but they were shattered when Australia scored five tries in the last game of the series. This was the first time the All Blacks have conceded five tries in a Test since the visit of the 1937 Springboks, and it shook their selectors as they sat down to choose the team for their tour of Britain, starting next month.

Greg Cornelsen, one of the Wallabies' loose forwards, scored four of Australia's five tries. This must have delighted his coach, Daryl Haberecht, who was 250 miles away in Wanganui recovering from a heart attack.

Tour match: Munster 12 New Zealanders 0, Limerick, 31 October

All Blacks legend is shattered by Ward and Munster

By John Mason

Large, craggy Irishmen – and small ones, too – were crying at Thomond Park, Limerick, yesterday. They were shedding tears of absolute joy in praise of the red-blooded deeds of 15 Munstermen, the first team to beat New Zealand in Ireland's history.

Not in their most extravagant of dreams beforehand did they seriously believe that Munster would succeed where every other representative Irish side since 1905 had failed.

Yesterday, at 4.34pm, those fond, hazy notions had become legendary truth. Munster beat the 1978 All Blacks by a goal and two dropped goals to nil, the first side to do so on this tour, and, for Ireland alone, etch their names in rugby's history books.

The All Blacks were unstinting in congratulations. 'Every man against us,' said Russ Thomas, the manager, 'lifted their game and kept it that way. I sincerely congratulate every one of them.'

The essence of victory was swift, shattering tackling. Even if gaps were prised open, mostly by Donaldson or Jaffray, another wave of defenders descended to rattle every bone in All Black bodies. That done, the ball was put on the ground and kept there.

Barrett, Dennison and the back row tackled everything that moved with fearsome relish. Often they went in so strongly that they were bruised and dazed in the process, but they went on and on doing so.

They had to, because for all the resolution of the others – especially Canniffe, the captain and scrum-half who must have played the game of his life – Munster would have been swamped. The All Blacks had sufficient possession to score a pile of tries but were not allowed to use it.

But – and there is an important 'but' which has to be noted – the All Blacks will not, I imagine, be awarding plus marks to Corris Thomas, the Welsh referee, who was inordinately generous in some areas, notably at the ruck and in sundry aspects of the offside law.

That said, the applause for Munster must ring out. The machine-gun staccato blasts of 'Mun-ster, Mun-ster' fuelled sore, weary bodies and inspired, in the final minutes, outside-half Ward, who was magnificent. It was the All Blacks who were stumbling, grey and tired.

[This was New Zealand's only defeat in 18 matches, the other 17 won.]

Tour International: Scotland 9 New Zealand 18, Murrayfield, 9 December

All Blacks write Grand Slam into tour history

By John Reason

New Zealand were defending for their lives to stop Scotland making a score either to draw or win this match at Murrayfield when right at the end they charged down a drop at goal by Ian McGeechan and hacked the ball the length of the slippery, rain-soaked field.

Bruce Robertson showed remarkable stamina and speed to outstrip the Scottish cover over the last 50 yards and slithered between the posts to score a try which Brian McKechnie converted.

That score, made in conditions of such gloom and rain that it looked as if the day of judgment had come, gave New Zealand victory by two goals and two penalties to a goal and a drop goal.

New Zealand thus beat all four of the home countries for the first time in their history.

1979

3 Feb Ireland register their highest score in Wales, but go down 24-21 at Cardiff.

16 Jul Flushed with their history-making victory in Auckland, France pop in to Papeete on their way home and beat Tahiti 92-12, Averous scoring 7 of their 20 tries.

1 Sep Argentina make it 4 wins out of 4 on their first tour of New Zealand, beating Bay of Plenty 32-12, with their splendid fly-half Hugo Porta contributing 20 (1C-3DG-3PG). [The Pumas go on to finish their tour with 6 wins and 3 defeats, including both internationals, with Porta scoring 84 of their 165 points. Porta plays in all 9 matches over 28 days and notches 10 drop goals.]

27 Oct It's that man Porta again, the Argentinian captain kicking 16 points, including another 3 drop goals, as the Pumas beat Australia 24-13 at Buenos Aires on the Wallabies' first visit to Argentina. [This is Australia's only defeat on their 7-match tour, and they tie the series with a 17-12 victory in the second international.]

16 Dec Beziers beat Montchanin 100-0, running in 21 tries, both French Club Championship records, while Michel Fabre's 11 tries is a world record for a first-class club match.

International Championship: Wales 27 England 3, Cardiff, 17 March

Wales crowned champions as England collapse

By John Reason

Wales took full advantage of a pathetic collapse in the England defence in the last 20 minutes to score 20 points and win both the Triple Crown and the international championship at Cardiff Arms Park.

This is the fourth year in succession that Wales have won the Triple Crown, which is a record, and they were helped to the championship by the resolution that England displayed and the good fortune they enjoyed when they beat France a fortnight ago.

Neither that resolution nor that fortune ever attended England's efforts in Cardiff, where for more than an hour they looked a thoroughly poor side playing one which was only marginally better.

At that stage the two sides had missed 11 kicks at goal between them, and Wales led narrowly by seven points to three. It could have been more, but Richards knocked on when he had only to catch the ball to score a try.

What is more, Wales had lost their captain, JPR Williams, with a gashed leg – and for the first and only time in the match England were attacking with enough spirit to create two scoring chances.

The almost inane way the England backs missed those chances, and the embarrassing poverty of their play immediately afterwards, settled the match psychologically.

The Welsh forwards squared their shoulders as if to say, 'Well, if they can't score from chances like those, they never will'; and the English forwards resigned themselves to the conclusion that their backs simply were not worth playing for anyway.

From that point Wales never looked back and picked up four of the easiest tries imaginable to win by two goals, three tries and a dropped goal to a penalty goal.

The championship table makes its own merciless comment on England's back play and goal-kicking. Even wooden-spoonists Scotland scored twice as many points.

[Despite an off-day with his goal-kicking – he missed 5 penalties – Bridgend centre three-quarter Steve Fenwick (pictured) converted a try with the last kick of the game to score the 2 points he needed to equal the International Championship record of 38 in a season, jointly held by R W Hosen (England, 1966-67), P Bennett (Wales, 1975-76) and AJP Ward (Ireland, 1977-78).]

John Player Cup Final: Leicester 15 Moseley 12, Twickenham, 21 April

Leicester squeeze through as Hare opens the door

By John Reason

Leicester came back to snatch victory in the last five minutes after being outplayed by Moseley for the first hour of an absorbing, spirited John Player Cup final.

Moseley, leading 12-6, missed a crucial penalty goal midway through the second half and then 'Dusty' Hare, the Leicester full-back, nibbled another three points out of the Moseley lead with his calm, precise goal-kicking.

That encouraged Leicester to raise their game and five minutes from the end Steve Kenney ran from a five-yard scrum to score a try. Hare converted to give last year's beaten finalists victory by a goal, two penalty goals and a dropped goal to a goal, a penalty goal and a dropped goal.

Moseley lost Barrie Corless and Derek Nutt through injury but had only themselves to blame for failing to put the issue beyond doubt in the first half and for failing to shut the door in Leicester's face in the last 20 minutes.

Tour International: Australia 12 Ireland 27, Brisbane, 3 June

Campbell answers critics

Ollie Campbell, Ireland's controversial replacement for fly-half Tony Ward, vindicated his selection by scoring 19 points as the Irish beat Australia 27-12 in the first Test in Brisbane yesterday. Campbell kicked four penalty goals, two conversions and a drop goal during the match.

Australia led 12-9 at half-time, but two tries in the second half by half-back Colin Patterson, and the accuracy of Campbell's boot, sent the tourists racing to victory.

Australia's points came from a try by winger Brendan Moon and two penalties and a conversion by fly-half Paul McLean.

A magnificent forward effort, with the help of Patterson's tigerish defence around the scrum and tactical kicking, gave Ireland the edge. They built their attack on 10-man rugby, rarely letting the ball out to the centres, while Australia ran the ball at every opportunity and, according to coach Dave Brockhoff, may have overdone it.

[Ireland won the international series 2-0 and lost only one of their 8 matches, 16-12 to Sydney.]

INTERNATIONAL CHAMPIONSHIP

	E	F	I	S	W	P	W	D	L	F	A	Pts
1 WALES	27-3	-	24-21	-	-	4	3	0	1	83	51	6
2 FRANCE	-	-	-	21-17	14-13	4	2	1	1	50	46	5
3 IRELAND	12-7	9-9	-	-	-	4	1	2	1	53	51	4
4 ENGLAND	-	7-6	-	7-7	-	4	1	1	2	24	52	3
5 SCOTLAND	-	-	11-11	-	13-19	4	0	2	2	48	58	2

TOURS (Tests)
Ireland in Australia: A12-I27, A3-I9
France in New Zealand: NZ23-F9, NZ19-F24
New Zealand in Australia: A12-NZ6
New Zealand in British Isles: S6-NZ20, E9-NZ10

Tour International: New Zealand 19 France 24, Auckland, 14 July

Bastille Day victory for France, but South Africa ban 'likely'

Yves Noe, manager of the French team in New Zealand, said in Auckland on Saturday night he did not believe his government would allow South Africa to make their scheduled tour of France later this year.

M Noe was speaking after France's magnificent 24-19 victory over the All Blacks at Eden Park in their last match in New Zealand.

The victory, on France's national holiday, Bastille Day, squared the two-Test series, New Zealand having won 23-9 in Christchurch the previous Saturday. Jerome Gallion justified his return to the side by scoring the first try; Alain Caussade, Averous and Codorniou scored the others, while Caussade added a dropped goal and a conversion and Jean-Michel Aguirre a penalty.

Stu Wilson and Graham Mourie scored tries for the All Blacks. Bevan Wilson added three penalties and a conversion.

[This was the first French side to taste international victory in New Zealand.]

Tour International: Australia 12 New Zealand 6, Sydney, 28 July

McLean sinks All Blacks

The New Zealand All Blacks went down to their first defeat in Australia since 1934 when they lost by 12 points to six in a torrid Test on Saturday.

A crowd of nearly 33,000 saw an absorbing struggle in which neither side managed to break through for a try, but Australian full-back Paul McLean landed three vital penalty goals from four attempts to clinch the issue. Tony Melrose showed remarkable maturity for a 19-year-old and his magnificent all-round display was capped with a finely angled drop goal during the first half.

The All Blacks' points were scored by full-back Bevan Wilson, who landed a penalty goal, and centre Murray Taylor, who dropped a goal.

Tour match: Newport 21 South African Barbarians 15, Rodney Parade, 27 October

Newport revival shatters tourists

By Arthurian

Newport ended their long sequence of 18 matches without victory by defeating the touring South African Barbarians in an excellent and often exciting match at Rodney Parade. A few hundred demonstrators outside the ground did not disturb the day and the tour ended in a triumph for the organisers and the tourists.

The match was watched by the South African Ambassador, Dawie de Villiers, a former Springbok captain. For Newport it was something similar to the Relief of Mafeking following their many months in the bondage of defeat at home and abroad.

Although the Barbarians scored three tries against two, it was only the goal-kicking in support of good forward play that carried the day for Newport, who eventually won by two goals and three penalties to three tries and one penalty.

Tour International: Wales XV 13 Rumania 12, Cardiff, 6 October

Proud Rumanians make their point against Wales

By John Mason

Viorel Morariu, the Rumanian tour manager, cheerfully declined to agree that he was disappointed with his country's single-point defeat by a Wales XV at Cardiff on Saturday. On the contrary, he said, he was proud.

The urbane, courteous Mr Morariu, who is also vice-president of the Rumanian Rugby Federation, congratulated Wales, fly-half Gareth Davies in particular, and looked forward to a time when there would be a Rugby Union World Cup.

Any lingering doubts about the rugby standing of the Rumanians were dispelled during an absorbing contest in which Wales had to play uncommonly well at times to ensure victory.

Remarkable resilience, organisation and spirit brought Wales, twice behind, a commendable win by a try, penalty goal and two dropped goals to a goal and two penalty goals – an impressive performance at this point of the season. Davies, besides dropping the goals, had an essential part in the build-up to the try. Morgan and Griffiths, the scorer, were major figures as well, but without Davies the attack would not have succeeded.

Rumania's try by Ionescu, cleverly shaped by the hooker Munteanu and Dumitru, was a beauty, and the thunderous goal-kicking of Constantin also helped to set up the distinct possibility of a magnificent victory. The astute Davies had other ideas.

Tour International: England 9 New Zealand 10, Twickenham, 24 November

Inhibited England bow to typical All Black grit

By John Mason

Within the scope of a limited tactical scheme, England's best was not good enough at Twickenham on Saturday. New Zealand, operating from a similarly restricted base, were a fraction better, the prize being victory by a point.

England might have sneaked a win had Hare kicked a fourth penalty goal with about 15 minutes remaining. No matter how welcome that would have been to Englishmen, it would not have been the right result.

By winning a drab, gritty, bitty contest by a try and two penalty goals to three penalty goals, New Zealand demonstrated their relentless driving determination at this level that enables them to disguise weaknesses which would undermine lesser teams.

England have to make and mend as well. But, for all their experience in this respect, their cobbling cannot always take the strain. They did not come apart at the seams, nor did they greatly alarm fairly ordinary opposition.

In Cusworth, the new outside half, England possess a footballer with much the same merits as Dunn, the All Black. New Zealand, apprehensive at what had happened the previous Saturday against the North at Otley, decided they had to do without Dunn.

England decided beforehand that they would kick for position, play tight to the forwards wherever possible, and attack from the 22 metres line. Cusworth's elusiveness at close quarters, it was felt, would be a further bonus.

In the event New Zealand (notably Taylor) kicked much better at halfback than England – and that is a relative statement because some of the kicking by both sides was downright poor. Too often the exchanges were stilted, wooden and muddled.

Scorers: England – Hare 3 penalty goals; New Zealand – R Wilson 2 penalty goals, Fleming try.

The 1980s

The great metamorphosis of rugby union began in the late 1980s, as growing commercialism accelerated the march of professionalism. A hugely successful first World Cup in 1987 and the proliferation of club leagues took rugby into a new and exciting era, but at the same time ensured that it would never be the same again.

The RFU, Canute-like, trying to stem the tide, were themselves largely responsible for the situation in England – an expansion of international and major club fixtures that made it increasingly impossible for the leading players to hold down a job while producing the standard of fitness and form required in what was rapidly becoming a big-money sport. Training hard perhaps five or six days a week is not conducive to the amateur status. Nor is the knowledge of huge sums of money pouring through the turnstiles or being channelled into the sport by eager sponsors. The players were bound to want a slice of the action. They were already getting it, by no means furtively, in the Southern Hemisphere. The push began in the Home Unions for a relaxation in the draconian amateur laws, at least to allow players to profit from ancillary activities such as writing and personal appearances.

The first serious moves towards such a revolution had been taken at the end of the 1982-83 season, when two prominent former England players, Bill Beaumont the captain, who had just retired, and Fran Cotton announced that they intended to accept royalties from books. This inevitably meant their exclusion from the 'administration, organisation or control of rugby football'.

The following season, while playing down persistent and loud rumours of 'boot money' – the surreptitious payment of players by manufacturers for wearing particular boots or other kit – as 'bar-room gossip', the RFU continued to encourage rampant commercialism in rugby by offering hospitality suites at Twickenham and courting sponsors like mad. At the same time, in France, a miserable turn-out (6,000) in Paris for the visit of an exciting Barbarians side to celebrate Racing Club's centenary convinced the French Union that the public wanted structured league or cup competition, and they immediately decided to install the latter kind – with 512 clubs – for 1983-84.

As Wales fell off their seventies pedestal and entered a long period in the wilderness, England flattered briefly to deceive at the start of the eighties, when Bill Beaumont led them to a famous Grand Slam. It was their last sniff of the championship for the rest of the decade, in which France won the title outright three times, including two Grand Slams,

and shared in another three. In 1984 Scotland won their first Grand Slam for 59 years, and Ireland's two championships (1982 and 1985) featured their first Triple Crowns since 1949.

England did enjoy one other triumph in the eighties, the defeat of New Zealand at Twickenham in 1983, albeit after Scotland had held the All Blacks to a draw in what was a hastily arranged short tour with a below-strength team. Still, it was some sort of revenge for the Lions' 4-0 whitewash in New Zealand earlier in the year.

In 1985 the International Board finally woke up to the fact that there were now more than a hundred countries playing rugby union and they set up a category of associate membership. They also took the momentous decision to organise a World Cup, a defensive but wise move, according to many commentators, to pre-empt the possible hijacking of world rugby by commercial interests setting up a pirate version.

The mid-eighties saw Australia begin to emerge as a force in world rugby, blessed as they were with the exceptional and unorthodox talents of wing three-quarter David Campese and an inspirational fly-half in Mark Ella. Whereas the 1982 Wallabies to the British Isles had beaten only Ireland, the 1984 tourists swept away each international side in turn to become the first Australians to achieve that particular Grand Slam.

But what of the game in the Home Unions? That Australian success had to be qualified, such was the state of British rugby. John Mason began his 1983 report on the John Player Cup final in *The Daily Telegraph*: 'After an English season of unacceptable muddle and misdirection, Bristol and Leicester . . . presented a timely reminder that a major rugby occasion does not have to be drab and cheerless, settled by whatever goal-kicking is permitted by a referee seizing upon some obscure technicality. The match will have served, too, as a handsome rebuke to that austere, ungenerous section within the game who believe that winning is everything and failure a heinous crime.' Strong stuff.

And John Reason's views on the state of British rugby emerged clearly in his comments in June 1986 on encroaching professionalism in the Southern Hemisphere:

'I have no doubt that the splitting of the game into two halves is fast approaching – a split to separate the Home Unions and what might be called the Away Unions. France are considering a French Barbarians tour of South Africa later this year. Australia and New Zealand, too, are sympathetic. It goes without saying that the strength of the Away Unions is that

Leading from the front: Bill Beaumont captained England to a memorable Grand Slam, clinched in style at Murrayfield.

they can play rugby football vastly better than the Home Unions, who cannot play the game for toffee, and who have little prospect of improving because the teaching of the game in our schools has been shot to pieces. It is most certainly not a time for the Home Unions to try to wave a big stick. To start with they do not have one, and the Board bye-laws do not provide them with one.'

Obviously, the continued absence from the international scene of the Springboks was proving an embarrassment for the IB. After the visit of the Lions and France to South Africa in 1980 and Ireland in 1981, the Springboks made their only tour of the decade, to New Zealand in 1981, and this was dogged by anti-apartheid demonstrations, with violence erupting outside the grounds at the three Tests. Even in the United States, where they played three matches on their way home, the Springboks were hounded from pillar to post by protesters. There was nowhere else for them to go. They entertained one

more touring party, England in 1984, before suffering complete isolation.

South Africa's need for international competition spawned rebel tours. Only money could provide the competition they craved. And as John Reason said, 'The [1986] tour of South Africa by Andy Dalton's New Zealand Cavaliers was professional from beginning to end.' It was blatantly obvious that players for this and a World XV tour in 1989 were 'bought in'. Yet a spineless, irresolute International Board still allowed them to remain in membership. As one delegate to a Board meeting in 1987 put it, 'There was a great deal of sympathy for the situation in which South Africa find themselves, of having probably the best rugby team in the world and not enough teams to play.' This, after New Zealand had won the first World Cup.

Certainly, the writing was on the wall for amateurism. But rugby would enter a new decade before 'bar-room gossip' became fact.

1980

2 Feb England owe their 17-13 victory over France, their first in Paris for 16 years and their first at the Parc des Princes, largely to the sheer dominance of their pack, in which Beaumont and Scott are outstanding.

3 May Richmond beat Rosslyn Park 34-18 in the final to win the Middlesex Sevens for the 5th time in 7 years and equal Harlequins' overall tally of 8 wins in the tournament.

20 Sep Thanks largely to 24 points from full-back Roger Blyth (3T-3C-2PG) on his retirement from top rugby, Wales (not awarding caps) open the WRU Centenary celebrations with a 32-25 victory at Cardiff over an Overseas XV made up of players from countries outside the International Board that have played against Wales.

8 Nov Despite 3 good wins on their 4-match tour of South Africa, France's 37-15 defeat by the Springboks at Pretoria in the only Test prompts John Reason of The Daily Telegraph to describe them as the worst French team he has seen.

29 Nov Wales-England beat Scotland-Ireland 37-33 in the Welsh RU Centenary match, producing a vastly entertaining spectacle at Cardiff for the Queen and Prince Philip, who see the glorious Gaels defeated by a Gareth Davies try in the final seconds.

INTERNATIONAL CHAMPIONSHIP

	E	F	I	S	W	P	W	D	L	F	A	Pts
1 ENGLAND	-	24-9	-	9-8		4	4	0	0	80	48	8
2=WALES	-	18-9	-	17-6	-	4	2	0	2	50	45	4
2=IRELAND	-	-	22-15	21-7		4	2	0	2	70	65	4
4 FRANCE	13-17	-	19-18	-	-	4	1	0	3	55	75	2
5 SCOTLAND	18-30	22-14	-	-	-	4	1	0	3	61	83	2

TOURS (Tests)
British Isles in South Africa: SA26-BI22, SA26-BI19, SA12-BI10, SA13-BI17
New Zealand in Australia: A13-NZ9, A9-NZ12, A26-NZ10
New Zealand in Wales: W3-NZ23
France in South Africa: SA37-F15

International Championship: England 9 Wales 8, Twickenham, 16 February

Brutality scars rugby's image as England head for 'slam'

By John Mason

England's victory over Wales by three goals to two tries was as miserable an advertisement for rugby football as the triumph of Scotland over France was encouraging. Success on a major sporting occasion need not equate with a degrading war of attrition.

Goodness knows what the uninitiated made of it or schoolboys newly introduced to the game (or their mothers, come to that). Goodness knows what the knowledgeable made of it. Too many people concerned have cause to be ashamed.

It was gratifying yesterday morning that the newly constituted disciplinary procedures were swiftly and sensibly carried through and that the decision of David Burnett, the referee, to send off Paul Ringer, for a late and dangerous tackle, hand and fingers extended, on Horton, was vigorously upheld .

Mr Burnett twice spoke to the captains, the first time after five minutes when he warned them about incidents of foul play. Still the nastiness simmered and the rugby suffered. So, too, did Wales in a match of 34 penalties.

As Wales received only a third of those awards and as the match hinged upon penalty goals, the last of which Hare kicked in the 41st minute of the second half, the only inference can be that the wounds to Welsh pride were self-inflicted.

That they were the better team was patently obvious. With 14 men for all but 13 minutes of 87 minutes 10 seconds' playing time, they out-thought and out-fought England and, to boot, scored two tries by turning opposition errors to rich profit.

International Championship: Scotland 18 England 30, Murrayfield, 15 March

Bold approach pays off as England achieve crowning glory

By John Mason

Boldness was England's friend at Murrayfield on Saturday. Victory over Scotland, as exciting as it was sweet, brought an avalanche of titles, of praise, and sincere congratulations from all opponents in the championship.

After two barren decades, the Red Rose of England for at least the next 10 months signifies Grand Slam winners, international champions and possession of the Triple Crown – achievements last gained en bloc 23 years ago.

On the fraternal front, the win by two goals, three tries and two penalty goals to two goals and two penalty goals permitted England to retain the Calcutta Cup in the 96th match with Scotland. It was a pleasure to be present.

Scotland, sagging at 0-16 after half an hour, and no better off at 3-19 by half-time, contributed wholeheartedly with a disregard for the possible pitfalls throughout a breathtaking second half. There were leaden England legs long before the finish.

In a bewildering build-up to the first try by Scotland, the ball was handled 14 times. No matter the forcefulness of England's tackling, possession was retained and even as, in the last stride, Renwick was held, Tomes, a lock, accepted the scoring pass.

Irrespective, though, of the compliments directed towards Scotland, the hymns and arias this time belong to England, to the players, the selectors and to that anonymous, patient and well-behaved band of loyal supporters. They were entitled to be vociferous.

Bill Beaumont, England's captain, who today, I trust, will be hurrying back to Edinburgh to attend his first Press conference as captain of the 1980 British Lions, politely decries suggestions that his leadership has taken England to the pinnacle long occupied by Wales. Modestly aware that the forwards allowed Woodward and Dodge, Horton and Hare, Carleton and Slemen, to undermine Scotland still further in a marvellous first half for England, Beaumont, has no illusions. He knows England played poorly against Wales – but they won.

Carleton's three tries, a figure only four players in England's history have exceeded in an international, were sensible examples of forthright, effective wing three-quarter play. The preliminaries satisfactorily set up, the speeding Carleton, having dropped his first pass, did the rest.

Woodward's balanced running and footwork, worthy of Jim Watt, enabled Slemen to score on the left. Hare's difficult conversion from the touchline took England to 12-0. Carleton's second try followed and still Scotland had had no ball to speak of.

England controlled scrum, ruck, maul, ruined Scotland's heel and permitted a miserlike parity at the line-out. Scotland's most useful possession in that period was a rebound from a post as Hare, now an astute international, missed a penalty.

The advance Scotland made indirectly led to Irvine's penalty goal which began his country's scoring. Hare, who landed two penalties, cancelled that out and at 19-3, England could decently wonder only what the eventual margin might be.

Scotland came to a similar conclusion, the outcome being a second half of sustained excitement and running. Carleton and Smith, helped importantly by Uttley and Scott, scored England tries. Tomes and the elusive Rutherford crossed for Scotland, Irvine kicking the conversions and a penalty.

England skipper Bill Beaumont is carried from the field shoulder high after his team had clinched the Grand Slam.

Tour Match: South African Invitation XV 19 British Lions 22, Potchefstroom, 21 May

Superb Slemen seals it for Lions

By John Mason

A try, the like of which cannot have been scored in a major match since the glorious encounter between the Barbarians and the All Blacks in 1973, saved the British Lions from defeat at the Olen Stadium, Potchefstroom, yesterday. The thunderclaps of applause re-echoed for minutes.

Those present had witnessed a sizeable slice of instant rugby football history. An unbroken bit of play, lasting 2 minutes 46 seconds, which included three rucks and 33 passes, ended in Mike Slemen scoring close to the posts for Clive Woodward to convert.

At least 10 players took part, apart from those involved in the rucks, several handling twice and some three times.

The distance covered is difficult to gauge because of the zig-zag approach and because once the opposition almost broke the rhythm by fly-kicking downfield. A conservative guess, however, would be twice the length of the pitch.

I must record also that as Hay finally fed Slemen for the last surge diagonally towards the post, this impartial critic leapt to his feet bawling approval. For the last 35 seconds the only entry in my notebook was an illegible squiggle.

As thumping hearts subsided, one realised that the Lions had established a vital psychological advantage with victory by a goal, a try and four penalty goals to a try and five penalty goals. The Invitation team were no mugs.

Tour International: Australia 26 New Zealand 10, Sydney, 12 July

Australia triumph by record margin

A devastating display by their back line swept Australia to a record 26-10 win over New Zealand in the third and deciding rugby union Test in Sydney on Saturday.

Australia won by four tries to one to achieve their biggest winning margin against the All Blacks and clinch their first home series triumph against New Zealand since 1934. Among the Australian heroes was Queensland winger Peter Grigg, who scored two tries on his Test debut, after being called in as a late replacement for the injured Mick Martin.

Australia's other points came from tries by Michael O'Connor and Peter Carson, two conversions and a penalty by Roger Gould and a dropped goal by Mark Ella. For New Zealand Bernie Fraser scored a try and Brett Codlin kicked two penalties.

Fourth Test: South Africa 13 British Isles 17, Pretoria, 12 July

O'Driscoll saves Lions pride from Test whitewash

By John Mason

The 1980 British Lions paraded a fair sample of their Jekyll and Hyde characteristics before winning the fourth Test against South Africa at Loftus Versfeld on Saturday.

Victory by a goal, two tries and a penalty goal to a try and three penalty goals was a tantalising glimpse of what might have been – should have been – in a remarkable series that the Springboks won by three matches to one.

It is impossible to quarrel with the overall result. South Africa won the international rubber, the yardstick by which a tour these days is judged, because they capitalised on opposition error and accepted most scoring chances presented – 11 to 7 in tries.

Only on Saturday did Beaumont's men make better use of opportunities created. They also kept South Africa on the retreat, front and back.

Yet, though South Africa looked a limited side in several areas, the spirit, initiative and opportunism that have decorated their efforts since May 31 in Cape Town, allowed them to greatly trouble the Lions.

The Lions, mind you, did co-operate generously. Despite immense forward superiority, muddling, mistakes and selfishness combined to suggest that for the first time in an international series in South Africa, the British Isles would go down 4-0.

Ultimately, the efforts of O'Driscoll, Robbie and Beaumont ensured that rugby logic prevailed and that the better team got back on course. The match-winning try came after Irvine, having ignored an overlap, was ankle-tapped by Pienaar. The ball was re-won and Robbie, Campbell twice, and Gravell set O'Driscoll surging for the posts for Campbell to convert.

Tour International: Wales 3 New Zealand 23, Cardiff, 1 November

Superb All Blacks trounce Wales in awesome display

By John Mason

Though the centenary celebrations were never likely to involve the heady delights of victory over New Zealand, there were few dissenting voices in Cardiff on Saturday. In defeat Wales acknowledged gracefully that they were outplayed.

The performance of the All Blacks, whose mix of individual and team skills stretched Wales to breaking point, was as awesome and inspiring as logic beforehand dictated it would be.

Sporting excellence comprises many factors. Not the least must be an easy command of basic requirements that eliminates needless error – the not-always-easy business of doing the simple things well.

In 15 days in Wales the tourists beat Cardiff, Llanelli, Swansea, Newport and the national team, scoring 16 tries.

At Swansea and again on Saturday at the National Stadium, New Zealand set standards no side in the world could have matched. Victory by two goals, two tries and a penalty goal to a penalty goal in the centenary international, sponsored by Crown Paints, pointed to the running sores endemic to parts of the game in Britain. There were lessons to be re-absorbed.

New Zealand do not kick away reasonable possession; they are not obsessed by the scrummage; forwards do not dominate the tactical approach; movement of the ball, and speed to it, are paramount; support play is supreme.

These qualities, unencumbered by the footling formations and complex complications that pass for back play in Britain, made an already auspicious occasion notable in the extreme. Nor need Welshmen mope, because many of the team did not cease in efforts to keep the ship afloat.

Holmes at all times was a massive comfort, but the support he got was flimsy in comparison.

1981

30 May Centre three-quarter Errol Tobias, who went to South America with the 1980 Springboks, becomes the first non-white player to be capped for South Africa in a full international when he plays in the first Test against Ireland, at Cape Town.

6 Jun Fly-half Naas Botha scores 3 drop goals and a penalty – all South Africa's points – in their 12-10 victory over Ireland to give the Springboks a somewhat fortuitous 2-0 series win.

6 Jun England beat Argentina 12-6 in Buenos Aires to take the international series 1-0, with one drawn, Rafter shackling Hugo Porta so efficiently that it had an effect on the great man's kicking.

26 Sep Romania's match with Scotland at Murrayfield is their first official international against a Home Union, a 12-6 defeat in which all the points are from penalty kicks, Irvine's 4 out of 4 enabling him to overtake the world record 207 held by Don Clarke (NZ).

26 Sep After their stormy passage through New Zealand, where their tour was dogged by anti-apartheid demos, the Springboks meet with much of the same when they play three games in the USA on their way home, the last, a representative match against the USA, having to be secretly moved (even the Press are not informed) to a hastily converted polo field in Glenville, NY, where a handful of spectators see them beat the USA 38-7.

24 Oct Playing two matches in Romania prior to their tour of France, the All Blacks win their first recognised international against the Romanians, who nevertheless enhance their growing reputation in defeat (14-6).

21 Nov The All Blacks beat France for the second Saturday in a row, to win the series 2-0, an impressive 18-6 victory against formidable opponents underlining the supremacy of New Zealand rugby. For Graham Mourie, it is his 11th successive victory in Europe as captain of the All Blacks, a sequence that began in Paris four years ago.

8 Dec Cambridge win the 100th University Match 9-6 on a blanket of snow at Twickenham to record their 44th victory and lead the series for the first time.

International Championship: England 12 France 16, Twickenham, 21 March

French masters leave no room for argument

By John Mason

France, having improved match by match, deservedly took the Grand Slam, the best rugby prize of all, by outwitting and outplaying England in gale force winds at Twickenham on Saturday.

On such an afternoon poise and precision, confidence and competence, were elusive allies that France harnessed to splendid effect; there can be no lasting grumbles.

It is true that France – who won by a goal, try and two dropped goals to four penalty goals – were awarded a try illegally when the wrong ball was used at a throw-in quickly taken. It is also irrelevant. Alan Hosie, the referee, made his decision as he saw fit; he was wrong, I am sure, but that is no cause for anyone to tear their hair. Bill Beaumont, England's captain, is insistent about that, so there ends the matter.

England's faults, when in advance everything appeared to favour victory and a shared championship with France, were more basic than the inability to cover a quick line-out throw – with or without the right ball.

All this France accomplished without recourse to the capricious benefit of the wind, of which they had the first use. England were pinned down by skill, commitment and alertness, the personification being the back row of Rives, Lacans and Joinel.

Beforehand, the realistic Beaumont, who had another storming match to add to those against Scotland and Ireland, pointed to the threat of Rives and his two musketeers. His pre-match summary of his principal rivals was borne out to the letter.

England, 16-0 down, had a windswept Everest to climb after the interval. Rose, once going for goal from 60 yards, took them to Camp Four with an assortment of penalty goals – four from eight attempts. The summit, though, belonged to France.

France's Gabernet (15) and Revazllier combine to stop England's Nick Jeavons.

John Player Final: Leicester 22 Gosforth 15, Twickenham, 2 May

Leicester attend to detail and make cup their own

By John Mason

So the John Player Cup will not only adorn Leicester's centenary dinner table next Friday but also any other occasion the club might choose. The trophy became Leicester's property soon after 4.30pm at Twickenham on Saturday.

In keeping with the careful attention to detail that symbolises the approach of the club's representatives on and off the field, arrangements were made then and there to insure the cup.

With a precision and purpose that left those of us who had doubts beforehand looking more than a fraction foolish, Leicester destroyed Gosforth in a manner which confirmed, without question, their status as England's outstanding club.

Leicester, troubled only for some 15 minutes soon after half-time, convincingly won the cup for the third successive season by two goals, a try and two penalty goals to a goal and three penalty goals. Gosforth's try came in the final seconds.

Last week Peter Wheeler, about to step down after five seasons of captaincy in two separate spells, identified the scrummage as the area crucial to the well-being of Leicester.

Cowling, who led Leicester out for his last senior match, and Redfern, the props, were as important in victory as any other section of a talented side.

What a pity – a mild word – that Johnson, the blindside flanker, was content with local rugby until relatively late in his career. No-one better typified the ability, seemingly inherent at Leicester, to meet the demands, indeed enjoy them, of the big occasion.

Nor would any account be complete without ringing applause for the contributions of Dodge in all respects, the cleverness of Cusworth and the dependability of Hare to collect points. Despite a hamstring twinge, Hare scored another 14 on Saturday, including the third try.

INTERNATIONAL CHAMPIONSHIP

	E	F	I	S	W	P	W	D	L	F	A	Pts
1 FRANCE	-	-	-	16-9	19-15	4	4	0	0	70	49	8
2=ENGLAND	-	12-16	-	23-17	-	4	2	0	2	64	60	4
2=SCOTLAND	-	-	10-9	-	15-6	4	2	0	2	51	54	4
2=WALES	21-19	-	9-8	-	-	4	2	0	2	51	61	4
5 IRELAND	6-10	13-19	-	-	-	4	0	0	4	36	48	0

TOURS (Tests)
Ireland in South Africa: SA23-I15, SA12-I10
Scotland in New Zealand: NZ11-S4, NZ40-S15
France in Australia: A17-F15, A24-F14
South Africa in New Zealand: NZ14-SA9, NZ12-SA24, NZ25-SA22
New Zealand in France: F9-NZ13, F6-NZ18

Tour International: Argentina 19 England 19, Buenos Aires, 30 May

Rafter brilliant as England hit back for draw

By John Mason

England, far from being the easy picking that had been widely forecast locally and overseas, gave Argentina a fearful fright at the Ferrocarril Oeste Stadium in Buenos Aires on Saturday. An English victory would not have been out of place.

The drawn match, 19 points each, means that next Saturday's international at the same ground should have the fervour and fury of a cup final – a one-off match in which the winners will take the series. England, I suspect, sense victory.

Though not securing the score that tied the match until the closing stages, England did lead until the stroke of half-time. Nor did their heads go down when they were trailing 4-10 or 13-19. In many respects it was Argentina who were struggling.

Less a period early in the second-half, the excellence of England's forwards shaped the game. At line-out, ruck, maul and scrummage, England won most of the ball they required and persistently spoilt (legally) Argentine possession.

Well as Beaumont, Pearce and Scott played, the outstanding forward was Rafter, on England's open-side. Maestro Beaumont, the captain, is not given to singling out players, but on this occasion, with absolute justification, he did. Rafter, he thought, was magnificent.

There was a point when England, on an overcast afternoon which was less humid than of late, might have won. On other occasions Hare, in all probability, would have converted the opening try and, late in the half, put over a penalty goal, admittedly at an angle but barely 30 yards from the posts.

No one, though, will be casting Hare a villain. Unlike Baetti, opposite, Hare did not falter under the high ball, nor did he have to scurry for position, and he tackled adequately.

Twice Carleton and Swift, for whom the ball did not run kindly as it had in his previous tour matches, should have been launched. Twice the ball stuck with laboured passing and, in Swift's case notably, England were left to wonder what might have been.

Tour International: Scotland 24 Australia 15, Murrayfield, 19 December

Shaw's frustration punch spurs Scots to fierce revival

By John Mason

Tony Shaw, Australia's captain, who punched Scottish lock Bill Cuthbertson in the face, knocking him to the ground, has apologised.

He said that he was extremely sorry for what had happened in the second half of Saturday's international at Murrayfield. The blow, said Shaw, was aimed because of frustration.

The blow was delivered at a break in play when Scotland were awarded a scrum. The Australians felt they should have had a penalty for a deliberate knock-on. Words were bandied and, according to Cuthbertson, he suggested where Shaw might go and what he might do; and the effect, once Cuthbertson was on his feet again, worked wonders for Scotland. They were revitalised.

That Shaw stayed for the final 20 minutes owes much to the charity of Roger Quittenton, the referee and an experienced member of England's panel. He considered that the punch was not premeditated, and he was well aware of the preliminaries.

For Cuthbertson and Shaw the episode is over. They left the field together, hands were shaken and apologies made. Shaw would do well to send Mr Quittenton a large Christmas card to his Sussex home. The offence plainly merited dismissal.

Tour International: New Zealand 25 South Africa 22, Auckland, 12 September

All Blacks savour 'bread of heaven'

By John Reason

New Zealand and South Africa fought out the decisive battle in the third and last game of their Test series at Eden Park, Auckland, on Saturday, while a crank in a light aircraft zoomed overhead, bombing the pitch with bags of flour, leaflets and smoke canisters.

It was an experience made even more memorable by the events on the field – which matched those going on around the ground, and above it.

This is what tends to happen when full-backs like Allan Hewson of New Zealand and Gys Pienaar of South Africa are involved in an international match.

Hewson and Pienaar are fairly typical of the current vogue in international full-backs. Both are gifted runners and spectacular counter-attackers, but they cannot be relied upon to catch the ball, or to tackle or to be in the right place at the right time.

This creates a situation which horrifies any self-respecting forward but entrances spectators. Throw in an hour of low-level strafing with flour and smoke bombs, and you have a combined entertainment that could reap more money at the box office than Star Wars'.

The Springboks gave New Zealand first use of the wind, which looked as if it was as unwise a decision as was that of the air-craft pilot, who decided to bomb downwind and found his accuracy suffering as a result.

New Zealand went off with such a hiss and a roar that they led 16-3 at half-time, and could have been out of sight if Hewson had approached the accuracy of the record-breaking Naas Botha as a goal-kicker.

By the time Colin Beck came out of the tunnel to replace du Plessis, one of the few smoke bombs which actually ignited was belching red fumes on one of the touchlines, and Beck burst through it onto the field like the Demon King.

His entrance seemed to unnerve the All Blacks. From that moment the Springboks dominated the game. As the match went into injury time, Ray Mordt scored his third try for South Africa to bring the scores level at 22-22.

Hardly a soul in Eden Park doubted that Botha would convert the try and win both the match and the series, even though it was a difficult kick. They were wrong, and within two minutes, Hewson was shaping to take a kick at goal to win the game for the All Blacks.

So New Zealand not only won the most remarkable game of international rugby that anyone is ever likely to see, but also the series 2-1.

Knight, the only international-class prop in New Zealand, is also the most accident-prone. On Saturday he was hit on the head by one of the aerial flour bombs. 'I've heard of Bread of Heaven,' he said afterwards, 'but this was ridiculous.'

Two protesters fall foul of the law.

1982

9 Jan The Wallabies' farewell is ruined as drifting snow, which has buried rows of seats, aisles and some terraces as well as affecting entrances and exits at Twickenham, causes the cancellation of their fixture with the Barbarians.

20 Feb Full-back Dusty Hare begins his sixth international career – he has been dropped five times since 1974 – by kicking 19 points, a record for an England player in Paris, to help England to their first victory of the season, 27-15 over France.

9 Apr Despite the referee playing 5 minutes short, the Barbarians equal their scoring record, set against Penarth in 1978, by beating the same side 84-16, crossing the home line 16 times, with Stuart Barnes notching up 24 points (1T-10C).

24 Apr It is only with less than 10 minutes to go in the Schweppes/WRU Challenge Cup final at Cardiff Arms Park, at 12-all, that Bridgend realise Cardiff's

try will decide the match if the scores remain level – too late, and their failure to cross the Cardiff line costs them the trophy.

9 May Stewart's Melville FP become the first guest side since 1949 (Heriot's FP) to win the Middlesex Sevens when they beat Richmond 34-12 in the final.

22 May A French XV are held to a 10-all draw by the USSR in Moscow, but win the FIRA Championship just the same, 2 points ahead of Italy.

4 Jul Scotland captain Andy Irvine celebrates his 50th cap (equalling the Scottish record) by leading them to their first ever full-international win in the Southern Hemisphere, a 12-7 victory over Australia at Ballymore (Brisbane).

11 Dec Llanelli flank forward David Evans scores the fastest try as a replacement in first-class rugby, scoring only 30 seconds after coming on against Ebbw Vale at Stradey Park.

---

1 February

Injured Beaumont to see specialist

By John Mason

Bill Beaumont, England's record-breaking captain, will see a specialist in Preston this morning to decide whether he should play against Ireland at Twickenham this Saturday. He has a head injury.

Later, Beaumont will join the England squad for a training evening at Stourbridge and discuss with the selectors the report of the specialist and, if relevant, his own thoughts on his

fitness. Beaumont, 30 next month, could not complete Saturday's Thorn EMI Championship final at Moseley, where Lancashire neatly rounded off their centenary season by beating North Midlands 7-3. Terry Morris accepted the trophy in Beaumont's absence.

[Beaumont did not make the Ireland match, and retired later in the season on medical advice.]

International Championship: Ireland 21 Scotland 12,
Dublin, 20 February

Campbell's kicks give Ireland Triple Crown

By John Mason

Athunderclap of applause greeted Ireland's players at their Dublin hotel on Saturday night, everyone running the gauntlet of delighted well-wishers, a heaving phalanx from pavement to foyer, from foyer to staircase.

Ollie Campbell, whose devastating contributions against Scotland could not only be measured by the 21 points he scored, an Irish record, was off the bus early. He looked tired, and slightly surprised by all the fuss.

For the first time since 1949 Ireland had won the Triple Crown. 'We'll bother about the Grand Slam a bit later on,' declared Ciaran Fitzgerald, Ireland's resolute new recruit among the international captains.

Everywhere, even among groups of Scotsmen, disappointed but refreshingly realistic in defeat, there was approval of Ireland's achievement: the logical outcome for efficiency, organisation and discipline, though the match itself was

---

Tour International: England 15 Australia 11, Twickenham, 2 January

England 'uplifted' by Colclough's mighty effort

By John Mason

England's forwards, greatly fortified by a fiery juggernaut called Maurice Colclough and stirringly led by Bill Beaumont, overpowered Australia at rain-ridden, squelchy Twickenham on Saturday. Victory, though not emphatic, was logical and satisfying.

Australian hands will be wrung because goals were not kicked and, for the third time in four internationals on this tour, because in losing they scored more tries than the winners.

There was a lengthy period when the relative inactivity of England's players in December was costing them dearly. With the aid of the breeze to come, Australia, beaten by a goal and three penalty goals to two tries and a penalty goal, could have seized the prize they cherish.

It was in this period, which spanned most of the first half, that Colclough was so impressive.

'Most of us felt ghastly after about 20 minutes,' said Beaumont afterwards. 'It was

a relief to see that Maurice was quite unaffected.' The captain, a genuinely modest person, dismisses his own efforts as 'just plugging away'. Beaumont has plugged away to such effect that his 11th victory in 20 internationals as England's captain is a record.

England also drew strength from the assured work of Steve Smith, a scrum-half who was first capped 10 years ago. By getting Smith back into international trim after a mid-career hiccough, Fran Cotton did England a splendid service.

Beaumont agreed that he did not have the undivided attention of all his team during his half-time tactical summary. Perhaps the Rugby Football Union should arrange a strip-tease at the South End for every match. Certainly England were uplifted.

[The last paragraph is an oblique reference to the unadvertised entertainment the match is perhaps best remembered for, streaker Erika Roe's uninhibited crossfield dash.]

INTERNATIONAL CHAMPIONSHIP

	E	F	I	S	W	P	W	D	L	F	A	Pts
1 IRELAND	-	-	-	21-12	20-12	4	3	0	1	66	61	6
2=ENGLAND	-	-	15-16	-	17-7	4	2	1	1	68	47	5
2=SCOTLAND	9-9	16-7	-	-	-	4	2	1	1	71	55	5
4=FRANCE	15-27	-	22-9	-	-	4	1	0	3	56	74	2
4=WALES	-	22-12	-	18-34	-	4	1	0	3	59	83	2

TOURS (Tests)
Australia in Great Britain: I12-A16, W18-A13, S24-A15, E15-A11
Scotland in Australia: A7-S12, A33-S9
Australia in New Zealand: NZ23-A16, NZ16-A19, NZ33-A18

memorable only for what victory entailed.

The other aspect which must yield universal pleasure is that the years of toil by Slattery, 33 last week and 55 caps, Keane, 33 and 42 caps, Orr, 31 and 34 caps, and Duggan, 31 and 33 caps, have been rewarded in the way players enjoy most.

As Campbell, who spent an often unnerving five minutes getting off the pitch at the end, insists, Ireland won because they presented the better team effort. Campbell dotted the i's and crossed the t's: his colleagues wrote the alphabet.

Campbell: record 21 points.

David Johnston takes the ball over for a Scottish try. Clive Rees (left) and Rhodri Lewis can only watch.

International Championship: Wales 18 Scotland 34, Cardiff, 20 March

Scotland destroy Welsh morale in crushing defeat

By George Mackay

Scotland waited 20 years to win at Cardiff, but when that victory came on Saturday it was so glorious, so complete and so sweet that it erased all the disappointments of those long, barren years. The Scots rewrote a fistful of records as they defeated Wales by four goals, a try and two dropped goals to a goal and four penalty goals.

It was Scotland's first win at Cardiff since 1962, Wales's first home defeat by championship rivals since 1968, and by 13 points the biggest tally ever conceded by Wales at Cardiff; the margin of five tries to one emphasised the totality of Scotland's success.

But it was a triumph not of figures but of spirit. The Scots were so much sharper, smarter and speedier than their rivals, playing a form of fast, inventive football which completely eclipsed the ponderous, stereotyped Welsh efforts.

The gulf in speed of thought was epitomised by Jim Renwick, at 30 winning his 47th cap and still not on a winning side away from home. He strode the midfield like a giant, ferocious in the tackle, swift to counterstrike. One try and a dropped goal were scant enough reward for Renwick's immense contribution in his finest performance for Scotland.

Tour Match: United States 0 England 59, Hartford, Connecticut, 19 June

Unbeaten England end in style

By John Mason

Americans, splendidly vigorous in efforts to avoid being second best at anything, reluctantly accept that their best rugby players are infants on the world stage. The babe is lusty, but a babe for all that.

England, systematically and efficiently, destroyed the Eagles, the national team, at Hartford on Saturday to complete an unbeaten North American tour of eight victories, 53 tries and 352 points.

The 34 points conceded included two tries only. In all respects England's leading players demonstrated to their opponents that fitness, enthusiasm and physical hardness are parts of the equation, not the total sum.

For about half-an-hour, to be generous, Saturday's match against a team that has been together since drawing with Canada (3-3) the previous weekend, did stretch England. The response by the touring party was awe inspiring – and again began up front.

Talented American individuals were no match for a capable team that claimed tries by Smith (2), Carleton, Swift (2), Scott (2), Rendall and Wheeler. The tidy Cusworth dropped a goal and Hare kicked nine goals from 11 attempts. Fittingly it was England's front row that scored the last two tries.

Hospitals' Cup Final: Westminster Hospital 16 St Mary's Hospital 6, Roehampton, 10 March

Westminster forwards surprise St Mary's

By Rupert Cherry

The Westminster forwards sprang a big surprise in the Hospitals' Cup Final at Roehampton yesterday, completely dominating the much fancied St Mary's and enabling their side to win handsomely.

It was only the third time in the 107 years of this competition, the oldest in rugby football, that Westminster have taken the trophy. They won previously in 1974 and 1975.

St Mary's had scored so freely and had run the ball so well in the earlier rounds that it seemed that Westminster, having struggled to beat the London in a replay, had little chance in the final.

Their pack, which included John O'Driscoll, a British Lion and Irish international with 15 caps, and Richard Thomas, a Cambridge Blue who plays for London Welsh, ordered things otherwise.

They pushed St Mary's in the scrums, driving yards forward, and won nearly all the rucks and mauls. So although Paul Jackson, the Harlequin, controlled the end of the line-out for St Mary's, most of the possession went to Westminster.

Tour International: South Africa 12 Jaguars 21, Bloemfontein, 3 April

Jaguars give South Africa a shock

Hugo Porta scored all the points for a team made up solely of Argentines, who scored the first South American victory on foreign soil in an official Rugby Test at Bloemfontein on Saturday.

The Jaguars were a transformed side from that crushed 50-18 by South Africa in the First Test a week before.

That was their only defeat in a seven-match tour in which they scored 219 points and conceded only 109.

In 1976 Argentina lost only 20-19 to Wales in Cardiff, and two years later they drew 13-13 with England at Twickenham. Jaguars' manager, Oscar Martinez-Basante, said on Saturday: 'We have touched heaven.'

Porta scored a try which he converted, kicked four penalties and dropped a goal. Gerber scored a try for South Africa, and Botha kicked the conversion and two penalties.

Tour International: New Zealand 33 Australia 18, Auckland, 11 September

Test record 26 points for Hewson

Allan Hewson, the New Zealand full-back, set a record for matches between International Board countries with 26 points as the All Blacks clinched the Test series 2-1 in Auckland.

He scored a try, dropped a goal and kicked five penalty goals and two conversions, but the key to New Zealand's victory was the dominance of their pack.

Graham Mourie, the captain, rated this the finest performance he has seen by an All Black side at home.

Roger Gould, full-back, opened the scoring for Australia in the second minute with a try after a fine move involving Mark Ella, Slack and Grigg, and converted.

Hewson kicked four penalties for New Zealand and Gould one for Australia, but a spectacular dropped goal by Hawker from 60 metres, followed by another penalty from Gould, gave the tourists a 15-12 half-time lead.

In the second half Hewson and Shaw scored tries for the All Blacks, both converted by Hewson; Hewson and Smith dropped goals, and Hewson kicked a penalty goal. Gould added a third penalty goal for Australia. The attendance, 52,000, was a record for a New Zealand-Australia match.

1983

5 Feb Dusty Hare hits 2 penalty goals in England's 13-all draw in Cardiff to take his international tally to 140, beating Bob Hiller's England record (138).

19 Mar France beat Championship leaders Wales 16-9 in Paris to share the title with Ireland, 25-15 victors over England, and Serge Blanco takes his seasonal tally to 36 points, a new French record (beating Guy Camberabero's 32 in 1967).

2 Apr South African centre Danie Gerber scores 4 of the Barbarians' 6 tries in their 32-all draw at Cardiff.

29 May Wales complete their 5-match tour of Spain with a 5th win, beating the Spaniards 65-16 in Madrid, having scored 275 points and 51 tries, and in the match at Valladolid on 21 May setting new records for Welsh representative sides by running in 15 tries in their 83-3 victory over a Castille/Leon XV.

4 Jun The British Lions contrive to lose the first Test at Christchurch 16-12, despite an appalling performance from the All Blacks full-back Allan Hewson, described by Sunday Telegraph rugby correspondent John Reason as having 'a game which almost defied belief ... not so

much uncertain under the high ball as out of sight..... I don't think that Hewson managed to get anywhere near an up-and-under that fell infield all afternoon, and yet in the last minutes of the match he confounded the crowd by catching a rare stray kick by Campbell and dropping a goal from the middle of the line-out.'

31 Jul Argentina shock Australia 18-3 in Brisbane, their forwards overwhelming the Wallabies pack to score 2 pushover tries against the head, both converted by Hugo Porta who adds another 6 points from a drop goal and a penalty. [A week later, in the 2nd international at Sydney, an inexplicable penalty try awarded by Welsh ref Clive Norling turns the game Australia's way and they win 29-13.]

31 Jul A South African XV beat an International Invitation XV 37-35 in Cape Town, scoring 7 of the match's 12 tries.

12 Nov The All Blacks twice blow 7-point leads at Murrayfield and cannot bear to watch as Dods just fails to win the match with a last-minute touchline conversion attempt, the result a 25-all draw.

17 Dec Clive Norling sends off 4 players, 3 from home side Treorchy, who go down 31-4 to Cardiff in the Welsh Cup.

Ian Smith (Leicester) goes over for a consolation try.

John Player Cup Final: Bristol 28 Leicester 22, Twickenham, 30 April

Bristol's trophy in final of style & polish

By John Mason

After an English season of unacceptable muddle and misdirection, Bristol and Leicester performed wonders for sagging morale by presenting a John Player Cup Final of style, polish and stomach-churning excitement at Twickenham, on Saturday.

Both clubs presented a timely reminder that a major rugby occasion does not have to be drab and cheerless, settled by whatever goal-kicking is permitted by a referee seizing upon some obscure technicality.

The match will have served, too, as a handsome rebuke to that austere, ungenerous section within the game who believe that winning is everything and failure a heinous crime. The priorities were re-established on Saturday.

Bristol's victory by three

goals, a try and two penalty goals to a goal, try and four penalty goals earned them the Cup for the first time in a competition that Leicester have dominated proudly for seasons. That pride has been well founded.

It was singularly appropriate that Leicester should share in a memorable match in the best-attended final there has been. A crowd of 33,000 roared approval, a great wall of sound echoing as Mike Rafter, Bristol's captain, received the Cup.

'Not a bad treble is it?' he said. 'A father for the first time, the County Championship and the Cup all in the same season...' – and with that a very happy Rafter dashed to the waiting bus and more protracted celebrations in the distant Bristol clubhouse.

International Championship: Ireland 22 France 16, Lansdowne Road, 19 February

Campbell establishes his record kingdom

By John Reason

With Serge Blanco scoring a marvellous try, kicking a thundering penalty goal, and generally playing like a delightful dream, France came back from the dead in the second half at Lansdowne Road and moved ahead 16-15 with only 15 minutes to go.

Considering they had been buried 15-3 in the first half by another avalanche from the elegant boot of Campbell, and Robert Paparemborde looked as if he had just gone 15 rounds with Marvin Hagler, this was a transformation to freeze the cockles and muscles of every Irishman's heart, not to mention his vocal chords.

The Irish rugby crowd has taken to singing 'Cockles and Mussels' as a herald of triumph in the same way that the Welsh sing 'Bread of Heaven'. Well, there is no accounting for tastes and at that stage Irish hopes looked anything but alive, alive-o.

France were very definitely in control and they looked capable of pulling right away. However, just when Ireland

appeared to be gone beyond recall, they were given the kiss of life, first by Belascain in the centre and then by scrum-half Berbizier.

Belascain attempted something as overcomplicated as it was unnecessary in an attacking position and saw Ireland hack and chase the ball the length of the field to score and regain the lead.

Even then France might have won, but Berbizier, who had been busily neutralising Blanco by playing like a dismal drain all through, made a bungle of two scoring situations and even Jean-Pierre Rives turned a ball back inside in the Irish 25 when he had a clear overlap on his left.

So it was that the final score was Ireland's and it was Ollie Campbell who put the final cross on France's grave. He kicked yet another penalty goal to give him 14 points in the match and in so doing he left Tom Kiernan's points scoring record for Ireland far behind in exactly one-third of the number of appearances.

INTERNATIONAL CHAMPIONSHIP

	E	F	I	S	W	P	W	D	L	F	A	Pts
1=FRANCE	-	-	-	19-15	16-9	4	3	0	1	70	61	6
1=IRELAND	25-15	22-16	-	-	-	4	3	0	1	71	67	6
3 WALES	13-13	-	23-9	-	-	4	2	1	1	64	53	5
4 SCOTLAND	-	-	13-15	-	15-19	4	1	0	3	65	65	2
5 ENGLAND	-	15-19	-	12-22	-	4	0	1	3	55	79	1

TOURS (Tests)

British Isles in New Zealand: NZ16-BI12, NZ9-BI0, NZ15-BI8, NZ38-BI6

Australia in France: F15-A15, F15-A6

New Zealand in British Isles: S25-NZ25, E15-NZ9

Tour International: New Zealand 38 British Isles 6, Auckland, 16 July

Lions out like lambs!

By John Reason

Without being in any way disrespectful to New Zealand, I do not think this really qualified as a Test match. It ought to be classified in the records as a walkover. The Lions simply scratched.

This was the worst defeat the Lions have ever suffered. It eclipsed by far the 34-14 defeat by South Africa in Bloemfontein in 1962. Suffered was the word, too. Not only did the Lions suffer, we all suffered with them.

The Lions were short of so many things. Commitment, hope, organisation, ability, clues, leadership, spirit, defence, ball – and you can take that last any way you like. Of guts, there were none. They did not even raise an effort. Neither did the All Blacks, come to that, but they did not have to.

They set up a much more positive tackle line than the Lions in defence and organised a tighter line-out than in the Third Test at Dunedin. They also picked up a couple of lucky bounces, but in the main they just coasted through a session of semi-opposed rugby and took the gifts that were on offer. They seemed almost as embarrassed as the sad, silent crowd at the ease with which they

helped themselves to points.

Victory gave the All Blacks the series by four matches to nil. It only puzzles me slightly that the analysis which led me to forecast precisely that result should have caused such anguish, particularly on the other side of the Irish Channel.

A few weeks ago it was said, to the vast amusement of some of us, that one of the Lions flown out as a replacement could play with equal facility on either side of the scrum. We felt that the word should have been 'futility'.

Well, the Lions showed in this match that they could play with equal futility on either side of the scrum, too. Except that a harder man than I might ask: What scrum? He might also ask: What line-out, too? There was none.

In their last match, the 1983 Lions were such a rabble that it was impossible to feel anger about what was happening. Just profound embarrassment and an immense sorrow as the last rites were performed in front of a crowd which sounded for all the world like mourners at a funeral instead of a triumphant mob acclaiming their gladiators.

All Black Stu Wilson leaves the Lions defence for dead.

Representative Match: Welsh XV 29 Japanese XV 24, Cardiff, 22 October

Dragon tail given twist

By John Reason

Japan counter-attacked so bravely and made space and ground with such death-defying precision of pass and such determination of support that they rattled Wales to the back teeth with three late tries. Oddly enough the Welsh crowd took them to their hearts. Some of the things Japan did and the risks they took would have given Ray Prosser a series of such massive coronaries that Pontypool would never have been the same again.

Never mind. Japan got away with it. They had cramped themselves unnecessarily early on and brought the ball back inside where they were swallowed by vastly bigger and stronger men, but as soon as they got those little

sewing-machine legs pumping away in the opposite direction and out towards the wings they made the Welsh passing look positively laboured by comparison.

If only Japan had produced tackling to match the bravery of their passing and the imagination of their line-out play – or even if they had been as remorselessly accurate as usual with their goal-kicking – they would have made Wales sweat even harder than they did.

Never mind again. Japan put the memory of that 82-6 mauling by Wales in Tokyo in 1975 far behind them and they left the Welsh selectors with tightly pursed lips as they contemplated the match in Rumania next month.

International Match: Rumania 24 Wales 6, Bucharest, 12 November

Wales in back seat as Rumania arrive

By Michael Heal

Rumanian rugby has come of age. Yesterday in Bucharest they emphatically displayed their superiority by outscoring a full Welsh side by four tries to nil and thus inflicting upon the Welsh their worst away defeat since 1969.

The margin of victory could have been even greater, but the normally lethal boot of fly-half Alexandru failed with three dropped goals and an easy conversion. Furthermore they had two tries disallowed for forward passes, one of which looked perfectly legal.

Fierce snowstorms early in the morning had given way to

crisp sunshine when Rumania kicked off in the magnificent August 23 Stadium in front of 22,000 spectators.

Wales were completely outplayed in the line-out where Rumania have four jumpers of six feet five and over. Wales did not select a specialist No.4 jumper and this left Mark Brown to battle manfully on his own at the tail. No wonder the line-out count went 37 to 18 in Rumania's favour.

Such were Rumania's ball-winning qualities and disciplined approach that, on this performance, they would be a match for anyone.

Tour International: England 15 New Zealand 9, Twickenham, 19 November

Wheeler and Youngs plot famous England win

By John Mason

Of the many significant events at Twickenham on Saturday, two stand out in addition to England's glittering prize of victory over New Zealand. Nick Youngs established himself as an international of repute and Peter Wheeler silenced carping critics.

How, asked a most distinguished former Welsh international beforehand in the car park, would England fare against New Zealand 'B'? Rather better, I suggested, than Wales had the previous week in

Bucharest. My fingers were tightly crossed.

The gentle ribbing from Vivian Jenkins was perfectly in order. He was right. England, though beating the best available New Zealand side, were playing their second team.

That said, it is permissible to applaud England's players and their astute advisers at practically every turn. So complete was their authority up front that mistakes and timidity elsewhere were, on the day, mostly irrelevant.

1984

4 Feb Scotland gain an emphatic 18-6 victory over England in the 100th clash between the two countries, the 92nd Calcutta Cup.

15 Feb Bristol's Alan Morley scores 2 tries against the Royal Navy to set a new world record of 313 for one club, overtaking the old mark of Andy Hill (Llanelli).

17 Mar With his score at Murrayfield, J-P Lescarboura becomes the first player to drop a goal in all four Five Nations matches in one season.

21 Apr Cardiff thrash the Baa-Baas 52-16 on Easter Monday, scoring 10 tries.

28 Apr Bath win the John Player Special Cup for the first time, taking the final 10-9 as Bristol's Stuart Barnes fails to convert a penalty from near the touchline with the last kick of the match. Thus Bristol captain Mike Rafter fails to emulate last season's 'spring double'.

12 May In a match played in intense heat, Grand Slam champions Scotland wilt in the second half in Bucharest and go down 28-22 to Romania after leading 19-12.

9 Jun An inexperienced England squad, missing several top players, complete their South African tour with their heaviest ever defeat, 35-9, in the 2nd Test at Johannesburg, Gerber scoring half the Springboks' 6 tries.

24 Jun All Black lock Andy Haden (39 caps), with 10 charges of breaching the amateur code hanging over him, declares himself unavailable for the tour of Australia and blasts the NZRFU, some members of whom he alleges 'appear bent on my destruction' and who appear 'only too pleased for me to play against the French and the Australians before administering their justice.'

3 Nov Australia, with an entertaining exhibition of running and handling, give England a lesson at Twickenham, where the drubbing would have been worse than 19-3 but for Michael Lynagh's uncharacteristically poor goal-kicking, although in the end he contributes 11 of their points (1T-2C-1PG).

15 Dec Wallaby captain Andrew Slack is chaired off the field at Cardiff after the tourists crown their Grand Slam triumph with a 37-30 victory over the Barbarians.

INTERNATIONAL CHAMPIONSHIP

	E	F	I	S	W	P	W	D	L	F	A	Pts
1 SCOTLAND	18-6	21-12	-	-	-	4	4	0	0	86	36	8
2 FRANCE	32-18	-	25-12	-	-	4	3	0	1	90	67	6
3 WALES	-	16-21	-	9-15	-	4	2	0	2	67	60	4
4 ENGLAND	-	-	12-9	-	15-24	4	1	0	3	51	83	2
5 IRELAND	-	-	-	9-32	9-18	4	0	0	4	39	87	0

TOURS (Tests)
England in South Africa: SA33-E15, SA35-E9
France in New Zealand: NZ10-F9, NZ31-F18
New Zealand in Australia: A16-NZ9, A15-NZ19, A24-NZ25
Australia in British Isles: E3-A19, I9-A16, W9-A28, S12-A37

Hongkong Sevens: Fiji 26 New Zealand 0, 1 April

Speedy Fiji thrash New Zealand

By George Mackay

Fiji swept to a record fourth victory in the Cathay Pacific Hongkong Sevens yesterday, serving up a final display that was dazzling in its combination of flair and pace. New Zealand, beaten 26-0, simply were overwhelmed, conceding five tries, three converted, without scoring.

The instinctive handling skills of these Fijians enabled them to retain possession by weaving intricate patterns, and they had the pace to go through a gap and make the break count.

Pluckily as New Zealand played, they were not in the same class as the Fijians, revelling in the opportunity to parade their rich talents before an appreciative crowd.

The star of the show was Sensivalati Laulau, a balding centre who toured Britain two seasons ago. He scored two sparkling tries, the second one putting the final flourish on the Fijian triumph.

Australia, winners for the past two years, were eliminated on the toss of a coin after drawing Saturday's group match with Canada.

Two of the British sides, Irish Wolfhounds and Public School Wanderers, reached the semi-finals. The Irish were beaten 12-10 by New Zealand after losing England fly-half Les Cusworth with a torn calf muscle.

Public School Wanderers, stirringly led by Andy Ripley, had looked impressive until they came up against Fiji in a semi-final, losing 4-12.

International Championship: Scotland 21 France 12, Murrayfield, 17 March

French panic as dogged Scots charge

By John Mason

Scotland's players, summoning a courage and resolution that conceivably they had been unaware they possessed, drove themselves to the sweetest of victories by securing the Grand Slam at Murrayfield on Saturday. The prize was richly deserved.

In ending the famine of 59 years without the prime spoils that the Five Nations' championship can offer, Scotland's fervent refusal to give way ultimately engineered the downfall of France, who were previously unbeaten.

For much of the first half and for a period in the second, the dazzling fluency of the French, it appeared, would overcome the dependable doggedness of the Scots. How and why that was not the case was a fascinating exposition of national characteristics.

Scotland, who on the hour were down 3-9, levelled at 12 each with 11 minutes or so remaining and scored twice more on the run-in to record a momentous victory by a goal and five penalty goals to a goal, penalty goal and dropped goal.

Whatever else happened – the departure of Gallion, scrum-half, to hospital 20 minutes into the second half was of extreme significance – the inability of the French to discipline themselves in moments of stress had a major bearing upon the result. The petulant Rives was silly.

Twice penalty kicks at goal were advanced because the French argued. Each time Dods, his right eye all but closed following a tackle he had made early on, kicked points that kept Scotland in close touch besides permitting a final surging rally to undermine suspect French temperament.

Without question, France were hard done by during a match that they dominated in the first half-hour – hard done by by their own frailties, a carelessness born of arrogance in the first instance and, subsequently, by churlish pettiness.

Perhaps the impeccable Gallion, knocked unconscious as he and two opposition forwards legally contested the ball, would have caused such eruptions, the marks of poor leadership, to be unnecessary. His replacement, Berbizier, was only ordinary in comparison at scrum-half.

Then there was the refereeing of Winston Jones, who, although he blew swiftly as a general rule and attended expertly to French line-out illegalities, was not consistent with the ball on the ground.

I am not impressed by the groans of the French, who became very foolish as the match slipped away from them at the end. I have sympathy for the Scots, who directed all energy to a physical confrontation within, less one flurry, acceptable limits.

But the final dissection of the match, for all the artistry of Gallion for France and the calmness of Dods, whose 50 points this international season establish a Scotland record, victory belonged to the Scotland pack, each and every man.

South Africa, 3 June

Craven praises Welsh vote

Danie Craven, the president of the South African Rugby Union, has hailed the Welsh Rugby Union's weekend vote to retain sporting links with his country as 'the most outstanding day of my life'. He said he hoped Wales would take up a standing invitation to follow England and tour South Africa.

Representatives of the 191 Welsh clubs affiliated to the WRU voted by five to one on Saturday to continue having links with South Africa. The special meeting was called after Mid Glamorgan County Council imposed sanctions because the WRU allowed the South African youth team to tour last year.

County Championship Final: Gloucestershire 36 Somerset 18, Twickenham, 31 March

Rafter plays lead in drama

By Richard Sharp

Gloucestershire produced a magnificent performance at Twickenham yesterday when they won the County Championship for the 15th time. In scoring six glorious tries at the headquarters of the English game, Gloucestershire showed a crowd of nearly 20,000 that when it comes to the County Championship they have no equals.

This was their 12th final in only 15 years and, although they have enjoyed many famous victories, this was surely their finest hour.

For skipper Mike Rafter, whose 32nd birthday it was, for George Wright, Gloucestershire's long-serving secretary, and for many other of their county stalwarts, it was a day to remember.

This year, the West Country's contribution to English rugby has not been fully recognised, so it was particularly appropriate that Gloucestershire should play so well in front of Messrs Morgan, Weston and Greenwood, who must now turn their attention to picking England's touring team.

Whatever the rights, or wrongs, of England's forthcoming visit to South Africa, all sportsmen will regret the need to leave Stuart Barnes, Gloucestershire's outside half, behind because of the prior requirements of Oxford University's examiners. He had a superb match, scoring a remarkable try and, as always, kicking with great skill.

Watching Gloucestershire yesterday, it was difficult to believe that only Blakeway has played for England this season. Rafter, Hesford and Gadd were far superior to the Somerset back row which contained two England men, Simpson and Hall.

Mike Rafter, who last April led Bristol to John Player Cup success, yesterday collected the County Championship for the second year in a row. At the end of the month he will be back at Twickenham again with Bristol for the John Player Cup Final.

Bledisloe Cup: Australia 24 New Zealand 25, Sydney, 18 August

All Blacks win thriller

New Zealand retained the Bledisloe Cup by defeating Australia 25-24 in a thrilling third and deciding Rugby Union Test Match at the Sydney Cricket Ground yesterday.

Australia took an early lead when Ella landed a penalty goal, but after ten minutes winger Clamp finished off a blind-side move after the All Blacks won a driving maul close to Australia's line.

New Zealand full-back Deans, who finished the match equal with Ella, landing five penalty goals and a conversion, kept New Zealand in the lead.

Deans and Ella swapped penalty goals until New Zealand scored their second try 10 minutes before the break, centre Stone finishing off a move by crashing over in the corner.

Following Campese's try and another Deans penalty goal, the All Blacks led 19-15 at half time.

Deans and Ella again swapped penalties early in the second half before Campese booted a long-range penalty goal to see Australia trailing by only one point.

Deans and Ella landed a goal apiece and Australia stormed into attack as time ran out. With only one minute to go Ella attempted to win the match for Australia with a hasty drop-goal attempt which swung wide.

Tour International: Scotland 12 Australia 37, Murrayfield, 8 December

Ella at his best as Wallabies do the 'slam'

By John Mason

On an afternoon when records tumbled like confetti, the Australians, on and off the field, did British and Irish rugby a service on Saturday. Amid the damp, sepulchral gloom of Murrayfield, a beacon-like message penetrated every dark corner.

The speed of the correctly timed pass will beat the man every time, and support will create space as well as time, that other precious commodity of games-playing at the highest level.

The Australians, in probably the most important match they have played, possessed those skills in such abundance that Scotland, last winter's unbeaten champions in domestic competition, were bundled aside in a splendid contest.

Victory by three goals, a try and five penalty goals to four penalty goals brought Australia a first tour Grand Slam in their history, 100 points in the four internationals, a try count of 12-1 and the largest win by them over a Home Union.

There were individual records to savour, too. It is astonishing to think that Michael Lynagh's 21 points – he kicked three conversions and five penalties, missing only a touch-line conversion – must on the day take second place.

Mark Ella's try early in the second-half, which also marked the point at which Australia slipped into overdrive, gave him the unique distinction of scoring a try in each of the tour internationals: a gloriously appropriate record for him to take into retirement.

While it is in order to applaud the achievements of so many for unceasing hard work and common sense, players and officials, I think it fair to say that Ella, above all, has propelled this friendly group to greatness.

Many other things have had to happen – leadership (Andrew Slack), motivation and organisation (Alan Jones), stability at scrum and line-out (the front five), the huge promise of the younger element, the monumental contributions of Roger Gould – but I believe Ella wins the accolade.

For all the elation that surrounded the euphoric awareness that the signal

Australian try scorers Mark Ella (left) and David Campese with captain Andy Slack (right) after the match.

home for the first time could be 'mission accomplished', Jones-the-coach, who has been a fund of incisive, searching, often controversial, often witty comment, was in a philosophical mood afterwards.

'I favour the Gucci outlook,' he said. 'Long after you've forgotten the price, you remember the quality.' Irrespective of the detailed analysis that must be made in Britain and Ireland, a more apt comment on Australian achievement would be difficult to find.

1985

2 Feb England scrape a 9-all draw at Twickenham thanks to a first-half aberration by French wing Patrick Estève, who is put clear by Sella, albeit from an obviously forward pass, but is tackled by Richard Harding as he tries to run round to the posts after crossing the try line and spills the ball. Irish referee David Burnett awards 15 penalty kicks against France in the second half to one against England.

13 Apr Nottinghamshire, Lincolnshire & Derbyshire, with their entire XV drawn from the Nottingham club and making their first appearance at Twickenham, lose the county final 12-9 to Middlesex, for whom Huw Davies drops the winner just after Simon Hodgkinson misses an easy kick at goal for the Three Counties.

22 May Scotland complete their tour of Canada (P5-W4-L1) with a 79-0 win over Alberta President's XV at Calgary, equalling their record winning margin (82-3 over Thailand in 1977) despite the referee's blowing for time after 75 minutes; Peter Dods, playing on the right wing, scores a record 43 points (4T-12C-1PG).

25 May The French club final produces a record number of points at the Parc des Princes, where Toulouse beat Toulon 36-22 after extra time.

2 Jun Having chalked up their biggest win in international rugby (48-13) against Japan at Osaka a week earlier, Ireland are made to fight in the 2nd and final Test in Tokyo, held 12-all at half-time before running out 33-15 winners, with centre Michael Kiernan scoring a record 25 points (2T-4C-3PG).

22 Jun Argentina beat France 26-16 in Buenos Aires (Porta 16pts), the tourists' first defeat. [France square the series a week later with a 23-15 win and finish the tour with a W6-L1 record.]

14 Sep Referee George Crawford walks off in the first half after a brawl in the Bristol-Newport game and a local referee takes over. [The two clubs are later censured by their respective unions.]

19 Oct Fiji are desperately unlucky to lose 16-15 to Ireland at Lansdowne Road where, late in the game, full-back Turuva, after chipping the ball over the last Irishman, is debatably adjudged to have knocked on. [Fiji later lose their other international 40-3 to Wales.]

27 Oct Japan, having lost the first international to France 50-0 a week earlier at Dax, finish their tour (P6-L6) with a heavier defeat, 52-0 at Nantes.

30 Oct Fiji beat Newport 7-6 but lock Savai is sent off and suspended for 6 weeks.

2 Nov The All Blacks, having beaten Argentina 33-20 in the first Test at Buenos Aires the previous week, score 4 tries in the 2nd Test to lead 21-12 at the interval, but the inevitable Hugo Porta, having kicked 4 penalties, drops 3 second-half goals to earn the Pumas a 21-all draw, and New Zealand lose their 100% record.

2 Dec South Africa call off next year's Lions tour.

INTERNATIONAL CHAMPIONSHIP

	E	F	I	S	W	P	W	D	L	F	A	Pts
1 IRELAND	13-10	15-15	-	-	-	4	3	1	0	67	49	7
2 FRANCE	-	-	-	11-3	14-3	4	2	2	0	49	30	6
3 WALES	24-15	-	9-21	-	-	4	2	0	2	61	71	4
4 ENGLAND	-	9-9	-	10-7	-	4	1	1	2	44	53	3
5 SCOTLAND	-	-	15-18	-	21-25	4	0	0	4	46	64	0

TOURS (Tests)
England in New Zealand: NZ18-E13, NZ42-E15

International match: England 22 Rumania 15, Twickenham, 5 January

Andrew's salts mask hangover

By John Reason

It seemed as if somehow there had been the most awful mistake, and the University match was being played a month late by teams in the wrong shirts.

Rob Andrew, the Cambridge, Surrey and England fly-half, ran the opposition kick-off out of defence and within a minute had started piling up points as if there was no tomorrow.

Bob Hesford won the line-out unopposed when England's counter-attack ran out of ground, and Andrew dropped a goal. Then, when Paul Dodge kicked ahead, Rory Underwood burst on to the ball and surely would have scored if he had not knocked on in an open field.

England forwards won every ball going for a quarter of an hour and their opponents, just like Oxford, looked as if they would have been exercised to beat the second team of any self-respecting first-class club. Admittedly, there was not quite as much snow around as there is at some University matches, although it had a jolly good try, but even the crowd of 30,000 looked about right. The member countries of the International Board may have decided that it is worth a cap to play against Rumania, but the crowd at Twickenham most definitely have not.

At the end of the day, the echoes of the last few years of the University match remained. A third or fourth division match, played with increasing ineptitude until it reached the point where it was first embarrassing, and then comical to watch.

Not only that, but Cambridge, sorry England, won. Andrew scored 18 points from six goals of one sort and another, and Simon Smith scored a try.

The only marginal difference was that, unlike Oxford, the Rumania forwards worked their way back into the game until it looked as if England might snatch defeat from the jaws of victory, but Smith's try at least saved that final humiliation.

International Championship: Scotland 15 Ireland 18, Murrayfield, 2 February

Ringland grabs glory for Irish

By Richard Sharp

In a game of fluctuating fortunes, Ireland scored a brilliant try in the closing stages to snatch as exciting a victory as one could wish to see.

When Dods, who scored 50 points in the International Championship last season, kicked his fourth penalty goal to make the score 15-12 in Scotland's favour, only four minutes from the end, it seemed all over for Ireland.

But Ciaran Fitzgerald's enterprising team had other ideas and they stormed back into the Scottish half. From a ruck on the left, Dean, who had a good match, made a lovely loop in midfield and

sent Ringland racing over for the winning score with only a minute of normal time remaining.

Kiernan, whose goal-kicking had been far from convincing early on, made amends now by converting triumphantly, to send the large contingent of Irish supporters wild with delight.

All credit then to Ireland. They had looked the better side in the first half and, in the second, they managed to score the only two tries of the match, both by Ringland. What is more, they were true to their coach's pre-match words and were prepared to run the ball from the start.

Donal Lenihan leads another Irish charge at Murrayfield, supported (left to right) by Fitzgerald, Orr and Bradley.

International Championship: Scotland 21 Wales 25, Murrayfield, 2 March

Wales' flashbacks to the glory days

Bevan condemns referee

By Michael Austin

Wales, offering tantalising reminders of their golden era in the 1970s, put together a high-speed, high-risk game so successfully under the inspiration of Mark Ring and David Pickering at Murrayfield on Saturday that a whitewash looms for Scotland.

Ring, brilliance personified at centre, and Pickering, celebrating new duties as pack leader with two tries, contributed handsomely to a match which was an undiluted thriller.

The way both sides played endeared them even to a neutral Englishman. Paxton's two opportunist tries stamped him as a No.8 of class even in defeat, and Scotland's season deserves a kinder epithet than 'grand slam to grand slump'.

Boldness banished soft options and handling superseded punting for safety as kindred Celts provided a salutary lesson for those who doubt the entertainment value of international rugby.

Execution scarcely matched boundless ambition, but for pure excitement this game had few peers in recent times, with the closeness of the scores and the lax refereeing of Rene Hourquet heightening the tension. The overall effect captivated a 60,000 crowd.

Wales, weighed down with mediocrity in past seasons, have sifted through their resources diligently amid criticism. Ironically, three prime forces, Davies, Moriarty and Morris, were not original choices in their positions.

Davies, who ended three years of international exile with a dropped goal after 43 seconds, fortified Wales with the relaxed authority of his line kicking, launched his backs expertly and even survived an unusually laboured service from Holmes.

Two Welsh scores stemmed from Scottish throws; Morris, a new cap, tapping down for Davies to drop a goal and Moriarty later deflecting a long throw by Deans for Pickering to score his second try and grant Wales a 54th-minute lead they did not relinquish.

Paxton's first try for Scotland, following a 65-yard kick and chase and exploitation of Lewis's fumble, was among the highlights of the day, but Wales, better organised in the backs and superior ball winners, were level at 9-9 by half-time.

The next 14 minutes produced 25 points, Paxton having begun the second half with a try after 13 seconds. During that bewildering spell Scotland led three times, twice through magnificent dropped goals by Rutherford.

Dods kicked Scotland's three goals from six attempts and Steven hit a post from 57 yards. The unflappable Wyatt landed five of his seven kicks for Wales, whose first try stemmed from Ring's sidestepping break and a pass to Davies which looked suspiciously forward.

After the match, Wales coach John Bevan condemned the refereeing of Rene Hourquet as 'diabolical'. Bevan said: 'He had no idea what was going on for half the time. I would

Referee Hourquet: criticised.

not entertain him refereeing my form three at school. He was totally incompetent and as bad for the Scots as he was for Wales. I have been tactful in my two and a half years as coach but I had to get this off my chest.'

International Championship: Ireland 15 France 15, Lansdowne Road, 2 March

Kiernan makes angry France pay the penalty

By John Mason

France's talented players lost friends in Dublin on Saturday. A wilful disregard for what is permissible meant that what should have been straightforward victory over Ireland became an unsatisfactory, often ill-tempered draw.

The French, notably Jacques Fouroux, the coach, have got to a point where the majority of decisions against them are greeted with a cynical shrug of the shoulders. They expect to be penalised. Fouroux, in loose translation, insisted that it was always the same when France encountered English-speaking referees. Neither understood the other. The situation never altered from match to match.

Monsieur Fouroux, I regret, is wrong. France are not the victims of some fiendish plot devised by English-speaking officials. The root cause is in their domestic game, where ball-winning illegalities, ball protection and the more subtle forms of obstruction go unpunished.

Ireland secured a draw in a bruising, extremely physical match because Michael Kiernan kicked five penalty goals from seven attempts. France scored two cracking tries, both of which Lescarboura, who also kicked a penalty goal, converted.

Kerry Fitzgerald, the referee, from Brisbane, had a testing introduction to international rugby in the northern hemisphere. Commendably he made it plain that he was in charge, his quick decisiveness preventing matters getting out of hand.

In the frantic closing stages, Ireland did enjoy the rub of the green. But by then any residual sympathy for the French had long since been spent. In the art of creating rods for their own backs, the French were masters.

UAU Final: Loughborough University 17 Durham University 15, Twickenham, 6 March

Oti's purple patch consoles Durham

By John Mason

Two scores in the final 10 minutes permitted Durham University to return home with heads held high after a mostly one-sided Universities Athletic Union rugby final against the holders, Loughborough, at Twickenham yesterday.

For a record 20th time since 1953 Loughborough secured the UAU title with a tidy display of thoughtful, well-organised teamwork. The minor alarms at the end were irrelevant.

Victory by a goal, two tries and a penalty goal to a goal and three penalty goals took Loughborough's total points from eight matches in this season's champion- ship to 289. They conceded 49. The game's most compelling personality, though, was wearing the palatinate purple of Durham and spent the first half on the right wing and the second on the left – which is where Chris Oti, the player concerned, did a lot of damage.

Oti, a generous 13 stone and not far off six feet, will have few illusions about his defence. But as an attacking force, with a little help from Hambly and Riley, Oti caused previously assured Loughborough men to appear extremely shaky. Burnhill cut Oti down once, but could not stop his try.

David Leslie, Scotland's captain, said: 'It's traditional that referees are not criticised, but sadly it's a tradition which is disappearing. He was the same for both sides and did his best.'

16 March

RFU end automatic ban

By John Mason

England's selectors will have to make character assessments as well as judgments of playing ability about potential international players next season.

After a five-year experiment, the RFU are to abandon the automatic 30-day suspension of players sent off. Nor will players be barred in that season from England selection.

'This decision,' says an RFU statement, 'was taken with some regret, as it had been hoped that the initiative taken by England regarding their potential international players would have been supported by other national Unions.'

In reaffirming their determination to punish severely misconduct on the field, the RFU declare that England will consider only those 'suitable to represent their country'. So a voluntary ban of sorts stays.

In some respects that is better than nothing. But as selectors, rightly, never discuss publicly why players have been dropped – or not chosen, if available – some uneasy 'no comment' days are likely.

And how Wales can rebuke an official for a sharp, honest opinion about a referee but condone the selection of men of violence is beyond my naive comprehension.

International Championship: Ireland 13 England 10, Dublin, 30 March

Irish nerve stretched but never broken

By John Mason

The fervent, often frantic business, of playing with the head carried Ireland to another defiant triumph in Dublin on Saturday. The prizes for victory over England were the Triple Crown and the international championship.

The most elementary analysis must disclose flaws, not all of them English, but the point is academic. Ireland won a heart-stopping match in little short of epic style.

Michael Kiernan's dropped goal, in the 40th minute of the second-half, was not so much the icing on the cake of a momentous season, as the cake itself – a rich, satisfying mix of ingredients carefully supervised.

Ireland's win, by a try, two penalty goals and the dropped goal to a try and two penalty goals, was logical, just and, if only for the passionate surge for victory in the last few minutes, thoroughly deserved. Touches of fortune do not matter.

Kiernan, Donal Lenihan, a mighty force, and Brian Spillane, the No.8, a bony, committed hunk of perpetual motion, were the core of the side which, for the 15th time,

was led with steadfast, heartening conviction by Ciaran Fitzgerald.

England, once more, achieved less than they promised. The pack were comfortable in much of their work, though not the line-out, and there was sufficient possession to cause Ireland's defence prolonged difficulties. Somehow, though, there was little impact.

England went ahead in the second minute when Andrew, from a long way out on the left, put over a penalty goal after Anderson had been offside at a line-out. Though he struck the ball well, Andrew missed his next three kicks, including two much closer to the posts.

The lead had lasted four minutes when Martin hurried his kick, Mullin charged it down and, barely having to alter course, ran on for the try. Kiernan's first penalty goal, after England had shuffled offside, permitted Ireland a half-time lead of 7-3.

An offside went unspotted in Underwood's scorching try 15 minutes into the second half. Andrew put England in front a second time when Dean must have set some sort of record, so far was he

offside. There were 23 minutes remaining.

England led for 16 of them until Dooley was judged to have come through a short line-out, and Kiernan slotted the goal. For the next seven minutes, Spillane and Lenihan were men possessed,

driving Ireland on.

There was a fearsome charge by Lenihan, brushing aside every attempt to kill the ball. The line-out was won and Kiernan, with two colleagues outside him, took the feed and dropped the most fateful of goals. Two minutes remained.

Headmaster will take charge of 'World Cup'

By John Mason

John Kendall-Carpenter, a Somerset headmaster, has been appointed chairman of the steering committee to organise Rugby Union's inaugural World Cup in Australia and New Zealand in the summer of 1987, it was announced in Paris yesterday.

After the annual meeting of the International Board, which has been in session all this week, he told me: 'Of the many matters discussed by the Board in the past few days, the new competition has to be a major part of rugby's future.

'It's essential that we get everything right, that the commercial aspects are developed in the best interests of the game, and that there are no financial flops. The Board must control the tournament in all respects.'

The Board had what was

described as 'a very full discussion' on the Cup feasibility study presented by Australia and New Zealand, who will act as the Board's agents in the detailed organisation and planning of the event.

Dr Roger Vanderfield, the Board's chairman, who is an Australian, said that many aspects of the proposed competition required further detailed consideration.

Dr Vanderfield's planned statement translates as meaning that the thorny nettle of South Africa's participation has not been resolved. But there has been a unanimous reiteration by the Board's other seven members that they want South Africa to be included.

Other decisions of the Board included the establishment of associate membership.

Try scorer Mullin (13) moves to pick up a loose ball.

12 April

Gareth Davies quits Wales

Gareth Davies, the Cardiff outside-half *(pictured)*, no longer wants to play international rugby. He was recalled by Wales this winter after being dropped three years ago.

Davies, a former captain, said the decision for the time being to leave the outside-half position open against England a week today, was the last straw. Even a phone call to him would have been appreciated.

Schweppes Welsh Cup Final: Cardiff 14 Llanelli 15, Cardiff, 27 April

Pearce grabs Llanelli glory

By Richard Sharp

Gary Pearce's dropped goal in the third minute of injury time enabled Llanelli to snatch victory in the Schweppes Welsh Cup at the National Stadium yesterday.

After a dull first half, dominated by penalty goals, this match blossomed into one of the most exciting finishes one could wish to see.

The lead changed hands five times in a remarkable second half when first one side and then the other nosed ahead. At the end of normal time, Cardiff were leading by two points and must have felt the Cup was theirs. But it was dashed from their lips as Llanelli made one final effort.

It was a remarkably accurate left-footed kick by Llanelli's No.8, Phil Davies,

which created the scoring position in the left corner. With the seconds ticking away, Llanelli won a set scrum near the Cardiff line. Pearce set himself up for the drop goal and, to the undisguised delight of thousands of Llanelli supporters, the ball soared between the posts.

There was just time for Gareth Davies to attempt a dropped goal at the other end, but the kick went wide of the mark and moments later the final whistle went.

The Llanelli supporters, unable to contain their excitement, rushed onto the field to acclaim their heroes, and May, their popular captain, was borne aloft in triumph.

Tour International: New Zealand 18 England 13, Christchurch, 1 June

Bewildered England pay harsh penalty

By John Reason

The England team of 1985 has nothing of the Bravura of that 1959 Lions team, but the fact remains that they did score two tries to nil against New Zealand at Lancaster Park and were only beaten by six thundering penalty goals kicked by Kieran Crowley, the All Black full-back.

England led until midway through the second half, and then their midfield

backs were not in the least convinced that they had advanced closer than 10 yards after Whetton had caught the ball at a line-out. Indeed, the England backs looked at the referee and looked at where they were standing and looked at the distant line-out as the referee penalised them. They raised their eyebrows and shrugged their shoulders and, inevitably,

17 April

New Zealand have put game above all

By John Mason

The decision of the New Zealand rugby authorities to tour South Africa in July and August is no surprise. But that their actions should be the source of such acrimonious dispute saddens them.

The New Zealand RFU Council, whose chairman is Cec Blazey from Canterbury, consider that a rugby tour, for example, of Great Britain no more indicates sympathy with or condonement of the policies of whatever political party is in power than a similar round of matches in South Africa.

But in view of the turmoil in New Zealand in 1981 when South Africa's players toured there, the Council's members have never pretended that the issues involved are not highly contentious and subject to extremes of behaviour.

The New Zealand Council make no judgements on the political regimes or the politics of the countries that they are invited to visit. They seek only not to break the law of their own country.

Mr Blazey, probably the most experienced and respected of administrators in the game worldwide, and a member of the International Board, told me in Paris recently that it was the duty of the 17-man council to listen to objections that the proposed tour of South Africa might raise.

The Council would listen to what the Prime Minister, Mr David Lange, had to say, to their own members and to the public. But in the end, the

decision whether to tour was theirs to be made only in the best interests of rugby football, their only elected brief.

The decision would have nothing to do with apartheid or the laws of another country. The tour was a meeting of games players, a challenge between men of varying beliefs, creeds and colours. It was as important as that, but it was nothing more than that.

Mr Blazey's committee is right in believing that sport is not the dustbin for the troubles of the world. Nor should New Zealand rugby be thought of as being solely responsible for the histrionics likely to ensue.

The Lions, who represent England, Wales, Scotland and Ireland, have accepted all invitations to tour South Africa, and England, after an RFU vote of 44-6 in favour, went there last summer. Those tours, in my experience, have created as much excitement in Britain as watching the tide come in.

The welcome changes of policy in South Africa in recent years – all right-minded people detest apartheid – have been aided immeasurably by a succession of bold, caring people in sport in that country.

Those officials and sportsmen of all races are sustained by the visits of those similarly involved from overseas. I do not defend the action of the New Zealand RFU Council. I applaud it.

Crowley kicked the goal.

Crowley's goal-kicking was about the only thing that went well for the All Blacks all day. They did not manage a decent drive until injury time; I have never seen them play so poorly.

Predictably, they annihilated England's one-man line-out in the first half, but delivered the ball so badly on a marshy ground made worse by drizzle that poor Kirk at scrum-half must have thought that he had climbed into the wrong-

coloured shirt. He took no end of stick.

It was a desperately poor game and the only thing in the least explosive about it was the bomb which the police found in the stand beforehand and which had to be detonated.

It made no more of a bang than the All Blacks, who might have been grateful for the fact that the expiring protest movement very nearly succeeded in pulling the plug on all communications out of Christchurch.

1986

18 Jan The boot dominates the two internationals: At Twickenham, in a game 'killed stone dead by the whistle' according to Wilf Wooller in The Sunday Telegraph, England fly-half Rob Andrew scores all his side's points in their 21-18 victory over Wales, starting with a 60-yard penalty goal and finishing with a left-footed drop goal deep into injury time, while Gavin Hastings marks his arrival on the international stage by scoring all 18 points (6PG) – a Scottish record – in their narrow win over France at Murrayfield. The only tries of the day are scored by the losers, Wales (1) and France (2).

15 Mar With the title at stake, France thrash a lacklustre England 29-10 in Paris, but must settle for a share of the Championship as Scotland scrape through somewhat luckily in Dublin.

12 Apr Warwickshire's captain and No.8 Graham Robbins scores 3 tries as they come back from 6-0 down to beat Kent 16-6 in the final of the Thorn-EMI County Championship at Twickenham; all his tries are 'not exactly pushovers' but are pushed near enough to put him within range of the line, and he has now scored over 30 such tries this season.

16 Apr Captained by Andy Slack (Aus), the International Board Centenary XV (comprising 7A-5NZ-2F-1SA players) beat the British Lions (S5-I5-W3-E2) 15-7 at Cardiff.

23 Apr Apart from their abortive attempt to stop the New Zealand Cavaliers tour of South Africa, the International Board, meeting in London, make several decisions. These include permitting payment for book, newspaper, radio and TV work provided statutory declarations not to play again have been completed; no major tour to be of more than 13 matches; and the end of the experimental law variation requiring play to stop if a player goes to ground in a maul – if the ball is immediately available play can continue, but if a scrum collapses play must stop.

26 Apr Cardiff, 28-9 up with 15 minutes to go, are shaken by a Newport revival in a splendid Schweppes Welsh Cup final, but hold out for a 28-21 victory.

3 May The Quins beat Nottingham 18-10 in the final of the Middlesex Sevens to equal Richmond's record of 9 wins.

10 May Bath (75%) have broken Pontypool's (72.22%) stranglehold by heading The Sunday Telegraph's 'original' English-Welsh merit table for 1985-86.

6 Jun Former Welsh coach and outside half John Bevan, 38, dies of cancer. A Barbarian who also played for Aberavon and Neath and was a British Lion in 1977, Bevan would have won more than his 4 caps in 1975 had not Phil Bennett been a contemporary.

21 Jun Michael Lynagh kicks an IB record 23 points in Australia's 27-14 win over France at the Sydney Cricket Ground.

INTERNATIONAL CHAMPIONSHIP

	E	F	I	S	W	P	W	D	L	F	A	Pts
1=FRANCE	29-10	-	29-9	-	-	4	3	0	1	98	52	6
1=SCOTLAND	33-6	18-17	-	-	-	4	3	0	1	76	54	6
3 WALES	-	15-23	-	22-15	-	4	2	0	2	74	71	4
4 ENGLAND	-	-	25-20	-	21-18	4	2	0	2	62	100	2
5 IRELAND	-	-	-	9-10	12-19	4	0	0	4	50	83	0

TOURS (Tests)

France in Australia & New Zealand: A27-F14, NZ18-F9
Australia in New Zealand: NZ12-A13, NZ13-A12, NZ9-A22
New Zealand in France: F7-NZ19, F16-NZ3

International Championship: Scotland 33 England 6, Murrayfield, 15 February

Scots break records as England reel

By John Mason

Scotland, fulfilling purposefully and excitingly every syllable of their pre-match message of intent, destroyed dazed, despairing England by a record Calcutta Cup margin in the Royal Bank international at Murrayfield on Saturday.

Records decorated Scotland's day of triumph at every turn, the prickly thorns of the thistle tearing at English hearts and confidence relentlessly. England lost the Battle of Hastings in 1066: nor did they do too well in the 1986 Murrayfield version.

Gavin Hastings kicked eight goals from eight attempts, the conversion of the third and final try pleasing him most because the scorer was his younger brother, Scott. Be warned England – there are two more rugby-playing Hastings brothers.

Of Scotland's victory by three goals and five penalty goals to two penalty goals, Gavin Hastings claimed 21 points, a new high. Scotland's previous individual record was set by him with 18 points against France a month ago. His 12 penalty goals this season are also a Scottish record.

Only against France in 1912 have Scotland recorded a larger winning margin, when the difference was 28 points. At that point in the rugby development of France, the feat would not have been unexpected.

But on Saturday, few believed beforehand, even those contemplating a Scottish victory, that England would be so comprehensively outplayed. Nor on the evidence of the first half alone did such catastrophic defeat appear likely.

The manner of the beating, however, left England's players and selectors in a state of bemused shock. They had travelled to Scotland in the expectation of victory, happy with the way preparations had gone and certain that the match would be played at a pace of their choosing. The big men would dominate.

Absolutely the reverse happened. England were made to appear medieval in their approach, light years removed from the athleticism and mobility exuding from every Scottish pore. Speed was the name of the game; the day of the donkey was over. In the end, regrettably, England degenerated into a disorganised, ineffective rabble, prey to the next humiliation that the marauding Scots cared to inflict. Here was South Africa 1984 and New Zealand 1985 all over again, bitter memories resuscitated.

The Hastings brothers, Scott and Gavin.

International Championship: Ireland 9 Scotland 10, Lansdowne Road, 15 March

Scotland are lifted by ill luck of the Irish

By Michael Austin

Ireland's resourceful backs and resurgent forwards can celebrate St Patrick's Day today knowing that their country's slide from champions to whitewashed wooden-spoonists is the season's most cruel irony.

Scotland, though strangely subdued, won by a try and two penalty goals to a goal and a penalty goal in an electric atmosphere at Lansdowne Road to share the championship title with France; but Saturday's moral victory belonged to Ireland.

The slender difference between top and bottom teams in the table has rarely been better illustrated. With a point separating the sides, two Irish aberrations during a ferocious late assault on the Scottish line tilted the game. A stamping incident involving Ringland was seen by the touch judge, and it deprived Kiernan of an easy penalty kick already awarded by Francis Palmade, the referee, who rescinded the decision.

Kiernan's authentic match-winning chance was with an angled 20-yard penalty, but it sailed across the posts on the headwind five minutes before a high-speed match of mistakes and counter-attacks was laid to rest.

Mick Doyle, Ireland's coach, said drily that the person handing out the luck to his side last season must have gone on holiday, and Colin Deans, Scotland's captain, sportingly confirmed this view.

The Daily Telegraph, 14 April

Top New Zealand players to tour South Africa

By John Mason

Andy Dalton, captain of the International Board's centenary squad for matches at Cardiff and Twickenham this week, will fly to South Africa next weekend to join a 12-match unofficial tour by New Zealand's leading players.

Dalton, the All Blacks captain and hooker, will be accompanied by seven of eight colleagues who flew into Britain on Friday for the centenary matches against the British Lions and a Five Nations XV.

A ninth New Zealander, John Kirwan, a wing three-quarter from Auckland, has refused to join the 30-strong party who will be assembling in South Africa throughout this week. They include eight Maoris.

Yesterday Dalton, who is in Cardiff, said he had no comment, official or unofficial, to make.

David Kirk, New Zealand's scrum-half and a doctor, who is due to take up a Rhodes scholarship at Oxford in the autumn, has also rejected an invitation to tour. He is not in Britain. The tour party otherwise comprises 28 of the 30 players originally chosen to

represent New Zealand in South Africa last summer.

That tour was cancelled following legal action by two members of clubs attached to the Auckland Rugby Union. The courts ruled that a tour of South Africa was contrary to the constitutional aims of the New Zealand Rugby Union and an interim injunction banning the tour was made the day before the rugby players were due to leave.

A spokesman for the New Zealand Rugby Union said in Wellington yesterday that the present proposed 12-match tour of South Africa was outside their control. The visit was unofficial and the players said to be involved have not sought permission to travel.

The tour party, including Mike Purcell, an American wing three-quarter, will be managed by Colin Meads, whose 133 matches for the All Blacks included 55 internationals, a New Zealand record. The coach is Ian Kirkpatrick, another All Black of renown who, like everyone else concerned, presumably will be banned after returning home in early June.

The Daily Telegraph, 22 April

All Blacks by any other name

By John Mason

The New Zealanders, whose unofficial tour party was completed by the arrival in Johannesburg of nine more players yesterday, including Andy Dalton, the All Blacks captain and hooker, will play their 12 matches as the Cavaliers.

The opening match is tomorrow against the Junior Springboks at Ellis Park, the venue for four games.

The tourists reiterated yesterday that they did not represent the New Zealand Rugby Union, that they should not be called All Blacks, and that the four 'Tests' were not official, even though they would be meeting the national team, the Springboks.

I hope the South African Rugby Board have informed

Dr Danie Craven, their president, who is in London for the annual meeting of the International Board, of that fact, because he did not seem to know about it last week.

New Zealand's self-styled Cavaliers, who have circumvented regulations about overseas tours by the simple expedient of ignoring the NZ RFU, also declared yesterday that they were aware that South Africa had political problems.

'But as sportsmen,' said a statement issued on their behalf, 'we emphasise it would be improper for us to comment on them. We are here to play sport and will not at any stage debate politics or answer politically slanted questions.'

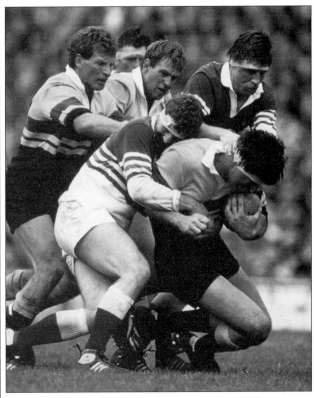

Steve Cutler drives forward for the Overseas Unions team.

Representative Match: Five Nations XV 13 Overseas Unions XV 32, Twickenham, 19 April

Nations not so united

By John Reason

Anyone who doubted that rugby union in the British Isles is in free fall and that it is without the moral and physical comfort of an unopened parachute must have gone away from Twickenham knowing the truth.

The Overseas pack annihilated the forwards chosen for the Five Nations. They cleaned them out in the line-out, they cleaned them out in support play and they had them under ceaseless pressure in the scrums.

Steve Cutler and Andy Haden did the damage in the line-out, very nearly the whole team did the damage in the loose, and Flippie van der Merwe, at way over or even weigh over 21 stone, looked as if he could hold the Five Nations scrum on his own.

Ian Eidman and Maurice Colclough, the British forwards most highly rated by France, would have made a difference and so would about 14 more Frenchmen. In the end, though, the forward superiority of the Overseas Unions was so crushing that the Five Nations backs simply

gave up. The Five Nations did lead 7-3 early on, but from that point the southern hemisphere scored 29 points without interruption and Naas Botha, South Africa's siege-gun kicker, was playing fly-half like he did when he was a boy.

He did let fly with a couple of screaming kicks off either foot early on, but as soon as he saw what his forwards were made of and what the Five Nations forwards were not made of, he began to work the midfield and cut back to the blind side to make use of the power of Daniel Gerber in the centre and the ferocious strength of John Kirwan, the young New Zealand wing.

The match, such as it was, did have a prologue and an epitaph. Kiernan kicked a penalty goal and scored a try after a scramble, and Ringland scored a try which Blanco converted in the last second of the match after an exquisite pass by Sella.

But as Blanco took the kick I could have sworn that I heard the strains of 'The Last Post' faintly in the distance.

International Board Meeting: London, 23 April

Craven warns professional game near

By John Mason

South Africa's rugby authorities were told yesterday to stop the unofficial 12-match tour by 30 of New Zealand's leading players, which began in Johannesburg last night. The organisers are the Transvaal RFU.

The South African Rugby Board, whose chairman is Dr Danie Craven *(pictured)*, have acknowledged responsibility for the tour and accept that the normal procedures for inviting players were not followed.

Dr Craven, who is also chairman of the International Rugby Board, which completed their annual general meeting yesterday in London, returned home last night convinced that professional rugby union was at hand. He also spoke of resignation.

In a wide-ranging, often emotional interview in the lower ground floor corridors of the East India and Sports Club, St James's Square, Dr Craven said that Transvaal had already been asked to call off the tour.

'They have told us, the South African Board,

that they can't. If we insist that they do, they will break away and there will be professional rugby union. That's not a possibility, that's a probability.

'The message is loud and clear for all to hear,' declared Dr Craven. 'I would rather resign and get out than be part of all that. If I go home and call off the tour, I might as well commit suicide now.'

Dr Craven, who has

directed South African rugby for more than 30 years after a distinguished playing and coaching career, insisted that there were three major companies in South Africa anxious to start professional rugby union.

[The following day Dr Craven, back in Johannesburg, revealed that an attempt to expel South Africa from the International Rugby Board because of the unofficial New Zealand tour had failed because some Board members were sympathetic still: 'Those members appreciate that the tour is essential to keep South African rugby alive and well. But there's no denying we broke the rules and action must be taken – as soon as possible.']

Tour match: Northern Transvaal 9
NZ Cavaliers 10, Pretoria, 26 April

Dalton has jaw broken

The unofficial New Zealand side touring South Africa overcame the loss of their captain Andy Dalton, who broke his jaw just before half-time, to beat Northern Transvaal, one of the strongest provincial states, 10-9 in Pretoria on Saturday.

The tourists, who scraped home against the Junior Springboks by 22-21 in their first match, escaped defeat when a penalty goal attempt by Naas Botha narrowly missed in the dying seconds.

[Dalton's jaw, apparently, was broken by a punch from Burger Geldenhuys – Welcome to South Africa!]

Representative Match: South Africa 24 New Zealand Cavaliers 10, Ellis Park, 31 May

Rowlands rapped: Setback in anger

By John Reason

Andy Dalton, the captain of the team of New Zealand All Blacks which has been touring South Africa, gave referee Ken Rowlands the most fearful public roasting after his team lost the final Test at Ellis Park and with it the series by three matches to one.

To a man, the New Zealand players and management were outraged by their treatment, and at the reception after the match Dalton said: 'I have always looked for honesty in a referee. We got less than that today. If you in South Africa say that was sour grapes, so be it. When the announcement came at half-time that Mr Rowlands was retiring as a referee, it was welcomed by us.'

The New Zealanders were thrown back almost the length of the field on four occasions and lost scoring positions through decisions against them and through arguing with the referee. There is no doubt that a strong tide flowed against the New Zealanders, but they did not help their own cause by indiscipline.

At one stage, the hooker, Hika Reid, lost his cool completely as the referee kept

drilling him between the eyes with a succession of ten-yard penalties for arguing, and it looked as if Reid tried to shoulder-charge him. Reid might well have been sent off the field.

Two players were sent off. Knight hit Smal in a ruck early on, and Smal flattened the New Zealand prop with a tremendous punch. The referee sent them off at once – but not to take, as Eddie Waring used to say, an early bath. They were sent to the cooler for five minutes.

Mr Rowlands said: 'I was told that the two countries use the system of sending players into the sin bin. I don't like it but it was appropriate on this occasion, because I would not have sent them off for the rest of the match.'

What of the rugby? The New Zealand forwards got better and better, and their backs and their goal-kicking got worse and worse. The Springbok defence was often a mess, but time and again the New Zealand backs turned inside when they had men to spare. Once they did it when they had a three-man overlap. The New Zealand forwards were worth four tries – their backs scored one.

John Player Special Cup Final: Bath 25 Wasps 17, Twickenham, 26 April

Cup joy for Bath: Wasps stamped out in swarm

By John Reason

Bath squeezed out four tries from a series of ferocious forward drives and attacking scrums to win the John Player Special Cup for the third year in succession after Wasps had astonished everyone at Twickenham with three sweeping counter-attacks which gave them a 13-0 lead.

Prop Paul Simpson played a prominent part in Bath's first three tries and then plunged to score himself after five successive scrums five yards from the Wasps line.

Wasps must have been heartbroken because, after spending the first 15 minutes defending for their lives, they had suddenly broken clear and flabbergasted Bath by scoring two tries and 13 points in ten minutes.

They owed much to the very New Zealand organis-

ation that their coach Derek Arnold has brought to their play, and, above all, to the precocity of Gareth Rees, their 18-year-old fly half. Rees is a Canadian schoolboy at Harrow, but there is nothing remotely callow about him. He is built like a tank, he is a shrewd footballer, and he is more than sufficiently under-awed to point out to international referees acting as touch judges just where opposing kicks have gone.

It was a character-building match of an intensity which English rugby badly needs, and that made it even harder to understand why the first-class clubs have been stalling so hard to try to prevent Rugby Union from introducing a full-scale league structure instead of the Merit Table nonsense.

The Daily Telegraph, 7 June

New Zealand snub tour men

None of New Zealand's All Blacks who played for the Cavaliers on the recent unofficial tour of South Africa will be chosen for the internationals against France and Australia, the New Zealand RUF have decided, writes John **Mason. The trial teams for the match against France on June 28 in Christchurch include only three capped players, led by David Kirk, the scrum-half and new captain. Australia play three internationals in New Zealand.**

The Sunday Telegraph, 8 June

Pro-Ams play on

By John Reason

The tour of South Africa by Andy Dalton's New Zealand Cavaliers was professional from beginning to end. I have no doubt about it. I admit I cannot prove it and I shall be very surprised if the New Zealand Rugby Union can either. We will not get at the truth until one of the players breaks rank and jumps the fence. That day will surely come.

In the meantime, I suspect that the New Zealand RU will be no more capable of proving breaches of the amateur regulations than they have been so conspicuously for the past 15 years, when a whole queue of their players has written books and articles about the game and somehow kept the money.

Closer to home, leading players in England and Wales have simply refused to answer the leading questions put to them. The secretariats of the two countries have shrugged their shoulders and given up.

From what I hear, New Zealand have virtually admitted already that they are powerless to take sanctions. They have now deferred their consideration of the matter until November.

Unfortunately, the International Board regulations in defence of amateurism are naive. Former secretary John Hart put it nicely when he said the intentions of the Board 'are imperfectly enshrined in law'.

Never forget the defence of amateurism is right at the core of the Board's very existence. So the message of last season's Australian tour here and of the happenings in South Africa of late is that the Board had better get its act together in a hurry.

The choice is stark. Either they redraft the international touring schedule to include South Africa or they face a backlash from the players themselves. And make no mistake, the players are on the verge of taking over. Andy Dalton and Andy Haden have proved that they can fill the gaps left open by the Board.

Tour International: Tonga 7 Wales 15, Nuku'alofa, 12 June

Welsh players hurt in Tonga punch-up

Two Welsh players were laid low in a brawl that marred the first international played by Wales in Nuku'alofa, the capital of Tonga, yesterday.

Penalty kicks gave Wales the foundation for their victory by 15 points to 7. The two sides scored a try each in a match dominated by forward play on a greasy pitch.

The punch-up in the **Tongan dead-ball area came 17 minutes after kick-off and left Phil Davies, the Welsh No.8, and inside-centre Adrian Hadley laid out on the ground.**

Hadley was stretchered off and replaced by Glenn Webbe, the Cardiff-born West Indian, winning his first cap and becoming the first black player to play a Test for Wales. Hadley was not seriously hurt.

Bledisloe Cup: New Zealand 9 Australia 22, Eden Park, 6 September

Australian win puts Meads' job on line

By Justin Rogers

The knives are out for Colin Meads, Cavaliers coach and All Black selector, as a follow-up to Australia's resounding win over New Zealand in Saturday's third Test at Eden Park.

It is only the fourth time this century the All Blacks have lost a series on their home soil.

Meads and fellow selector Tiny Hill, who are said to have out-voted coach Brian Lochore in pushing so many Cavaliers into the last two Tests, are certain to lose their jobs after the coming tour of France.

In a game played at a furious pace, the Wallabies scored two tries to nil as the All Blacks daringly tossed the ball about, even from their own line, in a complete change of character.

Australia led 12-6 at half-time, with a couple of Michael Lynagh penalty goals and a try by debutant full-back Andrew Leeds, converted from the touchline by Lynagh.

The All Blacks cut the deficit back to 12-9 with Crowley's third penalty – but then Lynagh slotted over a couple of penalty goals to give the Wallabies a nine-point cushion at 18-9 and take his points tally in Tests to exactly 200 in only three years.

David Campese, switched to his old spot on the wing, wound up a somewhat wretched tour by scoring his 21st try in only 26 Tests.

Tour International: France 16 New Zealand 3, Nantes, 15 November

France turn tables on the All Blacks with a vengeance

By John Mason

France, inspired by an awesome display of forward power, did more than beat the All Blacks at their own game in Nantes on Saturday. They destroyed them.

In practically every way, New Zealand were second best. It would be difficult to exaggerate how superior France were, except in converting that authority into points.

Victory by a goal, a try and two penalty goals to a penalty goal was France's fifth in 25 matches with New Zealand since 1906.

But not only statistically was this by some measure the most convincing.

From well before half-time – the scores were level at the break – it was obvious that the All Blacks, unbeaten in their seven previous matches on this tour, were heading for a mighty fall in their final game.

The champing noise from the VIP and Press benches of the splendidly appointed Beaujoire Stadium on the outskirts of Nantes was that of pre-match words, opinions and hats being eaten by the French, New Zealand and British, committee, players, journalists and Uncle Tom Cobley.

The roasting that Jacques Fouroux, France's coach, has received, culminating in defeat 19-7 the previous week in Toulouse, from all concerned was remarkable in its ferocity, even by French standards.

French rugby, in the words of Pierre Villepreux which I recorded last week, had lost its way. Traditional skills behind the scrum had been abandoned. It was impossible not to agree.

One week later, here were the French offering the same formula of forward strength, the same brand of percentage rugby – but with one important difference.

This time it was successful beyond the wildest dreams, so he declared, even of Fouroux.

1987

4 Apr With captain and scrum-half Richard Hill suspended, Mike Harrison leads a revitalised England to a 21-12 victory at Twickenham, denying Scotland the Triple Crown and saving England from a whitewash. Hill's replacement behind the dominant pack, Richard Harding, has an inspired match, and full-back Marcus Rose scores 17 points (1T-2C-3PG), to bring his aggregate to 41 (out of England's 48).

2 May Cardiff beat Swansea 16-15 after extra time at Cardiff Arms Park to win the Welsh Schweppes Challenge Cup final, their 5th success in 7 years.

2 May A Parc des Princes record crowd of 50,000 sees Toulon beat Racing Club de France 15-12 in the French Club Championship final.

25 Jul Fresh from their World Cup triumph, the All Blacks regain the Bledisloe Cup, beating Australia 30-16 in Sydney in a one-match series.

31 Oct After their disappointing World Cup, Argentina prove a different proposition on their own soil, holding the visiting Wallabies 19-all at the Velez Sarsfield Stadium, Buenos Aires, the inevitable Hugo Porta scoring 15 points

with a drop goal and 4 penalties.

1 Nov The All Blacks crush All Japan 106-4 in Tokyo in the 2nd unofficial international of their tour.

7 Nov Wales beat USA 46-0 at Cardiff in a match that causes outrage outside the WRU because they award full caps against one of the poorest teams in the World Cup who are without 11 of their first-choice squad.

14 Nov Arthur Jennings, a former member of the Fiji RU and manager of the South Seas Barbarians, a Fijian-based team who toured South Africa in September, is banned by the International Board for life from all rugby. Apparently, the South African Board had been misled into thinking the tour, which played multi-racial opposition, had been officially authorised.

8 Dec Led by the All Blacks' World Cup captain David Kirk at scrum-half, Oxford nevertheless are beaten 15-10 by Cambridge in the Varsity Match at Twickenham, where, according to Telegraph correspondent John Mason, C Oti's two tries 'transposed an already notable match into an event of lasting consequence and merit.'

International Championship: England 15 France 19, Twickenham, 21 February

The French Revolution: England are led bravely to the scaffold

By John Reason

As Dr Johnson said, the knowledge that you are going to be hanged in the morning does concentrate the mind wonderfully, and England went out at Twickenham with minds and bodies humming in their determination to avoid Rugby football's biggest drop.

The onslaught on the French, however, was started by Jim Fleming, the Scottish referee, rather than the England players. Marcus Rose kicked three penalty goals in 10 minutes and England led 9-0 thank you very much.

But France came back in the second half, just as they had against Wales at Parc des Princes, to score two tries and win the match.

The first try was a beauty. First they cut a hole with a delightful double scissors from the back of an attacking scrum, and then Eric Champ came off the back of that scrum to punch through in

midfield. The England defence was in shreds. Bonneval supported Champ, and the classy French winger scored so close to the posts that Berot had a simple conversion.

England gathered themselves for another effort, and their line-out jumpers gave Hill good possession. The England captain tried a version of the French double loop, but he is nothing like as dexterous as France's midfield players, and has nothing like the same eye for an opportunity. Instead of enabling one of his players to take off, the double loop crashed in flames and ended with the formidable Philippe Sella intercepting and running 65 yards to score.

Berot failed to convert, but he did kick a penalty goal from 50 yards when Rees was penalised at a ruck. France led 19-12 and England's white shirts looked appropriate for the waiting scaffold.

INTERNATIONAL CHAMPIONSHIP

	E	F	I	S	W	P	W	D	L	F	A	Pts
1 FRANCE	-	-	28-22	16-9		4	4	0	0	82	59	8
2=IRELAND	17-0	13-19	-	-		4	2	0	2	57	46	4
2=SCOTLAND	-	-	16—12		21-15	4	2	0	2	71	76	4
4=WALES	19-12	-	11-15	-	-	4	1	0	3	54	64	2
4=ENGLAND	-	15-19		21-12	-	4	1	0	3	48	67	2

TOURS (Tests)
New Zealand in Australia: A16-NZ30
For World Cup see pages 142-5.

For World Cup see pages 142-5.

International Championship: Ireland 17 England 0, Lansdowne Road, 7 February

Confident Irish put England under cloud

By Michael Heal

Even before the opening whistle, there was something unusual in the Dublin air, a giant cloud of Irish self-confidence. To be sure, this team would have won the championship last year instead of being whitewashed if all the matches had been stopped at half time!

That confidence was amply justified as they went the full distance and easily disposed of a desperately poor England side that lacked ball winners, strategy and cohesion.

England's problems stemmed from the line-out, where Lenihan, Glennon, Anderson and Matthews cleaned up. Poor Cusani never got a look in, and referee Hourquet was not prepared to help him.

Nor could England profit from their scrummaging. Syd Millar has transformed the Irish eight, and on countless occasions they disrupted England's hard-won ball at Simpson's feet.

Consequently, the Irish back row were always going forward, pressuring the England backs into panic

passing. If it had not been for heroic defence by Hall and Winterbottom, Ireland could have scored 30 points.

The conditions were wet and windy, with the ball like a piece of soap. All this contributed to a game which lacked any real flowing rugby. Both teams were content to disrupt rather than construct, and the game suffered as a spectacle, with high punts the order of the day.

The England backs had to feed off scraps, but the little that was seen of Harrison suggested that, with more ball, he could have posed a real threat.

Rose coped bravely with his defensive duties but had to retire near half-time after a heavy tackle from Carr. Barnes, who replaced him, had no real opportunity to demonstrate his attacking skills. Most worrying for England was skipper Hill's tentative and erratic performance, which made things extremely difficult for the rest of his backs.

Scorers: Kiernan 1T-1C-1PG, Matthews and Crossan tries.

France's Eric Champ sets up his team-mate Eric Bonneval for their first try during the international at Twickenham.

International Championship: France 28 Scotland 22, Paris, 7 March

Scots are outplayed but fight to the last

By John Mason

The lines of exhaustion were etched deeply on the faces of the Scotland forwards as, to a standing ovation, the team sought the ' relative calm of the dressing-rooms at the end of a superlative match at the Parc des Princes in Paris on Saturday.

Even the French, the balm of victory soothing the aches and pains of a match sympathetically refereed, were grateful that they no longer had to battle with resolute opponents who would not be subdued.

Daniel Dubroca, France's captain, summed up the occasion admirably. It was, he told French colleagues, an honourable day for Scotland, for France, and for rugby: honourable and hard.

The sordid pettiness and bullying sourness that England astonishingly believe to equate with spirit and backbone were refreshingly absent from this highly skilled, entertaining contest between France and Scotland.

Nor were the proceedings any the less vigorous or demanding than they should have been. Here and there, perhaps, bounds were exceeded, though ultimately there was time only to play rugby.

Everything happened at a pace which made wicked demands upon physical and mental resources. Scotland can be proud of their representatives and of Derrick Grant, the coach, whose instinctive reaction afterwards was to applaud in detail France's performance.

France won by four tries, a dropped goal and three penalty goals to a goal, a try and four penalty goals. For an hour they played thoughtful, efficient, attacking rugby that no one in Europe has matched since the great Wales team of a decade ago.

The value of Scotland's contribution can be judged in several ways. For once, though, the scoreline will suffice. Having been 7-22 down after 50 minutes, they finished at 22-28.

I believe France, who will be unchanged against Ireland on Saturday week, were a pace, a metre, a pass away from six other tries. Some of the play that did not yield points was breathtakingly inventive. Scotland defended marvellously! England: get that video tape.

RFU Statement: 9 March

RFU rap England after debacle

By John Mason

England, in an unprecedented public statement yesterday, told their players that the behaviour against Wales at Cardiff last Saturday was totally unacceptable.

Soon after the start Phil Davies, the Wales and Llanelli No.8, had his right cheekbone broken by a punch from Wade Dooley, the England lock, who is a community policeman in Blackpool.

England condemn without reservation the kicking and the punching as well as the many off-the-ball incidents that escaped the attention of the television cameras.

They offered no opinion yesterday as to who was to blame.

But they did accept that, on the penalty count alone (22-15), England — not Wales — were the principal aggressors.

England were penalised 12 times against Ireland and 16 times against France.

Dudley Wood, the secretary of the Rugby Football Union, said: 'There was a serious loss of discipline by players in both teams which cannot be condoned.'

Wade Wood, who said the people who knew him were well aware that what had happened was not in character as far as he was concerned, added that he was not proud of what he had done, especially as he was a policeman.

[The following week, the RFU made it clear to the England selectors that they would intervene if certain players were not dropped for the rearranged Scotland fixture, and Wade Dooley, Gareth Chilcott, Richard Hill and Graham Dawe were duly axed.]

International Championship: Wales 19 England 12, Cardiff, 7 March

Pride laid low as England lack discipline

By John Reason

Wales could not scrummage, their line-out ball was untidy, their line-kicking was worse than erratic and they did not construct one back movement in the entire match – but they never even remotely looked like losing to England at Cardiff Arms Park yesterday.

The sad truth is that Wales were awful and England were worse, and when last week I described the match in prospect as a Second Division contest I flattered the participants quite outrageously. This was not even a Third Division contest. It was non-League.

The conditions were dreadful. Bitterly cold rain and sleet slanted down the pitch. Wales played into the precipitations from the Arctic in the first half, but took a 12-9 lead, all the points coming from penalties. They went into half-time knowing that with the wind and the weather behind them they ought to have been as home and as dry as it was possible to be in those conditions.

While Wales were comforting themselves with these thoughts, we looked at each other in sheer disbelief that any international match of rugby football could be so poor.

The two packs were fighting each other from the first whistle, and the notion that anyone had managed to inculcate anything resembling discipline into the England pack would have made Ray Megson, the unfortunate Scottish referee, shake with laughter if he had not been so busy weeping.

In his three matches for England Graham Dawe has done some things that have been quite daft, and he has been more than lucky not to have been sent off the field. At Cardiff half the other England forwards joined him.

One of them was Wade Dooley, which surely was incautious to say the least because when you are 6ft 9in tall it's rather difficult to remain inconspicuous. The England forwards went so far over the top in the first quarter of an hour they looked as if they had been on pills. Sensibly, Wales kept their reaction to a minimum.

There were two casualties. Phil Davies, the Welsh No.8, had his right cheekbone fractured and had to be replaced by Richie Collins, and Steve Sutton had his nose broken apparently by Bob Norster's elbow. That, I hasten to add, did not break Davies' cheekbone.

After the interval, Stuart Evans scored an unconverted try for Wales, and Wyatt and Rose each added one more penalty kick. In the end, it was England's lack of discipline that cost them their last chance to salvage a shred of pride.

International Championship: Ireland 13 France 19, Lansdowne Road, 21 March

Cockerels and muscles: French slam door on Irish singing

By John Reason

Ireland went off with such a hiss and a roar in the cold clear sunshine that they scored two tries and 10 points in the first 13 minutes of this match at Lansdowne Road.

They drove the ball and drove it again to pull in the French loose forwards on both sides of the tight, and they did it so well that Trevor Ringland bounced past four men to score the first try and then Willie Anderson pulled off the burglary of the season by robbing that celebrated hit-man Laurent Rodriguez at the back of a French scrum.

Anderson fed the ball to Des Fitzgerald, who was charging forward like a bull; he slipped it to Philip Matthews, all legs and sinew, and when Matthews was brought down just short of the line Michael Bradley was close behind to take the ball and score.

Michael Kiernan converted one of the tries with a booming kick from the right touchline, so that in less than a quarter of an hour France had been bowled over for more tries than they reckon to concede in a season.

This forced the French to gather behind their line for the first emergency national assembly debate that I can recall for years and the ecstatic Irish crowd promptly launched into an enthusiastic rendering of 'Cockles and Mussels'.

This proved premature, and from that moment on it was much more a question of cockerels and muscles, and both of them were most decidedly French.

France came back with such fortitude and such resolution that they not only won the match and with it the international championship and the fourth grand slam in their history, but they also forced Ireland to produce one of the greatest defensive displays in modern times.

Twenty, ten, even two years ago, such resolution and such good old British phlegm would have been unthinkable from the French. They would have lost their temper with referee Clive Norling and his new Bubbles hair arrangement, they would have blown a fuse and blown the match with it.

But not now. Long before half-time Ireland were defending for their lives.

Somehow Ireland held out in the first half, and all France had to show for some super football was a penalty goal by Berot after a collapsed scrum. But early in the second half France did just what they had done against England and fairly piled up the points.

Haget won a line-out, Erbani and Rodriguez drove on, and Champ plunged over to score.

This season France has prospered in the line-out, an area in which they have been lightly regarded on the grounds that Berbizier cannot throw in for toffee and neither Haget nor Condom can jump.

Well, people who have been investing in condoms this winter have made a lot of money of late, and France's line-out shares have climbed to quite astonishing heights as a result of the efforts of the young lock from Biarritz. He and Haget and Champ wiped out Ireland in the second half. The last-named scored his second try after a reshuffle cause by injury to Blanco, and France were never headed again.

Below: A flying Irish tackle goes in on Eric Champ.

Tour match: Barbarians 16 New Zealand Barbarians 68, Cardiff, 1 April

Tourists destroy Barbarians

By John Mason

The New Zealand Barbarians wound up a five-match tour with a bit of style, as they had promised, against their parent club at Cardiff last night. They destroyed them.

A deluge of 12 tries swept away the Barbarians as they crashed to the heaviest defeat in their history. Three tries by the Barbarians were merely pinpricks.

A withering barrage of five tries, all of which were converted, in the opening 20 minutes by the New Zealanders left the Barbarians in a state of numbed shock.

The huge gulf in standards, application and efficiency – and a ruthless exposure of the ills besetting rugby in England and Wales.

Here were basic problems of technique, support and attacking intentions, plus exploitation of opposition weaknesses.

Jones, the New Zealanders' No.8, scored two of those early tries. Brewer scored the second and McGrattan, the loose-head, the fourth.

With four tries from the New Zealand forwards, the backs were anxious to join in the fun. Cooper, having kicked the conversions faultlessly, became bored at full-back, and came up for the fifth and sixth tries, taking two firm tackles at the line in the process of scoring his second.

The other New Zealand tries, several of which came from long range – involving backs and forwards alike – went to Bachop, Brewer, Kirk, Anderson (2) and Stanley.

Cooper, with 10 conversions and two tries, collected 28 points.

Women's RFU Club Championship Final: Wasps 19 Richmond 0, Twickenham, 11 April

Girls in Twickers approval

By David Grice

Headquarters seal of approval was finally bestowed on the girls yesterday when the Women's Rugby Football Union staged their own Championship final at Twickenham.

The familiar club names of Wasps and Richmond put the women's game firmly on the sporting map: the first time the fair sex had played in such august surroundings.

Wasps won through 19-0 with a performance which showed that, although the ladies may still have a lot to learn, they lacked for nothing in commitment and enthusiasm

Outside-half Karen Almond, Wasps' play-maker, would not have looked out of place in some men's teams I could mention, and kicked two conversions and a penalty. One of Wasps' tries was scored by their No.8 Sally Treadwell, whose father WT played for England in 1966.

John Player Cup Final: Bath 19 Wasps 12, Twickenham, 2 May

The Cup runneth over: Invasion mars Bath joy

By John Reason

Referee Fred Howard was told to abandon this John Player Cup Final three minutes before the end because the rabble who have attached themselves to the Bath club as so-called supporters made it impossible for play to continue.

Bath had come back from the dead to score two tries in the last 10 minutes, and each time they did so thousands of their camp followers swarmed over the pitch. They stole the match balls and refused to go away and left the referee with no alternative but to take the players off.

After the final try was scored, Mr Howard seemed to indicate to Jon Hall, the Bath pack leader, that there were three minutes still left to play. With the players waiting in the tunnel, the referee wanted to restart the match, which meant that some of the players had to recover the shirts they had already swapped with their opponents, but in the end he was told that it was impossible.

The referee was entitled to stop the game. The law states that he has the power to do so before time has expired if in his opinion the full time for any reason cannot be played, or if continuance of play would be dangerous.

Both options, therefore, were open to him. Bath duly won the cup for the fourth time in succession, which is a record, but all one can do is weep for the direction in which they are leading the club game in England and weep for Twickenham. They were the worst scenes of undiluted yobbery ever witnessed at the ground.

[The following day senior Tory MPs urged the RFU to take immediate action to prevent a repetition of the scenes at Twickenham, and warned that unless firm stewarding wass used to stop crowds invading the pitch, there would be no alternative to introducing fencing round the pitch at major rugby matches.]

Tour International: Argentina 27 Australia 19, Buenos Aires, 7 November

Porta record as Pumas shock Wallabies

Hugo Porta, Argentina's captain and outside-half, equalled his match record of 23 points, kicking the Pumas to a shock 27-19 **Second Test victory against Australia in Buenos Aires on Saturday after they had trailed 13-3 at half-time.**

Porta *(pictured below)* kicked five penalties, two dropped goals and a conversion of Mendy's try. Lynagh, Australia's captain, kicked three penalties and a conversion, Williams scoring two tries.

This was Australia's only defeat on their nine-match tour, but Argentina took the series 1-0, having drawn the first Test.

County Championship Final: Middlesex 11 Yorkshire 22, Twickenham, 11 April

Yorkshire can celebrate with blank cheque

By John Mason

Mike Harrison, the rugby-playing bank official who passionately believes that winning matches should also be a blank cheque for the enjoyment of the players and the entertainment of spectators, won more friends at Twickenham on Saturday.

As Harrison, England's World Cup captain, is employed by the 'action bank', the style of Yorkshire's victory over Middlesex in the Thorn-EMI county final was appropriate.

Before this season, captaincy, as far as Harrison, a wing three-quarter of stealth and speed, was concerned, was the job done by others. He is still slightly surprised that Yorkshire invited him to take charge in the first place.

The North division followed suit and so did England, having initially asked him to lead The Rest in the international trial at Twickenham in January. That is the only match Harrison has lost as captain – by a single point, too.

On Saturday, at windswept Twickenham, Middlesex twice led before Yorkshire, capitalising on a glut of possession in the middle period, pulled away to win by two goals, a try, and two penalty goals to two tries and a penalty goal.

International Board Meeting: Agen, 14 November

South Africa escape: Board expulsion fears prove groundless

From John Reason

South Africa's typically pessimistic fears that Agen might turn out to be Amen as far as their membership of the International Rugby Football Board is concerned have proved to be groundless.

For all the huffing and puffing done before the meeting about the unfortunate and absolutely pointless unofficial tour of South Africa by a Fiji-based team of South Pacific Barbarians, 'when it came to the crunch,' as one of the delegates said, 'there was a great deal of sympathy for the situation in which South Africa find themselves of having probably the best rugby team in the world and not enough teams to play.'

Accordingly, the IB have only suspended consideration of discussions about tours or matches involving South Africa until their next meeting in March.

That would still allow the IB to arrange tours to celebrate the centenary of Eastern Province and the 50th anniversary of Northern Transvaal which take place next year.

In addition, the Board will be able to discuss Australia's suggestion that they forego their tour by the British Lions in 1989 and give it to South Africa instead to celebrate the centenary of the South African Rugby Union.

As South Africa are now in their rugby close-season and they will not start playing again until next March, the ban has effectively no impact.

No one was more determined that South Africa should not be punished as if they were criminals for hosting an unimportant tour than Albert Ferrasse, the president of the French Rugby Federation and chairman of the International Board.

Ferrasse and Margaret Thatcher have exactly the same realistic view of sanctions. 'It will be our fault if rugby in South Africa is forced to go professional,' he says. 'It is abnormal that only rugby football is used to purify the conscience of Europe about South Africa.'

1987 World Cup

17 May Warming up for the World Cup on a wet, heavy Brisbane pitch, England's first opponents Australia, with a display that leads the England manager Mike Weston to describe their challenge as 'awesome, bordering on the terrifying', pile up their record international score in a friendly against South Korea – 65 points (13T-5C-1PG) against 18.

19 May Australia are established as World Cup favourites, ahead of New Zealand and France. Several former New Zealand players and some leading journalists have expressed the opinion that the mighty All Blacks have no better than an outside chance.

20 May Andy Dalton, just restored as All Blacks captain despite his involvement with the Cavaliers tour of South Africa, has had to withdraw from the World Cup with a hamstring injury.

22 May The World Cup opens in Auckland, where New Zealand pulverise Italy 70-6, a result that provides ammunition for those against the tournament. But while such one-sided games do not invalidate the principle of a

World Cup, they emphasise that there are not 16 rugby-playing nations of even remotely similar playing standards.

23 May While France and Scotland fight out their 20-all draw in Christchurch, the unseeded nations in Pool 4 provide an equally close finish at Hamilton, where Romania, 20-9 down with 20 minutes to play, come back to beat Zimbabwe 21-20 and top the table.

24 May Fiji, 'playing with purpose, commitment and showing brilliant ball skills,' surprise Argentina 28-9 at Hamilton in Pool 3, the only one without two IB countries.

29 May Welsh prop Stuart Evans, who has transformed their scrummaging since returning from injury, breaks a bone in his right foot in their victory over Tonga and is out of the tournament.

30 May Scotland beat their record score in internationals (35-10 against Wales in 1924) with their 60-21 win over Zimbabwe, while England also run up 60 points in their record 60-7 win against Japan. Ireland, after struggling to hold on

at 19-19 against Canada with 15 minutes to go, run out 46-19 winners.

2 Jun Mixed fortunes for Scotland's Hastings brothers against Romania in Pool 4. Scott's World Cup lasts less than 20 seconds owing to a hamstring injury, but Gavin, with 8 conversions (out of 9), a penalty goal and 2 tries himself, amasses 27 points, a world record for an international that stands for only a couple of hours before Didier Camberabero passes it for France against Zimbabwe with 30 points (3T-9C).

3 Jun Australia's faltering performance in beating Japan 42-23 at Concord Oval after trailing three times is jeered by the Sydney fans, who side with the underdogs, while none of the other second-rank powers manages to surprise England, Ireland or Wales, who all go through to the quarter-finals.

7 Jun Fiji, the only unseeded nation to reach the last eight, are beaten 31-16 by France, but centre Kaiava Salusalu is Player of the Match as the Fijians provide most of the excitement despite losing the forward battle.

10 Jun *The Daily Telegraph's* John Mason finds the omission of Roger Quittenton (England) and Clive Norling (Wales) from the list of referees being considered for the final and 3rd-place match 'inexplicable'.

13 Jun David Campese's try for Australia against France in the semi-finals is his 25th in Test matches, a new world record, beating Scotland's Ian Smith, who scored 24 in 32 Tests.

14 Jun Wales lock Huw Richards, playing against New Zealand in the semi-finals, is the first player to be sent off in the World Cup [he is suspended for a week], while All Black forward Michael Jones misses the Sunday fixture because of his religious beliefs.

16 Jun John Mason finds the appointment of Kerry Fitzgerald, a bank official from Brisbane, as referee for the final 'inexplicable', and slates the World Cup Referee Appointments Committee.

20 Jun In winning the Webb Ellis Trophy, the All Blacks have amassed 298 points in 6 matches, including 43 tries, while conceding only 52 points.

World Cup Pool 1: Australia 19 England 6, Sydney, 23 May

England's shortfall
Referee in try blunder

By John Reason

Most Australians feel New Zealanders have given them a great deal less than nothing down the ages. But chubby little Keith Lawrence, the New Zealand referee for England's opening World Cup match, more than made up for the shortfalls of history.

With the scores 6-6 midway through the second half, and Dean Richards and the rest of the England back-row skinning the Australian giraffes alive for the ball on the floor, Lawrence gave Australian winger David Campese a try after he had literally thrown the ball away in Peter Williams' tackle over the line.

Mr Lawrence did not see this and, sadly, he did not see much else either. He had a disastrous day, particularly in relation to offside, and some of the advantage he played came straight out of Alice in Wonderland.

All the referee did do was fall like a ton of bricks on

England in the line-out, and that presented Australia with a 19-6 advantage in penalty kicks, exactly the same as the score.

Australia were grateful for all the help they could get, because their allegedly awesome pack looked extremely vulnerable on the ground.

Not that England deserved to win. But they did make a nonsense of the lordly observations of Alan Jones, Australia's immensely entertaining coach, to the effect that his team is now operating at such a level that it ought to be able to play Beethoven from the sheet music.

Richards, Rees and Winterbottom really had a day to remember and Richards showed the world that he is not just a tiger at Leicester.

Webb, who had come on to make his debut when England lost Marcus Rose with concussion in the first five minutes, converted England's only try, scored by Harrison.

World Cup Pool 4: Scotland 20 France 20, Christchurch, 23 May

Injured Rutherford is out

Scotland's World Cup hopes were dealt a severe blow when injured fly-half John Rutherford was ruled out for the rest of the tournament. He was carried off after only six minutes of Scotland's opening match against France at Lancaster Park, Christchurch. Bob Munro, Scotland's manager, said Rutherford had suffered a serious tear in his right knee.

Scotland have relied heavily on the partnership between Rutherford and

scrum-half Roy Laidlaw in the past, and they had played a world record 34 times together before Saturday's match.

Although the Scots escaped with a draw against France, it was a match many thought they should have won, as they led 16-6 early in the second half. But it needed an injury-time try by Duncan in the right corner to save the Scots. The attempted conversion by Hastings faded across the face of the posts.

World Cup Pool 2: Ireland 6 Wales 13, Wellington, 25 May

Wales tame wind and Ireland

By John Mason

Wales, universally lambasted for being poor travellers, beat the wind and Ireland at Athletic Park to bring closer a Wales-England quarter-final at Brisbane.

The Welsh victory reflected the superiority of their forwards. Ireland were all at sea. The match, in comparison with what had gone before elsewhere in the World Cup, was an indifferent advertisement for standards in the Northern Hemisphere.

Despite the advantage of half a gale blowing behind them, Ireland had only a

couple of penalty goals by Kiernan at the break to show for their exertions.

In the second half, Jonathan Davies, always quick and often clever, ensured that Wales moved forward. The pack did their jobs as well. Paul Moriarty, the Wales No.8, was magnificent. It is a pity that in the only doubtful aspect of the match he should have been seen to trample upon Matthews.

Davies dropped two cheeky goals after Thorburn had landed a penalty, and Ring, handling twice, scored the only try.

World Cup Pool 2: Wales 40 Canada 9, Invercargill, 3 June

Davies puts Wales into last eight

Jonathan Davies, captain for the day, cut Canada to pieces with a remarkable display of attacking running as Wales cruised into the quarter-finals of the World Cup in Invercargill, New Zealand. Yet Canada had led 9-6 after playing down the wind in the first half, Rees kicking three penalty goals.

The chief beneficiary of the Davies magic was Ieuan Evans who ran in four tries from the right wing, equalling the post-war Welsh record of Maurice Richards. John Devereux was another mighty contrib-

utor in the centre, with a mixture of pace and power which unnerved the Canadian midfield

There was, however, a black mark for Giles, who was involved in an altercation with Stuart, his opposite number at scrum-half. Giles appeared to land a blow on Stuart, and the Canadian was taken from the field to have six stitches inserted above the right eye. De Goede, the Canadian captain, complained afterwards that the referee should have sent Giles off the field.

World Cup Quarter-Finals: New Zealand 30 Scotland 3, Christchurch, 6 June

Scotland out-Foxed

By John Reason

Grant Fox, New Zealand's fly-half, has now scored 95 points in five Tests – and in one of those he did not even kick at goal. At the rate Fox is scoring, he will break all the records in sight, real and ersatz, in about a year, and with the pack that New Zealand are developing, it looks as if South Africa could be fairly sure of blowing them out of the water.

I thought Scotland might inconvenience the All Blacks

in the tight, but they made increasingly less impression. Everything Scotland tried went wrong, chiefly because of pressure from the New Zealand defence. Scotland could not control the game anywhere.

The further the match went, the more goals Fox kicked and the more the power and the presence of the All Blacks became apparent. Whetton and Gallagher scored the New Zealand tries.

World Cup Quarter-Finals: Australia 33 Ireland 15, Sydney, 7 June

Ireland leave fight-back far too late

By a Special Correspondent

Australia yesterday at last revealed the style which has shot them to the top of the international rugby union rankings when they defeated Ireland to set up a World Cup semi-final with France. They piled up 24 points in the first 20 minutes at Sydney's Concord Oval and, although the Irish fought back gallantly to score two fine second-half tries, the match was effectively over from that early stage.

The Australians were furious over a first-half foul on scrum-half Nick Farr-Jones, who was hit very late by Irish flanker

Phil Matthews. The man regarded as the best scrum-half in the world was forced to go off after five minutes, suffering from a badly dislocated shoulder and concussion.

The foul inspired the Australians to throw off the insipid form they showed in the first round and finally start playing like potential world champions.

The Irish, whose knowledge of the offside rule appeared scanty, pulled themselves together towards half-time, but they never mastered the windy, wet conditions.

World Cup Quarter-Finals: England 3 Wales 16, Brisbane, 8 June

England at rock bottom and out

By John Mason

Even the Queensland skies wept yesterday at the sorry state of British rugby. England struck rock bottom in Brisbane, and Wales, though handing another drubbing to the old enemy, had no cause for complacency.

But, laboured as victory was, by far the more efficient team earned the privilege of opposing New Zealand in the semi-final on the same ground next Sunday. Wales needed to defend stoutly for a time, keep their heads and wait for England's mistakes, of which a large number were unforced.

England were dreadful. They were shorn of ideas, tactical appreciation, and what Clive Rowlands, the Wales manager, the sage of

Upper Cwmtyrch, graphically described afterwards as *calan* – the Welsh word for heart.

From the moment that the vociferous Welsh contingent at Ballymore gave a spirited rendering of 'Land of My Fathers', England back-pedalled, taking the wrong options with almost wilful intent.

The painful point was that England did not lack for possession. But all that ball was useless without control, as were the decisions to run before a satisfactory platform had been established up front. The three tries, all from English mistakes, were scored by Gareth Roberts, Robert Jones and John Devereux. New Zealand will not be quaking.

Welsh centre John Devereux salutes his try.

World Cup Semi-Finals: Australia 24 France 30, Sydney, 13 June

Frenchmen roar into final: Blanco try clinches victory

By John Reason

I never thought I would live to see a game to rival the one played between the Barbarians and the All Blacks at Cardiff in 1973, but this one did. It had a few more mistakes and not so many great players. And Australia in 1987 are not of the same class as New Zealand in 1973. But so much was happening in so many places for so much of the time that this game will be remembered as long as the World Cup is played.

What a pity that a miserable crowd of only 17,000 turned up to watch. The resilience of the French was remarkable. They came back from 9-0, 15-12 and 24–21 down, and were much the more inventive and exciting team all through. But for ages they did not get the reward that was their due, and other French teams, at other times, would have given up with broken hearts.

Australia went 6-0 up in the first eight minutes when Lynagh dropped a rifling goal from a line-out and kicked a penalty goal after Condom had collapsed a maul.

France then took over. Their forwards were mauling like lions, and the early departure of the brilliant Papworth with a knee ligament injury meant that France were left with nearly all the class behind the scrum.

Far from closing the gap, though, France saw it increased, Lynagh kicking a penalty goal from 57 yards. Then, ten minutes from half-time, he had a dolly of a kick from in front of the posts but missed it. France took a quick drop-out, and within a couple of minutes they had scored the try which turned the game and set it alight.

Coker, the Australian No.8, won the ball at a line-out, but had it ripped off him and Lorieux plunged over. Not only that, but Camberabero kicked the conversion from the touch-line. That meant that Australia led only 9-6 at half-time.

At the beginning of the second half, Sella finished off a marvellous move to score between the posts. Camberabero converted, and now France were ahead 12-9.

But then Grigg flipped a long pass back inside for Campese to score a try which Lynagh converted; 15-12. In the next minute Lynagh had another easy penalty kick to make it 18-12. He missed that, and France began to think that the gods might be on their side after all.

Blanco pulled in three defenders, like a sinuous black spider, before launching the sharp-footed Lagisquet on a scoring run. Again Camberabero converted, and when he kicked a penalty goal for offside, France led 21-15 and it looked as if Australia were dead and buried.

Not a bit of it. As this seething match went into the last quarter, Codey suddenly erupted from an attacking line-out and, with that tremendous man Rodriguez rubbing his eyes in disbelief at an unpunished knock-on, struggled over to score a try which Lynagh converted; 21-21.

Mesnel missed a drop at goal, Australia somehow held a brilliant French move and then, at the other end, Blanco made what looked like the mistake of a lifetime in front of his line, putting France in such trouble that they conceded a penalty in front of the posts which Lynagh kicked; 24-21.

Surely, we thought, that was the end. Not a bit of that, either. Camberabero kicked a penalty, which Champ could not bear to watch, after a late tackle. And then at the death, a surging move involving Champ, Lagisquet, Berbizier, Mesnel, Charvet, Berbizier again and Lagisquet again saw Rodriguez in support and Blanco forgetting his injured hamstring and going for his life and a try in the corner to put France in the final. Camberabero made sure with his second touch-line conversion.

Laurent Rodriguez: one of France's semi-final heroes.

World Cup Semi-Finals: New Zealand 49 Wales 6, Brisbane, 14 June

Wales are demolished by remorseless New Zealand

Wales, the last of the Home Unions in the competition, were ignominiously removed from the World Cup by a merciless New Zealand team that took no prisoners at Ballymore, Brisbane, yesterday.

Wales have been fiendishly unlucky. For various reasons they were missing five first-choice forwards for the semi-final. Against the Whettons and Shelfords of this world that is an impossible handicap.

New Zealand's tries went to Shelford (2), Drake, Kirwan (2), Alan Whetton, Stanley and Brooke-Cowden. Fox kicked eight goals from 11 attempts. John Devereux scored the Welsh try, which Thorburn converted.

The match will be remembered, however, for the miserable episode in the closing minutes when Richards, the Wales lock, was sent off for punching Gary Whetton. In the brawl that followed the incident, Richards was knocked semi-conscious by All Black No.8 Wayne Shelford, who should have been dismissed as well.

World Cup Third-Place Match: Australia 21 Wales 22, Rotorua, 18 June

Codey off: Wales leave it late

By John Mason

Wales, mischievously labelled the 49-ers after their crushing defeat by New Zealand, came from behind at the last gasp to secure third place in the 1987 World Cup by beating Australia yesterday.

From the fifth minute, Wales were playing against 14 men, a challenge that they fumbled and fretted about for the rest of a highly exciting but otherwise bumbling match.

Australia performed wonders while managing to create an impossible burden for themselves: some sort of 'macho' vanity was their undoing and, to a great degree, the Wallabies, I regret, forfeit sympathy. Codey, having been warned after barely a minute following a tussle with Roberts, waded in with his feet three minutes later, and off he went. His offence was more stupid than evil, the unthinking act of a self-styled 'hard man'.

Wales led three times and were behind twice, the second occasion for half an hour before Hadley, his path cleared by Thorburn, thundered into the corner. Still the agony was not over. From the left touchline, the crowd baying and the fifth minute of injury time about to begin, Thorburn had to convert the try to win the match.

Suddenly the bank behind the posts erupted and Wales were in front again. This time they stayed there.

World Cup Final: New Zealand 29 France 9, Auckland, 20 June

All Blacks on top of rugby world
France bogged down in final turn-off
By John Reason

As an exercise in turning off 600 million television viewers, New Zealand's victory in the first World Cup final in rugby history was almost without parallel.

Eden Park in Auckland produced the snore of the century. Perhaps that was not surprising. Once Scotland's John Rutherford had banjoed his knee, not one of the 15 teams left in the tournament had anything remotely resembling a top-class fly-half, and the best referee in the world, Clive Norling, was sent home with him.

With Australian referee Kerry Fitzgerald reluctant to apply the laws to any part of the proceedings, we had to go back to watching the grass grow and watching the All Blacks kick for position, kick up-and-unders, set up camp in the French 25 and play the blind-side all day long.

And watching Grant Fox, with his eternally deliberate six steps backwards, followed by two steps sideways before he wraps himself in his reverie of concentration, we were all bored to tears as he kicked another six goals.

We should have known it was going to be one of those days when we saw that the rains had left the going deep at Eden Park, which meant that no one would be able to run.

New Zealand kicked off, having been given the assistance of the wind and the sun by the French, and spent the whole of the next 25 minutes within about 15 yards of where the ball came down near the French 25.

Fox dropped a goal after 15 minutes and promptly lived up to his name by making such a mess of another drop kick that it took the French entirely unawares. Lagisquet, painfully on his own, fumbled the unintended grubber and Michael Jones erupted over the line to score.

Jones was brilliant. He was so much quicker than the French back row that he almost had to stop and wait for them. He has the hands of a centre, he jumps like a

All Black skipper David Kirk with the William Webb Ellis trophy.

decathlete and he tackles like a ton of bricks. Undoubtedly the player of the tournament.

Camberabero kicked a fine penalty goal for France early in the second half, but two more penalty goals by Fox took New Zealand 15-3 clear. Then a stunning tackle by Jones on Mesnel set up a ruck from which Kirk, Fox and Jones set up a blind-side try for Kirk.

Almost from the kick-off, Berbizier allowed Kirk to slip away on the inside. Three Frenchmen, including Sella and Blanco, fell over each other in tackling Kirk, and Shelford put Kirwan over in the corner.

That left Fox time to kick two more penalty goals for New Zealand, and in the last minute of the match Berbizier escaped to score a soft little try, which Camberabero converted.

By that time, we would have been glad of the diversion of an aeroplane dropping flour bombs, because Fox's idea of fly-half play is to stand absolutely still while shovelling the ball out. On a pitch as soft as that, it was a wonder he did not sink in up to his knees. No wonder New Zealand have no centres. But no doubt they will bear the pain. After all, they do have the World Cup and they know full well that their government will stop them being eaten alive by the Springboks.

1988

9 Mar St Ives are banned for 28 days by the Cornwall RU for having 16 players sent off in the last three seasons.

9 Apr Lancashire beat Warwickshire 23-18 to win the first Toshiba-sponsored County Championship.

23 Apr England beat Ireland 21-10 in the Dublin Millennium Challenge at Lansdowne Road, where the celebration is referred to as their 'Aluminium'.

7 May A world record crowd of 56,643 for a club match sees Llanelli beat Neath 28-13 at Cardiff to win the Schweppes Cup final.

15 May In the Australian Bicentennial Match at Sydney's Concord Oval, the Wallabies beat a World XV 42-38. Brian Smith, standing in for Michael Lynagh at outside-half, amasses 26 points (1T-5C-2DG-2PG) for Australia, his 9 successful kicks coming from 9 attempts.

21 May Scotland run in 5 tries as they beat Zimbabwe 31-10 in an international in Bulawayo, Peter Dods converting 4 of them and also kicking a penalty.

17 Jun Mosese Taga, 22, the Fijian loosehead prop sent off yesterday for punching England flanker Gary Rees in England's 25-12 win over Fiji in Suva, is banned for 28 days.

27 Nov The Wallabies finish a mixed tour on a high note with a 40-22 win over the BaaBaas at Cardiff, climaxed by a David Campese try in injury time in which he runs from midfield on the left, eluding four opponents with a series of dummies, swerves and changes of pace to earn a standing ovation from the crowd and his team.

6 Dec Oxford, packed with Southern Hemisphere stars, beat a strong Cambridge side 27-7 to record their biggest victory in the Varsity Match since 1909; their 5 Australians include outstanding full-back Robert Egerton (1T) and Wallaby fly-half Brian Smith (2T-2C), while their scrum-half is none other than David Kirk, who as All Black captain lifted the first World Cup last year.

INTERNATIONAL CHAMPIONSHIP

	E	F	I	S	W	P	W	D	L	F	A	Pts
1=WALES	-	9-10	-	25-20	-	4	3	0	1	57	42	6
1=FRANCE	10-9	-	25-6	-	-	4	3	0	1	57	47	6
3 ENGLAND	-	-	35-3	-	3-11	4	2	0	2	56	30	4
4=SCOTLAND	6-9	23-12	-	-	-	4	1	0	3	67	68	2
4=IRELAND	-	-	-	22-18	9-12	4	1	0	3	40	90	2

TOURS (Tests)
England in Australia: A22-E16, A28-E8
Wales in New Zealand: NZ52-W3, NZ54-W9
Australia in British Isles: E28-A19, S13-A32
New Zealand in Australia: A7-NZ32, A19-NZ19, A9-NZ30

The Daily Telegraph, 9 March

Cup affair costs Jeffrey place in Scottish seven

By John Mason

John Jeffrey, Scotland's World Cup back-row forward, was yesterday left out of the nine-man national squad for the New South Wales International Sevens in Sydney on April 1-2 for disciplinary reasons. Jeffrey has not been selected because of his part in the Calcutta Cup affair last Saturday. The cup, valued at £10,000, was damaged after being removed, temporarily, from an Edinburgh hotel.

Robin Charters, chairman of Scotland's selectors, said yesterday: 'He (Jeffrey) was the only player from our side that I know of being involved in the Calcutta Cup affair. That is the selectors' punishment for him – not being selected.'

The Scottish Rugby Union are carrying out a formal inquiry into the incident in which an England player was also involved. The trophy, as is usual, was on display at the post-match dinner and disappeared for two hours.

When the cup, which was minted in 1877 from silver rupees, the remaining funds of the then defunct Calcutta Rugby Club, was recovered, parts of it were compressed and dented. It is being repaired.

Dudley Wood, secretary of the Rugby Football Union, said yesterday: 'We shall be receiving a report from the Scottish Rugby Union in due course, which will be considered. I don't see us rushing into action.'

[Dean Richards, the England player involved, was later disciplined.]

International Championship: Ireland 9 Wales 12, Dublin, 5 March

Wales deserve Crown despite slips galore

By John Mason

The Triple Crown, without question this season, is back where it belongs. A score of agonising slips against Ireland in windy Dublin on Saturday cannot alter what Wales have achieved.

Should Celtic heads be modestly bowed at the prospect of adding the Grand Slam by beating France at Cardiff on Saturday week, Wales, thanks to Paul Thorburn, cannot be less than joint champions.

In the rough and tumble of a shapeless match, Ireland denied Wales, who were vastly superior territorially, the match-winning points until the fourth minute of time added for stoppages and injuries. Although victory by a goal, dropped goal and penalty goal to a goal and penalty goal was a just outcome, Ireland's tigerish tackling and well-organised cover did much to minimise deep-seated weaknesses.

Up front, Norster, the Wales lock, deserves for the umpteenth time the grateful thanks of his countrymen. He is also entitled to the protection the laws of the game permit. The illegalities began early on Saturday. Though Norster, the outstanding middle line-out forward in Europe, had re-asserted control of rugby's jungle by mid-way through the second half, some distinguished colleagues were distinctly made edgy by then.

Jones, similarly put out of stride by questionable means in the opening period, never did recover the poise of the past year. Davies, too, decided that attempted dropped goals – he missed four – would solve all problems. With sundry wrong options being taken by the back row, compounded in turn by mistakes elsewhere, Wales were less than cool.

However, the unfortunate Kiernan, so often Ireland's saviour, missed five of seven kicks, once striking a post. Thorburn, though winning the match at the last gasp, also had a harrowing time, failing with four of six kicks at goal in the second half.

International Championship: Wales 9 France 10, Cardiff, 19 March

Wales' stage fright

By John Mason

The Wales class of 1988 are not quite ready for the highest honours. In the drenching drizzle at Cardiff on Saturday during a tense, exciting match littered with errors, France were marginally more efficient at scoring points than Wales.

Wales, needing victory for the Grand Slam to end a 10-year drought or a draw to win the championship outright, fluffed their lines on a tacky, slippery banana-skin of a stage. Defeat by a try and two penalty goals to a goal and penalty goal was an anti-climax.

After the boldness of victory – and playing style – against England and the sustained skill and entertainment of the Scotland match, Wales have had to settle for a share of the championship with France, each country winning three matches.

Wales beat themselves. Early opportunities were not accepted. The squandering of early scoring chances – clear-cut and expertly created – ruined what could have been a rousing crescendo to a Welsh season in which the national team have disguised shortcomings shrewdly and thrived on the excellence of individuals.

But on the most important day in the careers of the 16 players called on by Wales, too many lost their way.

International Championship: England 35 Ireland 3, Twickenham, 19 March

Oti promises more as England turn corner

By Graham Tait

A rather bashful Chris Oti claimed after his hat-trick of tries had left Twickenham ecstatic on Saturday that England's supporters had yet to see the best of him. In the wake of England's superb six-try second-half showing, Trevor Ringland, of Ireland, one of the game's better tacklers, will be hoping to be a long way from Lansdowne Road when the teams meet again next month.

The sight of Oti hurtling down the left touchline will live in the memory for many a year. Poor Ringland may never forget those 40 minutes of sheer torture, with a jubilant crowd baying for more.

Over on the other side, Crossan experienced a similar painful lesson from Underwood, who at last opened his Twickenham account with two tries and a brilliant run that set up a third.

With the hordes of spectators still milling around long after the final whistle, Geoff Cooke, a beaming England manager, politely refrained from the 'O Ye Of Little Faith' thoughts that could not have been far from the surface. 'We have taken a lot of flak these last weeks, with the critics insisting that the backs can't play. I think we have proved our case.'

But amid all the euphoria, spare a thought for Nigel Melville. Fortune and the England captain have never been the closest of allies and, as his colleagues were revelling in their newly found confidence, the Wasps scrum-half was lying in the West Middlesex Hospital with a fracture at the base of the tibia and a dislocated ankle.

Melville always showed faith in Cooke's general plan of campaign. Sadly, he was not there to see such confidence justified and in particular to applaud the performance of Richard Harding, his half-time replacement, who never put a foot wrong.

After a mundane first half in which the England forwards had gradually asserted their authority, Ireland clung to the advantage of a dropped goal from Kiernan, and there was certainly little suggestion of deeds to come.

But after 36 seconds of the second half, Harding got Underwood underway, leading to England's first try, by stand-in captain Orwin, and then the cracks started to appear in the Irish defence. They were cut to ribbons by a complete all-round England display.

Courage League: Leicester 39 Waterloo 15, Leicester, 4 April

Leicester are first League champions after fitting climax

By John Mason

Leicester, finishing with a forthright flurry of points after an uneasy first half, became the first Courage League One champions in style yesterday.

Putting a series of uncharacteristic fumbles in a chilling, gusting wind behind them during a spirited second half, Leicester overran Waterloo, who had been level, 15-15, at the interval.

Victory by four goals, four penalty goals and a dropped goal to two goals and a penalty goal ultimately illustrated most of Leicester's virtues. Waterloo, too, helped to stage a fitting climax to England's first league season.

It was similarly appropriate that Paul Dodge, enthusiastically cheered by an 8,000 crowd, was presented with the Courage trophy. A broken kneecap had kept Dodge, the club captain, out of the team for most of the season.

Yesterday, he did not appear until the 35th minute, as replacement for Buttimore, who dislocated a shoulder.

Cusworth has been in charge in the absence of Dodge and, to a man, the Leicester players pushed their elected captain forward to receive the trophy from John Simpson, president-elect of the Rugby Football Union.

Cusworth, modestly, excluded all reference to himself, pointing instead to the two flank forwards and a greying full-back. They, he insisted, were the day's heroes – Wells, Thornley and Hare.

The remarkable Hare – adding 20 more points to reach 368 for the season – kicked eight goals from eight attempts, with four penalties and four conversions. He also presented scoring passes for two of the four tries.

That splendid contribution was capped only by the perpetual motion of Wells. Late on in a wearing match, Wells set up the ruck, won the ball and, 70 yards downfield, took the pass from the speeding Underwood to send Thornley over for Leicester's second try.

As Leicester did a lap of honour, Dean Richards declined his colleagues' offer of the trophy. The England No.8, disciplined last month for his part in the Calcutta Cup incident, moved rapidly in the other direction.

The Daily Telegraph, 22 April

New Zealand ban blow for World tour of South Africa: Series will go ahead says Craven

By John Mason

New Zealand's rugby authorities have joined Wales and Ireland in preventing their players from joining a World tour party in South Africa in August.

Russ Thomas, chairman of New Zealand's Rugby Union, said in Wellington yesterday that the proposed tour was not in the wider interests of New Zealand rugby. Invitations would not be passed on.

Grant Fox, the All Black outside-half and goal-kicker, said in Auckland that the New Zealand decision was an infringement of an individual's liberty and freedom of choice.

But Dr Danie Craven of the South African Rugby Board said the tour would still go ahead: 'Sure this is a great disappointment. But it's not the end of the world,' he said. 'It would have been better to have had All Blacks in the party, but they are still our friends and we will not break this friendship.'

France are the only leading rugby nation to have endorsed unconditionally the seven-match visit to mark the anniversary celebrations of Northern Transvaal and Eastern Province.

England, who discuss the matter again next Friday, are less than enthusiastic and Argentina, should their players be invited, are lukewarm. Scotland's attitude, too, may fall short of total opposition, but only because, like England, they are reluctant to stop individuals deciding for themselves

Once again the fond belief of the South African Rugby Board that they are about to return to the world rugby stage has been dashed.

They were ill-advised to bang the publicity drums so loudly last month.

John Player Special Cup Final: Harlequins 28 Bristol 22, Twickenham, 30 April

Salmon class sinks Bristol

By John Reason

Harlequins ran everything in a tumultuous match at Twickenham and shot into an 18-0 lead. But Bristol kicked up-and-unders all day long and came back so far and so quickly that they were once within a Quins fumble of taking the lead.

Simon Hogg, the Bristol fly-half, hit the cross-bar with a drop at goal. Jon Webb, the Bristol full-back, hit a post with a penalty kick. And when Richard Moon, the Harlequins scrum-half, thought it was time to take over as goalkeeper, referee Fred Howard took a dim view and awarded a penalty try, which Webb converted. This cut Quins' lead to 21-19.

When Richard Harding sent another kick spiralling into the tricky wind, the Quins looked as if they were about to be buried. So did Stuart Thresher, their full-back. But Thresher did not fumble.

Not only that, but he scraped the ball away to Davis, and the little winger started a glorious counter-attack which swept the length of the field. Harriman on the Harlequins right always had too much pace for Duggan on the Bristol left, and powerful support play by Salmon gave Carling the chance to battle over the line for his second try.

Little more than 10 minutes remained, and Bristol had lost their momentum. Webb kicked another penalty goal but, for the first and possibly only time in his life, Adrian Thompson, the Quins' makeshift fly-half, placed an attacking kick to such perfection that it nailed Bristol into a defensive position from which they could not escape.

Bristol's frustration then boiled over. In a silly outburst they conceded another penalty. That gave Salmon first the chance legitimately to take his time (John Olver had just been warned for time-wasting) and second the chance to score another three points. Salmon took both chances with the relish of the experienced player that he is.

That gave Harlequins the John Player Cup, and it made just as big a dent in Bristol's centenary celebrations as John Jeffrey and Dean Richards made in the Calcutta Cup.

It was the first time Harlequins had beaten Bristol since 1972.

Quins' John Olver celebrates their John Player Cup win.

Middlesex Sevens: Harlequins 20 Bristol 18, Twickenham, 7 May

Quins victory at the double

By Barrie Fairall

On their own lush Twickenham pitch, Harlequins completed a unique double when they ran away with the Middlesex Sevens yesterday – an encore to their stunning victory in the John Player Special Cup Final the previous weekend.

For their sins, it was the unfortunate Bristol who discovered once again that London Rugby is nothing to joke about. In successive weekends now, they have been on the receiving end of a side transformed. Is there no stopping Harlequins?

Apparently not. Because this latest victory brought them a hat-trick of titles in the Middlesex tournament, and they have now won here a record 11 times, after starting the ball rolling in 1926.

Mind you, this latest so-called 'designer seven' is a bit special from front to back, with the afternoon killer blows provided by Andrew Harriman, the flying son of a Nigerian Prince and a particular favourite of the crowd. Harriman sprinted clear for seven tries during the course of a lovely afternoon on which the enjoyment assumed the usual raucous proportions.

Indeed, we saw it all – from male and female streakers to the latest Mexican wave. On the pitch, a Harlequins victory appeared to be a mere formality.

That it was not was down to a spirited display from Bristol. They gave Harlequins a tremendous scrap to go down only 20-18 after being sixteen points adrift at the interval.

In the quarter-finals, finding a team-mate's dislodged contact lens proved to be Andy Ripley's last significant on-field contribution for Rosslyn Park before he walked away from first-class rugby after a career lasting almost 20 years. He received a moving ovation.

The Sunday Telegraph, 8 May

One-man game planned by Twickenham?

By John Reason

England's rugby players will be as disappointed as those in Scotland, Ireland and Wales to learn that they are not, after all, going to be allowed to accept invitations to play in the World XV touring South Africa.

Confusion arose after the Rugby Union's meeting last week when, after a garbled discussion late in a long day, some committee members left thinking that they had agreed that individuals should be allowed to play in South Africa.

So they are, but not for the World XV. The difference, you see, is that if they play for the World XV they will be going to make up a team!

You may well share my view that rugby players going to play anywhere always go to make up a team. You may also deduce, as I did, that perhaps the Rugby Union plan to initiate one-man rugby. That would be a novelty.

The truth is that the Rugby Union has now joined the ranks of appeasers. The RFU are frightened that hostile left-wing councils will withdraw their sports development officers.

Hopefully, the rugby players of England will react in the same way as our cricketers and those five rugby players in Wales who are investigating the possibility of taking legal action against the Welsh Rugby Union.

The Sunday Telegraph, 22 May

Home countries break through the TV barrier

By John Reason

John Burgess, president of the Rugby Union and now with the England team in Australia, says the new £5 million television contract negotiated with the BBC will give each of the four Home Unions a separate weekly magazine programme lasting 50 minutes.

Four different presentations from four different studio bases should increase the chances of an improved output. It will also be given a more attractive late-afternoon spot in the schedules rather than the lunch-time dustbin into which it has been consigned for years.

Burgess was at pains to stress that the Rugby authorities 'are much more concerned about marketing our game well than with the money we get for it'.

Tour International: New Zealand 52 Wales 3, Christchurch, 28 May

Wales hammered, but All Blacks 'made too many errors'

By John Mason

When Wayne Shelford, New Zealand's captain, insisted that the All Blacks had made too many mistakes, he was being perfectly serious. Passes had gone down and tries had been missed.

Such clinical assessment of another colossal presentation approaching playing perfection offers a clue to the 10-try decimation of Wales at Lancaster Park, Christchurch, on Saturday.

Shelford agreed that he was pleased with victory but that the errors bothered him. He felt 14 tries should have been scored.

Both Shelford and Alex 'Grizz' Wyllie, New Zealand's coach, offered consoling words for desolate Welshmen, most of whom were reduced to a numbed silence.

In many respects it was irrelevant that this was Wales who were humiliatingly thrashed by six goals and four tries to a penalty goal. The merciless dismantling of everything that British players and coaches have set out to achieve in the last decade possessed the shivery overtones of a public hanging.

But New Zealand, who on 14 June last year beat Wales 49-6 in the semi-finals of the World Cup, also created a gloriously simple, supremely efficient form of the game played throughout at a steady gallop.

There was something to admire at every turn, not least the forthright dispatch of outmoded ideas and attitudes in the Northern Hemisphere.

Wales were completely out of their depth. Evans and Bryant tackled constantly and Norster won some line-out ball in the middle. But the known skills of Davies and Robert Jones were sunk without trace, and, though not fully fit, Kirwan, New Zealand's right wing, toyed with Webbe at all times.

Kirwan (4), Wright (2), Shelford, Gary Whetton, Deans and Gallagher, late of St Joseph's, Lewisham, scored New Zealand's tries, Fox converting six. Michael Jones was not on the list, but, as he had a hand in everything else, that hardly mattered.

Tour International: Australia 22 England 16, Brisbane, 29 May

England waste chances to win 'league two' match

By John Mason

England, despite taking a 13-3 lead with two opportunist tries, fell to Australia in the second half of what can only be described as a 'world league two match' in Brisbane yesterday.

Should there be any doubts, league one status is reserved for New Zealand and probably South Africa. No other nations qualify.

The match, at Ballymore, Australia's international ground in Queensland, bore little comparison with the remarkable events at Lancaster Park, Christchurch, where Wales were humbled by New Zealand on Saturday.

England will be angry with themselves. They had a jumpy, nervous Australian team in trouble midway through the first half after breakaway tries by Underwood and Bentley and a conversion and penalty goal from Webb.

If the cool authority of Webb, England's outstanding player, had been matched by enough of his colleagues, there would be a different tale to tell. There were signs, but no consistency, and England were beaten by a try and six penalty goals to a goal, try and two penalty goals.

The Daily Telegraph, 31 October

Carling, 22, appointed England captain: Ackford, Harriman and Morris are capped

By John Mason

England, beaten twice in the summer series in Australia, go into battle against the Wallabies – for the third time in five months – with a new captain and three new caps at Twickenham on Saturday.

Will Carling, 22, the Harlequin centre, becomes England's fifth captain since last January. All being well, it is intended he should stay in command for at least three years.

The new caps are Dewi Morris, 24, the Welsh-born scrum-half who joined Liverpool St Helens this season, and two Harlequins – Andrew Harriman, 24, right wing, and Paul Ackford, 30, lock.

None of the newcomers was in Australia with England last summer, while Carling, who was completing his final year examinations at Durham University, arrived halfway through the tour.

Tour International: England 28 Australia 19, Twickenham, 5 November

Richards roars in and Underwood reaps the profit

By John Reason

With 20 minutes to go of a firecracker of a game, played in perfect conditions on the afternoon of Bonfire Night at Twickenham, England had twice hauled themselves out of pits they had dug for themselves and had pulled up to 13-13.

At that point, Australia dropped out long from their 25. It was nothing like the searching kick that has earned Australia such a reputation. But, for one moment, as Rob Andrew juggled with the ball, it looked as if they might get away with it. Andrew hung on, though, and shipped the ball off to Dean Richards. The England No.8 had been immense throughout, all muscle and aggression and power, and he took off through the Australian defence as if there were no-one in the way.

He burst through to clear water on the far side, and with Dave Egerton, Brian Moore and, inevitably, the perpetual Andy Robinson in support, England made room for Rory Underwood to have a cut on the left.

The Australia cover defence was tremendous, but Underwood rode it just long enough to score a try in the corner, which Jonathan Webb converted from the touchline.

That buried Australia, and an ecstatic England supporter stood up and bellowed above the hubbub: 'Dean Richards! I love you!'

Richards heard him and looked suitably coy. He had a fair bit of looking coy to do because, wherever he stood on the ground after that (and that was usually underneath the ball), the crowd just rose and roared a personal ovation.

England conceded far more of the throw than sides can normally afford against Australia, but Dooley, Richards and Egerton dug in so hard that they reduced Australia's throwing advantage of 37-14 to within one take of parity in possession.

Australia lost the game because they were trying to realise their coach Bob Dwyer's vision of running rugby. But the truth is that, with the single exception of David Campese, their backs are nowhere near good enough to do it.

1989

Laws Three replacements allowed instead of two.

17 Jun France give the All Blacks a fright in the first Test at Christchurch, reducing an 18-0 half-time deficit to 18-17 in 11 minutes before going down 25-17.

23 Jul The Lions conclude a triumphant tour of Australia with a 19-15 victory over an ANZAC XV (12A-3NZ), having won all 12 matches except the first Test.

4 Nov The Fijians finish a mixed tour (W3-D1-L4) of France (highlighted by a splendid 32-16 win over the powerful French Barbarians) and Britain (slammed 38-17 by Scotland but outscoring England B by 4 tries to 1 in a 20-12 victory) with a 58-23 thrashing at the

hands of England at Twickenham, having two three-quarters, Tevita Vonolagi and Noa Nadruku, sent off, while Rory Underwood's haul of 5 tries equals the England record set by Daniel Lambert in 1907 and brings him level with Cyril Lowe on 18 international tries.

25 Nov With a 21-10 victory over the Barbarians at Twickenham, the All Blacks complete a 100% 13-match tour of the British Isles, mainly Wales and Ireland.

12 Dec Cambridge win the Varsity match 22-13 over an Oxford side that causes raised eyebrows for its overseas content – 5 Australians, 2 South Africans, 2 Americans and 1 from Zimbabwe; the former women's college St Anne's provides 9 of their XV.

Berbizier scores the opening try for France.

International Championship: France 19 Scotland 3, Paris, 18 March

French blossom in the sunshine

By Michael Heal

Two weeks ago at Twickenham, the French lacked any kind of self-belief. Yesterday, encouraged by the prospect of yet another English defeat in Cardiff and with the sun on their backs, they never allowed the Scots to further their pretensions to the Five Nations Champion-ship, and in so doing secured the title for themselves.

The physical aggression of the home pack denied the Scots the opportunities on which they thrive, and ensured that most of the good ball was rolled back on the French side.

Although individuals like White, Sole, Gray and Calder caught the eye, their singular forays could not match the solidity and sense of purpose of the French pack.

Early skirmishing came to nothing, but the Scots had to tackle most. French frustration exhibited itself and Rodriguez was penalised

for punching Jeffrey. Dods exacted positive retribution with a penalty after 25 minutes.

This provoked the French into a more sustained and disciplined spell of attacking rugby. Although Gray was prominent in pilfering possession, it took committed defence to keep out thrusts from Lagisquet, Carminati, Rodriguez and Blanco.

The prize France deserved came in the 37th minute. From a scrum near the posts, Rodriguez picked up and fed Berbizier. With half a dummy, the French captain was over and Berot added the conversion.

The interval was the only respite Scotland had. On the resumption, Rodriguez fed Berbizier from a scrum near the 22. The foxy scrum-half drew the Scottish backs up on to him before planting a perfect kick over the line to make Blanco odds-on in the

INTERNATIONAL CHAMPIONSHIP

	E	F	I	S	W	P	W	D	L	F	A	Pts
1 FRANCE	-	-	-	19-3	31-12	4	3	0	1	76	47	6
2=ENGLAND	-	11-0	-	12-12	-	4	2	1	1	48	27	5
2=SCOTLAND	-	-	37-21	-	23-7	4	2	1	1	75	59	5
4=IRELAND	3-16	21-26	-	-	-	4	1	0	3	64	92	2
4=WALES	12-9	-	13-19	-	-	4	1	0	3	44	82	2

TOURS (Tests)

France in New Zealand: NZ25-F17, NZ34-F20
British Isles in Australia: A30-BI12, A12-BI19, A18-BI19
Australia in New Zealand: NZ24-A12
Australia in France: F15-A32, F25-A19
New Zealand in British Isles: W9-NZ34, I6-NZ23

International Championship: Wales 12 England 9, Cardiff, 18 March

Sorry England throw it away

By John Reason

Wales kicked the ball into the streaming skies and Robert Jones chipped, or rather slipped, the ball down the short side, and Rory Underwood made another of those painful mistakes in defence that cost England the game against Scotland. The one at Cardiff gave Wales six points and the match and spared them a face full of whitewash. It also deprived England of the Championship.

England led 9-6 at half-time without ever understanding how to play wet-weather rugby and maintain an attacking position, and when England kicked off in the second half Wales returned a diagonal kick to the open side.

There Underwood dropped the ball, and when Wales won the midfield scrum Paul Turner kicked an up-and-under which went too deep. Underwood caught the ball near his 25 but chose not to do the prudent thing and put the ball into touch or even run it there.

Instead he tried to make a fancy pass to Jon Webb even though Dewi Morris was blocking the pass to the England full-back. Predictably the ball went loose, and Wales hacked it over the line where Mike Hall was given the benefit of a doubt about the touchdown. Paul Thorburn converted.

That took Wales into the lead. Robert Jones kept them there, secure behind a solid scrum and content to sit on

the three-point advantage and keep England pegged in their half.

England had only once built up a position good enough to threaten a score and then Andrew dropped a goal which gave them the lead for the second time in the match.

Wales played the referee just as shrewdly as they used the elements. They knew that England carried more guns in the line-out, so they cheerfully turned that phase of the game into a shambles, and Mr Fitzgerald let them get away with it.

That shut England out of the game and extended the 26-year chasm since England last won in Cardiff.

To say that Mr Fitzgerald's refereeing of the line-out was the worst I have ever seen would be quite wrong in the literal sense because he did not referee the line-outs at all. Bodies and elbows were flying everywhere and players were taken out left and right. Mr Fitzgerald watched it with unblinking equanimity.

This cut away the platform on which England have built their season. Wade Dooley made little contribution and Paul Ackford was rendered almost invisible.

The referee did jump about a bit when Wales charged a scrum and Moore retaliated with his version of the Can-Can. That started a 20-second war which contained far more action than the rest of the match put together.

race for a try. Berot missed the conversion.

When Armstrong was penalised for killing the ball, Berot landed the penalty from the 22 to give France a healthy lead of 13-3.

A period of Scottish pressure came to nought as they squandered possession, and they soon paid for their

profligacy. From an innocuous position, Mesnel hoisted a high ball to the Scots 22. Sella claimed it, pirouetted and lobbed a pass to Andrieu, who found Lagisquet clear and the try was a formality. Berot converted splendidly from touch. With the game won, the French were able to relax.

Pilkington Cup Final: Bath 10 Leicester 6, Twickenham, 29 April

Barnes-storming Bath: Leicester lead slips

By John Mason

There is not a lot of Stuart Barnes, relatively speaking – more a case of quality than quantity, as Leicester ultimately discovered on Saturday. On an occasion in which the tightrope of taut nerves left even the most seasoned wondering where the safety net was, Barnes kept his head, and feet.

Bath's victory over Leicester in the final of the Pilkington Cup owed much to the coolness of Barnes, the club's captain and outside-half, in a contest as tense as it was absorbing.

Though the Bath sledgehammer was working overtime for much of the second half, the result was in considerable doubt until Fred Howard, the referee, decided emotions had been buffeted for long enough.

Leicester had led until the 29th minute of the second half when Bath drew level with a second penalty goal by Barnes. For another fraught nine minutes, with Bath in residence deep in enemy territory, Leicester tackled

Stuart Barnes goes over for the winning try.

tigerishly. Palmer was held, so was Sagoe. Hill added expertly to Leicester's troubles, and Simpson, the replacement No.8 after 52 minutes for the injured Egerton, allowed no respite either.

Somehow the Tigers coped until Barnes – all 5ft 6∞in and 11st 10lb of him – scurried down the short-side and burrowed successfully for the line and a try. Bath's sighs of

relief were thunderclaps. Barely three minutes remained, at the nerve-wracking end of which Bath, already the 1989 Courage League champions, could reasonably call themselves the best English club in the land.

Though Barnes, who suggested afterwards that the cup victory – Bath's fifth in six years – was even more satisfying than success in the

league, scored all his team's points, he was not the outstanding individual.

That particular contest was a close-run thing between Richards, Leicester's ubiquitous No.8, the Tiger who is a Lion, and Cronin, Bath's lock, whose next engagement is Scotland's tour of Japan.

Richards, I suppose, had the edge. To be back patrolling the edge of the box one moment as Barnes kicked, and the next to be ripping the ball away from someone as strong as Chilcott were tiny dazzling examples of the massive contribution he made.

Leicester's supporters in a full house of 58,000, a world record for a club match, were in fine voice, and when Hare, after two sighters, landed penalty goals in the 27th and 37th minutes, Twickenham's rafters rattled.

I swear I saw some blue and white favours doffed, too, for Hare is everyone's hero; a pleasant, easy-going bloke without an ounce of side. He trotted off into retirement without a backward glance, disappointed but not sad.

Schweppes Cup Final: Llanelli 13 Neath 14, Cardiff, 6 May

Mad moment mars Neath's Cup: Referee fails to stamp on brutality

By John Reason

The Welsh RFU or its representatives seem to be making an unfortunate habit of condoning unacceptable behaviour. Referee Les Peard's decision only to send Mark Jones, the Neath No.8, to the sin bin for 10 minutes for stamping on Laurence Delaney's face devalued the whole of this Schweppes Cup Final at Cardiff Arms Park.

If rugby football hopes to persuade its players and public that it is unequivocal about the need for discipline, Jones should have been sent off for good – or rather bad – and no option.

But back he was allowed to come, and his presence in the second half shored up a Neath pack which would have been very considerably pushed to survive in the tight. As it was, their

scrummage hung on and Kevin Phillips even won a priceless strike against the head in defence to bring off one of three crucial Neath saves when Llanelli were pressing for the winning score late in the game.

Above all, though, Neath took complete control of the line-out in the last half hour. So, almost every time Llanelli worked themselves into an attacking position, they lost it.

In the last minute, the same thing happened yet again, and two match-saving defensive mauls and two equally fine kicks pushed Llanelli back the length of the field.

So Neath won the Cup and gained revenge for their defeat by Llanelli last year. But they did owe their victory to the referee.

Representative Match: Japan 28 Scotland XV 24, Tokyo, 28 May

Scottish errors give Japan chance to make history

By John Menzies

Scotland's five-match tour to Japan finished ignominiously in Tokyo's Chichibu Stadium yesterday with the tourists on the wrong end of a five-one try count.

The hosts played some attractive rugby, with centres Kutsuki and Hirao dashing playmakers in helping their country to a first victory over an International Board country, although Scotland are not recognising the match as a full international and did not award caps.

The victory also vindicated the decision of the Japanese union not to allow their international squad to play in any of the previous four Scottish tour matches.

Richie Dixon, Scotland's coach, believed his side, playing again in intense humidity, made too many uncharacteristic errors. He

argued that the experience in the Scottish XV – there were 11 capped players – had hardly been evident from the mistakes made. He refrained from any criticism of the Japanese pack, three of whom – Oyagi, Kajiwara and Ohta – were warned for persistent infringement.

The Japanese forwards conceded the bulk of the 23 penalties awarded against their team, mostly through repeated killing of ruck ball. Scotland missed seven penalties at goal, five of the failures coming from Glasgow, who in his previous two matches had landed 25 kicks out of 30.

True, had Glasgow slotted his goals the Scots would have won, but that would be a gross over-simplification, as it was in other areas where the match was lost.

Lions into the arena: The Sydney Football Stadium.

Tour International: Australia 18 British Isles 19, Sydney, 15 July

Lions' pride at boiling point: Campese turns rabbit as he seeks the nearest hole

By John Mason

The British Lions, without a Test series victory in the three tours since 1974, held off a frantic, heart-stopping late challenge from Australia to win in Sydney yesterday.

The 39,401 spectators, plus one lively, most discerning stray rabbit, nibbled away nervously in the final nine minutes as the Wallabies, having been 12-19 down, got to within a point.

Brer Rabbit, who suddenly appeared on the field behind the posts, must have had Australian sympathies, not least for David Campese, who presented the Lions with what turned out to be the match-winning try.

Campese, the running, shooting star who so entranced English and Scottish audiences last winter, must have wished he could burrow a hole at that moment.

With the sort of maniac courage that wins medals on battlefields, Campese ran a ball back from behind his own line. A 25-yard drop-out would have sufficed for most.

But Campese is not most, and never has been. Suddenly, he realised that all was not well. There was a Lion bearing down, and Martin, his full-back colleague, was better placed for the clearing kick.

The switch was late, so was the pass, and poor Martin desperately reached back to his right for the ball. Inevitably, although he got a hand to it, down it went.

Evans arrived at full pelt, powered by seasons of high-pressure Sospan rugby at Llanelli's Stradey Park. Martin, off balance, could not recover in time as Evans roared past at his shoulder, the ball on the ground.

Evans, his instincts having driven him to the right place at the right time, dived elegantly for the ball, finishing at Campese's feet. The latter, head bowed and shoulders hunched, stared in disbelief at a triumphant Evans. Even the rabbit looked the other way.

That try – the only one the Lions could score despite a welter of possession for an hour – took the tourists to 13-12, a lead that Gavin Hastings extended with two more booming penalty goals.

Forward power was the single factor that produced victory for the Lions, who arrived in Australia in June having lost their last three series, in New Zealand (twice) and South Africa.

There was, of course, all-round excellence and unity. Sole, the loose-head, and Teague, the blindside flanker, were immense in everything they did. Teague won the award as the Player of the Series.

Much of the rest is history. Andrew kicked shrewdly in defence and attack – and tackled even better. So did Scott Hastings, once stopping Campese in his tracks. Guscott, too, played cleverly.

Hastings went on kicking goals, as did Lynagh, with three more. And Evans, with a little help from a great player, scored the most important try of his life.

Representative Match: South Africa 20 World XV 19, Cape Town, 26 August

Willie John's World side impresses South Africans

The predicted easy victory for the Springboks against an International XV on Saturday in Cape Town failed to materialise as Willie John McBride's invitational side gave the South Africans much harder competition than envisaged.

A one-point win left Morne du Plessis, the Springbok captain, praising the class of the visitors, particularly the French, who provided six of the side.

The match did not pass off without trouble: 36 anti-apartheid demonstrators were arrested in Cape Town several miles away from Newlands Stadium.

The South Africans, playing against foreign competition for the first time in three years, had to hold off a fierce late rally.

Rodriguez, the French No.8, had put the visiting side ahead with a try in the seventh minute, Charvet adding the conversion. But the Springboks, relying on a penalty and a conversion by Botha and a try by Knoetze in the 21st minute, took a 9-6 half-time lead.

South Africa extended their lead to 20-6 early in the second half when Smal and Botha scored tries, with Botha also contributing a penalty.

The visitors fought back with a try by Sella, but Charvet missed the conversion. A try by Williams, of Australia, and a conversion by Charvet in the final minutes failed to bring an unexpected win.

Willie John McBride, the international side's manager, commented: 'A brilliant game. Springbok rugby is still as strong as ever. They seem to get even bigger when they put on the green and gold.'

Saturday's match, watched by a crowd of 45,000, was the first international for South Africa since they played a rebel New Zealand side in 1986. Unlike that tour, this present visit is sanctioned by rugby's world ruling body.

Representative Match: France 27 Home Unions 29, Paris, 4 October

Hastings' bagful is difference between 'Lions' and France

By John Mason

The Lions, alias the Home Unions, march on – just. Thanks to Gavin Hastings, who scored 22 splendid points, France were narrowly beaten in Paris last night.

Having created a 14-point lead (23-9) early in the second half, the British and Irish team stumbled on the last lap. But for once Serge Blanco, France's full-back, proved fallible and, with Hastings collecting points as he pleased, France were in trouble until their big forwards got on top late in the second half.

Didier Camberabero, restored as France's outside-half, claimed 14 points in a fiercely contested second half. He, helped mightily by the forwards, and Berbizier, led the fightback, which ended with France's third try on the stroke of time. That made it 27-29 and the Lions were safe.

Hastings, Scotland's full-back, scored two tries, four penalty goals and a conver-sion as the Home Unions – wearing the colours of the Lions – held off a marvellous 18-point, second-half challenge by France. Though aware of the reluctance of the British and Irish authorities to give their blessing to a full-blooded Lions match, France were not bothering with such subtleties as they had so many other problems.

This was Hastings' benefit night, even when Blanco, complete with a masterly dummy, strolled round behind the posts for France's first try. Hastings, beating off three tackles, had the strength to reach the corner for the visitors' second try, and was on hand to support Guscott and Mullin for the second. He had already converted a try by Andrew and kicked two fine penalty goals.

Despite the accuracy of Camberabero – six goals from seven attempts, as well as France's late try – Hastings' contribution was enough.

The Daily Telegraph, 7 October

Wales to end all playing links with South Africa

By Edward Bevan

The clubs affiliated to the Welsh Rugby Union decided at a 2∞-hour special general meeting at Port Talbot last night to sever all playing links with South Africa. They overwhelmingly supported a motion proposed by the Union, who were disturbed by recent events surrounding the tour by an international squad to celebrate the South African Board's centenary.

The vote, carried by 276 to 113 with six abstentions, was in stark contrast to the decision taken in 1984, when 80 per cent of the membership supported playing links with the republic.

Wales therefore became the first country affiliated to the International Board to sever playing links with South Africa.

The motion proposed that 'for so long as any rugby player living in the republic is the victim of racial discrimination and the laws of that country, neither the WRU nor any of its member clubs will become involved in any matches organised under the authority of the South African Rugby Board.

'Nor will the Union, or any of its clubs, permit teams under the jurisdiction of the SARB to play in Wales.'

However, if Welsh players decide to play in South Africa, the Union have nothing in their constitution to say they cannot go there.

'Only the British Government have the power to withdraw passports," said Ken Harris, who chaired the meeting.

Clive Rowlands, the WRU president, stressed it was an amicable meeting and denied there had been any talk of further resignations.

Tour International: France 15 Australia 32, Strasbourg, 4 November

Campese has world at his feet

By Justin Rogers

Australia left France in tatters with a smashing victory in yesterday's first Test in Strasbourg as winger David Campese passed the world try-scoring record.

After trailing 6-12 midway through the first half, Australia's new-look team scored four tries to seal their first win in France since 1971.

Campese gives Carminati the slip.

With some bludgeoning defensive work, which stunned the 40,000 crowd at the Stade Meinau, Nick Farr-Jones and his gallant band became only the third Australian side to win a Test on French soil. It was France's biggest home defeat since the 25-3 thrashing by South Africa in Paris in 1952.

France had looked far more purposeful as they took a 12-6 lead through Didier Camberabero's three penalty goals and a dropped goal.

Australia had a single half-chance to score a try in the first half and Tim Horan grabbed it. Then, only five minutes after the resumption, Wallaby winger Ian Williams nipped in for a try.

With Australia leading 22-15 after Lynagh booted a couple of penalty goals, Campese notched his world record 34th Test try.

Horan supplied the coup de grace with his second try in the dying moments. Lynagh contributed 16 points to take his tally in 35 Tests to a stunning 445.

Tour International: Ireland 6 New Zealand 23, Dublin, 18 November

All Blacks continue their march of triumph despite pathetic 'Paddy O'Haka'

By John Mason

Willie Anderson, an employee of the Irish Rugby Union when he is not leading his country on the field, introduced his own version of the Paddy O'Haka to a packed audience in Dublin on Saturday.

The preliminaries involved the Ireland team linking arms on the halfway line at Lansdowne Road, facing a half-circle of All Blacks. As Wayne Shelford, New Zealand's captain, led his colleagues through the traditional pre-match Maori chant, Anderson, strategically placed in the middle, advanced a fraction faster than his team-mates – the line thus forming a shallow 'V'. Anderson did not stop until he was eyeball to eyeball with Shelford.

'I think he forgot to jump,' said Anderson ingenuously afterwards, referring to the climax of the haka. Shelford could not have moved an inch – there was not room.

I make no apology for presenting apparent trivia ahead of the rugby.

Anderson and company felt Ireland had scored a moral victory by such antics. Nothing could have been further from the truth. This idiotic, discourteous whistling in the dark, bordering on incitement, had a minimal effect upon the All Blacks. The first few minutes out of the way, there was a collective shrug of the shoulders and they got on with the game.

The challenge presented by the refereeing of Sandy MacNeill was largely ignored, too. While it was impossible for either side not to be affected by Mr MacNeill's difficulties, hostilities remained mostly within bounds.

The line-out was an unpoliced shambles, and offside in ruck and maul took on a new meaning. In such anarchy Ireland, awash with pride and passion, thrived.

New Zealand still scored three tries to nil, had one disallowed and were within inches of two, if not three, more. If ifs and ands were pots and pans and all the sea were ink...

Representative Match: England B 18 Soviet Union 10, Twickenham, 23 December

Plaudits go to two-try Soviet tourists

By John Reason

England can look forward to their best day against Wales for 100 years if David Leslie, the new Scottish international referee, climbs into the red shirts in his first international at Twickenham in February in the same way that he climbed into the red shirts in this match at Northampton. He tore into the well-meaning but legally uninfor-med Russians with such ferocity and such a lack of sympathy that in the first half they could have been forgiven for thinking that the cold war had started again.

Everything was against the Russians: The wind. The slope. The mud. The referee. The language. But the Russians stuck at it.

They turned round 18-0 down and, despite the fact that technically they are still wet behind the ears, they came back so strongly that they made England 'B' look distinctly tatty and had England coach Dick Best frowning about the lack of fitness and commitment.

With the crowd firmly on the side of the tourists and chanting 'Come on you Reds', the Russians scored two excellent tries in the second half and might have had a third.

The 1990s

Well, it all eventually came out into the open. With World Cups in 1991 and 1995, the intensification and expansion of league systems – Wales launched the Heineken Leagues in the 1990-91 season – and the new multi-racial body SARFU taking control of South African rugby, the drift towards professionalism continued to accelerate. No more could be asked of the top players without paying them.

Players were demanding more say in the control of the game and of their own destiny. When England captain Will Carling was sensationally sacked just before the 1995 World Cup for airing his views of the RFU a little too irresponsibly, he was soon restored to the helm by player power.

The day before the World Cup final, Rupert Murdoch's News Corporation announced that a massive 10-year broadcasting deal had been clinched with the three Southern Hemisphere countries, and Vernon Pugh, the outgoing chairman of the International Board, disclosed that Murdoch had made similar approaches to the Northern Hemisphere. But even then Pugh admitted there were still concerns among the 67 member unions of the IB at the increasing professionalism: 'They believe if it becomes pay for play it may be impossible for unions and the International Board to retain control. It's only New Zealand who have been pressing for a position where players are paid to play. The others favour, and New Zealand are happy to accept, a position where they continue to operate through their developing trust funds.'

But Will Carling was spot-on when he predicted, after the World Cup, that in November England would compete as fully-paid professionals against the Springboks, who, he said, were 'as good as professionalised'. There were no half measures, no stepping-stones. When it happened, on 27 August, it was pay for play. Rugby went open – hook, line and sinker.

Things began to happen quickly, as some of the big clubs adopted soccer-like attitudes. In September, Newcastle United FC chairman Sir John Hall took over Courage League Two rugby union club Newcastle Gosforth and quickly made England fly-half Rob Andrew the 'Kevin Keegan' of rugby, signing him on a five-year contract believed to be worth £750,000. The financial details were admitted to be 'quite staggering', but were kept under wraps as Andrew soon began recruiting other stars.

New Zealand were the first union to remove all anti-League barriers, the only major issue left unresolved when the floodgates opened. They were happy to welcome back players who had switched codes. At home, there was no doubt that Wales, who

had suffered a haemorrhage of its top stars to Rugby League, would do the same, and, sure enough, Jonathan Davies was soon back at Cardiff from Warrington.

The RFU's first decision was to announce that the game below international level in England would remain amateur for another season, but members of the national squad were promised around £40,000 for the season's six internationals. The top clubs in Wales signalled a football-style breakaway.

The RFU became deeply involved in disputes in 1996, with the other Home Unions for arranging their own television deals – an action that has threatened England's status in the Five Nations Championship – and with the clubs, a long-running battle that was apparently settled in May. Serious internal bickering still festered, however.

With all these rows and revolutions going on in the nineties, it is not surprising that the most extensive overhaul of the laws in the history of the game, effected in 1992, has taken a back seat. More than forty changes were made in an effort to speed up the game, some of them experimental. The points value of the try was increased from 4 to 5, and up to four replacements for injured players now permitted.

Meanwhile, on the field of play, Australia confirmed that they had joined the giants of world rugby when in 1991 they annihilated Wales, crushed England and beat New Zealand comprehensively, all in Australia, before repeating their victories to win the World Cup. England, Grand Slam champions at home, gave the Wallabies a hard game in the final at Twickenham, and went on to chalk up further Grand Slams in 1992, 1995 and 1996, while once-mighty Wales, despite a title win in 1994 on points difference (a method finally adopted in 1993), suffered many humiliating defeats by associate members of the IB and sadly seemed to be slipping into a lower division of world rugby.

England's home triumphs, first under Geoff Cooke and then under Jack Rowell, gave them the belief that they could live with the Southern Hemisphere giants, and indeed they shared in the pickings as South Africa began to find her feet again when returning to world rugby in 1992. England also defeated the 1993 All Blacks (who earlier that year had beaten the Lions 2-1), and went on to share a series 1-1 in South Africa in 1994. Then came the World Cup in South Africa, and a dramatic victory over Australia in the quarter-finals fired English hopes of world domination.

But they reckoned without the single most extraordinary phenomenon of modern rugby, the massive Tongan-born wing three-quarter Jonah

Will Carling meets President Nelson Mandela before the South Africa versus England international in Pretoria, 1994.

Lomu, who came at them like a runaway train in the first 12 minutes of their semi-final and removed them from the tournament. Yet in an emotional final, the Springboks managed to keep the ball away from Lomu and they beat the All Blacks in extra time.

South Africa's was a popular victory, celebrated charmingly by their leader Nelson Mandela. But later in the year, there were signs that the Springboks were returning to their ruthless, cynical attitude of yesteryear when, in the first 'professional' international, against Wales at Ellis Park, their lock Kobus Wiese cold-bloodedly took out Welsh line-out specialist and dangerman Derwyn Jones in the first few minutes with a punch behind the referee's back.

A new, highly successful tournament in 1996 was the Super 12 competition in the Southern Hemisphere, between states and provinces. But one movement in rugby that was proceeding out of the limelight was the advance of the women's game, with a rapid rise in the number of clubs, and, at international level, the establishment of their own World Cup in 1991, when it was won by the United States.

Perhaps the most startling sight of the nineties so far – apart from Lomu in full flight – was Wigan Rugby League Club taking part in, and winning, the Middlesex Sevens, in between getting the better of English club champions Bath in a two-match challenge played respectively under the two rival codes.

When rugby went open, there were celebrations of victory and there were fears. There was also a great deal of uncertainty. It was impossible to forecast how this historic upheaval would affect the game. But there was no doubt in anyone's mind that the tremors would be felt at international level, at club level and at grass-roots level for some time to come. Rugby would never be the same again.

1990

Laws The International Board allows earnings from certain ancillary activities, including advertisements and endorsements not rugby-related.

24 Mar With their 14-8 defeat in Ireland, Wales suffer their first Five Nations whitewash.

7 Apr Dewi Morris scores a hat-trick of tries as Lancashire beat Middlesex 32-9 to win the last County Championship sponsored by Toshiba.

22 Apr In Twickenham's first Sunday game, the Rugby for Romania fund-raising match sees the Four Home Unions beat the Rest of Europe 43-18.

12 May The Quins win their fifth Middlesex Sevens on the trot, beating Rosslyn Park 26-10 in the final.

20 May England Veterans beat Belgium 14-4 in Brussels to become the first winners of the European Rugby Classic, a tournament for over-33s between Five Nations countries and Belgium.

24 May Romania's 12-6 victory in Auch is their first win over France in France.

26 May Racing Club beat Agen 22-12 after extra-time in the French Club final, their backs providing extra entertainment

for the crowd at Parc des Princes by wearing pink bow ties and garish shorts.

27 May Australia drop star try-scorer David Campese from the forthcoming Test against France after he delays his return from playing club rugby in Italy for Milan.

8 Jul Australia chalk up their record win, 67-9 over the USA at Brisbane, with Michael Lynagh equalling his record 24 points set two weeks earlier against France.

4 Aug Argentina beat England 15-13 in Buenos Aires to tie the series 1-1 and send England home with a W3-L4 tour record. All Argentina's points in the Tests are scored by wing three-quarter H Vidou, with 9 penalty goals.

10 Nov Serge Blanco wins his 81st cap for France in their 30-12 defeat by New Zealand in Paris, equalling the world record set by Mike Gibson (Ireland and Lions).

11 Dec Oxford beat Cambridge 21-12 in the Varsity match after a much-publicised internal controversy that saw their Irish captain, Mark Egan, ban four players from selection, including Australian internationals Brian Smith (last year's captain) and Troy Coker.

INTERNATIONAL CHAMPIONSHIP

	E	F	I	S	W	P	W	D	L	F	A	Pts
1 SCOTLAND	13-7	21-0	-	-	-	4	4	0	0	60	26	8
2 ENGLAND	-	-	23-0	-	34-6	4	3	0	1	90	26	6
3 FRANCE	7-26	-	31-12	-	-	4	2	0	2	67	78	4
4 IRELAND	-	-	-	10-13	14-8	4	1	0	3	36	75	2
5 WALES	-	19-29	-	9-13	-	4	0	0	4	42	90	0

TOURS (Tests)

Scotland in New Zealand: NZ31-S16, NZ21-S18

France in Australia: A21-F9, A48-F31, A19-F28

Australia in New Zealand: NZ21-A6, NZ27-A17, NZ9-A21

New Zealand in France: F3-NZ24, F12-NZ30

International Championship: Wales 19 France 29, Cardiff, 21 January

Seven-month ban for banished Moseley

By John Reason

Kevin Moseley, the Welsh lock, has been banned from playing any rugby for seven months after being sent off the field for stamping on Marc Andrieu's head in Saturday's international at Cardiff.

A disciplinary meeting convened by the International Board met after the match and its decision was announced by Ireland's Ronnie Dawson, who was the chairman.

Moseley's transgression was the second of two fateful moments of indiscipline among the Welsh forwards in the first half, and cost Wales a real chance of beating a disappointing French team.

Wales had just regained the lead with Thorburn's third penalty goal when Griffiths, the Welsh loose head, threw a punch on the open side of the maul following the restart. Four

minutes later, as the French drove in support of a thrust by Andrieu, Moseley stamped on the prostrate winger.

Both incidents occurred in the full view of English referee Fred Howard. He gave a penalty kick against Griffiths and he sent Moseley off. No-one except Moseley was disposed to argue about either decision. The first presented Camberabero with another three points, enabling France to level the match at 9-9. The second scuppered the Welsh line-out, took the edge off their capable scrum, presented France with the blind side and lost the match.

Even after Moseley had departed, the Welsh scrum was not unduly inconvenienced. And Wales had a real hero in Robert Jones, their captain. He was everywhere. There is not

---

International Championship: England 34 Wales 6, Twickenham, 17 February

Quiet men's triumph: England slam the Welsh as never before

By John Reason

Wales spent most of their match preparation wondering how they could out-think, out-manoeuvre, or possibly even inconvenience Paul Ackford and Wade Dooley in the line-out, only to be dismantled by the England scrum at Twickenham.

This was a triumph for the quiet men of the England pack, Paul Rendall and Jeff Probyn, and for the noisy little chunk of determination between them, Brian Moore.

Rendall, particularly, exacted a fearful price for David Young's decision to turn professional and sign for Leeds in the Rugby League. Wales brought Laurence Delaney into the scrum in Young's place and he had one of the most miserable afternoons inflicted on an international prop forward.

Moore was nearly scalped by an early head injury, but he stole two heels against the head in the first half, with Wales in all sorts of difficulty,

whereas England won their own put-in with such undisturbed authority that Richard Hill, at scrum-half, was able to polish his fingernails while he wondered what to do next. Wales won only one scrum in the entire half, whereas England won 11.

If the England midfield backs had not kicked so many attempted long diagonals out on the full, instead of peppering Welsh full-back Paul Thorburn with up-and-unders in the swirling wind; if the referee had given England a penalty try for a collapsed scrum instead of a penalty kick; or if England full-back Simon Hodgkinson had not dropped a couple of passes with overlaps and tries on offer, England would have scored 50 points. As it is, England's 34 points is a record for them against Wales.

Scorers – England: Carling, Underwood 2, Hill tries; Hodgkinson 3 conversions, 4 penalty goals. Wales: Davies try, Thorburn conversion.

---

much of him, but no-one covered with more determination in defence. He even got stuck into the heavy stuff – so essential against France – of taking their forwards head on as they tried to drive. It was a remarkable performance.

It was Jones' quick-wittedness that made Wales' try soon after Moseley was sent off. From a quick tap-kick, he stabbed

a kick ahead for Titley to chase, fly-hack and score.

But Wales' 13-9 half-time lead was lost immediately when Sella scored after jumping above Thorburn to take a high kick by Camberabero. Thanks to their numerical superiority, France were able to survive crises of line-out and scrum, and thanks largely to Sella and Lafond they ran out easy winners.

International Championship: Scotland 13 England 7, Murrayfield, 17 March

Scotland find crowning glory as England are body-slammed

By John Reason

Ferociously determined tackling and some canny scrum manoeuvring won Scotland every prize on offer in European rugby yesterday.

The International Championship, the Grand Slam, the Triple Crown and the Calcutta Cup all fell into the hands of the successful Scots.

It is true that Simon Hodgkinson, the England full-back, could not reproduce the brilliant kicking he had shown in the first three matches of the Championship. He missed a difficult conversion in the first half, but much more important he missed two penalty goals downwind in the second half.

Those would have given England an ill-deserved draw after Craig Chalmers, Scotland's fly-half, had kicked three penalty goals in the first half. But without doubt it was a passage of defence late in the first half, when Scotland cleverly responded at a succession of scrums five yards from their line, which won the match.

England had just scored a try through Jeremy Guscott to pull up to 6-4 and they then laid siege to Scotland's line. England nearly pushed Scotland over their line, but

Stanger: Vital try.

the scrum kept going down. Twice England were given penalty kicks when they were probably expecting a penalty try.

As Oscar Wilde might have said, one collapsed scrum might be regarded as unfortunate, but three really did merit the firing squad.

England hesitated about whether to give the ball to the backs when scrumming and whether to kick for goal or take tap-kicks when Scotland were penalised. In the end England did neither and finished up falling between every stool.

In the end, too, to a huge roar of relief from the crowd, Scotland hacked the ball clear to the 25 and were reprieved.

England started the second half with an absolute disaster. Scotland's kick-off went out of

the field on the full. England chose to scrum back in the middle of the field, and Moore struck the ball like a rocket. But Teague never has been a scrummage No.8 in the way that Dean Richards is, and the ball cannoned back into the Scottish scrum.

Courage League: Wasps 24 Saracens 6, Sudbury, 28 April

Andrew is the catalyst as Wasps snatch title

By John Mason

Paul Rendall, sage of Wasps, merciless Hanging Judge of the Players' Court and Peerless Prop Forward of The Realm, was right after all. The best time to top the league, he said, was at 4.30pm on the last Saturday.

That, give or take a minute, was what the Wasps, who had never won a national competition, did with considerable precision this weekend.

The title of Courage League champions, 1990, sits easily on accommodating shoulders after a sweeping victory over Saracens by two goals and three tries to a goal at Sudbury.

Though several influential Wasps insist they came from nowhere to take the title, they do themselves less than justice, not least because of an overwhelming victory over Gloucester in October. Not too many sides put 29 points on Gloucester and win easing up.

Over eight months and 11 matches, Wasps have demons-

trated that a combination of lively forwards and dextrous backs – Clough and Lozowski were supreme – is enough to win England's premier competition. They proved it several times over against Saracens on a pitch that was puffing so much dust that the spinners would have had a field-day.

Chief 'spinner', as has been the case since he came storming into the Lions' camp last June with a point or so to prove, was Rob Andrew, their captain. He was the catalyst, the agent in producing change in others without undergoing change himself; alert, quick and with hands stickier than toffee paper.

Wasps' only defeats were at Quins and Bath, but they would not have won the title had Gloucester won on Saturday. In the event, Gloucester never looked like winning at Nottingham, and their 12-3 defeat left them in second place, ahead of Bath and Saracens.

That gave Scotland the put-in. Jeffrey took it off the back, Armstrong slipped it to Gavin Hastings, and he placed the most perfect chip for Stanger to score in the corner with the England defence nowhere.

England never really looked like making up the deficit.

Pilkington Cup Final: Bath 48 Gloucester 6, Twickenham, 5 May

'Awe-inspiring' Bath light a path for rest to follow

By John Mason

Bath's frolic in the sun at Twickenham on Saturday was mighty close to rugby perfection. In the ruthless application of team skills, they set fresh standards that must become the heady summit for every club in the land. They were superb.

There was a shining efficiency to everything that Bath, winners of the Pilkington Cup for the sixth time in seven years, attempted. Their victory in their 50th cup match by five goals, three tries and two penalty goals to a goal set all manner of records – highest score in the final, biggest winning margin, most tries. Since failing to qualify for the 1982-83 competition, they have lost once only in seven seasons of cup rugby – 32 wins from 33 matches. In the 50 ties overall, they have won 38 and scored 984 points against 448.

Nothing they have done previously can match their Twickenham performance in which, for about half an hour, Gloucester were in reasonable contention. Only when kicking goals did Bath waver. Though converting the first try from the left-hand touch, Barnes missed three conversions and three penalty goals before permitting

Halliday to convert the final try from in front of the posts.

The awareness that Bath could have scored 60 points or more has already sent Richter Scale tremors around the English leagues. Keith Richardson, Gloucester's coach, whose pre-match assessment warned of mountains to be climbed, spoke for most of Bath's opponents, past and future, when he said: 'This time, Bath played to their potential, offering an all-round game of such excellence that no English club can at present get anywhere near. The awe-inspiring thought is that they have the personnel and presence to improve further.'

The less well known members of the team, Swift in the lead, blended expertly with Barnes, Guscott and company to provide object lessons in two essentials of the game: ball retention and decision-making.

Not even Gadd's stupidity, when kicking Egerton in the head, could more than marginally detract from a marvellous occasion in which Bath demonstrated why they are formidable champions. Gadd, Gloucester's flanker, was sent off with 24 minutes' purgatory for his colleagues remaining. Bath kindly stopped at 48 points.

Schweppes Challenge Cup Final: Neath 16 Bridgend 19, Cardiff, 5 May

Kembery dismissal sours Neath triumph

By Edward Bevan

Andrew Kembery, the Neath second row, became the first player to be sent off in a Welsh Cup final when he was dismissed by referee Clive Norling at Cardiff Arms Park yesterday for stamping.

Nevertheless, Neath recorded their second successive Cup triumph and a unique treble, having won the Welsh unofficial championship and the Merit Table. But the incident soured their most successful season ever.

Afterwards, Ron Waldron, the Neath and Wales coach, said Kembery would almost certainly be withdrawn from the Welsh squad to tour Namibia later this month.

The 20-year-old was sent off 16 minutes into the second half on the advice of touch judge Les Peard, who caught him stamping in a ruck, ironically on one of his own players. Norling did not see the incident, but had no hesitation in pointing to the dressing-room.

Kembery now has the distinction of holding two Cup final records – the youngest player to appear in one and the first to be dismissed from one.

Neath took a 12-0 lead after 38 minutes with a try by Martyn Morris, converted by Thorburn, who also kicked a penalty, and a dropped goal from Jason Ball. Bridgend reduced the arrears just before the interval with an unconverted try by scrum-half Kevin Ellis.

In the second half, Bridgend outside-half Aled Williams dropped goals either side of Kembery's dismissal. But the depleted Neath proved the stronger side and a try by scrum-half Chris Bridges two minutes from time sealed their victory.

Tour International: Australia 48 France 31, Brisbane, 24 June

Excesses to follow an austere diet

By John Mason

Australia and France, with a little help from Clive Norling, the referee, turned international rugby upside-down in Brisbane yesterday, in an astonishing match involving 79 points, 10 tries and 17 separate scores, excluding conversions.

To view such prolific excess after a month's diet of the more austere percentage game in New Zealand invoked an attack of rugby indigestion – the colic of over-indulgence encouraged by chronic neglect of standard defensive chores.

French coach Jacques Fouroux said nothing would have pleased him better than to have been 'a mere spectator'. Joe French, the Australian Rugby Union president, said he had never seen a match of that calibre anywhere in the world. I must disagree. The Australia-France match was a highly enjoyable mess with peaks of achievement that make viewing of the match tape compulsory – but a muddle. If Australia do not tighten matters in New Zealand in July, they will have problems.

The desire to move the ball was admirable, and had suited the Scots well against the All Blacks the previous afternoon. But there was also an efficiency and composure about that and much of the rest of the operation that would have made the frills of yesterday's match at Ballymore impossible in New Zealand.

As Mr Norling was also in cheerful disarray, it was an afternoon to remember. Two of the tries should not have been allowed – Lacombe (France) dropped the ball before touching down and Little (Australia) ran onto a huge forward pass.

There were no penalties for the opening 22 minutes, and while there was a legitimate penalty try to follow, the Nelsonian Norling eye had to work overtime to maintain the flow.

Other tries were scored by Carozza, Cornish, Gavin and Campese for Australia, Armary and Blanco (2) for France. Lynagh converted all six Australian tries and kicked four penalties, while Camberabero kicked three conversions and three penalties for France.

Tour International: New Zealand 21 Scotland 18, Auckland, 23 June

Scotland are not satisfied with second best

By John Mason

Scotland's Grand Slam team are within an ace of leading the world – and until they do, the management are not satisfied. The pinnacle for David Sole the captain, Ian McGeechan, coach, and Duncan Paterson, manager, the hard-headed trio who will shape Scotland's 1991 World Cup challenge, must be as undisputed rugby kings.

Substantial steps to achieve so laudable an ambition were taken at Eden Park amid Auckland's squally showers on Saturday, irrespective of a second defeat in an international series of spectacular movement, spirited entertainment and, in the case of the All Blacks, an unrelenting will to win.

No-one in the Scottish party, whose rugby reservoir is about a tenth of the size of that available to New Zealand, where rugby union is the national game, is the slightest bit mollified by having shared in a memorable series.

'Encouraging, yes,' said McGeechan. 'Successful, no. We lost the series 2-0. What happened must be a source of pride and a tremendous benefit to our younger players. But we still lost.'

McGeechan's words were echoed throughout the squad, who were unbeaten in their provincial matches – in itself a rare feat for a touring side in New Zealand.

For an hour in the wind and rain on the soapiest of pitches and with a wet ball that at times had a mind of its own, Scotland gave the world champions, unbeaten for the previous 20 matches, the hardest of times. Only Australia, once, have got any closer – the draw at Ballymore, Brisbane, two years ago – since New Zealand lost 16-3 to France at Nantes in November 1986.

In the finish, Scotland, despite scoring two tries to one, were out-Foxed. In 22 internationals for New Zealand, beginning against Argentina in 1984, Grant Fox has scored 363 points, including Saturday's tally of 17: five penalty goals and a conversion for a 100 per cent record in the most adverse of conditions.

It mattered not a hoot where the kick was taken, the touch line, as it were, only increasing the challenge.

For Scotland, Gavin Hastings kicked splendidly, including one goal downwind from 65 metres plus. But not even he could match the ice-cool efficiency of Grant Fox's kicking.

With tries from three-quarters Stanger and Moore, Scotland got to the brink of the most joyous of victories. But being world champions also means the ability to absorb pressure. And New Zealand managed that superbly throughout.

Representative Match: Wales 24 Barbarians 31, Cardiff, 6 October

Wales still go cap in hand for wider vision and enterprise

By John Mason

Adrian Davies, who is in his third year reading geography at Cambridge, returns to his university studies this week as a fully fledged Welsh international, complete with a handsome rich red-and-white braided cap.

A boyhood ambition achieved, the badge of sporting honour and prowess will be dearly treasured. Deep down though, Davies, who came on as replacement centre for Mark Ring early in the second half against the Barbarians, knows that the symbolic cap – players get one only – will not be quite what it appears.

By much the same token, the new entry in the record books of 21 points for Paul Thorburn, the highest individual total in an international by a Welshman, does not ring with the resonance that such a feat should be due.

The unpalatable verdict on Saturday's events at Cardiff, where the Barbarians won by three goals, a try and three penalty goals to a goal, a dropped goal and five penalty goals, is that Wales

need to turn many more corners before they even reach the crossroads. They fell to a scratch Barbarians side, less than half of whom are first choice for their countries.

Why such a match, which was sponsored by Scottish Amicable, should attract caps – for playing against, to borrow from an astute colleague, 'the good people of Barbaria' – will remain a mystery, the solution to which should lie with Ron Waldron, the Welsh coach. He sought caps in the interests of team unity and confidence, and the WRU agreed.

The Barbarians played by choice a loose game awash with risk. At times a form of rugby teasing was evident, which meant that foolhardiness ruled.

Even then, Wales could not extract retribution. Nick Farr-Jones, the Barbarians captain, said afterwards that the scratch team had played far better against England the previous Saturday and lost by two points, an opinion he capped laconically by saying, 'Draw your own conclusions.'

Tour International: New Zealand 9 Australia 21, Wellington, 18 August

Australia end four-year run by All Blacks

By Justin Rogers

Australia's heroic defensive work ended a 50-match unbeaten run by the All Blacks with a shock victory in yesterday's third Test at Wellington's Athletic Park.

It was the first time the New Zealanders had failed to score a try since their last defeat, which was against France in Nantes four years ago.

With powerful southerly wind gusts at their backs in the first half, the All Blacks threw everything at the Australian defensive line, but could lead only 9-6 at the interval.

The Wallabies grabbed the lead in the second minute of the second half when hooker Phil Kearns plunged over for a try after Gary Whetton's line-out take was bumped out of his hands by Australian prop Tony Daly. Michael Lynagh's conversion from the touchline made it 12-9, but Australia had to hang on grimly as the All Blacks launched one attacking raid after another, until Lynagh kicked a 45-yard penalty goal to make it 15-9 midway through the second half.

Australian skipper Nick Farr-Jones, his back red-lined with stud marks, was quick to admit afterwards: 'It was the defence that won us the game.'

Of the Wallabies, Kearns

emphasised he will be the successor to All Black hooker Sean Fitzpatrick in World XVs, half-back Farr-Jones was back to his devastating best, and centres Tim Horan and Anthony Herbert were brick walls in defence.

Sam Scott-Young, a last-minute inclusion when flanker Brendan Nasser's eye gash ruled him out five hours before the game, was a one-man destructive missile, aimed at hounding the All Blacks into errors. He saved a certain try by ripping the ball from the hands of All Black flanker Mike Brewer as he was plunging over the line from the back of a line-out.

The All Blacks, who retained the Bledisloe Cup with a 2-1 series win, made an uncharacteristic number of errors, many of them from passes that went astray, and dropped ball in the tackle.

Alex Wyllie, the New Zealand coach, said: 'Australia took their opportunities and we didn't. They're improving all the time, and they'll be a team to watch in the World Cup next year.

Relishing the better supply of ball from his forwards, fly-half Lynagh regained much of his old poise and kicked six goals in a row, after missing his first attempt, for a personal tally of 17 points.

Tour International: England 51 Argentina 0, Twickenham, 3 November

Hodgkinson record caps England romp

But sent-off Mendez earns only notoriety in Pumas thrashing

Ten minutes from the end of a one-sided match at Twickenham, Federico Mendez, Argentina's 18-year-old loose-head prop, was sent off for flattening Paul Ackford with such a devastating punch that the England lock had to be helped from the pitch, buckling at the knees.

Last night Mendez was given a four-week ban by the disciplinary committee of the International Board, which excludes him from the rest of the tour, after England were named as being guilty of

'provocation'.

Argentina had sent for schoolboy Mendez as a replacement for Lonardi, sent off and suspended after their first match, against Ireland 'B'. Mendez then enjoyed a storming début against Ireland, but he must learn that when your team is already dead and buried and losing 33-0 ten minutes from the end of a match, and a scuffle breaks out, there is no point in turning a gentle hand-bagging into a nuclear war.

Mendez (on ground, centre) settles the score with Ackford.

Mendez had just turned up at outside centre and had put in a run far more penetrating than anything managed by his backs, but he then took exception to being trodden on by Jeff Probyn. When Mendez had digested this, he stood up and let fly at the nearest white

shirt available. This happened to contain the 6ft 6in Ackford, who never saw the punch.

Admittedly this is an era of confetti caps, but the 23 points scored by England full-back Simon Hodgkinson, who converted 10 of 11 kicks, was a record for one match.

1991

13 Mar St Mary's beat London 15-8 in the Hospitals' final to equal Guy's record of 30 cups.

30 Mar After a 46-34 victory over East Midlands earlier in the month, the Barbarians continue the celebration of their centenary season, 100 years almost to the day since their first match at the Arms Park, by beating Cardiff 42-25, recording their highest-ever score there.

11 May London Scottish end Harlequins' five-year run in the Middlesex Sevens, coming back from a 12-4 first-half deficit in the final to beat them 20-16.

25 May With a largely experimental side, Scotland go down 24-19 to Canada in New Brunswick to end their 6-match tour with a defeat after winning the first 5 matches, including a 41-12 victory over the USA. This is Canada's first victory

over an IB country, and the 8 penalty goals by their captain and full-back Mark Wyatt is an international record.

20 Jul When the scoreboard is hit by lightning during a violent electrical storm, the 2nd Test between the USA and France at Colorado Springs is abandoned just after the interval, with France, having won the first 41-9 at Denver, leading 10-3.

27 Jul Australia emerge as a serious World Cup threat with their biggest win over England, 40-15 at Sydney, 20 points coming from the boot of Lynagh, who in the process becomes the first player to amass 600 points in internationals, while Campese and Ofahengaue each score 2 of the Wallabies' 5 tries. England conclude their much-criticised pre-World Cup tour with a W3-L4 record, although they do beat Fiji 28-12 in the only other Test.

INTERNATIONAL CHAMPIONSHIP

	E	F	I	S	W	P	W	D	L	F	A	Pts
1 ENGLAND	-	21-19	-	21-12	-	4	4	0	0	83	44	8
2 FRANCE	-	-	-	15-9	36-3	4	3	0	1	91	46	6
3 SCOTLAND	-	28-25	-		32-12	4	2	0	2	81	73	4
4=IRELAND	7-16	13-21	-	-	-	4	0	1	3	66	86	1
4=WALES	6-25	-	21-21	-	-	4	0	1	3	42	114	1

TOURS (Tests)

Wales in Australia: A63-W6
England in Australia: A40-E15
New Zealand in Australia: A21-NZ12
Australia in New Zealand: NZ6-A3

The Daily Telegraph, 21 January

Carling denies money behind players' revolt

Report by John Mason

International Championship: Wales 6 England 25, Cardiff, 19 January

Welsh Dragon slain in its lair at last

By John Reason

England have waited for what seems like all eternity, 28 years in fact, to beat Wales once more in Cardiff. Now they have done it. The score says that they did it easily, that they ended up lolling in an armchair polishing their fingernails and toying with a hopelessly outclassed opposition.

That only goes to show just how misleading a score can be, and no-one knows better than Paul Thorburn, the Welsh captain, how much closer it might have been. Three times in the first half, when England were only three or six points ahead, Thorburn missed kicks at goal which, by his standards, should have been formalities.

Meanwhile, Simon Hodgkinson, the England full-back, pale and almost frail compared with the forthright red-headedness of Thorburn, got on with his coaxing and steering style of kicking: 3, 6, 9, 12, 15, 18. Six penalty goals, all placed with calm efficiency, and there were England 18-6 ahead without ever having done anything really well.

The game was nearly over and England made sure that it was, by concentrating on

the one thing that they did consistently well – the forward drive.

A clever chip-kick by scrum-half Richard Hill drove Wales into their left corner, where England set themselves up for a five-yard scrum. As the scrum wheeled slightly to the left, to the open side, Dean Richards, the England No.8, waited and waited with the ball at his feet for exactly the right moment to pick it up. As soon as he did, the England forwards got into a driving group much quicker than the Welsh forwards were able to position themselves to defend.

The ball was slipped from one man to the next in the arrowhead, Mike Teague looped in from the blindside and was driven over the Welsh line for the only try of the match. The game was over and the Cardiff crowd knew it. They did not even bother to whistle and jeer as Hodgkinson took the kick at goal.

As it happened, he missed. But he soon stroked over his seventh penalty goal, and no Englishman has ever done that against Wales in Cardiff. Indeed, he broke the world record for most penalties in an international.

English rugby slipped deeper into a morass of confusing half-truths yesterday as officials sought to quell a pay rebellion led by an agent on behalf of leading players.

A bitter row stemmed from the refusal of England's players, supported by the management, to be interviewed on television or attend a post-match press conference after their 25-6 triumph over Wales.

Will Carling, England's captain, yesterday rejected angrily claims that the decision not to give media interviews was because of money. 'No-one,' he said, 'has the right to say that we were wanting money. That's not true.'

Carling's categorical denial can only mean that a score of wires have been crossed. According to the players, Instyle Promotions, the players' agents, were acting without the knowledge or consent of their clients.

The BBC confirmed yesterday that Instyle – run by Bob Willis, the former England cricketer, his brother David, and other partners – had asked for a fee of £5,000 to cover availability for post-match interviews for the rest of the international season.

A BBC spokesman said yesterday: 'We were approached at the beginning of last week and asked to make payment for interviews with England players. The approach was made by the Willis brothers.'

Despite the BBC statement, Carling remained adamant that his non-appearance at the post-match press conference, organised by the Welsh Rugby Union, had nothing to do with money. He had stayed away following a team decision not to talk about the match for 24 hours.

Carling said: 'When we play Scotland at Twickenham next month, there will be interviews. I am not going to ask *The Daily Telegraph* for money for an interview – I would not dream of doing so.

'This had nothing to do with finance. I accept that we may have made a mistake, but I also have to say that some players are fed up with being bothered by some of the press at their homes and in their offices. They are being rung up at all times and they don't like it.

'We have got to do something about this and try to find some guidelines for all concerned. We've no quarrel with most of the media and want to co-operate.'

International Championship: France 36 Wales 3, Paris, 2 March

Blanco's coup de grace slays ragged Welsh

By Charles Randall

Blanco in the thick of the action at Parc des Princes.

To the pounding beat of the Dax jazz band high in the terraces, Wales were torn to pieces on an overcast afternoon in Paris. Like a macabre dance with the Devil, they staggered to their heaviest defeat in Five Nations rugby, conceding six tries and losing to France for the ninth consecutive time.

Wales, from 1908, managed 15 successive wins over France, who were then a fledgling rugby nation, and it is becoming to look as though the wheel will turn the full circle – with Wales themselves returning to the ranks of beginners.

The Parc des Princes bowl echoed to the chant of 'Blan-co, Blan-co' as the teams appeared, and Serge Blanco answered the call with an early try, his 33rd for France.

At the final whistle, the massed chant echoed again as Blanco wrapped up his joyous afternoon with a touchline conversion to complete Wales' humiliation.

Blanco, at 32, had insisted that this would be his final Five Nations appearance in Paris, and his 84th appearance for France must have been one of his most satisfying.

Hong Kong Sevens: Fiji 18 New Zealand 14, 24 March

Prayers pay off for triumphant Fijians in Sevens

By Michael Calvin

Any event where the average spectator is reckoned to consume 10 jugs of beer is guaranteed to be tinged with unreality. But at its best, as when Fiji defeated the Barbarians in a semi-final of stunning speed and fluctuating fortune, the Cathay Pacific Hong Kong Bank Sevens captures the spirit of rugby. It encourages the crowd to share the fundamental thrill of running with a ball.

It is also a folk festival, where lovelorn Scots broadcast marriage proposals over the public address system, Americans frolic in plastic George Bush masks and expatriate Britons from the Gulf dance in the aisles. Everyone jeers Australia.

'It's an amazing event,' said Will Carling, who did his best to court public approval by leading the Barbarians to a 16-6 quarter-final victory over the Australians. 'If they don't like you they boo. It's as simple as that.'

True to tradition, the Barbarians' preparation consisted of two training sessions and several Happy Hours in the hotel bar. They struggled to beat Germany in their opening match, but once they learned to exploit the

---

International Championship: England 21 France 19, Twickenham, 16 March

England fulfil their dreams as French fall at last throw

By John Mason

For the moment, England's players, management and back-up team deserve to enjoy the vanity of victory. A first Grand Slam for 11 years demands celebration – and the recognition of the sustained capabilities of the best side in the 1991 championship.

In treasuring so rare an achievement for English rugby in recent years, the occasion was given a further dimension of scalp-tingling excitement – or was it apprehension? – by the inventive daring of France, who won universal admiration but not the match.

If the analogy of the sturdy shire horse in competition with the thoroughbred racehorse is less than kind to England, possibly the more acceptable version would be the no-nonsense feet-on-the-ground battering ram versus the subtle, spring-heeled swordsman.

What cannot conceivably be in dispute is that the Save and Prosper Grand Slam decider between England and France at Twickenham on Saturday will be fondly remembered as an epic struggle expertly refereed and crammed full of drama, high skill and pulsating entertainment.

If that were not sufficient on an afternoon of slate-grey skies and a worsening dripping drizzle, the French presented a rapt full house with two tries of superlative quality. Fact made a monkey of fiction yet again.

Satisfying as the counter-thrust which culminated in Rory Underwood's 27th international try was, for once England's record-breaking wing three-quarter has to be among the also-rans.

Twice Twickenham caught

its collective breath as France ran the ball out from behind their own line, soaring into areas momentarily unguarded. The results were two tries of startling ingenuity and invention by Saint-Andre and Mesnel – and a match that will be enshrined in the folklore of the game.

Blanco, Lafond, Sella and Camberabero in the 12th minute, and Berbizier, Sella and Blanco in the 79th, created tries of which dreams are made.

The first covered 100 metres or more, beginning when Blanco ran the ball back from a failed penalty-goal kick by Hodgkinson.

The second, with England sitting comfortably on a 21-13 lead deep in French territory, Grand Slam sweaters and ties at the ready, started with Berbizier in-field on the north-west side of the pitch and finished in the south-east corner with Mesnel mesmerising Hill with jink, shuffle, body lean and change of pace.

Camberabero converted from the touchline, and the cup was all but dashed from eager English lips.

Yet for all the expertise of the tries, England's victory by a goal, dropped goal and four penalty goals to two goals, try and penalty goal was their third in succession over France.

The England forwards made everything possible, though they, too, have good cause to be immensely grateful to Hodgkinson, who weighed in with another 14 points – his 60 in the Championship this season breaking Jean-Patrick Lescarboura's record of 54 – and to Underwood, whose 43rd cap matched Tony Neary's all-time English record.

---

pace of Jeremy Guscott and Andrew Harriman, they quickly improved.

There was no shame in being beaten 22-14 by Fiji after leading at half-time. The Fijians tackle with the ferocity of sumo wrestlers, but run with the languid ease of Carl Lewis.

The Fijian players stood in a reverent semi-circle before each match while a village elder took prayers. In an

increasingly cynical rugby world, they provided a reminder of lost innocence.

The tone of the final, however, was set by each side conducting a war dance in the centre of the pitch. The All Blacks retrieved an early eight-point deficit, came from behind again to level the match at 14-14, but lost to a try by substitute Timoci Waingolo in the final move of the match.

Heineken League Premier Division: Neath 16 Pontypool 9, The Gnoll, 13 April

Thomas goes scouting as Neath gain new Welsh prize

By David Roberts

While Neath finally clinched the one point they needed to take the inaugural Heineken League Premier Division title and bank a cheque for £23,000, Brian Thomas, their new rugby supremo, was out and about scouting for talent to bolster next season's title defence.

Two days into his 10-year contract, reputed to be worth £36,000 per annum, the first full-time paid rugby administrator in the Welsh game was over the Severn Bridge watching Bath playing Newport in a second-team game. There was no real need for him to have been at The Gnoll, because with two games left to play after this one the title was already in the bag for the Welsh All Blacks.

Having scooped an unprece- dented treble last season – the Schweppes Cup, the Merit Table title and the unofficial Welsh championship – everyone expected Neath to carry off the first Premier Division crown. With only two defeats in 16 league games to date, they have been by far the most consistent team in the division, but securing the title has been a bigger struggle than many thought.

It has been a long hard season down at The Gnoll, especially as so many of their players were involved with Welsh teams. Add to that their losing three internationals – Allan Bateman, Mark Jones and Rowland Phillips – to rugby league early in the winter and they have shown remarkable resilience to match the pre-season predictions.

County Championship Final: Cornwall 29 Yorkshire 20 (aet), Twickenham, 20 April

Cream of Cornwall rises to top

By John Mason and Brendan Gallagher

THE unforgettable sight of an entire black and yellow clan going right off their collective trolley must rank as the enduring memory of a wonderful season for English rugby.

Like bees to a honey pot, Cornwall's magnificent supporters swarmed onto the Twickenham pitch as referee Roger Quittenton's final whistle announced their first county championship since 1908.

Twickenham visibly recoiled as Trelawny's Army, more than 30,000 strong, embarked on the mother of all parties. Back in Cornwall, another 400,000 delirious followers watched the game incredulously on television. The Cornish love their saints, but nobody can actually recall a miracle live on TV before.

Cornwall was a madhouse last week. Over 200 coaches were requisitioned, and special trains and planes were chartered as the exodus began. Fuelled by Newquay Steam, the local brew, they travelled in hope and expectation.

Whatever else Cornwall and their joyous supporters proved at Twickenham, they deserve grateful thanks for demonstrating that intense competition, unbridled enjoyment and responsible behaviour can go hand in hand.

There must be consoling applause, too, for the definitive contribution of Yorkshire, whose outnumbered devotees, at 16-3 up with 15 minutes remaining, could be excused for checking that celebration bottles were in place.

But Yorkshire conceded a penalty goal for collapsing the scrum, and could not contain Cornwall fly-half Nancekivell *(pictured right)* as he burrowed in for two late, late tries. A missed conversion of the second meant extra time, with the score 16-16.

Champion, with half Cornwall not daring to look, gave them the lead with a penalty goal. Then Bassett added a fresh dimension to wing three-quarter play when he joined a tumbling scrum to score in the corner.

What with a Peters try in the manner of a marauding No.8, plus a Champion conversion, Cornwall had

---

Women's World Cup Final: England 6 USA 19, Cardiff, 14 April

US take first women's cup

By David Roberts

England, outpaced and outmanoeuvred, failed in their attempt to win the inaugural women's World Cup at Cardiff Arms Park yesterday.

The United States deservedly took the trophy by scoring three tries in a 12-minute burst in the second half. Long before that, England had failed to capitalise on the ample possession their bigger pack gave them, and their heads began to drop when

Chris Harju kicked a penalty goal just before half-time to reduce the deficit to 6-3.

Once the dynamic flanker Claire Godwin had scored twice within two minutes after the interval – tries which would not have been out of place in the men's game – England had no way of getting back into the game against the fierce tackling and greater commitment of the Americans.

Pilkington Cup Final: Harlequins 25 Northampton 13 (aet), Twickenham, 4 May

Quins' trophy by a whisker

By John Reason

Northampton took such a fearful drubbing in the line-out that the illustrious Harlequin backs ought to have had enough ammunition to win this Pilkington Cup Final at Twickenham by 30 points. But the Saints achieved one of the defensive miracles of the season and sent the bookmakers into ecstasies by leading for much of the time and by forcing the match to extra time.

Admittedly, Northampton were much assisted by the lack of variation in the Quins' play. Nevertheless, David Pears, the Harlequins fly-half, was given exactly three times as much of the ball as his opponent, John Steele.

Any pack that delivers 42 prime bits of possession to its backs in the course of an afternoon is entitled to bleat a bit about having to scramble a

draw in the last five minutes of normal time. But that's what happened. Thornycroft, on the Northampton left wing, missed Harriman, who ran on to score in the corner. So with five minutes left Pears had a kick from the touchline to win the match ... but missed it.

The Quins kicked off in extra time deep into Northampton's right corner where they won their opponents' throw for the 12th time in the match. Once again they drove to set up an attacking scrum, and from that, Simon Halliday took a short pass from Pears and forced his way over the line for a try which Pears converted.

This finally knocked the stuffing out of Northampton, and Quins added another try through scrum-half Glenister, also converted.

scored 26 points without reply until the immaculate Harrison escaped in the final seconds.

It mattered not two hoots that slickness, style, efficiency and method did not meet

every test, or that some players would be hard pressed to get into a League One club's second team. The 1991 ADT County Championship final already claims a unique place in rugby's folklore.

The United States team pictured with the Women's World Cup trophy after defeating England in the final at Cardiff.

Tour International: Australia 21 New Zealand 12, Sydney, 10 August

Australia top of the world

By Justin Rogers

AUSTRALIA'S thundering forwards beat the All Blacks at their own game in Sydney to confirm their new-found status as favourites for the World Cup this autumn.

New Zealand were taken aback by the ferocity of Australian assaults in the second half of the first of two Tests to decide the Bledisloe Cup.

The teams had been locked at 9-9 at the interval, but for once the All Blacks came off second best in the tight, rucks and mauls, and in the lineouts where lock John Eales announced himself as a future world figure.

New Zealand, beaten only once in 20 previous internationals, were not helped by the almost unthinkable – Grant Fox failing with two first-half attempts at goal in just over a minute.

After the aperitif of a match against Wales and the entree offered by England, Nick Farr-Jones' warriors attacked the All Blacks with the urging of a full house of 41,565. 'We attacked them at their strength,' said flanker Simon Poidevin.

The All Blacks drew first blood in the 17th minute, when Fox's well-placed kick eluded both Campese and All Black winger John Timu. To the horror of the Australians, Ian Jones, the tall All Black second-row forward, followed up to plunge on the ball for a try, which Fox converted from the touchline.

Within two minutes, the issue was squared when the ball bounced over the New Zealand line from a lineout and there was Australia's No.8, Tim Gavin, to pounce for a try. Fox and Lynagh exchanged penalties before half-time.

The ferocity of the Australian assaults up front took the sting out of the All Blacks in the second half, and two Michael Lynagh penalty goals enabled Australia to slip away to a 15-9 advantage.

Then, with a quarter of an hour remaining, winger Rob Egerton swept in for a spectacular try which sealed one of Australia's most memorable rugby victories in years.

Spotting the open space, Lynagh, the fly-half, hoisted the ball deep behind All Black winger John Kirwan. Suddenly, the opportunist Egerton, socks down around his ankles, was flying up the left wing and, before Kirwan could respond, had plucked the ball out of the air and sprinted clear to plant it behind the posts, giving Lynagh the simplest of conversions. New Zealand's only response was a late Fox penalty goal.

[Two weeks later, in Auckland, the All Blacks threw the World Cup into the melting pot again, with a merited 6-3 win to retain the Bledisloe Cup, although the match developed into a kicking duel between the world's two leading international scoring machines – Fox kicked 2 out of 5, Lynagh only 1 out of 7.]

Tour International: Namibia 15 Ireland 6, Windhoek, 20 July

Irish are embarrassed

IRELAND slumped to a 15-6 defeat by Namibia in the first Test in Windhoek where lock Brian Rigney was ruled out of the rest of the tour with a knee injury.

Donal Lenihan is to be called out as a replacement while Brendan Mullin and Simon Geoghegan also finished with thigh injuries and will remain in Windhoek for treatment.

Namibia made the ideal start when fly-half Jaco Coetzee slotted a drop goal from 30 metres before full-back Andre Stoop scored a try which Coetzee converted.

Referee Clive Norling awarded Ireland a penalty try against the retreating Namibian scrummage, which Mullin converted, but Coetzee later added two penalties.

[Ireland lost the other Test a week later 26-15 to complete a disastrous tour. Namibia, formerly South-West Africa, were not in the World Cup draw, but had slammed qualifiers Italy and Zimbabwe twice each.]

Tour International: Australia 63 Wales 6, Brisbane, 21 July

Wales tumble from top level into obscurity: Wallabies score 12 tries

By John Mason

WALES, even more accident prone than Humpty Dumpty, tumbled headlong into the obscurity of the also-rans of world rugby in the oppressive heat of mid-winter Brisbane yesterday.

From the moment Michael Lynagh, Australia's outside-half, who collected another 23 points to add to the 564 already to his international credit, hoisted a high ball in the second minute, Wales were doomed.

Paul Thorburn, the Wales captain and full-back, who had time to recall most of his 301 international points before the ball came down, dropped it. Back it rolled over the Welsh goal-line, and Horan, the Wallaby centre, was first to the loose ball to score the try.

There were 11 more tries to follow in the 15th, 17th, 25th, 48th, 51st, 55th, 59th, 68th, 72nd, 76th and 79th minutes. Had Lynagh not missed eight of 15 kicks at goal, the rout, if only mathematically, would have been even worse.

The statistics of misery, though, count for little on this occasion – and explain nothing. In the expanding Welsh catalogue of failure for recent seasons, Ballymore '91 was infinitely more alarming than other falls from grace. The World Cup is three months away and bemused Wales are not remotely ready.

This time, plain for all to see, was a continuing sequence of shoddy teamwork, muddled thinking and, alas, incompetence. If there was a coherent game plan, Wales disguised it embarrassingly well – their only success in an afternoon of unpalatable home truths.

Even the Ballymore crowd, not known for their sympathetic treatment of visiting teams, either national or domestic, grew tired of gloating. Instead they indulged in an uncoordinated form of the Mexican wave, the clumsiness of their efforts being on a par with Welsh attempts to stem the Australian tide.

Had Emyr Lewis and Mike Hall not been playing, goodness knows what the Welsh fate would have been.

Though both tackled and tackled, the worst nightmares of the tour party, already heightened by the 13 tries conceded the previous week in the 71-8 thrashing by New South Wales, were realised.

Scorers – Australia: Tries Horan, Lynagh 2, Ofahengaue, Kearns 2, Roebuck, Gavin 2, Campese, Egerton, Little; Lynagh 6 conversions, 1 penalty goal. Wales: Penalty goal Thorburn; dropped goal A Davies.

1991 World Cup

29 Sep World Cup betting has Australia as 11-8 favourites, with the All Blacks at the marginally longer odds of 6-4. Only three other countries are given much chance of winning, England and France at 7-1 and Scotland at 9-1, after which it is 100-1 Ireland and 150-1 both Wales and Western Samoa, who are both in Australia's pool. Anyone fancying a flutter on Japan or the USA can get 5,000-1.

1 Oct The Irish players finally sign their World Cup contracts, having settled their dispute with the IRU over a 'misunderstanding' in which the squad believed the contracts, mainly concerning amateurism, were not worth signing as the activities of players from other countries had 'rendered them virtually invalid'.

4 Oct Argentina put up a good performance against favourites Australia, surprising them with the strength and technique of their scrummage before going down 32-19, while France's 30-3 defeat of Romania owes much to the inability of kicker Niculai Nichitean (7 of 8 kicks missed) to come to terms with the despised synthetic RWC ball.

6 Oct Records fall in Ireland's 55-11 defeat of Zimbabwe, Brian Robinson setting a new Irish record of 4 tries, while Ralph Keyes, winning only his 2nd cap, registers a record 23 points (4C-5PG).

8 Oct Jon Webb scores an England record 24 points (1T-4C-4PG) in their 36-6 victory over Italy at Twickenham, where the penalty count (37-10) is higher than the points scored. Referee Brian Anderson (Scotland) later tempers England No.8 Dean Richards' accusations of cheating against the Italians by declaring that none of their 37 penalties was for foul play, although he did consider sending off an Italian for persistent infringement.

9 Oct Scotland, with 9 changes, and Ireland ensure their quarter-final places with comfortable victories over the Pool 2 minnows, and Canada also go through by beating Romania.

13 Oct Wales, requiring the miracle of a small (3-0) Argentinian win over Western Samoa to stay in the Cup, soon have their hopes dashed as the Pacific Islanders emerge 35-12 victors; the Samoan lock Ma'taafa Keenan and Argentinian second-row Pedro Sporleder are sent off for fighting. At Leicester, a capacity 16,200 crowd give the hitherto villainous Italians a standing ovation after their gallant, exciting performance in the 31-21 defeat by a chastened New Zealand, obliterating the sad memories of Twickenham.

19 Oct Scotland burst the South Sea bubble with a thoroughly professional 28-6 dismantling of the Western Samoans at Murrayfield to earn a place against England in the semi-finals.

20 Oct New Zealand's 29-13 victory over far-from-disgraced Canada sets up a needle semi-final with Australia.

29 Oct French coach Daniel Dubroca, who resigned last week having admitted to verbally abusing referee David Bishop after the quarter-final with England, hints he might return, adding: 'He [Bishop] was laughing as he walked in the players' tunnel. That made me mad, and I stopped him by putting my hand on his chest to tell him I was not happy with his refereeing.'

World Cup Pool 1: England 12 New Zealand 18, Twickenham, 3 October

Crash landing for sweet chariot

By John Mason

IT WAS business as usual for world champions New Zealand, who wore England down under gun-metal grey skies at Twickenham yesterday. Not, perhaps, the ideal start to a World Cup seeking universal appeal, but the job, for all that, was expertly done.

By denying England possession for long periods, besides snatching important line-outs against the throw-in, New Zealand steadily built the foundations of victory by a goal and four penalty goals to three penalty goals and a dropped goal.

Amid the often drab nuts and bolts of a game unnecessarily complicated by rugby union's obscure laws, half a dozen individuals stood out – Rob Andrew and Jonathan Webb for England, and Michael Jones, Graeme Bachop, John Kirwan and, inevitably, Grant Fox, who kicked another 14 points to take him to 495 in internationals.

Of these, flanker Jones, playing his first full match for more than a month, scaled heights reserved only for the expert of experts. Irrespective of his try, which killed off England's challenge, Jones was the personification of athletic power.

England, for all the unremitting hard work of Winterbottom, had no-one to match Jones for support play, intelligent lines of running or, in the second-half, the sheer menace of his lurking power.

World Cup Pool 3: Wales 3 Australia 38, Cardiff, 12 October

Australians douse feeble Welsh fire

By John Mason

AUSTRALIA, though barely out of second gear, thrashed threadbare Wales. Devoid of everything but a dogged determination to hang on somehow, Wales were totally eclipsed.

Five second-half tries by Australia left rugby union in Wales in a fearful state. Having been on the back foot throughout the opening period, Wales saw the dam burst in the second as Australia's running backs exploited the gaps as large as the Nullabor Plain.

What with full-back Marty Roebuck and David Campese, who took his international try total to 43, a world record, adding their pennyworth, Wales were sunk with scarcely a trace.

The Princess of Wales chose a red and white ensemble. The colours of the day, though, were the green and gold of Australia.

World Cup Pool 3: Wales 13 Western Samoa 16, Cardiff, 6 October

World Cup exit door beckons for Wales

By John Mason

THE 10-year humiliating descent of Wales to the lower reaches of the world game is almost complete. By the end of the week the once proudest rugby nation in the world, winners of five Triple Crowns and three Grand Slams of the Seventies, are likely to be among the also-rans of the Nineties.

Defeat by Western Samoa at the Arms Park, Cardiff, in their opening match in the World Cup yesterday was the unkindest, harshest blow of all in what has been a decade of dithering in the committee room and disgrace on the field.

But, unlike in Australia in July, at least yesterday the Wales team went down honourably. Emyr Lewis, who moved from flanker to No.8 as injuries disrupted the Welsh pack, battled mightily.

The Western Samoans tackled with a clattering relish that not only stopped opponents in their tracks – time after time players in possession, or circling for the high ball, were knocked back yards, the ball spilling loose as the unfortunate recipient of the tackle attempted to get breath back into a bruised body.

That this was the greatest day in the history of the game in the islands, there can be no doubt – it is their first win over an International Rugby Board country.

Stephen Bachop (Western Samoa) in control.

Yet, amid all the deserved congratulations and resounding back-slapping for a famous victory in a tremendous match, Wales were fiendishly unlucky. The try that in all probability has consigned them to the pre-qualifying section of the 1995 World Cup, should not have been awarded.

French referee Patrick Robin was unsighted when awarding a try to To'o Vaega, Western Samoa's centre, 36 seconds into the second half. In fact, Robert Jones, the Wales scrum-half, was first to the ball over the line to deny the score.

The conversion took Western Samoa, a dozen of whose team live and work in New Zealand, to 9-3, and a sigh of sadness at the demise of the men in red enveloped a ground barely two-thirds full. Either the absentee Welshmen knew something in advance or had no heart for a wake.

World Cup Pool 2: Scotland 24 Ireland 15, Murrayfield, 12 October

Unseen Calder delivers decisive blow

By John Reason

AN UNDETECTED short-arm shot by former Scotland and British Lions captain Finlay Calder, which laid out Irish full-back Jim Staples, had a decisive bearing on this match at Murrayfield.

Ireland were leading 15-9, and their forwards were going so well that they looked comfortably in control, when Staples successfully marked a high kick. In doing so he was legitimately tackled by Tony Stanger, the Scottish right wing, but was then felled by Calder following behind.

Staples took a long time to recover. By that time he had dropped two more high balls and Scotland had won the match.

That was a thoroughly unsavoury affair, but it has to be said that Ireland dug such a large hole for themselves that Scotland were able to bury them and thereby make certain of a home quarter-final next Saturday.

World Cup Quarter-Finals: Ireland 18 Australia 19, Lansdowne Road, 20 October

Australians count cost of last-gasp win against Irish
Campese and Farr-Jones both doubtful for semi

By Charles Randall

THE genius of David Campese lit up this magnificent quarter-final at Lansdowne Road, which Australia won with a try four minutes from time. But Campese finished the match limping and is due to have tests today on his right ankle, while Farr-Jones' fitness also remains suspect.

Ireland, beaten cruelly by Lynagh's late try, could take credit in defeat for whipping up the best contest of the tournament, helping to soothe memories of that televised chessboard violence between France and England the previous day. The Dublin game proved to the armchair millions that rugby football can offer more than wall-to-wall Garryowens and a hit record for Dame Kiri.

Francis was again the key man in the Irish line-out, and Smith, at hooker, could hardly have had a more effective all-round match for his country. But it was Australia's backs who shaded the game, making every attack count, and the try tally of three to one suggested, rightly, that many people's favourites deserved their success. Campese, in his 62nd international, emphasised his value by scoring two lovely tries and gave Lynagh the chance to snatch the late winner in the corner.

Ireland's committed performance, with seven minutes remaining, seemed to have brought about the upset of the tournament. That was when Hamilton sprinted 45 yards for an extraordinary try, Keyes converting from wide out to put Ireland 18-15 ahead.

But in the few minutes remaining, Australia forced a set-scrum back upfield, and Horan and Little cut through. Campese was caught, but Lynagh followed up to break a thousand Irish hearts.

World Cup Quarter-Finals: France 10 England 19, Parc des Princes, 19 October

Sucker punch floors France
England set up showdown with Scots

By John Mason

NOT even lurid tales of assaults on the referee as the teams left the field could spoil England's moments of triumph in a match in which victory was everything.

Whatever reservations there might be about the way in which it was done, the incontrovertible fact is that resolute, single-minded England beat nervy, inefficient France on every count.

The reward for successfully playing the percentages, as well as recognising scoring opportunities, was a World Cup semi-final with Scotland at Murrayfield this Saturday.

For France, at odds with themselves let alone England, there was little but disarray, dissension and, for coach Daniel Dubroca and prop Pascal Ondarts, disgrace.

Nor did Serge Blanco, a pale, irritable imitation of a marvellously gifted player, endear himself in what presumably was his farewell match.

England, understandably, were well pleased with themselves. The forwards cleared the trail, captain Carling had an outstanding match in every respect, and with a touch of class at the precise moment from Guscott England had won a prize which I, for one, believed to be beyond their reach.

Skinner, who should have a gold medal for one tackle alone on Cecillon, did exactly as the selectors required in his roving blind-side flank role, and, in the last quarter, Ackford ruled the line-out in a way which will have set the alarms ringing north of the border.

The tattoo that French fists beat on Heslop's chin in the opening minutes after he had pursued his own high kick set unbelievable standards. Blanco, piqued at being challenged after calling a mark, joined in vigorously after Champ had let fly. The Bishop lectures began early, and so did the penalty kicks for Webb.

With the score locked at 10-10 in the second half and extra time looming fast, Ondarts, to his fury, was penalised for seeking the ball illegally, and Webb's third penalty goal crept over the bar.

England made quite sure, driving Lafond over the line as he caught another high, hanging kick. Carling, as ever, was first up, and his try, converted by Webb, was entirely appropriate.

Michael Lynagh: late try rescued Australia in Dublin.

Rob Andrew makes the crucial drop goal at Murrayfield.

World Cup Semi-Finals: Scotland 6 England 9, Murrayfield, 26 October

Andrew drops England into the final as blunder of Hastings dooms Scots

By John Reason

A DROPPED goal by Rob Andrew gave England their ticket to the World Cup final after a dreadful error by Scottish full-back Gavin Hastings.

With the scores level at 6-6 midway through the second half, Hastings missed a penalty kick in front of the England posts.

Hastings had kicked so well throughout the World Cup, and in this match, that it seemed inconceivable that he could miss. But the ball flew dramatically wide.

England then squared their shoulders and their forwards took such relentless control in the last 20 minutes that Scotland spent the whole time fighting for their lives. If they had not done it so effectively, England would have pulled clear away.

Rory Underwood nearly squirmed in for a try on England's left, and half a dozen times the England scrum looked to be on the verge of scoring a push-over try.

The scrum collapsed as often as not, but the referee looked no more likely to award England a penalty try than he had earlier in the half

when the Scotland pack was broken just to the left of their posts and pulled the scrum down as a last resort.

England were given a penalty kick on that occasion and Jon Webb brought some comfort to what had been a miserable afternoon for him by kicking the goal from point-blank range.

But that only brought the scores level. England still needed another score to win and reach the World Cup final. They got it from the last of a series of attacking scrums, two of which collapsed with no more stringent award than another put-in to England.

From that final scrum Andrew dropped the goal. The England supporters erupted with joy, and England led for the first time in the match.

England were never threatened after that. The only inconvenience they suffered was when Skinner predictably had his white-socked toes trodden on after losing a boot and finishing the match without it. Quite properly he did not dare go off the field to put it back on.

World Cup Semi-Finals: Australia 16 New Zealand 6, Lansdowne Road, 27 October

Waltzing Campese leads All Blacks a merry dance

By John Mason

DAVID CAMPESE, eagerly aided and abetted by 14 other Australians, brought a sparkle back to rugby in the twinkling of a few star-studded strides in Dublin yesterday.

In routing the peddlers of caution, the purveyors of the unimaginative and second-rate, the extraordinary Campese also brought down New Zealand, the world champions.

Victory by a goal, try and two penalty goals to two penalty goals took Australia storming through to next Saturday's final of the Rugby World Cup at Twickenham, where steadfast England will resolutely guard their territory.

While Campese's skilled contributions were essential to the Wallaby cause, victory was a well-organised, spirited team effort, so competently carried out that, against the All Blacks of all teams, Australia could afford to coast a shade in the second half. New Zealand were dispatched to the third place play-off with scant ceremony.

I am not sure that mere words can convey the shimmering skills of Campese, who pursues magical paths of his own making. The opening try was sufficient to titillate the palate. Quite what Campese, nominally right wing, was doing far out on the left, goodness knows. But as the ball came shooting back from a ruck at speed and scrum-half Farr-Jones, his right knee heavily protected, rifled it fast and low to his left, it was Campese there, reaching for the pass and attacking the ball to such effect that it took him beyond the first line of defence. Then, with the adrenalin pumping and the try-line in his sights, Campese pinned back his ears and went. The crowd, even some of those sporting black favours, erupted.

When Campese struck again, so relaxed and assured was he against

some of the best players in the world, he might have been on a training run. Full-back Crowley, hastily summoned from New Zealand for this match because of injuries, moved in to gather a Lynagh chip as it bounced at thigh height.

Even as Crowley swung in for the ball, Campese, leaning forward, swept it up without breaking stride. Horan came tearing up on the left, and Campese, swaying one way and then the other, sensed that Horan had switched outside him. Still, he leaned inwards as if making for the posts at a diagonal. Then came the cheekiest of flips over his right shoulder, the ball hanging in the air for a fraction as if willing Horan to run on to it. He did – at speed again – and though there was one more challenge to come he dived in for a try close to the posts.

There was a semblance of known All Black form to end the half. But Australia met every defensive demand and already it looked as if the Wallaby management could decently begin to make arrangements for a London hotel this week.

Lynagh's second penalty goal settled the match with some 20 minutes remaining. It was an uncanny feeling to see the men in black reduced to states of panic that I, for one, have not previously seen in a New Zealand representative team.

How they must have wished their silver-tongued management could have persuaded Michael Jones to have taken part. Such are his religious beliefs that Jones, the world's most astute flank forward, will not play on a Sunday.

Yesterday's convincing defeat was the end of an era in New Zealand rugby. Australia's march to Twickenham has been a just reward for a team who believe in the virtues of attacking rugby which, properly played, requires all 15 players to be involved.

World Cup Final: England 6 Australia 12, Twickenham, 2 November

Australia's triumph

England bang head against yellow brick wall

By John Reason

FROM the moment midway through the first half when Tony Daly scored a try which was converted by Michael Lynagh, it always looked as if Australia would win the World Cup final at Twickenham. It has to be said, though, that the result would have been a lot closer if referee Derek Bevan had decided that a deliberate knock-on by David Campese late in the game was worth the award of a penalty try.

Winterbottom's attempted pass to Underwood was knocked abruptly upfield. If the pass had been,made, there was not too much space between Underwood and the Australian line, and Campese has never been quick enough to catch England's left wing. The referee took a long time to make his decision. He finally gave England a penalty, which Webb kicked

But Australia were fortunate. Had the referee awarded a penalty try and had the try been converted, England would still have been 12-9 down. At that stage, though, there was just enough time for England to have some prospect of making another score.

Apart from that overlap balked by Campese – and he cheerfully accepted the booing that followed – England found themselves frustrated at every turn. They tried a stream of switch moves, but few of them reached the gain line against such an uncompromising defence. When the ball was stopped, Poidevin did some priceless retrieving for Australia.

Australia had some sizeable problems of their own. Their midfield, admittedly in a blustery wind that made kicking difficult, missed touch far too often when they really needed to make it. And their line-out got into a real mess in the second half when they needed another score for insurance. They called a succession of five, four and three-man line-outs and did not win the ball from any of them.

But England lost just about the most important line-out of the match. Horan, the Australian centre, broke out of defence with a loose ball and with Campese at his shoulder England were casting round desperately for a few lifeboats,

Campese holds the trophy.

even though the Australians had 70 yards to run.

Campese decided to kick ahead, and there is not much doubt that he would have scored if the ball had taken a kindly bounce. His progress when he tried to regather looked as if it was impeded by Guscott, but Australia held the attacking position and, when Ofahengaue won the ball at the tail of a line-out a few yards from England's line, Australia's two props sandwiched the ball between them and drove over the line, Daly securing the touchdown.

Lynagh had already given Australia the lead after 27 minutes, when England were penalised at a line-out. It was a long kick in that wind, but he gave it a thoroughly good thump and saw it sail over from 45 yards.

Midway through the second half, Webb, whose kicking had been as bad as against Scotland, kicked a penalty goal to the enormous relief of the crowd. But in no time Dooley was penalised after a line-out and, kicking down the wind, Lynagh drove home a superb penalty goal from 50 yards.

That was effectively game, set, match and World Cup. Australia led 12-3 and not much more than 10 minutes remained.

After the controversial Campese knock-on and Webb's penalty goal, the closest England got to a score was when Lynagh, trying to run the ball, was caught by Underwood with a most tenacious tackle. But England knocked on when they tried to develop the attacking position. Somehow that was entirely appropriate.

RUGBY UNION WORLD CUP 1991

(NB: The pool matches each carry a total of 4pts – 3 for a win, 2 for a draw and 1 for a loss)

Pool 1

3 Oct	Twickenham	NEW ZEALAND	18	ENGLAND	12
5 Oct	Otley	ITALY	30	USA	9
8 Oct	Gloucester	NEW ZEALAND	46	USA	6
8 Oct	Twickenham	ENGLAND	36	ITALY	6
11 Oct	Twickenham	ENGLAND	37	USA	9
13 Oct	Leicester	NEW ZEALAND	31	ITALY	21

Pool 1	P	W	D	L	F	A	Pts
1 NEW ZEALAND	3	3	0	0	95	39	9
2 ENGLAND	3	2	0	1	85	33	7
3 ITALY	3	1	0	2	57	76	5
4 USA	3	0	0	3	24	113	3

Pool 2

5 Oct	Murrayfield	SCOTLAND	47	JAPAN	9
6 Oct	Lansdowne Road	IRELAND	55	ZIMBABWE	11
9 Oct	Lansdowne Road	IRELAND	32	JAPAN	16
9 Oct	Murrayfield	SCOTLAND	51	ZIMBABWE	12
12 Oct	Murrayfield	SCOTLAND	24	IRELAND	15
14 Oct	Belfast	JAPAN	52	ZIMBABWE	8

Pool 2	P	W	D	L	F	A	Pts
1 SCOTLAND	3	3	0	0	122	36	9
2 IRELAND	3	2	0	1	102	51	7
3 JAPAN	3	1	0	2	77	87	5
4 ZIMBABWE	3	0	0	3	31	158	3

Pool 3

4 Oct	Llanelli	AUSTRALIA	32	ARGENTINA	19
6 Oct	Cardiff Arms Park	WESTERN SAMOA	16	WALES	13
9 Oct	Pontypool	AUSTRALIA	9	WESTERN SAMOA	3
9 Oct	Cardiff Arms Park	WALES	16	ARGENTINA	7
12 Oct	Cardiff Arms Park	AUSTRALIA	38	WALES	3
13 Oct	Pontypridd	WESTERN SAMOA	35	ARGENTINA	12

Pool 3	P	W	D	L	F	A	Pts
1 AUSTRALIA	3	3	0	0	79	25	9
2 W SAMOA	3	2	0	1	54	34	7
3 WALES	3	1	0	2	32	61	5
4 ARGENTINA	3	0	0	3	38	83	3

Pool 4

4 Oct	Béziers	FRANCE	30	ROMANIA	3
5 Oct	Bayonne	CANADA	13	FIJI	3
8 Oct	Grenoble	FRANCE	33	FIJI	9
9 Oct	Toulouse	CANADA	19	ROMANIA	11
12 Oct	Brive	ROMANIA	17	FIJI	15
13 Oct	Agen	FRANCE	19	CANADA	13

Pool 4	P	W	D	L	F	A	Pts
1 FRANCE	3	3	0	0	82	25	9
2 CANADA	3	2	0	1	45	33	7
3 ROMANIA	3	1	0	2	31	64	5
4 FIJI	3	0	0	3	27	63	3

Quarter-finals

19 Oct	Parc des Princes	ENGLAND	19	FRANCE	10
19 Oct	Murrayfield	SCOTLAND	28	WESTERN SAMOA	6
20 Oct	Lansdowne Road	AUSTRALIA	19	IRELAND	18
20 Oct	Lille	NEW ZEALAND	29	CANADA	13

Semi-finals

26 Oct	Murrayfield	ENGLAND	9	SCOTLAND	6
27 Oct	Lansdowne Road	AUSTRALIA	16	NEW ZEALAND	6

Third-place match

30 Oct	Cardiff Arms Park	NEW ZEALAND	13	SCOTLAND	6

FINAL

2 Nov	Twickenham	AUSTRALIA	12	ENGLAND	6

AUSTRALIA Roebuck; Campese, Little, Horam, Egerton; Lynagh, Farr-Jones (capt); Daly, Kearns, McKenzie, McCall, Eales, Poidevin, Coker, Ofahengaue
Scorers T: Daly; C: Lynagh; PG: Lynagh 2
ENGLAND Webb; Halliday, Carling (capt), Guscott, Underwood; Andrew, Hill; Leonard, Moore, Probyn, Ackford, Dooley, Skinner, Teague, Winterbottom
Scorer PG: Webb 2

INDIVIDUAL SCORING

Most points in tournament	68	RP Keyes (Ire)
	66	MP Lynagh (A)
	61	AG Hastings (S)
Most tries in tournament	6	DI Campese (A)
	6	J-B Lafond (F)
Most points in a match	24	JM Webb (E, v Italy)
	23	RP Keyes (Ire, v Zimbabwe)
Most tries in a match	4	BF Robinson (Ire, v Zimbabwe)
	3	TJ Wright (NZ, v USA)
	3	I Tukalo (S, v Zimbabwe)
	3	J-B Lafond (F, v Fiji)

FAIR PLAY AWARD

Zimbabwe: No penalties conceded for fouls or dangerous play.

1992

4 Mar Records fall at Old Deer Park as St Mary's register their 31st Hospitals' Cup triumph to surpass the long-standing Guy's record. It is also a record sixth win in succession, and their 49-0 defeat of UCH/Middx equals their own points record in the final.

25 Apr The World XV, in New Zealand to celebrate the NZRU Centenary, lose the series 2-1, going down 26-15 to the All Blacks in Auckland after winning 28-14 in Christchurch and losing 54-26 in Wellington.

16 May Rupert Moon, the former England B scrum-half who last autumn opted for an international career with Wales, has an outstanding match in attack and defence as Llanelli retain the Schweppes Cup with a 16-7 win over Swansea. After setting up Llanelli's first try in the 7th minute, he then scores the second, midway through the second half, before applying the coup de grace in the final minute with a sweetly timed drop-goal. Llanelli's 8th win in 21 years means the cup will now remain permanently in Stradey Park's museum, as the sponsors have withdrawn their support.

6 Jun Ireland, having lost a great chance to record their first win over the All Blacks last week, are thrashed 59-6 at Wellington in the last game of their tour (W3-L5).

19 Jul France win the 2nd World Students Cup, beating New Zealand 21-9 at Rovigo, Italy.

19 Sep Auckland, holders since 1985, complete their 8th successful defence of the Ranfurly Shield this season with a 25-16 victory over North Harbour at Eden Park, taking their remarkable winning run to 56 matches.

INTERNATIONAL CHAMPIONSHIP

	E	F	I	S	W	P	W	D	L	F	A	Pts
1 ENGLAND	-	-	38-9	-	24-0	4	4	0	0	118	29	8
2=FRANCE	13-31	-	44-12	-	-	4	3	0	1	75	62	4
2=SCOTLAND	7-25	10-6	-	-	-	4	2	0	2	47	56	4
2=WALES	-	9-12	-	15-12	-	4	0	1	3	40	63	4
5 IRELAND	-	-	-	10-18	15-16	4	0	1	3	46	116	0

TOURS (Tests)
Ireland in New Zealand: NZ24-I21, NZ59-I6
Scotland in Australia: A27-S12, A37-S13
New Zealand in Australia: A16-NZ15, A19-NZ17, A23-NZ26
New Zealand in South Africa: SA24-NZ27
Australia in South Africa: SA3-A26
South Africa in France & England: F15-SA20, F29-SA16, E33-SA16
Australia in British Isles: I17-A42, W6-A23

International Championship: England 24 Wales 0, Twickenham, 7 March

England slam door, quietly

By John Reason

NOT SINCE the days of Wavell Wakefield in 1924 has a country won all four matches in the Five Nations Championship for two years in succession, and England duly accomplished that feat once more by winning this match against Wales.

However, there was nothing remotely as final or as dramatic as a slam in what occurred at Twickenham. The door closed so quietly that the noise was barely perceptible, and to use the word grand in any associated context would be to insult the English language.

Even to call it a small slam would be an overstatement, because both teams were so lacking in finesse and missed so many tricks that for long periods it looked as if everyone on the field was playing *misère*.

Wales were nothing like big enough, good enough, quick enough or fit enough, but, though England won without being remotely threatened, they made so many mistakes and became stuck in such a deep rut for so long that it seemed as if Wales would escape with a defeat as modest as 15-0.

In the last 10 minutes, though, Wales pointlessly tried to run the ball out of defence, or they kicked so badly that they presented England with such a series of scoring opportunities that, hard as they tried, they could not help adding two more scores.

The last, a penalty goal by Jonathan Webb, took his season's tally to 67 points, a championship best, breaking the record set by last season's England full-back, Simon Hodgkinson.

Scorers: Carling, Skinner, Dooley tries; Webb 3 conversions, 2 penalty goals.

International Championship: France 13 England 31, Paris, 15 February

England close to greatness
Gallic marbles take French leave

By John Mason

IGNORE, if that is possible, the rows and ructions. This was a mighty performance by England in a match which, for an hour at least, had a score of sublime moments.

That was before the French self-destruct button was pressed by, among others, Gregoire Lascube, the loose-head, and Vincent Moscato, the hooker turned prop. Both were sent off – and at least one other could have followed.

When a rugby player, tears cascading down his cheeks, is screaming at the top of his voice before a scrum packs down, the knife-edge of acceptable competitive behaviour is precariously balanced. Several marbles, I fear, had taken French leave.

That, and a great deal more, is what confronted England's players in the final 20 minutes or so of another imperious victory on Saturday, the fifth in succession over France, three of them in Paris.

In so many ways it was difficult to decide for whom to be most sorry – England, denied their true ration of glory; referee Stephen Hilditch, confronted by anarchy; or Pierre Berbizier, France's coach, whose brave new world fell to tiny pieces.

There has to be sympathy, too, for Philippe Sella, France's captain, who went off reluctantly 16 minutes into the second half as a result of an accidental clash of heads with Rob Andrew, who had already departed for stitches. When Sella was on the field, discipline and *le fair play* reigned, even though a penalty try had been conceded.

I could accept French grumbles about that decision because the collapsed scrum appeared more accidental than deliberate. For all that, Mr Hilditch was ideally placed to make a judgment. From that point on, temperatures rose.

When Sella retired, England led 18-7: two Webb penalty goals, plus conversions of the penalty try and a superlative try of his own, against a smartly taken try and penalty goal by Viars, the 20-year-old on the left wing.

Scrum-half Galthie thereafter took charge of the French team, whose forwards were already hunting illegally. Gouging of eyes and nostrils and the twisting of testicles sorely tried English discipline. The slide towards madness and mayhem was inexorable.

Some irresponsible French players had assassinated what could have been one of the sport's great games. That it very nearly was, in spite of everything, says much for the quality of England's play and, it cannot be stressed too strongly, the potential of France's better players.

Tempers flare at Parc des Princes: Moscato (2) was sent off.

Collisions, replacements, and fights showered the pitch like confetti. The crowd hooted, booed and whistled and, though Penaud charged down a kick by Carling for a try at the posts, the final scenes ruined all hopes that the *entente* had been mended.

Another penalty goal by Webb, taking him to 55 points in three matches, and a try for the admirable Morris tied the bows of victory which, amid the hysterical fury, the stamping of Lascube and the head-butting of Moscato, was less sweet than it deserved to be.

The Daily Telegraph: Wellington, 17 April

England condemn new ruck and maul rules

By John Mason

MORE than 40 sweeping law changes aimed at banishing the penalty-ridden, slow-coach version of rugby football were adopted by the International Rugby Board yesterday.

But further changes at line-out, maul and ruck, most of which were condemned by England's players and management, will be experimental variations for a year.

The other changes, including five points for a try instead of four, are mandatory next season – or, as far as Australia, South Africa and New Zealand are concerned, in mid-season, including incoming tours if the visiting country agrees.

The law-makers, roundly condemned by Brian Moore, England's hooker, on the nonsensical grounds that they have not played for 40 years, have decided that when a maul – ball in hand – grinds to a halt, or the ball becomes unplayable, the team not in possession at the start of the maul should put the ball into an ensuing scrum. The ruck – ball on the ground – attracts the same experimental variation except when the referee is unable to determine the team responsible.

The five members of the IRB's laws committee sifted more than 300 proposals and amendments covering 78 closely typed pages. Their decisions, together with the previously announced siting of the 1995 World Cup in South Africa, became the principal business of the Board's annual meeting which ended here yesterday.

In addition to Moore, neither Geoff Cooke, England's manager, nor Dick Best, the coach, were greatly impressed by the experimental ruck and maul variations, which have been in force at under-19 level in England this season.

Cooke said: 'It puts the responsibility on the ball-carrier but gives an incentive to the tackler. Players will be encouraged to go to the ground when tackled to form a ruck, which goes against the whole purpose of staying on your feet to play rugby.'

Best said: 'I can see the thinking but I think it's stupid. You are encouraging people to get on the wrong side of mauls and to cheat.'

Moore said: 'If people get into wrong positions inadvertently, there will be such a desperate desire to get

out of them because they need the ball, I think it could increase violence.'

Gavin Hastings, however, was purring with delight. Told that, when a penalty is kicked directly into touch, the same team will have the throw-in, Hastings, the glint in his eyes revealing those Murrayfield touch-flags in the

distant corners already beckoning, said, with a grin: 'Tell Mooro we're not all hookers ....'

Generally, the handful of professional club coaches, the men who lead the way in exploiting the laws to suit their teams, welcomed the changes, though not without reservation.

Courage League Championship: Bath 32 Saracens 12, Bath, 25 April

Bath's euphoria muted by Cassell sending-off

By Brendan Gallagher

BATH'S justifiable euphoria at retaining the Courage League Championship could not disguise their genuine concern at the undeserved 41st-minute dismissal of Saracens flanker Justyn Cassell, who could now miss the England B tour of New Zealand this summer.

Saracens had just kicked off in the second half when Cassell was tackled by Andy Robinson, who then clung on to his legs as a second ruck developed upfield. As Cassell, anxious to rejoin the action, vigorously attempted to extricate himself, a boot undoubtedly made contact with the Bath captain's face.

Referee George Seddon, who was unsighted, waved away Robinson's immediate protestations of Cassell's innocence and based his decision on the word of touch-

judge Barry Lucas. Cassell, 24, is arguably the outstanding newcomer to first-class rugby this season. A design consultant, he was recently made redundant because of his determination to take six weeks off for the New Zealand tour.

All this rather detracted from one of Bath's proudest days, a second successive league title during a period of transition, achieved despite the deducted point for fielding an unregistered player against London Irish. They win on points difference from Orrell, who had the title in their grasp two weeks ago before an injury-time dropped-goal by Huw Davies allowed Wasps to steal the match from them and, ultimately, deprive them of the title.

[Cassell was reprieved and went to New Zealand.]

Pilkington Cup Final: Bath 15 Harlequins 12, Twickenham, 2 May

Barnes drops last-second bombshell to crack Quins

By John Reason

STUART BARNES, the Bath fly-half, dragged triumph from what had been something of a disaster for himself when he won the Pilkington Cup by dropping a goal with the last kick of extra time after an absolutely tremendous match.

It was one of the few kicks that Barnes had hit reasonably well all afternoon. What made it even more uncharacteristic was that he was given the ball from a short line-out won by Nigel Redman.

It was a wonder Barnes was able to overcome his surprise, because Paul Ackford had come out of retirement and had so dominated the line-out for the Harlequins that he cleaned Bath out – soap, sponge, flannel, pumice stone, tide mark and all.

The crippling misfortune

Stuart Barnes celebrates with Jeremy Guscott after his winning drop-goal.

which seemed to have befallen the Quins when Skinner and Langhorn were sent off the

field a week ago turned out to be the best thing that could have happened to them. Langhorn could never have monopolised the line-out like Ackford.

What is more, Russell came in to play such a ferocious game in the tight-loose that he was not all that far behind Winterbottom, his captain.

With some impressive handling grafted almost posthumously onto his game by his coach, Dick Best, Winterbottom has had the best season of his career. It was cruel when Barnes dashed the Cup from his grip.

The extra periods were littered with poor kicking, Hill and Barnes making mistakes for Bath, while Quins, still looking likely

winners, saw Pears and Challinor each make a mess of two drop-goal attempts.

Barnes, at the last, however, did not. Redman won a line-out and, as referee Howard stood poised to blow the final whistle, Barnes completed the most brazen theft of the season. Thirty exhausted players and 60,500 enthralled, privileged spectators followed the curling, rolling flight of the ball, itself seemingly in the last stages of terminal tiredness, as it limped over the bar.

Scorers – Bath: Try, De Glanville; Conversion and 2 penalty goals, Webb; Drop goal, Barnes. Quins: Try, Winterbottom; Conversion and 2 penalty goals, Pears.

Bledisloe Cup: Australia 19 New Zealand 17, Brisbane, 19 July

Australia in second call for Loe to be disciplined

By Justin Rogers

FOR THE second time in two Tests, the Australian Rugby Union will call for the New Zealand tour management to take action against prop forward Richard Loe.

Yesterday, Loe broke diminutive winger Paul Carozza's nose with an elbow smash as Australia took a 2-0 lead in the Bledisloe Cup series with this win over the All Blacks at Ballymore.

'If Loe gets out of this one he's a miracle man,' declared Bob Dwyer, the Australian coach. 'It was late and it was cowardly – a disgrace to the game.'

A fortnight ago, New Zealand tour officials dismissed a call for Loe to be disciplined after Australia's Sam Scott-Young had needed 15 stitches in a head gash.

Television viewers saw Loe smash his elbow into Carozza's face as he lay defenceless on the turf after scoring the first of his two tries. French referee Patrick Robin, whose view was obscured, was powerless to act after the touch judge told him that he had missed the incident.

Victim Carozza was Australia's match-winner. Watched by a crowd of 27,506, he drove through a tackle by giant rival John Kirwan to score the decisive try with only eight minutes to go. It was Australia's fifth win over the All Blacks in the last six matches, their first triumph over New Zealand in Brisbane and the 10th straight victory since last August's 6-3 loss to the All Blacks at Eden Park.

[Loe was not disciplined by the All Blacks tour management and helped New Zealand win the final Test. But he was later suspended from the game for gouging in domestic rugby.]

Tour International: South Africa 3 Australia 26, Newlands, 22 August

Springboks in major rethink after drubbing by Wallabies

By John Reason

THIS WAS a slogging dog-fight in the rain and the muddy trenches of Newlands, but at the end South Africa knew that they will have to go back to the drawing-board to recover their leading place in the world of rugby. It was the biggest defeat in their history.

John Williams, the Springbok coach, admitted the changed situation. Ten days earlier, he had said that, old as his players were, he felt they were still the best in the country.

The disaster duly arrived just as his rugby excellency the Argentine ambassador forecast it might. Hugo Porta also felt that a disaster might be necessary for the health of Springbok rugby, because it would blow away any complacency.

Well, this game showed that South Africa are so out-dated and ponderous in the forwards and so blunt and dull at half-back that they looked as if they could have played for a week without ever threatening to score a try.

Afterwards Williams accepted the evidence: 'We will now have to reconsider our options very thoroughly as far as selection is concerned. Our game in South Africa is out of date.'

Lynagh kicked three penalties for the Wallabies and converted one of their three tries, scored by Carozza (2) and Campese – his 50th in internationals.

South Africa's only score was a penalty by their captain, Naas Botha. The veteran outside-half acknowledged the significance of the result and its implications both for his team and himself. The feeling is that he will retire.

The Daily Telegraph: 28 July

All Blacks welcomed in South Africa: New badge for Springboks

NEW ZEALAND, galvanised by a late resurgence in Australia, arrived in South Africa for their first official visit since 1976 to a warm welcome. About 400 supporters greeted the All Blacks on their arrival in Johannesburg, with captain Sean Fitzpatrick describing the reception as emotional and moving.

Only two players among a squad of 30 have played in the Republic before. Grant Fox (outside-half) and Steve McDowell (loose-head prop) were members of the rebel Cavaliers tour party in 1986.

South Africa's return will be symbolised by a new badge. The Springbok – the old emblem of the white-dominated SA Rugby Board – is linked with four protea flowers. The protea was the badge and nickname of the old coloured union in the Republic.

Tour International: South Africa 24 New Zealand 27, Johannesburg, 15 August

Springboks finish on false high despite loss

By John Reason

The Springboks line up for their anthem at Ellis Park.

SOUTH Africa came back into international rugby with such a storming finish against New Zealand that the match ended in a tumult of exultation.

Little more than 10 minutes earlier, the All Blacks were leading 27-10. If they had played half as well as they should have done with their control of possession and position, their score would have been well up into the 40s.

The magnificent stadium at Ellis Park was then a very quiet and reflective place. South Africans brood when a Springbok pack is demolished as this one was in the line-out and in the loose. Then, though, one of those accidents occurred that start a chain of events which blur the memory of much of what has gone before. Referee Sandy MacNeill, of Australia, made a clattering mistake.

He did not see Robert du Preez, the Springbok scrum-half, knock the ball on at least a yard prior to centre Piet Muller's try, which Naas Botha converted with a magnificent kick.

Those seven points gave the Springboks just the kick-start they needed to make the match look much closer than it was, and to finish with a score which all the knowing people in South African rugby admit flattered their team.

[A row developed before the match when the crowd sang the South African anthem through the two-minute silence for peace and democracy, under the impression that neither anthem would be played, because the African National Congress do not accept the traditional one. Then the anthems were played, so the crowd sang their anthem again.

The ANC threatened to stop the two remaining matches of Australia's concurrent tour, furious with the crowd's 'spiteful behaviour'. But ANC president Nelson Mandela admitted it was impossible to dictate what a rugby crowd should think.]

The Daily Telegraph: 30 September

France's call for 'black Bok' refused

By Nick Cain

THE South Africans arrived in Paris yesterday to begin their tour of France and England, and they immediately became involved in controversy by disclosing that the French government had insisted that a black player be included in their party of 36.

Abie Malan, the South African manager, said that the request – a fax message two hours before departure – had been rejected. 'Our players are selected according to their ability,' he said. 'They always have been and they always will be. We were, at the least, surprised by the French government's attitude.'

The request for the symbolic inclusion of a black player came from Frederique Bredin, France's minister for sports and youth.

Tour International: England 33 South Africa 16, Twickenham, 14 November

England tame Springboks

By John Reason

SOUTH AFRICA ran out of steam in the second half to such an extent that what had been a surprisingly sturdy forward effort collapsed almost completely, and with it their defensive organisation fell in ruins. The result was England's third ever win over the Springboks, and by far their biggest.

The Springboks' scrum were always comfortable on a wet day but they allowed Dewi Morris to steal a try when scrum-half Garth Wright missed a pick-up from one of their own heels and they conceded two more from set-piece chip kicks.

Jeremy Guscott took the first as easily as if he was picking an apple in an orchard all by himself, and Will Carling scored the second after Theo Van Rensburg, the Springbok full-back, had taken his eye off the ball and had dropped it on his own line. Jon Webb, the England full-back, converted two of the tries and kicked a penalty goal, and so England turned a 16-11 deficit at half-time into something of a second-half stroll.

The Springboks were markedly short of fitness by current international standards. Yet all England had to comfort them in the first half was a try scored by Tony Underwood. Rory Underwood picked up a loose ball from a ruck and stood calmly acting as a pivot while his brother doubled round him to take the scoring pass

and slide over in the corner.

Webb had kicked an early penalty goal for England, but in reply Naas Botha kicked two for South Africa. What is more, no sooner had Underwood Minor scored his try than Botha put his team back in the lead with a remarkable dropped goal. He calmly did a U-turn in midfield, for all the world as if he was Mr Heseltine or Mr Major, and hooked the ball back with unerring accuracy between the posts.

Nor was that all. Before the half was over, England's travails in the line-out began to look really serious when they lost a throw on their own line and Tiaan Strauss drove through to score. Botha converted

Leading 16-8 and controlling the scrummage put-in 9-1, and winning their own line-out throw almost unchallenged, the Springboks looked to be in forbidding control of the match. England, therefore, were more than grateful when Webb managed to pull three points back with a penalty goal just before half-time.

However, as soon as the second half started, it was clear that someone had been tampering with the machinery, because South Africa's wheels promptly fell off. England found themselves winning line-outs as fast as they had lost them in the first half, and they ran up their 22 points without reply.

[Naas Botha later confirmed that he is to retire from rugby.]

The Daily Telegraph: 5 November

South Africans return to England after 22 years

By John Mason

SOUTH AFRICA, whose last representative match in England was on 31 January 1970, end 22 years and nine months of rugby union boycott in Britain when they meet the Midlands at Welford Road, Leicester, today, the first of four tour matches.

The South Africans arrived on Sunday from France, where five of nine matches were won, including the first international in Lyon. France squared the series the following week in Paris. The England leg of the tour, which culminates in the international at Twickenham on Saturday

week, was in doubt last week after withdrawals of support in South Africa by the National and Olympic Sports Congress and the African National Congress.

After 48 hours of behind-the-scenes diplomacy, the ANC reaffirmed that the tour should go ahead without militant protest.

Abie Malan, South Africa's manager, stressed again yesterday that the team were in England to play rugby, not politics.

[South Africa beat Midland Division 32-9 and had victories over England B and Northern Division before losing the Test.]

Tour International: France 20 Argentina 24, Nantes, 14 November

Pumas march to a historic victory

By Charles Randall

ARGENTINA flew out of Nantes yesterday, leaving their French hosts in a state of shock. The Pumas had won in France for the first time, at the same Beaujoire Stadium that witnessed the taming of the All Blacks in 1986 – the height of French rugby history now followed by the depths.

This victory ranks with Argentina's one other great moment abroad, when they beat Australia 18-3 in Brisbane in 1983.

The Pumas deserved their win and they departed far happier than the South Africans two weeks before them. They made their tackles count, and Santiago Meson, a medical student from Tucuman, kicked seven penalty goals from nine attempts to win the match, playing the game of his life at full-back.

France scored three tries to Argentina's nil, with Philippe Sella scoring his 26th for his country 10 years to the day

since making his international début, also against Argentina. That might make the scoreline seem an injustice, but this was, in fact, an undoubtedly inept performance by the French and a blow between the eyes for Pierre Berbizier, the national coach.

The Pumas showed unexpected mental resilience. They maintained their composure after a cruel early set-back when Martin Teran's try under the posts was controversially ruled out.

France immediately went 15-3 ahead. Puma sides from the past might have buckled after this turn around in fortunes. But Meson's beautifully composed goal-kicking punished the over-anxious French forwards for frequent infringements in loose play. His first success arrived after one minute and his seventh 12 minutes from time, which put Argentina 21-20 ahead. A dropped goal from Arbizu clinched matters.

1993

20 Mar France beat Wales 26-10 in Paris and, thanks to England's shock defeat in Dublin, take the Five Nations without recourse to the newly instituted points difference 'tie-breaker'. This is France's 12th successive win over Wales, whose try by Nigel Walker, the international hurdler winning his second cap, is their first at Parc des Princes for 10 years.

4 Apr Infighting leaves the WRU in turmoil as the 25-strong general committee are sacked after two votes by representatives of the 212 clubs, and treasurer Glanmor Griffiths, having previously resigned, is reappointed.

9 Jun Wales conclude their 100% 6-match tour of southern Africa, which includes wins over Zimbabwe (35-14 and 42-13) and Namibia (38-23), with a 56-17 thrashing of the South African Barbarians, and Neil Jenkins, having appeared at centre, full-back and fly-half in the 3 internationals, takes his points tally to 89, a Wales tour record.

12 Jun Scotland, travelling without most of their first-choice players, lose their 100% record in the last match of their South Pacific tour, going down 28-11 to Western Samoa at Apia, having beaten Fiji 21-10 and Tonga 23-5 in their other internationals.

17 Jul The All Blacks beat world champions Australia 25-10 at Dunedin in a one-off Bledisloe Cup match.

17 Jul Despite losing their home leg 15-10 to Fiji, Tonga qualify for the World Cup finals (1995) for the first time, having won 24-11 in Suva last month.

16 Oct Wales run up their highest score in an international, beating Japan 55-5 at Cardiff, with Ieuan Evans scoring their fastest ever international try, in 45 seconds. Japan's try, coming at the end, is scored by wing three-quarter Ian Williams, former Oxford Blue and Australian international.

6 Nov The Wallabies' brilliant 24-3 victory at the Parc des Princes is their biggest winning margin over France and squares the 2-match series.

10 Nov The All Blacks, with their midweek side, cruise to an 84-5 victory over South of Scotland, their highest total on tour in the British Isles, surpassing their 63-0 win over Combined Hartlepool Clubs in 1905. Captain and flanker Zinzan Brooke scores 4 of their 12 tries.

20 Nov New Zealand beat Scotland 51-15 at Murrayfield, their highest total for a full international in Europe, and the most points Scotland have conceded in a Test.

INTERNATIONAL CHAMPIONSHIP

	E	F	I	S	W	P	W	D	L	F	A	Pts
1 FRANCE				11-3	26-10	4	3	0	1	73	35	6
2* SCOTLAND		15-3			20-0	4	2	0	2	50	40	4
3* ENGLAND		16-15		26-12		4	2	0	2	54	54	4
4* IRELAND	17-3	6-21				4	2	0	2	45	53	4
5 WALES	10-9		14-19			4	1	0	3	34	74	2

* Points difference introduced to determine placings

TOURS (Tests)

British Isles in New Zealand: NZ20-BI18, NZ7-BI20, NZ30-BI13
France in South Africa: SA20-F20, SA17-F18
Australia in New Zealand: NZ25-A10
South Africa in Australia: A12-SA19, A28-SA20, A19-SA12
Australia in France: F16-A13, F3-A24
New Zealand in British Isles: S15-NZ51, E15-NZ9

International Championship: England 16 France 15, Twickenham, 16 January

England rebound to victory
Hunter swoops as goalposts deny France
By John Reason

WITH full-back Jon Webb all over the place under the high ball in the swirling wind, and two tries having been conceded in the first 20 minutes, England were looking both uncomfortable and unconvincing. But late in the first half they enjoyed a pot full of jam.

They scored a try from a penalty kick by Webb which rebounded off the far post, the ball coming back perfectly into the path of Ian Hunter, who was the only England back really following up. It bounced perfectly for him as well. All he had to do was catch it at a comfortable waist height and keep running to score. It was the only try that England scored or even looked like scoring.

Webb made the conversion and also made himself feel a whole lot better after the disasters that had gone before. As it turned out, that try and that kick also won the match.

Late in the game, when France wanted only two points to gain the win they deserved, Didier Cambero-bero hit England's crossbar with a drop at goal, and so did scrum-half Aubin Hueber. The rebounds came back just as handily for England as when Webb's kick hit the post.

Obituary: *The Daily Telegraph*, 5 January

Dr Danie Craven
'Doc' made men cringe but was best of them all

John Reason pays a tribute to Mr Big of rugby

Danie Craven did what he always wanted to do. He died with his boots on. They were big boots, too. The biggest in the world of rugby. For more than 40 years, no other rugby man anywhere on earth could have come anywhere near to filling them.

At a function in Bordeaux last October at the start of the Springbok tour of France, he paid his last respects to his country's rugby. And now we are paying ours to him. Two long overnight flights in the space of four days by a man in his 80s who had had three heart operations was a trip he should never have made. He had undoubtedly contributed to his premature death.

At that time, he spoke about the administrative reconstruction he was supervising in South African rugby, and when I leapfrogged ahead to 1994, to the end of his joint presidency with Ibrahim Patel, of the New South African Rugby Football Union, he looked up with a puckish smile.

'I'll be dead by then,' he said. The Doc knew he was going to die of a heart attack. The only thing he got wrong was the date, and he got that wrong by about 40 years.

Many years ago, he said every male member of his family had died of heart attacks before they were 50, and he had made all his dispositions on the assumption that he would do the same. By then he was already 15 years in credit.

He used those years as no-one else could have done. He and he alone made it possible for South Africa to re-enter the world of international rugby, and his efforts to end apartheid helped all the other sports in his country.

Before all the political turmoil, he had been one of South Africa's greatest scrum-halves. He coached the Springboks in the British Isles in 1951-52, and a few years later took his place on the International Board as one of South Africa's representatives.

In battling to end apartheid in South Africa, he not only went to Zambia to talk to the then banned African National Congress, but subsequently made no secret of it.

After he was elected president of the South African Rugby Board, he had to fight off many attempted palace revolutions. He won every one, even though he had to carve up South African rugby into much smaller pieces in order to dilute the power of the great unions.

The Doc was determined to stay alive to watch South Africa's return to Twickenham. 'When we have done that,' he said, 'we will know we are back.' He should have saved his strength to go to London for that match – the great leap forward. Bordeaux was just a small step along the road.

'I know,' he said. 'I know.' Again came that grin. 'The trouble is that when you get old you start making mistakes. It was just the same when I was a player.'

International Championship: Wales 10 England 9, Cardiff, 6 February

Ferocious-tackling Wales bask in glory after smothering champions

By John Mason

THE charitable view would be that victory for Wales did them far more good than the single-point defeat did harm to England. Perhaps. Of its multitudinous facets, though, international sport is rarely about charity, especially when the opposition at a heaving, melodious Arms Park, Cardiff, are English.

For Wales, even more than the 80 draining minutes it took to smother-tackle into oblivion well-founded England hopes of a record third successive Grand Slam, the greatest joy was in one factor above all others. In a nerve-jangling win of great significance, Wales proved they are a force again.

The Welsh roll of honour, which had half a dozen players, led by Gibbs, Mike Rayer and Gareth Llewellyn, jostling for pole position, must begin with Ieuan Evans, the captain and right wing – and try-scorer.

The man who nudged David Campese, the world's leading international try-scorer, into error to secure a Test series win for the Lions in Australia in 1989 turned his Svengali-like attentions this time to Rory Underwood, England's record try-scorer and most capped player.

Half-time beckoning fast and England 9-3 ahead, Underwood was late in realising the danger as he moved back to cover a Welsh clearance. Evans, accelerating and kicking on, left him standing before completing the most satisfying dive of his career for the try. Neil Jenkins converted and Wales led 10-9.

Having in the last three matches conceded 83 points to England (24-0, 25-6 and 34-6), Wales defended mightily.

With England, whose previous run of defeats lasted 28 years, losing in Cardiff again, it was like old times, except that Wales will not win the Grand Slam ... will they?

International Championship: Ireland 17 England 3, Dublin, 20 March

Elwood steers Ireland to famous victory

Curtain down on golden English era

By John Mason

DUBLIN, the city of mussels and muscles, was alive'o with the satisfying sound of much munching on a long Saturday evening, of the English having to eat many thousands of words.

Ireland's forwards took England to the cleaners and Eric Elwood, the newest and brightest of outside-halves to grace the Five Nations Championship for a while, made absolutely certain that that is where they stayed.

In the rough and tumble of a match in which, unusually, the pace appeared to get faster and faster, Ireland were magnificent. Neither was their strength confined to the dedicated, bull-like pursuit of the ball.

There were a score of deft touches from Michael Bradley, the captain and scrum-half, either in tidying up or, when attacking the short side, adding to England's discomfort. There was the athleticism and alertness of Brian Robinson, the No.8, and the unceasing belligerence, energies finely channelled, of Mick Galwey, the lock.

Best of all, there was the menace and sophistication of Elwood, who, more than anyone on the day, had that precious commodity of time in which to do things, the true mark of the outstanding player.

Elwood, his soaring dropped goals in the 43rd and 76th minutes plus penalty goals in the 28th and 45th, pushed England to the precipice. The try in the final seconds by the mighty Galwey toppled them over it.

England's defeat gifted the Five Nations Championship to France, 26-10 victors over Wales in Paris, without resort to the slide-rule.

World Sevens Final: England 21 Australia 17, Murrayfield, 18 April

Harriman in crowning glory

By John Mason

ANDREW HARRIMAN *(pictured)*, the prince of speeding wings, led England, the outsiders, to an astonishing 21-17 victory over Australia in the final of the Melrose Cup at a chilly, rainswept Murrayfield yesterday.

In paying tribute to the self-belief and team spirit of his colleagues, Harriman played down his part – 62 points, including a handsome bag of 12 tries, the tournament record. Nick Beal, England's principal goal-kicker, finished with 70 points.

For starters, on the third and final day of the inaugural Rugby World Cup Sevens, England, with a little bit of help from gallant Ireland, disposed of the much-vaunted challenge from the South Seas.

With co-favourites Western Samoa and Fiji out of the way, England, making their tackles count in tight situations, worked unceasingly for the sweetest win of a wearing three days which involved 10 matches, 34 tries and 227 points.

Harriman soared away in the opening seconds, going outside Campese and holding off the chasing Constable. Sheasby sent Dallaglio in for the second try and a third came from Rodber. Beal's three conversions had England 21 points ahead of Australia.

With Lynagh scoring in the corner and Campese going clear on the left, Australia were in business. Expert juggling and support allowed Taupeaffe to score and with Lynagh's conversion that was 21-17. One fraught minute later, with England scrambling the ball into touch, it was over.

Courage League: Saracens 13 Bath 19, Southgate, 24 April

Bath scale heights to claim title: Barnes the inspiration

By John Mason

BATH'S barely convincing victory over businesslike Saracens was a long time coming. Down 13-11, ahead late on, Bath, as ever, owed much to Stuart Barnes. It was his penalty goal, difficult enough to cause the nerves to flutter, that restored their lead.

Barnes dealt smartly, too, with the preliminaries to the final try, which had its origins in his steepling kick to the full-back. The ball, perfectly struck, acutely placed, hovered just long enough to allow Jeremy Guscott to make the clattering tackle, and Phil de Glanville and Jonathan Callard, the makeshift left wing, did the rest. In the glittering course of Bath's dedicated accumulation of the silverware through the years – seven John Player or Pilkington Cups plus two doubles of cup and league – Barnes has never been far removed from the planning and the execution, though in one of those cup wins he was among the opposition, clad in the blue and white of Bristol.

Bath needed the win. Wasps beat Bristol 7-6 and finished level on 22 points with Bath, both having lost only one match. Bath's points difference, however, 355-97, was far superior to Wasps' 186-118.

Middlesex Sevens: Wasps 26 Northampton 24, Twickenham, 8 May

Wasps pair cruise to success

By Rupert Bates

WASPS pairing Lawrence Dallaglio and Laurence Scrase did not have far to go for the Save and Prosper Middlesex Sevens at Twickenham, as home to these two Kingston University students is a houseboat on the Thames at Strawberry Vale.

They also shared in Wasps' remarkable triumph in the sevens final when, sapped by the burden of bruising wins over Wellington and Western Samoa, they came back from 19 points down to snatch the title in the dying seconds against Northampton.

Dallaglio, 20, who was in the England side which won the World Cup Sevens at Murrayfield, has not yet broken into the Wasps' first XV pack, but he goes on the England Under-21 tour to Australia this summer as an open-side flanker.

The Wasps' forwards at Twickenham – Dallaglio, Paul Volley, whose extra-time try beat the Samoans in the semi-final, and Mike White – were burly minders to the canny playmaker Adrian Thompson and electric-paced runners Mike Friday, Phil Hopley and John Abadom, who due to injury was replaced by Scrase for the final.

Tour International: New Zealand 7 British Isles 20, Wellington, 26 June

Jubilant Lions maul fumbling All Blacks

By John Reason

The All Blacks always go to their matches suitably dressed for a funeral, but this time they went to their own. The British Isles buried them to square the series at 1-1. The Lions forwards won so much ball from the line-out that, if their midfield had done anything more adventurous than kick up-and-unders or kick for position, they could well have scored 40 points.

No wonder the Lions backs want Stuart Barnes at outside-half, because they know the All Blacks are paranoid about the pace of Jeremy Guscott and Rory Underwood and Ieuan Evans on the wings. Some hope now. Barnes is not best pleased.

As a result, the only try the Lions scored came when this rabble of a New Zealand pack were trying to drive the ball, but, just as they reached clear water, Sean Fitzpatrick dropped it.

Dewi Morris, the Lions scrum-half, snatched it up and flicked it out to Guscott. The field was broken to smithereens. New Zealand's back row were miles away, and the world's smoothest runner just set up the remains of the defence and made a couple of yards for Underwood.

Against Auckland, Underwood had given Kirwan – now little more than the skeleton of what he used to be – a start and turned and caught him in 15 yards. Here at Wellington he left him for dead and streaked away to score in the corner.

That try was what the Southern Hemisphere call the game-breaker because it took the Lions ahead 17-7 and New Zealand had nothing like enough time to catch up.

Heaven knows, the Lions selectors did their best for the All Blacks by leaving their three best props at home and almost giving the scrummage as a present to New Zealand.

But the All Blacks were not even good enough to take advantage of that, because Jason Leonard philosophically moved across to tight-head and stood there quite untroubled all through.

It was not an occasion for triumphalism. Rather it was one of sadness. Remembering the All Blacks' great days, the only decent thing to do was bare your head, put your right arm across your chest and suggest that cremation might be more appropriate so that in future the teams could play for the Ashes of New Zealand rugby.

[The following week the Lions, 10-0 up at half-time, were beaten 30-13 by an All Black side who finally did justice to their reputation.]

WRU SWALEC Cup Final: Llanelli 21 Neath 18, Cardiff, 8 May

Referee Simmonds apologises after error gives Llanelli victory

By Edward Bevan

GARETH SIMMONDS, one of Wales's three international panel referees, apologised to Neath after allowing Emyr Lewis' winning dropped goal which enabled Llanelli to become the inaugural holders of the SWALEC Cup.

The points were awarded contrary to the laws that came in this season. The goal came following a free kick, but the laws state the ball must first be touched by the opposition.

The goal, 24 minutes into the second half, allowed Llanelli to regain the lead 21-18 and they held on to win the WRU Cup for the third successive year and also achieve the league and cup double. Mr Simmonds awarded Llanelli a tapped penalty, which was quickly taken by Rupert Moon. His pass was gathered by Lewis in front of the posts, and the kick was perfectly judged.

Mr Simmonds said that Neath full-back Paul Thorburn had questioned his decision, but having made it and admitting his mistake, he could not change it.

Neath also criticised Mr Simmonds for allowing Llanelli their second try, when Nigel Davies allegedly played the ball from the ground after a tackle, and for ignoring an obstruction on Jamie Reynolds near the end which would have given Paul Thorburn a chance to level the scores with a penalty. Certainly Neath were unlucky.

Gareth Llewellyn, the Neath captain and man of the match, was an outstanding inspiration to his team. Llanelli were indebted to Colin Stephens' accurate place-kicking and Ieuan Evans' opportunism on the right wing. Evans, named last week as the Welsh player of the year, scored two tries and broke JJ Williams' record of 40 tries in the Welsh Cup.

Celebrations for Gavin Hastings and fellow Lions Rory Underwood (left) and Rob Andrew.

Tour International: South Africa 17 France 18, Johannesburg, 3 July

French lesson for Springboks

By Deon Viljoen

THE schooling of South Africa, recently allowed back into the honours class of international rugby union, is far from complete. Of all the frailties exposed by France in this first floodlit Test in the republic, temperament was the most critical at Ellis Park on Saturday evening.

Thus, from the summit reached through James Small's lightning try in the sixth minute, the Springbok challenge deteriorated to the point where Uli Schmidt conceded the last of many penalties in stoppage time by petulantly punching French flank Laurent Cabannes. He was extremely fortunate not to be sent off by English referee Ed Morrison.

By comparison, France played with supreme composure, worthy of the Five Nations title, even when they were eight points down in as many minutes.

The European champions failed to breach the South African defence, but the victory margin – two dropped goals and four penalties to a try and four penalties – clinched the series following the 20-20 draw in the first Test in Durban.

Tour International: Australia 19 South Africa 12, Sydney, 21 August

Farr-Jones bids farewell at high spot for Wallabies

By Justin Rogers

The cheers came rolling down from the giant stands of the Sydney football stadium to acclaim Phil Kearns and his Wallabies after they had demolished the Springboks 19-12 in yesterday's series decider.

Kearns held up the trophy and told the record crowd of 41,877: 'One of the great rugby players played his last game today. Thanks very much, Nick Farr-Jones. You're a champion.'

This was the signal for an ovation for the former Australian captain who produced yet another whole-hearted performance in his 63rd and final Test after a thigh injury had seemed likely to rule him out earlier in the week.

He said later: 'I was very choked up during the anthem because it was a very special

day for me. This Australian team is like a brotherhood, a family, and although I'm leaving it, I'll always be attached by some sort of umbilical cord.'

If the crowd reaction was anything to go by, the judges who voted David Campese as man-of-the-match and Kearns as player-of-the-series got it right. Campese might not have produced the zip-zip attacking with which he set alight the 1991 World Cup, but for sheer mastery of all the rugby-playing skills, he can rarely have bettered yesterday's display.

His long, raking kicks for territory invariably arrowed home, he caught the ball with aplomb, and he invariably took the right option. If there was such a degree as Mastery of Rugby, he would be given it with honours.

Tour International: Wales 24 Canada 26, Cardiff, 10 November

Wales humbled by Welsh Canadian: Last-ditch try earns Canada victory

By John Mason

A TRY by Canada lock Al Charron 40 seconds from time floored Wales in an exciting but penalty-ridden international at the Arms Park, Cardiff, last night.

Despite an international world record of eight penalty goals by Neil Jenkins, Wales – though leading three times – could make little of a gritty Canada team who never wilted.

Inspired by Welsh Canadian Gareth Rees, who kicked 16 points, the proud visitors were consumed by a burning ambition to be recognised as a force in the world's big league.

For Wales, it was a bitter disappointment: they were made to look very ordinary for long periods in a match

in which the penalty count topped 40.

There were no tries on the Welsh agenda; in contrast, Canada (who also kicked four penalty goals) scored two tries. Concerted pressure brought the first, a fraction fortuitously for Ian Stuart, the captain, but the second was a beauty – mass handling right and left, the ball quickly re-won and moved quickly.

Charron was the scorer, making it 24 points each, and the dependable Rees kicked the conversion to secure a famous victory and remind Wales what they had probably missed when his father, Alan, decided to emigrate from Llantrisant to British Columbia.

Tour International: England 15 New Zealand 9, Twickenham, 27 November

England steal All Black thunder: Joseph in trampling incident

By John Mason

THERE were not the expected Kiwi capers at Twickenham on Saturday after the annihilation of Scotland last week. Instead of plucky England, the best of the Brits, bowing heads respectfully to their superiors, it was the men in black, the team who set the world's standards, that had to tug the forelock. They did not enjoy the experience.

England won on four counts: self-belief, ruthless first-time tackles, ball retention and gain-line protection. New Zealand, seeking to play the same way, found for the first time on tour that they were consistently shut down. Only John Timu got away and, given a fraction of an inch, a try then would have turned the match.

The All Blacks are entitled to wail at life's iniquities in that for all the expertise of Kyran Bracken, England's new scrum-half, and Victor Ubogu in getting across to cover Timu as he hurtled along the touchline, neither brought him down.

Timu finished well inside the corner flag, only to discover that touch-judge Stephen Hilditch had ruled a foot in touch, a tiny, muddy scar straddling the touch-line made by the toe of Timu's right boot. Hilditch was right, a fact Timu acknowledged graciously later.

All England heaved a huge sigh of relief and marvelled at Ubogu's despairing dive that momentarily took Timu off balance and fractionally out of play. Tight-head props covering across to make corner-flag tackles. Whatever next?

Jon Callard, on his début, fanned the flames of English fires with penalty goals in the 16th, 28th, 49th and 70th minutes. Rob Andrew, in manner and appearance the coolest person on the field, scooped over a dropped goal in the 61st minute, and England, who never led by more than six points, could afford to let New Zealand play all the catch-up rugby.

Those England penalties were awarded for a late tackle by Eroni Clarke on Will

Kyran Bracken: impressive at scrum-half for England.

Carling, for offside by Arran Pene and Zinzan Brooke, and for some grubby work by Jamie Joseph. Someone, preferably New Zealand's management, needs to tell Joseph to clean up his act.

There was no excuse for Joseph's trampling on Bracken's right ankle early on. The flank forward seems to think that sly viciousness off the ball is acceptable behaviour. Bracken, who was on crutches yesterday, said: 'Having now seen the match video, I realise that what happened could have been avoided. At the time I thought it was an accident.'

With Matthew Cooper, New Zealand's principal goal-kicker, unable to play, the goal-kicking passed to Jeff

Wilson, who learnt more about the twin impostors of success and failure, winning and losing, in a painful hour on Saturday than at any other time in his tender 20 years and four weeks. He missed goals in the 20th, 23rd, 39th, 73rd and 75th minutes and finished a haunted figure. His goals in the 47th, 51st and 63rd minutes (offsides and over the top), which at best took New Zealand to 9-12, were of little consolation.

[The All Blacks won their two remaining matches to finish with a W12-L1 tour record, but their failure to make public the disciplinary action taken against Joseph for the trampling incident led to the sacking of manager Neil Gray on their return.]

1994

21 Mar Jack Rowell takes over at the helm for England in place of Geoff Cooke.

18 May The Irish tour Down Under begins with a slaughter – of Western Australia – by 68-4, a record for Ireland. [The rest of the tour is a disaster, Ireland winning only once more and losing 6, including the 2 Tests.]

4 Jun While England are thrashing the Springboks in South Africa, other touring Five Nations countries fare less well, France and Scotland losing in the Americas, 18-16 to Canada (only Test) and 16-15 to Argentina respectively

11 Jun Humiliated in the first Test, the Springboks stage a great comeback in Cape Town to defeat England 27-9 and tie the series. It is their first home victory since they beat a makeshift World XV in 1989. In other Tests today, Wales beat Canada 33-15 but Scotland are defeated 19-17 in Buenos Aires to lose the series 2-0, having won only one of their six games.

18 Jun Italy give the Wallabies a scare in Brisbane before succumbing 23-20 in the first Test. [A week later, Italy complete their tour with a 20-7 defeat in the 2nd Test, but they win all 6 provincial games.]

25 Jun In a debilitating 100°F, Wales understandably lose 34-9 to Western Samoa in Apia, finishing their tour in

anti-climax after wins over Canada, Fiji and Tonga.

17 Sep Ieuan Evans overhauls the Wales try-scoring record set by Gerald Davies and Gareth Edwards with his 21st try, the only one of the match at Bucharest, where Romania are beaten 16-9 in a World Cup seeding match.

27 Oct Hong Kong, although failing to qualify from their Asian World Cup group, beat Singapore by a world record score in Kuala Lumpur, 164-13, with their 26 tries, Ashley Billington's 50 points (10 tries) and Jamie McKee's 17 conversions all world Test records.

19 Nov The Princess Royal opens the new £44m Murrayfield, where 63,500 see Scotland thrashed 34-10 (5 tries to 1) by the rampant Springboks, who record their first win in Britain in 8 Tests spread over 4 tours since 1961.

3 Dec The BaaBaas, selecting from 7 countries, score a famous 23-15 victory at Lansdowne Road over the Springboks, who finish their tour with an impressive W11-L2 record.

10 Dec Outside-half Rob Andrew kicks 12 out of 12 to score 30 points (6C-6PG) at Twickenham, equalling Didier Camberabero's world Test record, as England win 60-19 against Canada, recent victors over both Wales and France.

INTERNATIONAL CHAMPIONSHIP

	E	F	I	S	W	P	W	D	L	F	A	Pts
1 WALES		24-15		29-6		4	3	0	1	78	51	6
2 ENGLAND			12-13		15-8	4	3	0	1	60	49	6
3 FRANCE	14-18		35-15			4	2	0	2	84	69	4
4 IRELAND				6-6	15-17	4	1	1	2	49	70	3
5 SCOTLAND	14-15	12-20				4	0	1	3	38	70	1

TOURS (Tests)
England in South Africa: SA15-E32, SA27-E9
Ireland in Australia: A33-I13, A32-I18
France in New Zealand: NZ8-F22, NZ20-F23
South Africa in New Zealand: NZ22-SA14, NZ13-SA9, NZ18-SA18
South Africa in British Isles: S10-SA34, W12-SA20

International Championship: England 15 Wales 8, Twickenham, 19 March

Rampant England fall short
Wales miss Grand Slam but take title
By Paul Ackford

INTERNATIONAL rugby is worth watching after all. The 100th match between England and Wales was fit to set before a Queen. She was there, too. It was the best match of the championship by far, as good an exhibition of flat-out, attacking rugby as has been played all season, and proved once and for all that England can play a wide game under the new laws. Geoff Cooke, in his final match as manager, was seen off in style.

For Wales a hollow victory of sorts. They were crowned Five Nations champions, but the ultimate prize, the Grand Slam, was never within their grasp.

England held all the cards. Ian Hunter at full-back was security itself under the high ball and ran riot through the Welsh defence on more occasions than was decent. Dean Richards played up to his normal standards, and there is no greater compliment than

that. Tony Underwood re-emerged as an international wing, and looked a threat virtually every time he got the ball. There was also the power of Jason Leonard and Victor Ubogu. And if you had said before the match that Rob Andrew would be criticised for doing too much himself, you would have been carted off to the madhouse.

England turned round at half-time 7-3 up, and the only question was whether they could get the 16-point margin that would make them outright champions. At the start of the second half they were playing as well as they have done at any time in the last three seasons, stringing together play after play with cohesion and imagination.

Wales could not even get close. But, 15-3 down, they refused to capitulate, and a try by Nigel Walker with five minutes to go settled the championship.

International Championship: Scotland 14 England 15, Murrayfield, 5 February

Last kick by Callard fells Scots

By Paul Ackford

SCOTLAND came to this match with their reputation in tatters. They left, defeated but unbowed, to a standing ovation from a Murrayfield crowd which had witnessed their rebirth. England were lucky to snatch victory. For large chunks of this match they were outclassed, out-thought and out of it. But their championship hopes are still alive thanks to that heart-stopping last-minute penalty kicked by Jonathan

Callard (*pictured above*).

England had started so well, and enjoyed most of the early luck. When Callard kicked a penalty goal to bring them the lead after four minutes, it looked as if they would run away with the match.

Then all change. It was as if Scotland had flicked a switch. Their line-out found itself. They started winning the bobbling ball and they found self-belief and passion.

When Rob Wainwright scored the only try of the match after a Rory Underwood fumble, it unsettled England and mistakes began to creep in. Scotland were now in the driving-seat, and got their just reward three minutes into the second half when Gavin Hastings kicked a penalty goal to put them 8-3 ahead. They trapped England in their 22 and the clock was ticking.

Eventually, it took captain Will Carling to make a stand, with a wonderful break, leading to a penalty, which Callard kicked. Another soon followed to make it 9-8 to England.

Hastings and Callard then exchanged penalties, so with six minutes left England were again a point ahead.

Then Shade Munro won his umpteenth line-out and Townsend hit a drop-kick, the ball hovering tantalisingly over the crossbar until it dropped the right side for Scotland. The roar could have been heard in Watford.

But with seconds to go, Scotland handled the ball on the floor to give Callard the chance. It was the last kick of the game and everyone knew it. The silence at Murrayfield as he stroked the ball between the posts was deafening.

Women's World Cup Final: England 38 United States 23, Edinburgh, 24 April

Pack power gives England joy
US women bring flair to World Cup

By Peter Donald

ENGLAND relentlessly and successfully pursued their pre-match plan of forward domination in beating the US by five goals and a penalty goal to four tries and a penalty goal in the final of the Women's World Cup at Raeburn Place in Edinburgh yesterday.

A crowd approaching 4,000 cheered them on as they avenged their defeat by the Americans in the final of this event three years ago, but the losers also earned friends with their exciting brand of back play.

The match followed the pattern predicted by both camps, with England relying heavily on a strong, well-drilled pack and the Americans turning their fast three-quarters loose whenever possible. These tactics brought them two superb tries in the last three minutes, but by then England had stretched their lead to comfortably winning proportions and, while none of the American tries was converted, the sure-footed Karen Almond converted all five England tries. Her kicking from hand was equally impressive, time and again repulsing promising attacks with long returns.

It is an indication of England's forward power that they held the ball in the scrum and moved it almost a dozen yards in earning two penalty tries when the tired opposition collapsed the scrum close to their goal line. Almond added the conversions to her third-minute penalty goal, but the Americans kept in touch with tries by Jen Crawford and Patti Jervey, whose speed left the defence stranded.

The handling of the American backs was certainly one of the exciting features of the match, and Jos Bergman picked up one almost impossible pass from her toes before sending Jervey in for the second of those scores.

Trailing by just seven points, they were still very much in contention, but then a smart bout of handling by the England backs sent Jane Mitchell in for a try which Almond converted from near the left touchline.

Bergman raised American hopes with a penalty goal four minutes into the second half, but England stretched their lead to 31-13 with another try arising from their scrum control, which saw them encamped on the US line.

England wave the flag after becoming world champions.

Middlesex Sevens Final: Bath 19 Orrell 12, Twickenham, 14 May

Callard try clinches Bath Triple Crown

By Brendan Gallagher

BATH, whose preparation consisted of an hour's mid-week training, completed an unprecedented Triple Crown by defeating Orrell 19-12 to add the Save & Prosper Middlesex Sevens to their League and Cup double.

Jonathan Callard scored the winning try in a sparkling final to become the first Bath captain to lift the Russell-Cargill Memorial Cup.

Bath had taken an early lead through Ed Rayner only for the outstanding Jim Naylor to reply with a vintage try. Audley Lumsden then went over for Bath, but back came gritty Orrell through Paul Johnson to level the scores before Callard's decisive strike.

England's team of the season had progressed to the final via a fraught but exciting first-round victory over London Scottish (28-26), followed by more comfortable wins over Loughborough University (24-0) and Saracens (19-0). Lumsden clocked up six tries, while Ian Sanders and Callard provided the invention and guile.

Orrell's traditional virtues of solid tackling and industry were enhanced by the skill and pace of England Under-21 colleagues Naylor and Austin Healey.

After accounting for the much-fancied Bristol 17-12 in extra time, their indomitable spirit prevailed in successive 10-7 triumphs over Fiji Spartans and Rosslyn Park.

The competition attracted 48,000 spectators, although as the weather deteriorated many sought refuge in their cars or hospitality tents.

In the opening round, holders Wasps were unceremoniously dumped 17-5 by Saracens, and Northampton, runners-up last season, lost 26-12 to Rosslyn Park.

Super Ten Provincial Championship Final: Natal 10 Queensland 21, Durban, 14 May

Natal fall to Lynagh

By John Reason

MICHAEL LYNAGH, just returned from playing in Italy, kicked three late goals to make sure Queensland overcame Natal 21-10 to win the Southern Hemisphere's Super Ten Provincial Championship.

Early in the match Lynagh had outflanked the Natal defence and made Queensland's two tries with shrewd diagonal kicks for his wingers. Tim Horan, the Australian centre, was carried off late in the game with a dislocated kneecap.

It was a dire match, but Jack Rowell, the England manager, took a charitable view of Natal, who will play England next Saturday, praising their loose forwards and the sharpness of their backs. John Connolly, the coach of Queensland, is in no doubt that Natal will find it hard to compete with England in the line-out and that South Africa will have the same problem.

However, any coach who can afford to leave John Eales out of his team and keep him on the bench as a reserve lock cum No.8 and, even more astonishingly, as a reserve goal-kicker, is in a position of unique strength.

In my estimation Eales is the most important player in the Southern Hemisphere, and apart from his remarkable talents as a forward he is eighth in the Super Ten list of points scorers because of his goal-kicking.

Natal scrum-half Robert du Preez starts another attack.

Tour International: South Africa 15 England 32, Pretoria, 4 June

Springboks blown apart
Carling's tourists come good at last: Record for Andrew

By Paul Ackford

HOLD the obituaries, England are alive and kicking. This was only the second victory in six matches, but who cares? All through the tour England had been looking to the Tests. This was the reason they were here. 'Judge on these matches,' they said.

And we scoffed. There was no way their laboured approach could triumph on the high veld. How wrong we were. England blew South Africa out of the water with as good a 50 minutes of rugby as they have played in a long, long time. And Rob Andrew went into the record books with 27 points, the highest total for an individual in an international in England's history, eclipsing Jonathan Webb's 24 points against Italy in the World Cup.

England were super-efficient. Several players had their best games on tour just when it mattered, and they got off to a wonderful start, catching South Africa cold.

Phil de Glanville was a revelation, Dewi Morris was firing on all cylinders, but head and shoulders above them all stood Tim Rodber. The big flanker had the game of his life. Whenever a ball needed to be won on the floor, he was first to it. He won crucial line-outs, put in huge tackles and raced around the pitch.

After five minutes Andrew kicked his first penalty and England were playing at their pace, their tempo, everything on their terms. South Africa simply did not get into the game. They were 20 points down after 15 minutes. They had no platform up front, no cohesion behind.

The other factor which was crucial was that for the first

Tim Rodber on the charge for England, with Brian Moore.

time in South Africa, England were allowed to play. For years England have criticised Southern Hemisphere referees for their liberal approach to the ruck, ball and line-out, but they welcomed New Zealand's Colin Hawke with open arms.

Brian Moore and Ben Clarke climbed into the rucks, Martin Bayfield bumped and barged in the line-out. It was Test rugby with no holds barred, Defensively, too, England excelled. Carling and de Glanville sewed up the midfield, Clarke covered acres and Dean Richards dealt with anyone coming round the fringes.

England's two crucial scores came within three minutes of each other during the first half. From a midfield

maul, Morris fed Andrew, who drifted across the field in front of the posts before turning the ball inside to Tony Underwood. Clarke was on hand to continue the move and made the line.

Then came the killer blow. Rodber won a line-out, Andrew had a look down the blindside, decided nothing was on, and hoisted a huge kick. André Joubert made the fateful mistake of staying on the ground instead of competing for the ball in the air and Andrew gathered it as he followed up his own kick.

At 23-6 at the interval it was simply a question of holding out for the second period. It was only as England's lungs collapsed at 5,500ft that the home side came back into the game.

Tour Match: Eastern Province 13 England 31, Port Elizabeth, 7 June

Rodber sent off but cleared for Test: Callard's ugly head injury

By John Mason

JONATHAN Callard, who left the pitch bleeding profusely and needed 25 stitches in his forehead, was one of the casualties on an acutely depressing list last night after a thoroughly unpleasant match in which Tim Rodber, the England flanker, and Eastern Province's Simon Tremain were dismissed for fighting.

Callard suffered his injuries as a direct result of being trampled. Dean Ryan, the midweek captain, retired early on with a broken thumb and Graham Rowntree was also replaced, concussed.

The comings and goings, for whatever reasons, did nothing for the final midweek match of the tour which, should anyone be interested, England won well.

Rodber becomes only the second England player to have been sent off. The other was Mike Burton – dismissed in 1975 against Australia in Brisbane – who, ironically, was present to witness all this

last night as a BBC Radio summariser. Rodber can consider himself to be very fortunate to be cleared by a disciplinary panel to play in the second Test on Saturday. But Dick Best, the England coach, said afterwards: 'Tim was punched three times on the floor and retaliated. He is very upset at being sent off and feels amazed at being singled out.'

Rodber, who was on as a replacement, had previously asked the referee to take firmer control – a legitimate request as he was England's acting captain at the time. The match was ugly throughout, and England players were incensed by the Callard incident. But the failure of the RFU to suspend Rodber for the Test makes it difficult for them to protest to their hosts about the player guilty of twice raking Callard's face – his only punishment was a midfield kick to touch and the throw-in.

Tour International: New Zealand 8 France 22, Christchurch, 26 June

Benetton makes Sella's day
By Ron Palenski

FRENCH CENTRE Philippe Sella celebrated becoming the first player to play 100 internationals yesterday in dream style – with victory over New Zealand in the first Test.

Someone should have told the All Blacks that when there is a moment of special passion for the French, they are even more formidable than usual. The last time they beat the All Blacks in New Zealand was on Bastille Day in 1979. Yesterday it was Sella's day.

This was not a victory founded on French flair; it was founded on hard driving forward play, big men at line-outs and tactical kicking by the scrum-half and fly-half. It was also about taking chances when they presented themselves, such as the two

dropped goals by Christian Deylaud and the one by Jean-Luc Sadourny, and especially the try by Philippe Benetton.

The try was a gem. All Black full-back John Timu ran out of support in an attack on the left wing, was robbed of the ball, and Thierry Lacroix kicked through for the opposite wing. Philippe Saint-Andre beat Frank Bunce to the ball but was pushed into touch. Somehow, though, he freed the ball to Benetton and no All Black laid a hand on him.

After leading 9-3 at half-time and adding another penalty soon after, the converted try to make it 19-3 sealed the All Blacks' fate, and it was of little consequence that Bunce grabbed a try at the end.

Tour International: New Zealand 20 France 23, Auckland, 3 July

All Blacks stunned by late French try

By Ron Palenski

FRANCE beat the All Blacks for the first time in a rugby series yesterday thanks to a try that swept the length of the field.

The New Zealanders, their wagons circled after their first-Test defeat in Christchurch a week ago, were an infinitely better team here and had the match won everywhere but on the scoreboard.

The All Blacks had the bullocking forwards to retain possession – though lacked the backs to make quality use of it – and they led 20-16 until two minutes from time.

Then French full-back Jean-Luc Sadourny scored a try that ranks alongside Gareth Edwards' heart-stopper for the Barbarians against the All

Blacks in 1973, or Serge Blanco's try against Australia in Sydney in 1987 that gained France a place in the first World Cup final.

'It was a counter-attack from the end of the world – a true image of French rugby,' said captain Philippe Saint-Andre.

It was Saint-Andre who fielded a kick from New Zealand fly-half Stephen Bachop 15 yards from the French line, allowing France to sweep downfield in a combination of desperation and flair. The ball raced through eight pairs of hands before Sadourny scored, ending a move that laid the All Blacks' defence bare and snatching victory.

Tour International: New Zealand 13 South Africa 9, Wellington, 23 July

Guilty Le Roux sent home after ear-biting

By Ron Palemski

SOUTH AFRICA lost the Test, the series and the services of prop Johan Le Roux, who was sent home in disgrace last night after biting New Zealand captain Sean Fitzpatrick's left ear during the second Test in Wellington.

After the match, Fitzpatrick, with blood dripping from the ear, would not comment on the Le Roux incident, which was caught by television cameras.

Fitzpatrick drove Le Roux back off a ruck and the All Black captain was left face-down on the ground, with Le Roux poised over him. Television pictures replayed to the 38,000 spectators showed the South African bending down with his face close to Fitzpatrick's ear.

Fitzpatrick then jerked convulsively away, jumped up and talked animatedly to referee Brian Stirling, one hand holding his ear and the other pointing at Le

Roux. All Black manager Colin Meads would not comment, but New Zealand officials were expected to cite Le Roux under the New Zealand Rugby Union's disciplinary procedures within the stipulated 24-hour period.

In international rugby's most notorious ear-biting incident, Australian hooker Ross Cullen was sent home from the Wallabies' tour of Britain and Ireland in the winter of 1966-67 for biting Oxford University prop Ossie Waldron. Cullen never played rugby again.

The incident cast a pall over a match that otherwise was one of the most entertaining internationals to be played in New Zealand for years and a marked contrast to the dour first Test.

New Zealand's tries, by wing John Timu and No.8 Zinzan Brooke, were both the result of Springbok errors. All the other points came from penalties.

Bledisloe Cup: Australia 20 New Zealand 16, Sydney, 17 August

Australia clinch a thriller to complete first unbeaten season

By Peter FitzSimons

A SINGLE moment determined the fate of the entire Test match between Australia and New Zealand at the Sydney Football Stadium yesterday, and rewrote the record books at the same time.

It needs, though, to be viewed in context. In a match which was ferociously contested from the opening whistle, the Wallabies had stormed to a 17-3 lead, been pegged back to 17-16 and edged away again to 20-16.

Then it happened. With barely four minutes to go, with the game poised delicately in Australia's favour, the ball came into the hands of the All Black winger Jeff Wilson, on the burst.

Only 25 metres out from the Australian line, he jinked down the right touchline, inside his opposing winger, outside the first of the despairing Australian cover defence, and then set full and glorious sail for the line. At stake was not only the Test

match, but sporting history. Fifteen metres to go now.

If he scored, this All Black side would escape the ignominy of being the first New Zealand side of the modern era to lose more matches than they had won in a season. If he didn't, the 1994 Wallabies would be the first in history to have an unbeaten season.

Two metres to go. The line yawned before him.

There remained just one chance for the Wallabies: the Australian scrum-half, George Gregan, who was covering across hard. In desperation, Gregan launched himself across the last two metres into Wilson and hit him hard. So hard that even in the process of scoring the try, the ball was jarred loose from Wilson's hands, spilled forward, and the game was lost for New Zealand.

Australia held on to take the Bledisloe Cup after a fitting climax to a marvellous game, which displayed Test rugby at its best.

World Cup Qualifier: Wales 29 Italy 19, Cardiff, 12 October

Jenkins kicks record as Wales brush aside Italy

By Brendan Gallagher

NEIL JENKINS, a veritable goal-kicking machine from Pontypridd, became the highest scorer in Welsh international rugby history at the tender age of 23 when his 24-point haul ensured victory over a defiant Italy at Cardiff Arms Park last night.

Jenkins landed seven penalties and a dropped goal to increase his total to 308 points, four more than Paul Thorburn's old record. It was a remarkable performance from the nerveless outside-half, who has accumulated his total in 28 internationals. Yet again he produced a match-winning display when his side

most needed it – as Wales were far from impressive.

Victory ensures that they finish top of the European qualifiers' seeding group and guarantees their place in Group C at next year's World Cup in South Africa. This will entail playing New Zealand, Ireland and the Asian qualifiers.

It was an incredible 12th international this year for Wales, whose other points came from a Nigel Davies try. Diego Dominguez, who had scored all Italy's points against Romania with eight penalty goals, kicked another 14 points.

1995

18 Feb Scotland earn their first ever win at Parc des Princes and their first in Paris since 1969 thanks to a last-gasp try scored when Townsend slips an underarm pass to Gavin Hastings, who races clear unchallenged to cross under the posts and convert to make it 23-21.

15 Apr Cardiff, though not calling on a single player from the side that virtually clinched the Heineken title in midweek, rewrite the record books with a 75-33 mauling of the BaaBaas, running in a record 11 tries for this fixture to go with the record points haul.

6 May Bath respond to premature obits with a dazzling 36-16 victory over Wasps in the Pilkington final, Tony Swift scoring their clinching try, his 27th in the Cup and his last in Bath colours.

18 May The Five Nations committee confirm the establishment of a European Cup for clubs, beginning this autumn with an abbreviated pilot tournament (it is too late for the RFU to alter their season's structure) followed by a full competition in October 1996.

4 Aug Plans for a professional World Rugby Circus, allegedly supported by Kerry Packer, are in tatters as South Africa's World Cup winning squad reject his overtures.

2 Sep The first 'pro' international, in which South Africa beat Wales 40-11 at Ellis Park, is marred by two moments of madness. Wales' replacement hooker Garin Jenkins is sent off a minute from time for flooring Joost van der Westhuizen and is

The stormy South Africa–Wales international: Welsh No.8 Taylor confronts Pienaar.

banned for 30 days, as is Springbok lock Kobus Wiese, who knocks line-out specialist Derwyn Jones senseless after just 3 minutes with a haymaker that escapes the referee's eye but is caught by TV, and he is cited after the match by officials. [Wiese is later fined about £9,000 by the SARFU.]

31 Oct Former Wales international Jonathan Davies MBE is transferred back to Cardiff from rugby league club Warrington in a deal thought to be worth nearly £90,000.

11 Nov In a match of passion and incident, France gain a famous 22-15 victory over the All Blacks at Toulouse in a howling gale.

18 Nov A drab England are outclassed 24-14 by South Africa at Twickenham, while Scotland are held 15-15 by Western Samoa at Murrayfield and France are slaughtered 37-12 in Paris by New Zealand, who tie the series. But Ireland beat Fiji 44-8 at Lansdowne Road.

The Sunday Telegraph: 19 February

Prop banned as red card shows up law loophole

JOHN DAVIES, the Wales tight-head prop, in becoming the first player to receive a red card in international rugby, inadvertently triggered a legal debate.

The Neath forward was banned for 60 days last night after being dismissed by French referee Didier Mené for kicking Ben Clarke as the England flanker was on the ground at a ruck. There followed a near farcical situation as Wales captain Ieuan Evans questioned what would happen at set scrums as Wales had lost one of their props.

'At first he shrugged his shoulders,' said Evans. 'Then he said we could change a player, so I made sure we got someone on as quickly as possible. Will [Carling] said it was fine by him.'

Eventually, Wales brought on Hugh Williams-Jones and took off flanker Hemi Taylor, a situation that is not legislated for in rugby's laws.

Bob Weighill, secretary of the Five Nations committee, said: 'There is nothing in law to govern a front-row player being sent off. This is something that is now exercising the minds of the International Board members.

'This incident has shown a loophole in the laws that will be closed at the meeting of the IB next month.'

International Championship: Wales 9 England 23, Cardiff, 18 February

England lay ghost of Cardiff to set up Grand Slam finish

By Paul Ackford

HOODOO? What hoodoo? England and Rory Underwood laid the ghost of Cardiff and took another giant step towards a third Grand Slam in five years. It was far from pretty, and a big step down from the majestic performances against Ireland and France, but in its way it was just as effective.

Wales had a thoroughly miserable afternoon. John Davies, the prop, was sent off for kicking an opponent, they were disrupted by an unfortunate sequence of injuries, and a leaky defence conceded three tries, including the first at Cardiff by an England back since 1987 as Rory Underwood raced over for a score mid-way through the second half.

All Cardiff was waiting to see how England would cope with the early questions, but the England line stood firm, and Rory Underwood exorcised the nightmare of two years ago, snuffing out the danger this time when Ieuan Evans threatened to race clear.

Wales took the lead after six minutes, when Neil Jenkins kicked the first of his three penalty goals, out of four attempts. But three minutes later they lost full-back Tony Clement, concussed, and he was replaced by Bridgend's Matthew Back.

At this point England looked rusty, but gradually the pieces fell into place. Bayfield plucked a ball out of the air at last after 20 minutes, the forwards took charge and Victor Ubogu picked up and drove over for his first international try. Andrew converted to give England a 7-3 lead, and increased it by another three points with a penalty.

Then Wales, crucially, missed two gilt-edged chances after a penalty attempt by Jenkins rebounded off a post.

The sides exchanged penalties before Wales signed their own death warrant when Jenkins found Clarke, the only man on the pitch who was unmarked, from a 22 drop-out. Setting off like a startled rabbit, Clarke was eventually dragged down, but Carling continued the move and Rory Underwood went over in the corner for the first of his tries. His second came, after another Jenkins penalty, when England stepped up a gear and he finished another multi-handling raid.

England's old faithful, Dean Richards, became the world's most capped No.8 yesterday, and celebrated with another storming performance. England are head and shoulders above any other team in Europe at the moment and all eyes are turning to South Africa to see how good they are on a global stage.

INTERNATIONAL CHAMPIONSHIP

	E	F	I	S	W	P	W	D	L	F	A	Pts
1 ENGLAND		31-10		24-12		4	4	0	0	98	39	8
2 SCOTLAND		26-13			26-13	4	3	0	1	87	71	6
3 FRANCE			21-23	21-9		4	2	0	2	77	70	4
4 IRELAND	8-20	7-25				4	1	0	3	44	83	2
5 WALES	9-23		12-16			4	0	0	4	43	86	0

TOURS (Tests)
Bledisloe Cup: NZ28-A16, A23-NZ34
Wales in South Africa: SA40-W11
New Zealand in France: F22-NZ15, F12-NZ37
South Africa in England: E14-SA24

International Championship: England 24 Scotland 12, Twickenham, 18 March

Andrew's golden boot cuts down flower of Scotland

Inspired kicking seals Grand Slam

By Paul Ackford

THEY wanted a real test and they got one. England snapped up their third Grand Slam in five years, but they were made to fight every inch of the way. All that talk of annihilation was so much hot air.

They triumphed because their pack did just enough to subdue a Scottish eight, and they had golden boots himself, Rob Andrew (*pictured right*), who kicked them to victory with his seven penalties and a dropped goal. Andrew shot past Jonathan Webb's record with his second kick to become England's leading points scorer, and his tally of 24 equalled the record for an individual in a Five Nations Championship match.

The man can do no wrong. In the previous three matches he made folk sit up and take notice with his running and handling game; yesterday he booted Scotland off the park. He was afforded the opportunity because Scotland were under so much pressure that they were forced to concede a succession of penalties. They competed magnificently and were never totally overwhelmed, but they lacked the beef when it mattered.

The die was cast in the first few minutes. Martin Bayfield caught the first line-out and the pack swarmed round. They paused, gathered their collective wills and tried to march Scotland back. For line-out read scrum, because the script remained the same at the initial scrummage. Dean Richards held the ball at the back and the front row heaved and groaned to roll Scotland back.

But neither quite came off. The drive from the line-out was fractured and the scrum slewed sideways, and it was a telling comment on the whole match. England had the upper hand but never complete control.

Scotland, to their credit, never wavered. Underdogs they might have been, but they fought like Rottweilers. Weir had a storming first 20 minutes, before he was hauled back by Bayfield and Martin Johnson, who got better and better with every minute, and Iain Morrison and Rob Wainwright asked questions of England's defence around the fringes.

But the pick of the bunch, as ever, was Gavin Hastings at full-back. In the early frantic exchanges he caught the bombs and returned them with interest.

But 20 minutes from full time, Rory Underwood banged a speculative kick downfield, which caused Gavin Hastings to turn. Instead of seeking the safety of touch he found Weir, but the lock could not get those long legs moving fast enough, and he was caught in front of the posts. It gave Andrew his sixth successful penalty and England the all-

important cushion of nine points.

Gavin Hastings reduced the deficit to six two minutes later, but then Andrew re-established the lead with a huge dropped goal and the match was over. Guscott nearly brought the house down with a surging run right at the end of the match, but the try remained elusive.

England will be delighted with their defensive display, which was intelligent and organised all afternoon. If Catt led the way, Rory Underwood was close behind him. His tackling was ferocious.

So thoughts now turn to South Africa and the World Cup. England travel with hope and expectation, having done enough this season to send a few shudders down the spines even of world champions Australia.

Hong Kong Sevens: New Zealand 35 Fiji 17, 26 March

New Zealand steal show

By Brendan Gallagher

ENGLAND, hugely popular but ultimately unsuccessful debutants here, could only watch in admiration as the Southern Hemisphere generally, and New Zealand in particular, staged a stunning exhibition of running and passing on the final afternoon of the Cathay Pacific Hongkong Bank Invitation Sevens.

New Zealand, featuring the awesome power of Jonah Lomu and the well-honed skills of Eric Rush, beat Fiji 35-17 to retain their title, and royally entertained a capacity 40,000 crowd at the Hong Kong stadium.

The Tongan-born Lomu, still only 19, scored two tries in the final and was undoubtedly the tournament's top player.

England were far from disgraced in losing 26-0 to Australia in the quarter-finals. Their tackling was comparable to that famous World Cup triumph in 1993, but the blistering pace of Andy Harriman was, alas, missing, although the former England wing proved a splendid manager.

Courage League: Leicester 17 Bristol 3, Welford Road, 29 April

Richards stakes all for Leicester

By Paul Ackford

IT took Leicester precisely four minutes to turn the carnival atmosphere before kick-off into a riot of celebration. That was how long it took Stuart Potter to score the first try of the match and set Leicester on the path to glory and the league title, their first since 1988.

The Leicester faithful never had a moment's doubt that Bristol would be swept aside. Chants of 'Deano, Deano' echoed round the ground as the great man hopped, skipped and jumped his way on to the pitch.

If ever one man is responsible for the success of a team it is Richards. Socks down, sleeves cut off, he led from the front for the umpteenth time this season, and it was especially appropriate that he was the only one of Leicester's six World Cup men who was eligible to play, the other five – the Underwood brothers, Martin Johnson, Neil Back and Graham Rowntree – honouring their agreement to play just two League games in April.

He has been a club man throughout his career and his decision to return early with damaged ribs against Bath and risk long-term injury, and possibly his World Cup place, was the factor which swung the championship Leicester's way. It was typical of the man, and the Leicester club and his colleagues owe him a huge debt of gratitude.

[As it happened, the title-winners for the last four years, Bath, who needed not only to win but also to overturn a points difference of 13, suffered their first home defeat of the season, losing 18-13 to Sale.]

The Sunday Telegraph: 7 May

SACKED: Will Carling pays ultimate price for outspoken attack on RFU

By Paul Ackford

IN a move of unbelievable crassness, the Rugby Football Union have relieved Will Carling of the England captaincy. As decisions go, it stinks. Whatever you may think of Carling as an individual, the indisputable fact remains that he has led England out of the rugby wilderness. Appointed in November 1988, he has guided England to three Grand Slams in five seasons as well as a World Cup final in 1991. Under his command, the England side are in such fine fettle that they set off for South Africa on May 17 as joint favourites with Australia to lift the World Cup.

Carling is England's, and world rugby's, most successful captain. He has been capped 55 times and has led his country on 48 occasions. Of those, 37 games have been won, one drawn and 10 lost.

The RFU took the decision late on Friday night following Thursday's screening of the Channel 4 programme *Fair Game*, in which Carling described the RFU committee as '57 old farts'. Carling swears his remarks were made off camera and were meant as a light-hearted, throwaway line. Whatever the context, the comments were ill-judged and naive for one who has held the captaincy as long as he has and who is so well versed in media practices. But the RFU were stupid to take the matter so seriously and react in the way that they did.

Carling is devastated by the news. Bewildered and upset, he said: 'I am totally shocked. I was asked to phone Dennis Easby, the RFU president, late last night, and he told me I was not fit to represent England as captain. There is nothing I can do about it. The decision has been made and I am just going to concentrate on the World Cup and give the new man all the help I can.'

The news came as a complete shock to Carling and the sporting world. On Friday afternoon I talked to Dudley Wood, secretary of the RFU, who said then: 'The RFU could suspend Carling, but I don't see the slightest possibility of such a thing happening.' Later that evening Wood was proved conclusively wrong when the officers of the Union gathered at the East India Club to debate the matter.

It is exactly the type of club and the type of meeting of which Carling and several senior members of the England team have been openly critical. No briefcases are allowed in the bar and the dress code is jacket and tie at all times, even on the hottest days. In that archaic environment, the decision was taken to demote Carling to the role of foot soldier.

It was a decision which, perversely, gave weight to Carling's flip comments. For the RFU to act in such a heavy-handed, prissy way, refusing to accept Carling's public apology, is merely to confirm the player's opinion of them. Any administration so sensitive to criticism cannot be wholly sound.

[Two days later, after sustained pressure from players and commentators to change his mind, and statements from two possible successors, Rob Andrew and Dean Richards, that they would decline the captaincy, Easby relented and reinstated Carling as captain. The two then posed for photographers.]

The Daily Telegraph: 24 June

Murdoch's grand slam with £340m rugby deal

By John Mason, in Johannesburg

RUPERT Murdoch has clinched the largest rugby union deal in history: a 10-year £340 million broadcasting contract with the three main rugby unions in the Southern Hemisphere.

The agreement, which follows his £300 million plan to revolutionise rugby league around the globe, raised immediate fears among European rugby unions that the days of the amateur game might finally be at an end.

Mr Murdoch's News Corporation has negotiated for an annual six-match Test series, home and away, between New Zealand, South Africa and Australia, creating a Home Nations-style championship for the other side of the world.

His television and broadcasting rights will also cover all representative provincial matches in those countries as well as incoming tours from Britain and France. The sum involved, at £34 million a year, dwarfs the £32 million which the BBC and Mr Murdoch's Sky TV paid to screen the Five Nations and English club games from 1994 and 1997.

The leading so-called amateur players in the three countries, who at present cannot be paid directly, are bound to benefit.

Louis Luyt, one of the principal negotiators, who is also chairman of South Africa's World Cup organising committee, announced the broad outline of the deal on the eve of the 1995 Rugby World Cup final between South Africa and New Zealand at Ellis Park, Johannesburg.

He said yesterday: 'For some time rugby union has appeared to be threatened by other codes, almost like an injured impala limping through the bushveld with lions nearby. This agreement allows these three unions to retain control of their destinies.'

Tony Hallett, the incoming secretary of the Rugby Football Union, said in Johannesburg: 'This will drive a hole through amateurism. We must redefine the boundaries of professionalism.' Dennis Easby, the RFU president who was recently embroiled in the 'old farts' row with Will Carling, said: 'I see no harm in players being rewarded for off-the-field activities which promote the game. I hope, though, that we don't have a system of match fees and contracts.'

Brendan Gallagher writes from Pretoria:

VERNON PUGH, the outgoing chairman of the International Board, last night admitted that Rupert Murdoch's News Corporation had already made approaches about backing a Northern Hemisphere tournament similar to the £340 million deal involving South Africa, New Zealand and Australia.

Pugh congratulated the Southern Hemisphere countries on their 10-year broadcast deal and added: 'They have done us an enormous favour in a game where money is very important. They have raised the stakes and set a marker for us to aim at.'

He then said that News Corporation were interested in making a bid for the Five Nations Championship, adding: 'No harm can come to the game from this kind of financial windfall.'

Bledisloe Cup: Australia 23 New Zealand 34, Sydney, 30 July

Lomu sets standard

By Peter Fitzsimons

IT WAS the Jonah Lomu show all over again. Running, swerving, charging over the top of all opposition, Lomu palmed off defenders with insolent ease and scored. He was named man of the match as the All Blacks registered their second successive win over the Wallabies, 34-23, to win the Bledisloe Cup.

After only one minute and 20 seconds of play, Lomu gathered the ball on the left touchline and set off towards the line. In, out, over, and all of the above three times over, he was at last brought to ground 10 metres from the Australian line ... but not before he got a pass away that resulted in a try for centre Frank Bunce.

The All Blacks went on to score five tries in the game, three of which Lomu set up, and one of which he scored. He was simply unstoppable, and Wallaby coach Bob Dwyer rightly said: 'I don't think that there has ever been anyone like him.'

For the rest of it, it was an entertaining game with the Wallabies somehow managing a 13-12 lead at half-time despite everything, before the All Blacks powered away.

David Campese, starting the game as a reserve, came off the bench in the second half to replace the injured Damien Smith, but was no sooner on the field than Lomu ran over the top of him for the easiest of tries.

The Daily Telegraph: 28 August

The Daily Telegraph: 22 September

Andrew joins Newcastle in £750,000 deal

By John Mason

ROB Andrew became rugby union's best-paid professional yesterday when he was appointed Newcastle United Sporting Club's first rugby development director.

Andrew, 32, who has played 70 times for England, has signed a five-year contract believed to be worth £750,000.

The announcement, which follows the decision to end restrictions on players' pay, was made at a news conference at St James's Park, home of Newcastle United, which took Newcastle Gosforth rugby club under its wing 17 days ago. Andrew's appointment could spark off more high-profile signings. His brief is to turn Newcastle into 'one of the foremost clubs in Europe'.

'We've got the Kevin Keegan of rugby,' said Sir John Hall, chairman of Newcastle United. 'Rob will do for the game here what Kevin has done for football.'

Andrew, a Cambridge rugby and cricket Blue from Richmond, North Yorks, has played for Wasps for 10 years, and will be eligible for them for the next seven weeks. He must serve a 120-day qualification period before he can represent Newcastle Gosforth in the league.

RU chiefs finally kick amateurism into touch

By David Millward

AFTER more than a century as an amateur sport, Rugby Union finally bowed to the inevitable and turned professional yesterday.

Players will be allowed to be paid for participating in the sport at all levels as a result of the decision taken by the International Rugby Football Board at a three-day meeting in Paris.

In doing so, Rugby Union joined other one-time bastions of amateurism – tennis and athletics – in converting itself into an 'open sport'. The decision was described as 'momentous'and 'challenging' by Tony Hallett, the Secretary of the Rugby Football Union. But Barry John, the former Welsh fly-half, condemned the move as 'calamitous'.

The changes announced yesterday in a five-point statement will sweep away all regulations governing amateurism. The reforms, which pave the way for a transfer system, player contracts and win bonuses, are the culmination of almost 20 years of creeping professionalism in the game.

The implementation of the board's decision will be left to its 67 members. Scotland, Wales and Ireland are expected to announce their position within 48 hours.

England, where the 60 top players are expected to be put under contract and paid by a sponsor, will formalise its approach at a special meeting of the RFU over the next few weeks.

The changes are a reflection of the way in which the sport has changed since the Seventies, when players were not only unpaid but banned from making money even indirectly from the game – for example, writing their memoirs or writing for newspapers. But by the early Eighties under-the-counter payments – such as 'boot money' from kit manufacturers and inflated expenses – became increasingly commonplace.

In recent years rules have been relaxed across the world. Top English players have been allowed to endorse products, providing they are not wearing rugby kit when doing so. In the Southern Hemisphere the rules were even more relaxed, with star players being given well-paid coaching and administrative sinecures.

The board has acted as the sport's commercial pulling power has become more evident in the wake of the successful World Cup tournament in South Africa.

In doing so, it has attempted to draw up a formula which it hopes will harmonise the approach of the Northern and Southern Hemispheres and enable the sport to foil attempts by the Australian media chiefs Rupert Murdoch and Kerry Packer to poach its stars.

It was their involvement which brought the issue to a head, according to Vernon Pugh, who led the team that produced the board's report.

Speaking on Radio Four's *The World This Weekend*, he said: 'I don't think we had an alternative, and we do have a very strong belief we can properly control the game for the future.'

But while Louis Luyt, South Africa's leading rugby administrator, described the Paris decision as 'a total victory', Bill Bishop, the president of the RFU, admitted he was 'taken aback' by the scale of the changes.

'It's a momentous day in the history of the sport, but it's a sad day at the same time. The game will never be the same again. Hopefully we can hold on to what is good about it.'

Under the board's blueprint, clubs will be free to pay their players. But with only about 10 – including Bath, Leicester, Bristol and Harlequins – believed to have the resources to do so, there are fears that the gap between the the elite and the rest will widen.

1995 World Cup

26 May Scotland and captain Gavin Hastings rewrite the record books with their 89-0 victory over Ivory Coast: the highest score and biggest winning margin in the World Cup finals, the highest individual points haul, 44 (4T-9C-2PG), and Scotland's highest ever score.

26 May Tongan flanker Feleti Mahoni is sent off for stamping on a French forward and will take no further part in the competition. [Video evidence later appears to suggest the referee got the wrong man.]

27 May England's World Cup campaign gets off to a shaky start, rescued by the boot of Rob Andrew who scores all their points in a 24-18 win over Argentina, from 6 penalties and 2 drop goals, as the Pumas score the only two tries. Meanwhile Bridgend wing Gareth Thomas, at 20 the baby of the party, celebrates his début with a hat-trick of tries as Wales get off to a flying start with a 57-10 victory over Japan, Neil Jenkins contributing 22 points (5C-4PG). But Ireland are flattened by the awesome power of 21-year-old All Black Jonah Lomu, as New Zealand cruise to a 43-19 victory.

30 May Gavin Hastings scores another 31 points (1T-1C-8PG), equalling the international record of 8 penalties, as Scotland beat Tonga 41-5. He now has 198 points in 11 World Cup games, eclipsing Grant Fox's record of 170. South Africa, with 11 changes from the side victorious over Australia, are somewhat subdued in their 21-8 win over Romania, who show a marked improvement after their depressing 34-3 defeat by Canada. Four teams have now booked their places in the quarter-finals – South Africa, Scotland, France and Western Samoa, who edge past Argentina 32-26, snatching victory in a thrilling match with a try 5 minutes from time.

31 May England score their first tries, one each by the Underwood brothers, as a pedestrian display sees them scrape past Italy 27-20 and into the quarter-finals. New Zealand are also through after their 34-9 success over Wales.

3 Jun A try in the third minute of injury time by France's right wing Emile Ntamack, in one of the matches of the tournament, denies Scotland victory and condemns

them, barring miracles, to a quarter-final with the rampant All Blacks. In the other Pool D match, Ivory Coast wing Max Brito suffers a serious injury against Tonga that has left him with both legs and an arm paralysed. [Shortly after, surgeons confirm he will be paralysed for life.]

3 Jun At Port Elizabeth, with South Africa coasting to an easy win over Canada with six minutes to go, the match suddenly develops into an extraordinary touch-line brawl, and Irish referee David McHugh sends off 3 players, captain Gareth Rees and Rod Snow of Canada and Springbok hooker James Dalton [all 3 receiving 30-day bans].

4 Jun New Zealand, without Lomu, Mehrtens and 10 others of the XV that whacked Wales, rewrite the record books with their 145-17 victory over Japan, the highest ever World Cup (finals) tally. Newcomer Simon Culhane marks his debut by succeeding with 20 out of 21 attempts and setting a world record with 20 conversions in his 45 points (1T-20C). With Dean Richards fit again, England impress in beating Western Samoa 44-22.

5 Jun Further to Saturday's Port Elizabeth fracas, the RWC disciplinary authority slaps an immediate 3-month ban on Springbok wing Pieter Hendriks for kicking and punching, with 2 months for Canada's full-back Scott Stewart, the player accused of starting the brawl.

10 Jun The first black Springbok, Chester Williams, brought back to the South African squad as a replacement for the banned Hendriks after a remarkable recovery from a torn hamstring, grabs 4 tries as the Springboks slam Western Samoa 42-14, but has to share the headlines as the pundits slam the Samoan display as 'sporting terrorism' (Stuart Barnes in *The Daily Telegraph*). The Samoans in turn slam the referee (Scot Jim Fleming) and there are allegations of persistent 'racist' baiting against Springbok scrum-half Joost van der Westhuizen.

11 Jun England are the only Home Union to reach the semi-finals, at the expense of Australia, where, back home Down Under, a news presenter warns, 'Listeners may find some of the following material offensive.'

The Irish celebrate Popplewell's opening try.

World Cup Pool C: 4 June, Ireland 24 Wales 23, Johannesburg

Ireland's jolly green giants live to fight another day

By Brendan Gallagher

AN ENTHRALLING last 20 minutes, totally out of character with an otherwise appalling match, resulted in Ireland booking a quarter-final place against France in Durban on Saturday. On yesterday's showing here, though, Philippe Saint-André and his team will hardly be quaking in their boots.

Terry Kingston's side deserved to win by virtue of

World Cup Pool A: South Africa 27 Australia 18, Cape Town 25 May

Hosts off to joyous start

By John Mason

THE hastily painted banner read 'Forget the rhino, save the wallaby', its bearers grinning hugely with delight. The script was in bold red letters, though the message was already plain enough. Australia, the world champions, had been handsomely seen off by South Africa in the opening match of the 1995 Rugby World Cup.

From the moment that the Navy band struck up Anchors Aweigh to begin the pre-match ceremonial, South Africa, the rainbow nation, was in joyous mood. Victory in a sense was a happy bonus. Long before Joel Stransky's 22 points had nailed Australia well and truly to the floor, the mood was euphoric. President Nelson Mandela was given a thunderous reception and he, too, expertly responded to the affection and humour.

Supreme statesman that he is, the president, a small,

upright, neat figure, his temples flecked with grey, recognised instantly that the light touch would be appropriate. 'Your presence,' he told the 416 players from 16 nations, plus some 40,000 visitors from overseas, 'affirms the unity in diversity, the humanity in healthy contest, that our young democracy has come to symbolise. South Africa keenly appreciates your love and support. South Africa opens its arms and its heart to embrace you all.'

The finale of the splendidly simple opening involved seven groups of girls and boys forming in separate groups in front of a slightly raised stage. When they knelt, the formation spelt 'Welcome'. Behind them all the hundreds, including the Navy band, lined up to form the outline of South Africa's coast.

The rugby could not have possibly gone wrong after that.

outscoring their opponents three tries to two, but for an hour it was desperately poor fare and the 35,000 Ellis Park crowd knew it. The game did not take off until the final whistle loomed and players of known quality started to perform with the passion of those who wished to avoid returning to work tomorrow morning.

Wales chipped away at Ireland's lead, but the unforgiving clock ran down remorselessly and their second try in the fourth minute of injury time came too late to affect the outcome.

World Cup Quarter-Finals: France 36 Ireland 12, Durban 10 June

Irish battered into submission

By Paul Ackford

WHERE was it? All that fire and passion which we were promised. Ireland went down with barely a whimper, strangled by a French team who grabbed them by the scruff of the neck and refused to let go.

It was a strange occasion. Perhaps it was the half-empty stadium, the crowd in shirt sleeves or the fabulous weather, but it did not feel like a quarter-final of the World Cup.

France did not give a damn. At the end of the contest, the team gathered in a circle to salute their victory and pledge commitment to the cause. It was a sure sign that they are fast generating the spirit which makes them a much stronger side away from home.

This was a much different France from the team who slid past Scotland. The backs played second fiddle to the forwards, who earned them the victory. It was an astonishing performance. France outplayed Ireland in the tight, shading the scrap for possession 42-34, and in the loose the margin was an even more devastating 50-18.

Thierry Lacroix equalled the international world record of eight penalties in his 26-point tally. He scored four of them in the first half, which finished 12-12, Ireland having led four times from Elwood penalties.

The second period was generally a disaster area for Ireland, Lacroix scoring another four penalties before converting a Saint-André try. Wing Emile Ntamack hammered the final nail in their coffin, intercepting a pass and running 95 yards to score.

World Cup Quarter-Finals: England 25 Australia 22, Cape Town 11 June

Andrew leaves it late to topple Australia

By John Mason

ROB ANDREW'S soaring, sweetly-struck dropped goal allowed England to squeeze past world champions Australia in the final minute of a tense, nerve-jangling World Cup quarter-final yesterday. An English dream for which everyone had been working for four years had come true.

England, having started splendidly, played ducks and drakes with the nerves of their most devoted followers. A relatively comfortable 13-3 lead after 20 minutes subsided to 13 points each in the opening minute of the second half.

No praise can be too high for the work of scrum-half Dewi Morris, whose enthusiasm and refusal to concede an inch was a glowing example of everything that a competitor should present in this arena. He, Andrew, of course, and Martin Bayfield ensured that the Newlands shoot-out went England's way – bull's-eye and bulldog.

Michael Lynagh kicked the first of his five penalty goals in the second minute. Andrew followed suit in the sixth and ninth minutes. England's try came from a long way back and, ironically, Australia were attacking, ball in hand.

Sport being a cruel taskmaster, it was Lynagh who dropped the ball. Eager English hands seized upon it, Andrew to the fore. The raid swung to the right: Andrew to Jeremy Guscott to Will Carling. At that point the midfield was blocked and Guscott delayed his pass to the last possible moment.

By then, right wing Tony Underwood was in full stride, running on to a flicked pass that may have been forward. Head back, knees pumping, he stepped up a gear to sweep round the cover and there was time and room to finish close to the posts. Andrew converted and, tantalisingly, the semi-finals beckoned.

English nerves were sorely tried, not least by lock John Eales, who had a remarkable match – a true athlete and competitor. Lynagh kicked a late penalty goal to end the half, and immediately afterwards it was his chip high to the left-hand corner that for the first time exposed an English defensive frailty.

Mike Catt, making his only mistake, and Tony Underwood attempted to cover but Damian Smith, Australia's large left wing, was quicker and stronger. As he reached for the ball, Smith turned and rolled through the tackle, landing over the goal-line for Lynagh to convert from touch.

Suddenly English roses were not in bloom. Two more penalty goals by Lynagh put Australia ahead, only for Andrew to peg back the Wallabies: 13-16; 16-16; 19-16; 19-19; 22-19 and, in the 76th minute, 22-22. Andrew's fifth penalty had squared matters again; extra-time loomed.

Lynagh twice ran the ball when a dropped goal might have been the better option. Another penalty award, this time on England's left. Up stepped Catt to drill the ball to touch; England's throw at the line-out.

The telescopic reach of middle jumper Bayfield, the RFU's player of the year, plucked the ball out of the air. His colleagues converged and England's pack rumbled downfield. At scrum-half Dewi Morris' barked command, the release was swiftly efficient. The ball thumped into Andrew's cricketer hands and back went the right foot, some 40 metres from goal and two minutes and 36 seconds into time added-on. The rest is history.

World Cup Quarter-Finals: New Zealand 48 Scotland 30, Pretoria 11 June

Hastings and Scotland go down with all guns firing

By Brendan Gallagher

SCOTLAND, determined that Gavin Hastings should not be embarrassed on his farewell to international rugby, dug deep into reserves of pride and courage before finally conceding a gloriously entertaining quarter-final at Loftus Versfeld.

Only Australia have scored 30 points against the All Blacks before, and no side have achieved that total and still lost to New Zealand. Scotland went down with all guns firing, as you would expect from any side with Hastings at the helm.

After the inevitable dressing-room TV interview, the loyal Scottish supporters demanded that the Scotland captain re-emerge after his 61st and final appearance. An impromptu lap of honour followed, ending with Hastings being chaired off to thunderous applause.

The game exploded into life when the incomparable Jonah Lomu created a try, the like of which is rarely seen in international rugby. Collecting the ball 65 yards out, he cruised around Craig Joiner, a former Scottish schools sprint champion, and dismissed the challenges of Scott and Gavin Hastings before gifting the touchdown to Walter Little.

The All Blacks ran in six tries altogether, Lomu scoring one himself, Little getting his second, with Mehrtens, after a 70-yard run, Bunce and Fitzpatrick notching one apiece. Mehrtens, exuding remarkable confidence for a 22-year-old playing only his fourth Test, converted all six and also hit two penalty goals.

Scotland's points came from tries by Doddie Weir (two) and Scott Hastings, all converted by Gavin Hastings, who also kicked three penalty goals.

Last gasp: Rob Andrew sends over the winning drop goal.

14 Jun Springbok full-back André Joubert makes a remarkable recovery from a broken hand and will play in the semi-finals, while Van der Westhuizen, still recovering from the blow to the throat he received from Samoan full-back Mike Umaga (cited and banned for 60 days after a similar 'tackle' on Joubert), is well enough to refute the allegations of racism and biting made against him.

17 Jun Torrential rain delays the first semi by 90 minutes at Durban, where South Africa eventually splash their way to the final at the expense of France.

18 Jun Jonah Lomu justifies all the hype and steamrollers England to defeat. Former England coach Geoff Cooke describes the 6ft 5in 20-year-old Tongan-born winger as a 'human rhinoceros'.

22 Jun In the 3rd-place play-off match, England suffer their first defeat by France in 9 matches since 1988, and will now have to pre-qualify for the 1999 World Cup. Meanwhile, a newly emerging volcanic island off Tonga has been named after Jonah Lomu.

23 Jun With the whole rugby world looking ahead to tomorrow's final, Rupert

Murdoch drops his £340m bombshell – a 10-year contract with the Southern Hemisphere rugby nations that surely spells the end of the amateur game.

24 Jun South Africa's historic and emotional victory marks the culmination of an extraordinary tournament in which the Springboks were swept along on a wave of national celebration and unity.

Lomu shrugs off a despairing tackle by Rob Andrew.

World Cup Semi-Finals: New Zealand 45 England 29, Cape Town 18 June

World Cup Semi-Finals: South Africa 19 France 15, Durban 17 June

Joubert the hero as Springboks finish singing in the rain

By Paul Ackford

RUGBY World Cup should strike up a special medal to commemorate the efforts of 31 players who salvaged a potentially disastrous afternoon. In atrocious conditions which tested their resilience and skills to the limit, they produced a thrilling climax which was more than a rain-sodden crowd had a right to expect.

In the end the Springboks held on for a place in the final next Saturday and probably just about deserved to on the balance of play, but it was desperately close.

With seconds to go, Abdel Benazzi fastened onto a kick, dived full length and slid toward the Springbok goal-line. Agonisingly for France he was inches short, but the drama was not over. France were awarded a scrum. Twice they went for the big shove, once when half their back line came in to help their forwards. On the third occasion their World Cup hopes were obliterated when they ran it wide and Thierry Lacroix was gang-tackled by half of South Africa.

The debate will rage whether this game should have been played at all. The pitch was a lake in places, and to call the bounce of the ball a lottery would be a gross understatement. At times the ball stopped dead in a puddle, at others it skidded an extra 15 or 20 metres.

Andre Joubert was the one player who was able to cope with the conditions. His kicking out of hand as the last line of defence was marvellous, and every time he popped into the line to send skidding kicks in behind the French backs, the alarm bells sounded. His performance was especially compelling because he played the entire match with a broken thumb.

Scorers – S Africa: Kruger 1T, Stransky 1C-4PG. France: Lacroix 5PG.

Lomu's powerhouse display shatters England's dreams

By John Mason

EVERYTHING the rugby world warned that Jonah Lomu would do to Grand Slam England, he did. He began with a try after 70 seconds, followed with three more, and at all times had seasoned opponents in a state of impotence, if not panic.

It was a hair-raising marvel of a performance from this 6ft 5in giant of a man blessed with a strength and physical presence way beyond his 20 years. From the kick-off at a full house Newlands it was: 'Good afternoon, Tony Underwood. Here I am to make your life a misery for the next 79 minutes 50 seconds.'

At the start a dummy line-up by the All Blacks on the right had England covering in the wrong places. Lomu, the lay preacher's son from Tonga via South Auckland, was in business instantly, thundering in pursuit of a soaring ball well to New Zealand's left. The alarm bells were at full decibel even before the opening try.

But it was not just the youngest Underwood who had a recurring nightmare in attempting to stop 18st 8lb Lomu, a runaway potting shed in boots. Will Carling, Mike Catt, Tim Rodber, Dewi Morris and Dean Richards discovered that the genuine, well-timed tackle was not sufficient to do more than momentarily slow an athletic mountain.

The sorry outcome was that England conceded more points than they have ever done previously. The try-count finished at 6-4 to New Zealand, not much of a consolation for England, a team striving to lead the world.

Whenever in that opening 20 minutes of ice-cool, calculating rugby New Zealand cared to employ Lomu, England were in trouble. Perhaps not paralysed, they were Lomu-lised, well and truly. If New Zealand do not win the World Cup at Ellis Park next Saturday against South Africa, there will have to be a stewards' inquiry.

In defying all the tenets of a team game, here was one player who spent the semi-final of the 1995 World Cup reducing a previously competent, well-drilled England team, seeking an 11th consecutive victory, to bedraggled also-rans. It was embarrassing; it was also inspiring, a sporting occasion to treasure.

During that opening quarter New Zealand scored three tries, kicked a penalty goal and, in a kind of sporting leg-pull, as if for a dare, No.8 Zinzan Brooke dropped a long goal, the first by a forward in international history, from the range that allowed Rob Andrew to topple Australia last week. If it had not added so much to English doom and despondency, it would have been permissible to laugh.

Scorers – New Zealand: Tries, Lomu 4, Kronfeld, Bachop; Conversions, Mehrtens 3; Penalty goal, Mehrtens; Dropped goals, Z Brooke, Mehrtens.
England: Tries, R Underwood 2, Carling 2; Conversions, Andrew 3; Penalty goal, Andrew.

World Cup Final: 24 June, Johannesburg

Extra-special Springboks keep a date with destiny

By Paul Ackford

South Africa 15 New Zealand 12 (aet: 9-9 at 80 minutes)

SOUTH Africa were destined to win this World Cup, it was written in the stars. No side could have had a harder path to tread. They faced the world champions in their first match, overcame floodlight failure, the sending-off of James Dalton and the citing of Pieter Hendriks at Port Elizabeth, and played a semi-final in Durban in torrential rain.

Nothing disturbed their momentum, and even the best team in the competition by far, New Zealand, were unable to deny them the celebrations which a country craved. After the final whistle, their hugely impressive and modest captain, Francois Pienaar, said: 'We did not have 63,000 fans behind us today, we had 43 million South Africans.'

He was right, and the memories of President Nelson Mandela dancing a jig before the first game of the competition and waving his Springbok cap after the last match will live with me for the rest of my life.

Joel Stransky won it for them. Eighty minutes could not settle the match, neither could the first period of extra time, but Stransky gave South Africa a crucial three-point winning margin three minutes into the final period of drama. From a scrum he hoisted a huge up-and-under which Zinzan Brooke knocked on. The position was on the 22, slightly to the right of the posts, and all of South Africa knew what Stransky was going to attempt.

On the first occasion the scrum slewed sideways, but the Springboks pack regrouped and managed to provide a stable platform for Stransky to attempt the dropped goal. Graeme Bachop tried to intercept the path of the ball, Andrew Mehrtens raced up to block the kick, but Stransky ignored everyone and struck the ball cleanly between the posts to leave a nation delirious.

It was a compulsive match, rarely living up to the expectations of free-flowing rugby, but of its kind it was a classic. Neither side managed to get more than three points ahead, and the tension as the game built towards its memorable climax was unbearable.

Joel Stransky: phenomenal.

That South Africa were able to keep the lid on an astonishingly talented All Black team is a tribute to the resolve and courage of the entire team. They tackled like demons and the All Blacks were never able to create the space and continuity to launch their dangerous backs.

Jonah Lomu was the name on everyone's lips before the game, but he rarely had the opportunity to get out of the starting-blocks, faced as he was with two or three pumped-up Springbok defenders. In the end the All Blacks asked too much of Lomu; he was given the ball and told to work a miracle, and in the biggest game of his life he could not deliver.

Aside from their defence the Springbok pack had a wonderful match. They shared the line-outs but held a discernible edge in the scrums, and the work of Pienaar, Ruben Kruger and Mark Andrews was crucial.

Time and again the back row trio killed All Black attacks or started some of their own, and when they appeared to falter there was always the massive presence of Kobus Wiese and Balie Swart to add weight to the move.

The other impressive figure in the Springbok pack was Chris Rossouw, who played like a man possessed and suffered nothing in comparison with the All Black captain, Sean Fitzpatrick.

Bolt on to this display the phenomenal kicking of Stransky, who slotted three penalty goals and two dropped goals, the midfield tenacity of Japie Mulder and Hennie Le Roux – who snuffed out the All Black centres – and the inevitable peerless display of Andre Joubert at full-back, and you you get some idea of why the Springboks edged home.

RUGBY UNION WORLD CUP 1995

(NB: The pool matches each carry a total of 4pts – 3 for a win, 2 for a draw and 1 for a loss)

Pool A

25 May	Cape Town	SOUTH AFRICA	27	AUSTRALIA	18
26 May	Port Elizabeth	CANADA	34	ROMANIA	3
30 May	Cape Town	SOUTH AFRICA	21	ROMANIA	8
31 May	Port Elizabeth	AUSTRALIA	27	CANADA	11
3 June	Stellenbosch	AUSTRALIA	42	ROMANIA	3
3 June	Port Elizabeth	SOUTH AFRICA	20	CANADA	0

Pool A	P	W	D	L	F	A	Pts
1 SOUTH AFRICA	3	3	0	0	68	26	9
2 AUSTRALIA	3	2	0	1	87	41	7
3 CANADA	3	1	0	2	45	50	5
4 ROMANIA	3	0	0	3	14	97	3

Pool B

27 May	East London	WESTERN SAMOA	42	ITALY	18
27 May	Durban	ENGLAND	24	ARGENTINA	18
30 May	East London	WESTERN SAMOA	32	ARGENTINA	26
31 May	Durban	ENGLAND	27	ITALY	20
4 June	East London	ITALY	31	ARGENTINA	25
4 June	Durban	ENGLAND	44	WESTERN SAMOA	22

Pool B	P	W	D	L	F	A	Pts
1 ENGLAND	3	3	0	0	95	60	9
2 W SAMOA	3	2	0	1	96	88	7
3 ITALY	3	1	0	2	69	94	5
4 ARGENTINA	3	0	0	3	69	87	3

Pool C

27 May	Bloemfontein	WALES	57	JAPAN	10
27 May	Johannesburg	NEW ZEALAND	43	IRELAND	19
31 May	Bloemfontein	IRELAND	50	JAPAN	28
31 May	Johannesburg	NEW ZEALAND	34	WALES	9
4 June	Bloemfontein	NEW ZEALAND	145	JAPAN	17
4 June	Johannesburg	IRELAND	24	WALES	23

Pool C	P	W	D	L	F	A	Pts
1 NEW ZEALAND	3	3	0	0	222	45	9
2 IRELAND	3	2	0	1	93	94	7
3 WALES	3	1	0	2	89	68	5
4 JAPAN	3	0	0	3	55	252	3

Pool D

26 May	Rustenburg	SCOTLAND	89	IVORY COAST	0
26 May	Pretoria	FRANCE	38	TONGA	10
30 May	Rustenburg	FRANCE	54	IVORY COAST	18
30 May	Pretoria	SCOTLAND	41	TONGA	5
3 June	Rustenburg	TONGA	29	IVORY COAST	11
3 June	Pretoria	FRANCE	22	SCOTLAND	19

Pool D	P	W	D	L	F	A	Pts
1 FRANCE	3	3	0	0	114	47	9
2 SCOTLAND	3	2	0	1	149	27	7
3 TONGA	3	1	0	2	44	90	5
4 IVORY COAST	3	0	0	3	29	172	3

Quarter-finals

10 June	Durban	FRANCE	36	IRELAND	12
10 June	Johannesburg	SOUTH AFRICA	42	WESTERN SAMOA	14
11 June	Cape Town	ENGLAND	25	AUSTRALIA	22
11 June	Pretoria	NEW ZEALAND	48	SCOTLAND	30

Semi-finals

17 June	Durban	SOUTH AFRICA	19	FRANCE	15
18 June	Cape Town	NEW ZEALAND	45	ENGLAND	29

Third-place match

22 June	Pretoria	FRANCE	19	ENGLAND	9

FINAL

24 June	Johannesburg	SOUTH AFRICA	15	NEW ZEALAND	12

SOUTH AFRICA Joubert; Small (97 Venter), Mulder, Le Roux, Williams; Stransky, Van der Westhuizen; Du Randt, Rossouw, Swart (68 Pagel), Wiese, Strydom, Pienaar (capt), Andrews (90 Straeuli), Kruger
Scorers PG: Stransky 3, DG: Stransky 2
NEW ZEALAND Osborne; Wilson (55 Ellis), Bunce, Little, Lomu; Mehrtens; Bachop (Strachan, temp); Dowd (83 Loe), Fitzpatrick (capt), Brown, Jones, Brooke RM, Brewer (40 Joseph), Brooke ZV, Kronfeld
Scorers PG: Mehrtens 3, DG: Mehrtens

INDIVIDUAL SCORING

Most points in tournament	112	T Lacroix (F)
	104	AG Hastings (S)
	84	AP Mehrtens (NZ)
Most tries in tournament	7	MCG Ellis (NZ)
	7	JT Lomu (NZ)
Most points in a match	45	SD Culhane (NZ, v Japan)
	44	AG Hastings (S, v Ivory Coast)
	31	AG Hastings (S, v Tonga)
	30	MCG Ellis (NZ, v Japan)
Most tries in a match	6	MCG Ellis (NZ, v Japan)
	4	AG Hastings (S, v Ivory Coast)
	4	JT Lomu (NZ, v E)
	4	CW Williams (SA, v W.Samoa)

1996

9 Jan Saracens, currently in the nether regions of Courage League One, sign outside-half Michael Lynagh, the Australian world record holder with 911 points from 72 internationals, who is contracted to Italian club Treviso until mid-May.

14 Jan The RFU's plans for professionalism are left in turmoil as a meeting in Birmingham is abandoned in chaos and acrimony after the rank and file vote overwhelmingly to hold another special general meeting to debate and vote specifically on the matter. Earlier, the RFU received another slap in the face with the election, as chairman of the new streamlined executive committee, of Cliff Brittle, who will wake up tomorrow as the most powerful man in British rugby.

21 Feb John Devereux, capped for Wales at both codes, becomes the first player to commit himself professionally to both sports, agreeing to play union for Sale in the winter and league for Widnes in the summer.

22 Feb Gloucester forward Simon Devereux is jailed for 9 months for an incident last season in a second-team game when he broke Rosslyn Park flanker Jamie Cowie's jaw, an injury that left him hospitalised for 5 days and out of the game for 8 months.

6 Mar England tight-head prop Jason Leonard is cleared of allegations that he punched Scotland captain Rob Wainwright in the Calcutta Cup match, the video evidence being inconclusive.

1 Apr Quins chairman Roger Looker mounts a scathing attack on the RFU, especially its executive committee chairman Cliff Brittle, warning of a possible split with the clubs if the RFU do not get their act together in talks to establish a competitive structure for the fledgling professional sport.

3 Apr Neath beat Aberavon 95-17, running in 15 tries, in a Heineken League match.

16 Apr The Five Nations committee slate the RFU's decision to go it alone in negotiating future TV rights as 'wholly unacceptable' and warn that the other member unions will be asked to 'consider the future format of the Five Nations Championship'.

19 Apr A controversial decision of the High Court, in the first case brought against a referee, rules that the official, Mr Michael Nolan, 'failed to exercise reasonable care and skill' in preventing scrum collapses. The rugby player paralysed as a result of a collapsed scrum in an Under-19 match in 1991, Mr Ben Smoldon, was claiming more than £1m damages, which will be assessed later. The ruling could have far-reaching consequences for other sports as well as rugby.

20 Apr Gloucestershire defeat Warwickshire 17-13 at Twickenham in the CIS County Championship final to equal Lancashire's record of 16 titles.

Pilkington Cup Final: Bath 16 Leicester 15, Twickenham, 4 May

Referee steps in to shoot angry Tigers: Back in trouble

By Paul Ackford

AND SO an extraordinary season ended with an extraordinary incident. With one minute of normal time remaining, referee Steve Lander awarded Bath a penalty try after Leicester had persistently infringed in their attempt to stop Bath's last-ditch effort.

Leicester were devastated. As Lander blew the final whistle, Neil Back, their flanker, was so incensed that he pushed Lander in the middle of the back with both hands and the referee fell to the ground.

Other Leicester players remonstrated and Brian Campsall, the touch judge,

had to escort Lander off the pitch.

Back's reaction was a disgrace. Whatever the provocation, however distraught he must have felt, there is no place for behaviour of that kind on a rugby pitch.

After Matt Poole's try, which gave Leicester a 15-9 lead with five minutes remaining, Bath launched wave after wave of attack. Each time Bath looked like breaking through, Leicester infringed, either for offside or deliberately killing the ball, and after the fourth time, when Catt again went close, Lander penalised Leicester.

International Championship: England 28 Ireland 15, Twickenham, 16 March

England find answer with the old routine

By Paul Ackford

SO ENGLAND are top of the heap once more. Not in a way everyone expected, but, after a season when the critics and the crowd have occasionally given them a hard time, the players will not mind that one little bit. In the end the margin of victory against Ireland was insignificant. Wales's one-point defeat of France was enough to gift England the Five Nations title as well as the Triple Crown. It was the first time I can remember a Twickenham crowd cheering a Welsh victory.

But, true to form, England ended a roller-coaster season with as many questions as answers. For the first time in six outings we saw them start in fluid vein. It was wonderful to watch and the crowd roared their approval. The first 20 minutes produced more movements, invention and risk-taking than the rest of the season put together, but it was Old England who finally subdued Ireland. Not quite the up-the-jumper stuff which dominated Scotland, but hard-nosed, controlled driving play led by Dean Richards, Ben Clarke, Lawrence Dallaglio and Garath Archer.

England, however, still have a lot of work to do before their running game embarrasses better sides than Ireland. Fly-half Paul Grayson kicked 23 points, but the balance sheet in other areas was less impressive.

We had to wait until three minutes from the end before we had a glimpse of what England, at their best, can offer. Jon Sleightholme ripped Ireland apart to score his first Five Nations try, and in the process sent a packed stadium delirious. It was the reason why it is right to be critical of England's earlier effort. When they play like this we sup with the gods.

Will Carling's match ended 34 minutes after the start, when he limped off with a badly sprained right ankle. His replacement, Phil de Glanville, looks a good bet, and Carling without the captaincy may find it hard to hold his place in Jack Rowell's side.

But whatever happens to Carling, he can rest easy in the knowledge that he has led England to another major triumph. Five Nations rugby is much derided at times, but the title is devilishly hard to win.

Jonathan Callard had a kick in front of the posts which he converted to give Bath their 10th win in their 10th knock-out final.

Leicester, for huge chunks of time, dominated the ball and the territory with a pack of forwards who were simply outstanding. But Bath probably deserved their

victory simply because of their all-round approach. Despite intolerable pressure, they always sought to attack.

The controversy should not detract from another incredible Bath double. They are simply the best club in Great Britain.

[Back received a 6-month ban from the RFU.]

INTERNATIONAL CHAMPIONSHIP

	E	F	I	S	W	P	W	D	L	F	A	Pts
1 ENGLAND			28-15		21-15	4	3	0	1	79	54	6
2 SCOTLAND	9-18	19-14				4	3	0	1	60	56	6
3 FRANCE	15-12		45-10			4	2	0	2	89	57	4
4 WALES		16-15		14-16		4	1	0	3	62	82	2
5 IRELAND				10-16	30-17	4	1	0	3	65	106	2

TOURS (Tests)

Wales in Australia: A56-W25, A42-W3
Scotland in New Zealand: NZ62-S31, NZ36-S12

29 Apr Scotland tight-head prop Peter Wright is fined £2,000 by the SRU for breaches of contract, half for failing to meet fitness standards set by the coaching staff and half, presumably, for bringing the game into disrepute – examination of the video of the Calcutta Cup match found Wright stamping on England No.8 Dean Richards.

4 May Down 22-9 in the SWALEC Welsh Cup final at Cardiff with 30 minutes left, Pontypridd, having gifted Neath two of their four tries, stage a remarkable comeback, with a try from Paul John and two late ones from Geraint Lewis adding to Neil Jenkins's 14 point haul for a 29-22 victory.

18 May The BaaBaas beat an Ireland XV 70-38 in the Dublin 'Peace International', running in 10 tries, all converted by Bath full-back Jon Callard.

20 May The RFU reject out of hand concessions offered by England's top clubs in the long-running dispute about the competitive and financial structure of the new pro game in England. EPRUC (English Pro RU Clubs) have expressed complete frustration at trying to negotiate with RFU chairman Cliff Brittle, and the hawks among the clubs believe UDI is the only answer.

21 May The RFU/Clubs dispute reaches crisis point as the top clubs are advised to split from the union.

24 May The clubs and the RFU finally make peace, neither claiming victory.

25 May The new, highly successful Southern Hemisphere Super 12 competition is brought to a suitably thrilling conclusion as Jonah Lomu inspires Auckland to a 45-21 victory over Natal in the final in Auckland.

25 May The RFU's National Playing committee grant Jack Rowell a stay of execution as England coach provided he brings new blood into the national set-up and ends the international careers of Will Carling (33), Jeremy Guscott (34), Rory Underwood (36) and Dean Richards (36), in order to have at least 20 of the 26

World Cup squad sorted out by the end of next season.

8 Jun Wales return to the killing fields of Brisbane, where their 56-25 defeat by Australia stops just short of a massacre this time.

15 Jun Like Wales last week, Scotland are blown away by opponents who are faster, fitter and more powerful, going down 62-31 in Dunedin to the All Blacks, a record score against Scotland. Four of New Zealand's 9 tries are scored by 20-year-old Christian Cullen, their slightly built but electrically fast full-back who ran in 3 on his début against Western Samoa last week.

Rugby Challenge: Wigan 82 Bath 6, Maine Road, Manchester, 8 May

Wigan in league of their own: Bath emptied

By John Whalley

WIGAN took the first leg of what they hope will be a historic inter-code treble without having to break sweat last night. It would no longer surprise many people if they went on to win the Middlesex Sevens on Saturday and followed that up by defeating Bath under rugby union rules in the return clash on May 25.

The first meeting between club sides from the rival codes in over a century was always going to be more about occasion than a competitive event. It was probably just as well. Bath, as so many League sides have found to their cost over the last 10 years, could not cope; Martin Offiah

inevitably made his mark, scoring six of Wigan's 16 tries.

The power and speed of Wigan was always going to be decisive, but Bath contributed heavily to their own problems early on with some suspect handling and a poor kicking game which ensured Wigan would always have sufficient territory to lay foundations for their predicted rout.

The loudest cheers, however, were saved for Jon Callard's try in the 48th minute, with the England full-back adding the goal. But though Bath never lacked spirit, they also never looked like breaking through again, while Wigan were able to score at will.

John Mason writes: Teaching old dogs new tricks is a fraught exercise. Bath's terriers did their best against Wigan, the best of the rugby league breed, on a unique occasion – the public bonding of the two rugby codes in a match, the staging of which only a few months ago would have been claimed to be anything from unnecessary to impossible. Bath possessed neither the stamina nor the expertise to make more than occasional dents in the masterly authority of rugby

league's wizards. Here were England's rugby union champions, the club who have won 16 of the 22 trophies available since 1984, very much on the back foot, often confused, always on the rack, and finally slaughtered.

[Wigan did indeed win the Middlesex 7s, chalking up victories over Richmond, Quins and Leicester before coming from 15-0 down to beat Wasps 38-15 in the final. But Bath salvaged some pride at Twickenham, winning the union leg of the Challenge 44-19.]

The Daily Telegraph, 11 June

Sky deal threat to rugby 'jewel'

By Colin Randall

THE Five Nations championship, the key event in the British rugby union calendar, was threatened yesterday when England defied Irish, Scottish and Welsh opposition to sign an exclusive £87.5 million television deal with BSkyB.

Under the five-year contract announced at Twickenham, fans without access to Sky will not be able to watch England internationals live from the 1997-98 season.

Although the Rugby Football Union insisted that it remained 'wholeheartedly committed' to the championship, its decision was taken in the full knowledge that it could lead to England's exclusion.

Signs of a rift in the English camp emerged when Cliff Brittle, the RFU chairman, said that it made 'no sense whatever' to

jeopardise the Five Nations. Mr Brittle, who said that he had been excluded from talks because of his views, is taking legal advice and consulting colleagues before deciding on his next move.

BSkyB is believed to have offered separate deals totalling £96 million to the Welsh, Irish and Scottish unions. The three unions say that England broke an agreement to negotiate as a four-nation unit. The French tend to negotiate separate television contracts and do not share the others' anger.

Fred McLeod, the vice-president of the Scottish Rugby Union, said he was sad that rugby's 'jewel in the crown should be put at risk through greed'. The Triple Crown and Calcutta Cup were equally under threat.

The Bath defence struggles to cope as former All Black Va'aiga Tuigamala looks to break through.

Index